"Mark's book *Africa's Top Wildlife Countries* is spot on! Mark was with us in Mombo for the release of our first rhinos back into the Okavango after being poached out of Botswana completely in the 80s. With the release of these animals, Mombo becomes the first place in Botswana to complete the whole 'big five' potential. As a conservationist and filmmaker I am delighted by this. As a citizen of Botswana I am proud that we have conquered the poaching issue and can now enjoy the recovery of the bush to its original glory. As an adult I breathe a sigh of relief that we may just be able to look the next generation in the eye. I encourage you to travel to Africa to experience first-hand all it has to offer. Your traveling to Africa ensures that there is money for conservation. *Africa's Top Wildlife Countries* is the perfect guidebook to help plan that adventure."

Dereck and Beverly Joubert
Authors of *Hunting in the Moon — The Lions of Savuti* and *The African Diaries*
Producer of the films *Eternal Enemies: Lions and Hyenas* (National Geographic), *Whispers — an Elephants Tale* (Disney), and *The Stolen River* and *Zebras: Patterns in the Grass* (National Geographic)

"This book is just what any new and experienced traveler to Africa requires. It shows the diversity of the continent's wildlife and wildlife experiences in a truly unique and complete approach. A good reference guide for the repeat traveler!"
Solly Moeng
General Manager, South African Tourism

"*Africa's Top Wildlife Countries* is a great resource for planning a safari or vacation to Tanzania's fabulous parks, reserves, beautiful coast and exotic islands. The detailed descriptions of the hotels, safari lodges and camps are very helpful in requesting the right accommodations for you."
Mr. Peter Mwenguo
Managing Director, Tanzania Tourist Board

"*Africa's Top Wildlife Countries* is a 'must have' for anyone thinking of traveling to that great continent. It provides invaluable information that will enable the reader to experience the very best from what is sure to be the trip of a lifetime. As someone who has experienced Africa well over a dozen times and returns annually, I find this reference the best on the market today. Don't go without it!"
Ron Magill
Miami Metro Zoo

"There are a number of excellent travel guides that offer in-depth information on a variety of individual countries in Africa, but none that can begin to rival the latest edition of *Africa's Top Wildlife Countries.* This is due to the simple fact that Mark Nolting personally visits Africa at least twice a year; this love affair has been ablaze for over twenty-five years. During this time he has moved from an intrepid explorer to one of North America's most reputable tour operators, sending the lion share of safari visitors to this diverse continent. There are many reasons 'The Africa Adventure Company' holds poll position in this field, the most pertinent being a particularly in depth knowledge of every safari destination, camps, lodges, guides and small, personalized hotels. Over the years exceptionally strong relationships have been forged with the people on the ground who facilitate these lifetime experiences. Mark is in touch with Africa on a daily basis and offers you a travel guide to 16 countries with the most comprehensive and up-to-date information on safari travel through Africa."
Garth Thompson
Author of *A Guide's Guide to Guiding*

"When it comes to Africa trips, Mark Nolting is the man. He's the first guy I call, and his book *Africa's Top Wildlife Countries* is the first one I reach for."
David Noland
Contributor to *National Geographic Adventure* and author of *Outside Adventure Travel: Trekking*

"As a safari tour leader to Africa for the past 17 years, the only book I need is Mark Nolting's *Africa's Top Wildlife Countries.* It is my 'Bible' for planning my photo safaris, and I recommend it to anyone considering a wildlife safari to sub-Sahara Africa."
Richard L. Henning
Safari Leader

REVISED AND EXPANDED

AFRICA's
Top Wildlife Countries

SIXTH EDITION

By
Mark W. Nolting

Global Travel Publishers, Inc.

AFRICA'S TOP WILDLIFE COUNTRIES
(Sixth Edition, completely revised and updated)

Copyright:	2003 © by Mark W. Nolting
ISBN:	0-939895-10-2
Edited by:	Alison V. H. Nolting
Proofread by:	Betsy Lampe and Kinda Blomberg
Cover and Interior Design by:	Chris Pearl
Maps by:	Ken Perna and Chris Pearl
Published by:	Global Travel Publishers, Inc.

Enquiries should be addressed to: Global Travel Publishers, Inc.. P.O. Box 70067, Ft. Lauderdale, FL 33307-0067, U.S.A., Telephone (954) 491-8877 or (800) 882-9453, Facsimile (954) 491-9060. Email safaribooks@aol.com

International Standard Book Number
0-939895-10-2
Library of Congress Cataloging-in-Publication Data
Nolting, Mark, 1951-
    Africa's top wildlife countries / by Mark W. Nolting,--6th ed., rev. and expanded.
    p. cm.
    Includes bibliographical references (p.).
    ISBN 0-939895-10-2 (alk. paper)
    1. Wildlife watching--Africa, Sub-Saharan--Guidebooks. 2. Safaris--Africa, Sub-Saharan--Guidebooks. 3. National parks and reserves--Africa, Sub-Saharan--Guidebooks. 4. Africa, Sub-Saharan--Guidebooks. I. Title.

QL337.S78 N65 2002
916.7'0433--dc21

2002034183

Printed in the United States of America
Distributed by Publishers Group West.
Exclusive distributor to East and Southern Africa:
Russell Friedman Books CC, PO Box 73, Midrand 1685, South Africa
Tel: +27 11 7022300 • Fax: +27 11 7021403 • email: rfbooks@iafrica.com

The Africa Adventure Company

Dear Reader:

I developed a strong passion for Africa on my first visit to this amazing continent over 25 years ago. Perhaps I was drawn to the "Cradle of Mankind" by a subconscious desire to travel back to the land of our roots — to see the continent's landscape, to hear the sounds and savor the smells that would evoke impressions of "what the world was once like." Since then I have returned countless times and have enjoyed traveling with and sharing my love for Africa with my wife and our two children.

As President of The Africa Adventure Company, I have also had the pleasure over the last 17 years of sending many people from all walks of life on photo safaris. Why do so many people wish to go to Africa, and why do so many return time and time again after experiencing a well-planned safari? Many seek the wonderful, pristine wilderness in which wildlife still abounds in a natural and exciting environment. Others seek contact with vast, open spaces and traditional African cultures, which can have a meaningful effect on the human spirit — stirring and stimulating the senses, relaxing and revitalizing the mind. Visiting Africa means going back in time and feeling the thrill of experiencing something entirely different from the world in which we live.

One of the main allures of Africa is that you can find adventure there. When you go on a game viewing activity, you never know what you're going to see or what is going to happen. Every safari is exciting. With the right assistance and guidance from an expert in African travel, it doesn't matter if you go on a tented or lodge safari, a luxury or participation safari, a hot-air balloon ride, a walking safari, a canoe safari or go white-water rafting — there's no finer adventure!

There is no better time to venture to Africa than the present, because more and more of the world's wildlife is becoming threatened. We may be the last generation to see Africa in its true glory — huge herds of wildlife and tribal cultures living unaffected lifestyles.

Going on a photographic safari is a donation, in itself, toward conserving African wilderness regions and wildlife, because tourism gives jobs and economic incentives to preserve wildlife to governments and many people who live near the reserves. Tourism, if properly managed, can influence change for the good — allowing the next generation the opportunity to enjoy the same adventures. A safari to Africa could be the most enjoyable and rewarding environmental donation you will ever make!

Sincerely,

Mark W. Nolting, *President*
The Africa Adventure Company

P.S. To plan your safari with us and for more information on The Africa Adventure Company, please see the following pages.

DEDICATION

To my two sons, Miles and Nicholas,

through whose eyes I have been blessed in

experiencing yet another wonderful dimension

of Africa – and of life.

AN INVITATION:

Before booking your trip to Africa, contact us at
The Africa Adventure Company
toll-free at 1-800-882-9453

(U.S.A. and Canada) or (954) 491-8877

on the web at www.AfricanAdventure.com

or email us at noltingaac@aol.com
to discuss the many safari options we have to offer.
Call today — my expert staff and I would love to
assist you in planning your safari!

The Africa Adventure Company

Dear Adventurer:

With so much information readily available on the internet, many prospective travelers are overwhelmed and, indeed, confused over the wide range of safari options available.

This is where the expertise of The Africa Adventure Company staff is invaluable. They can help clarify the important issues and guide you through the information quagmire to the best safari experience (and away from the marginal ones) — separating the marketing "hype" from reality. Because The Africa Adventure Company does not own any camps or lodges in Africa, they are free to recommend the properties that will provide you with the best experience, based on your interests.

"The key," explains Mark, "is to understand the personal experience an individual wants to have in Africa and to match that experience with the optimum itinerary, one that is specifically designed to the traveler's needs, wants and desires. This can best be accomplished only if the person advising the traveler has extensive on-site experience in all the top safari countries. No amount of office training can substitute for actually having been there.

"Once we have a good feeling for what our clients want," Mark continues, "we then recommend the African countries that can best provide that experience, along with the best parks and reserves within those countries. Only then do we pick a few safari options or create special itineraries for our clients to consider, and we add specific hotels, lodges, camps, or mobile tented accommodations, and safari activities that we feel would be of greatest interest to them. Doing anything less would be compromising the best interests of our clients.

"We frankly feel we are the best company in the world for discerning travelers who are looking to join small group safaris or those who prefer private safaris to Africa. Our books demonstrate our level of knowledge on the subject. Our passion for Africa and our overwhelming desire to provide life-changing, exciting experiences for travelers says the rest.

"Our goal, adds Mark, "is not to have you travel with us on a safari — it is for you to become a member of our extended "family" — to have you book return safaris with us to Africa again and again. The only way to accomplish that goal is to give you the best possible experience and value the first time around.

Prices of programs begin at around $3,500 per person (land and air from North America) for a 12-day safari.

Dispense with the uncertainties of traveling to Africa. Save yourself and your energies for the thrill of your African adventure ... let Mark and the friendly safari advisers of The Africa Adventure Company go to work for you, just as they have done for many happy, satisfied "safariers."

It's easy to start planning your safari. Simply call toll-free (from the United States and Canada), 1-800-882-9453 (1-800-882-WILD) or (954) 491-8877, fax us at (954) 491-9060. Email us directly at noltingaac@aol.com, or visit our website at www.AfricanAdventure.com and email us a completed questionnaire. You'll soon be off to Africa!

The Africa Adventure Company

5353 N. Federal Hwy., Suite 300, Ft. Lauderdale, FL 33308 U.S.A.
Tel: (954) 491-8877
Tel. Toll-Free (USA & Canada): 1 (800) 882-9453
Fax: (954) 491-9060
Email address: noltingaac@aol.com
Visit our website at www.AfricanAdventure.com

Other Books by Mark W. Nolting

African Safari Journal

Fourth Edition

The *African Safari Journal* is the perfect book to take on safari as it is a wildlife/botany guide, trip organizer, safari directory, phrasebook, safari diary, map directory and wildlife checklist all in one! (See page 685 for details.)

CONTENTS

CALL OF THE WILD

CALL OF THE WILD

Feature films like *The Serengeti* (Imax), *Out of Africa*, *African Queen* and *Gorillas in the Mist*, along with countless documentaries, have kindled in the hearts of many people the flame of desire for travel to Africa.

A visit to Africa allows you to experience nature at its finest — almost devoid of human interference, living according to a natural rhythm of life that has remained basically unchanged since the beginning of time.

At our deepest roots, the African continent communicates with our souls. Travelers return home, not only with exciting stories and adventures to share with friends and family, but with a better understanding of nature, a feeling of accomplishment, increased self-confidence and broader horizons from having ventured where few have gone. Here's the kind of adventure about which many dream but few experience!

Having visited Africa once, you will want to return again and again to the peace, tranquility and adventure it has to offer. In this book, I invite you to explore the reasons for this ceaseless pull as we journey to some of the most fascinating places on earth.

The time to visit Africa is now. Despite a network of large wildlife reserves, Africa's poverty threatens natural habitats and the wildlife

they contain, as people look for ways to get ahead. Only viable eco-tourism initiatives — where local communities reap benefits from foreign income generated by lodges and entry fees to parks — can provide an alternative to short-term poaching, the growing of subsistence crops on marginal land, or selling out to multinational companies that transform entire landscapes in sterile mono-cultures. Most of Africa's people cherish their rich cultural background, yet they also yearn for material development. The challenge is to make room for both. Many of the localities featured in this book will provide you with an opportunity to see wildlife in abundance and also to meet people whose ancestors have been co-existing with nature for thousands of years. But the pressure is on, and the time to go is now, while Africa can still deliver all that it promises — and more!

Africa has such a tremendous variety of attractions that most everyone can find something fascinating to do. In addition to fabulous wildlife, the continent boasts one of the world's largest waterfalls (Victoria Falls), the world's longest river (the Nile), the world's largest inland delta (the Okavango), the world's largest intact volcanic caldera (Ngorongoro), the world's highest mountain that is not part of a range (Kilimanjaro) and beautiful cites like Cape Town. Africa is also home to some of the world's last and largest animal migrations.

Africa is huge. It is the second largest continent on earth, covering over 20% of the planet's land surface. More than three times the size of the United States, it is also larger than Europe, the United States and China combined. No wonder it has so much to offer!

HOW TO USE THIS BOOK

Africa's Top Wildlife Countries highlights and compares wildlife reserves and other major attractions in the continent's best game viewing countries.

Most people travel to Africa to see the large and spectacular wildlife, unique to this fascinating continent, in its natural surroundings. In addition to lion, elephant, rhino and giraffe, there is an amazing array of other large mammals, as well as spectacular birds and a tapestry of compelling cultures. The finest safaris are not only those that provide the thrill of seeing the big mammals, but also explore the whole ecosystem and capture the true spirit of the African wilderness —

SOUTH, EAST AND CENTRAL AFRICA

making your visit an exciting and educational experience. The combination of unforgettable adventures, great food, service, accommodations and meeting interesting people is the perfect formula for the trip of a lifetime!

This book is based on over 25 years of first-hand experience and makes planning your adventure of a lifetime easy. It is designed to help you decide the best place or places to go in Africa to do what you want to do, when you want to do it, in a manner of travel that suits you.

Using the easy-to-read **When's The Best Time To Go For Game Viewing** chart (see inside front cover), you can conveniently choose the specific reserves and country(ies) that are best to visit during your vacation period. From the **What Wildlife Is Best Seen Where** chart (see inside back cover), you can easily locate the reserves that have an abundance of the animals you wish to see most. From the **Safari Activities** chart (see page 43), you can choose the reserves that offer the safari options that interest you most. From the **Rainfall and Temperature** charts (see pages 58-59), you can decide how best to dress for safari and have an idea of what weather to expect.

The **Safari Glossary** (see page 633) contains words commonly used on safari and defines words used throughout the book. English is the major language in most of the countries covered in this guide, so language is, in fact, not a problem for English-speaking visitors.

The **Safari Pages** (a safari directory - see page 591) provide a veritable gold mine of difficult-to-find information and sources on Africa, including in-depth discussions on birdwatching, fishing, photography, and what to wear and take on safari. The **Suggested Reading List** (see page 641) includes over 100 publications on the wildlife, cultures, landscapes and history of sub-Saharan Africa.

The safari countries are divided between East and Central Africa and Southern Africa and, in general, appear in their order of desirability as safari destinations. The most important safari countries are Tanzania, Kenya and Uganda in East Africa, and Botswana, Zimbabwe, Zambia, Namibia and South Africa in Southern Africa.

To get the most out of this book, first read through this introduction ("Call of the Wild"). Next, read the chapter or chapters on the countries that you feel offer the kind of experience you are looking for in Africa. Then call us at The Africa Adventure Company (toll-free 1-800-882-9453 in the United States and Canada or 954-491-8877 from other countries) to discuss your thoughts. We will match the experience you are looking for with a fabulous safari program — putting you on track to experience the safari of your dreams.

WHAT IS A SAFARI LIKE?

"Alephaant, allephanntt," the Masai softly said as he escorted us to dinner one evening. Neither of us could understand him until he shined his flashlight on a tree-sized elephant browsing not 50 feet (15 m) from where we stood. It was then I realized why we were requested to wait for the spear-wielding Masai, who was assigned to our tent, to escort us to dinner. The pathway to the dining tent was covered with giant pizza-sized footprints that were not there 45 minutes earlier.

The intimate dining tent was filled with people from the four corners of the earth, reveling in camaraderie and sumptuous cuisine by candlelight. An excellent selection of wines and desserts complemented the meal.

After dinner we sat around a roaring fire, listening to bush lore from our entertaining host. The night was alive with the sounds and scents of the Africa we had dreamed of — the untamed wilderness where man is but a temporary guest and not a controller of nature. Only then did we retire to our comfortable, deluxe tent with ensuite bathroom to sleep the gentle sleep that comes with a sigh of contentment.

What is a typical day on safari? Most safaris are centered on guests participating in two activities per day, such as morning and afternoon game drives in four-wheel-drive (4wd) vehicles or minivans. A game drive consists of having your guide drive you around a park or reserve in search of wildlife. Your guide helps you to interpret and understand what you are seeing in the bush.

Most activities last two to five hours and are conducted when the wildlife is most active: early in the morning (often before breakfast), just after breakfast, in the late afternoon and at night (where allowed by park authorities). Midday activities might include spending time in a "hide" observing wildlife, lazing around the swimming pool, reading, visiting a local village or school, birdwatching or viewing game as it passes by your tent or lodge, or taking a nap. After an exhilarating day on safari, many guests return to revel in the day's adventures over exquisite European or Pan-African cuisine in lodges and camps that range from comfortable to extremely luxurious.

The kind and quality of experience you may have on safari vary greatly from country to country, and even from park to park within the same country. For instance, going on safari in East Africa (Kenya and Tanzania) is almost always completely different from going on safari in Southern Africa (Botswana, Zimbabwe and Zambia).

Simply watching wildlife from a vehicle anywhere in Africa is an experience in itself. However, more and more people prefer to personally experience more from the safari than simply watching animals.

How can that be accomplished? By choosing a safari that includes parks and reserves that are not crowded and offer more of a feeling of being in the bush. Choose reserves that allow you to participate in activities that make you a more integral part of the safari, like walking, boating and canoeing. Choose smaller camps and lodges that are unfenced and that allow wildlife to walk freely about the grounds.

Depending on the park or reserve, safari activities might include day game drives, night game drives, walks, boat safaris, canoeing, kayaking, white-water rafting, ballooning, hiking, mountain climbing, fishing, horseback riding, African elephant-back riding — the options are almost endless. See "Safari Activities" and the **Safari Activities Chart** which follow.

In terms of the long-term future of Africa's wildlife reserves, it is important to consider selecting a lodge destination from which local people benefit in tangible ways. To be guided by or to meet happy people from various cultures, and to learn about their customs, will greatly enhance your trip to Africa.

Another excellent way to get the most out of your adventure is to have a private safari arranged for you. Why? A private safari immediately becomes *your* safari. You do not have to bow to the wishes of the majority of the group or a strictly set itinerary of group departures. With your guide, you are basically free to explore your own interests, spend as much time as you want photographing particular animals, and generally do things at a pace that suits you.

To gain a better understanding of what you might experience on safari, I suggest you read the trip reports in "Bush Tails" (see page 675).

DISPELLING MYTHS ABOUT TRAVEL ON THE "DARK CONTINENT"

Many prospective travelers to Africa seem to think that, if they go on an African safari, they may have to stay in mud or grass huts or little pup tents, eat strange foods and have dozens of vaccinations. Nothing could be farther from the truth!

Almost all of the top parks and reserves covered in this guide have deluxe or first class (Class A+, A or A/B by our grading system) lodges or camps (with ensuite bathrooms) that serve excellent food, specifically designed to cater to the discerning traveler's needs. Going on safari can be a very comfortable, fun-filled adventure!

Many prospective travelers to Africa have voiced their fear of being overwhelmed by mosquitoes and other insects or the fear of encountering snakes on safari. However, most travelers return pleasantly surprised, having found that insects or snakes are a greater problem in their own neighborhoods than on safari.

The fact is that most safaris do not take place in the jungle, but on open savannah during the dry season, when the insect populations are at a minimum. In addition, the best time to go on safari, for most of the countries, is during their winter, which is when many snakes hibernate. Also, many parks are located over 3,000 feet (915 m) in altitude, resulting in cool to cold nights, further reducing the presence of any pests. In any case, except for walking safaris, most all of your time in the bush will be spent in the safety of a vehicle or boat. Although some vaccinations are recommended, they are actually not required for travel to many of the top wildlife areas.

ECOTOURS

Several years ago, the terms "ecotour" and "ecotourism" hit the travel industry like cholesterol hit the food industry. Many new companies have sprung up to claim that their new ecotours are eco-friendly and implying that they have pioneered this type of travel. However, many tour companies have been conducting eco-sensitive tours for years, without the eco-hype.

Ecotours have a very low impact on the environment. Travelers take photos and leave little more than footprints. True ecotourism ensures that the local people, who living adjacent to parks and reserves, benefit directly from tourism in such a way that they have a positive incentive to preserve wildlife and the environment; CAMPFIRE projects in Zimbabwe and camps like Ndumo and Rocktail Bay (South Africa), Damaraland (Namibia) or Klein's Camp (Tanzania) are excellent examples of the ecotour strategy. For additional information on conservation and ecotourism, please see "Conservation in Africa" in "The Safari Pages."

SECURITY

Since September 11th, concerns over security have become an issue for some travelers. I know of no incidents where tourists traveling in the top wildlife countries covered in this guide were affected by the Gulf War, trouble in the Middle East, or, to date, the war in Afghanistan. Kabul, for instance, is closer to London than it is to Johannesburg (5,000 miles/8000 km). In addition, safari camps and lodges cater to people from all over the world and are, in almost all cases, owned by non-American or non-British companies. One of the safest places in the world has to be in the African bush!

CHOOSING ACCOMMODATIONS

There is a great variety of styles and levels of comfort in accommodation available in the major cities and while on safari, and they range from simple bungalows to extravagant suites with private swimming pools. Options include hotels, lodges, small camps with chalets or bungalows, houseboats, fixed tented camps and mobile tented safaris.

The type of accommodation included in a tour of Africa will have a major influence on the type of experience and adventures you will have on safari.

An important factor to consider when choosing accommodations or a tour is the size of the lodge or camp. In general, guests receive more personal attention at smaller camps and lodges than at larger ones.

Large properties tend to stick to a set schedule, while smaller properties are often more willing to amend their schedules according to the preferences of their guests. However, larger accommodations tend to be less expensive, which makes tours using the larger ones more affordable.

Many larger lodges and permanent tented camps (especially in Kenya) are surrounded by electrical fences, allowing guests to move about as they please without fear of bumping into elephant and other dangerous wildlife. Travelers (including myself) who enjoy having wildlife roaming about camp should seek properties that are not fenced; these lodges and camps are best for travelers who want to experience nature at close quarters.

Many properties in Kenya and Tanzania have 50-200 beds (while several have under 20 beds), whereas most camps in Botswana, Zambia and Zimbabwe have 20 beds or fewer.

HOTELS AND HOTEL CLASSIFICATIONS

Many African cities, such as Nairobi (Kenya), Harare (Zimbabwe), Johannesburg and Cape Town (South Africa) have four- and five-star (first class and deluxe) hotels that are comparable to lodging anywhere in the world, with air-conditioning and ensuite facilities, swimming pools and one or more excellent restaurants and bars.

Hotels are categorized as Deluxe, First Class and Tourist Class. The phrases "ensuite facilities," "facilities ensuite" and "ensuite rooms" mean bathrooms (toilet and basin plus shower and/or bathtub) are connected to the sleeping rooms/tents. "Private facilities" means that bathrooms are exclusive to guests but are not connected to the sleeping rooms/tents. "Separate facilities" means that bathrooms are separate from the sleeping quarters, and may, in some cases, be shared by guests from more than one room/tent.

DELUXE: An excellent hotel, rooms with ensuite bathroom (toilet plus shower and/or bathtub), air-conditioning, one or more restaurants that serve very good food, and that feature a swimming pool, bars, lounges, room service — all the amenities of a four- or five-star international hotel.

FIRST CLASS: A very comfortable hotel, rooms with ensuite facilities, air-conditioning, at least one restaurant and bar, and most have a swimming pool.

The Victoria Falls Hotel, the grand colonial style of a bygone era.

TOURIST CLASS: A comfortable hotel with simple rooms with ensuite facilities, most with air-conditioning, a restaurant and bar, and most with a swimming pool.

LODGES AND CAMPS

Lodges that range from comfortable to deluxe (many have swimming pools) are located in or near most parks and reserves. Many lodges and camps are located in wildlife areas 3,000 feet (915 m) or more above sea level, so air-conditioning often is not necessary.

There is often confusion over the term "camp." A camp often refers to lodging in chalets, bungalows or tents found in a remote location. Camps range from very basic to extremely plush. Deluxe camps often have better service and food, and most certainly a truer safari atmosphere, than large lodges and hotels.

Permanent tented camps (sometimes also called fixed tented camps) are camps that are not moved. Aside from generally having better food and service than lodges, guests of tented camps have more of a "safari" experience. They are less isolated from the environment than those who stay in a lodge, and can, for instance, hear the sounds of the wild from inside their tent because the walls are made of canvas. Mobile tented camps are discussed below under "Types of Safaris."

Lounge setting of a camp or lodge, designed with local materials.

LODGE AND CAMP CLASSIFICATIONS

Lodges and tented camps are classified as Class A+ to F. Accommodations have been primarily graded on facilities, food and service. However, the overall experience, including quality of the guides and management as well as the location of the properties and quality of game viewing, have also, in some cases, been taken into account. For instance, a lodge that might be rated "A+" for accommodations but is in a poor game-viewing area might be rated "A".

Keep in mind that a lower-class accommodation may be preferable over a higher-class one if the lower-class option offers better guides and management, a better location and/or preferable activities.

CLASS A+: An extremely luxurious lodge or permanent tented camp (five-star) with superb cuisine and excellent service, most all with swimming pools, and some with private "plunge" pools (small swimming pools) for each chalet or tent. Lodges and chalets are air-conditioned, while tents are usually fan-cooled.

CLASS A: A deluxe lodge or tented camp, most with swimming pools, excellent food and service, large nicely appointed rooms or tents with ensuite facilities, comfortable beds and tasteful decor; the

A typical "Class A" permanent tented camp accommodation.

lodges may have air-conditioning and the tents are usually fan-cooled.

CLASS A/B: An excellent lodge or tented camp with very good food and service, ensuite bathrooms, and many have swimming pools. The rooms/tents are of good size but perhaps not as large as "Class A" properties.

CLASS B: A comfortable lodge or camp with good food and service, ensuite bathrooms, and many have swimming pools

CLASS B/C: Most often, a "Class B" property is one that is very rustic or somewhat inconsistent in the quality of accommodation, food and service, most with ensuite bathrooms.

CLASS C: A simple lodge with private bathrooms; a tented camp, chalet or bungalow with ensuite, private or shared facilities and fair food and service; or a "Class B" structure with fair to poor food or service.

CLASS D: A basic lodge or tented camp (lodges, chalets, bungalows and tents seldom have ensuite or private bathrooms) or a "Class C" structure with poor food or service. There may be a restaurant, or it may be "self-catering."

Dining on safari is one of the highlights!

CLASS F: A very basic lodge or tented camp with separate bathrooms; often self-catering (no restaurant).

FOOD ON SAFARI

Excellent cuisine, along with interesting local dishes, are served in the top hotels, lodges, camps and restaurants. French cuisine is primarily served in Rwanda, the Congo and Burundi. European cuisine predominates in the other countries covered in this guide. However, some of the more expensive lodges now produce a combination of "Pan-African cuisine" — innovative recipes and ingredients from across the continent, and international fare. Restaurants serving cuisines from all over the world may be found in the larger cities in Africa.

Most international travelers are impressed with the quality of the food and drink served on their safari. The fresh air will give you a healthy appetite. Typical meals include:

Breakfast — Usually fruit and cereal, eggs, bacon and sausage, toast and preserves, tea and coffee

Lunch — Assorted cold meats and salads with cheeses and bread

Dinner — Normally three courses, with an appetizer or soup, main entree and vegetables, and a dessert. Class A+ (and some Class A) lodges and camps may serve four or more courses.

Some safari camps and lodges will provide a light breakfast of tea, coffee, rusks (hard biscuits traditionally served in southern Africa), and cereal in the early morning. Brunch is served at about 11:00 a.m. and follows a game drive or other activity. Tea, coffee, cake and biscuits (cookies) are served at about 3:30 p.m. Following the afternoon game activity, guests return to the lodge for a delicious dinner.

GAME VIEWING

While on safari, you will enjoy the attention and input of one or more guides, whose job is to make sure that you have a safe, enjoyable and enlightening experience. Although you will be in capable hands, the more you know before setting off, the more you will get out of the experience.

Background reading is perhaps the most important, although speaking to somebody who has been to the area that you intend to visit can be invaluable in giving you an idea of what you might experience. This book is packed with information on the best safari destinations on the continent, as is the companion, *African Safari Journal*, and there are several other useful books available.

Your desire to visit Africa may very well have been triggered by a *National Geographic* or a David Attenborough documentary film. This is all very well, but you should not expect to see everything in the way in which the films, the best of which take years to make, depict. Part of enjoying your safari is having a realistic expectation, and you should always remember that wildlife is just that, it's wild! With the exception of the most common birds and herbivorous mammals, nothing can be guaranteed on safari — and that, really, is the thrill of it. It is the anticipation and chance that makes getting up each morning, and driving around each bend, so enthralling.

Get to know what the animals you can expect to see in a particular area look like by purchasing a good field guide, such as *African Mammals* by Jonathan Kingdon (Academic Press), well in advance. A few nights of bedtime browsing — or a few hours on the airplane

— will give you a head start. Obtain good maps of the countries and areas you'll be visiting, and read up on the local cultures. This will not only increase your awareness of the geography before and during your visit, but will better enable you to relate your experiences to family or friends when you return. For a catalog of difficult-to-find maps and reference guides on Africa, please see the catalog at the back of this book.

It is most important to develop a good relationship with your guide from the outset. Bear in mind that a good guide will know not only the area and its wildlife, but the best ways to reveal them to you. Make sure that you state your expectations clearly from the word go, and do not be shy to get involved in each day's routine, when appropriate. If you have seen enough lions for one day, for example, let your guide know that you would like to look for other species, or perhaps ask him or her to just park at a scenic lookout so that you can enjoy the space and serenity of the wilderness while enjoying a cool drink.

It is vital that you do not spend your whole safari charging about looking only for big game. The idea is to get an understanding and appreciation for the whole ecosystem, of which termites and fig trees play as big a role as elephants and lions. Developing an interest in birds, reptiles and trees means that you'll never be bored, for wherever you stop or pause, there will be something fascinating to see. The most pitiful thing to come across on safari is someone who has spent all day in the bush and says that he has "seen nothing"!

Consideration for wildlife should always take priority on safari. Good guides and trackers are sensitive to wildlife and approach particular species only to a certain distance. On the other hand, there are guides who believe that the best view is the closest view. Unfortunately, such an approach often prompts animals to stop their natural behavior and depart the scene. It is far better to watch a mother cheetah peacefully suckling her cubs from a hundred yards than it is to drive alongside the animals and perhaps force them to stop feeding and retreat. Lion and elephant are generally more tolerant of close approaches by vehicles than other animals, but even then, it is preferable to always allow wildlife to move in whichever direction it pleases and not for it to be compromised by safari vehicles. If you

feel that your guide has approached an animal too close
know that you would be more comfortable giving the an
space. One of the richest wildlife experiences is to watc.. animals
from a comfortable distance, and then depart without having been
detected.

Ask your guide to switch off the vehicle engine periodically, so you
can hear the sounds of the bush. It is quite remarkable just how many
birds and other creatures make an appearance if you'll simply stop,
listen and wait. Many guides detect leopards and other predators by
listening out for the distinctive alarm calls of monkeys, squirrels and
francolin.

Getting to know animal tracks adds another dimension to your safari,
and a good guide or tracker will point out the different species and
any interactions that can be "read" in the sand.

If you are staying at a lodge or permanent tented camp, in most cases
the game drives and other activities have been scheduled during the
best wildlife viewing times. Invariably, the heat of the day is spent
resting at the camp, because most animals are relatively inactive
between 11:00 a.m. and 3:00 p.m. If you are on safari in a national
park, it is often worthwhile to spend the midday hours quietly
parked at a waterhole because rhino, elephant and others may arrive
to bathe or quench their thirst.

An excellent pair of binoculars is more important than a good camera; each person on safari should have his or her own pair. For additional advice, please see "Safari Tips" in the "Safari Pages."

TYPES OF SAFARIS

LODGE AND PERMANENT TENTED CAMP SAFARIS
Lodge safaris are simply safaris that use lodges or permanent tented
camps as accommodations. Some safaris mix lodges with tented
camps or camps with chalets or bungalows, providing a greater range
of experiences for their guests.

MOBILE TENTED CAMP SAFARIS
Private and group mobile tented camp safaris are, in my opinion, one
of the best ways to experience the bush and a great way of getting off
the beaten track.

Sleeping tents used on a typical First Class Mobile Tented Camp Safari.

Seeing hippo grazing by your tent at night or elephant walking through your camp by day is an experience not to be missed! When under the protection of a professional guide, this is not as dangerous as it might sound. Animals will not try to enter a closed tent unless tempted by the smell of food. If you keep the tent flaps closed at night and you don't have food in your tent, you are generally just as safe as if you were staying in a bungalow or chalet. Tanzania, Zimbabwe and Botswana are excellent countries for mobile tented safaris; Kenya, Zambia and Namibia are also good destinations for this type of safari.

Mobile tented safaris range from deluxe to first class, midrange, limited participation and participation safaris. You may join a group departure or have a private safari, depending on your interests and budget. **Warning**: some tour operators advertise their mobile tented camp safaris as "luxury" when they actually operate them on a first class or even a midrange level (ie. small tents with shower and toilet tents separate from the sleeping tents). Instead of stating the actual internal floor dimensions of the tent, some operators give the size of the fly sheet over the tent, which is very misleading. Be sure to be perfectly clear as to what services they provide!

Deluxe Mobile Tented Camp Safaris
Deluxe mobile tented camp safaris are the epitome of mobile safaris. The sleeping tents are large (approx. 12-by-18 ft./4-by-5.5 m in floor

area) and have ensuite bush (bucket) showers and bush (short-drop) toilets. Food and service are excellent. Camp attendants take care of everything, including the delivery of hot water for your shower. Campsites are private and usually set in remote areas of parks and reserves, providing a true *Out of Africa* experience. For a party of four, the cost generally ranges from $400-$850 per person per day.

First Class Mobile Tented Camp Safaris

These are similar to deluxe safaris except that the tents are a little smaller (approx. 8-by-12 ft./2.5-by-3.5 m), yet very comfortable; less expensive cutlery and crockery may be used, there are not quite as many staff, and there is usually a bush shower (hot water) and bush toilet tent attached to the back of each sleeping tent. The food and service is still very good, and private campsites are used. For a party of four, the cost is around $300-$400 per person per day, depending on the country and season.

Midrange Mobile Tented Camp Safaris

Comfortable (and less expensive) midrange mobile tented safaris are available in a number of countries. Like deluxe and first class mobile tented safaris, camp staff take care of all the chores. The difference is that the tents are smaller (approx. 8-by-8 ft./2.5-by-2.5 m) but are still tall enough in which to stand. The food and service are good, and guests from one to three sleeping tents may share one separate toilet tent and one separate shower tent (with hot water). Private or group campsites may be used. For a party of four, the cost is usually around $200-$250 per person per day.

Limited Participation Mobile Tented Camp Safaris

On these safaris, the guide usually has one camp attendant to do the heavy work, while guests are expected to assist in some camp chores. Bow-type nylon tents (approx. 8-by-8 ft./2.5-by-2.5 m) are often used, and you usually camp in group campsites. Rates are usually around $150-$200 per person per day.

Full Participation Mobile Tented Camp Safaris

On full participation mobile tented safaris, participants are required to help with all of the camp chores. Group campsites with basic (if any) facilities are often used.

A group on a scheduled departure, Southern Africa.

The advantage is price. Participation camping safaris are almost always less expensive than lodge safaris. However, these are recommended for only hardy travelers with previous camping experience or with a sense of adventure. Most participants are under 45 years of age. Hot showers are usually available most nights, but not all. The cost is usually under $100 per person per day. The problem with these low-end safaris is that the guiding is often marginal at best, greatly compromising the quality of the experience.

GUIDED DRIVING OR MOBILE SAFARIS
Driving safaris are simply safaris in which guests are driven by their driver/guide from reserve to reserve. You generally have the same guide throughout the safari, who should have very good knowledge of all the parks and reserves to be visited.

Driving safaris are usually less expensive than flying safaris (see below). However, travelers should take into account the amount of time it takes to get from reserve to reserve, the quality of the roads and whether or not there will be something enroute that will be of interest to them, and compare that to the cost of doing some or all flying on their safari.

FLYING SAFARIS
Flying safaris are safaris in which guests are flown to or near the wildlife reserves that are to be visited. They are then usually picked up at the airport or airstrip upon arrival and driven to their camp or lodge — which is usually a game drive in itself.

Flying between wildlife parks is part and parcel of the experience.

Guides and vehicles are based at the camps and lodges at which guests will be staying. A real advantage is that the resident guides should have intimate knowledge of the area because they are usually based in the same camp for the season.

This type of safari is very popular in Botswana, Zimbabwe, Zambia, Namibia, Kenya and Tanzania. Time that would normally be spent on the road driving between the parks and reserves may instead be spent game viewing — the primary reason why most people travel to Africa in the first place!

FLY/DRIVE SAFARIS

As the name implies, these safaris are a combination of some driving and some flying. The general idea is to fly over areas that are not interesting to drive or that you have already covered on the ground, and drive through the areas that have the most to offer. This is an excellent option in northern Tanzania, for instance, where safariers may be driven from Arusha to Tarangire, Lake Manyara, Ngorongoro Crater and the Serengeti, and then fly back to Arusha instead of driving the same route back.

GROUP SAFARIS

Group safaris are, in many cases, a more cost-effective way of experiencing the bush than private safaris (see below). Group safaris usually have scheduled departure dates. The key for group safaris in Africa is to be sure the group size is small. Group size preferably

Traveling as a group?

should be limited, in my opinion, to 12 or fewer passengers, whereas a maximum of six to eight is preferable.

It never ceases to amaze me the number of tour operators that tout that their maximum group size is limited to only 16, 24 or 30 members. With such large groups, passengers in the lead vehicle see game, while those in the vehicles that follow eat dust. A great deal of time is wasted getting under way and time schedules are very inflexible. Large group tours may be fine for Europe or Asia, but they have no place in the African bush!

PRIVATE SAFARIS

For those who wish to avoid groups, a private safari is highly recommended for several reasons.

An itinerary can be specially designed according to the kind of experience YOU want, visiting the parks and reserves YOU wish to see most, and traveling on dates that suit YOU best.

You may spend your time doing what you want to do rather than having to compromise with the group. If you wish, you may socialize with other travelers at mealtimes and still have the flexibility to do what you want on your game activities.

For instance, if you find a leopard up a tree with a kill, yc
five minutes or five hours at that location — it's up to yot

What few people realize is that, in many cases, a private safari need
not cost more than one with a large group. In fact, I have sent many
couples and small groups on private safaris for not much more (and
sometimes less) than the cost of group safaris from other tour operators who offer the same or often inferior itineraries.

If you find that difficult to believe, call, email or write us with what
you have in mind, and we'll be happy to send you an itinerary (see
introduction pages).

SPECIALIST GUIDED SAFARIS

In various parts of the continent, the idea of going on safari with a
specialist guide is gaining popularity. Recognized experts in particular subjects, such as elephants, predators, birds, nature photography
or trees, lead or accompany a safari — concentrating on the aspect
that they have most knowledge of, but also providing a good all
round safari. Book authors, respected conservationists, photographers and artists are among the personalities who lead such safaris,
but a growing number of local, resident guides are becoming specialists on particular aspects of their own environment. The additional experience gained by having one of the top guides in Africa
lead your safari is almost priceless.

HONEYMOON SAFARIS

There is no more romantic setting for a honeymoon than an African
safari. Most honeymooners begin with a few days to relax and recov-
er from the wedding in a five-star hotel or beach resort — then it's off
on safari!

Honeymoon safaris, like all safaris, can include as plush or rustic
accommodations, as you wish. Most camps and small lodges have a
"honeymoon tent" or "honeymoon suite" on the premises to ensure
maximum privacy. Please keep in mind that most tented camps and
small lodges have two single beds per room/tent, so be sure to have
your tour operator let them know you are indeed honeymooners.

The epitome of a honeymoon safari, in my opinion, is a private
mobile tented and lodge safari, with a private guide. Tenting at a
remote, private campsite is truly the *Out of Africa* experience!

Mark, Alison, Miles and Nicholas Nolting on a family game drive, Masai, Mara.

My romantic honeymoon included visiting Victoria Falls and Hwange National Park (Zimbabwe), a private reserve near Kruger National Park, Rovos Rail and Cape Town (South Africa), and the Seychelles. What an exciting way to begin a life together!

FAMILY SAFARIS

More and more parents and grandparents are taking their children and grandchildren on safari. Seeing nature in all its abundance as a child is an experience that cannot be underestimated. As of this writing, our son Miles is eight years old, and has been on five safaris; Nicholas is five and has been on three safaris. We have thoroughly enjoyed experiencing Africa through their eyes. Needless to say, the kids have also had a wonderful time filled with exploration and adventure!

In most cases, the best option for families is a private safari with your own vehicle(s) and guide(s). You may travel at your own pace and choose camps and lodges that offer amenities, like swimming pools, that will provide the kids with some play time as well as help them burn off some of that endless energy they seem to possess. In addition, visits to local schools and villages provide insights into how children of their own age live in the countries you are visiting — and will hopefully make them more thankful for what they have!

Most guides, camp and lodge staff love to have children visit, and they go out of their way to make kids and the parents feel welcome. Be sure to plan into your trips some activities that your children enjoy.

Many of the smaller camps and lodges in Africa have minimum age restrictions (ranging from seven to 16 years of age) while most of the larger camps and lodges have no restrictions at all. Some camps and lodges have minimum age restrictions (12 or 16 years old) for activities offered, such as walks in the bush with professional guides and canoeing. However, if, for instance, your family or group takes over the entire lodge, camp or canoe safari departure, or if you do a private mobile safari, you can, in most instances, get around the minimum age requirements. As some safari camps and lodges cater to a maximum of six to 20 guests, taking over a camp may be easier than you think. Just try to book your safari well in advance to ensure availability.

SELF-DRIVE SAFARIS
In Africa, self-drive safaris are a viable option for general sightseeing in countries such as South Africa that have excellent road systems. However, self-drive safaris into wildlife parks and reserves are, in general, not a good idea for several reasons.

One major disadvantage of a self-drive safari is that you miss the information and experience that a professional driver/guide can provide. A good guide is also an excellent wildlife spotter and knows when and where to look for the animals you want to see most. In many cases, he or she can communicate with other guides to find out where the wildlife has most recently been seen. This also leaves you free to concentrate on photography and game viewing instead of worrying about the road, and it eliminates the anxiety of the possibility of getting lost.

Self-drive safaris, especially ones requiring 4wd vehicles, are most often more expensive than joining a group safari. Gas (petrol) is generally several times the cost of what it is in North America. Vehicle rental costs are also high, and the driving is often on the left side of the road.

Finally, self-drive safaris by people without extensive experience in the bush can be dangerous. Lack of knowledge about wildlife and the bush can result in life-threatening situations.

Game viewing from a mini-van with a pop-top roof.

Carnet de Passage is required by most countries to take your own vehicle across borders without paying import duty or leaving a deposit with customs; a carnet must be purchased before arrival.

An International Driver's License is required by some of the countries covered in this book. Contact the tourist offices, consulates, or embassies of the countries in which you wish to drive for any additional requirements.

OVERLAND SAFARIS
Overland safaris may cover several countries and last from around six weeks to nine months. Participants usually take care of all the chores and sleep in small pup tents. In addition to the initial cost of the trip, travelers must contribute to a "food kitty." Because many of these safaris originate in Europe, where they load up with supplies, only a small amount of the money spent for the safari reaches the local people. A lack of local infusion of funds places this type of safari very low on the ecotourism scale.

SAFARI ACTIVITIES
Africa can be experienced in many exciting ways. What follows are a number of types of safari activities. For additional information, refer to the country or countries mentioned.

Close up encounter with elephant in a roof-hatch vehicle.

GAME DRIVES

The type of vehicle used on game drives varies from country to country.

Open vehicles usually have two or three rows of elevated seats behind the driver's seat. There are no side or rear windows or permanent roof, which provides you with unobstructed views in all directions and a feeling of being part of the environment instead of on the outside looking in. This is my favorite type of vehicle for viewing wildlife — especially on flying safaris in southern Africa. Open vehicles are used in Botswana, Zambia, Zimbabwe, southern Tanzania, South Africa and some reserves in northern Tanzania, Kenya, and Namibia.

In vehicles with roof hatches or pop-top roofs, riders may stand up through the hatch for game viewing and photography. If the vehicle is full, riders usually must take turns using the hatches, making tours that guarantee window seats for every passenger (a maximum of six or seven passengers in a nine-seat minivan) imperative. These vehicles are primarily used in Kenya, Tanzania and Uganda. Roof-hatch vehicles in these countries are actually more practical than open vehicles, because reserves in these countries usually get some rainfall 12 months of the year. On driving safaris in southern Africa, roof-hatch vehicles are often preferred because they offer more protection from rain, sun and wind.

Wildlife viewing, and especially photography, is more difficult where closed vehicles are required.

Game viewing by open vehicle.

NIGHT GAME DRIVES

Many African animals, including most of the big cats, are most active after dark, and night game drives open up a whole new world of adventure. Much of the actual hunting by lion and leopard happens after nightfall; therefore, night drives probably provide your best chance to observe these powerful cats feeding or even making a kill. Vehicles are typically driven by your guide, and an assistant (tracker) carries a powerful spotlight. By driving slowly and shining the beam into the surrounding bush, the eyes of animals are reflected back to the spotlight bearer, and it is then possible to stop and take a closer look. When an infra-red filter is used on the beam, most animals behave in a completely natural manner (providing the occupants of the vehicle keep quiet and still) and marvelous views can be enjoyed.

Leopard, lion, hyena, bushbabies, aardvark and especially smaller carnivores, such as genets, civets and honey badgers, would be among the highlights of a night game drive, with nocturnal birds, such as owls and nightjars, adding to the experience.

Night drives are conducted in national parks in Zambia and Malawi, and in private concessions or private reserves in Botswana, Kenya, Namibia, Tanzania, South Africa and Zimbabwe.

SAFARI ACTIVITIES
Vehicles•Night Game Drives•Walking Safaris•Boat Safaris•Canoe Safaris

COUNTRY	PARK OR RESERVE	VEHICLE TYPE ALLOWED			NIGHT DRIVES	WALKING SAFARIS	BOAT SAFARIS	CANOE (C) MOKORO (M)
		OPEN	HATCHES	CLOSED				
EAST & CENTRAL AFRICA								
TANZANIA	Arusha		✔			✔		
	Lake Manyara		✔					C
	Tarangire		✔		1	1, 5		
	Ngorongoro		✔			5		
	Serengeti	4	✔		1	1, 5		
	Selous	✔				✔	✔	
	Ruaha	✔				✔		
	Ndarakwai&Sinya	✔			✔	✔		
KENYA	Masai Mara	4	✔		1	1		
	Laikipia Reserves	✔			✔	✔		
	Samburu		✔			1		
	Ol Donyo Waus, Campi ya Kanzi	✔			✔	✔		
	Other Parks		✔					
UGANDA	Murchison Falls		✔				✔	
	Queen Eliz.abeth		✔			✔	✔	
	Bwindi		✔			✔		
	Kibale		✔			✔		
	Ruwenzori Mts.					✔		
RWANDA	Volcano					✔		
SOUTHERN AFRICA								
ZIMBABWE	Chizarira	✔				✔		
	Hwange	3			1, 2, 3	✔		
	Mana Pools	3			1	✔	1	C
	Matusadona	3			1, 3	✔	✔	C
BOTSWANA	Chobe	✔					✔	
	Moremi	✔			1	1, 2	✔	M, 2
	Okavango Delta	✔				✔	✔	M
	Linyanti	✔				✔	✔	C, 2
ZAMBIA	S. & N. Luangwa	3			3	✔		
	L. Zambezi	3			3	✔	✔	C
NAMIBIA	Etosha	3	3		1	1		
S. AFRICA	Kgalagadi			✔				
	Kruger	6			✔	1, 6	1, 6	
	Private Reserves	✔				✔	✔	

1: Activity is conducted on the outskirts of the park or reserve.
2: Activity is conducted at a few camps within the reserve.
3: Licensed tour operators only.
4: Open vehicles are used by some camps in the reserve.
5: Activity is conducted in certain areas of the park reserve.
6: Activity is conducted by National Parks.

WALKING SAFARIS

Walking safaris put you in closest touch with nature. Suddenly your senses come alive — every sight, sound and smell becomes intensely meaningful. Could that flash of bronze in the dense brush ahead be a lion? I wonder how long ago these rhino tracks were made? Can that herd of elephant ahead see or smell us approaching?

Walking safari in Southern Africa (Zambia).

Accompanied by an armed wildlife expert or Professional Guide, walking safaris last anywhere from a few hours to several days. The bush can be examined up close and at a slower pace, allowing for more attention to its fascinating detail than a safari by vehicle.

Participants can often approach game quite closely, depending on the direction of the wind and the cover available. This is experiencing the excitement and adventure of the bush at its best. Zambia and Zimbabwe are the top countries for walking safaris. Walking is also available in some parts of Botswana, Namibia, Tanzania, Kenya, Uganda and South Africa.

BOAT/CANOE/KAYAK/MOKORO SAFARIS

Wildlife viewing by boat, canoe, kayak or mokoro fr
lakes often allows you to approach wildlife as close o̲ ᴜᵥₑᵢᵢ ᴄⁱₒser
than by vehicle.

Game viewing and birdwatching by **boat** is available in:

- Chobe National Park, Linyanti and the Okavango Delta (Botswana)
- Along the shores of Lake Kariba including Matusadona National Park, and on the Zambezi River upstream from Victoria Falls and downstream from the Kariba Dam, including areas adjacent to Mana Pools National Park (Zimbabwe)
- Upstream from Victoria Falls and along Lower Zambezi National Park (Zambia)
- Liwonde National Park (Malawi)
- In KwaZulu-Natal at reserves like Phinda on the fringe of Lake St. Lucia (South Africa)
- On the Rufiji River in the Selous Game Reserve (Tanzania), and
- On the Kazinga Channel in Queen Elizabeth National Park and on the Victoria Nile in Murchison Falls National Park (Uganda)

Canoe safaris are, in my opinion, one of the most exciting ways of experiencing the bush. Paddling or silently drifting past herds of elephant frolicking on the river's edge, and watching herds of buffalo and other game cross the river channels in front of you are a few examples of what you may encounter.

Canoe safaris from three to nine days are operated along the Zambezi River below Kariba Dam on both the Zimbabwe and Zambia sides of the river. Wildlife is best in the area along Mana Pools National Park (Zimbabwe) and Lower Zambezi National Park (Zambia). This is definitely one of my favorite of all African adventures. Motorboats are not allowed along Mana Pools National Park; however, they are allowed along the Lower Zambezi National Park.

Short excursions are also available upstream from Victoria Falls (Zimbabwe), along Matusadona National Park (Zimbabwe) and Kafue National Park (Zambia).

One- to three-day **kayak** safaris are operated along Zambezi River in Zambezi National Park upstream from Victoria Falls, Zimbabwe.

Mokoro safaris from a few hours to several days in length are available in the Okavango Delta (Botswana). A mokoro is a flat-bottomed, dugout canoe used in the watery wilderness of the Okavango Delta. Although these craft may appear unstable, there is no better way to experience the beauty and tranquility of this spectacular wetland. Experienced polers pilot the mokoro through channels of papyrus and floating fields of water lilies, each with two passengers still and safe aboard.

PHOTOGRAPHIC (PHOTO) SAFARIS

The term "photo safari" generally means any kind of safari except hunting safaris.

In its strictest sense, a photo safari is a safari during which you are escorted by a professional wildlife photographer, especially for the serious photographer. These safaris are mainly about learning wildlife photography and getting the best photos possible. These are recommended only for the serious shutterbug.

The best option by far for the serious photographer is to have a private vehicle and guide (see "Private Safaris" above). Group safaris generally move too quickly from place to place, allowing insufficient time to get the best shots. For additional information, see the "Photography" section in the "Safari Pages."

BALLOON SAFARIS

At 5:30 in the morning, we were awakened by steaming hot coffee and tea brought to our bedsides by our private tentkeeper. We were off at 6:00 for a short game drive to where the hot-air balloons were being filled. Moments later, we lifted above the plains of the Masai Mara for the ride of a lifetime.

Silently viewing game from the perfect vantage point, we brushed the tops of giant acacia trees for close-up views of birds' nests and baboons. Most animals took little notice, but somehow the hippos knew we were there. Maybe it was our shadow or the occasional firing of the burners necessary to keep us aloft.

Our pilot was entertaining and knowledgeable of the ecosystem we flew over, and pointed out a variety of large birds flying along side us and plains game, as well as a cheetah. We had the opportunity to see part of the Great Serengeti Migration from the air — an awesome sight indeed!

Our return to earth was an event in itself. About an hour after lift-off, our pilot made a perfect crash landing. By the way, all landings are crash landings, so just follow your pilot's instructions and join in the fun.

Minutes later, a champagne breakfast appeared on the open savannah within clear view of herds of wildebeest, buffalo and zebra. Our return to camp was another exciting game drive, only a little bumpier than the trip out.

Hot-air balloon safaris are available in Kenya in the Masai Mara Game Reserve, at Taita Hills near Tsavo West National Park, in Serengeti National Park (Tanzania), near Namib-Naukluft National Park (Namibia) and in Pilanesberg Nature Reserve (South Africa).

GORILLA SAFARIS
Gorilla trekking is one of the most exciting adventures you can have on the "dark continent" and is certainly one of the most exciting experiences of my life.

Mountain Gorillas now number about 300 individuals that live in the cool, forested heights of the Virunga Volcanoes, which straddle three countries — Rwanda, Uganda and the Democratic Republic of the Congo. This is the region in which renowned but controversial primatologist Dian Fossey undertook her studies.

Because the respective governments do value the great apes for the foreign currency that they attract, efforts to conserve the remaining gorillas and provide opportunities to view them are good.

A few hundred miles (km) to the north of the Virungas is Uganda's Bwindi Impenetrable National Park, which provides a refuge for some 300 gorillas of a different sub-species. Security at Bwindi has been intensified following a tragedy in 1999 (several tourists were killed), and this is currently regarded as the safest locality in Africa for getting close to gorillas.

Gorillas are perhaps the most charismatic of all animals, and a close encounter with a free-ranging family in their forest home will never be forgotten. A typical experience involves a hard, uphill slog

White–water rafting - Class 5 - Zambezi River.

through mud in the company of two guides, several porters and an armed guard or two. Habituated family groups are located, and you'll then sit quietly and watch as they feed and go about their business. Due to the threat of their contracting potentially fatal human diseases, the group of no more than six visitors in Uganda and eight in Rwanda is encouraged to keep a fair distance from the gorillas. Given the physical exertion required, gorilla trekking is recommended only for safariers in good hiking condition. Nevertheless, a large and growing number of people have been inspired to visit these peaceful relatives of mankind, and permits are at a premium in terms of both cost and availability.

Gorillas are currently best seen in Bwindi Impenetrable Forest (Uganda) and Parc des Volcans in Rwanda. At the time of this writing, gorilla trekking in the Congo is not recommended, due to lack of security. Permits for gorilla trekking are limited; gorilla safaris should be booked well in advance.

CHIMPANZEE TREKKING
Chimpanzee trekking, like gorilla trekking, can be exciting beyond words. Chimp trekking is best in Mahale Mountains National Park and Gombe Stream National Park (Tanzania), and Kibale Forest National Park (Uganda).

WHITE-WATER RAFTING

For white-water enthusiasts and newcomers alike, the Zambezi River (Zambia/Zimbabwe) below Victoria Falls is one of the most challenging rivers in the world. Some rapids are "Class Five" — the highest class runable. Rafting safaris from one to eight days are available. No previous experience is required. Just hang on and have the time of your life! See the chapter on Zimbabwe for more details.

ELEPHANT-BACK SAFARIS

For years only available in Asia, elephant-back is a fabulous way to explore the bush. Clients may ride well-trained African elephants, which are much larger than Indian elephants, in the Okavango Delta (Botswana), and near Victoria Falls and Matobo National Park (Zimbabwe).

HORSEBACK SAFARIS

Game viewing by horseback is yet another intriguing way to experience the bush. Horseback safaris from three to 10 days in length are conducted in the Okavango Delta (Botswana), from a half day to 10 days in length on the Nyika Plateau (Malawi) and up to 16 days in length in Kenya. These safaris are for only serious riders who can canter and who would enjoy spending six or more hours in the saddle each day.

Half- or full-day horseback safaris are available in Matobo National Park, Mutirikwe Recreational Park, Nyanga and Victoria Falls (Zimbabwe), Maputaland Coastal Forest Reserve and Cape Town (South Africa), near Mt. Kilimanjaro (Tanzania) and several private reserves in Kenya.

BIRDWATCHING

If you are not already a keen birdwatcher, there is a good chance that you will be converted before the end of your safari. Birdwatching in Africa is almost beyond belief. Some countries have recorded over 1,000 different species and some parks over 500. The strident, sometimes beautiful calls of many birds will form a continual "soundtrack" to your African safari, add to the atmosphere and provide lasting memories.

The wonderful thing about birds is that they are present just about everywhere, all the time. The surroundings of camps and lodges are always good localities for birdwatching because a variety of species have become used to the presence of people, and many birds will appear on the scene if you simply sit quietly on your veranda. Game drives are constantly punctuated by views of large or colorful birds, and, if you take the time, numerous less-dramatic species.

Most reserves in Africa are simply heaven for birdwatchers. The best times for birdwatching are often the opposite of the best times for big game viewing. Birdwatching, however, is good year-round in many regions. For additional information, please see "Birdwatching Tips" in the "Safari Pages."

MOUNTAIN CLIMBING
Africa has mountains to challenge the tenderfoot and the expert alike. Mt. Kilimanjaro (Tanzania), 19,340 feet (5,895 m) in altitude, is the highest mountain in Africa, followed by Mt. Kenya at 17,058 feet (5,199 m). The Ruwenzoris, or Mountains of the Moon (Uganda/Congo), are the highest mountain chain in Africa, rising to 16,762 feet (5,109 m). All of these mountains lie within a few degrees of the equator yet are snowcapped year-round. Hiking through fascinating and unique Afro-alpine vegetation found on all of these mountains gives you the feeling of being on another planet. With over 20,000 climbers a year, Mt. Kilimanjaro is by far the most popular of the three peaks.

SCUBA DIVING AND SNORKELING
Kenya, Tanzania, South Africa, Mauritius and the Seychelles offer excellent coral reef diving in the warm waters of the Indian Ocean. Lake Malawi offers a fascinating freshwater dive experience.

The Malindi-Watamu Marine National Reserve is probably the best choice in Kenya, and Pemba Island is the best choice in Tanzania.

The northern Natal coast of South Africa has excellent coral reefs, while the Southern Cape offers the ultimate underwater thrill of diving with great white sharks!

Mauritius and the Seychelles offer numerous coral reefs and a variety of dive options.

FISHING

Africa has some very fine fishing to offer — from excellent deep-sea fishing off the east coast of the continent to great inland lakes that boast some of the largest freshwater fish in the world.

The best areas for **deep-sea fishing** are found off the coast of Kenya and Tanzania and in the Mozambique Channel. Game fishing these areas can be particularly rewarding, and, in fact, one of the marlin world records comes from the coast of Mozambique. The Seychelles and Mauritius also offer very good fishing. The Seychelles, in fact, is considered one of the top bonefishing destinations in the world.

Freshwater fishing for tigerfish (great fighters) or Nile Perch (often weighing over 100 lbs./45 kg) as well as other species across the continent can be very exciting. While fishing, you may watch elephant cross a channel, listen to hippo grunting and watch a variety of kingfishers and herons fly by — adding another dimension to the sport that can be found nowhere else in the world! For more in-depth coverage, please see the "Freshwater Fishing" in the "Safari Pages."

STAR GAZING IN THE SOUTHERN HEMISPHERE

Breathtaking views of the night sky are a typical feature of clear nights in African wilderness areas. A cloudless night provides a glorious opportunity to become familiar with several interesting constellations and noteworthy stars, as well as up to five planets. One or more of the planets Venus, Jupiter or Mars will be visible at any given time. The Milky Way is quite astounding when viewed through binoculars! For maps of the summer and winter skies of the southern hemisphere, obtain a copy of the *African Safari Journal*.

OTHER SAFARI ACTIVITIES

Additional options for the special-interest traveler include anthropology, archeology, art, backpacking, mountain biking and camel safaris.

Miles Nolting reading up on Swahili in his *African Safari Journal*.

COST OF A SAFARI

The cost per day is most dependent upon how comfortably you wish to travel (the level of accommodation), the remoteness of the safari, type of transportation used, whether you're on a private safari or on a group tour, and the countries involved. Deluxe accommodations and transportation are normally more expensive in countries off the beaten track than in the more popular tourism spots.

For example, deluxe (Class A) safari camps in Botswana are often more expensive than Class A lodges in Kenya. Camps in Botswana and Zimbabwe cater to smaller groups and are generally situated in more remote locations, and charter aircraft are often used to reach them.

Transportation is more costly in Tanzania, for instance, than in South Africa because in Tanzania gas (petrol) is more expensive and poor roads mean greater wear and tear on vehicles.

As in Europe and other parts of the world, general-interest tours cost less than tours with more unique itineraries. Getting off the beaten track may dip a bit more into the wallet, but many travelers find it well worth it.

For current costs on package tours and tailor-made itineraries, contact The Africa Adventure Company (see introduction pages). For tips on selecting a safari company, see "Booking a Safari" in the "Safari Pages".

LANGUAGE

English is widely spoken in all the countries featured in this book except Burundi, Rwanda and the Congo, where French is the international language.

The *African Safari Journal* (see our catalog) has illustrations of 175 mammals, birds, reptiles and trees, along with words and phrases in French, Kiswahili (Kenya, Tanzania), Shona (Zimbabwe), Setswana (Botswana) and Zulu (Southern Africa). Your guide will love it if you start naming the animals you spot in his native language!

WILDLIFE

HABITATS

Animals are most often found in and nearby the habitats in which they feed or hunt. These habitats fall roughly into four categories — savannah, desert, wetlands and forest.

Savannah is a very broad term that refers to dry land that can be open grasslands, grasslands dotted with trees, or wooded areas.

ANIMALS BY HABITAT AND DIET

The animals listed below are classified according to the habitat where most of their time is spent. Most animals are listed in order of size by weight.

SAVANNAH/ SAVANNAH WOODLAND

GRAZERS	BROWSERS	CARNIVORES
White Rhino	Black Rino	Lion
Eland	Giraffe	Hyena (three species)
Zebra	Nyala	Cheetah
Roan Antelope	Bushbuck	African Wild Dog
Gemsbok (Oryx)	Gerenuk	Jackal (three species)
Topi	Duiker, Grey	Serval
Hartebeest	Dikdik	Bat-Eared Fox
Wildebeest	Elephant	Mongoose (many species)
Tsessebe		Genet (two species)
Warthog		Caracal
Reedbuck		
Grant's Gazelle	Grant's Gazelle	
Impala	Impala	
Springbok	Springbok	
Thomson's Gazelle	Thomson's Gazelle	
Klipspringer	Klipspriinger	
Steenbok	Steenbok	

FOREST

OMNIVORES	BROWSERS	CARNIVORES
Gorilla	Elephant	Leopard
Chimpanzee	Colobus Monkey	Serval
Syke's Monkey	Bongo	Genet
	Bushbuck	
	Duiker (several species)	

WETLANDS

BROWSERS	CARNIVORES
Hippopotamus	Crocodile
Buffalo	Otter
Sitatunga	

DESERTS

See savannah grazers, browsers and carnivores above

MAJOR WILDLIFE AREAS BY HABITAT
P - Primary Habitat S - Secondary Habitat (R) - Riverine   (L) - Lake
EAST AND CENTRAL AFRICA

COUNTRY	WILDLIFE AREA	SAVANNAH	FOREST	WETLAND
TANZANIA	Arusha (N.P.)		P	S
	Lake Manyara	S	S	P(L)
	Ngorongoro Crater	P	S	S (L)
	Serengeti	P		S(R)
	Tarangire	P		S(R)
	Mt. Kilimanjaro		P	
	Selous	P		S(R)
	Ruaha	P		S(R)
	Mikumi	P		
	Gombe Stream		P	S (L)
	Mahale Mountains		P	S (L)
KENYA	Nairobi (N.P.)	P		
	Amboseli	P		S
	Tsavo	P		
	Masai Mara	P		S(R)
	Mt. Elgon		P	
	Aberdare		P	
	Mt. Kenya		P	
	Meru	P	S	
	Lake Navaisha			P (L)
	Lake Nakuru	S		P (L)
	Lake Bogoria			P (L)
	Lake Baringo			P (L)
	Samburu	P		S(R)
	Lewa Downs	P		
	Laikipia	P		
UGANDA	Murchison Falls	P	S	S(R)
	Queen Elizabeth N .P.	P	S	S(L)
	Bwindi		P	
	Kibale Forest		P	
RWANDA	Volcano N. P.		P	
CONGO	Virunga (Rwindi area)	P		S (L)
	Virunga (other areas)	S	P	
	Kahuzi-Biega		P	

MAJOR WILDLIFE AREAS BY HABITAT
P - Primary Habitat S - Secondary Habitat (R) - Riverine   (L) - Lake
SOUTHERN AFRICA

COUNTRY	WILDLIFE AREA	SAVANNAH WOODLAND	FOREST	WETLAND	DESERT
Botswana	Okavango Delta	S		P	
	Moremi	P		S	
	Linyanti	P		S	
	Savute	P			
	Chobe	P		S(R)	
	Makgadikgadi	P			
	Nxai Pan	P			
	Kalahari Desert	S			P
Zimbabwe	Hwange	P			
	Matusadona	S		P (L)	
	Mana Pools	S		P (R)	
	Matobo Hills	P			
	Chizarira	P			
	Gonarezhou	P			
Zambia	South Luangwa	P		S(R)	
	North Luangwa	P		S(R)	
	Lower Zambezi	S		P(R)	
	Kafue	P		S	
	Lochinvar	S		P	
Malawi	Liwonde	S		P(R)	
Namibia	Etosha	P			S
	Caprivi	P		S(R)	
	Damaraland				P
	Skeleton Coast				P
	Namib-Naukluft				P
South Africa	Kruger	P			
	Private Reserves (Kruger)	P			
	Hluhluwe Umfolozi	P			
	St. Lucia	S	S	P(L)	
	Phinda	P	S	S(R)	
	Kgalagadi Trans-Frontier Pk.				P

Grazers (grass-eaters) and carnivores (meat-eaters) adept at hunting in savannah are most easily found here. Savannah supports the densest concentration of larger mammals as well as innumerable conspicuous birds, and it is the favored situation for safari lodges, camps and routes.

Deserts have little or no standing water and very sparse vegetation. Many desert animals do not drink at all but derive water from only the plants they eat and the condensation formed on them. Some savannah grazers and carnivores can be found in the desert. Much of the wildlife in deserts is specially adapted for the extreme climatic conditions.

African forests are thickly vegetated, often with an understory of ferns and shrubs growing to between three and 10 feet (1-3 m) in height, shorter trees 20-50 feet (6-15 m) high, and a higher canopy reaching to 150 feet (45 m) or more.

It is more difficult to spot animals in forests than in the other habitats. Forest herbivores (plant-eaters) are browsers, preferring to feed on the leaves of plants and fruits that are usually found in forests. Carnivores have adapted to a style of hunting in which they can closely approach their prey under cover.

Wetlands consist of lakes, rivers and swamps, which are often part of a larger savannah or forest habitat. Many rivers wind through savannah regions, providing a habitat within a habitat. Wetlands are good places not only to see wetland species, but also other habitat species that come there to drink.

The **Eco Map** (see page 270 of the color insert pages) shows the location of different eco-zones.

The animals listed in the **Animals by Habitat and Diet** chart (see page 54) are classified according to the habitat where most of their time is spent — their most dominant habitat. The animals are listed in order of size by weight.

The major parks and reserves listed in the **Major Wildlife Areas By Habitat** charts (see pages 55-56) are classified according to their most dominant habitats.

AVERAGE MONTHLY TEMPERATURES
Min/Max in Fahrenheit
EAST AFRICA

CITY	JAN	FEB	MAR	APR	MAY	JUN	JUL	AUG	SEP	OCT	NOV	DEC
Dar-es-salaam	77/88	76/87	76/89	74/87	72/85	68/85	66/84	66/84	68/84	68/86	73/87	76/88
Dodoma	66/86	66/85	64/84	64/84	62/83	57/82	57/79	57/81	59/85	63/88	64/89	65/88
Kigoma	67/81	68/82	68/82	67/82	68/83	67/82	63/833	65/85	67/86	69/85	68/81	67/80
Nairobi	55/78	56/80	58/78	58/76	56/73	54/70	51/70	52/71	53/76	55/77	56/74	55/75
Mombasa	75/88	76/88	77/89	76/87	75/84	74/83	71/81	71/81	72/83	74/85	75/86	76/87
Kampala	65/84	65/83	64/82	64/81	63/79	63/78	63/78	62/78	63/81	63/82	62/81	62/81
Kabale	49/76	50/76	50/75	51/74	51/73	50/73	48/75	49/75	50/76	51/75	50/73	50/73
Kigali	43/68	48/68	46/68	43/68	41/68	37/68	41/68	39/70	37/70	48/68	37/68	39/68
Bujumbura	66/83	66/83	66/83	66/83	66/83	65/85	64/85	65/87	67/89	68/87	67/83	67/83

SOUTHERN AFRICA

Harare	61/79	61/79	59/79	56/79	50/75	45/71	47/75	54/80	58/84	60/84	60/82	61/79
Victoria Falls	65/85	64/85	62/85	57/84	49/81	43/76	42/77	47/82	55/89	62/91	64/90	64/86
Hwange	64/85	64/84	62/85	56/83	47/80	47/76	40/76	45/81	54/88	61/90	64/89	64/85
Kariba	71/88	71/88	69/88	65/87	58/84	53/80	52/79	57/84	67/91	74/95	74/93	7289
Mana Pools	71/89	71/89	70/89	67/88	62/85	57/81	56/81	59/86	66/92	73/97	74/95	72/91
Bulawayo	61/82	61/81	60/80	57/80	50/75	46/70	46/71	49/75	55/82	59/86	61/85	61/83
Maun	66/90	66/88	64/88	57/88	48/82	43/77	43/77	48/82	55/91	64/95	66/93	66/90
Lusaka	63/78	63/79	62/79	59/79	55/78	50/73	49/73	53/77	59/84	64/88	64/85	63/81
S. Luangwa	68/90	68/88	66/90	64/90	66/88	54/86	52/84	54/86	59/95	68/104	72/99	72/91
Windhoek	63/86	63/84	59/81	55/77	48/72	45/68	45/68	46/73	54/79	57/84	61/84	63/88
Swakopmund	54/77	54/73	54/73	59/77	59/77	64/82	59/82	59/82	54/77	54/77	54/77	54/77
Johannesburg	59/79	57/77	55/75	52/72	46/66	41/61	41/61	45/66	48/72	54/75	55/77	57/77
Durban	70/82	70/82	68/82	63/79	55/75	50/73	50/73	54/73	59/73	63/75	64/77	68/81
Cape Town	61/79	59/79	57/77	54/73	50/68	46/64	45/63	45/64	46/66	50/70	55/75	59/77

AVERAGE MONTHLY TEMPERATURES
Min/Max In Centigrade
EAST AFRICA

CITY	JAN	FEB	MAR	APR	MAY	JUN	JUL	AUG	SEP	OCT	NOV	DEC
Dar-es-salaam	25/32	25/32	24/32	23/31	22/29	20/29	19/28	19/28	19/28	21/29	23/31	24/31
Dodoma	18/29	18/29	18/28	18/28	16/28	15/27	13/27	14/27	15/29	17/31	18/31	18/31
Kigoma	19/27	20/27	20/27	19/27	19/28	188/29	17/28	18/29	19/30	21/29	20/27	19/26
Nairobi	12/25	13/26	14/25	14/24	13/22	12/21	11/21	11/21	11/24	14/25	13/24	13/24
Mombasa	24/32	24/32	25/32	24/31	23/28	23/28	22/27	22/27	22/28	23/29	24/29	24/30
Kampala	18/28	18/28	18/27	18/26	25/17	26/18	26/18	26/17	27/17	27/17	27/17	27/17
Kabale	9/24	11/24	11/24	11/24	11/23	10/23	9/23	10/23	10/24	11/24	11/24	10/24
Kigali	6/20	9/21	8/20	6/20	5/20	3/20	5/20	4/21	3/21	9/20	3/20	4/20
Bujumbura	19/28	19/28	19/28	19/28	19/28	18/29	18/29	18/29	18/31	19/32	20/31	19/29

SOUTHERN AFRICA

Harare	17/27	17/27	15/27	13/27	10/24	8/22	7/22	8/24	12/27	14/29	16/28	16/27
Bulawayo	17/28	17/28	16/27	14/27	10/24	8/22	8/22	10/24	12/28	15/30	16/31	16/29
Victoria Falls	18/29	17/29	17/29	14/29	9/27	5/24	7/27	12/31	16/32	18/31	18/31	18/30
Hwange	18/29	18/29	17/29	14/29	9/27	5/24	5/25	7/27	12/31	16/32	18/32	18/30
Kariba	22/31	21/31	21/31	19/31	15/29	12/27	11/26	14/29	19/33	23/35	24/34	22/32
Mana Pools	22/32	21/32	21/32	20/31	17/29	14/27	13/27	15/30	19/34	23/36	23/35	22/33
Maun	19/32	19/31	18/31	14/31	9/28	6/25	6/25	9/28	13/33	18/35	19/34	19/34
Lusaka	17/26	17/26	17/26	15/26	13/25	10/24	10/23	12/25	15/30	18/31	18/30	18/28
S. Luangwa	20/32	20/31	19/32	18/32	19/31	12/30	11/29	12/30	15/35	20/40	22/37	22/33
Windhoek	17/30	17/29	15/27	13/25	9/22	7/20	7/20	8/23	12/26	14/29	16/29	17/31
Swakopmund	12/25	12/23	12/23	15/25	15/25	18/28	15/28	15/28	12/25	12/25	12/25	12/25
Johannesburg	15/26	14/25	13/24	11/22	8/19	5/16	5/16	7/19	9/22	12/24	13/25	14/25
Durban	21/28	21/28	20/28	17/26	13/24	10/23	10/23	12/23	15/23	17/24	18/25	20/27
Cape Town	16/26	15/26	14/25	12/23	10/20	8/18	7/17	7/18	8/19	10/21	13/24	15/25

AVERAGE MONTHLY RAINFALL
in Inches
EAST AFRICA

CITY	JAN	FEB	MAR	APR	MAY	JUN	JUL	AUG	SEP	OCT	NOV	DEC
Dar-es-salaam	2.6	2.6	5.1	11.4	7.4	1.3	1.2	1.0	1.2	1.6	2.9	3.6
Dodoma	6.0	4.3	5.4	1.9	0.2	0	0	0	0	0.2	0.9	3.6
Kigoma	1.5	2.5	4.9	8.3	6.2	1.8	0.7	0.9	1.3	2.2	4.3	3.4
Mombasa	1.1	0.8	2.4	7.7	12.7	4.7	3.5	2.6	2.6	3.4	3.8	2.4
Kampala	1.8	2.4	5.1	6.9	5.8	2.9	1.8	3.4	3.6	3.8	4.8	3.9
Kabale	2.4	3.8	5.2	4.9	3.6	1.2	0.8	2.4	3.7	3.9	4.4	3.4
Kigali	3.5	3.5	4.1	6.5	4.9	1.0	.3	.8	2.4	3.9	3.9	3.5
Bujumbura	3.7	4.4	4.8	4.9	2.3	0.4	0.3	0.4	1.5	2.5	3.9	4.4

SOUTHERN AFRICA

CITY	JAN	FEB	MAR	APR	MAY	JUN	JUL	AUG	SEP	OCT	NOV	DEC
Harare	7.7	7.1	4.5	1.2	0.5	0.2	0	0.1	0.3	1.2	3.8	6.4
Bulawayo	5.6	4.4	3.3	0.8	0.4	0.1	0	0	0.2	0.8	3.3	4.9
Victoria Falls	6.6	5	2.8	1.0	0.1	0	0	0	0.7	1.1	2.5	6.8
Hwange	5.7	5.1	2.3	0.8	0.1	0	0	0	0.1	0.8	2.2	5.0
Kariba	7.5	6.2	4.4	1.2	0.2	0	0	0	0	0.7	2.9	6.9
Mana Pools	8.7	7.1	4.2	1.0	0.2	0	0	0	0	0.5	2.3	9.1
Maun	4.3	3.2	2.8	1.0	0.3	0.1	0	0	0	1.2	2.0	3.8
Lusaka	9.1	7.6	5.7	0.7	0.2	0	0	0	0	0.4	3.6	5.9
S. Luangwa	7.7	11.3	5.6	3.6	0	0	0	0	0	2.0	4.3	4.3
Windhoek	1.7	2.0	2.2	1.1	0.2	0.1	0.1	0.1	0.1	0.4	0.9	1.0
Swakopmund	0.5	0.5	0.5	0.4	0.4	0.4	0.3	0.4	0.4	0.6	0.6	0.4
Johannesburg	4.5	3.8	2.9	2.5	0.9	0.3	0.3	0.2	0.1	2.7	4.6	4.3
Durban	5.1	4.5	5.3	4.2	2.0	1.2	1.4	1.7	2.4	3.9	4.5	4.6
Cape Town	0.6	0.7	0.7	2.0	3.5	3.3	3.5	3.1	2.0	1.4	0.5	0.6

AVERAGE MONTHLY RAINFALL
in Millimeters
EAST AFRICA

CITY	JAN	FEB	MAR	APR	MAY	JUN	JUL	AUG	SEP	OCT	NOV	DEC
Dar-es-salaam	66	66	130	292	188	33	33	26	31	42	74	91
Dodoma	152	110	138	49	5	0	0	0	0	5	24	92
Kigoma	123	128	150	130	44	5	3	5	19	28	143	135
Nairobi	39	65	125	211	158	47	15	24	32	53	110	87
Mombasa	25	19	65	197	320	120	90	65	65	87	98	62
Kampala	47	61	130	175	148	73	45	85	90	96	122	99
Kabale	58	97	130	125	92	28	20	58	98	99	110	87
Kigali	90	90	105	165	125	25	7	20	60	100	100	90
Bujumbura	95	110	121	125	56	11	5	11	37	65	100	115

SOUTHERN AFRICA

CITY	JAN	FEB	MAR	APR	MAY	JUN	JUL	AUG	SEP	OCT	NOV	DEC
Harare	196	179	118	28	14	3	0	3	5	28	97	163
Bulawayo	143	110	85	19	10	3	0	0	5	20	81	123
Victoria Falls	168	126	70	24	3	1	0	0	2	27	64	174
Hwange	145	129	57	20	3	0	0	0	2	21	56	127
Kariba	192	158	113	30	4	1	1	0	1	18	74	175
Mana Pools	221	181	107	26	4	0	0	0	1	13	59	231
Maun	110	80	70	25	7	3	0	0	0	30	50	95
Lusaka	232	192	144	18	3	0	0	0	0	11	92	150
S. Luangwa	195	287	141	91	0	0	0	0	0	50	108	110
Windhoek	43	53	56	28	5	3	3	3	3	10	23	26
Swakopmund	12	15	12	10	10	10	7	9	11	15	16	11
Johannesburg	112	96	74	61	23	8	8	5	3	69	117	109
Durban	130	114	135	107	54	31	36	43	61	99	114	117
Cape Town	15	18	18	50	90	85	90	80	50	36	13	15

How much closer can you get?

Many of these wildlife areas are composed of more than one habitat, so consult the text of this book for in-depth descriptions. Keep in mind that savannah and forest animals may visit wetland habitats to drink and that many forest animals are more easily seen on the open savannah.

A well-rounded safari includes visits to several types of habitats and parks, which gives the visitor an overall picture of wildlife and ecosystems.

Use the **What Wildlife Is Best Seen Where** chart (see the inside of the back cover) as a guide in finding the major parks and reserves that are most likely to have the animals you are most interested in seeing on safari.

An endangered wild dog pup.

WHEN'S THE BEST TIME TO GO?

The **When's The Best Time To Go For Game Viewing** chart (see the inside of the front cover) shows, at a glance, when you should go to see the greatest numbers or concentration of large mammals in the countries, parks and reserves of your choice. Alternatively, the chart shows the best places to go in the month(s) in which your vacation is planned. In other words, how to be in the right place at the right time!

For example, your vacation is in February and your primary interest is game viewing on a photographic safari. Find the countries on the chart in which game viewing is "excellent," "good," or "fair" in February. Turn to the respective country chapters for additional information and choose the ones that intrigue you the most. In this example, for instance, northern Tanzania would be an excellent choice. Use this chart as a general guideline because conditions vary from year to year. Timing can make a world of difference!

The fastest running land mammal is the cheetah.

In most cases, the best game viewing, as exhibited on the chart, also corresponds to the dry season. Wildlife concentrates around water holes and rivers, and the vegetation is less dense than in the wet season, making game easier to find. There are, however, exceptions. For instance, the Serengeti migration (to the north and west) often begins at the height of the rains in Tanzania.

During the rainy season, the land is often luxuriously green and the air clear. People interested in scenery or who have dust allergies may want to plan their visits shortly after the rains are predicted to have started or soon after the rains are predicted to have stopped. Game may be a bit more difficult to find, but there are usually fewer travelers in the parks and reserves, which adds to the overall quality of the safari.

Many camps and lodges offer low-season rates, making travel during those times economically attractive. The low season in Kenya and Tanzania is April-May (except for Easter) and November, while in Botswana the "Green Season" (offering the lowest rates) is generally December-March and the low season is April-June and November. South Africa's high season is September-April.

Generally speaking, game viewing is best in Kenya and Tanzania mid-December-March and July-September, while the best game viewing in Zimbabwe, Zambia, Malawi and South Africa is June-October. Good game viewing in Botswana can be found year-round.

Young cubs are such fun to watch - usually up to some kind of mischief!

Another advantage of traveling during the low season, especially if you visit the more popular parks and reserves in Kenya and Tanzania, is that there will be fewer tourists. In fact, one of my favorite times to visit Tanzania and Kenya is in October and early November.

In summary, the best time for you to go may be a combination of the best time to see the wildlife that interests you most (large mammals vs. birds), the relative costs involved (low or high season), and when you can get vacation time.

The **Temperature and Rainfall Charts** (see pages 58-59) give average high and low temperatures and average rainfall for each month of the year for a number of locations. Keep in mind that these are average temperatures; you should expect variations of at least 7°F (5°C) from the averages listed on the chart. Also keep in mind that at higher altitudes you should expect cooler temperatures. This is why many parks and reserves in Africa can be warm during the day and cool to cold at night. The most common packing mistake safariers make is not bringing enough warm layers of clothing!

AFRICA'S TOP WILDLIFE COUNTRIES

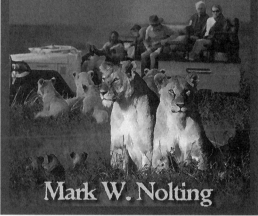

Mark W. Nolting

EAST AND CENTRAL AFRICA

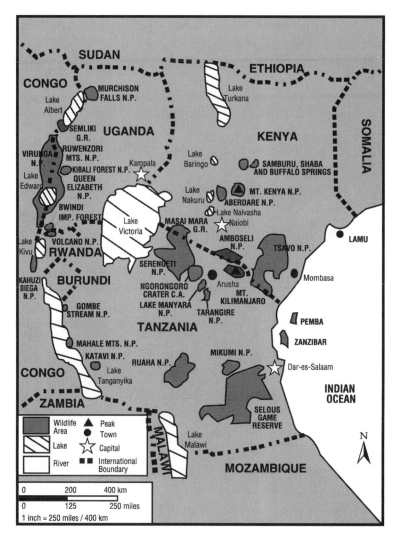

SUDAN

ETHIOPIA

CONGO

MURCHISON
FALLS N.P.

Lake
Albert

Lake
Turkana

SEMLIKI
G.R.

UGANDA

KENYA

RUWENZORI
MTS. N.P.

VIRUNGA
N.P.

KIBALI FOREST N.P.

Kampala

Lake
Baringo

SAMBURU, SHABA
AND BUFFALO SPRINGS

SOMALIA

QUEEN
ELIZABETH
N.P.

Lake
Edward

Lake
Nakuru

MT. KENYA N.P.
ABERDARE N.P.

BWINDI
IMP. FOREST

Lake
Victoria

Lake Naivasha

VOLCANO N.P.

Lake
Kivu

RWANDA

MASAI MARA
G.R.

Naiobi

AMBOSELI
N.P.

TSAVO N.P.

LAMU

KAHUZI
BIEGA
N.P.

BURUNDI

SERENGETI
N.P.

NGORONGORO
CRATER C.A.

Arusha

Mombasa

GOMBE
STREAM N.P.

LAKE MANYARA
N.P.

MT.
KILIMANJARO

TARANGIRE
N.P.

PEMBA

TANZANIA

ZANZIBAR

MAHALE MTS. N.P.

KATAVI N.P.

RUAHA N.P.

MIKUMI N.P.

CONGO

Lake
Tanganyika

Dar-es-Salaam

INDIAN
OCEAN

ZAMBIA

SELOUS
GAME
RESERVE

	Wildlife Area	▲	Peak
	Lake	●	Town
	River	★	Capital
		▪▪	International Boundary

MALAWI

Lake
Malawi

N

MOZAMBIQUE

0   200   400 km

0   125   250 miles

1 inch = 250 miles / 400 km

TANZANIA

THE LION'S FEAST

On a game drive you will most often see lion either lying in the shade, too sleepy to raise their heads, or grouped around a recent kill, eating their "share."

It may seem that, since the females do most of the hunting (males often do assist in bringing down large prey such as buffalo and giraffe), the females should be the first to gorge. However, this is not the lion's pecking order. The males will select their preferred contents, usually the lungs, liver and kidneys, followed by the rump, and will move up toward the head. Skin and hair are also eaten, which gives the lion the roughage it needs. When food is plentiful, the females and cubs will feed next. However, there are usually lots of cat fights, snarls, hisses and arguments during feeding, with the males expressing their views in roars. The males will retire, satisfied (of course); the females survive on the remains. Cubs will go hungry during periods of food shortage, or they can even be killed in the scramble for food.

Male lions feed first as they need all their strength to protect their territories from invading and nomatic lions. If they can defend their territories the females and cubs within that territory will be safe.

If a small pride is feeding together on a kill, the dominant male will control who eats where and what. Any females or cubs that overstep this order will be disciplined by a snarl or with a slap of the paw. Inevitably, the younger cubs will try all sorts of tricks to distract the male, who will usually tolerate these antics. He is not as fierce as he appears.

When they have finished their feast, lions will either wander off for a drink or begin grooming themselves, and all becomes peaceful, once again, in the lion pride.

TANZANIA

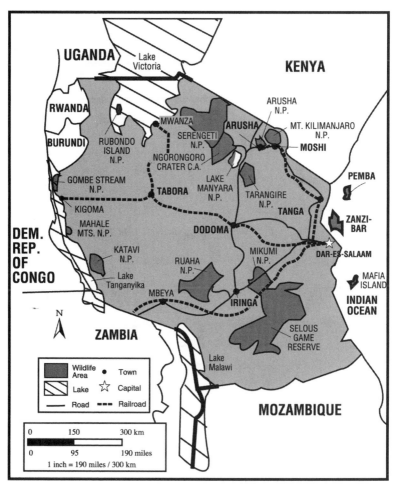

FACTS AT A GLANCE

Area: 364,864 sq. mi./945,000 sq.km
Approximation size: Texas plus Oklahoma, or France
Population: 35 million
Capital: Nominal: Dodoma (pop.est.2,000,000;
Functional: Dar es Salaam
(pop. est. 1.4 million)
Official Language: Swahili; English widely spoken

TANZANIA

Between Africa's highest mountain (Kilimanjaro) and Africa's largest lake (Victoria) lies one of the best game viewing areas on the continent. This region also includes the world's largest unflooded intact volcanic caldera (Ngorongoro) and the most famous wildlife park (the Serengeti). To the southeast lies one of the world's largest game reserves — the Selous.

Volcanic highlands dominate the north, giving way southward to a plateau, then semidesert in the center of the country and highlands in the south. The coastal lowlands are hot and humid with lush vegetation. One branch of the Great Rift Valley passes through Lakes Manyara and Natron in northern Tanzania to Lake Malawi (Lake Nyasa) in the south, while the other branch passes through Lakes Rukwa and Tanganyika in the west.

Heavy rains usually occur in April and May and lighter rains in late October and November. Altitude has a great effect on temperature. At Arusha (4,600 feet/1,390 m) and the top of Ngorongoro Crater (7,500 feet/2,285 m), nights and early mornings are especially cool. Tanzania's highest temperatures occur December-March and are lowest in July.

Some scientists debate that East Africa was the cradle of mankind. Some of the earliest known humanoid footprints, estimated to be 3.5 million years old, were discovered at Laetoli by Dr. Mary Leakey in 1979. Dr. Leakey also found the estimated 1.7-million-year-old skull *Zinjanthropus boisei* at Oldupai (formerly Olduvai) Gorge in 1957.

From as far back as the tenth century, Arabs, Persians, Egyptians, Indians and Chinese were involved in heavy trading on the coast. The slave trade began in the mid-1600s and was abolished in 1873.

British explorers Richard Burton and John Speke crossed Tanzania in 1857 to Lake Tanganyika. Speke later discovered Lake Victoria, which he mistakenly thought was the source of the Nile.

The German East Africa Company gained control of the mainland (then called German East Africa) in 1885, and the German government held it from 1891 until World War I, when it was mandated to Britain by the League of Nations. Tanganyika gained its independence from Britain in 1961, and Zanzibar gained its independence in December 1963. Zanzibar, once the center of the East African slave trade, was ruled by sultans until they were overthrown in January 1964. Three months later, Zanzibar formed a union with Tanganyika — the United Republic of Tanzania.

There are 120 tribes in Tanzania. Bantu languages and dialects are spoken by 95% of the population, with Swahili the official and national language. Over 75% of the people are peasant farmers. Export of coffee, cotton, sisal, tea, cloves and cashews bring 70% of the country's foreign exchange. Tourism is now one of the country's top foreign exchange earners.

WILDLIFE AND WILDLIFE AREAS

Reserves cover over 95,000 square miles (250,000 km²) of area; only a few countries on earth can boast having a greater amount of land devoted to parks and reserves. The 13 national parks, 17 game reserves and one conservation area comprise over 15% of the country's land area. In total, over 25% of the country has been set aside for wildlife conservation. Tanzania's great variety of wildlife can be at least partially attributed to its great diversity of landscapes, with altitudes ranging from sea level to 19,340 feet (5,895 m).

Tanzania is one of the best wildlife countries in Africa for mobile tented camp safaris. Vehicles with roof hatches or pop-tops are used on safari. If accompanied by a national park guide, walking is allowed in Arusha, Mt. Kilimanjaro, Gombe Stream, Ruaha, Mahale Mountains and Rubondo Island National Parks, and the Selous Game Reserve. Areas for walking have recently been designated in

Tarangire National Park and the Serengeti, and more areas are expected to be opened. Walking is also allowed in the Ngorongoro Conservation area (but not within the Ngorongoro Crater itself) if accompanied by a conservation ranger.

The best weather for viewing game in northern Tanzania is June-March. January, February, July and August are the busiest months. Heavy rains can fall in April and May, during which time travel in 4wd vehicles is highly recommended. Advantages of traveling in April and May include lower rates, fewer tourists, and great game viewing in some parks, such as the Serengeti and Ngorongoro Crater. Light rains usually fall October-November, but, in fact, have little negative effect on game viewing. A little rain is nice because it helps drop the dust out of the air, and the bush turns from brown to green. In southern Tanzania the best months for game viewing are July-October.

The country contains 35 species of antelope and over 1.5 million wildebeest — over 80% of the population of this species in Africa. The calving season for wildebeest is from mid-January to mid-March.

THE NORTH

This region, from Mt. Kilimanjaro in the east to Serengeti National Park in the west, is the area most visited by tourists and boasts the country's most famous parks.

Some visitors reach Arusha, gateway to the area, by flying directly in to Kilimanjaro International Airport. Others fly into Nairobi (Kenya) and then take a one-hour flight to Kilimanjaro or a four- to five-hour drive via Namanga to Arusha, or they fly into Dar es Salaam and then take an hour's flight to Kilimanjaro or Arusha airports. Kilimanjaro International Airport is located 34 miles (54 km) east of Arusha and 22 miles (35 km) west of Moshi, and has a bank, bar, shops and a restaurant.

The "Northern Circuit" includes Arusha National Park, Tarangire National Park, Lake Manyara National Park, Ngorongoro Conservation Area, Oldupai Gorge and the Serengeti National Park.

NORTHERN TANZANIA

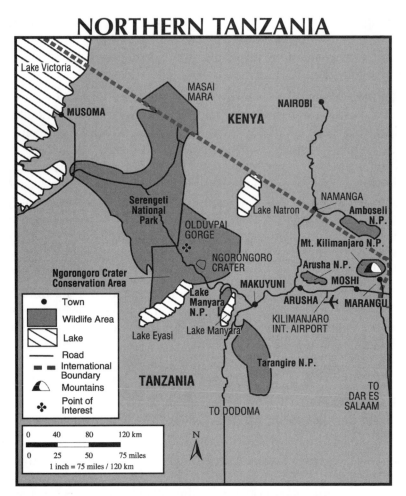

From Arusha the Northern Circuit runs 45 miles (73 km) west on a good tarmac road, across the gently rolling Masai plains with scattered acacia trees, to Makuyuni. You can then either continue on the main road toward Dodoma for another 20 miles (32 km) to Tarangire National Park or turn right (northwest) to Mto wa Mbu (Mosquito Creek) on a dirt road that is currently being paved.

Enroute you pass many Masai bomas (villages) and Masai in their colorful traditional dress walking on the roadside, riding bicycles, herding their cattle and driving overloaded donkey carts.

Masai herding cattle.

Masai Morani completing the circumcision ritual are sometimes seen clad in black with white paint on their faces. They leave the village as children for a period of training and instruction by elders and return as men.

Mto wa Mbu is a village with a market filled with wood carvings and other local crafts for sale. Be sure to bargain. If you take a few minutes to walk into the village behind the stands, you will get a more realistic (and less touristic) view of village life.

Continuing west, you soon pass the entrance to Lake Manyara National Park. The road then climbs up the Rift Valley escarpment past huge baobab trees and numerous baboons looking for handouts (please do not feed any wild animals). Fabulous views of the valley and Lake Manyara Park below can be seen. Next you pass through beautiful cultivated uplands, the village of Karatu and other small villages, past the turnoff to Lake Eyasi, and on up the slopes of the Crater Highlands to Ngorongoro Crater. The road then follows the rim of the crater and finally descends the western side of the crater to Oldupai Gorge and Serengeti National Park.

ARUSHA

This town is the center of tourism for northern Tanzania and is situated in the foothills of rugged Mt. Meru. Named after a sub-tribe of the Masai, the Wa-Arusha, it is located on the Great North Road midway between Cairo and Cape Town. Makonde carvings and other souvenirs are available in the numerous craft shops at the center of town. Walking around the **Arusha Market**, located behind the bus station, is an interesting way to spend a few hours.

 ACCOMMODATION: Also see "Accommodation" under "Arusha National Park."

DELUXE: * *Arusha Coffee Lodge*, located near the Arusha Airport on a coffee plantation, has 21 rooms with large ensuite bathrooms with separate shower and bath, telephones, mini bar, ceiling fans and fireplaces. There is massage facility available alongside a swimming pool, and 24-hour room service. * *Mountain Village* has recently been renovated and has 62 bungalows with ensuite facilities, swimming pool and conference center. The lodge is set in lovely gardens and is located 6 miles (10 km) east of Arusha overlooking Lake Duluti. * *Moivaro Lodge*, situated outside of Arusha on a coffee plantation, has 23 double (or triple) cottages with ensuite facilities and a swimming pool. * *Safari Spa*, situated in a valley between Kilimanjaro and Mount Meru, has cottages with ensuite facilities, fitness center, sauna, steam room, jacuzzi, and swimming pool. Polo matches are often played on the grounds.

FIRST CLASS: * *Karama Lodge*, located about 3 miles (5 km) from Arusha, consists of 12 bungalows with ensuite bathrooms, and it is built on stilts. On a clear day there are spectacular views of Mt. Meru and Mt. Kilimanjaro. * *Dik Dik Hotel* has nine bungalows with two double rooms in each bungalow, with ensuite facilities, and a swimming pool. Horseback riding and fishing are available. * *Rivertrees Guest Farm* is a country-style hotel with four rooms with ensuite facilities, set in tranquil gardens and farmland, situated midway between Arusha and Kilimanjaro airport. * *Ngare Sero Mountain Lodge* is a farmhouse situated on the slopes of Mt. Meru, with rooms that have private facilities. * *Mt. Meru Hotel* is a 200-room hotel with ensuite facilities and a swimming pool.

TOURIST CLASS: * *The Impala Hotel* has 125 rooms, including several suites, with ensuite facilities and a swimming pool. * *New*

ARUSHA NATIONAL PARK

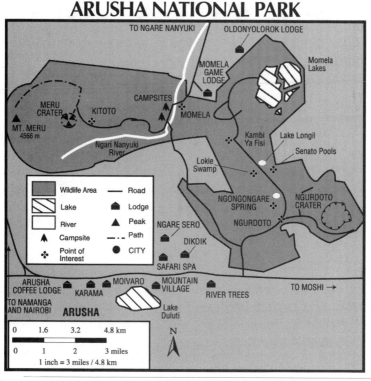

Arusha Hotel, located in the center of town, has 72 rooms with ensuite facilities. * *Hotel 77* has 250 rooms with ensuite facilities.

ARUSHA NATIONAL PARK

This highly underrated park is predominantly inhabited by forest animals, while in the other northern parks, savannah animals are the more prevalent. Arusha National Park is the best place in northern Tanzania to spot black-and-white colobus monkeys and bushbuck and to photograph larger species with Mt. Kilimanjaro or Mt. Meru in the background. Early mornings are best for this because Mt. Kilimanjaro is less likely to be covered with clouds.

This 53-square-mile (137-km²) park is actually the merger of three regions: Meru Crater National Park, Momela Lakes and Ngurdoto Crater National Park. The wide range of habitats, from highland rain forest to acacia woodlands and crater lakes, hosts a variety of wildlife. Armed park guides are required to accompany you for walks in the western part of the park or for climbing Mt. Meru; guides are available at Park Headquarters at Momela Gate.

Black-and-white colobus monkey.

On the open grassland near the entrance to the park, Burchell's zebra are often seen. High in the forest canopy of the Ngurdoto Forest is a good place to find blue monkeys and black-and-white colobus monkeys. Olive baboons are common and red duiker are sometimes seen.

Walking is not allowed in the 2-mile- (3-km) wide Ngurdoto Crater, which is, in essence, a reserve within a reserve. However, there can be good views (especially in the early morning) of the crater, Momela Lakes and Mt. Kilimanjaro.

Driving north from Ngurdoto, you pass Ngongongare Spring, the Senato Pools (sometimes dry) and Lokie Swamp and are likely to see common waterbuck and maybe Bohor reedbuck. Buffalo are often seen around Lake Longil.

As you continue past Kambi Ya Fisi (hyena's camp), the landscape becomes more open, and elephant and giraffe can be seen. Hippo and a variety of waterfowl can be seen at the shallow, alkaline Momela Lakes.

From Kitoto, a 4wd vehicle is needed to reach Meru Crater. The sheer cliff rises about 4,920 feet (1,500 m) and is one of the highest in the world.

At the base of Mt. Meru, you may encounter elephant and buffalo.

Kirk's dikdik, banded mongoose and klipspringer can also be seen in the park. On one visit we saw giraffe lying down – very unusual indeed! The best time to visit for game viewing is June-March.

Over 400 species of birds have been recorded, with Hartlaub's turaco, red-fronted parrot and brown-breasted barbet among the species not easily found elsewhere in northern Tanzania.

Mt. Meru (14,977 feet/4,566 m) is an impressive mountain that is classified as a dormant volcano; its last eruption was just over 100 years ago. The mountain can be climbed in two days, but it is more enjoyable to take three days, which allows more time for exploration.

On the morning of the first day of a three-day climb, walk for about three hours from Momela Gate (about 5,000 feet/1,500 m) to Miriakamba Hut. In the afternoon, hike to Meru Crater. On the second day, hike three hours to the Saddle Hut, and in the afternoon walk for about one and one-half hours to Little Meru (12,530 feet/3,820 m). On day three, reach the summit and return to Momela Gate.

The best months to climb are June-October and late December-February. Bring all your own gear and make your reservations in advance.

The turnoff to the park entrance is 13 miles (21 km) east of Arusha and 36 miles (58 km) west of Moshi. Continue another 7 miles (11 km) to Ngurdoto Gate. Walking is allowed in the western part of this park where there are a number of hikes and picnic sites to enjoy when accompanied by a park ranger.

ACCOMMODATION IN THE RESERVE – CLASS F: One self-service resthouse (five beds) is located near Momela Gate.

ACCOMMODATION NEAR THE RESERVE – CLASS A/B: *Oldonyolorok Lodge* is a small lodge with six bungalows (doubles) and ensuite facilities.

CLASS C/D: * *Momela Game Lodge*, located just outside Arusha National Park, has 57 rooms with ensuite facilities.

CAMPING: One campsite is located near Ngurdoto Gate, in the forest, and three are at the foot of Tululusia Hill. All have water, long-drop toilets and firewood.

NDARAKWAI RANCH

Ndarakwai is a 10,000 acre (4,000 hectare) private wildlife reserve located on the northwest slopes of Mt. Kilimanjaro about one and a half hours' drive from Arusha. The area is dominated by acacia woodlands. There is permanent water on the ranch – a key element in making it a haven for wildlife – especially in the dry season.

Activities include day and night game drives in open vehicles, escorted walks with armed guides, and visits to Masai villages that are far off the tourist track.

During a morning game drive we saw a large herd of lesser kudu (this is one of the best places for lesser kudu in East Africa), eland, bushbuck, gerenuk, Defassa waterbuck, Burchell's zebra, Thomson's gazelle, impala, baboon and vervet monkey. In the afternoon, we encountered lesser kudu, eland, ostrich and other game. On a night-drive we spotted marsh mongoose, bushpig, springhare and bush duiker. Elephant are prevalent in the dry seasons.

 ACCOMMODATION – CLASS B: * *Ndarakwai Ranch* has 10 permanent tents on platforms under thatch, with bush (bucket) showers and ensuite flush toilets.

SINYA

The Sinya region is Masailand bordering the southwestern corner of Amboseli National Park in Kenya. Mt. Meru lies to the southwest and Mt. Kilimanjaro to the southeast. This area of hills and acacia woodland has seldom been visited by tourists until recently.

Unlike at Amboseli, one seldom if ever encounters other tourists on this Tanzania side of the border. From the time we left Namanga until the time we left the region, we encountered no other vehicles.

There is no permanent water in the area except for a few boreholes used by the Masai for their livestock. In addition to seeing resident game, wildlife can be seen traversing the area, moving to and from permanent water in Amboseli National Park to permanent water on the slopes of Mt. Kilimanjaro.

Two Masai morani joined us on two game drives during which we spotted lesser kudu, African wild cat, eland, cheetah, elephant, Masai giraffe, dikdik, impala, dwarf mongoose and Burchell's zebra.

Young Masai after his traditional initiation.

Game viewing in Sinya is good; however, its major attraction may be that it offers very good opportunities for a non-touristic, cultural experience with the Masai.

Sinya is about an hour and a half drive from Namanga and about a two-hour drive from Arusha.

ACCOMMODATION – CLASS B: * *Campi ya Tembo* has eight tents with ensuite bucket showers and flush toilets.

TARANGIRE NATIONAL PARK
Large numbers of baobab trees dotting the landscape give the park a prehistoric look, the likes of which I have never seen. This 1003-square-mile (2,600-km²) park has a different feel to it than any other northern park — and an eerie feeling at that, making it one of my favorites.

Tarangire is the best park on the northern circuit to see elephant. Several years ago while in the park I met Cynthia Moss, author of *Elephant Memories* and *Portraits in the Wild* (Chicago University Press), who told me that she had identified over 500 individual elephants within the park during one week!

Fewer tourists visit this park than Manyara, Ngorongoro and Serengeti, allowing a better opportunity to experience it as the early explorers did — alone. This park should not be missed; wildlife

TARANGIRE NATIONAL PARK

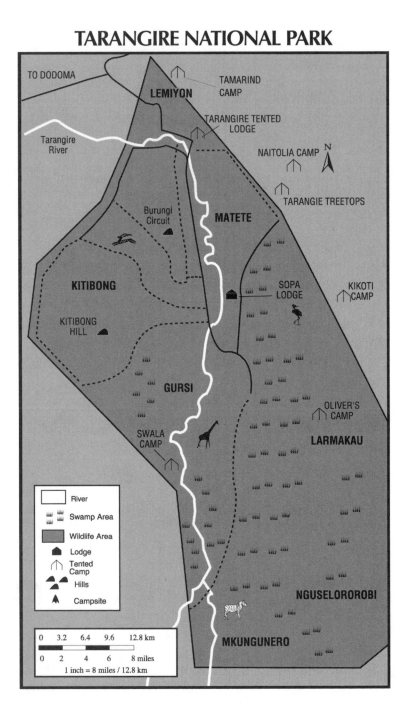

TO DODOMA

LEMIYON

TAMARIND CAMP

TARANGIRE TENTED LODGE

Tarangire River

NAITOLIA CAMP

N

TARANGIE TREETOPS

Burungi Circuit

MATETE

KITIBONG

SOPA LODGE

KIKOTI CAMP

KITIBONG HILL

GURSI

OLIVER'S CAMP

SWALA CAMP

LARMAKAU

River

Swamp Area

Wildlife Area

Lodge

Tented Camp

Hills

Campsite

NGUSELORORROBI

| 0 | 3.2 | 6.4 | 9.6 | 12.8 km |

| 0 | 2 | 4 | 6 | 8 miles |

1 inch = 8 miles / 12.8 km

MKUNGUNERO

Kikoti Tented Camp, located in an area outside of Tarangire where walking is allowed.

viewing is excellent, especially from July to November, when many animals concentrate near the only permanent water source in the area — the Tarangire River and its tributaries.

At the beginning of the short rainy season (November), migratory species including wildebeest and zebra, soon followed by elephant, buffalo, Grant's gazelle, Thomson's gazelle and oryx, begin migrating out of the park. However, as most migration routes have been cut off from the expansion of man's presence, many of these animals are, in fact, remaining in the park and few are migrating out of the park or far beyond the park's borders, also making December-February a good time to visit. Giraffe, waterbuck, lesser kudu and other resident species remain in the park. The migratory animals that do manage to leave the park usually return at the end of the long rains in June.

On a recent two-day visit during November we saw over 600 elephant, several prides of lion, leopard in a tree with an impala kill, eland, oryx, along with a variety of other antelope. The game viewing was excellent!

Tarangire wildlife populations include approximately 30,000 zebra, 25,000 wildebeest, 5,000 elephant, 5,000 buffalo, 5,000 eland, 2,500 Masai giraffe and 1,000 oryx. Other prominent species include

Tarangire may be the best park in Africa for seeing lions in trees.

Grant's and Thomson's gazelle, hartebeest, impala, lesser and greater kudu, reedbuck and gerenuk. Lion and leopard are frequently seen. Cheetah and spotted hyena are also present, as are the banded, slender, dwarf and marsh mongoose. African wild dog may also be seen.

The **Lemiyon region**, the northernmost region of the park, is characterized by a high concentration of baobab trees that is unmatched by any park I've seen. This unique landscape is also dotted by umbrella acacia trees, as well as some open grasslands and wooded areas. Elephant, wildebeest and zebra are often seen. Visitors with little time for game viewing may want to concentrate on the Matete and the Lemiyon areas, including the Tarangire River.

The **Matete region** covers the northeastern part of the park and is characterized by open grasslands with scattered umbrella acacia and baobab trees and the Tarangire River. Lion, fringe-eared oryx and klipspringer are seen quite often. Bat-eared fox are also present.

On the 50-mile (80-km) **Burungi Circuit**, you pass through acacia parklands and woodlands. You are likely to see a number of species, including elephant, eland and bushbuck.

The eastern side of the **Kitibong area** is a good place to find large herds of buffalo. The eastern side is mainly acacia parklands, and the western side is thicker woodlands.

The **Gursi section** is similar to the Kitibong area with the addition of rainy season wetlands, which are home to large populations of water birds.

The **Larmakau region**, located in the central eastern part of the park, has extensive swamps. **Nguselororobi**, in the south of the park, is predominantly swamp with some woodlands and plains. The **Mkungunero section** has a few freshwater pools and a variety of bird life.

On one visit, we spotted eland, giraffe, buffalo, a few lion, oryx, elephant, impala, Grant's gazelle, zebra, hartebeest, warthog, baboon and ostrich.

Elephants have destroyed many baobab trees. A baobab tree with a huge hole through the center of its trunk — literally eaten through by elephant — can be seen near Tarangire Safari Lodge.

Game viewing is excellent during the dry season from July-October, and is, in fact, good year-round. Well over 300 species of birds have been recorded at Tarangire, with lappet-faced vulture, yellow-necked spurfowl, Fischer's lovebird, white-bellied go-away bird, rosy-patched bushshrike and ashy starling among the characteristic species. Bird watching is best December-May. During the rainy seasons, some roads become impassable.

ACCOMMODATION – CLASS A/B: * *Tarangire Sopa Lodge* has 75 rooms with ensuite facilities and a swimming pool. * *Swala Camp* is a permanent tented camp, located on the western side of the park, with 12 tents with ensuite facilities, and swimming pool. * *Tarangire Safari*

Lodge is set on high ridge overlooking the Tarangire River, and has 35 tents (doubles) and six bungalows (triples) with private facilities and a large swimming pool.

CLASS B/C: * *Oliver's Camp*, located inside the eastern border of the reserve overlooking a swamp, has nine tents with private bush showers and long-drop toilets. Day game drives and walking safaris are offered within the park.

ACCOMMODATION ON THE PERIPHERY OF THE PARK – CLASS A: * *Kikoti Camp* is a 20 bed luxury permanent tented camp, with ensuite facilities, perched high on a ridge on the eastern periphery of the park only 4 miles (7 km) from the park gate. Activities include day game drives into the park, nature walks with a Masai guide, escorted mountain biking, night game drives outside the park and visits to local villages. * *Tarangire Treetops Camp* is set in a private reserve just outside the border of the park, about an hour and a half drive from the park entrance. Each of the 21 tents has bathroom facilities ensuite, and it features a deck built around one of the trees. Activities offered outside the park include walking, night game drives as well as mountain biking.

ACCOMMODATION – CLASS B: * *Tarangire Tamarind Camp* is a 20-bed tented camp with ensuite bucket showers and long-drop toilets. It is located near the park's main entrance. Activities include nature walks with a Masai guide in the immediate area and a night game drives. * *Naitolia Camp*, located in a private concession area north east of the park, has four stone and grass cottages with ensuite toilets and bucket showers, and one tree camp (used only in the dry season). Walking safaris and night game drives can be arranged from this camp.

CAMPING: There are campsites with no facilities.

LAKE MANYARA NATIONAL PARK

Once one of the most popular hunting areas of Tanzania, this 125-square-mile (325-km²) park has the Great Rift Valley escarpment for a dramatic backdrop. Two-thirds of the park is covered by alkaline Lake Manyara, which is situated at an altitude of 3,150 feet (960 m).

The turnoff to Lake Manyara is past Mto wa Mbu on the road from Makuyuni to Ngorongoro Crater, about 75 miles (120 km) west of Arusha.

Despite its comparatively small size, the park has five distinct vegetation zones and a remarkable diversity of wildlife. From the crest of

Communicating by bush telegraph.

the Rift Valley to the shores of the lake, the varied topography and soils support characteristic plants and animals. The first zone reached from the park entrance is ground-water forest that is fed by water seeping from the Great Rift Wall, with wild fig, sausage, tamarind and mahogany trees. Elephant prefer these dense forests, as well as marshy glades. The other zones include the marshlands along the edge of the lake, scrub on the Rift Valley Wall, open areas with scattered acacia, and open grasslands.

Manyara, like Tarangire National Park (Tanzania) and Ishasha in Queen Elizabeth National Park in (Uganda), is well known for its tree-climbing lions, which can be found lazing on branches of acacia trees. Some people believe that lions climb trees in Manyara and Tanangire to avoid tsetse flies and the dense undergrowth while they remain in the cool shade. They also believe that lions of the Ruwenzori National Park in Uganda climb trees to gain a hunting advantage. Finding lion in the trees in Lake Manyara is rare, so don't set your heart on it – look at it as an unexpected bonus.

Manyara features large concentrations of elephant and buffalo. Other wildlife includes common waterbuck, Masai giraffe, zebra, impala, baboons and blue monkeys.

Some 450 species of birds — including an astonishing total of over 40 varieties of birds of prey — have been recorded, which makes

LAKE MANYARA NATIONAL PARK

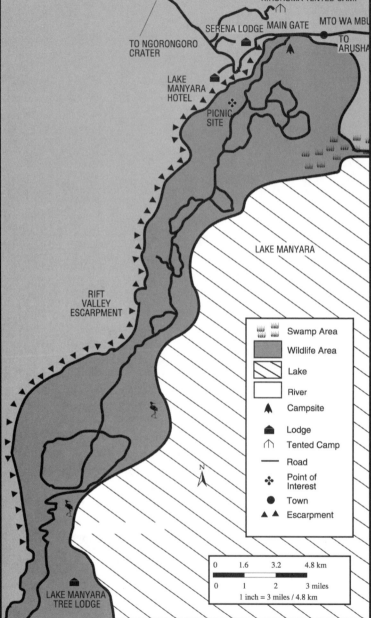

KIRURUMA TENTED CAMP

MTO WA MBU

SERENA LODGE   MAIN GATE

TO NGORONGORO
CRATER

TO
ARUSHA

LAKE
MANYARA
HOTEL

PICNIC
SITE

LAKE MANYARA

RIFT
VALLEY
ESCARPMENT

	Swamp Area
	Wildlife Area
	Lake
	River
	Campsite
	Lodge
	Tented Camp
	Road
	Point of Interest
	Town
	Escarpment

N

0	1.6	3.2	4.8 km
0	1	2	3 miles

1 inch = 3 miles / 4.8 km

LAKE MANYARA
TREE LODGE

Manyara one of Tanzania's best birdwatching localities and one of the world's most impressive raptor havens. Among the exciting birds regularly seen are saddle-billed stork, crowned eagle, southern ground hornbill, silvery-cheeked hornbill, grey-hooded kingfisher, long-tailed fiscal, spotted morning thrush and black-winged red bishop.

The level of the lake fluctuates with rainfall, and it rose to its highest level in over 30 years in 1998, when El Nino rains caused flooding in northern Tanzania. When the lake is high, the fish population increases and pelicans and storks flourish. At lower levels, the salinity of the water increases, and vast flocks of lesser and greater flamingo feed on brine shrimp and algae in the shallows.

The traditional migration route from Lake Manyara to Tarangire National Park has been all but cut off by villages. Nevertheless, much of the wildlife is resident year-round, making this a good park to visit any time. The best time to visit is December-March and June-October A 4wd vehicle is recommended for travel in April and May.

On one visit we encountered a pride of lion lying only a few yards (meters) from the road. Later, as we were rounding a bend, we almost ran right into two huge bull elephants that were sparring with tusks locked, pushing each other from one side of the road to the other, trumpeting and kicking up mounds of dust in their fight for dominance.

Birds spotted included white-breasted cormorant, red-billed oxpecker, African spoonbill, lesser flamingo, white pelican, grey-headed gull, wood sandpiper, black-winged stilt, white-faced duck, white-crowned plover, blacksmith plover, long-toed plover, avocet, water dikkop, cattle egret, common sandpiper, painted snipe and sacred ibis.

Other activities offered in and near the park include canoeing, abseiling (rappelling), and mountain biking.

Roads in the northern part of the park are good year-round and four-wheel drive is not needed, although in the rainy season some side tracks may be temporarily closed. Four-wheel-drive vehicles are sometimes necessary in the more remote southern part of Lake Manyara.

ACCOMMODATION – CLASS A: * *Lake Manyara Tree Lodge*, located in the southwestern area of the park in a mahogany forest, has 10 luxury treehouses with facilities ensuite and a swimming pool. * *Lake Manyara Serena Lodge*, magnificently set on the Rift Valley Escarpment overlooking the park and the Rift Valley 1,000 feet (300 m) below, has 67 rooms with ensuite facilities and a swimming pool. The hotel offers walks along the Rift Valley escarpment, mountain biking, abseiling, rock climbing and canoeing.

ACCOMMODATION – CLASS A/B: * *Kirurumu Camp* is set on the escarpment overlooking the Rift Valley, outside the reserve, and has 20 tents covered by thatched roofs, with ensuite facilities. Short nature walks around the area as well as hikes down the escarpment to Mtu wa Mbu village are offered.

ACCOMMODATION – CLASS B/C: * *Lake Manyara Hotel*, set on the escarpment overlooking the park, has 100 rooms with ensuite facilities and a swimming pool.

ACCOMMODATION – CLASS C/D: * *Migunga Camp* is located near the park and has eight tents with ensuite chemical toilets and communal showers.

CLASSES D & F: * *National Park Self-Service Bandas* (10 doubles) are located near the park entrance. Some bandas have private facilities and everyone shares a communal kitchen.

CAMPING: Two campsites are located near the park entrance, both with toilet and shower facilities. One campsite is situated within the park with no facilities; this site requires a special permit.

ACCOMMODATION BETWEEN LAKE MANYARA AND NGORONGORO CRATER – CLASS A/B: * *Kifaru Safari Lodge*, a converted farmhouse located on a working coffee, vegetable, flower seed and dairy plantation, has 10 rooms and two family cottages with ensuite facilities (24 beds), a swimming pool and tennis court. You may explore the farm and environs and, perhaps, visit a village on the property. * *Plantation Lodge*, set in lovely gardens on a coffee farm near Karatu, has 12 rooms with facilities ensuite and a swimming pool. * *Gibb's Farm* has 19 rooms with ensuite facilities. Walks to nearby waterfalls can be arranged.

LAKE EYASI

Lake Eyasi lies on the southern border of the Ngorongoro

Conservation area and is Tanzania's largest soda lake. The remote region is seldom visited by travelers and is home for the Hadzabe Bushmen and the Datoka tribe. Here you can have a much truer picture of tribal life than in the more touristed areas.

Hadzabe Bushmen are traditional hunter-gatherers who speak a "click" language similar to the Bushmen of southern Africa. The men hunt in the early mornings and afternoons with bows and arrows. Poison arrows are used for large game and non-poison arrows for birds and small game. The women gather wild fruits, roots and tubers.

Hunting with the Bushmen is one of the most exciting cultural experiences you can have in Africa. During a recent visit we followed five Bushmen hunters on an early morning hunt. During the next two hours of walking and running with them, they attempted to shoot a few birds and antelope, but were unsuccessful. Finally, they shot a baboon out of the top of a tree, built a fire and cooked it on the spot. We then returned to their village, where the meat was shared among their families.

That afternoon we visited a family of the Datoka, a tribe similar to the Masai, that herd cattle and goats. Their diet primarily consists of meat, milk, and blood. The family slaughtered a goat and cooked it while our guide showed us around their boma.

Only travelers with a keen interest in culture should venture here. If you visit the area, please do your part in helping them maintain their culture by not giving the Bushmen or the Datoka any clothing or other western articles. Your guide will know what is appropriate.

Lake Eyasi is about a three-hour drive from the Karatu - Ngorongoro Crater road.

 ACCOMMODATIONS: None

Camping: Campsites are available.

NGORONGORO CRATER CONSERVATION AREA
Ngorongoro Crater is the largest unflooded, intact caldera (collapsed cone of a volcano) in the world. Known as the eighth wonder of the world, its vastness and beauty are truly overwhelming, and it is believed by some to have been the proverbial Garden of Eden. Many

There are more than 7 lion prides resident in the Ngorongoro Crater.

scientists suggest that before its eruption, this volcano was larger than Mt. Kilimanjaro.

Ngorongoro contains possibly the largest permanent concentration of wildlife in Africa, with an estimated average of 30,000 large mammals. In addition, this is one of the best reserves in Africa in which to see black rhino.

Large concentrations of wildlife make Ngorongoro Crater their permanent home. Game viewing is good year-round. Because there is a permanent source of fresh water, there's no reason for much of the wildlife to migrate as it must do in the Serengeti.

Ngorongoro Crater itself is but a small portion of the 3,200-square-mile (8,288-km²) Ngorongoro Conservation Area, a World Heritage Site that is characterized by a highland plateau with volcanic mountains as well as several craters, extensive savannah and forests. Altitudes range from 4,430 to 11,800 feet (1,350 to 3,600 m).

Ngorongoro Crater is about 12 miles (19 km) wide and its rim rises 1,200-1,600 feet (365-490 m) off of its expansive 102-square-mile (265-km²) floor. From the crater rim, elephant appear as small dark specks on the grasslands.

NGORONGORO CRATER

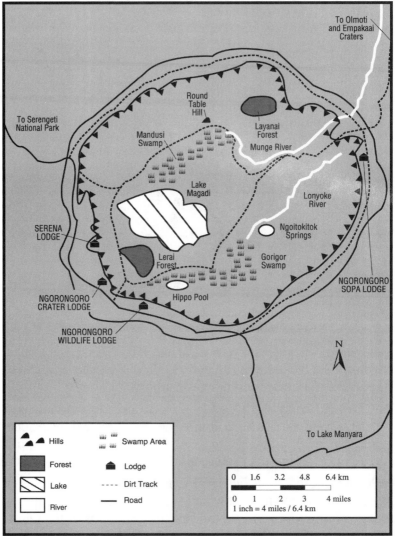

To Olmoti
and Empakaai
Craters

Round
Table
Hill

Layanai
Forest

Munge River

To Serengeti
National Park

Mandusi
Swamp

Lake
Magadi

Lonyoke
River

SERENA
LODGE

Ngoitokitok
Springs

Lerai
Forest

Gorigor
Swamp

NGORONGORO
CRATER LODGE

Hippo Pool

NGORONGORO
SOPA LODGE

NGORONGORO
WILDLIFE LODGE

N

To Lake Manyara

Hills		Swamp Area	
Forest		Lodge	
Lake		- - - - Dirt Track	
River		Road	

0	1.6	3.2	4.8	6.4 km
0	1	2	3	4 miles

1 inch = 4 miles / 6.4 km

The steep descent into the crater along winding roads takes 25-35 minutes from the crater rim. The crater floor is predominantly grasslands (making game easy to spot) with two swamps fed by streams, and the Lerai Forest. The walls of the crater are lightly forested. You may descend on a road beginning on the western rim or on the eastern rim. Once on the floor, your driver will more than likely turn left on a dirt road and travel clockwise around the crater floor.

Ngorongoro Crater Lodge.

Lake Magadi, also called Crater Lake and Lake Makat, is a shallow soda lake near the western rim entry point of the crater that attracts thousands of flamingos and other water birds.

The dirt road continues past Mandusi Swamp. Game viewing is especially good in this area during the dry season (July-October) because some wildlife migrates to the fresh water. Hippo, elephant and reedbuck, among many other species, can usually be found here.

You then come to Round Table Hill, which provides a good view and excellent vantage point to get your bearings. The circular route continues over the Munge River, the source of which is in the Olmoti Crater north of Ngorongoro Crater, to Ngoitokitok Springs. From there, you journey past Gorigor Swamp, fed by the Lonyokie River, to the Hippo Pool, which is probably the best place to see hippo.

The Lerai Forest, primarily composed of fever trees (a type of acacia), is a good place to spot elephant and waterbuck and, if you are very lucky, leopard. There are two picnic areas here with long-drop toilets and running water. The exit only road that climbs the wall of the crater is behind the forest. The road from the eastern rim can be used as both a down and up road into the crater.

On my most recent visit we saw three lion, hippo and black rhino within one hour on the crater floor. On another game drive we saw a variety of wildlife including two black rhino and one of the large tusker elephant that we found near the Lerai Forest. On a full-day's game drive during a another visit, we saw seven black rhino (including one mother with her baby), 27 lion, several golden jackal, a spotted hyena, numerous elephant, buffalo, zebra, wildebeest, flamingo, kori bustard, bat-eared fox at their den an ostrich guarding the eggs in her nest. Later we spotted a leopard crossing the rim road around the crater. Bull elephant are also found in the wooded areas and on the slopes of the crater. Cheetah are present, but there are no giraffe, topi or impala.

Close to 400 bird species have been recorded in and around the Ngorongoro Crater. Birds commonly encountered on the Crater floor are kori bustard, northern anteater chat, rufous-naped lark, rosy-breasted longclaw, superb starling and rufous-tailed weaver, as well as host of waterfowl and waders. A different avifauna thrives on the forested crater rim and misty highlands, with augur buzzard, golden-winged sunbird, malachite sunbird, tacazze sunbird, Schalow's turaco, white-eyed slaty flycatcher and streaky seedeater all being common.

At the picnic sites, vervet monkeys are very aggressive in getting at your food. Black and yellow-billed kites (predatory birds) habitually make swooping dives at lunch plates out in the open, and it is advisable to eat inside your vehicle! Once you've enjoyed your food, you'll be able to stretch your legs by walking around without being harassed by the kites. Camping has not been allowed on the crater floor since 1992.

One important thing to remember: game is not confined to the crater; wildlife is present throughout the conservation area, including near hotels and lodges. This I learned the hard way on my first visit to Ngorongoro over 25 years ago. One evening, just outside the Ngorongoro Wildlife Lodge, I walked blindly to within 20 feet (6 m) of three large buffalo. One buffalo appeared as if it were going to charge, but fortunately it ran off. *Welcome to Africa!* I thought, relieved beyond words.

The Serengeti Plains cover the western part of the conservation area. Game viewing in this region bordering the Serengeti National Park is best between December and May, when the Serengeti migration is usually in the area.

Ngorongoro Crater is about 112 miles (180 km) west of Arusha. An airstrip is located farther along the crater rim, but fog often keeps it closed in the mornings. Four-wheel-drive vehicles are required for game drives into the crater, and guests must be accompanied by a licensed guide or ranger.

Since this is classified as a conservation area and not a national park, wildlife, human beings and livestock exist together.

Ground cultivation is not allowed. The Masai are allowed to bring in their cattle for the salts and permanent water available on the crater floor, but they must leave the crater at night.

An interesting excursion — for the adventurous and hardy only — is to take the beautifully scenic drive past **Olmoti Crater** through Masailand to the 10,700-foot- (3,260-m) high **Empakaai Crater**, situated 20 miles (32 km) northwest of Ngorongoro Crater on a road that is difficult (and sometimes impossible) to negotiate, even with a 4wd vehicle. **Ol Doinyo Lengai** (10,600 feet/3,231 m) — an active volcano and holy mountain of the Masai — Lake Natron and possibly even Mt. Kilimanjaro may be seen. Hiking Olmoti Crater and Empakaai Crater is allowed if you are accompanied by an armed wildlife guard.

About 30 miles (50 km) west of Ngorongoro Crater and a few miles off the road to the Serengeti is **Oldupai Gorge**, site of many archeological discoveries, including the estimated 1.7-million-year-old *Zinjanthropus boisei* fossil. The fossil is housed in the National Museum in Dar es Salaam.

A small museum overlooks the gorge itself, and a guide there will tell you the story of the Leakeys' research and findings. For a small tip, the guide will take you down into the gorge and show you where the *Zinjanthropus boisei* fossil was found.

The vast flat plains around Oldupai Gorge and west toward Ndutu and the Naabi Hills are underlain with volcanic ash, which promotes the growth of highly nutritious annual grasses. These plains are the principle breeding grounds of the one and a half million Serengeti wildebeest, which drop their calves in January or February and feed on the lush but short-lived grasses. When the rains come to an end, the wildebeest move north and the plains bake under the relentless sun.

To the north of Oldupai are the **Gol Mountains**, a range of jagged hills and deep valleys where great numbers of griffon vultures nest and the elusive striped hyena may sometimes be seen. At the western end of the Gols, the huge monolith of **Nasera Rock** is a striking landmark and — if you have the energy to climb to the top — allows for breathtaking views across the endless wilderness.

 ACCOMMODATION – CLASS A+: * *Ngorongoro Crater Lodge*, set on the southwestern rim of the crater, has three separate camps: North and South Camp, each with 12 suites and Tree Camp with 6 suites. Each stilted suite is elegantly furnished with full ensuite facilities and butler service.

ACCOMMODATION – CLASS A: * *Ngorongoro Serena Lodge*, situated on the western rim of the crater, has 75 rooms with ensuite facilities. Escorted walks are offered. * *Ngorongoro Sopa Lodge*, located on the eastern rim of the crater, has 92 suites with ensuite facilities and a swimming pool. There is a down-and-up access road into the crater nearby.

CLASS B: * *Ngorongoro Wildlife Lodge*, a 78-room hotel with ensuite facilities, has a wonderful view of the crater.

CAMPING: Campsites are located on the crater rim.

SERENGETI NATIONAL PARK

The Serengeti is Tanzania's largest and most famous park, and it has the largest concentration of migratory game animals in the world. It is also famous for its huge lion population and is one of the best places on the continent to see them. The park has received additional notoriety through Professor Bernard Grzimek's book, *Serengeti Shall Not Die* (Hamish Hamilton) and the feature film *Serengeti* (IMAX).

Serengeti is derived from the Masai language and appropriately means "endless plain." The park's 5,700 square miles (14,763 km²) makes it larger than the state of Connecticut. Altitude varies from 3,120 to 6,070 feet (950 to 1,850 m).

SERENGETI NATIONAL PARK

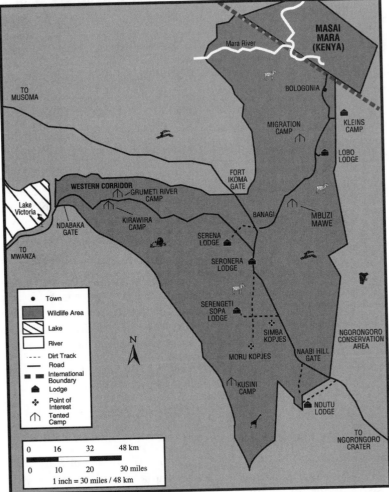

The park, a World Heritage Site, comprises most of the Serengeti ecosystem, which is the primary migration route of the wildebeest. The Serengeti ecosystem also includes Kenya's Masai Mara National Reserve, bordering on the north; the Loliondo Controlled Area, bordering on the northeast; the Ngorongoro Conservation Area, bordering on the southeast; the Maswa Game Reserve, bordering on the southwest; and the Grumeti and Ikorongo Controlled Areas, bordering on the northwest. The "western corridor" of the park comes within 5 miles (8 km) of Lake Victoria.

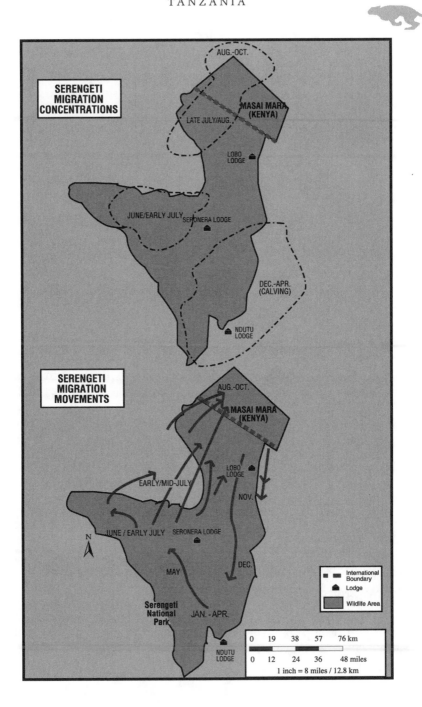

Luxury mobile tented accommodations.

Nearly 500 species of birds and 35 species of large plains animals can be found in the Serengeti. The park may contain as many as 1.5 million wildebeest, 500,000 zebra, 300,000 Grant's gazelle, 250,000 Thomson's gazelle, 120,000 impala, 70,000 topi, 20,000 buffalo, 9,000 eland, 8,000 giraffe, 1,000 lion and 800 elephant.

Most of the Serengeti is a vast, open plain broken by rocky outcrops (kopjes). There is also acacia savannah, savannah woodland, riverine forests, some swamps and small lakes.

The north is more hilly, with thick scrub and forests lining the Mara River, where leopards are sometimes spotted sleeping in the trees. Acacia savannah dominates the central region, with short- and long-grass open plains in the southeast and woodland plains and hills in the western corridor.

It is impossible to predict the exact time of the famous **Serengeti migration** of approximately 1.3 million wildebeest, 200,000 zebra and 300,000 Thomson's gazelle, which covers a circuit of about 500 miles (800 km).

African architecture – Serengeti Serena.

The key element in understanding of "The Greatest Wildlife Show on Earth" is that it follows the general "rainfall gradient" across the ecosystem, with lower rainfall in the southeast (short-grass plains) and higher rainfall in the northwest. The migration moves from Kenya back to the short-grass plains of the Serengeti and Ngorongoro Conservation area once the short rains have begun (usually in late October-November), and after the short-grass plains have dried out (usually in May), the migration moves northwest to higher rainfall areas and areas of permanent water — and fresh grass.

From December-May wildebeest, zebra, eland and Thomson's gazelle usually concentrate on the treeless short-grass plains in the extreme southeastern Serengeti and western Ngorongoro Conservation Area near Lake Ndutu in search of short grass, which they prefer over the longer dry-stemmed variety. This is the best time to visit the Serengeti. In April and May, the height of the rainy season, a 4wd vehicle is highly recommended.

Other species common to the area during this period are Grant's gazelle, eland, hartebeest, topi and a host of predators including lion, cheetah, spotted hyena, honey badger and black-backed jackal. Kori

A picnic set up at Kleins.

bustard, secretarybird, yellow-throated sandgrouse and rufous-naped lark are resident birds of the open plains, which attract large numbers of migratory Montagu's and pallid harriers (from Europe) between September and March.

During the long rainy season (April-May), nomadic lions and hyena move to the eastern part of the Serengeti. The migration, mainly of wildebeest and zebra, begins in May or June. Once the dry season begins, wildebeest and zebra must migrate from the area. There is no permanent water, and both of these species must drink on a regular basis.

The rut for wildebeest is concentrated over a three-week period and generally occurs at the end of April, May or early June. After a gestation period of eight and one-half months, approximately 90% of the pregnant cows will give birth on the short-grass plains within a six-week period between the mid/end of January and February. Zebra calving season is spread out over most of the year, with a slightly higher birth rate December-March. The best time to see wildebeest and zebra crossing the Grumeti River is in June/early July and November.

Wildebeest move about six to 10 abreast in columns several miles long toward the western corridor. Zebra do not move in columns but in family units.

Leopards are commonly seen in the Seronera Valley.

As a general rule, by June the migration has progressed west of Seronera. The migration then splits into three separate migrations: one west through the corridor toward permanent water and Lake Victoria and then northeast; the second due north, reaching the Masai Mara of Kenya around mid-July; and the third northward between the other two to a region west of Lobo Lodge, where the group disperses. At present, there are few roads in the region where the third group disperses; however, this may change.

During July-September, the Serengeti's highest concentration of wildlife is in the extreme north. The first and second groups meet and usually begin returning to the Serengeti National Park in late October; the migration then reaches the central or southern Serengeti by December.

Short-grass plains dominate the part of the Ngorongoro Conservation Area bordering the Serengeti. As you move northwest into the park, the plains change to medium-grass plains and then into long-grass plains around **Simba Kopjes** north of Naabi Hill Gate. Topi, elephant, Thomson's and Grant's gazelle, bat-eared fox and warthog are often seen here.

The Great Serengeti Migration.

There are two saline lakes in the south of the park, **Lake Masek** and **Lake Lagaja**, known mainly for their populations of lesser and greater flamingos.

SERONERA

The **Seronera Valley** is located in the center of the park and is characterized by large umbrella thorn trees — the archetypal image of the African savannah. Game is plentiful, and the area is famous for lion and leopard. Other wildlife includes hyena, jackal, topi, Masai giraffe and Thomson's gazelle. This is the best part of the park to find cheetah, especially in the dry season. In the wet season, many cheetah are found in the short-grass plains. They are, however, found throughout the park.

Banagi Hill, 11 miles (17 km) north of Seronera on the road to Lobo, is a good area for Masai giraffe, buffalo and impala. Four miles (6 km) from Banagi on the Orangi River is a hippo pool.

A unique way to experience the Serengeti is by hot air balloon. Guests are transferred from the Serengeti Sopa, Serengeti Serena and Seronera lodges to the balloon launch site near Maasai Kopjes in time for a dawn takeoff. Your pilot may fly you, at times, over 1,000 feet off the ground for panoramic views, and at other times at a very low altitudes for great game viewing and photographic opportunities. The flight lasts about an hour, depending on wind conditions. After landing, guests enjoy a champagne breakfast.

LOBO

From Banagi northward to Lobo and the Bologonja Gate are rolling uplands with open plains, bush, woodlands and magnificent kopjes. This is the best area of the park to see elephant. Forests of large mahogany and fig trees are found along the rivers where kingfishers, fish eagles and turacos can be seen. Other wildlife found in the Lobo area includes grey bush duikers and mountain reedbuck. Large numbers of Masai giraffe are permanent residents.

Large herds of wildebeest are often in the region from August until the rains begin, usually in November. During this period, many wildebeest drown while attempting to cross the Mara River.

While game viewing in the Seronera Valley, one December morning, we found leopard and watched a large running herd of zebra splash through a marsh swamp in the soft morning light. Under some nearby bushes, a pride of five lion looked on in total disinterest as they continued their morning snooze. Later we drove around the Moru Kopjes and found a lone lion sunning himself on a rock, surrounded by the magnificent spectacle of the larger herds of wildebeest and zebra on the grassy plains.

On another visit, only an hour after stepping off the charter flight at the Seronera airstrip, we saw leopards mating in clear sight on a kopje. Other game spotted in a 24-hour period included Masai giraffe, elephant, lion, spotted hyena, black-backed jackal, klipspringer, dikdik, bushbuck, buffalo, topi, Bohor reedbuck and steenbok.

On yet another visit, we watched a pride of lion with five cubs play for hours. Later we came upon a fire in the northern Serengeti, where hundreds of storks were feeding on the insects that were fleeing the flames.

WESTERN CORRIDOR

Beginning 3 miles (5 km) north of Seronera, the western corridor road passes over the Grumeti River and beyond to a central range of hills. Eighteen miles (29 km) before Ndabaka Gate is an extensive area of black cotton soil, which makes rainy season travel difficult. This area is best visited June-October, during the dry season. Colobus monkeys may be found in the riverine areas. Other wildlife includes eland, topi, impala, dikdik, hippo and crocodile. The area is known for its huge crocodiles, which reach 20 feet in length. I saw one specimen that was 17 feet long and about 1,500 pounds! In this remote region of the Serengeti, we also saw a mother cheetah with six cubs, along with a variety of other game.

The granite kopjes or rocky outcrops that dot the plains are home to rock hyrax, Kirk's dikdik and klipspringer. Banded, dwarf and slender mongoose are occasionally seen nearby. Verreaux's eagle are sometimes sighted near the Moru Kopjes.

Three species of jackal live in the Serengeti: black-backed, side-striped and golden. Side-striped jackal are rare, golden jackal are usually found in the short grass plains and black-backed jackal are quite common. The six species of vultures found in the park are white-backed, white-headed, hooded, lappet-faced, Ruppell's and Egyptian.

At the time of this writing, the border with Kenya between Serengeti National Park and the Masai Mara is officially closed, and is expected to remain closed. There is a dry-weather road (often impassable in the rainy season) from Mwanza and Musoma (Lake Victoria) to the west through Ndabaka Gate. The main road from the Ngorongoro Conservation Area via Naabi Hill Gate is open year-round.

Vehicles must stay on the roads within a 10-mile (16-km) radius of Seronera, Lobo, Kirawira and Grumeti (Western Corridor), as well as around Simba Kipjes, Moru, Naabi and Gol Kopjes. Off-road driving is usually allowed in the rest of the park, making a safari with a 4wd vehicle all the more attractive. Travel in the park is allowed only from 6:00 a.m. until 7:00 p.m. Visitors may get out of the vehicle in open areas if no animals are present. Do stay close to the vehicle, and keep a careful lookout.

From July to September, when one arm of the migration is usually in the Masai Mara in Kenya, consider concentrating your time in either the Western Corridor or the northern Serengeti. At that time, wildebeest and zebra may be more concentrated in the Masai Mara (Kenya), but you will most certainly encounter a fraction of the tourists in the Serengeti than you would in the Masai Mara. Having those expansive Serengeti Plains almost to yourself is a priceless experience for travelers who are looking for more out of a safari than just seeing animals.

Park Headquarters are located at Seronera, while the park staff housing is located at Ft. Ikoma, outside of the park.

ACCOMMODATION – CLASS A: * *Kirawira Camp,* located in the western corridor approximately 55 miles (90 km) west of Seronera and 6 miles (10 km) east of the Kirawira Ranger Post, has a classic Victorian atmosphere, with 25 luxury tents with ensuite facilities and a swimming pool. * *Grumeti River Camp,* located in the Western Corridor 53 miles (85 km) west of Seronera Lodge and 31 miles (50 km) east of Lake Victoria, has 10 tents with ensuite facilities and a plunge pool. * *Kusini Camp,* located in the southern Serengeti, has 12 tents with ensuite facilities scattered around a rock formation, and a swimming pool. *Serengeti Serena Lodge,* set on a hill overlooking the Serengeti Plains about 18 miles (29 km) northwest of Seronera Lodge, has 66 rooms with ensuite facilities and a swimming pool.

ACCOMMODATION – CLASS A/B: * *Migration Camp,* located 14 miles (22 km) west of Lobo Lodge, has 16 tents with ensuite facilities and a swimming pool. *Serengeti Sopa Lodge,* located 25 miles (40 km) southwest of Seronera Lodge and 60 miles (96 km) from Naabi Hill Gate, has 75 suites with ensuite facilities and a swimming pool.

CLASS B: * *Mbuzi Mawe Camp* is located on a kopje between Seronera and Lobo in a wilderness zone where walking is allowed. The camp consists of tents with ensuite facilities. * *Lobo Wildlife Lodge,* located in the north of the park 43 miles north of Seronera, is uniquely designed around huge boulders and has a swimming pool carved out of solid rock. All 75 double rooms have ensuite facilities. * *Seronera Wildlife Lodge,* situated in the center of the park 90 miles (145 km) from Ngorongoro Crater, has 75 double rooms with ensuite facilities.

ACCOMMODATION ON THE PERIPHERY OF THE PARK – CLASS A: * *Kleins Camp* is situated in a 25,000-acre (10,000-hectare) private reserve bordered on the west by Serengeti National Park and the north by the Masai Mara in Kenya. Each of the 10 thatched cottages are made from local rock and have ensuite facilities. Day game drives, night game drives to spot nocturnal creatures and active predators, guided bush walks and visits to local Masai are offered.

CLASS A/B: * *Speke Bay Lodge*, located on the southeastern shore of Lake Victoria, 10 miles (15 km) from the Serengeti National Park and 78 miles (125 km) north of Mwanza has eight thatched bungalows on the lakeshore, with ensuite facilities. Fishing, boat excursions and mountain biking are offered.

CLASS B: * *Ndutu Safari Lodge* is a rustic lodge with 34 rooms (doubles) with ensuite facilities, located on the edge of the park in Ngorongoro Conservation Area.

CAMPING: Campsites are available at Seronera, Ndutu, Naabi Hill Gate, Moru Kopjes, Kirawira and Lobo. Camping in other areas requires permission from the warden and higher fees. It is best to book well in advance.

LAKE NATRON REGION

This is a remote wilderness with limited wildlife, a few scattered Masai settlements, rugged sand tracks and no tourist infrastructure. You may encounter Masai tribesmen as they tend their herds of cattle, visit the waterfalls and see the inland cliffs that are home to thousands of Ruppell's vultures.

Located between the Ngorongoro Conservation Area and the Kenya border, **Lake Natron** is a shallow, alkaline lake approximately 38 miles long and 15 miles wide (60-by-25 km). This remote lake is one of East Africa's largest breeding areas for both lesser and greater flamingos.

South of Lake Natron is **Oldoinyo Lengai**, the only active carbonatite volcano in the world and holy mountain of the Masai. This steep mountain takes about 10 hours to climb and return to its base.

RUBONDO ISLAND NATIONAL PARK

Located in the southwestern part of Lake Victoria, the main attractions of this 93-square-mile (240-km^2) island are sitatunga (indigenous) and small groups of chimpanzees. Walking is allowed and the wildlife that may be seen includes black-and-white colobus monkey, giraffe, bushbuck and otters. There are no large predators. Nearly 400 species of birds have been recorded, including storks, herons, ibises, kingfishers, bee-eaters, flycatchers and an abundance of fish eagles.

In addition to the main island, there are about a dozen small islands that make up the park. Habitats include papyrus swamps, savannah, open woodlands and dense evergreen forests. Visitors, accompanied by a guide who is usually armed, may walk along forested trails in search of wildlife or wait patiently at a number of hides. The best time to visit is November-February. A few boats are available for hire.

Flying by air charter is the only easy way to get to the park. An airstrip is located at Park Headquarters. From Mwanza, it is a seven-hour drive by vehicle and a two-hour boat ride by one route and a 10-hour drive and half-hour boat ride by another route. Visitors are not allowed to bring their vehicles to the island.

ACCOMMODATION – CLASS A/B:* *Rubondo Island Camp* has 10 tents under thatch with ensuite facilities and a swimming pool. Activities include fishing, walks in search of chimpanzees and other wildlife, and birdwatching.

ACCOMMODATION – CLASS F: Two self-service bandas are available; bring your own food.

CAMPING: Sites are available, but bring your own supplies.

MT. KILIMANJARO NATIONAL PARK

Known to many through Ernest Hemingway's book *The Snows of Kilimanjaro* (Arrow), Mt. Kilimanjaro is the highest mountain in the world that is not part of a mountain range, and it is definitely one of the world's most impressive mountains. Kilimanjaro means "shining mountain"; it rises from an average altitude of about 3,300 feet (1,000 m) on the dry plains to 19,340 feet (5,895 m), truly a world-class mountain. On clear days, the mountain can be seen from over 200 miles (320 km) away.

The mountain consists of three major volcanic centers: Kibo (19,340 feet/5,895 m), Shira (13,650 feet/4,162 m) to the west and Mawenzi (16,893 feet/5,150 m) to the east. The base of the mountain is 37 miles (60 km) long and 25 miles (40 km) wide. The park is a World Heritage Site and covers 292 square miles (756 km^2) of the mountain above 8,856 feet (2,700 m). The park also has six corridors that climbers may use to trek through the Forest Reserve.

Hikers pass through zones of forest, alpine and semidesert to its snow-capped peak, situated only three degrees south of the equator.

It was once thought to be an extinct volcano, but due to recent rumblings, it is now classified as dormant.

Climbing Mt. Kilimanjaro was definitely a highlight of my travels. For the struggle to reach its highest peak I was handsomely rewarded with a feeling of accomplishment, fabulous views of the African plains, and many exciting memories of the climb. In fact, with over 22,000 climbers a year, Kilimanjaro is second only to the Everest and Annapurnas areas in Nepal in popularity as a trekking destination outside of Europe.

Kilimanjaro may, in fact, be the easiest mountain in the world for a climber to ascend to such heights. But it is still a struggle for even fit adventurers. On the other hand, it can be climbed by people from all walks of life who are in good condition and have a strong will. Mind you, reaching the top is by no means necessary; the flora, fauna and magnificent views seen enroute are fabulous.

A Christian missionary, Johann Rebmann, reported his discovery of this snow-capped mountain, but the Europeans didn't believe him. Hans Meyer was the first European to climb Kilimanjaro, doing so in 1889.

The most unique animal in this park is the Abbot's duiker, which is found in only a few mountain forests in northern Tanzania. Other wildlife includes elephant, buffalo, eland, leopard, hyrax, and black-and-white colobus monkeys. However, very little large game is seen.

Birdlife is sparse but interesting, with bronze sunbird, red-tufted malachite sunbird, alpine chat and streaky seedeater not uncommon. You might see augur buzzard and white-necked raven soaring above you, and you may even be lucky enough to see the rare bearded vulture.

The best time to climb is January-March and June-December during the drier seasons when the skies are fairly clear. November and December can be wet due to the short rains, while the temperatures in July and August can be quite cool. April and May should be avoided because of heavy rains and overcast skies.

From April to May, during the long rainy season, the summit is often covered in clouds, with snow falling at higher altitudes and rain at lower altitudes. The short rains (October-November) bring afternoon thunderstorms, but evenings and mornings are often clear.

Many routes to the summit require no mountaineering skills.

Mountaineers wishing to ascend by technical routes may wish to get a copy of *Guide to Mt. Kenya and Kilimanjaro* (Mountain Club of Kenya), edited by Iain Allan.

The Park Headquarters is located in Marangu, about a seven-hour drive from Nairobi, or two hours from Arusha. Children under 10 years of age are not allowed over 9,843 feet (3,000 m).

Travelers wishing to see Mt. Kilimanjaro, but who do not wish to climb it, may do so (provided the weather is clear) from within the park, from Arusha National Park or Amboseli National Park (Kenya).

Zones
Mt. Kilimanjaro can be divided into five zones by altitude: (1) cultivated lower slopes, (2) forest, (3) heath and moorland/lower alpine, (4) highland desert/alpine and (5) summit. Each zone spans approximately 3,300 feet (1,000 m) in altitude. As the altitude increases, rainfall and temperature decrease; this has a direct effect on the vegetation each zone supports.

The rich volcanic soils of the **lower slopes** of the mountain around Moshi and Marangu up to the park gate (6,000 ft./1,830 m) are intensely cultivated, mostly with coffee and bananas.

The forest zone (5,900-9,185 ft./1,800-2,800 m) receives the highest rainfall of the zones, with about 80 inches (2,000 mm) on the southern slopes and about half that amount on the northern and western slopes. The upper half of this zone is often covered with clouds, and humidity is high, with day temperatures ranging from 60 to 70°F (15 to 21°C). Don't be surprised if it rains while walking through this zone; in fact, expect it.

In the lower **forest**, there are palms, sycamore figs, bearded lichen and mosses hanging from tree limbs, tree ferns growing to 20 feet (6 m) in height, and giant lobelia which grow to over 30 feet (9 m). In the upper forest zone, giant groundsels appear. Unlike many East African volcanic mountains, no bamboo belt surrounds Kilimanjaro.

Black-and-white colobus and blue monkey, olive baboon and bushbuck may be seen. Elephant, eland, giraffe, buffalo and suni may be seen on the northern and western slopes. Also present but seldom seen are bushpig, civet, genet, bush duiker, Abbot's duiker and red duiker.

Zone three, a **lower alpine zone** ranging from 9,185 to 13,120 feet (2,800 to 4,000 m), is predominantly heath followed by moorlands. Rainfall decreases with altitude from about 50 inches to 20 inches (1,250 to 500 mm) per year. Giant heather (10-30 feet/3-9 m high), grasslands with scattered bushes and beautiful flowers, including "everlasting" flowers, protea and colorful red-hot pokers, characterize the lower part of this zone.

You then enter the **moorlands** with tussock grasses and groups of giant senecios and lobelias — weird, prehistoric-looking Afro-alpine vegetation that would provide a great setting for a science fiction movie. With a lot of luck, you may spot eland, elephant, buffalo or klipspringer.

The **highland desert/alpine zone** is from around 13,120 to 16,400 feet (4,000 to 5,000 m) and receives only about 10 inches (250 mm) of rain per year. Vegetation is very thin and includes tussock grasses, "everlasting" flowers, moss balls and lichens. The thin air makes flying too difficult for most birds, and the very few larger mammals that may be seen do not make this region their home. What this zone lacks in wildlife is compensated for by the fabulous views. Temperatures can range from below freezing to very hot, so be prepared.

The summit experiences **arctic conditions** and receives less than 4 inches (100 mm) of rain per year, usually in the form of snow. It is almost completely devoid of vegetation.

Kibo's northern summit is covered by the Great Northern Glacier. On Kibo there is an outer caldera about one and one-half miles (2.5 km) in diameter. Uhuru peak is the highest point on the outer caldera and also the highest point on the mountain. Kilimanjaro's glaciers are shrinking and trends in global warming suggest that the mountain may lose most of its ice peak in the foreseeable future.

Within the outer caldera is an inner cone that contains the Inner or **Reusch Crater**, which is about .5 mile (1 km) in diameter. Vents (fumaroles) spewing steam and sulfurous gasses are located at the

Terrace and the base of the crater. Within the Inner Crater is an ash cone with an ash pit about 1,100 feet (335 m) across and about 400 feet (120 m) deep.

ROUTES

In regards to routes, Kilimanjaro is divided into two halves by a line running north/south between Barafu Camp and Kibo Hut. All climbers who ascend on the Machame, Shira, Lemosho, and Umbwe routes must descend on the Mweka route. All climbers who ascend on the Rongai and Marangu routes must descend on the Marangu Route. The Marangu Route is the only two-way route; all other routes are one way only. Climbers from the Rongai and Marangu routes only meet climbers from the other routes on the Kibo Crater rim. This system is effective in reducing the impact of large numbers of climbers on all routes, except for the Marangu Route.

Climbers on the Machame, Shira, Lemosho, and Umbwe routes may approach the summit via the Western Breach or may skirt around to Barafu and climb up to Stella Point.

Climbing Kibo Peak via the routes described below requires no mountaineering skills. A guide for each climbing party is required. Porters are highly recommended. The Marangu and the Machame routes are the most popular, carrying 85% of all climbers, while the Shira Plateau, Lemosho, Rongai and Umbwe routes are much less used. Climbers stay in basic mountain huts on the Marangu Route and in small portable mountain tents carried by porters on the other routes.

Your porters will bring fuel (kerosene or gas) for cooking and heating because cooking with firewood has been banned. The national park guides are not qualified to lead glacier- or ice-climbing routes. The services of a professional guide must be arranged in advance.

The park has a rescue teams based at the Park Headquarters, on the eastern edge of the Shira Plateau, and another beneath Barafu Campsite, and there is a ranger post at Rongai Camp 1.

MARANGU ROUTE

The Marangu Route is the least expensive route to climb and is second in popularity only to the Machame Route. Marangu has hut accommodations with separate long-drop toilets, and is the second easiest (most gradual) route to the summit (Rongai is the easiest).

This route may be completed in five days, but it's best to take six days, spending an extra day at Horombo hut to allow more time to acclimatize to the altitude. The huts are dormitory-style with common areas for cooking and eating.

Most climbing tours originate in Nairobi, Arusha or Kilimanjaro Airport and last seven or eight days. The night before and the night after the climb are usually spent in the village of Marangu or in Arusha.

DAY ONE: MARANGU (6,004 ft./1,830 m) to MANDARA HUT (8,856 ft./2,700 m) — FOUR-FIVE HOURS. ALTITUDE GAIN: 2,854 feet (870 m).

An hour or so is spent at Park Headquarters at Marangu Gate handling registration and arranging the loads for the porters. Try to leave in the morning to allow a leisurely pace and to avoid afternoon showers. The trail leads through the forest and is often muddy.

Mandara has a number of small wooden A-frame huts that sleep eight persons each, four to a room, and a main cabin with a dormitory upstairs and dining room downstairs, for a total of 60 beds. Kerosene lamps, stoves and mattresses are provided.

DAY TWO: MANDARA to HOROMBO HUT (12,205 ft./3,720 m) — FIVE-SEVEN HOURS. ALTITUDE GAIN: 3,346 feet (1,020 m).

On day two, you pass through the upper part of the rain forest to tussock grassland and fascinating Afro-alpine vegetation of giant groundsels and giant lobelias to the moorlands. Once out of the forest, you begin to get great views of the town of Moshi and Mawenzi Peak (16,893 feet/5,149 m). If you can spare an extra day for acclimatizing, Horombo is the best hut for this. There are some nice day hikes that will help you further acclimatize. Kibo is too high to allow a good night's sleep. Horombo has 120 beds and is similar to but more crowded than Mandara.

**DAY THREE: HOROMBO HUT to KIBO HUT (15,430 ft./4,703 m) —
FIVE-SIX HOURS. ALTITUDE GAIN: 3,225 feet (983 m).**

On the morning of day three, the vegetation begins to thin out to open grasslands. You pass "Last Water" (be sure to fill your water bottles because this is the last source of water). The landscape becomes more barren as you reach "the saddle," a wide desert between Kibo and Mawenzi Peak. Kibo Hut does not come in view until just before you reach it. Kibo Hut has 58 beds and is located on the east side of Kibo Peak.

With the wind-chill factor, it can be very cold, so dress warmly. This is the day many hikers feel the effects of the altitude and may begin to experience some altitude sickness. Most people find it impossible to sleep at this height because of the lack of oxygen and the bitter cold, not to mention the possibility of altitude sickness. Get as much rest as you can.

**DAY FOUR: KIBO HUT to GILLMAN'S POINT (18,635 ft./5,680 m) and
UHURU PEAK (19,340 ft./5,895 m) AND DOWN TO HOROMBO HUT
— TEN-TWELVE HOURS.**

Your guide will wake you shortly after midnight for your ascent, which should begin around 1:00 a.m. Be sure not to delay the start; it is vital that you reach the summit by sunrise. The sun quickly melts the frozen scree, making the ascent all the more difficult.

The steep ascent to Gillman's Point on the edge of the caldera is a grueling four- to five-hour slog up scree. Hans Meyer Cave is a good place to rest before climbing seemingly unending switchbacks past Johannes Notch to Gillman's Point.

From Gillman's Point, Uhuru Peak is a fairly gradual climb of 705 feet (215 m) in altitude. It will take another hour to hour and a half. Uhuru Peak is well marked, and there is a book in which you may sign your name.

If you are still feeling strong, ask your guide to take you down into the caldera to the inner crater, which has some steam vents. You return to Gillman's Point by a different route.

The feeling of accomplishment upon reaching the summit, as I said, is one of the highlights of my life. I was amazed at the tremendous size of the glaciers so close to the equator.

KILIMANJARO ROUTES

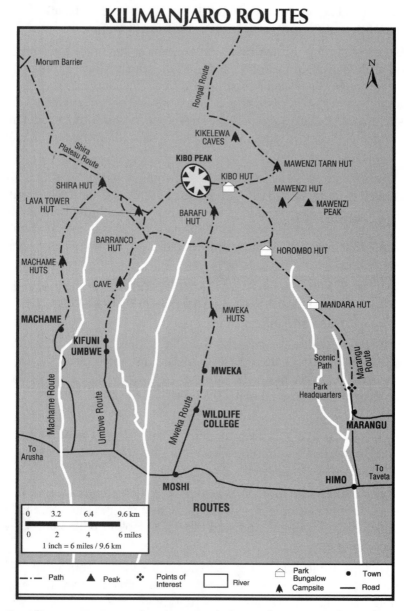

Standing over 16,000 feet (4,900 m) above the surrounding plains, the view was breathtaking in every direction. Sunrise over Mawenzi is a beautiful sight. You truly feel that you're on the top of the world!

KIBO PEAK

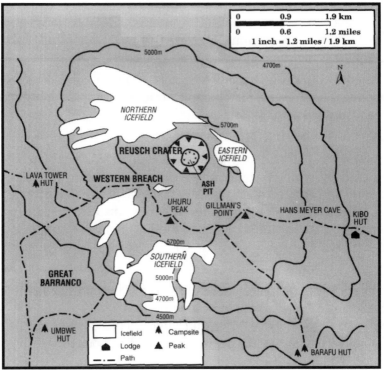

The author at Uhuru Peak, Mt. Kilimanjaro.

Shortly after sunrise, you begin the long walk down the mountain to Kibo Hut for a short rest, then continue onward to Horombo Hut. Provided you are not completely exhausted, the walk down is long but pretty easy going. From Gillman's Point to Horombo takes about four hours and from Uhuru Peak, about five.

The entire descent is made in two days, and your knees take a hard pounding; you may want to wrap your knees with elastic bandages or use elastic knee supports.

DAY FIVE: HOROMBO HUT TO MARANGU

Another long day of hiking as you descend past Mandara Hut to Park Headquarters, where you receive a diploma certifying your accomplishment. Many climbers then spend the night in hotel in Marangu or Arusha and have the pleasure of sharing their experiences with unwary visitors planning to begin their Kilimanjaro adventure the following day.

Machame Route

This is the most popular and one of the most beautiful routes up the mountain. It is also one of the steepest routes. The park gate is located a few miles above Machame village. Hike four to six hours through rain forest to Machame Huts (9,843 ft./3,000 m).

The following day you hike five to seven hours to the defunct Shira Hut (12,467 ft./3,800 m) on the Shira Plateau (see Shira Plateau Route for description of the area). Continue hiking about four hours to Lava Tower Hut. From Lava Tower Hut there are two choices to reach Uhuru Peak. One route is via the Western Breach with an overnight at Arrow Glacier (15,744 ft./4,800 m) before reaching the Inner Crater and onward to Uhuru Peak, and then descending on the Mweka Route to Mweka Hut. The other route option is to continue along the Southern Summit Circuit path to Barranco and Barafu before climbing to Uhuru via Stella Point (18,811 ft./5,735 m).

Rongai (Nale Moru) Route

This route is also accessible from Kenya via the border crossing at Tarakea. Some climbers spend a few nights at camps in private reserves such as Ol Donyo Waus or Camp ya Kanzi in the Chyulu Hills or in Tsavo West National Park, before beginning the climb.

This little-used, unspoiled route with panoramic views of Amboseli and the Chuyulu Hills (Kenya) is also the easiest ascent route because of the steady gradient and the short distance to reach Kibo Hut for the summit attempt. It can be climbed in five days, however, six days are recommended to aid acclimatization and increase your chances for success. If coming from Kenya, meet your Tanzanian operator across the border at Tarakea. From Marangu Gate, drive two hours to the village of Nale Moru (6,396 ft./1,950 m), where you will hike on a path through maize (corn) fields before climbing through a forest sheltering a variety of wildlife, including the Kilimanjaro colobus monkey. The hike takes 3-4 hours. The campsite is on the edge of the moorland zone (8,530 ft./2,600 m) with views of the Kenyan plains. The next morning ascend for 6-7 hours to the "Second Cave," toward the peaks of Mawenzi, and camp in a sheltered valley near Kikelewa Caves (11,320 ft./ 3,450 m). On the third day, take a short but steep 3-4 hour hike to Mawenzi Tarn (14,210 ft./4,330 m), situated beneath the towering spires of Mawenzi. This afternoon you will have a chance to hike up to 15,088 feet (4,600 m) to further help your body acclimatize. On day four, cross the saddle between Mawenzi and Kibo to reach School Campsite (15,580 ft./4,750 m) — a hike of 4-5 hours. On the fifth day, begin the steepest and most difficult part of the ascent at 12:00 a.m. Hike slowly on a switchback trail through loose volcanic scree to the crater rim at Gillman's Point (18,635 ft./5,680 m) at approximately 6:00 a.m. Continue to Uhuru Peak (19,340 ft./5,895 m) — a three-hour roundtrip hike. Descend down to Kibo hut for a short rest and then onward to Horombo Hut for the night. The following day you will depart on your six-hour downhill hike to the Marangu gate.

Shira Plateau Route

This is a very scenic and yet seldom-used route, providing great views of Kilimanjaro and the Rift Valley and probably the best wildlife viewing on the mountain. This and the Lemoshe are the most varied and among the longest of the routes on the mountain. A 4wd vehicle is needed, and the roads may be impassable in the rainy seasons.

Drive north from the Moshi-Arusha road at Boma la Ng'ombe to Londorossi Gate, located on the western side of Kilimanjaro. From the gate it is usual to continue by vehicle on a 4wd road for a few miles (kilometers) to an altitude of around 9,000 feet (2,700 m). Then hike four to five hours up to the western edge of Shira Plateau and continue to Shira 1 Camp (11,480 ft./3,500 m) for the night. The track ends shortly thereafter, at 12,200 feet (3,720 m) at the Murram Barrier. It is advisable to hike and not be driven all the way to the barrier — to assist in acclimatization. Hike three to four hours to complete the crossing of Shira Plateau, usually via the rock formations around Shira Cathedral, to Shira Hut (12,595 ft./3,840 m.) It is a good idea to spend two nights at Shira Hut to acclimatize before continuing on. You may take acclimatization hikes to spectacular rock formations on the edge of Shira Caldera or a longer hike toward Moir Hut, which give excellent views of the Northern Icefields.

From Shira Hut it is about a four-hour hike to the remains of Lava Tower Hut. The vegetation changes on the Shira Plateau are fabulous as you walk through open grasslands and moorlands dotted with giant senecios, over 30 feet (9 m) high, and past the impressive Shira Cone, Cathedral and Needle Peaks. From Lava Tower Hut follow the directions from the Machame Route for optional routes to the summit.

Lemosho Route

Next to the Umbwe Route, this is the least-used route and requires a minimum of seven days. As with the Shira Plateau Route above, drive to the Londorossi Gate. Then drive to Lemosho Glades and hike through the rainforest to Forest Camp (8,000 ft./2,440 m). On the second day, take a full day's hike into the Shira Caldera, a high grassy plateau, to Shira One Campsite (11,500 ft./3,500 m). On day 3, trek for 3-4 hours across the Shira Plateau to Shira 2 Campsite (12,200 ft./3,700 m). Those who feel strong can take an acclimatizing trek to Shira Cathedral. On Day 4, hike seven hours down the Barranco Valley over 15,000 feet (4,570 m). This is great for acclimatization. Next go to the camp at Barranco Wall (12,900 ft./3,940 m.). On day 5, climb up Barranco Wall (14,000 ft./4,270 m). On Day 6 trek to Barafu Camp (16,000 ft./4,600 m). On Day 7, begin trekking up the scree slopes just after midnight to Stella Point on the rim and onward to Uhuru Peak. Return to Barafu Camp and continue your descent to Mweka Hut (10,170 ft./3,100 m). On Day 8, hike to Mweka Gate.

Umbwe Route

The Umbwe Route is very steep and strenuous. The route begins at Umbwe (about 4,600 ft./1,400 m), a village 10 miles (16 km) from Moshi. Walk two miles to Kifuni village and into the forest. Follow the path for another 3.5 miles (5 km) and then branch left into a mist-covered forest until you reach the forest cave (Bivouac #1) at 9,515 feet (2,900 m), six to seven hours from Umbwe. Overhanging ledges extending about 5 feet (1.5 m) from the cliff provide reasonable protection for about six people; however, it is recommended you use your own tents. Water is available, but not close by.

Continue through moorlands and along a narrow ridge with deep valleys on either side. The thick mist and vegetation covered with "Old Man's Beard" moss creates an eerie atmosphere. The second caves at 11,483 feet (3,500 m) are still another two- to three-hour hike from Bivouac #1. The vegetation thins out, and you branch right shortly before arriving at Barranco Hut (12,795 ft./3,900 m) about two hours later.

From Barranco you can backtrack to the fork and turn right (north) and hike for three hours to where Lava Tower Hut (15,092 ft./4,600 m) used to stand. From there, the climb is up steep scree and blocks of rock to the floor of the crater and Uhuru Peak via the Great Western Breach. The climb from Lava Tower Hut to the caldera takes about nine hours. An alternative from Barranco Hut is to traverse the mountain eastward and follow the Summit Circuit path to Barafu Camp. Descend via the Mweka Route, regardless of the summit routes used.

Summit Circuit

There is a circuit between 12,139 and 15,092 feet (3,700 and 4,600 m) completely around the base of Kibo Peak. Horombo, Barranco and Moir Huts are on the circuit, while Lava Tower, Shira, Kibo and Mawenzi Huts are on side trails, not far from the circuit. A tent is needed since there is no hut on the northern side of Kibo. Be sure to bring a well-insulated pad for your sleeping bag.

EQUIPMENT CHECKLIST

The better equipped you are for climbing Mt. Kiimanjaro, the higher your chances of making the summit. When it comes to clothing, the "layered effect" works best. Bring a duffel bag to pack your gear in for the climb. Wrap your clothes in heavy garbage bags to keep them dry. Keep the weight under the porter's maximum load of 33 pounds (15 kg). Here's a suggested checklist of items to consider bringing:

CLOTHING

- ☐ Gortex jacket (with hood) and pants, and a light raincoat
- ☐ polypropylene long underwear - tops and bottoms, medium and heavy weight
- ☐ wool sweater (one or two)
- ☐ Gortex gaiters (to keep the scree out of your boots at higher altitudes)
- ☐ tennis shoes or ultralight hiking boots (for lower altitudes)
- ☐ medium-weight insulated hiking boots for warmth and to help dig into the scree during the final ascent
- ☐ heavy wool or down mittens with Gortex outer shell and glove liners
- ☐ several pairs of wool socks and polypropylene liner socks
- ☐ several pairs of underwear
- ☐ track or warm-up suit (to relax and sleep in)
- ☐ long trousers or knickers (wool or synthetic)
- ☐ light, loose-fitting cotton trousers
- ☐ shorts (with pockets)
- ☐ wool long-sleeve and cotton long sleeve shirts
- ☐ T-shirts or short-sleeve shirts
- ☐ turtleneck shirt
- ☐ down vest
- ☐ balaclava (wool or synthetic)
- ☐ wide-brimmed hat or cap for protection from the sun
- ☐ bandana
- ☐ wool hat
- ☐ sleeping pad (for all routes except the Marangu Route)

MISCELLANEOUS

- [ ] day pack large enough to carry extra clothing, rain gear, two plastic water bottles (1 liter/quart each), camera and lunch
- [ ] sleeping bag (rated at least 0° F (-18° C)
- [ ] pocket flask for summit climb
- [ ] flashlight with extra bulb and batteries (some prefer head lamps)
- [ ] light towel
- [ ] sunglasses and mountaineering glasses
- [ ] camera and film
- [ ] strong sunblock
- [ ] protective lip balm, such as Chapstick brand
- [ ] body lotion (otherwise skin may get dry and itchy)
- [ ] water purifiers
- [ ] duffle bag
- [ ] half-dozen heavy garbage bags in which to wrap clothes
- [ ] toilet paper
- [ ] moist towelettes
- [ ] pocket knife with scissors
- [ ] granola bars, trail mix and sweets that travel well
- [ ] powered drink mix

BASIC FIRST AID KIT

- [ ] malaria pills
- [ ] moleskin and second skin
- [ ] plastic bandage strips, such as Band-Aid brand
- [ ] elastic bandages
- [ ] gauze pads (4" X 4")
- [ ] diuretics (diamox) - by prescription from your doctor
- [ ] broad-spectrum antibiotics (pills) - as above
- [ ] laxative
- [ ] antihistamine tablets
- [ ] antibiotic cream
- [ ] antidiarrheal preparation - Imodium or Lomotil
- [ ] iodine
- [ ] aspirin or acetaminophen for headache/muscle pain
- [ ] throat and cough lozenges
- [ ] decongestant (can be found in combination with antihistamine tablets)

Huts

Mandara, Horombo and Kibo Huts are described under the Marangu Route above. The other huts are prefab metal huts, either 10 or 15 feet (3 or 4.5 m) in diameter in varying states of disrepair; most are basically uninhabitable. Many of the wooden floors have been ripped up and used for firewood. Tourists are not allowed to sleep in any of the huts on the mountain (other than Mandara, Horombo and Kibo) so you must plan on sleeping in your own tent and let the guides and porters use the huts. Drinking water should be filtered, treated and/or boiled, because some sources on the mountain are polluted.

* MAWENZI HUT (15,092 ft./4,600 m): From "The Saddle" on the Marangu Route, just after passing East Lava Hill, hike 1 1/4 (2 km) miles east-northeast on a marked path to the hut at the base of the West Corrie. Mawenzi Hut sleeps five and is about a three-hour hike from Horombo or Kibo Huts. There are no toilets. Mawenzi Peak should be attempted only by well-equipped, experienced mountaineers.

* MAWENZI TARN HUT (14,206 ft./4,330 m): This hut is situated northeast of Mawenzi Hut; it is an easy hike around the foot of the peak. There are toilets there, and water is also available.

* MWEKA HUTS (9,515 ft./2,900 m): There are two large huts. There is a stream nearby.

* BARAFU HUT (15,092 ft./4,600 m): There is no water.

* BARRANCO HUT (12,795 ft./3,900 m): There is a bivouac site about a 600-foot walk above the hut under a rock overhang. A stream is located nearby.

* MOIR HUT (13,780 ft./4,200 m): This hut is located on the northwest side of Kibo north of the Shira. There is water nearby.

Climbing Tips

There are a number of ways to increase your chances of making it to the top. One of the most important things to remember is to take your time. *Polepole* is Swahili for "slowly," which is definitely the way to go. There is no prize for being the first to the hut or first to the top.

Pace yourself so that you are never completely out of breath. Exaggerate your breathing, taking deeper and more frequent breaths than you feel you actually need. This will help you acclimatize and help keep you from exhausting yourself prematurely, and it will help lower the chances of developing pulmonary or cerebral edema.

Ski poles make good walking sticks; they can be rented at Park Headquarters and are highly recommended. Bring a small backpack to carry the items to which you wish to have quick access along the trail, such as a water bottle, snacks and a camera. Most importantly, listen to what your body is telling you. Don't overdo it! Many people die each year on the mountain because they don't listen or pay attention to the signs and keep pushing themselves.

On steep portions of the hike, use the "lock step" method to conserve energy. Take a step and lock the knee of your uphill leg. This puts your weight on the leg bone, using less muscle strength. Pause for a few seconds, letting your other leg rest without any weight on it, and breath deeply. Then repeat. This technique will save vital energy that you may very well need in your quest for the top.

Some climbers take the prescription drug Diamox, a diuretic which usually reduces the symptoms of altitude sickness; but, there are side effects from taking the drug, including increased urination. You should discuss the use of Diamox with your doctor prior to leaving home.

Drink a lot more water than you feel you need. High-altitude hiking is very dehydrating, and a dehydrated body weakens quickly. Climbers should obtain 4-6 quarts (4-6 liters) of fluid daily from their food and drinks. Consume foods such as soups, oatmeal porridge, and fresh fruits to supplement water and other liquids. Climbers should drink until the color of their urine is clear.

Most hikers find it difficult to sleep at high altitude. Once you reach the hut each afternoon, rest a bit, then hike to a spot a few hundred feet in altitude above the hut and relax for a while. Acclimatizing even for a short time at a higher altitude will help you get a more restful night's sleep. Remember, "Climb high, sleep low!"

Consume at least 4,000 calories per day on the climb. This can be a problem. Most climbers lose their appetite at high altitude. Bring along trail mix (mixed nuts and dried fruit), chocolate, and other goodies that you enjoy, to supplement the meals prepared for you.

Forget about drinking alcoholic beverages on the climb. Altitude greatly enhances the effects of alcohol. Plus, alcohol causes dehydration. A headache caused by altitude sickness can be bad enough without having a hangover on top of it.

Park Headquarters is located in Marangu, 29 miles (47 km) from Moshi, 63 miles (101 km) from Kilimanjaro Airport and 75 miles (120 km) from Arusha.

Equipment is available for rent from Park Headquarters and Kibo and Marangu Hotels, but it may not be of top quality. If possible, I recommend that you bring your own gear.

ACCOMMODATION NEAR MARANGU – TOURIST CLASS:
* *Nakara Hotel*, located 1.5 miles (2 km) from the Marangu Gate, has 19 rooms with ensuite facilities. * *Protea Capricorn Hotel*, located 1.5 miles (2.5 km) from the Park Gate, has 20 rooms with ensuite bathrooms. * *Kibo Hotel*, situated less than a mile (1.6 km) from Marangu village, has rooms with ensuite facilities (150 beds). * *Marangu Hotel*, located a mile and a half (2.4 km) from Marangu village, is a rustic lodge with 29 double rooms with ensuite facilities.

THE SOUTH

The "Southern Circuit" of wildlife reserves includes the Selous Game Reserve, Ruaha National Park and Mikumi National Park. The Selous and Ruaha are less visited than the northern Tanzania parks and offer a great opportunity to explore wild and unspoiled bush.

SELOUS GAME RESERVE

This little-known reserve happens to be the second largest game reserve in Africa, and it is a World Heritage Site. Over 21,000 square miles (55,000 km²) in area, the Selous is more than half the size of the state of Ohio, twice the area of Denmark and three-and-three-fourths times larger than Serengeti National Park. Unexploited and largely unexplored, no human habitation is allowed in this virgin bush, except at limited tourist facilities.

The Selous is a stronghold for over 50,000 elephant, 150,000 buffalo (herds often exceed 1,000), and large populations of lion, leopard,

Open game drive vehicle in the Selous.

Lichtenstein's hartebeest, greater kudu, hippo, crocodiles, and numerous other species, including giraffe, zebra, wildebeest, waterbuck, African wild dog, impala and a small number of black rhino. Colobus monkey can be found in the forests along the Rufiji River. Over one million large animals live within its borders. Over 350 species of birds and 2,000 plant species have been recorded.

Almost 75% of this low-lying reserve (360-4,100 ft./110-1,250 m) is composed of miombo woodlands, with a balance of grasslands, floodplains, marshes and dense forests.

Morning walks accompanied by an armed ranger and guide are popular and are conducted by all the camps. Fly camping for a few nights, as well as portered safaris up to two weeks in length, are also available.

This reserve can give you the feeling of exploring the bush for the first time, because you will encounter few other visitors during your safari.

The Rufiji River, the largest river in East Africa, roughly bisects the park as it flows from the southwest to the northeast. The Rufiji and its tributaries, including Great Ruaha and Luwego, have high concentrations of hippo and crocs. Fish eagles are numerous.

Exploring the Rufiji River, its channels, swamps and lakes by boat is another great way to view game and experience the reserve. You

Selous Safari Camp, a comfortable permanent tented camp.

should consider adding the Selous onto a northern Tanzania itinerary, because game viewing by boat is not possible in the Serengeti, Ngorongoro, Lake Manyara or Tarangire. Fishing is also popular.

On our last visit, we encountered numerous lion, including two females and four cubs on a Defassa waterbuck kill, a pack of wild dogs, large herds of elephant, eland, buffalo and giraffe, banded mongoose, Defassa waterbuck, and very healthy blue wildebeest that I classified as almost handsome. Bird life was prolific; our sightings on a boat game drive included African spoonbill, black-winged stilt, fish eagle, gray heron, great white egret, little egret and open-billed stork.

All photographic safari activities are restricted to the northern 20% of the reserve. The best time to visit the reserve is during the dry season, June-November. Game viewing from December to February is good, although it is quite hot during that period. During the rainy season, many of the roads are impassable and wildlife is scattered. The reserve is usually closed from March to May.

Most visitors fly to the Selous by group or private air charter from Dar es Salaam, while others charter in from Arusha, Zanzibar or other parks. Access by road is difficult and only possible in the dry season.

ACCOMMODATION: The camps are located about 160-235 miles (260-380 km) from Dar es Salaam, requiring a 6- to 12-hour drive in a 4wd vehicle. All camps have private airstrips and flying is highly recommended.

CLASS A: * *Selous Safari Camp*, a luxury tented camp set on the banks of the Rufiji River, has 12 tents with ensuite facilities and a swimming pool. The camp also has a "dungo," a large elevated platform overlooking the Rufiji River for relaxing and watching game and bird life during the midday. Game drives, escorted walks, boat safaris, fishing and fly camping and multi-day walking safaris are offered. * *Sand Rivers* has eight luxury chalets with ensuite facilities and a swimming pool. Game drives, walks, boat safaris, fishing, multi-day walking safaris with fly camping and long-distance portered walking safaris (up to two weeks) are offered.

CLASS A/B: * *Rufiji River Camp*, a comfortable tented camp with 15 tents (doubles) with ensuite facilities, offers game drives, fishing, walking and boat safaris.

CAMPING: Sites are available.

RUAHA NATIONAL PARK

Ruaha, known for its great populations of elephant, buffalo, greater and lesser kudu, hippo, crocs and magnificent scenery, is one of the country's newest and best national parks, and because of its location, it is one of the least visited.

Ruaha's scenery is spectacular, and its 5,000-square-mile (12,950-km²) area makes it almost as large as Serengeti National Park. The landscape is characterized by miombo woodland with rocky hills on a plateau over 3,300 feet (1,000 m) in altitude. Park elevation ranges from 2,460 feet (750 m) in the Ruaha Valley to the 6,230-foot (1,900-m) Ikingu Mountain in the west of the park.

The Great Ruaha River, with its impressive gorges, deep pools and rapids, runs for 100 miles (160 km), close to the park's eastern boundary, and it is home to many hippo and crocodiles. The black rocks of the riverbed contrasted against the golden grass on the riverbank dotted with baobab trees is a beautiful sight indeed. This is an excellent area for walking.

The dry season, June-November, is the best time to visit the park, when game is concentrated along the Ruaha River. Large numbers of greater and lesser kudu, elephant, wildebeest and impala can be seen, along with eland, sable antelope, roan antelope, buffalo, Defassa waterbuck, ostrich and giraffe. Lion, leopard, spotted and striped hyena, black-backed jackal, bat-eared fox and African wild dog are also present in significant numbers. Black rhino are present but seldom seen. Over 400 species of birds have been recorded.

On our most recent visit, we saw 25 greater kudu, two eland and herds of buffalo and zebra on the drive from the airstrip to the camp alone. Other game spotted included leopard, lion, elephant, lesser kudu and a pack of wild dog that ran right through our camp!

In addition to morning and afternoon excursions, midday game viewing in this park can also be very productive because wildlife can be seen walking to and from the river.

During the wet months of December to March, wildlife is scattered, but viewing is still good. Game viewing from February to June is difficult due to high grass.

The park is about a two and a half hour charter flight from Dar es Salaam, or a two-hour drive from Iringa, through the villages of Mloa and Idodi and across the Ruaha River via the Ibuguziwa Ferry. Park Headquarters and an airstrip are located at Msembe, 70 miles (112 km) from Iringa and 385 miles (615 km) from Dar es Salaam.

 ACCOMMODATION – CLASS B: * *Jongomero Camp*, located on the banks of the Jongomero Sand River in the southwestern section of Ruaha, has eight tents with flush toilets and bucket showers. The camp specializes in day long game drives to the remote areas of Ruaha. * *Ruaha River Camp*, located in the park 6 miles (10 km) south of Msembe, has 29 stone-and-thatch bandas and tents in a natural setting, most with ensuite facilities. * *Mwagusi Safari Camp* has eight tents under thatch with ensuite bathrooms, bucket showers and flush toilets. Game drives in open vehicles and walks are offered.

CLASS F: * *National Park Rondavels* (self-service) are situated at Msembe.

CAMPING: Campsites are available.

MIKUMI NATIONAL PARK

Mikumi is the closest park to Dar es Salaam (180 miles/288 km), and it takes about four hours to drive on tarmac from Dar es Salaam via Morongoro.

The park covers 1,247 square miles (3230 km²) and borders the Selous Game Reserve to the south along the Tazara Railroad line, which runs down to Zambia and divides the park.

The park is dominated by the Mkata River floodplain, swamps and grasslands dotted with baobab trees and miombo woodlands at an average altitude of 1,800 feet (550 m) above sea level. Elephant, buffalo, lion, hippo, zebra, wildebeest and Masai giraffe are prevalent. Sable antelope, common waterbuck, Lichtenstein's hartebeest, eland, Bohor reedbuck and impala may also be seen. Black-and-white colobus monkey are frequently seen in the south of the park.

During a two-day stay, we saw elephant, zebra, six lion, giraffe, buffalo, impala, ground hornbill and guinea fowl, among other species. There is a variety of bird life, because Mikumi is in the transition zone between north and south.

The long rains are from March to May and the short rains from November to December. Rainfall within the park ranges from 20 to 40 inches (510 to 1,070 mm) yearly.

It is difficult to say when the best time is to visit Mikumi. Unlike most parks, wildlife concentrates in this park during the wet season, when the vegetation is the thickest, making game viewing more difficult. Fewer animals are present in the dry season, but the ones present are easier to spot. Lion and elephant are two mammals that are more likely to be seen in the dry season. Considering this, the best time to visit is June-February.

This park is open all year, although some roads are closed during the rainy season. There is an airstrip, gas (petrol) station and garage at Park Headquarters.

ACCOMMODATION – CLASS A/B: * *Vuma Hill Tented Camp* has luxury tents under thatch and set on platforms with ensuite facilities and a swimming pool.

ACCOMMODATION – CLASS B/C: * *Mikumi Wildlife Lodge* has 50 double rooms with ensuite facilities and a swimming pool.

CLASS D: * *Mikumi Wildlife Camp* has self-contained bandas and a restaurant and bar.

CAMPING: Campsites are available.

THE WEST

LAKE TANGANYIKA

Lake Tanganyika forms much of the western border of Tanzania and is indeed an "inland sea." This is the world's longest lake (446 mi./714 km) and the world's second deepest lake (over 4700 ft./1,433 m). Only Lake Baikal in Russia is deeper, at over 5,700 feet (1,738 m). More than 400 species of fish inhabit Lake Tanganyika's clear waters. Easiest access to the lake in Tanzania is by flying to Kigoma.

KIGOMA

Kigoma is the country's major port on huge Lake Tanganyika. From there you can catch a steamer to Burundi or Zambia. Kigoma is the closest town to Gombe Stream National Park and many travelers stay there while in transit to and from the park. Kigoma can be reached by air, by road or by a two-and-one-half-day train ride from Dar es Salaam.

Ujiji, a small town 6 miles (10 km) south of Kigoma, is where the line, "Dr. Livingstone, I presume?" was spoken by Stanley in 1872. Buses run there regularly from the Kigoma Rail Station.

 ACCOMMODATION – FIRST CLASS: * *Kigoma Hilltop Hotel*, located just outside Kigoma on the edge of Lake Victoria, has 30 air-conditioned cottages with ensuite bathrooms.

TOURIST CLASS: * *Aqua Lodge*, located 50 yards (50 m) from the lake, has nine rooms with private facilities.

GOMBE STREAM NATIONAL PARK

Gombe Stream is the setting for Jane Goodall's chimpanzee studies and her films and books, including *In the Shadow of Man* (Houghton Mifflin). The remote 20-square-mile (52-km²) park is situated along the eastern shores of Lake Tanganyika 10 miles (16 km) north of Kigoma in remote northwestern Tanzania.

This tiny park covers a thin strip of land 3 miles (5 km) wide and stretches for 10 miles (16 km) along Lake Tanganyika. A mountain range ascends steeply from the lake at an altitude of 2,235 feet (681 m) to form part of the eastern wall of the western branch of the Great Rift Valley, rising to 5,000 feet (4,524 m).

Thick gallery forests are found along Gombe Stream and many other permanent streams in the valley and lower slopes of the mountains. Higher up the slopes are woodlands with some grasslands near the upper ridges.

The experience of seeing chimpanzees in the wild is by far the major attraction of this park. Other primates include red colobus monkey, blue monkey and baboon. Other wildlife of note includes buffalo, Defassa waterbuck and leopard.

Chimpanzees can usually be found around the research station and are quite habituated to humans. Two-hour morning and afternoon hikes into the forest searching for chimps can be arranged. The Kakombe Waterfall is worth a visit. There is also a nice walk along the lake shore northward from the guest house.

You can reach the park by water taxi (about three hours) from Ujiji or Kigoma.

ACCOMMODATION – CLASS F: There is a basic, self-service guest house and one hostel with separate facilities. Book well in advance or bring a tent, because the guest house may be full. Only basic supplies are available in Kigoma.

CAMPING: Allowed on special request.

MAHALE MOUNTAINS NATIONAL PARK

Like Gombe Stream, the main attraction of this remote park, which was only gazetted in 1985, is to be able to walk among large populations of chimpanzees. The chimps have been studied by Japanese researchers for more than 35 years, and now many chimps have been habituated to humans.

Located about 95 miles (150 km) south of Kigoma, this 609-square-mile (1,577-km²) park is situated on the eastern shores of Lake Tanganyika. The Mahale Mountains, featuring deep ravines, permanent streams and waterfalls, run through the center of the park, forming the eastern wall of the Great Rift Valley — with altitudes up to

Greystoke (Mahale) Tented Camp.

8,075 feet (2,462 m) above sea level. The western side of the mountains, where the chimp trekking occurs, is primarily composed of semitropical rain forest with brachystygia (semideciduous) woodland on the ridges and montane forest at higher altitudes.

Trekking in the park occurs in the range of the M Group, which as of this writing consists of 57 individuals that have been habituated to human presence. Once found, trekkers can watch them naturally go about their normal daily activities from often just a few yards (meters) away.

In addition to over 1,000 chimpanzees, the park is also home to eight other species of primates, including red colobus monkey and Angolan black-and-white colobus monkey. Other wildlife includes bushbuck, otters, banded mongoose, Sharpe's grysbok and blue duiker.

Seasons are fairly predictable. The main dry season usually runs from mid-May to mid-October, with mid-December to mid-February also being quite dry. Rainy seasons are usually mid-October to mid-December and mid-February to mid-May. Nights are often cool and rainfall ranges from 60 to 100 inches (1,500 to 2,500 mm) per year. The best time to visit is during the two dry seasons mentioned above.

There is no easy way to reach this seldom-visited park except by air charter from Nairobi, Dar es Salaam, Arusha or any Tanzanian park. To reach Mahale by boat from Kigoma (not recommended), take the weekly steamer MV Liemba for eight to 10 hours to the village of Lagosa (Mugambo). You usually arrive in the middle of the night and must be transferred ashore. From there you may be able to charter a boat for a three-hour ride to Kasoge (Kasiha village) in the park. Small boats from Kigoma make this journey in about 16 hours. The park cannot be reached by vehicle.

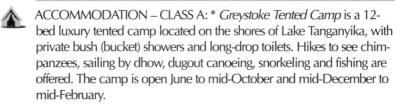

ACCOMMODATION – CLASS A: * *Greystoke Tented Camp* is a 12-bed luxury tented camp located on the shores of Lake Tanganyika, with private bush (bucket) showers and long-drop toilets. Hikes to see chimpanzees, sailing by dhow, dugout canoeing, snorkeling and fishing are offered. The camp is open June to mid-October and mid-December to mid-February.

CLASS F: There are two small resthouses, but you will need to bring your own food, crockery and cutlery, bed linens and stove. No supplies are available in the park.

CAMPING: Camping sites are available.

KATAVI NATIONAL PARK

This undeveloped 1,545-square-mile (4,000-km²) park is located between the towns of Mpanda and Sumbawanga on the main road running through western Tanzania from north to south.

Lake Katavi and its extensive floodplains are in the north of this park, which is about 2,950 feet (900 m) above sea level. To the southeast is Lake Chada, which is connected with Lake Katavi by the Katuma River and its extensive swampland. Miombo woodlands dominate most of the dry areas, except for acacia woodlands near Lake Chada.

Wildlife includes hippo, crocs, elephant, zebra, lion, leopard, eland, puku, roan antelope and sable antelope. Herds of several thousand buffalo are sometimes seen. Over 400 species of birds have been recorded.

The long rains are March-May. The best time to visit is July-October.

 ACCOMMODATIONS – CLASS B: * *Chada Tented Camp* is a seasonal camp with four comfortable tents with bush showers (hot water) and bush (long-drop) toilets. Activities include game drives, walks and optional fly-camping.

CLASS F: There are only a few huts for shelter. Very basic hotel accommodation is available in Mpanda and Sumbawanga.

CAMPING: Sites are available in the park. Campers must be self-sufficient, as there are no facilities.

THE COAST

DAR ES SALAAM

Dar es Salaam, which means "haven of peace" in Arabic, is the functional capital, largest city and commercial center of Tanzania. Many safaris to the southern parks begin here. Among the more interesting sights are the harbor, National Museum, Village Museum and the Kariakoo Market. Ask at your hotel about traditional dancing troops that may be performing during your stay.

Once the German capital, hub of the slave trade and end point of the slave route from the interior, **Bagamoyo** is an old seaport 46 miles (75 km) north of Dar es Salaam. Fourteenth century ruins, stone pens and shackles that held the slaves can be seen.

 ACCOMMODATION – FIRST CLASS: * *Hotel Sea Cliff*, situated on the northeastern point of the Msasani Peninsula 14 miles (22 km) from the international airport, has 86 rooms with facilities ensuite, restaurant, bar and swimming pool. * *Sheraton Hotel* has 250 air-conditioned rooms with ensuite facilities, two restaurants, and a bar, swimming pool and health club. * *Holiday Inn*, located in the city center, has 154 rooms with ensuite bathrooms, two restaurants and cocktail lounge.

TOURIST CLASS: * *The New Africa Hotel*, situated in the heart of Dar es Salaam's shopping and banking district, has 119 air-conditioned rooms and seven suites with ensuite facilities, two restaurants, two bars,

 a casino and business center. * *The Kilimanjaro Hotel* is a large, air-conditioned hotel with ensuite facilities, a swimming pool and a fabulous view of the harbor. * *Oyster Bay Hotel* is 4 miles (6 km) from town on the coast and has rooms with ensuite facilities.

ACCOMMODATION NEAR DAR-ES-SALAAM – LUXURY: * *Amani Beach Club*, situated on the coast south of Dar es Salaam, has 10 luxury air-conditioned cottages, each with garden terrace and hammock overlooking the Indian Ocean, and swimming pool.

ACCOMMODATION – FIRST CLASS: * *Ras Kutani Beach Resort*, located on a beautiful, remote beach 17 miles (28 km) south of Dar es Salaam, has 25 rooms with ensuite facilities. Wind surfing, sailing, snorkeling, deep sea fishing and horseback riding are offered. Easiest access is by air charter. Humpback whales can sometimes be seen from shore. Access is by a 10-minute charter flight or one hour road transfer from Dar es Salaam.

ZANZIBAR

Zanzibar and its sister island, Pemba, grow 75% of the world's cloves. A beautiful island, Zanzibar is only 22 miles (35 km) from the mainland — a 25-minute, scheduled charter flight from Dar es Salaam or a 90-minute hydrofoil ride.

The narrow streets and Arabic architecture of historical Zanzibar City are exceptionally mystical and beautiful on a moonlit night. Main attractions include the **Zanzibar Museum**, former British Consulate, **Arab Fort**, the **Anglican Cathedral** built on the site of the old slave market, **Sultan's Palace**, clove market and Indian bazaar. Livingstone's and Burton's houses are near the picturesque Dhow Harbour, where 20-30 large Arab dhows can often be seen having their cargos loaded or unloaded.

Antique shops stocked with Arab clocks, kettles, brass trays, Zanzibar beds, carved doors and frames have special atmospheres all their own.

The **Spice Tour** travels north of Stone Town and includes a visit to one or more spice gardens and farms. Various spices and plants, including cinnamon, cloves, nutmeg, vanilla, ginger and black pepper, along with fruits such as tamarind, guava, rose-apple and several types of mango and bananas, may be seen, touched and smelled.

View of the Indian Ocean from the Zanzibar Serena Inn.

Good restaurants include Blues at the Zanzibar Serena Inn, and The Fisherman, located near the Tembo Hotel in Stone Town.

The more pristine coral reefs off Zanzibar offer a superb diving or snorkeling experience. In addition to a mind-boggling diversity of brightly colored reef fish, dolphins, green turtles and the largest of all fishes — the harmless whale shark — are fairly numerous in the waters around Zanzibar.

For a taste of what Zanzibar was like prior to the arrival of the traders, sultans and farmers, a visit to **Jozani Forest** is highly recommended. This small patch of remaining forest — mostly palm, pandanus and mahogany trees — is home to the unique Zanzibar red colobus, one of Africa's rarest and most endangered primates. Among birds, the equally rare Fischer's turaco may also be seen at Jozani, along with paradise flycatcher, banded wattle-eye and numerous other species.

ACCOMMODATION IN ZANZIBAR TOWN — DELUXE: * *Zanzibar Serena Inn*, located on the waterfront in Stone Town, has 52 rooms (most with private balconies) with ensuite facilities, seafront restaurant, bar and swimming pool. Guests have access to a beautiful private beach.

ACCOMMODATION — TOURIST CLASS: * *Dhow Palace*, located in the heart of Stone Town about 300 yards (300 m) from the waterfront and has 16 tastefully decorated rooms with ensuite facilities and rooftop restaurant (no alcoholic beverages served), with panoramic views of Stone Town. * *Tembo Hotel* has 32 air-conditioned rooms with ensuite facilities, restaurant (no alcoholic beverages served), and a swimming pool. From its waterfront location, ships are constantly seen, passing enroute to and from the harbor. * *Emerson's* is a very basic hotel situated in the heart of Stone Town on a narrow alleyway, and it features a restaurant on the roof. Some of the 10 rooms have ensuite facilities.

ACCOMMODATION ON THE BEACH — DELUXE: * *Sultan's Palace* is an exclusive resort situated on the southeast coast about 36 miles (60 km) from Zanzibar Airport, set on a beautiful beach. The hotel has 15 large, air-conditioned cottages with ensuite bathrooms, including five Imperial Suites and four smaller Ocean Suites, restaurant, bar and swimming pool.

FIRST CLASS: * *Karafuu Hotel Village,* located on the east coast of Zanzibar about a 90-minute drive from the airport or Stone Town, has 92 air-conditioned rooms in bungalows with ensuite facilities, five restaurants, two bars, sports and entertainment facilities, and swimming pool. * *Blue Bay Beach Resort* is situated on a fine, white-sand beach on the east coast of Zanzibar, a 25-minute drive from Stone Town. This 25-acre property has 88 air-conditioned rooms and suites in two-story bungalows with ensuite bathrooms, two restaurants, two bars and a large swimming pool. Scuba diving and water sports are offered. **Breezes Beach Club,* located on the east coast near the village of Bwejuu, about an hour's drive from Zanzibar airport, has 70 ensuite bedrooms in two-story bungalows set on an unspoiled beach, two restaurants, two bars, conference facility, fitness center, flood-lit tennis court, disco and scuba diving center. * *Ras Nungwi Beach Hotel,* located about 36 miles (60 km) north of Zanzibar Airport on the northern tip of the island, has 16 rooms and four chalets (some of which are air-conditioned) with facilities ensuite, two restaurants, bar, swimming pool, PADI Dive Center, deep-sea fishing, water skiing and windsurfing. **PlanHotel Mapenzi Beach Resort,* located on a beautiful beach on the east coast 28 miles (45 km) from the airport, has 60 spacious rooms (20 with air-conditioning) with ensuite facilities, two restaurants, three bars, tennis courts and a swimming pool. Activities include mountain biking, archery, snorkeling, beach volleyball, table tennis, wind surfing, canoeing and deep-sea fishing. * *Protea Mbweni Ruins Hotel,* located on the west coast of the island and a 15-minute drive from Stone Town, has 12 sea-facing, air-conditioned rooms with ensuite facilities, restaurant, bar and swimming pool.

TOURIST CLASS: * *Matamwe Bungalows*, located on cliffs overlooking the northeast coast, has 12 bandas, most with ensuite facilities, and a restaurant.

CHUMBE ISLAND CORAL PARK

Located 6 miles (10 km) by boat from Stone Town, this nature reserve offers forest and marine nature trails, over half a mile (1 km) of protected reef, great bird watching and snorkeling. Over 40 species of birds, including the endangered roseate tern, have been recorded on the island, and 370 families of fish have been identified on the colorful reefs that drop off to about 50 feet (16 m).

FIRST CLASS: * *Chumbe Island Lodge* offers seven palm-thatched bungalows with ensuite facilities set in the forest and facing the ocean. Each bungalow has solar-powered lights and is equipped to catch, filter and solar-heat its own water for warm showers. This lodge has recently won prestigious environmental awards for its sensitive ecotourism.

MNEMBA ISLAND

Mnemba is an exclusive island located 2 miles (3 km) northeast of the Zanzibar mainland. The island is only 1 mile (1.5 km) in circumference and is idyllic for anyone who wants to truly get away from it all.

Mnemba's reefs are among the best around Zanzibar, and, along with a bewildering variety of spectacular reef fish, encounters with green turtles and whale sharks are fairly common. Humpback whales pass through the straits between Mnemba and the mainland, and pods of common dolphins are seen almost daily. The huge coconut crab is an occasional visitor and the charming little ghost crabs are abundant on the pearly white beach. A variety of birds roost on Mnemba's secure sandbanks, including crab plovers, dimorphic egret, lesser crested tern and a host of Eurasian migratory waders.

ACCOMMODATION – DELUXE: * *Mnemba Island Lodge* is an exclusive island getaway with 10 thatched beach cottages with ensuite facilities. This is "barefoot luxury" at its finest. Wind surfing, big-game fishing, skiing, snorkeling and scuba diving are available. The lodge is an hour by road, followed by 20 minutes by boat from Stone Town.

PEMBA ISLAND

Pemba is located 16 miles (25 km) north of Zanzibar Island near the Kenyan border and offers some of the best scuba diving and deep-sea fishing in all of sub-Saharan Africa. The Pemba Channel runs between Pemba and the mainland with depths up to 2,625 feet (800 m). Sheer underwater walls drop 150-600 feet (45-183 m) just off the coastline. Divers often see eagle ray, grouper, tuna and a variety of tropical fish.

Access to the island is by boat transfer to Pemba Harbor (Mkoani) or by a 20-minute scheduled or private charter flight.

 ACCOMMODATION – FIRST CLASS: * *Fundu Lagoon*, set on 3 miles (4.5 km) of private beach, has 20 bungalows (some on the beach and some of the ridge), a restaurant, two bars and a PADI Dive Center. Activities include snorkeling, scuba diving, sailing, fishing, water skiing and kayaking.

TOURIST CLASS: * *Manta Reef Camp* has 11 comfortable rustic cabins, completely open in the front and built on raised platforms with ensuite facilities, and a dive shop. Scuba diving and snorkeling are offered.

MAFIA ISLAND

A 40-minute flight south from Dar es Salaam, this island offers some of the best big-game fishing in the world. Species caught include marlin, sailfish, tuna and shark. The diving is also very good.

 ACCOMMODATION – FIRST CLASS: * *Polepole Lodge* has 12 rooms with facilities ensuite and a restaurant.

ACCOMMODATION – TOURIST CLASS: * *Kinasi Camp* is a small lodge (20 beds) with ensuite facilities, and is set on a hillside overlooking Chole Bay. Scuba diving, snorkeling, sport fishing, sailing and wind surfing are offered. Other activities include excursions to historic sites, villages, forests, secluded beaches and bays. * *Mafia Island Lodge*, located on Chole Bay, has 40 rooms with ensuite facilities. Scuba diving, snorkeling, deep-sea fishing, water skiing, sailing and motor boating are offered.

KENYA

THE HUNTING CHEETAH

Cheetah generally hunt only by day and are observed in pursuit of their prey more than any other large carnivore. They are most active early in the morning and in the late afternoon (some may even hunt at midday, when the lion and hyena are most likely sleeping).

As animals of the open grassland, the color markings of the cheetah help with the stalking process. If motionless, the cheetah may be obscured, since the underpart of its body is in shadow, making the lighter, lower part as dark as the upper body. This makes it difficult for the cheetah's prey to notice its spots. The stalking process may take from a few minutes to several hours as the cheetah approach to within 100 yards (100 m) of their prey. From that vantage point, they prepare for their attack.

That is when you see the speed of the cheetah. The acceleration from 0 to 45 mph (0 to 70 km/h) in a couple of seconds is made possible by its huge strides, which are six times the length of its body. At three strides per second, their hind feet strike the ground far in front of their head to reach a top speed of 70 mph (110 km/h). The cheetah uses its tail as a rudder to help it keep its balance at such high speeds.

As sprinters, cheetah have up to 15 seconds to catch their prey. Maximum speed may not be reached, however, since the cheetah must often slow down to swerve and follow the zigzag path of its prey. At high speed, cheetah also have to judge the timing of their strike. They either swipe the legs out from under their prey with a front paw, or hook a dew claw into the animal's side.

KENYA

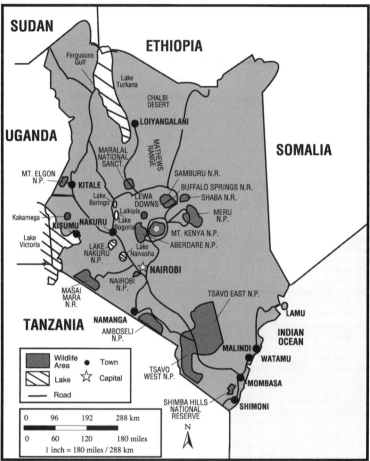

FACTS AT A GLANCE

AREA: 224,960 sq. mi. / 582,750 sq. km
APPROXIMATE SIZE: Texas or France
POPULATION: 30.4 million
CAPITAL: Nairobi (pop. est. 2 million)
OFFICIAL LANGUAGE: Kiswahili and English

KENYA

The word "safari" is Swahili for "a journey," and Kenya is where it all began. Hemingway immortalized the safari experience, although he was a sport and trophy hunter rather than a naturalist or photographer.

Joy Adamson was among the group of expatriates, in the 1960s and 1970s, whose endeavors to conserve African wildlife captured the world's attention. The writings of Karen Blixen, and the adaptation of her classic book *Out of Africa* into a motion picture starring Robert Redford and Meryl Streep, helped establish Kenya as a great safari destination in the modern era.

Visitors to Kenya can enjoy game viewing, birdwatching, hot-air ballooning, mountaineering, scuba diving, freshwater and deep-sea fishing, and numerous other activities.

Kenya is well known for the magnificent Serengeti Migration (shared with Tanzania) of more than one million wildebeest and zebra in the Masai Mara and for the colorful Masai, Samburu and other tribes that contribute so much to making this a top safari destination.

Kenya has one of the most diversely majestic landscapes on the continent. The Great Rift Valley, with the steep-walled valley floor dropping as much as 2,000-3,000 feet (610–915 m) from the surrounding countryside, is more breathtakingly dramatic here than anywhere else in Africa.

The eastern and northern regions of the country are arid. Most of the population and economic production are in the south, which is

Samburu Morani.

characterized by a plateau that ranges in altitude from 3,000 to 10,000 feet (915 to 3,050 m), sloping down to Lake Victoria in the west and to a coastal strip to the east.

Over half the country is Christian, although many people still retain their indigenous beliefs. There is a Muslim population concentrated along the coast. The Masai are found mainly to the south of Nairobi, the Kikuyu in the highlands around Nairobi, the Samburu in the arid north, and the Luo around Lake Victoria.

Bantu and Nilotic peoples moved into the area before Arab traders, who arrived on the Kenyan coast by the first century A.D. The Swahili language was created out of a mixture of Bantu and Arabic and became the universal trading language.

The Portuguese arrived in 1498 and took command of the coast, followed by the Omani in the 1600s and the British in the late nineteenth century. Kenya gained its independence within the British Commonwealth on December 12, 1963. Key foreign exchange-earners are tourism, coffee, tea and horticulture (flowers and vegetables exported to Europe, especially in the European winter).

A family outing.

WILDLIFE AND WILDLIFE AREAS

Kenya is one of the best countries on the continent for seeing large amounts of wildlife. In addition, lodge safaris, where guests are driven from park to park, are generally less expensive here than in Tanzania, Botswana or Zimbabwe. Prices are even more attractive in Kenya's low season (April, May and November). Game viewing is still quite good in the low season due to the excellent visibility of the open plains of the Masai Mara and other reserves.

Kenya's well-known parks can become crowded in high season. However, it is possible to get away from the crowds in some of the splendid private reserves or the less popular national parks. Many private reserves cater to a maximum of 12-24 guests in luxury accommodations and offer activities not allowed within the parks, such as night game drives and escorted walks. Ol Donyo Waus and Campi Ya Kanzi, for instance, each cover 250,000 acres (100,000 hectares) and cater to no more than 16 guests. You can also visit the major reserves at times other than during peak seasons. Booking a

The Norfolk Hotel, Nairobi.

safari with a private vehicle and guide is a great way to maximize the quality of your game viewing experience.

The Kenya Wildlife Services, formed to monitor the national parks and reserves, has instituted changes that have reduced poaching and limited the building of new lodges and camps in parks and reserves.

The Masai Mara is the best reserve in Kenya for wildlife viewing and should, if at all possible, be included in your itinerary, unless you will be touring the Serengeti National Park in Tanzania at the times of the year when the Serengeti Migration is more concentrated there.

In general, game viewing is best during the dry seasons, mid-December-March and July-early October. Wildlife is easiest to spot in the Masai Mara, Amboseli and Nairobi National Parks, which have vast wide-open plains. Samburu/Buffalo Springs National Reserves and Lewa Downs are the country's best northern reserves and are also excellent for game viewing.

The country is an ornithologist's paradise, with over 1,000 species of birds recorded within its borders. Greater and lesser flamingos migrate along the Rift Valley and prefer the alkaline lakes of Magadi,

Elmenteita, Nakuru, Bogoria or Turkana. Lakes Naivasha and Baringo are freshwater lakes. Birdwatching is good year-round, but is perhaps best between September and March when many species of Eurasian migratory birds are present alongside the breeding residents.

Flying safaris are available to many of the parks and reserves. Unique, camel-back safaris are operated in the north, where guests spend time riding these "ships of the desert" and walking down dry riverbeds.

THE SOUTH

NAIROBI

Nairobi, situated at altitude of about 6,000 feet (1,830 m), means "place of cool waters" in the Masai language.

The **National Museum** of Nairobi features the Leakey family's paleo-anthropological discoveries, botanical drawings and the original tribal paintings of Joy Adamson. Studying the taxidermy displays of birds and wild animals will help you identify the live game while on safari. Across from the museum is the **Snake Park**, exhibiting over 200 species of the "well-loved" reptilian family. At the **Municipal Market** in the center of town on Muindi Mbingu Street, vendors sell and produce unusual and beautiful curios (be sure to bargain). The **Railroad Museum** will be of interest to railroad enthusiasts. The **Nairobi Race Course** has horse racing on Sunday afternoons (in season); the track is an excellent place for people to watch and meet a diverse cross section of Nairobians.

One of the more popular dining and disco spots is the Carnivore, famous for its beef and game meat. The Horseman, located in the suburb of Karen, is also excellent. The Tamarind is known for excellent seafood. The Minar and Haandi are possibly the finest of Kenya's great Indian restaurants. The Thorn Tree Cafe is a renowned meeting place for travelers on long safaris who leave messages on a bulletin board; it is one of the best spots in town for people-watching. Other excellent restaurants include Alan Bobbies' Bistro and the Red Bull. The most happening disco in Nairobi these days is The Pavement in Westlands.

Other attractions include the **Bomas of Kenya**, which features daily performances of ethnic dances and 16 varying styles of Kenyan homesteads. At the **Giraffe Centre,** guests can learn more about the Rothschild's giraffes and even feed them from an elevated platform. The **Karen Blixen Museum** is also an interesting attraction, featuring many of this famous author's personal possessions on display in her restored home. The **African Butterfly Research Institute** (ABRI), located near the Karen Blixen Museum, has a "butterfly flight house," a great shop and restaurant. The trained team at the **Daphne Sheldrick Elephant Orphanage** have brought sick, abandoned elephants back to health and released them into the wild at Tsavo East National Park. Using a milk formula she created, Daphne was the first person to successfully bottle-raise an orphaned milk-dependent elephant.

ACCOMMODATION – DELUXE: * *Norfolk Hotel*, a landmark in Nairobi and a member of the "Leading Hotels of the World," has traditional safari atmosphere, a swimming pool, the fabulous Ibis Grill, and an open-air bar that is especially popular on Friday nights. All rooms are air-conditioned with ensuite facilities. . * *Nairobi Serena Hotel*, located a 10-minute walk from town, is also a member of the "Leading Hotels of the World," and has 200 air-conditioned rooms with ensuite facilities, business center, conference facilities, gym and a large swimming pool. * *Grand Regency Hotel* is a 300-room high-rise hotel with ensuite facilities and a swimming pool, restaurant, rooftop lounge, conference center and casino. * *Nairobi Safari Club* is an air-conditioned, all-suite hotel (146 rooms) with ensuite facilities and a health club and swimming pool

FIRST CLASS: * *Hilton International* is centrally located and has 329 air-conditioned rooms with facilities ensuite and a swimming pool. * *Inter-Continental Hotel*, near the center of town, has a swimming pool, 440 air-conditioned rooms with ensuite facilities and a casino. * *New Stanley Hotel*, located in the center of town, has 240 air-conditioned rooms with ensuite facilities.

TOURIST CLASS: * *Boulevard Hotel*, located on the edge of town, is set in lovely gardens and has 70 rooms with ensuite facilities and a swimming pool. * *Fairview Hotel*, set on 5 acres of gardens just over a mile (2 km) from the city center, has 103 rooms and 11 apartments with ensuite facilities. * *Landmark Hotel*, located just outside the city center, has 124 rooms with ensuite facilities. * *Mayfair Court Holiday Inn* has

 108 rooms with ensuite facilities, two swimming pools, a restaurant and a casino.

ACCOMMODATION OUTSIDE OF NAIROBI – DELUXE: * *Safari Park Hotel*, located 7 miles (11 km) from the city center in a quiet, country setting, has 228 rooms with ensuite facilities, a huge swimming pool, tennis and squash courts and several restaurants — all in a lush garden setting. * *The Windsor Golf and Country Club*, located 11 miles (17 km) outside Nairobi, is a colonial-style hotel with 130 rooms with ensuite facilities, an 18-hole golf course, tennis courts, and a health club and gymnasium.

FIRST CLASS: * *Ngong House*, located in the suburb of Langata, has four elevated log cabins set in beautiful natural gardens, with ensuite facilities and excellent food. * *Giraffe Manor*, located in the suburb of Langata, is famous for having Rothschild's giraffes roaming about the property, often sticking their heads through open windows looking for handouts. This unique lodge has three bedrooms with and two without ensuite facilities. * *Karen Blixen Cottages*, situated 20 miles (32 km) from Nairobi and a half mile (1 km) from the Karen Blixen Museum, has 16 suites with ensuite bathrooms, restaurant, bar and swimming pool. * *Macushla House*, a private guesthouse located near Giraffe Manor, which is just a 20-minute drive from downtown Nairobi, caters to a maximum of 10 guests in rooms with ensuite facilities and swimming pool.

THE "LUNATIC EXPRESS"

The service and standard of accommodations on this overnight train between Nairobi and Mombasa has, unfortunately, deteriorated over the last several years, and at this point should be considered only by hardy travelers. Dinner and breakfast are served on this journey that passes Mt. Kilimanjaro in the night. There are departures three times a week from both Nairobi and Mombasa.

NAIROBI NATIONAL PARK

Nairobi National Park is only 8 miles (13 km) south of Nairobi, and has an abundance of game including lion, cheetah, hippo and a variety of antelope — a bit of everything except elephant. The park has one of the highest concentrations of black rhino in Africa, with a current population of over 60.

Most of the park is open plains with areas of scattered acacia bush.

AMBOSELI NATIONAL PARK

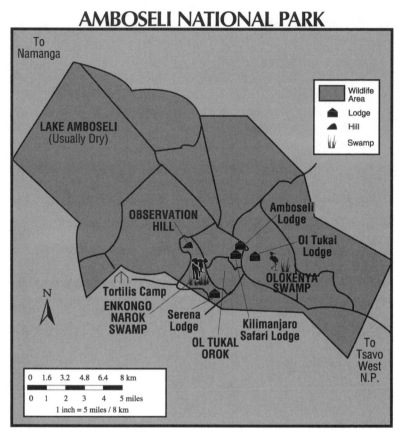

The permanent Athi River is fringed by yellow-barked fever trees, and there is a small patch of highland forest dominated by crotons. An impressive list of birds has been recorded, but occurrence is seasonal for many species. Among the characteristic varieties are ostrich, secretary bird, black-headed heron, augur buzzard, little bee-eater and Jackson's widowbird.

There is something very strange about being in the midst of wild game while still within sight of a city skyline. Altitude ranges from 4,950 to 5,850 feet (1,500 to 1,785 m) above sea level.

The Animal Orphanage, a small zoo near the main park entrance, cares for hurt, sick or stray animals. The side of the park facing Nairobi is fenced. A 4wd vehicle is recommended in the rainy season.

Mt. Kilimanjaro makes for a fantastic background when photographing wildlife.

AMBOSELI NATIONAL PARK

Set on the Tanzanian border, Amboseli is one of the most scenic of Kenya's wildlife reserves. Every vista is dominated by the majestic, snow-capped peak of Kilimanjaro in neighboring Tanzania. The grandeur of this imposing feature provides a superb backdrop for photographing and viewing big game.

Amboseli is perhaps best-known for its abundant (over 1,000) and approachable elephants — the subject of several documentary films and researcher Cynthia Moss' classic book *Elephant Memories* (University of Chicago Press).

Amboseli National Park covers 150 square miles (390 km²) and averages about 3,900 feet (1,190 m) in altitude. Elephant and giraffe are easily found, and many visitors enjoy photographing them as they pass in front of majestic Mt. Kilimanjaro. The mountain seems so close, but it is actually located in Tanzania, more than 30 miles (48 km) from the park.

The park lies in the rain shadow of Kilimanjaro and receives, on average, just 12 inches (300 mm) of rain per year. Interestingly, however, subterranean water draining off the northern slopes of

Tortilis Camp, Amboseli National Park.

Mt. Kilimanjaro surfaces in Amboseli in the form of freshwater springs. These springs are a major draw-card for wildlife, and the surrounding papyrus beds are an attractive habitat for wetland species. The dominant habitat is acacia-commiphora scrub or woodland, much of it on rocky, lava-strewn plains.

A dry and ancient lakebed occupies the western part of the reserve, but when it fills after heavy rain it can be a huge attraction for birds. Over 400 bird species have been recorded here, including three varieties of sandgrouse, rosy-patched bushshrike, Taveta golden weaver and purple grenadier. In addition to the plain's game typical of East Africa, the arid-adapted gerenuk, lesser kudu and fringe-eared oryx may been seen.

From Nairobi, travel south across the Athi Plains inhabited by the Masai pastoralists. Visitors enter the park on a badly corrugated road from Namanga and pass Lake Amboseli (a salt pan), which is bone dry except in the rainy seasons, eastward across sparsely vegetated chalk flats to Ol Tukai. Mirages are common under the midday sun.

Approaching the center of the park, the barren landscape turns refreshingly green from springs and swamps fed by underground runoff from the overshadowing Mt. Kilimanjaro. These swamps give life to an otherwise parched land, providing water for nearby grass-

A room with a view of Mt. Kilimanjaro.

lands and acacia woodlands and attracting a profusion of game and waterfowl. Superb starling, red-and-yellow barbet and silverbird are amongthe bush birds in residence.

Large herds of elephant and buffalo are often seen around the swamps, especially at **Enkongo Narok Swamp,** where it is easy to obtain photos of animals (especially elephant) in the foreground and Mt. Kilimanjaro in the background. Early morning is best, before Kilimanjaro is covered in clouds; the clouds may partially clear in late afternoon.

Observation Hill is a good location from which to get an overview of the park. There is a pretty good chance of spotting cheetah, giraffe and impala, but oryx and gerenuk are less likely to be seen. Game viewing is best from mid-December to March (also best views of Kilimanjaro) and from July to October.

To limit destruction to the environment, driving off the roads is forbidden, and heavy fines are being levied against those who break the rules. Please do not ask your driver to leave the road for a closer look at wildlife. The park is about 140 miles (225 km) from Nairobi.

ACCOMMODATION – CLASS A: * *Tortilis Camp* is located just outside the reserve and has 17 luxury tents with ensuite facilities and a swimming pool. Day games drives within the park, and night game drives and walks in their concession area outside the park, are offered.

CLASS A/B: * *Amboseli Serena Lodge*, located in the south of the park, is a lodge with 96 rooms with ensuite facilities and a swimming pool.

CLASS B: * *Ol Tukai Lodge* has 80 rooms with facilities ensuite and a swimming pool.

CLASS C: * *Amboseli Lodge* has 112 rooms with facilities ensuite and a swimming pool.

CAMPING: Campsites are located outside the park on Masai land, 4 miles (6 km) past Observation Hill. No facilities exist except long-drop (pit) toilets. Bring your own water.

OL DONYO WUAS

Ol Donyo Wuas is set on a 250,000-acre (100,000-hectare) Masai Group Ranch (part of the Amboseli ecosystem) in the foothills of the Chyulu Range, halfway between Tsavo West and Amboseli National Park. Guests of the lodge have panoramic views of Mount Kilimanjaro and exclusive access to the ranch.

On game drives during my last visit we saw Masai giraffe, oryx, Grant's gazelle, eland, bush duiker, dikdik, Coke's hartebeest, black-backed jackal and serval, among other game. Lion, cheetah and elephant may also be seen. On horseback we cantered among herds of zebra and wildebeest and came fairly close to giraffe, oryx and eland. This is certainly one of the best places for horseback riding in East Africa.

Easiest access is by a 50-minute charter flight from Nairobi.

 ACCOMMODATION – CLASS A: * *Ol Donyo Wuas* accommodates guests in seven thatched luxury cottages with open fireplaces, verandas and ensuite facilities. Day and night game drives in open vehicles and escorted walks with excellent resident guides, Masai visits, horseback rides ranging from an hour's ride to multi-day safaris, and fly camping are offered.

CAMPI YA KANZI

Campi Ya Kanzi is located on a 250,000-acre (100,000-hectare) Masai Group Ranch surrounded by Chyulu, Tsavo and Amboseli National Parks, and stretching to the foothills of Mount Kilimanjaro. The landscape is quite varied from lush forests to riverine forest and savannah grasslands, as the altitude ranges from 3,000-6,900 feet (900-2,100 m). Wildlife includes elephant, lion, cheetah, lesser kudu, fringe-eared oryx, gerenuk and mountain reedbuck. Over 400 species of birds have been recorded. Easiest access is by a 50-minute charter flight from Nairobi.

 ACCOMMODATION – CLASS A: * *Campi Ya Kanzi* has six luxury tents under thatch, set on raised wooden decks with verandahs and ensuite bathrooms. Activities at this family-run lodge include day and night game drives, escorted walks with the Masai trackers, Masai cultural visits, and excursions to Tsavo West, Chyulu and Amboseli national parks. There are lovely views of Mt. Kilimanjaro from the camp.

TSAVO WEST NATIONAL PARK

Halfway between Nairobi and Mombasa lie **West** and **East Tsavo National Parks**, which together with **Chyulu Hills National Park** total 8,217 square miles (21,283 km²). Large herds of over 100 elephant are part of the massive population of over 15,000 in Tsavo West and East combined. The park has a number of large prides of lion and a good leopard population. Also present are caracal, giraffe, zebra and a variety of antelope.

Acacia and Commiphora woodland dominates the landscape, with ribbons of taller trees along the Galana, Tsavo and other rivers. The graceful doum palm, with its forked trunk, is a common sight. The many enormous baobab trees provide plenty of breeding cavities for barbets, starlings, parrots, rollers, kestrels and owls.

Less wildlife is usually seen here than in Amboseli National Park; however, the park's rugged terrain is quite impressive in itself.

Tsavo West National Park is predominantly semi-arid plains broken by occasional granite outcrops. Lava fields are located near Kilaguni Lodge. Altitudes range from 1,000 feet (305 m) to nearly 6,000 feet (1,830 m) in the Ngulia Mountains located in the northern region of the park.

TSAVO NATIONAL PARK

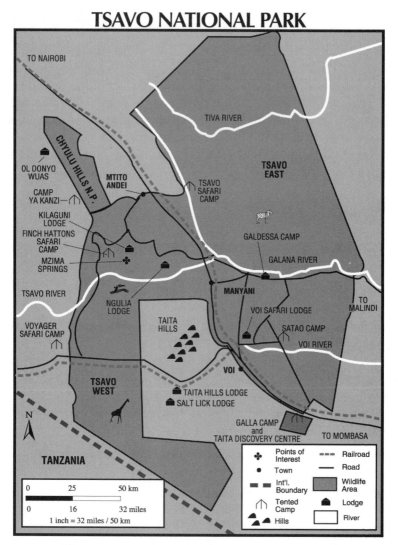

From the **Mzima Springs** underwater viewing platform, located just south of Kilaguni Lodge, visitors may be lucky enough to watch hippo swim in the clear waters among the crocs and fish. Otters also inhabit these waters. The best viewing is early in the morning. Kilaguni Lodge is about 180 miles (290 km) from Nairobi.

ACCOMMODATION – CLASS A: * *Finch Hattons Safari Camp* overlooks a hippo pool, and has 35 tents with ensuite facilities and a swimming pool.

CLASS A:/B: * *Severin Safari Camp* has 20 unique octagonal ensuite tents overlooking a waterhole and Mt Kilimanjaro beyond.

CLASS B: * *Kilaguni Lodge* has 50 rooms with facilities ensuite and a swimming pool. * *Ngulia Lodge* has 52 rooms with ensuite facilities and a swimming pool.

CLASS D: * *Ngulia Safari Camp* is located near Ngulia Lodge and has self-service bandas. * *Kitani Lodge* is located near Mzima Springs and has self-service bandas.

CAMPING: Campsites are available at Kitani, Kamboyo and Kangechwa and at the following park gates: Mtito Andei, Chyulu (Kilaguni), Kasigau and Tsavo. Chyulu has showers and toilets; the other campsites have basic (if any) facilities.

ACCOMMODATION NEAR TSAVO NATIONAL PARK – CLASS B/C: * *Voyager Safari Camp* overlooks a hippo pool and has 16 tents with ensuite showers and long-drop toilets. The camp is situated just outside the southwestern boundary of the park and offers day and night game drives, walks and excursions to Lake Chala.

CLASS D: * *Kasigau Bandas* are operated and hosted by the local community.

TSAVO EAST NATIONAL PARK

Tsavo East is mostly arid bush dotted with rocky outcrops that are traversed by seasonal riverbeds lined with riverine forest. Tsavo East is generally hotter and drier, as it lies at a lower altitude (about 1,000 ft./305 m) than its western counterpart. The 3,000 square miles (7,770 km²) south of the Galana River is the main region open to the public.

Substantial numbers of elephant, lion, cheetah, Masai giraffe, lesser kudu and other large mammals occur, as well as a small number of highly endangered hirola (Hunter's hartebeest), which were relocated here in 1996 and seem to be holding their own. Among the interesting dryland birds are vulturine guineafowl, orange-bellied parrot, white-bellied go-away bird and golden-breasted starlings.

East Tsavo's only permanent water hole is at Aruba Dam, and the drive from Voi makes for a good game drive. Just north of Voi is an isolated hill, Mudanda Rock, another good spot for game. The scenic drive along the Galana River often produces sightings of hippo and crocs.

View of the Galana River from Galdessa Camp.

Tsavo East receives fewer visitors than Tsavo West; wildlife is generally more heavily concentrated in Tsavo West. Voi is about 210 miles (340 km) from Nairobi.

ACCOMMODATION – CLASS A: * *Galdessa Camp,* situated on the banks of the Galana River, takes a maximum of 16 guests in eight luxury tented bandas under thatch with ensuite bathrooms. Activities include day and night game drives and walking safaris. Black rhino have been reintroduced locally.

CLASS B/C: * *Satao Camp* has 32 tents with ensuite flush toilets and bush (bucket) showers. * *Voi Safari Lodge,* in the hills above the town of Voi, has 52 rooms with facilities ensuite, a swimming pool and photographic hide.

CLASS C: * *Patterson's Camp,* set along the banks of the Athi River in this historical "man-eaters" area of the park, has 20 spacious tents with ensuite facilities.

CLASS D: * *Tsavo Safari Camp,* located 15 miles (24 km) from Mtito Andei Gate on the Athi River, has 30 tents and six bandas with facilities ensuite.

CAMPING: Campsites are available at Voi, Sala and Buchuma Gates. There are few or no facilities.

Taita Discovery Centre.

 ACCOMMODATION NEAR THE PARK– CLASS A: * *Kalinda*, set on the banks of the Athi River at the edge of the park, has six cottages (one of which has a private jacuzzi), with verandahs, ensuite facilities and a swimming pool. Activities include day and night game drives, walks, escorted game walks and fishing.

WITHIN THE TSAVO ECOSYSTEM

The **Tsavo Kasigau Wildlife Corridor** is a wildlife conservancy in the making, encompassing an enormous 380,000-acre (152,000-hectare) stretch of unspoiled private wilderness that is nestled between Tsavo East and West. This area forms a vital corridor route for a population of almost 1,000 elephants as they disperse between the Galana River in Tsavo East and south to Lake Jipe in Tsavo West.

Located within this ecosystem is the Taita Discovery Centre, dedicated to the environmental education of foreigners and Kenyans alike through their participation in a variety of community service programs. It is also the motivating epicenter for the testing and establishment of a variety of environmentally based micro-enterprises including aquaculture, apiculture, sericulture and many more.

 ACCOMMODATION – CLASS B: * *Taita Hills Lodge* and *Salt Lick Lodge* are situated between the southern extensions of Tsavo East and West Parks, about 240 miles (390 km) from Nairobi. * *Salt Lick Lodge*, built on stilts to enhance viewing of wildlife visiting the salt lick, has 64 rooms with facilities ensuite and a swimming pool. * *Taita Hills Lodge* has 60 rooms with ensuite facilities, a swimming pool and golf course.

MASAI MARA NATIONAL RESERVE

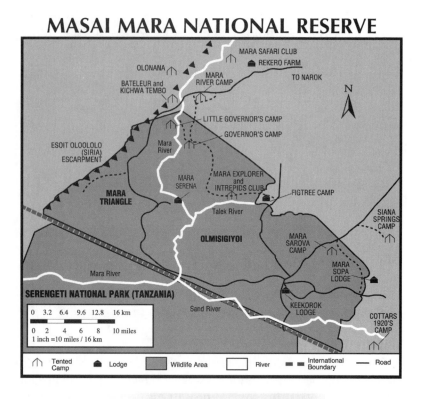

Walking with Masai is possible at certain camps and lodges.

CLASS C: * *Galla Camp* has six tents with ensuite bathrooms, and it sits on a rock kopje overlooking a waterhole. Guides and resident researchers assist guests in "service learning" activities from the Taita Discovery Centre.

CLASS C and D: * *The Taita Discovery Centre* has four ensuite rooms for adults and volunteers, and four dormitories with eight beds each for students with separate facilities. The center is a popular destination for volunteers wanting to participate in wildlife conservation projects for extended periods of one to six months at a time.

MASAI MARA NATIONAL RESERVE

This is undoubtedly the finest wildlife area in Kenya. All of the big game is here: elephant, lion, leopard, cheetah and buffalo are prevalent, along with a small population of black rhino. Other commonly sighted species include zebra, wildebeest, Thomson's gazelle, Defassa waterbuck, eland and Masai giraffe. This is the only place in Kenya where topi are common.

Masai Mara National Reserve, a northern extension of the Serengeti Plains (Tanzania), is located southwest of Nairobi and covers 590 square miles (1,530 km²) of open plains, acacia woodlands and riverine forest along the banks on the Mara and Talek Rivers, which are home for many hippo, crocs and waterfowl.

One of the best places to look for wildlife is in the Mara Triangle in the western part of the reserve, which is bounded by the Siria (Esoit Oloololo) Escarpment rising about 1,000 feet (305 m) above the plains on the west, by the Tanzanian border to the south and by the Mara River to the east. A multitude of savannah animals can be found on these open grasslands and other areas to the northwest of the reserve.

The western part of the Mara is less crowed than the eastern part of the reserve. Most adventurers visiting the camps in the western part of the reserve fly into the Mara, while most people visiting the lodges and camps in the eastern Mara are driven into the reserve.

Lion are distributed throughout the park. Cheetah are most often seen on the short-grass plains. Black rhino are most concentrated in the Olmisigiyoi Region in the center of the park, in the northwest and in the extreme eastern parts of the park; and are now starting to forage in the Mara Triangle.

The best time to visit is during the migration, from approximately July to October when great herds of wildebeest (1.4 million) and zebra (250,000) reside in the Mara and northern Tanzania before returning to Serengeti National Park. During the migration, prides of 40 or more lion may be seen. From the southern Serengeti of Tanzania, a major portion of the migration moves northwest toward Lake Victoria, then north across the Mara River into Kenya in search of grass, usually returning to Tanzania in late October. The best time to witness large numbers of wildebeest and zebra crossing the Mara River is from mid/late July to mid/late September. However, as the park teems with resident wildlife, game viewing is, in fact, good year-round.

On our most recent visit, we saw lion, cheetah, thousands of wildebeest and zebra, and the unforgettable experience of witnessing part of the migration crossing the Mara River! We patiently sat at the river's edge for four hours and were handsomely rewarded for our patience. On another visit we saw a mother leopard and two cubs with their kill in a tree, several cheetah, numerous prides of lion, thousands of wildebeest and zebra, a large breeding herd of elephant and a variety of other game.

The Mara is a paradise for birds and birdwatchers. Over 400 species have been recorded, with grassland and wetland birds especially well represented. Martial eagle, long-crested eagle and bateleur are common, while large numbers of vultures follow the great migration of wildebeest and zebra, feeding on the remains of those that die of exhaustion, old age or predator attacks. The Mara River and some of its tributaries are forested along their banks, providing ideal habitat for exciting birds such as Ross's turaco, black-and-white-casqued hornbill, blue flycatcher and the narina trogon.

In the **Mara Triangle** and the northwestern part of the park, 4wd vehicles are recommended. There are at least two flights a day from Nairobi that serve the park. Keekorok Lodge is located about 170 miles (275 km) and the Mara Serena about 210 miles (340 km) from Nairobi.

Balloon safaris are very popular and certainly a unique way of experiencing Africa. On my last balloon safari we flew from Little Governor's Camp over part of the great migration and saw a variety

Bush breakfast a la "Out of Africa".

of wildlife. The pilot was extremely entertaining as well as knowledgeable of the flora and fauna enroute. The champagne breakfast that followed was great fun for the entire group.

Fishing safaris by private air charter to **Mfangano Island, Rusinga Island** and **Takawiri Island** on Lake Victoria are available from all the camps (book in advance).

ACCOMMODATION – All lodges and camps listed below either conduct hot-air balloon safaris or will take you to where one is being offered. Many guests fly into the Mara (highly recommended) and are taken game viewing in 4wd vehicles (preferably) or minivans. Most camps and lodges are a five- to six-hour drive from Nairobi.

ACCOMMODATION IN THE RESERVE – CLASS A+: * *Mara Explorer,* situated on the Talek River in the middle of the Mara, has 10 luxurious tents with facilities ensuite. Activities include game drives, walking safaris outside the reserve and visits to Masai communities.
Governor's Ilmoran Camp is located within the reserve, and has 10 huge tents lining the winding banks of the Mara River — all with ensuite bathrooms. Group morning and afternoon game drives and walks on the periphery of the reserve are offered.

One of the tents at Mara River Camp.

ACCOMMODATION IN THE RESERVE – CLASS A: * *Mara Intrepids Club* is situated on the Talek River and has 27 tents with four-poster beds, ensuite facilities and a swimming pool. Walks are offered in the adjacent Masai land. * *Little Governor's Camp*, located in the northwest part of the park on the Mara River, has 17 tents with facilities ensuite. Guests reach the camp by crossing the Mara River. Walks are offered outside the reserve. * *Governor's Camp*, located a few miles from Little Governor's Camp on the Mara River, has 38 tents with ensuite facilities and excellent food and service. Walks outside the reserve are offered. * *Mara Serena Lodge*, set on a hill in the central western part of the park, has 78 rooms with private facilities and a swimming pool. Because it is set far from any other camps or lodges, guests encounter very few other vehicles. The view from the lodge of the expansive plains below is spectacular.

CLASS A/B: * *Mara Simba Lodge* has 36 rooms with facilities ensuite and private verandas overlooking the Talek River, and a swimming pool. * *Governor's Private Camp* caters to private parties of up to 16 guests in tents with ensuite flush toilets and bush (bucket) showers.

CLASS B: * *Keekorok Lodge* is an old-style lodge with 72 rooms and 12 cottages with ensuite facilities and a swimming pool. * *Sarova Mara Camp* has 75 tents with ensuite facilities and a swimming pool.

Cottars 1920's Mara Safari Camp.

 ACCOMMODATION ON THE PERIPHERY OF THE RESERVE – CLASS A+: * *Bateleur Camp* at Kichwa Tembo, situated on the western border of the Mara, has nine luxuriously furnished tents with facilities ensuite. Morning and afternoon game drives, night game drives on a private concession, guided walks and Masai visits are offered. * *Cottars 1920's Mara Safari Camp*, set outside the eastern border of the reserve on a private concession, accommodates up to eight clients in authentic, spacious white canvas tents, and it incorporates original safari antiques from the 20s. Each tent has a dressing room and bathroom (old-fashioned tub), a main bedroom and private verandah. Game drives are conducted in the reserve and are also provided on the concession along with walking and fishing.

CLASS A: * *Kichwa Tembo* has 40 tents and two thatched rondavels with ensuite facilities and swimming pool. Escorted walks, Masai village visits, day and night game drives in a private concession area are offered. * *Olonana*, set on the banks of the Mara River, has 12 luxury tents built on wooden platforms with ensuite facilities.

CLASS A/B: * *Mara River Camp* is located on the banks of the Mara River and one of the smaller camps with only 16 tents with ensuite facilities, and it provides excellent guides. * *Siana Springs* has 38 tents with facilities ensuite, and a swimming pool. Walks and day and night game drives are offered. * *Bush Tops* is a private home accommodating 10 guests in thatched bungalows with ensuite facilities. Game drives, escorted walks and fly camping are offered. * *Mara Sopa Lodge*, located on the eastern border of the park high on a ridge overlooking the Mara near Ololaimutiek Gate, has 72 rooms with facilities ensuite and a swimming pool.

CLASS B/C: * *Fig Tree Camp,* located on the Talek River, has 30 basic chalets and 30 tents with facilities ensuite and a swimming pool. Walks and day and night game drives are offered.

CAMPING: Sites are located outside the park along the Talek River.

THE WEST

KAKAMEGA FOREST

Kakamega is the eastern-most remnant of the great West African rain forests that once stretched the width of Africa. There are 4 miles (7 km) of walking trails through a forest that includes some of Africa's greatest hard and soft woods, including Elgon Teak, red and white stink woods, and several varieties of Croton.

Kakamega is an ornithologist's dream, alive with different species of birds — some are found only in this part of Kenya. Avifauna specialties include great blue turaco, African gray parrot, blue-headed bee-eater, black-and-white casqued hornbill, emerald cuckoo, black-billed and Vieillot's black weavers, Chubb's cisticola, Turner's eremomela, joyfull greenbul, Luhder's bushshrike, honeyguide greenbul, Uganda woodland warbler, yellow-bellied wattle-eye and chestnut wattle-eye. Black-and-white colobus monkey, blue monkey and red-tailed monkeys may also be seen.

 ACCOMMODATION – CLASS B: * *Rondo Retreat* has four rooms in the main house (originally built in the 1920s) and four cottages with two to four rooms each, some with ensuite facilities.

MT. ELGON NATIONAL PARK

Seldom visited, this 65-square-mile (169-km²) park is a huge, extinct volcano shared with Uganda, and at 14,178 feet (4,321 m) it is the second highest mountain in Kenya. Mt. Elgon also has the giant Afro-alpine flora found on Mts. Kenya and Kilimanjaro.

The forests are often so thick that a full-grown elephant could be standing 20 feet (6 m) from the road and not be seen. Buffalo, waterbuck and bushbuck are more likely to be spotted.

Mount Elgon is of great botanical interest and offers a wealth of Afro-alpine plants on the high-altitude moorlands. Giant podocarpus, olive and juniper trees form a dense forest on the mid-slopes, where

Balloon Safari over the Masai Mara.

epiphytic orchids and lichens abound. The spectacular black-and-white colobus and blue monkey are the most common primates, while small numbers of giant forest hog feed on the forest floor. The cliffs and caves are home to lanner falcon, scarce swift and hill chat, while keen birdwatchers can look for the elusive bar-tailed trogon and Doherty's bushshrike in the dense forest.

Kitum and Makingeny Caves are unique; they were partially formed by the resident herds of elephant. Small herds often enter the caves near dusk to spend several hours in the company of thousands of bats, mining salts with their tusks. Makingeny is the largest, but Kitum is more frequently visited by elephants. During our visit, elephant droppings were everywhere, foreshadowing the real possibility of their sources being inside.

To explore the caves, be sure to bring two or more strong flashlights. Access to the park is difficult in the rainy season, when 4wd vehicles are recommended. There are no huts on the mountain, and campers must bring their own tents. The park is 255 miles (360 km) from Nairobi.

ACCOMMODATION – CLASS D: * *Mount Elgon Lodge*, situated less than a mile (1.5 km) before the park entrance, has 17 rooms with private facilities.

CAMPING: Several campsites and self-service bandas are available in the park.

ACCOMMODATION NEAR THE RESERVE – CLASS B/C: * *Lokitela Farm* is located on the foothills of Mt. Elgon, 11 miles (19 km) from the town of Kitale. Up to 24 guests are accommodated in the main house and in lodge cottages. The 874-acre (350-hectare) farm primarily produces milk and maize, along with a number of other crops. Over 300 species of birds have been recorded on the farm.

LAKE VICTORIA

Lake Victoria is the largest lake in Africa and the second largest freshwater lake in the world (Lake Superior is the largest). The lake is approximately 26,650 square miles (69,000 km²) in size and is bordered by Kenya, Tanzania and Uganda.

Fishing for the giant Nile perch is excellent; the largest one taken from the lake was reported to weigh 520 pounds (236 kg)! Nile perch weighing in excess of 100 pounds (45 kg) are sometimes caught.

Unfortunately, the Nile perch is not native to Lake Victoria. It was introduced in the 1950s and is a major predator of indigenous fish, some of which have become extinct. In recent years, the gigantic lake has also been plagued by the rapidly spreading water hyacinth, an aquatic plant from tropical America that has blanketed much of the water surface and starved it of oxygen. This has had grave consequences for aquatic wildlife as well as for local fishing communities.

Over 100 species of birds have been recorded on the islands. Spotted necked otters may also be seen.

Easiest access to the island camps in the lake is by air charter from the Masai Mara or from Nairobi.

 ACCOMMODATION – CLASS A/B: * *Rusinga Island Club* has five cottages with ensuite facilities. Fishing, boating, birdwatching, water skiing, wind surfing and visits to Luo fishing villages are offered. * *Mfangano Island Camp*, just a 40-minute charter flight and 15-minute boat ride from the Masai Mara, has seven cottages with ensuite facilities. Fishing, boating, birdwatching and visits to Luo fishing villages are offered.

CLASS B/C: * *Takawiri Island Resort* has four cottages, each with two rooms, and ensuite facilities. Fishing, sailing, wind surfing, birdwatching and visits to local villages are offered.

KISUMU

Kisumu, located on the shores of Lake Victoria about 215 miles (345 km) from Nairobi, is the third largest city in Kenya, with a population over 125,000.

ACCOMMODATION – TOURIST CLASS: * *Imperial Hotel* has 87 rooms (most of them air-conditioned) with ensuite facilities.

THE MOUNT KENYA CIRCUIT

ABERDARE NATIONAL PARK

This 296-square-mile (767-km²) park of luxuriant forest includes much of the Aberdare (renamed Nyandarua) Range of mountains.

The park can be divided by altitude into two sections. A high plateau of undulating moorlands with tussock grasses and giant heather lies between Ol Doinyo Lasatima (13,120 ft./3,999 m) and Kinangop (12,816 ft./3,906 m). This region affords excellent views of Mt. Kenya and the Rift Valley. Black rhino, lion, hyena, buffalo, elephant, eland, reedbuck, suni, bushpig and, very rarely, the nocturnal bongo can be seen.

On the eastern slopes below lie the forested hills and valleys of the Salient, home to black rhino, leopard, elephant, buffalo, waterbuck, bushbuck, giant forest hog, and black-and-white colobus monkey.

The park is also rich in birdlife, including many species not easily seen elsewhere. The moorlands and montane forest are home to Jackson's and Moorland francolins, Aberdare cisticola and Cape eagle owl, as well as various eagles and buzzards. Several species of dazzling sunbirds, the ecological equivalents of the American hummingbirds, occur on the mountains and are frequently seen in the gardens of the various camps and lodges.

Night temperatures range from cool to freezing, as most of the park lies above 9,800 feet (2,988 m). A 4wd vehicle is required for travel within the park. The Ark and Treetops are about 110 miles (175 km) from Nairobi.

ACCOMMODATION: Guests of two tree hotels, Treetops and the Ark, are entertained by a variety of wildlife visiting their water holes and salt licks.

CLASS B: * *The Ark,* a "tree hotel" overlooking a water hole, has small rooms with ensuite facilities (104 beds total), a glass-enclosed main viewing lounge, outside verandas on each level (floodlit for all-night game viewing) and ground-level photo hide. The area near the Ark is a rhino reserve. Game drives in the Salient are offered. Guests usually have lunch at the Aberdare Country Club before transferring to the Ark and are transferred back to the Aberdare Country Club by 9:00 the following morning to depart to their next safari destination. Children under seven are not allowed. * *Aberdare Country Club* has 50 rooms with ensuite bathrooms, sitting areas and log fireplaces.

CLASS B/C: * *Treetops,* the first of the "tree hotels" (on stilts), is older and more rustic than the Ark. Only the suites have ensuite facilities. Guests usually have a buffet lunch at the Outspan Hotel before transferring to Treetops and are returned to the Outspan by 9:00 the following morning to continue their safari. Children under seven are not allowed.

CAMPING: Only by special permission from the warden. Beware of lions.

ACCOMMODATION NEAR ABERDARE NATIONAL PARK – CLASS B: * *Sangare* is a 6,500-acre (2,600-hectare) ranch set in the foothills of the Aberdare Mountains with views of Mt. Kenya in the distance. Six tents with ensuite facilities are set on the shoreline of a small lake. Game drives, walks and horseback riding are offered. The camp is conveniently located near Aberdare National Park and the Solio.

SOLIO RANCH AND WILDLIFE SANCTUARY

This private 18,000-acre (7,200-hectare) rhino sanctuary has approximately 140 black rhino and white rhino. On my last visit I in fact saw a black rhino with the largest horns I think I have ever seen!

Other wildlife includes lion, leopard, cheetah, hippo, oryx, and a variety of plain's wildlife and birdife. The reserve is situated near Aberdare National Park, a three-hour drive from Nairobi or a 20-minute private air charter from Nanyuki. A visit to the Solio can be easily combined with a visit to Aberdare National Park.

 ACCOMMODATION: None (see "Aberdare National Park" above).

Sangare, Aberdare Mountains.

MT. KENYA NATIONAL PARK

Kenya's highest mountain and the second highest on the continent, Mount Kenya lies just below the equator, yet it has several permanent glaciers.

Mt. Kenya's two highest peaks, **Batian** (17,058 ft./5,199 m) and **Nelion** (17,023 ft./5,188 m), are accessible by about 25 routes and should be attempted only by experienced rock climbers. **Point Lenana** (16,355 ft./4,985 m) is a non-technical climb that is accessible to hikers in good condition and is best climbed in the dry seasons. January-February is the best time to go, when views are the clearest and temperatures are warmer on top; July-October is also dry but colder. Vegetation changes are similar to those described for the Ruwenzori Mountains (see the Congo) and Mt. Kilimanjaro (see Tanzania).

Rock-climbing routes on the south side of the mountain are in best condition from late December to mid-March, while routes on the north side are best climbed from late June to mid-October. Ice routes are best attempted during the same periods but on opposite sides of the mountain. Howell Hut (17,023 ft./5,188 m), located on the summit of Nelion, sleeps two.

Although rarely seen, climbers should be on the lookout for buffalo and elephant. Other wildlife that may be encountered includes leopard, duiker, bushbuck, giant forest hog, Syke's monkey and colobus monkey.

Overlooking part of the Mt. Kenya region.

Because climbers can ascend to high altitudes very quickly, Mt. Kenya claims more than half of the world's deaths from pulmonary edema. My climbing partner had symptoms of pulmonary edema after reaching Austrian Hut (15,715 ft./4,790 m), and we had to abandon our attempt of Batian Peak and return to lower altitudes. Therefore, a slow, sensible approach is recommended.

The world's highest altitude scuba diving record was shattered at Two Tarn Lake (14,720 ft./4,488 m), one of more than 30 lakes on the mountain. The previous record of 12,500 feet (3,811 m) was set at Lake Titicaca in Bolivia. In addition, climbers are occasionally seen ice skating on the Curling Pond below the Lewis Glacier.

Naro Moru Route

The Naro Moru Route is a steep, quick route up the mountain. The climb to Point Lenana normally takes two or three days up and one or two down. The first night is often spent at Naro Moru Lodge or, better yet, at the Met — Meteorological Station — (10,000 ft./3,050 m) to assist altitude acclimatization.

From Nairobi, drive 105 miles (168 km) to Naro Moru, then 10 miles (16 km) on a dirt road to the park gate (7,874 ft./2,400 m). You may be able to drive to the Met Station, unless the rains have washed out the road.

From the park gate, it is a three and one-half hours (6 mi./10 km) hike through conifer, hardwood and bamboo forests to the *Met Station*. Beware of buffalo enroute. The Met Station has self-service bandas with mattresses, cooking facilities, long-drop toilets and water. To help you acclimatize, consider hiking for about an hour up to the tree line (10,500 ft./3,200 m) in the afternoon, returning well before dark.

From the Met Station, hike through the **Vertical Bog**, a series of muddy hills with patches of tussock grass. To keep your boots dry, you may want to wear tennis shoes through the bog. Cross the Naro Moru River and continue to **Teleki Valley**, where Mt. Kenya's peaks finally come in clear view (if it is not cloudy). After leaving the tree line, vegetation will change to tussock grass and heather moorlands with everlasting flowers, giant groundsel and giant lobelia that sometimes exceed 30 feet (9 m) in height.

From the Met Station, it takes about six hours to reach *Mackinder's Camp* (13,778 ft./4,200 m), which has a brick lodge and campsites. *American Camp* (14,173 ft./4,320 m), a camping spot one hour from Mackinder's Camp, is used by some campers who bring their own tents. Water is available from a nearby stream.

Austrian Hut (15,715 ft./4,790 m) is a three- to four-hour hike from Mackinder's Camp. Another hour is usually required to gain the additional 640 feet (195 m) in altitude needed to reach Point Lenana, only a half-mile away.

Austrian Hut is bitterly cold at night and is most often used by technical rock climbers attempting Nelion or Batian Peaks. Many climbers wishing to conquer Point Lenana begin from their camps in the Teleki Valley (Mackinder's) long before sunrise, reaching Point Lenana shortly after sunrise and return to Teleki Valley for the night. The view from Point Lenana is the clearest and one of the most magnificent panoramas I've seen from any mountain — and well worth the effort!

Around the Peaks

From Mackinder's Camp, it is a two- to three-hour hike to *Two Tarn Hut* (14,731 ft./4,490 m). You may stop for the night or continue for another three or four hours over two passes exceeding 15,000 feet to *Kami Hut* (14,564 ft./4,439 m), located on the north side of the peaks. From Kami Hut, it is a five- to six-hour hike up the north ridge of

Point Lenana or directly to Austrian Hut. Return via the Naro Moru Route described above. Due to the path's continuous gain and loss of altitude, this is a very strenuous hike — the equivalent of climbing to Point Lenana two or three times!

Chogoria Route

This is the most scenic route on the mountain. From the Chogoria Forest Station on the eastern side of Mt. Kenya, hike or drive 10 miles (16 km) to *Bairunyi Clearing* (8,858 ft./2,700 m) and camp. You may choose to continue for another 4 miles (6 km) (4wd vehicle required) to *Meru Mt. Kenya Lodge* (9,898 ft./3,017 m) and stay in its self-catering bandas.

Hike through hagenia forest to *Urumandi Hut* (10,050 ft./3,063 m), owned by the Mountain Club of Kenya. Room for camping is available nearby. *Minto's Hut* (14,075 ft./4,290 m) is about a six-hour hike from *Meru Mt. Kenya Lodge*. Space for tents is available nearby. *Two Campsites*, situated a mile beyond Minto's Hut, is another good place to camp.

Austrian Hut is a four-hour hike from Minto's Hut. Some climbers descend using the Naro Moru Route.

The access road to the Chogoria Forest Station is very bad, so allow plenty of time for the drive.

Sirimon Route

The Sirimon Route is a long, slow route up the mountain.

Ten miles (16 km) past Nanyuki on the Nanyuki-Timau Road, turn right on a dirt road and drive 6 miles (10 km) to the park gate. Sirimon is the least used and most strenuous of the three major routes on Mt. Kenya.

The northern side of the mountain, much drier than the western side (Naro Moru Route), has no bamboo or hagenia zone. Acacia grasslands cover much of the northern slopes, and zebra and a variety of antelope are likely to be seen.

Although the track continues up to the moorlands to about 13,000 feet (3,960 m), it is better to make your first camp around 8,000-9,000 feet (2,440-2,745 m) so you can acclimatize. There is another campsite at 10,990 feet (3,350 m), 5 miles (8 km) from the park gate. About a mile (1.5 km) farther is *Judmeier Camp* (operated by the Mountain

Mountain Lodge, Mt. Kenya area.

Rock Hotel). *Liki North Hut* (13,090 ft./3,990 m) is about a four-hour hike from Judmeier. Another four-hour hike brings you to *Shipton's Cave Campsite* (13,450 ft./4,100 m). *Shipton's Camp* (operated by Bantu Lodge) is a little farther up the mountain. Austrian Hut is a five-hour hike from Shipton's Cave.

Lone climbers are not usually allowed to enter the park. Little equipment is available in Kenya, so bring whatever you need. For climbing tips and equipment checklist, see "Mt. Kilimanjaro" in the chapter on Tanzania.

ACCOMMODATION NEAR THE PARK – CLASS A: * *The Mount Kenya Safari Club* is located on the slopes of Mt. Kenya, outside the national park near Nanyuki, about 140 (224 km) miles from Nairobi. It was partially owned by actor William Holden and became one of the most famous "country clubs" in Africa. The spacious gardens are frequented by many species of exotic birds. Facilities include swimming pool, Irish Pub, nine-hole golf course, and very comfortable rooms, suites and luxury cottages with fireplaces (264 beds total). The Animal Orphanage contains a number of rare species, such as zebra duiker and bongo. High-altitude flights around the peaks of Mt. Kenya in a Beaver aircraft are available. Game drives are *not* conducted on the property.

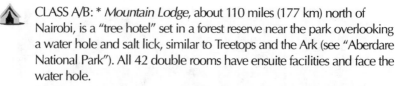

CLASS A/B: * *Mountain Lodge*, about 110 miles (177 km) north of Nairobi, is a "tree hotel" set in a forest reserve near the park overlooking a water hole and salt lick, similar to Treetops and the Ark (see "Aberdare National Park"). All 42 double rooms have ensuite facilities and face the water hole.

CLASS B: * *Lake Rutundu Cottages* is a rustic yet comfortable fishing lodge set on a small tarn (mountain lake) at 10,200 feet (3,100 m) altitude. Guests are accommodated in two cedar cabins with ensuite facilities and hot tub. The lodge is self-catering, but most tour companies will provide full-service catering. The trout fishing is some of the finest in the world! Best access is by charter flight to Africa's highest airstrip, at 11,000 feet (3,355 m).

CLASS B/C, D & E: * *Naro Moru River Lodge*, located below the entrance to the park, has chalets (Class B/C) with ensuite facilities and rustic, self-service cabins (Class D & E). Climbers often stay here before and after their attempts at Mt. Kenya's peaks. Trout fishing is good.

CLASS C/D: * *Mountain Rock Hotel* has a few simple chalets in a patch of forest near Naro Moru.

CAMPING: Camping is allowed at the *Naro Moru Lodge* and at sites in the park.

OL PEJETA RANCH

This 110,000-acre (44,000-hectare) private game reserve of savannah and riverine forest has a variety of wildlife, including black rhino, reticulated giraffe, buffalo, Grevy's zebra, oryx, Coke's hartebeest and Thomson's gazelle. Walks, day and night game drives, boat rides and camel rides are offered. There is also a chimpanzee sanctuary/rehabilitation center. A 4wd vehicle may be necessary to reach the camp from the main road during the rains.

ACCOMMODATION – CLASS A/B: * *Sweetwaters Tented Camp* has 25 large tents with ensuite facilities facing a water hole, and a swimming pool. The camp is located 150 miles (240 km) north of Nairobi. * *Ol Pejeta Ranch House*, with six luxury ensuite bedrooms, was restored to the former farmhouse glory of its previous owner, Lord Delamere, by tycoon Adnan Kashoggi. The house is available for private parties.

MERU NATIONAL PARK

Meru is best known for Elsa, the lioness of Joy Adamson's *Born Free*, which was rehabituated to the wild. This 300-square-mile (870-km²) park is located east of Mt. Kenya, 220 miles (355 km) from Nairobi (via Nanayuki or Embu).

The swamps are host to most of Meru's 5,000 buffalo, sometimes seen in herds of more than 200, and a number of elephant. Oryx, eland, reticulated giraffe and Grevy's zebra are plentiful on the plains, where lion and leopard are also most likely to be seen. Lesser kudu, gerenuk and cheetah can be found along with hippo and crocs within the Tana River area.

Over 400 species of birds have been recorded, including palm nut vulture, African finfoot, Pel's fishing owl, violet woodhoopoe, and the spectacular golden-breasted starling, which move about in small flocks.

ACCOMMODATION – CLASS A: * *Elsa's Kopje* is built on Mughwango Hill, the site of George Adamson's first camp in Meru. There are eight cottages with ensuite bathrooms and open verandahs overlooking the plains, and a swimming pool. Game drives are taken in open 4wd vehicles, and walks are offered.

ACCOMMODATION – CLASS C: * *Leopard Rock* is a 60-bed lodge with ensuite facilities, and swimming pool. Guests are offered game drives, walks and fishing.

CLASS F: *Self-service bandas* are located at Park Headquarters and at Leopard Rock.

CAMPING: Sites are available at Murera Gate and Park Headquarters.

THE RIFT VALLEY

Stretching some 4,000 miles (6,500 km) from the Red Sea to the Zambezi River, the Rift Valley is one of the most distinctive ruptures on the Earth's surface, and one of the few geological features than can be seen from the moon. The Rift Valley is thought to have begun to form some 40 million years ago, at a time when mankind's ancestors emerged onto the African savannahs. The slow rending apart of the Earth's crust also led to the formation and eruption of many volcanic mountains along or adjacent to the Rift Valley. The Rift Valley is split

A view of Lake Elementeita, a Rift Valley lake.

into two arms: the Eastern Arm, which cuts through the center of Kenya, and the Western Arm, which forms the border between Uganda and the Democratic Republic of the Congo. A chain of beautiful lakes have formed along the length of the Rift Valley, and when combined with sheer cliffs and acacia flats, they make for breathtaking scenery.

LAKE MAGADI REGION
Lake Magadi is a soda lake near the Tanzanian border. Nearby is Shompole — a 35,000-acre (14,000-hectare) conservancy surrounded by a 140,000-acre (56,000-hectare) group ranch on the Tanzanian border near Lakes Magadi and Natron, about 75 miles (120 km) south of Nairobi.

 CLASS A/B: * *Shompole*, set on the edge of the Nguruman Escarpment, has six tents with ensuite bathrooms and private plunge pools. Actitivites include day and night game drives, escorted walks, visits to Lake Natron and fly camping.

LAKE NAIVASHA
Lake Naivasha, located just 55 miles (89 km) northwest of Nairobi, is one of the most beautiful of Kenya's Rift Valley lakes, and it features fringing papyrus beds, secluded lagoons and the picturesque Cresent Island. It is a favorite spot for picnics and water sports for Nairobi residents, and it is a birdwatcher's paradise. African fish eagles occur in abundance. Waterfowl, plovers, sandpipers, avocet, terns, kingfishers, storks and ibis are plentiful. This is a freshwater lake with a sus-

pected underground outlet, so it is less attractive to flamingos, which prefer soda lakes.

Take a boat ride to **Crescent Island** and walk around this game-and-bird sanctuary, which is host to zebra, giraffe, waterbuck , several antelope species and a few camels.

 ACCOMMODATION – CLASS A: * *Loldia House*, a cattle ranch located on the northern side of Lake Naivasha, accommodates up to 10 guests in rooms at the main house and a cottage with ensuite facilities.

CLASS A/B: * *Longonot Game Ranch* has three double rooms with ensuite facilities. Horseback riding is the main attraction. * *Crater Lake Camp*, set on a crater lake southeast of Lake Naivasha on the Ndabibi Estate, accommodates guests in 10 tents with ensuite facilities. Day and night game drives and walks are offered.

CLASS B: * *Lake Naivasha Country Club* is a beautifully landscaped hotel with 51 rooms with ensuite facilities and a swimming pool. Sunset cruises are offered and a special Sunday afternoon tea is served.

CAMPING: * Fisherman's Camp has a restaurant, bar and a wide-screen TV, and is popular with Nairobi residents.

HELL'S GATE NATIONAL PARK
Located to the south of Lake Naivasha, this ruggedly scenic park covers 26 square miles (68 km²) of high cliffs and scattered grassy areas. The deep gorge is great for hiking and for spotting raptors. Klipspringer, mountain reedbuck, eland, giraffe, and Grant's and Thomson's gazelles may also be seen. Cliff-dwelling birds such as Verreaux's eagle and Ruppell's griffon vultures breed here, and rare lammergeyer or bearded vulture were reintroduced during the year 2000.

 ACCOMMODATION: See "Lake Naivasha" above.

LAKE ELMENTEITA
Lake Elmenteita is a shallow, alkaline lake located between Lakes Naivasha and Nakuru. The lake only holds surface water for a brief period after heavy rain, and it rapidly evaporates. A white soda crust covers much of the lake. A number of hot springs feed permanent lagoons on the fringes of the lake — very attractive to a host of birds.

Up to 50,000 lesser flamingos may feed here, and the uncommon great white pelican, avocet and chestnut-banded plover are breeding residents. The sparse, open bushland surrounding the lake is home to Grant's and Thomson's gazelle, as well as Rothchild's giraffe.

ACCOMMODATION – CLASS C/D: * *Lake Elmenteita Lodge* has 33 rondavels with ensuite facilities. Nature walks and ox-wagon rides to the lakeshore are offered.

LAKE NAKURU NATIONAL PARK

Lake Nakuru National Park encompasses the alkaline lake of the same name and is frequently visited by hundreds of thousands (sometimes more than a million) of greater and lesser flamingos — and more than 400 bird species in all. Located 100 miles (160 km) northwest of Nairobi on a fair road, the park covers 73 square miles (188 km²) — most of which is the lake itself.

Nakuru has been declared a black rhino sanctuary and has a fair number of these endangered animals. A small population of white rhino has been reintroduced from South Africa. Other wildlife includes lion, leopard, Rothschild's giraffe (introduced), waterbuck, reedbuck, hippo, baboon, pelican, and cormorant. The lake is an important stopover for thousands of migratory wading birds that head to and from Europe each year.

ACCOMMODATION – CLASS B: * *Sarova Lion Hill Lodge* is located in the park and has air-conditioned cottages (150 beds total) with ensuite facilities and a swimming pool.

CLASS C: * *Lake Nakuru Lodge* has rooms and cottages (120 beds) with ensuite facilities and a swimming pool. Horseback riding just outside the park and nature walks within the park are offered.

CAMPING: Campsites with running water are available in the park.

ACCOMMODATION NEAR LAKE NAKURU – CLASS A: * *Deloraine* is an old, colonial home set on a 5,000-acre (2,000-hectare) farm, with six rooms with ensuite facilities, tennis court and swimming pool. Horseback riding is offered.

CLASS A/B: * *Gogar Farm House*, a picturesque colonial farm owned by the same family for almost 100 years, has six rooms with ensuite bathrooms, tennis court and large swimming pool. Walks on the farm, birdwatching and horseback riding are offered.

NYAHURURU (THOMPSON'S) FALLS

Thompson's Falls is located at 7,745 feet (2,360 m) altitude about 115 miles (185 km) from Nairobi, above the Rift Valley between Nanyuki and Nakuru.

 ACCOMMODATION – CLASS C/D: * *Thompson's Falls Lodge* is a rustic country hotel; rooms have private facilities.

LAKE BOGORIA NATIONAL RESERVE

Lake Bogoria National Reserve, located north of Nakuru, has numerous hot springs and geysers along the lakeshore. Thousands of flamingos frequent this alkaline lake, as do greater kudu on the steep slopes of the lake's eastern and southern shores.

 ACCOMMODATION – CLASS C/D: * *Lake Bogoria Lodge* has 45 rooms with ensuite facilities.

CAMPING: Campsites are available with no facilities.

LAKE BARINGO

Lake Baringo, a freshwater lake located 20 miles (32 km) north of Lake Bogoria, is a haven for a colorful and mixed variety of bird life (over 400 species recorded). There is a sporting center for waterskiing, fishing and boating.

The early morning boat ride along the lakeshore and a walk below the cliffs were two of the finest birdwatching excursions I've experienced. I was also entranced by hippo, crocodile, fishermen and villages along the shore.

 ACCOMMODATION – CLASS B: * *Island Camp* is located in the center of Lake Baringo on Ol Kokwa Island. All tents have ensuite facilities. Take a walk and you may see a few waterbuck and meet the Njemps tribespeople who also inhabit the island. Boat safaris and water sports (beware of hippo and crocs) are available. * *Lake Baringo Club* has 52 rooms with ensuite facilities and a swimming pool. Boat and fishing trips are offered.

CLASS F: * *Betty Robert's Campsite*, situated on the lakeshore, has bandas.

CAMPING: * *Betty Robert's Campsite*.

A stunning panorama from Loisaba.

THE NORTH

LAIKIPIA

Laikipia, located north of the Aberdares and northwest of Mt. Kenya, is a wild and sparsely populated region considered to be the gateway to Kenya's Northern frontier. Much of Laikipia is covered by large, privately owned ranches that cover a wide range of landscapes from high plains to low forested valleys. On most ranches, cattle share the land with free-ranging wildlife. Some are sanctuaries were created by local communities, which have combined small farms and grazing land into large group ranches — some of which are active in significant conservation programs. These community ranches are great places to learn about traditional cultures. A visit to one of these private ranches is a highly recommended as a way to get off the beaten path.

Borana Ranch, Ol Malo Ranch, Loisaba Ranch, Ol Ari Nyiro Ranch and Mugie Ranch are located in Laikipia. Although Lewa Downs, Il'Ngwesi and Tassia are technically outside Laikipia, I have included them in this section because they offer similar experiences.

Sabuk

This wilderness area, located in Northern Laikipia, has plains, valleys, acacia forest and wild olive forest. Kudu, zebra, eland, elephant, giraffe, gazelle, and, of course, the predators, leopard, lion and cheetah are found here.

ACCOMMODATION – CLASS A: * *Sabuk Lodge* has five beautiful stone -and-thatch cottages with ensuite bathrooms and private verandahs overlooking the Ewaso Nyiro River Gorge below. Day and night game drives, escorted walks, and walking/camel safaris as well as fly camping with Lailipiak Maasai warriors as your guides are available.

Loisaba Ranch

Loisaba is a 65,000-acre (26,000-hectare) ranch located on the northern edge of the Laikipia Plateau. Day and night game drives, escorted walks, fly-camping, horseback riding and helicopter rides are offered.

 ACCOMMODATION – CLASS A: * *Loisaba Lodge*, perched on the edge of a cliff overlooking Mt. Kenya in the distance, has seven chalets with private verandas and ensuite facilities, a swimming pool and tennis court.

Borana Ranch

Borana is a 35,000-acre (14,000-hectare) ranch located in the Laikipia area about 6,500 feet (2,000 m) above sea level. Elephant, lion, buffalo, greater kudu and klipspringer and a variety of antelope may be seen. The activites are day and night game drives, escorted walks, horseback riding and camel riding.

ACCOMMODATION – CLASS A: * *Borana Lodge* is set on the edge of the escarpment and has six luxury chalets with ensuite facilities and a swimming pool.

Ol Malo Ranch

Ol Malo Ranch, located along the Uaso Nyiro River on the edge of Kenya's North Eastern Province, covers 5,000 acres (2,000 hectares). Day and night game drives, escorted walks, overnight fly-camping and camel treks are offered.

During my last visit we saw lion, giraffe, greater kudu, elephant and a variety of other game while on game drives and on walks.

 ACCOMMODATION – CLASS A: * *Ol Malo Lodge*, located on an escarpment with dramatic views of the bush below, has four beautiful chalets with ensuite bathrooms with large tubs, and a swimming pool.

Ol Ari Nyiro Ranch

The ranch is a rhino sanctuary, and Mukutan Retreat is owned by Kuki Gallmann, author of *I Dreamed of Africa* (Penguin Books).

The lodge is built on the edge of a gorge on the top of the Rift Valley wall, and it overlooks Lakes Baringo and Bogoria.

The bush is quite thick, which makes game viewing a bit difficult. The real attraction is spending time with Kuki herself; however, she does not guarantee that she will be at the lodge. Only one group of guests is accommodated at a time.

 ACCOMMODATION – CLASS A: * *Mukutan Retreat* has three stone-and-thatch cottages with ensuite facilities.

Mugie Ranch
Mugie Ranch is situated on the northern end of the Laikipia Plateau at 6,000 feet (1,830m) above sea level.

 ACCOMMODATION – CLASS A: * *Mutamaiyu* has four luxury cottages with ensuite facilities, and it offers day and night game drives, guided walks, camel and donkey treks, cultural visits, horseback riding and clay pigeon shooting.

Lewa Downs
Located between Mt. Kenya and Samburu National Reserve, the privately owned, scenic 45,000-acre (18,000-hectare) Lewa Wildlife Conservancy has a variety of wildlife, adapted to the semi-arid environment, including a large black and white rhino population (Lewa is a rhino sanctuary), elephant, lion, leopard, cheetah, reticulated giraffe, Grevy's zebra, buffalo, hartebeest, bushbuck, gerenuk, Gunther's dikdik and Somali ostrich. Lewa is one of the few places in Kenya where the rare, semi-aquatic sitatunga antelope and African wild dog are sometimes seen, and we were fortunate to have seen sitatunga on our last visit!

During a previous visit we spotted Beisa oryx, Grant's gazelle, a large herd of elephant and a few smaller herds, Mt. Kenya hartebeest and Somali ostrich, among other species.

Horseback riding, hiking, camel riding, day and night game drives in open 4wd vehicles and a cultural visit to the nearby Il N'gwesi Masai tribal community are offered. The Lewa Wildlife Conservancy is a unique experiment in wildlife conservation and community development and is a not-for-profit organization.

Beautiful scenery in the northern region.

 ACCOMMODATION – CLASS A: * *Wilderness Trails* accommodates up to 16 guests in luxury cottages with ensuite facilities and a swimming pool. * *Ngarie Niti* is a large two-bedroom stone house with two separate cottages with ensuite facilities.

CIASS A/B: * *Lewa Safari Camp* has 12 tents, set on elevated platforms with ensuite facilities, and a swimming pool. Day and night game drives, walks, horseback and camel riding are offered. A cultural visit to the nearby Il N'gwesi Masai tribal community is a highly recommended option.

Il'ngwesi

The Il'ngwesi Conservation Area is adjacent to Lewa Downs. Wildlife includes a variety of species that have adapted to dry conditions, including oryx, reticulated giraffe, Grevy's zebra, gerenuk and dikdik.

 ACCOMMODATION – CLASS B: * *Il'ngwesi* has six bandas with ensuite bathrooms and a swimming pool. The lodge has a covered viewing platform and offers cultural visits and camel safaris.

Tassia

Tassia is owned and managed by the Lekurruki Community Conservation Group Ranch. Walks, Masai cultural visits and game drives are the main activities.

ACCOMMODATION – CLASS B: * Tassia Lodge has six rooms with ensuite bathrooms, and a plunge pool. The lodge is booked on an exclusive-use basis.

SAMBURU NATIONAL RESERVE

This relatively small (64 sq. mi./165 km²) but excellent reserve of scrub desert, thornbush, riverine forest, and swamps along the Ewaso Ngiro River is situated north of Mt. Kenya and the Laikipia region.

Elephant and lion are plentiful, as are Beisa oryx, reticulated giraffe, gerenuk, Grevy's zebra and other species adapted to an arid environment. Leopard are often seen.

Birdlife is strikingly colorful and abundint, with golden-breasted starling, white-headed mousebird, sulphur-breasted bushshrike and a variety of weaver birds. Larger birds include the blue-necked Somali ostrich, martial eagle, Egyptian vulture and vulturine guineafowl.

Samburu, probably the best-known reserve in northern Kenya, is located about 220 miles (355 km) north of Nairobi. Under special arrangement, walking may be offered just outside the reserve.

 ACCOMMODATION – CLASS A: * Samburu Intrepids Camp has a swimming pool and 25 luxury tents, each with a private terrace and facilities ensuite. * Larsen's Tented Camp, situated on the banks of the Ewaso Ngiro River, has 13 double and four huge suite tents, all with facilities ensuite (34 beds total).

CLASS B: * Samburu Lodge, located on the banks of the Ewaso Ngiro River, has rooms, cottages and tents (75 units) with private facilities and a swimming pool. This lodge also baits for crocs and leopard.

CAMPING: Campsites are located along the north bank of the Ewaso Ngiro River between the West Gate and Samburu Lodge. Public sites have long-drop toilets.

BUFFALO SPRINGS NATIONAL RESERVE

Buffalo Springs is a 50-square-mile (131-km²) reserve located south of the Ewaso Ngiro River, which serves as its northern border with Samburu National Reserve. The unusual doum palm, the only palm

SAMBURU, BUFFALO SPRINGS AND SHABA

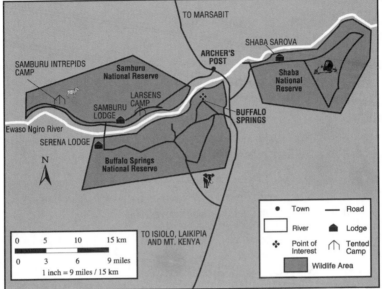

tree species whose trunk divides into branches, grows to over 60 feet (19 m) in height in this arid park. Wildlife is similar to what is seen in Samburu National Reserve.

On a two-hour game drive, we encountered oryx, gerenuk, Grant's gazelle, waterbuck, Somali ostrich and two large herds of elephant. Baboon are often found drinking at the springs.

 ACCOMMODATION – CLASS A/B: * *Samburu Serena Lodge,* situated on the banks of the Ewaso Ngiro River, has 52 rooms with facilities ensuite and a swimming pool. The lodge baits for crocs and leopard.

CAMPING: Campsites have no facilities.

SHABA NATIONAL RESERVE

The turnoff to the entrance to Shaba National Reserve is located east of Samburu National Reserve, 2 miles (3 km) south of Archer's Post. The Ewaso Ngiro River forms the reserve's northwestern border and flows through the western part of the reserve.

This 92-square-mile (239-km^2) reserve is characterized by rocky hills and scattered thornbush. Volcanic rock is present in many areas. Mt.

Shaba, a 5,320-foot- (1,622-m) high volcanic cone, which the park was named after, lies to the south of the reserve.

Shaba has recently become famous for hosting the 2001 "Survivor" television series.

A marsh in the center of the reserve is a good spot to look for wildlife. During a short visit to this rugged, rocky park, we spotted oryx, gerenuk, common waterbuck, Grant's gazelle, dikdik and ostrich.

Wildlife is less abundant and cannot be approached as closely as in the Samburu and Buffalo Springs National Reserves. However, there is much less traffic in this reserve.

ACCOMMODATION ——CLASS A/B: * *Shaba Sarova Lodge*, situated on the Ewaso Ngiro River, is a resort-style lodge with 85 rooms with facilities ensuite, and a huge swimming pool.

CAMPING: Ask at the gate.

MARALAL NATIONAL SANCTUARY

Maralal National Sanctuary, located northwest of Samburu and 95 miles (153 km) north of Nyahururu (205 mi./330 km from Nairobi) near the town of Maralal, has zebra, buffalo, eland, impala and hyena.

Leopard are baited and are seen just before sunset from a blind near the Maralal Safari Lodge. We were fortunate to see two of these fascinating creatures during our visit.

ACCOMMODATION – CLASS C: * *Maralal Safari Lodge* has 12 cottages with fireplaces and ensuite facilities, a swimming pool and a waterhole.

CLASS F & CAMPING: * *Yare Safaris Hostel* and Campsite, located 2 miles (3 km) south of Maralal, has bandas, dormitories and campsites.

MATHEWS RANGE

Located northwest of Samburu National Reserve, this remote wilderness area with lush green vegetation rises above the surrounding semi-desert lowlands. Elephant, lion, buffalo, greater kudu, waterbuck and other game may be seen, and over 100 bird species have been recorded. The real attraction of this area is its stark beauty, remoteness and opportunity for a cultural interaction with the

Camel trekking in Northern Kenya.

Samburu. Camel safaris are operated in the area. Access to the region is by air charter or 4wd vehicles, which are necessary in this region.

ACCOMMODATION – CLASS A/B: * *Desert Rose*, perched on a cliff high up on the remote Mount Nyiru, has five houses with open-air bathrooms. The camp offers remote cultural interactions, forest walks up Mt. Nyiru and exciting camel treks. Easiest access to the camp is by an approximately 100-minute charter flight from Nairobi.

CLASS B * *Kitich Camp* is situated on a private concession of over 150,000 acres (60,000 hectares) in the southern part of the Matthews Range at an altitude of 4,300 feet (1,300 m). It has six tents with ensuite long-drop toilets and bucket showers. Walks in the forests with local Samburu tribesmen, game tracking, swimming in nearby natural rock pools and visits to Samburu villages are offered.

LAKE TURKANA

Sometimes referred to as the Jade Sea because of its deep green color, Lake Turkana is a huge inland lake surrounded by semi-desert near the Ethiopian border, three days of hard driving over rough terrain or a few hours by air charter from Nairobi.

Formerly named Lake Rudolf, this huge lake, which is over 175 miles (280 km) long and 10–30 miles (16–48 km) wide, is set in a lunar-like landscape of lava rocks, dried-up river beds and scattered oases.

The brown Omo River flows from the Ethiopian Highlands into the northern part of the lake, where the water is fairly fresh but becomes increasingly saline further south due to intense evaporation. The presence of puffer fish implies that the lake was at one time connected to the Mediterranean Sea by the River Nile.

One of the continent's largest populations of crocodile is found here. Because the bitter alkaline waters render their skins useless for commercial trade, crocodile are not hunted and grow to abnormally large sizes. Although the water is very tempting in such a hot, dry climate, swim only at your own risk!

Forty-seven species of fish live in the brackish waters, seven of which are found nowhere else. This is a very worthwhile location for keen birders, as aquatic birds abound. Expect to see pink-backed pelican, greater flamingo, spur-winged plover and African skimmer. Up to 100,000 little stint winter here on their annual migration from northern Europe. In the dry scrublands, birds that are absent or seldom seen elsewhere in Kenya include the swallow-tailed kite, fox kestrel, Abyssinian roller, star-spotted nightjar and Jackson's hornbill.

Fishing is a major attraction at Turkana. Nile perch, the world's largest freshwater fish, can exceed 400 pounds (180 kg). Tigerfish, however, put up a more exciting fight. The El Molo tribe, the smallest tribe in Kenya (about 500 members), can be found near Loiyangalani.

Central Island National Park, a 2-square-mile (5-km²) island containing three volcanic cones, is the most highly concentrated breeding ground of crocodile in Africa. Excursions to **South Island National Park**, also volcanic and full of crocodile, are available from the Oasis Lodge.

Easiest access to the park is by small aircraft. Four-wheel-drive vehicles are necessary. Loiyangalani is about 415 miles (665 km) and Ferguson's Gulf is about 500 miles (805 km) north of Nairobi.

 ACCOMMODATION – CLASS C: * *Lobolo Camp* has six tents under thatch with verandahs and ensuite showers and long-drop toilets. The camp is located near Eliye Springs, almost halfway up the western shore of Lake Turkana. Activities include visiting the Turkana and Merille tribes, Koobi Fora, the crocodile-breeding colony on Central Island, the Omo Delta and fabulous fishing. Access is by a two and a half hour charter flight from Nairobi. * *Oasis Lodge*, located on the southeastern shore of the lake at Loiyangalani, has 24 basic cottages with facilities ensuite, two swimming pools, fishing boats and equipment for hire. Excursions to South Island National Park are available.

CLASS D: * *El Molo Lodge* has bandas. There are also self-catering bandas at Koobi Fora.

CAMPING: At El Molo Lodge, Sunset Strip Campsite and El Molo Bay.

CHALBI DESERT

The Chalbi Desert is home to 30,000 nomadic Gabra Tribesmen, who are still living an unaffected lifestyle in an untouched, harsh wilderness, east of the southern part of Lake Turkana. The Gabra water their goats, oblivious of the visitors, at oases and deep wells set on the edge of the Dida Galgalu plains.

The Kalacha Oasis is a natural spring attracting jackals, ostrich, sandgrouse and other wildlife.

ACCOMMODATION – Accommodation – CLASS B: * *Kalacha Community Bandas*, a unique community project with the Gabra people, consists of four bungalows set among the palm trees of the Oasis with ensuite facilities and swimming pool.

THE COAST

MOMBASA

Mombasa is the second largest city in Kenya, with a population of over 600,000. Situated on an island, 307 miles (495 km) from Nairobi on a paved road, it is a cultural blend of the Middle East, Asia and Africa.

The **Old Harbour** is haven for dhows carrying goods for trade between Arabia and the Indian subcontinent and Africa, especially from December-April. **Kilindini**, "place of deep water," is the modern harbor and largest port on the east coast of Africa.

Built by the Portuguese in 1593, **Fort Jesus** now serves as a museum. The **Old Town** is Muslim and Indian in flavor, with winding, narrow streets and alleys too narrow for cars. The tall, nineteenth century

Dhows at sunset.

buildings with hand-carved doors and overhanging balconies, and small shops of Old Town and Fort Jesus are best seen on foot.

Mombasa is the best place in Kenya for excellent Swahili food. The Tamarind Restaurant, located just north of Mombasa, and the Nomad Restaurant, located in Diani Beach, serve excellent seafood.

The city of Mombasa has no beaches, so most international visitors stay on the beautiful white sand beaches to the south or north of the island. Nyali Beach, Mombasa Beach, Kenyatta Beach and Shanzu Beach is just to the north of Mombasa, while Diani Beach is about 20 miles (32 km) to the south.

Most beach hotels on the coast offer a variety of water sports for their guests, including sailing, wind surfing, water skiing, scuba diving and snorkeling on beautiful coral reefs.

ACCOMMODATION IN MOMBASA – TOURIST CLASS: * *Castle Hotel,* located on Mombasa Island, has 60 simple rooms with facilities ensuite.

ACCOMMODATION JUST NORTH OF MOMBASA – DELUXE: * *Serena Beach Hotel* has 150 air-conditioned rooms with facilities ensuite, a swimming pool and tennis, scuba diving and other water sports. * *Nyali Beach Hotel* has 235 air-conditioned rooms with ensuite facilities and minibars and a disco, nightclub and swimming pool.

A fashionable beach resort near Mombasa.

Voyager Beach Resort, located on Nyali Beach, has 233 spacious cabins with ensuite facilities, restaurant, 3 swimming pools, tennis courts, health center, dive center, watersports and children's Adventure Club.

FIRST CLASS: * *Whitesands Hotel* has 346 air-conditioned rooms with ensuite facilities, a swimming pool, tennis and water sports. * *Mombasa Beach Hotel* has 150 air-conditioned rooms with ensuite facilities, a swimming pool, and tennis courts.

ACCOMMODATION JUST SOUTH OF MOMBASA – DELUXE: * *Leopard Beach Hotel*, located on 30 acres along Diani Beach, has 160 rooms and suites with ensuite bathrooms, four restaurants, bar, swimming pool, business center, massage and beauty parlor, floodlit tennis courts, scuba diving and water sports center. * *Alfajiri*, one of the finest guest houses on the Kenya coast, accommodates eight guests in four bedrooms with ensuite facilities, dining room, kitchen, lounge and a large veranda overlooking the Indian Ocean. In addition, the Main House has five air-conditioned bedrooms with ensuite facilities. * *Diani Reef Hotel* has 304 air-conditioned rooms with facilities ensuite and swimming pool, dive school and tennis courts. * *Pinewood Village* has 20 private villas with ensuite facilities and private chefs. *Indian Ocean Beach Club*, set on a beautiful beach, has 100 air-conditioned rooms with ensuite facilities, a swimming pool, tennis, squash, scuba diving and water sports.

FIRST CLASS: * *Diani House,* set on 12 acres (5 hectares) of forested garden along 820 feet (250 m) of beachfront, has four rooms with private verandahs and ensuite facilities, and a single room with shared facilities. Snorkeling, fishing, windsurfing, visits to the local market and walks in the Kaya Kinondon and the Jadini Forest are available. * *Jadini Beach Hotel* has 152 air-conditioned rooms with private facilities and a swimming pool.

TOURIST CLASS: * *Africana Sea Lodge* has 158 air-conditioned rooms with ensuite facilities and a swimming pool.

CAMPING: Campsites available at *Twiga Lodge* (Tiwi Beach) and *Dan's Trench* (Diani Beach).

SOUTH OF MOMBASA

SHIMBA HILLS NATIONAL PARK

This 74-square-mile (192-km²) reserve of rolling hills and forests is located an hour's drive south of Mombasa and 10 miles inland. At 1,500 feet (460 m) above sea level, this is a good place to cool off from the heat of the coast. From the park there are magnificent views of the Indian Ocean, and Mt. Kilimanjaro can even be seen on exceptionally clear days.

Wildlife includes elephant and buffalo and occasional sightings of genet, civet, serval, leopard and roan antelope. This is the only park in Kenya with sable antelope.

ACCOMMODATION – CLASS B: * *Shimba Hills Lodge* is a three-story "tree hotel" with 80 beds, overlooking a floodlit water hole.

ACCOMMODATION NEAR THE RESERVE – CLASS B: * *Mukurumuji Tented Camp,* set in the privately owned Sable Valley Sanctuary overlooking Shimba Hills Reserve, has four basic but comfortable tents under thatch with ensuite facilities. Activities include day trips into Shimba Hills and to the Mwaluganje Elephant Sanctuary.

KISITE MPUNGUTI MARINE RESERVE

Kisite Mpunguti Marine Reserve is situated near the small fishing village of Shimoni ("place of the caves"), where slaves were held before shipment, near the Tanzanian border far from the mainstream of tourism. Delightful boat excursions to **Wasini Island**, an ancient Arab settlement across a channel from Shimoni, and snorkeling excursions are available.

The **Pemba Channel**, just off of Shimoni, is one of the world's finest marlin fishing grounds.

 ACCOMMODATION – TOURIST CLASS: * *Pemba Channel Inn and Fishing Club* accommodates up to 14 guests in bungalows with ensuite facilities. Boats are available for hire for deep-sea fishing. The inn is closed from April 1 to July 31st. * *Shimoni Reef Lodge* has 10 basic thatched cottages with ensuite facilities, a swimming pool and a PADI Dive Center.

NORTH OF MOMBASA

MALINDI-WATAMU MARINE NATIONAL RESERVE

Malindi-Watamu Marine National Reserve encompasses the area south of Malindi to south of Watamu, from 100 feet to 3 nautical miles (30 m to 5 km) offshore, and it has very good diving and snorkeling. During a recent visit we snorkeled in the park and were very impressed by the clarity of the water and the great variety of tropical reef fish.

 ACCOMMODATION IN WATAMU – FIRST CLASS: * *Hemingway's* is a 175-bed hotel with ensuite facilities, swimming pool and charter boats for deep-sea fishing and diving. * *Turtle Bay Beach Club* has 154 air-conditioned rooms with ensuite facilities.

MALINDI

Malindi, located 75 miles (120 km) north of Mombasa (two hours by car), has numerous beach hotels, nightclubs and shops. The International Bill Fishing Competition is held here every January.

On our last visit we went out for a fun day of fishing on the *Albatros* and caught 10 wahoo weighing over 40 pounds each!

The **Sokoke Arabuko Forest** is Africa's northernmost brachystegia forest and Kenya's last remaining area of extensive lowland forest. The forest contains a variety of interesting wildlife, including Adder's duiker, bushy-tailed mongoose, golden-rumped elephant shrew, the Sokoke scops owl, the Sokoke pipit and Clarke's weaver.

The **Gedi Ruins**, last inhabited in the thirteenth century by about 2,500 people, is a mystery in that there are no Arabic or Swahili records of its existence.

ACCOMMODATION – FIRST CLASS: * *Indian Ocean Lodge* is an exclusive, personable lodge with only six fan-cooled suites with facilities ensuite and a swimming pool. The lodge is set on a point over looking the Indian Ocean and receives tropical breezes year-round. Activities include (at no additional charge) snorkeling in the marine park, boating down the shore to secluded beaches for picnics, shopping in the local markets, nature walks into Sokoke Arabuko forest and visits to the Gedi Ruins led by qualified guides. Deep-sea fishing is available right from the lodge on the *Albatross* at an additional charge, and scuba diving is available through nearby resorts.

TOURIST CLASS: * *Driftwood Beach Club* has 27 bandas (some air-conditioned) with ensuite facilities and a swimming pool.

CAMPING: * *Silversands Campsite* is 1 mile (2 km) north of town.

LAMU

Swahili culture on the island of Lamu has changed little in the past few hundred years on the island of Lamu. The only two motorized vehicles on the island are owned by a government official, but plenty of donkey carts provide substitutes. Narrow, winding streets and a maze of alleyways add to the timeless atmosphere. Many travelers have compared Lamu to a mini-Katmandu.

The **Lamu Museum** has exhibits of Swahili craftwork. Of the more than 30 mosques on Lamu, only a few are open to visitors. The best beaches are at **Shela,** a 45-minute walk or short boat ride from the town of Lamu to the Peponi Beach Hotel. **Matondoni** is a fishing village where dhows, fishing nets and traps are made. Numerous attractions are also found on nearby islands.

The best way to reach the island is to fly. Driving is not recommended because the road from Malindi is very rough and may be impassable in the rainy season.

ACCOMMODATION – FIRST CLASS: * *Peponi Beach Hotel,* a pleasant beach resort, is located about 1 mile (2 km) from the town of Lamu. All 25 rooms are fan-cooled and have facilities ensuite. * *The Island Hotel,* located in the center of Shela Village, has 14 fan-cooled rooms with ensuite facilities.

TOURIST CLASS: * *Lamu Palace Hotel* has air-conditioned rooms (50 beds) with ensuite facilities and is located 200 yards (200 m) from the jetty. * *Petley's Inn* has been a landmark since the nineteenth century. The hotel has a rustic atmosphere and rooms with private facilities.

ACCOMMODATION IN THE REGION OF LAMU – FIRST CLASS:
* *Kiwayu* is situated on a peninsula 30 miles (50 km) northeast of Lamu in the Dodori National Reserve on a beautiful beach. There are 18 large, fan-cooled but simple cottages with private verandahs (with hammocks) and ensuite facilities set right on the beach. Activities include snorkeling, wind surfing, sailing, water-skiing, deep-sea fishing, game drives in the Dodori National Reserve and visits to local Bajuni villages.
* *Kipungani Bay*, set on the southern end of Lamu Island, has 15 cottages with ensuite facilities and a swimming pool. Water-skiing, sailing, deep-sea fishing and snorkeling are offered.

UGANDA

THE NESTING GORILLA

Gorillas are diurnal and on the move constantly within their home range. They find themselves at a different location each night, where they meticulously build their beds (nests) and sleep.

The nests do not appear to offer any decent protection from the rain or cold. Building them seems to be an activity that has continued from their evolutionary past, a time when they were more arboreal.

Females take time and care in the construction of their nests and will frequently build on the ground instead of in trees. The lightweight youngsters may make their nests in trees. Tree nests last longer than those on the ground and can be found from five months to a year after being built.

Males, who are not as careful as females in building their nests, have been observed trying to snuggle into the nest of a female and child to get out of the rain. Hollow tree trunks are good protection from the rain, and they will use them when they can, sometimes lining the nest with moss.

An average nest built by females takes between three to five minutes to construct. They begin by breaking the tips of nonfood vegetation, like *lobelia*, and weave them in a semicircle around their bodies, like the rim of a bathtub, using the leaves as a lining on the bottom. The tasty nettles, thistles, celery and bamboo shoots gorillas like to eat do not make a comfortable mattress for them.

Youngsters make a great pretense at nest building. They begin at about 18 months and practice until they are between three and four years old. They bend and break the pliable stems into their laps, stand up and then quickly try to sit down on them, holding on with their hands. However, their small, light bodies cannot weigh down the springy stems. Signs of frustration are numerous while they learn to master the art of building the rim, and they use the leafy portion for a mattress. The babies will try to mimic, but their beds are usually a flimsy pile of leaves.

UGANDA

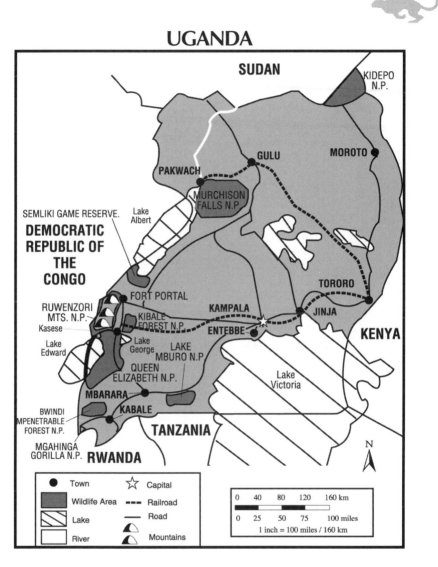

FACTS AT A GLANCE

AREA: 93,050 sq. mi. / 241,000 sq. km
APPROXIMATE SIZE: Oregon or Great Britain
POPULATION: 22 million
CAPITAL: Kampala (pop. est. 2.5 million)
OFFICIAL LANGUAGE: English

UGANDA

Uganda, once the "Pearl of the British Empire in East Africa," is one of the most beautiful countries on the continent. One-sixth of its area is covered by water. Along its western boundary lie the Ruwenzori Mountains, Africa's highest mountain range, and Ptolemy's fabled "Mountains of the Moon." The Ugandans claim the source of the Nile is at Jinja, where it leaves Lake Victoria.

The climate in Uganda is similar to Kenya except that Uganda is wetter. The driest times of the year are December-February and June-July, and the wettest is from mid-March to mid-May, with lighter rains October-November.

English is spoken as widely here as in Kenya or Tanzania. The main religions are Christianity and Islam.

In the eighteenth century, the Kingdom of Buganda became the most powerful in the region. Together with three other kingdoms, and several native communities, it was made a British Protectorate in 1893 and achieved independence in 1962.

Over 90% of the population is employed in agriculture, with coffee as the major export.

Uganda has been politically stable for over ten years. Nature-based tourism grew steadily in the 1990s, but collapsed almost overnight in 1999 when eight tourists were killed while tracking gorillas at the Bwindi Impenetrable Forest National Park. The security situation at Bwindi and other parks on Uganda's border with the Democratic

Republic of the Congo was beefed-up after the incident and a permanent army presence has made it safe for travelers. Gorilla trekking at Bwindi is once again so popular that safaris should be booked well in advance.

WILDLIFE AND WILDLIFE AREAS

Uganda's tremendous diversity of wildlife is due to its situation at the junction of the East African savannahs, the West African rainforests and the semi-arid Sahelian zone of North Africa. There are 10 national parks and 15 wildlife reserves, but most are much smaller than those in Tanzania or Kenya. Clever planning of the parks and reserves has, however, resulted in most of the different habitats being conserved, enabling visitors to enjoy a wide variety of wildlife and nature experiences.

Primates, including gorillas, large numbers of chimpanzees and an array of smaller monkeys are a major attraction. The endemic Uganda kob (a beautiful antelope), as well as lion, leopard, elephant and giraffe inhabit the savannahs while the great wetlands are home to large numbers of hippo and crocodile.

Gorillas remain the greatest international attraction, and there is nothing comparable to the thrill of a close encounter with these magnificent, peaceful apes. Travelers from all over the world venture to Bwindi to experience these magnificent animals in their native environment.

Relative to its size, Uganda is the richest country for birds in Africa, with over 1000 species in an area the size of Great Britain. A wealth of hornbills, turacos, barbets, sunbirds, kingfishers, weavers and storks are present, as well as the bizarre and much sought-after shoebill.

A real advantage of parks in Uganda is that they are not anywhere near as crowed as those in Kenya or Tanzania. You meet very few other vehicles on game drives — in some cases, you even have the parks almost to yourself!

NORTHERN AND WESTERN

MURCHISON (KABALEGA) FALLS NATIONAL PARK

This park is named after the famous falls where the Victoria Nile rushes with tremendous force through a narrow, 20-foot-wide (6-m) rock gorge to crash onto the rocks 150 feet (45 m) below. Fish dazed by this fall are easy prey to one of the largest concentrations of crocodile on the continent.

Located in northwestern Uganda, this park covers approximately 1,500 square miles (3,885 km²) of predominantly grassy plains and savannah woodlands, with altitudes ranging from 1,650 to 4,240 feet (500 to 1,292 m). Riverine forest with giant tamarind trees lines some parts of the Victoria Nile, which traverses the park from east to west.

In addition to Murchison Falls, a highlight of the park is the three-hour, 7-mile (11 km) boat trip from Paraa-Sarova Lodge to the foot of the falls. Numerous crocodile and hippo in the river and along its banks, as well as buffalo, elephant, and prolific birdlife (over 400 species) including red-throated bee-eater, piapiac, silverbird and black-headed gonolek.

Another great excursion is a six-hour launch trip from Paraa-Sarova Lodge to the delta where the Victoria Nile flows into Lake Albert. Shoebills (whale-headed storks) are a popular feature of this trip.

The park is also home to Rothchild's giraffe, Defassa waterbuck, oribi, hartebeest and Uganda kob. The Rabongo Forest has a population of chimpanzees. Record Nile perch over 200 pounds (90 kg) have been caught in the Nile. Some of the best fishing is just below Karuma Falls and Murchison Falls.

The easiest time to spot animals is January-February; the short dry season from June to July is also good. From March to May, the landscape is more attractive, but the wildlife is less concentrated.

Park headquarters and the most extensive road system for game viewing are near the Paraa Lodge. The Buligi Circuit arrives at the confluence of the Albert and Victoria Niles. Waterfowl are especially abundant, as is a variety of game. Fuel is usually available at the Paraa-Sarova Lodge.

ACCOMMODATION – CLASS A/B: * *Nile Safari Camp,* set on the south bank of the Nile River on the western edge of the park, has six tents and two chalets with ensuite facilities and a swimming pool. * *Sambiya River Lodge,* located on the Sambiya River 23 miles (20 km) from the falls, has 32 brick bandas with ensuite facilities. * *Paraa-Sarova Lodge* has 56 rooms and two suites with ensuite facilities.

CLASS F: * *Paraa Rest Camp* has simple bandas, long-drop toilets and bucket showers.

CAMPING: Several sites available.

SEMLIKI GAME RESERVE

Formerly called the Toro Game Reserve, this 85-square-mile (220-km²) reserve of grassland, savannah, forest and wetland habitats is bordered by Lake Albert to the north and the Ruwenzori Mountains to the southwest.

The tropical lowland forest conserved in this park is ecologically linked to the Congo basin and provides a very different Ugandan wildlife experience. The giant hardwood trees and tangled undergrowth of the forest are home to many fascinating mammals such as Africa's smallest ungulate- the tiny pygmy antelope, which is hardly bigger than a hare. While elephant and chimpanzee occur, primates such as the gray-cheeked mangaby, red-tailed monkey and De Brazza's monkey are more readily seen.

Other wildlife includes Uganda Kob (the most common large mammal), buffalo, leopard, lion, hyena, bushbuck, waterbuck, reedbuck, duiker, forest hog and warthog.

The reserve is an absolute paradise for birdwatchers, with 35 of the so far 385 species occurring nowhere else in East Africa. Specials such as the chestnut owlet, white-crested hornbill, African piculet and fiery-breasted bushshrike attract enthusiastic observers from far and wide.

The park has an airstrip and is about a six-hour drive from Kampala, a three-hour drive from Queen Elizabeth National Park and a two-hour drive from Kibale Forest National Park.

RUWENZORI MOUNTAINS

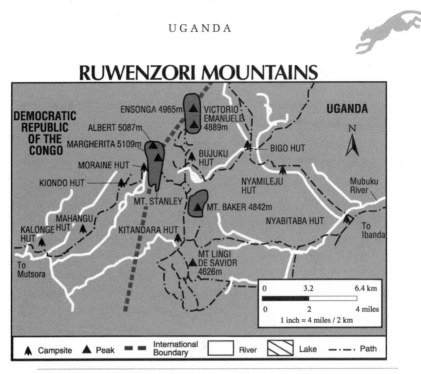

ACCOMMODATION – CLASS A/B: * *Semliki Lodge* has eight tents with ensuite facilities and a swimming pool. Activities include night game drives, chimpanzee tracking, boat trips on Lake Albert, fishing for Nile perch, tilapia and tiger fish, and visits to Nkusi Waterfalls.

RUWENZORI MOUNTAINS NATIONAL PARK

This is the highest mountain range in Africa and home of the legendary "Mountains of the Moon." They rise 13,000 feet (3,963 m) above the western arm of the Rift Valley to 16,762 feet (5,109 m) above sea level, just north of the equator, and are usually covered in mist. See "Ruwenzori Mountains" in the chapter on the Congo for a general description. The only mountains that are higher are Mt. Kilmanjaro and Mt. Kenya.

Hikers in good condition can enjoy walking a strenuous circuit for six or seven days that rise to over 13,000 feet (3,963 m) in altitude through some of the most amazing vegetation in the world. Walking routes trace the lower slopes and it is a region of great biological beauty. Successive zones of distinct vegetation ring the six major massifs of the Ruwenzori with woodland, evergreen forest, bamboo, boggy heath-land and afro-alpine moorland in a sequence up the slopes. Large mammals are few, but the Ruwenzori colobus, giant forest hog and yellow-backed duiker may be encountered. The exquisite Ruwenzori turaco is fairly common, while the Ruwenzori batis and bamboo warbler are found nowhere else in Uganda.

The main trailhead begins near Ibanda. Drive 6 miles (10 km) north from Kasese on the Fort Portal road, then turn left (west) for 8 miles (13 km). The mountain huts take up to 15 people. It is best to bring all your own gear, although equipment may be available for hire.

The Central Circuit

On day one, a dirt road from Ibanda runs 3 miles (5 km) to the Park Headquarters at Nyakalengija (5,400 ft./1,646 m). There is a five-hour hike past village huts, into the park and onward to Nyabitaba Hut (8,700 ft./2,652 m). You may be lucky enough to see black-and-white colobus monkeys or the Rwenzori turaco. Many climbers prefer staying in a nearby rock shelter instead of the hut. Water and firewood are not available near the hut. Tent spaces are located nearby.

Day two is the most grueling of the circuit. Climbers hike five or six hours past a bamboo forest to Nyamileju Hut (10,900 ft./3,322 m) and a nearby rock shelter. Time and energy permitting, you may continue hiking through a bog in the giant heather, lobelia and groundsel zone for about an hour to John Mate Hut (11,200 ft./3,414 m).

On day three, hikers must traverse a muddy bog to Bigo Hut (11,300 ft./3,444 m). A rest is recommended before continuing through Upper Bigo Bog to Bujuku Lake, where there are views of Mt. Baker, Mt. Stanley and Mt. Speke, to Bujuku Hut (13,000 ft./3,962 m). From John Mate Hut to Bujuku Hut should take about five to six hours. Technical climbers attempting Mt. Speke often use this hut as a base.

On day four, the hike crosses Groundsel Gully towards Scott Elliot Pass to Elena Hut (14,700 ft./ 4,372 m). Elena is the base camp for climbing Margarita Peak, which requires two more days, previous permission from National Parks and the proper equipment (crampons, ice axe, ropes, etc.). As you hike over Scott Elliot Pass you enter the alpine zone of limited vegetation, but with fabulous views of Margarita Peak, Mt. Baker, Elena and Savoia Glaciers. From there, the trail continues to Lake Kitandara and Kitandara Hut (13,200 ft./4,023 m) and then goes on to Kabamba Rock Shelter (12,400 ft./3,779 m). The hike from Bujuku Hut takes about five hours.

On day five, hike to Freshfield Pass and then descend past the rock shelters at Bujongolo and Kabamba (an optional overnight stop) onward to Guy Yeoman Hut (10,700 ft./3,261 m). The hike to Guy Yeoman Hut takes six to seven hours.

On day six, there is a five-hour hike down to Nyabitaba Hut, with an optional overnight stop, or you may choose to finish the journey with a three-hour hike to the park gate.

The Rwenzori Mountains have two rainy seasons, from March-May and September-mid-December. The best time to climb is mid-December through February and June through August during the dry season. However, no matter when you climb, you will still get wet. Wood fires are prohibited, so be prepared to use paraffin or gas stoves.

For information on climbing the summits and glaciers, I recommend the books *East Africa International Mountain Guide*, by Andrew Wielochowski (1986), and *Guide to the Ruwenzori*, by Osmaston and Pasteur (1972), both published by West Col Productions in England. Maps of the area include "The Central Ruwenzoris" with a scale of 1:250,000 and "Margherita" with a scale of 1:50,000.

ACCOMMODATION – CLASS C/D: See "Kasese" below.

CLASS F: A few dormitory huts are available from RMS at Ibanda. Many of the huts on the hiking trails are in poor condition but are in the process of being renovated. Bring a ground sheet and insulated pad for your sleeping bag. Because not all of the huts are in good repair, it is best to bring your own tent.

KIBALE FOREST NATIONAL PARK

This 296-square-mile (766-km²) park consists of lowland tropical rain forest, tropical deciduous forest, marshes, grasslands and crater lakes, and is the best place in Uganda for chimpanzee trekking.

In addition to escorted walks, the park offers a Chimpanzee Habituation Experience. The program starts at 6:00 a.m., from the time the chimpanzees leave their nests until slightly before dark, which allows guests to observe the chimps nesting and de-nesting as well as their other daily activities.

QUEEN ELIZABETH NATIONAL PARK

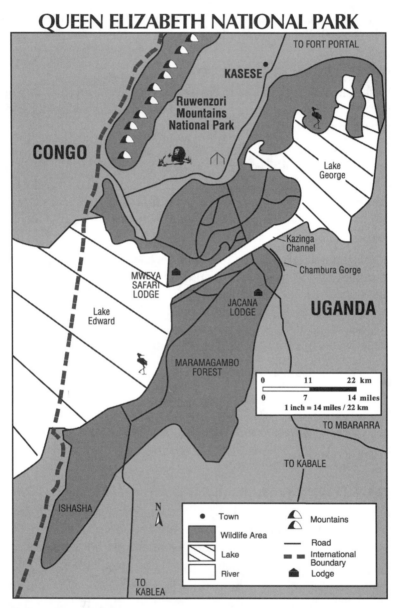

Kibale is home to 10 other species of primates, including black-and-white colobus monkey, red colobus, gray-cheeked mangabey and red-tailed monkey. Some of the other wildlife species include blue duiker, Harvey's red duiker, bushbuck, bushpig and over 100 species of butterflies.

Over 300 species of birds have been recorded, and experienced local guides - with their knowledge of calls and behavior - are invaluable in this challenging bird watching environment. Green-breasted pitta, black bee-eater, white-headed woodhoopoe and the tiny chestnut wattle-eye are among the possible delights for keen observers.

The park is located northeast of Queen Elizabeth National Park, 22 miles (35 km) south of Fort Portal.

ACCOMMODATION – CLASS B: * *Mantana Safari Camp* is a permanently based luxury mobile camp with seven tents with ensuite bush shower (hot water) and long-drop toilet, located 2 miles (3 km) from the park. * *Ndali Lodge*, located in a delightful setting on a crater lake a 45-minute drive from the park, has eight cottages with ensuite facilities.

QUEEN ELIZABETH NATIONAL PARK

The park contains about 770 square miles (1,995 km^2) of tremendous scenic variety, including volcanic craters and crater lakes, grassy plains, swamps, rivers, lakes and tropical forest. The snowcapped Ruwenzori Mountains lie to the north and are not part of the park itself. The park is being extended to give migratory species more protection as they move to and from Virunga National Park in the Congo.

A two-hour launch trip on the **Kazinga Channel**, which joins Lakes Edward (Lake Rwitanzige) and George, affords excellent opportunities for viewing hippo and a great variety of waterfowl at close range. Truly marvelous photographic opportunities present themselves from the boat. The launch trip departs from just below Mweya Lodge and should not be missed.

The Katwe-Kikorongo area in the north of the park has several saline lakes.

The **Chambura Gorge**, located on the northeast boundary of the park, has a population of chimpanzees. Trekkers descend from the savannah into a tropical rain forest within the gorge where turacos, hornbills and flycatchers abound.

South of the Kazinga Channel, the **Maramagambo Forest** is home for large numbers of chimpanzees, black-and-white colobus monkeys, the rare red colobus monkeys, blue monkeys, red-tailed monkeys and baboons. The **Ishasha** region in the south of the park is famous for its tree-climbing lions.

Mweya Safari Lodge is situated on a high bluff.

Elephant are present, as well as buffalo, leopard, sitatunga, giant forest hog, Uganda kob, topi and Defassa waterbuck.

Interestingly enough, there are no giraffe, zebra, or impala or rhino, and only a few crocodile have been sighted in the Kazinga Channel, while none have been seen in Lakes Edward or George. The crocodiles are believed to have been killed long ago by volcanic activity.

An astonishing total of 547 bird species have been recorded here, one of the highest figures for any single protected area in the world. Twelve species of kingfisher, including the giant (the world's largest) and the dwarf (the world's smallest) are to be seen on waterways, in forest, and in the open savannah. There are 17 varieties of nectar-feeding sunbirds, flocks of red-throated bee-eaters, gangs of crow-like piapiacs, families of spectacular Ross's turacos in fruiting trees, and the rare, prehistoric-looking shoebill, which may be sighted along the shores of Lake George and in the Ishasha region.

From Kampala, the park is 260 miles (420 km) via Mbarara and 285 miles (460 km) via Fort Portal. A landing strip is located at Mweya for light aircraft; larger planes can land at Kasese.

CLASS A/B: * *Mweya Safari Lodge* is situated on a high bluff overlooking the Kazinga Channel and Lake Edward. All 46 rooms and suites have ensuite facilities.

ACCOMMODATION – CLASS B: * *Jacana Lodge,* situated in the Maramagambo Forest, has wooden cabins with ensuite facilities.

CLASS F: * *Institute of Ecology Hostel.*

CAMPING: Sites are available near Mweya Lodge and along the Kazinga Channel.

KASESE
Kasese is the largest town situated near Queen Elizabeth National Park and Ruwenzori National Park, and it is a good place to purchase supplies. Kasese can be reached by train or by road from Kampala.

 ACCOMMODATION – CLASS C/D: * *Margherita Hotel* has rooms with private facilities and is located 2 miles (3 km) out of town.

SOUTHERN

BWINDI IMPENETRABLE FOREST NATIONAL PARK
The major attraction of the 127-square-mile (330-km²) Bwindi Impenetrable Forest is the population of over 300 gorillas known to inhabit the park, that are in fact a different sub-species (yet to be named) from the mountain gorillas of Rwanda.

Bwindi is a forest of enormous hardwood trees, giant ferns, tangled undergrowth and hanging vines - the quintessential equatorial jungle. The size and altitudinal range of montane and lowland forests at Bwindi support more species of trees, ferns, birds and butterflies than any other forest in East Africa. It is also the only one which contains both chimpanzees and gorillas.

As of this writing, only two groups may be visited by up to six tourists per day. The Mbare Group (Group M) consists of about 15 gorillas, including one silverback. The Habinyanja Group (Group H) consists of 20 gorillas, including one silverback. The Nkuringo Group is presently in the process of being habituated by skilled trackers and, hopefully, will be suitable for visitation soon. Once found, visitors spend one hour with the gorillas.

Silverback gorilla from the H group, Bwindi National Park.

Gorillas form themselves into fairly stable groups of 3–40. They are active by day and sleep in nests at night.

Gorillas eat leaves, buds and tubers (like wild celery), and are continuously on the move, foraging for their favorite foods. They eat morning and afternoon, interspacing their dining habits with a midday nap.

Searching for gorillas can be likened to an adventurous game of "hide and seek" in which the guides know where they were yesterday but must find their trail again today and follow it. Finding gorillas can almost be guaranteed for those willing to hike one to four hours or more in search of them.

Each group of visitors is led by a park guide, an armed guard and one tracker. Porters may be hired to carry lunch, drinks, etc., and to assist anyone who may wish to return early.

The search often involves climbing down into gullies, then pulling yourself up steep hills by holding onto vines and bamboo. Even though the pace is slow, you must be in good condition to keep up; the search may take you to altitudes of 3,800 to over 6,500 feet (1,160-1,982 m) or more. While this sounds difficult, almost anyone in good physical condition can do it.

The guide looks for nests used the night before, and then tracks them from that spot. Once the gorilla group has been located, he then calms them by making low grunting sounds and imitates them by picking and chewing bits of foliage. Juvenile gorillas are often found playing and tend to approach within a few feet of their human guests. Occasionally, our guides had to keep them from jumping into our laps!

Adult females are a little more cautious but may still approach within several feet. The dominant male, called a silverback because of the silvery-grey hair on his back, usually keeps more than 20 feet (6 m) from his human visitors.

In terms of sensitivity towards the great primates and to afford you the best chances of a close and relaxed encounter, simple gorilla-viewing "etiquette" is critical. Never make eye contact with a silverback. If a silverback begins to act aggressively, look down immediately and take a submissive posture by squatting or sitting, or he may take your staring as aggression and charge. The key is to follow the directions of your well-trained guide. Gorillas are herbivores (vegetarians) and will not attack a human unless provoked. Your guides will instruct you not to touch the gorillas because they are susceptible to catching human colds and diseases.

Use 400 ASA film or higher, because gorillas are often found in the shadow of the forest. You will probably want to "push" 400 ASA to 800 ASA to get enough light. Many trekkers use 1000 and 1600 ASA films. Flash photography is not allowed because it will startle the

Bwindi Mantana Safari Camp.

gorillas. Bring several rolls of film on the trek — you very well may need them! Videos and digital cameras are highly recommended because they produce good results in low-light conditions. After spending up to 60 minutes visiting with these magnificent animals, visitors descend to a more open area for a picnic lunch.

Mornings are almost always cool and misty; even if it doesn't rain, you will undoubtedly get wet from hiking and crawling around wet vegetation. Wear a waterproof jacket or poncho (preferably Gortex), leather gloves to protect your hands from stinging nettles, waterproof light- or medium-weight hiking boots, to give you traction on muddy slopes and to keep your feet dry, and a hat. Bring a waterproof pouch for your camera and plenty of film, a water bottle and snacks. Do not wear bright clothes, perfumes, colognes or jewelry, because these distractions may excite the gorillas.

Visiting the gorillas is one of the most rewarding safaris in Africa. The park fees, which are among the highest in Africa, go toward the preservation of these magnificent, endangered creatures.

Other primates resident in the Bwindi forest include chimpanzee, black-and-white colobus monkey, red colobus monkey, grey-cheeked mangabey, L'Hoest's monkey and blue monkey. Other wildlife includes elephant, giant forest hog and duiker. Among the 345 species of birds recorded are the great blue turaco, yellow-eyed black flycatcher, Lühder's bushshrike, vanga flycatcher, black-faced rufous-warbler, black-throated apalis, and elusive green broadbill.

Park Headquarters is based at Buhoma, a three-hour drive (67 mi./108 km) from Kabale. Because trekkers must be at the park by 8:30 a.m., it is necessary to overnight at a nearby guesthouse or permanent tented camp. Neither children under 15 years of age nor contagiously ill adults are allowed near the gorillas.

ACCOMMODATION – CLASS A: * *Gorilla Forest Camp* is a permanent tented camp, situated near the park at Buhoma, with eight tents with ensuite facilities.

ACCOMMODATION – CLASS B: * *Mantana Safari Camp* is a permanently based luxury mobile camp with ensuite bush shower (hot water) and long-drop toilet.

CLASS C: * *Volcanoes Bwindi Camp*, located about half a mile (1 km) from Park Headquarters, has eight tents with separate bush showers and short-drop toilets. * *African Pearl Guest House* has simple rooms with shared facilities.

CLASS D: * *National Park bandas* have rooms with separate facilities.

CAMPING: Campsites are available near the park entrance.

MGAHINGA GORILLA NATIONAL PARK
Mgahinga Gorilla National Park is situated on the slopes of Mts. Muhabura and Gahinga in the southwestern corner of Uganda, bordering Rwanda and the Congo.

A joint commission has been set up by Uganda, Rwanda and the Congo to protect the mountain gorilla in the Virunga Mountains where the borders of the three countries meet, and despite human conflict over the past decade, the population of gorillas has actually undergone a slight increase.

Because family troops have not been habituated and since families range across the political borders, Gorillas are much less likely to be sighted here than in Bwindi.

While gorilla tracking is the main activity in this 12-square-mile (34-km²) reserve, other mammals such as the rare golden monkey (a sub-species of the blue monkey), buffalo, black-fronted duiker, leopard, golden cat and serval may be encountered.

Birdlife is not prolific, however, gems such as the red-tufted mala-chite sunbird, white-starred robin and Ruwenzori turaco may be observed in this highland region.

ACCOMMODATION – CLASS C: * *Mount Gahinga Rest Camp* has four rondavels and three tents with private facilities

CLASS D: * *Traveller's Rest,* situated about a two-hour drive from the park, has eight rooms and two suites with ensuite facilities. Many travel-ers taking day trips for gorilla trekking in Parc des Volcans in Rwanda overnight here.

CAMPING: By permission of the landowner. There are no facilities.

KABALE
Kabale is Uganda's highest town, situated in a beautiful area called "The Little Switzerland of Africa" in southwestern Uganda.

ACCOMMODATION – TOURIST CLASS: * *White Horse Inn* has rooms with private facilities. * *Victoria Inn* has basic rooms, some with ensuite facilities.

LAKE MBURO NATIONAL PARK
Lake Mburo National Park is located in southwestern Uganda between Masaka and Mbarara. This approximately 200-square-mile (520-km²) park is named after the largest of the park's 14 lakes.

Located in the rain shadow between Lake Victoria and the Ruwenzori Mountains, the park is characterized by open plains in the north, acacia grassland in the center and lakes and marshes in the south. It is bounded by the Kampala-Mbarara road on the north, Lake Kachera on the east and the Ruizi River on the west.

Herds of zebra, impala (found nowhere else in Uganda) and buffalo enjoy this habitat, and the wetland system around the lake is home to the aquatic sitatunga antelope and hippo. Other game includes leopard, eland, reedbuck, topi, bushbuck and klipspringer.

Birds more typical of dryer Tanzanian savannah such as emerald-spotted dove and bare-faced go-away bird occur alongside lilac-breasted roller and pennant-winged nightjar. The lake's edge is busy with the feeding activities of herons, storks, cormorants, ducks and pelicans.

The park is a good place to overnight when driving between Bwindi and Kampala.

ACCOMMODATION – CLASS B: * Mantana Tented Camp has eight tents with ensuite bush showers and toilets. Game drives and escorted bush walks are offered.

CLASS F: * Park bandas with shared facilities are available.

CAMPING: Campsites are available in the park.

ACCOMMODATION NEAR THE RESERVE – CLASS D: * Lake View Hotel and the * Katatumba Resort are located in Mbarara.

KAMPALA AND ENTEBBE

Kampala, the capital of Uganda, is built on seven hills. Points of interest include the **Uganda Museum** and the **Kasubi Tombs of the Kabakas** — a shrine to the former Baganda kings and a fine example of Baganda craftsmanship.

For thrill seekers wanting a close encounter with the mighty River Nile, enthralling **white-water rafting** adventures operate from near the town of Jinja, east of Kampala.

The international airport is at Entebbe, about an hour's drive from Kampala.

ACCOMMODATION – DELUXE: * Lake Victoria Hotel is located near Entebbe airport overlooking Lake Victoria. The hotel has 99 rooms and suites with facilities ensuite, swimming pool, health club and restaurant. * Kampala Sheraton Hotel, situated in an attractive park setting, has 302 rooms (rooms on the first floor are air-conditioned) with private facilities, a health club, several restaurants and a swimming pool. * Grand Imperial Hotel is located in the center of town and has 80 air-conditioned rooms with ensuite facilities, a swimming pool, health club, shops and restaurants.

FIRST CLASS: * *Nile Hotel* contains the International Conference Center and has 85 air-conditioned rooms with ensuite facilities. * *Hotel Equatoria* has rooms (most of them are air-conditioned) with ensuite facilities.

TOURIST CLASS: * *Fairway Hotel* has ensuite facilities and overlooks the Kampala Golf Course.

NGAMBA ISLAND (CHIMP ISLAND)

Ngamba Island Chimpanzee Sanctuary is situated in Lake Victoria 45–60 minutes by boat from Entebbe Pier. The tropical 100-acre (40-hectare) island is home to approximately 35 orphaned chimpanzees, which are free to roam the forest during the day and return to the holding facility at night.

Chimpanzee viewing is the main activity. There are two daily viewing times during which you can watch the chimps being fed. A raised viewing platform allows you to view the chimps very closely and provides great photographic opportunities. Day visits and overnight stays are allowed but must be booked in advance.

Swimming, kayaking, bird watching, sunset cruises and fishing are other optional activities.

 ACCOMMODATION: CLASS B: *Ngamba Island Camp* has four tents set on raised wooden platforms with ensuite facilties.

RWANDA

THE NILE CROCODILE

Crocodiles are opportunistic feeders and have adapted techniques for acquiring their diet of fish, water birds, terrapins, water monitors and smaller animals. They attack smaller animals from the shoreline and drag them into deeper water to drown them before feeding. A valve at the back of their throat closes when they have an animal within their jaws, and it prevents them from swallowing water and drowning themselves. As reptiles, crocodiles are cold-blooded, and they regulate their body temperature by basking in the sun in the early mornings and afternoons, cooling off in the water during mid-day and returning at night to the warmer water. Interestingly, they lay their eggs in the sand along the riverbanks, and the difference of a few degrees in temperature within the incubated nest under the sand will determine whether the hatchlings are male or female. Crocodiles spend their time either underwater, floating just below the surface — with only the nostrils and eyes showing — or basking on sandbanks. While underwater, they can slow their heart rate to one beat per minute, thereby conserving oxygen. They are known to ingest stones, which act as ballast to counteract the buoyancy of their lungs. During a night safari, you may see the red, reflected eyes of the crocodile on the top of the water, waiting...

RWANDA

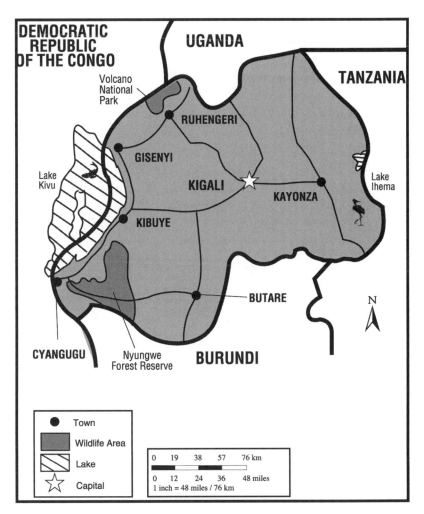

FACTS AT A GLANCE

AREA: 10,160 sq. mi. /26,638 sq. km
APPROXIMATE SIZE: Maryland or Belgium
POPULATION: 10 million
CAPITAL: Kigali (pop. Est. 3-4 million)
OFFICIAL LANGUAGES: Kinyarwanda, French and English

RWANDA

Appropriately called "The Country of a Thousand Hills," Rwanda is predominantly grassy uplands and hills, with altitudes above sea level varying from a low of 3,960 feet (1,207 m) to Mt. Karisimbi, the highest of a range of extinct volcanoes in the northwest, which reaches 14,786 feet (4,507 m). Lake Kivu forms part of the border with the Congo and is one of the most beautiful lakes in Africa.

Also called "The Country of Perpetual Spring," Rwanda's comfortable climate is temperate and mild with an average daytime temperature of 77°F (25°C). The main rainy season is from mid-February to mid-May, and the shorter one is from mid-October to mid-December.

Almost all (97%) of the people live in self-contained compounds and work the adjacent land. Over half of the population is Christian (most of which are Catholic), though many people follow traditional African beliefs. Hutu (Bahutu) and Tutsi (Batusi) tribes make up the majority of the population. The Tutsi have long dominated the Hutu farmers in a feudal system analogous to that of medieval England. The system was based on cattle and its size was surpassed in Africa only by Ethiopia.

Because of its physical isolation and fearsome reputation of its people, Rwanda was not affected by the slave and ivory trade from Zanzibar in the 1800s. The area became a German protectorate in 1899 and in 1916 was occupied by the Belgians.

Following World War I, Rwanda and Burundi were mandated by the League of Nations to Belgium as the territory of Ruanda-Urundi. Full independence for Rwanda and Burundi was achieved on July 1, 1962.

In 1994, a civil war (actually begun in 1990) between the Hutus and the Tutsis resulted in over a million deaths and even more refugees fleeing to neighboring Congo and Tanzania. The Tutsi forces were victorious, and many refugees have returned.

As of this writing, security in Rwanda has stabilized considerably, and international tourists are returning to gorilla trek in Parc National des Volcans and to visit other areas of the country. Before visiting Rwanda, be sure to check the current security situation.

High population density is at the root of Rwanda's economic problems. Almost all arable land is under cultivation. Coffee is the country's major export.

French, English, and Kinyarwanda are widely spoken, and Kiswahili is spoken in the major towns and regions close to the borders of Uganda and Tanzania. Tourism is an important foreign exchange earner for the country.

WILDLIFE AND WILDLIFE AREAS

Mountain gorilla trekking in Volcano National Park is by far Rwanda's major international attraction. After the release of the feature film, *Gorillas in the Mist,* about the late Dian Fossey's pioneering work habituating the gorillas, interest in gorilla trekking reached new heights.

THE WEST

VOLCANO NATIONAL PARK
(PARC NATIONAL DES VOLCANS)

Volcano National Park is home to the mountain gorilla, first documented by Europeans in the early 1900s. The peaks of the Virunga Mountains, heavily forested extinct volcanoes, serve as a border with the Congo and Uganda and are part of the watershed between the Congo and Nile river systems.

The 48-square-mile (125-km²) park supports several vegetation zones, from lush bamboo stands to luxuriant mountain forest to Afro-alpine. From 8,500 to 11,000 feet (2,590 to 3,350 m), primary forest is dominated by hagenia trees growing 30-60 feet (9-18 m) in height. Hagenia have twisted trunks and low branches covered with lichen, out of which epiphytic orchids, moss and ferns often grow.

VOLCANO NATIONAL PARK

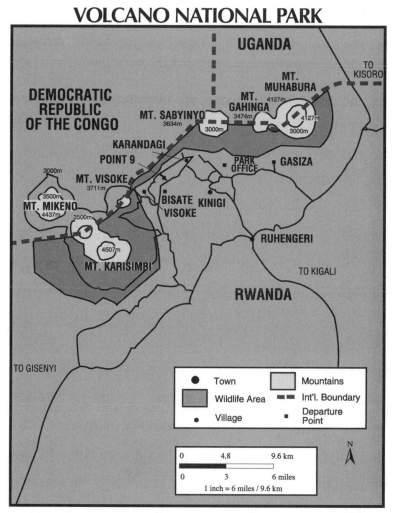

Volcano National Park borders both Virunga National Park in the Congo and the Mgahinga Gorilla National Park in Uganda. The park receives a high amount of rainfall, over 70 inches (1,800 mm) per year. Daytime temperatures at Park Headquarters average about 70°F (21°C).

Other wildlife in the park includes the golden monkey (a rare sub-species of blue monkey), black-fronted duiker (very common), bush-buck and buffalo. Over 90 species of birds have been recorded, including spectacular mountain turacos (the Rwenzori turaco is the most common) and forest francolin.

The mountain gorilla grows to over 6 feet (2 m) in height and weighs more than 440 pounds (200 kg). For a description of gorilla trekking, see the "Bwindi Impenetrable Forest" section of the chapter on Uganda. The four gorilla groups currently acclimated for tourist visits are Group Sabyinyo, Group Susa, the Amahoro Group and Group 13. Group Sabyino, Group Susa and the Amahoro Group may be visited by up to eight tourists each day, while Group 13 may be visited by a maximum of six tourists per day.

As of this writing, the makeup of the gorilla groups were as follows: the Susa Group — 35 members including two silverbacks; The Sabyinyo Group — 13 individuals including the largest of the silverbacks; The Amahroro Group — 14 members including one silverback; Group 13 — 11 members including one silverback (it had 13 members during the 1980s, when the group was habituated). Visitors to Group Amahoro meet at Bushororo; Group Susa meet at Gashinga or Cundura; Group Sabyinyo gather between Karandaryi and Ayindishyira; Group 13 at Ayindishyira.

Children under 15 years of age are not allowed to visit the gorillas. Permits must be purchased in advance in Kigali, and a copy of the first three pages of a visitor's passport must be presented at the time of purchase.

Check-in at Park Headquarters is between 7:00 and 8:00 a.m., near Kinigi village, which is a 20-minute drive from Ruhengeri. Be sure to have your voucher before making the 30- to 40-minute (up to 10-mi./16-km) drive to departure points where the searches begin. Visitors must meet their guides at the designated departure points no later than 9:00 a.m.

The most popular time to visit the gorillas is during the dry seasons, which occur mid-June-September and December-March.

It is difficult to get to the park and departure points unless you join a tour (the best option) or rent your own vehicle (expensive). There is no public transportation from Ruhengeri to the Park Headquarters or to the trek departure points.

Mountain Climbing
Hiking in the beautiful Virunga Mountains is an adventure in itself. Trails lead to the craters or peaks of the park's five volcanoes, upward through the unique high vegetation zones of bamboo, hagenia-hyper-

icum forests, giant lobelia and senecio, and finally to alpine meadows. Views from the top, which overlook the lush Rwandan valleys and into the Congo and Uganda, are spectacular.

Some travelers spend a day or two of gorilla searching interspersed with hikes to one or more of the volcanoes.

Karisimbi (14,786 ft./4,507 m), which is occasionally snowcapped, is Rwanda's highest mountain. It is the most arduous ascent, requiring two days from the Visoke departure point. The night may be spent in a metal hut at about 12,000 feet (3,660 m).

Visoke (12,175 ft./3,711 m) has a beautiful crater lake and requires four hours of hiking, up a steep trail from the Visoke departure point, to reach the summit . The walk around the crater rim is highly recommended. Allow seven hours for the entire trip.

Lake Ngezi (9,843 ft./3,000 m), a small, shallow crater lake, is the easiest hike in the park; it takes only three to four hours round-trip from the Visoke departure point.

Sabyinyo (11,922 ft./3,634 m) can be climbed in five to six hours, starting at Park Headquarters near Kinigi. A metal hut is located just before you reach the lava beds. The final section is along a narrow rocky ridge with steep drops on both sides.

Gahinga (11,398 ft./3,474 m) and **Muhabura** (13,540 ft./4127 m) are both reached from the departure point at Gasiza. The trail rises to a hut in poor condition on the saddle between the two mountains. Gahinga's summit can be reached in four hours, while two days are recommended to reach the summit of Muhabura.

A park guide must accompany each group, but porters are optional. Should you encounter gorillas on your hike, you may not leave the path to follow them. You may only track gorillas if you have previously purchased the proper permits.

Unfortunately, as of this writing, hiking in these mountains is not considered safe and may, in fact, not be allowed.

 ACCOMMODATION – FIRST CLASS: See "Gisenyi," below. Gisenyi is about two hours by road to the gorilla trek points.

TOURIST CLASS: * *ASOFERWA Guest House*, located within the park, has 15 simple rooms with ensuite facilities. * *Hotel Muhabura* is a very rustic hotel with 10 simple rooms and two pavilions with bathrooms ensuite, and a bar and dining room. The hotel is located about 10 miles (16 km) from Park Headquarters, which takes about 20 minutes to drive. *Travelers Rest*, located in Kisoro, Uganda, has basic rooms with ensuite facilities. Some travelers overnight here and visit Parc des Volcans on day trips.

CAMPING: Campsites at Park Headquarters are near Kinigi, and cold shower and toilet facilities may be available. Beware of thieves.

GISENYI

Gisenyi is a picturesque resort on the northern shores of beautiful Lake Kivu. Lake Kivu has some nice, white beaches and is believed to have little or no bilharzias (a disease). Crocodiles are absent from the lake due to volcanic action, eons ago, that wiped them out. Beware, however, of rising sulpher gas, which can be fatal.

 ACCOMMODATION – FIRST CLASS: * *Hotel Izuba* has 68 double rooms and four suites with ensuite facilities and is a 90-minute drive from Volcano National Park. Situated on Lake Kivu, the hotel has a swimming pool, tennis courts and solarium. * *Hotel Palm Beach* has 22 rooms, some with ensuite facilities, and is located on the lakeshore drive.

KIBUYE

Kibuye, located on Lake Kivu midway between Gisenyi and Cyangugu, is a small town with an attractive beach. Be sure not to miss the over-330-foot- (100-m) high **Ndaba Waterfall** (Les Chutes des Ndaba), not far from Kibuye.

 ACCOMMODATION – TOURIST CLASS: * *Centre Bethanie Mission* has 24 rooms, half of which have facilities ensuite. * *Kibuye Guest House* is located on Lake Kivu and has 18 double rooms with private facilities, tennis courts and sports activities on the lake.

NYUNGWE FOREST RESERVE
(LA FORET DE NYUNGWE)

The Nyungwe Forest is one of the most biologically diverse, high-altitude rain forests in Africa. Located in southwestern Rwanda and bordering the country of Burundi, this 375-square-mile (970-km^2)

reserve is home for 13 species of primates including a rare sub-species of black-and-white colobus monkey (documented in groups of several hundred), L'Hoest's monkey, blue monkey, grey-cheeked mangabey and chimpanzee.

In addition to a variety of butterflies and orchids, more than 275 species of birds have been recorded. Some of the over 250 species of trees and shrubs grow to over 165 feet (50 m) in height. This mountainous reserve has a variety of habitats, including wetlands, forested valleys and bamboo zones. Elevation ranges from 5,250 to 9,680 feet (1,600 to 2,950 m).

Although Nyungwe Forest Reserve is situated at a lower altitude and receives less rain than Volcano National Park, hiking is more difficult in Nyungwe. The vegetation at Nyungwe is much thicker, and many slopes are steeper, if not impossible, to ascend. Colobus and the other primates may be difficult to approach closely.

 ACCOMMODATION – TOURIST CLASS: * ORTPN Guesthouse, located on the southwest edge of the forest, has 15 basic rooms with ensuite facilities.

CAMPING: Campsites are available at the Park Headquarters in the middle of the forest.

BUTARE

Located in southern Rwanda, not far from the border with Burundi, Butare is the intellectual capital of Rwanda. There you will find the **National Museum** (good archeology and ethnology exhibits) and the **National University** and **National Institute of Scientific Research** (ask about folklore dances). Several craft centers are located in villages within 10 miles (16 km) of Butare. The **Ballet National du Rwanda** is located in Nyanza, 22 miles (35 km) from Butare.

 ACCOMMODATION – TOURIST CLASS: * Hotel Credo has 25 rooms with ensuite facilities, tennis court and swimming pool. * Hotel Faucon has 13 rooms with ensuite facilities. * Hotel Ibis has 15 rooms with ensuite facilities.

Impala.

CENTRAL AND EAST

KIGALI

The capital of Rwanda, Kigali is the commercial center of the country. A number of very good restaurants are located in the first class hotels.

ACCOMMODATION – FIRST CLASS: * *Hotel des Mille Collines* has 113 rooms with ensuite facilities and a swimming pool. * *Hotel Umubano*, located a few miles outside the city center, has 100 rooms with ensuite facilities, swimming pool and tennis courts.

TOURIST CLASS: * *Hotel Isimbi,* located in the center of Kigali, has 26 rooms with ensuite facilities. * *Hotel Chez Lando*, situated in the suburb of Remera, has 32 rooms with ensuite facilities. * *Hotel Alpha* is also located in Remera and has 40 rooms with ensuite facilities. * *Hotel Okapi*, located in the center of Kigali, has 24 rooms with ensuite facilities.

Seeing eye to eye on safari.

Part of a zebra migration, Kenya.

The leopard has to be the most beautiful of all the cats.

Mother cheetah and cub, Masai Mara.

Early morning, black rhino, Solio in Kenya.

Portrait of an elephant.

Reaching up high.

Morning walk on the African plains.

Game viewing from a vehicle in East Africa.

Lilac-breasted roller, a favorite bird of many who see it on safari.

Viewing platform for an egret.

Fish eagle swooping down to catch a fish.

Flamingoes in Ngorongoro Crater.

East Africa tented camp, Little Governors.

Luxury mobile camping – sleeping tent.   The ambiance of a luxury mobile tented camp.

East Africa tented room, Mara Explorer.

East African lodge, Mara Serena.

Dining with a view, Mana Pools.

Dining on a deck at Ngorongoro Crater Lodge.

A bush dinner, Samburu.

So many stories are shared around the campfire.

Southern Africa – tented camp lounge area.

Southern Africa – permanent tented camp bedroom.

Southern Africa – the boutique-style accommodations (A+) at Mombo Tented Camp.

A visitor in camp at Little Mombo, Botswana.

Rovos Rail crossing the bridge at Victoria Falls, from Zambia into Zimbabwe.

The changing colors of the Namib-Naukluft dunes.

The Waterfront of Cape Town, with Table Mountain in the background, Cape fur seal in the foreground.

Mt. Kilimanjaro attracts more than 20,000 mountain climbers a year.

Elephant patrol in Damaraland.

Warming up on a cold morning.

Hippo popping up from under the floating plants.

White rhino at Ongava Reserve, Namibia.

Leopard cooling off, Botswana.

The Serengeti Migration crossing the Mara River.

Canoeing the Lower Zambezi River is one of the true adventures in Africa!

A breeding herd of elephant on the move, Okavango Delta.

Open vehicle game drive, Botswana.

H group – Bwindi, Uganda.

Mother and cub in perfect lighting for photography!   Portrait of a leopard.

Days old leopard cub.

Young Masai after a ceremony.

Her ornate hairstyle indicates that
this Himba lady is married.

Masai – so beautifully color coordinated.

Bushman from Namibia.

Wild dogs beginning their evening hunt.

Healthy, wealthy and wise.

Sunset on the Luangwa River, Zambia.

Memories to take back from Africa, Mana Pools.

ECO MAP OF EAST, CENTRAL AND SOUTHERN AFRICA

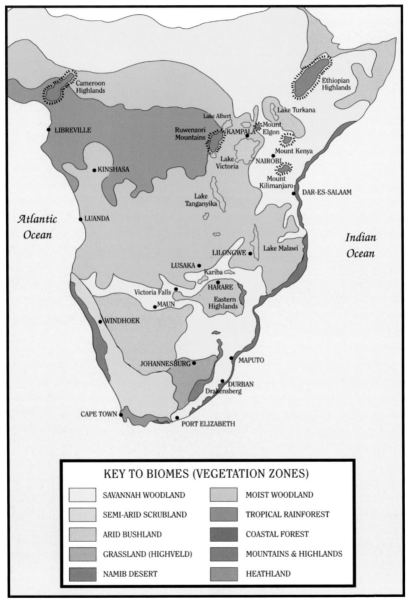

Cameroon
Highlands

Ethiopian
Highlands

Lake Turkana

LIBREVILLE

Lake Albert

Ruwenzori
Mountains

KAMPALA

Mount
Elgon

Mount Kenya

KINSHASA

Lake
Victoria

NAIROBI

Mount
Kilimanjaro

DAR-ES-SALAAM

Atlantic
Ocean

LUANDA

Lake
Tanganyika

Indian
Ocean

LILONGWE

Lake Malawi

LUSAKA

Kariba

Victoria Falls

HARARE

Eastern
Highlands

MAUN

WINDHOEK

JOHANNESBURG

MAPUTO

DURBAN
Drakensberg

CAPE TOWN

PORT ELIZABETH

KEY TO BIOMES (VEGETATION ZONES)

	SAVANNAH WOODLAND		MOIST WOODLAND
	SEMI-ARID SCRUBLAND		TROPICAL RAINFOREST
	ARID BUSHLAND		COASTAL FOREST
	GRASSLAND (HIGHVELD)		MOUNTAINS & HIGHLANDS
	NAMIB DESERT		HEATHLAND

DEMOCRATIC
REPUBLIC OF THE CONGO

THE AQUATIC HIPPO

Amphibious, roly-poly hippos spend most of the day in the water, ambling off at dusk or night to graze. They may, however, be seen out of the water during the day.

Their partially webbed toes assist in both walking on muddy riverbeds and swimming. They are nature's natural dredgers; they displace sand and silt in riverbeds and estuaries, which ensures a continuous flow of water. The paths that they stamp while moving between channels, increases the flow of fresh water to swamps.

Hippos make a display by flapping their tails, which sends their dung flying into the water or onto riverside vegetation. This spreads organic nutrients for fish and is a natural fertilizer for plant life. Some fish swim with the hippo and feed off algae growing on their skin.

Their barrel-like bodies have a natural buoyancy in the water, and only their noses, eyes and ears extend above the surface. Hippos often stand on the bottom and let their front legs rise until their heads reach the surface.

When disturbed on land, they will run to water (the safe haven) and submerge, and they may hold their breath for up to six minutes. They close both their nostrils and ear flaps while underwater and, upon surfacing, will blow open their nostrils and twitch open their ear flaps. Babies are often seen gulping for air before disappearing underwater, where they rest on their mothers' backs.

A content hippo is a grunting hippo. Open, displayed jaws are a sign of aggression or annoyance. An even happier hippo is one that is able to feed his sweet tooth on fresh green grass at a bush camp or nearby sugarcane field!

D.R. CONGO (EAST)

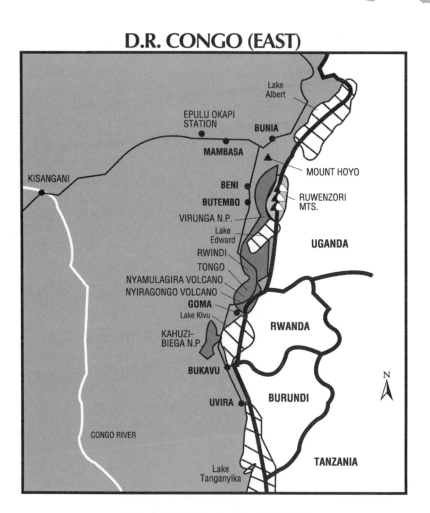

FACTS AT A GLANCE

AREA: 905,365 sq. mi./ 2,344,885 sq. km
APPROXIMATE SIZE: USA east of the Mississippi River or 10 times the size of Great Britain
POPULATION: 52 million
CAPITAL: Kinshasa (pop. est. 3.5 million)
OFFICIAL LANGUAGE: French
NATIONAL LANGUAGES: KiSwahili, Tshilbua, Kokongo, Lingala

DEMOCRATIC REPUBLIC OF THE CONGO

The Democratic Republic of the Congo (D. R. Congo), formerly the Republic of Zaire, is the third largest country in Africa. The name Zaire came from the Kikongo word *nzadi*, meaning "river." The Congo River, the tenth longest river in the world, winds 2,880 miles (4,600 km) through the Congo basin, the world's second largest drainage basin (the Amazon is the largest), and finally empties into the Atlantic Ocean.

Of all the countries listed in this guide, the Congo is closest to Tarzan's Africa. You can very easily imagine him swinging on a vine right in front of you as you travel through this country, which is visited more by adventurers than tourists.

Kivu Province, the most beautiful region of the D. R. Congo, holds the country's most exciting attractions. This province is situated along the western borders of Rwanda and Uganda in the region of the great lakes: Lakes Tanganyika, Kivu, Edward and Albert. This is an important agricultural area with large tobacco, coffee, tea and banana plantations. The only paved road in the Kivu Province runs north from Goma to the Kabasha Escarpment.

Due to the altitude, much of the region has an agreeable Mediterranean-type climate. In general, the best time to visit the eastern D. R. Congo is during the dry seasons from December to February and mid-June to August.

Of the 200 or so tribal or ethnic groups in the D. R. Congo, four-fifths are Bantu. Physically, tribal groups range from the tall nomadic herders from the north to the smaller Mbuti hunter-gatherers in the densely forested regions. About 80% of the population is Christian, with the balance embracing Muslim or traditional native beliefs.

The Congo remained virtually unknown until Henry Morton Stanley traveled from East Africa to the mouth of the Congo River (1874-1877). Belgian King Leopold II claimed the so-called Congo Free State as his personal property until he ceded it to Belgium in 1907. It was then renamed the Belgian Congo. Zaire achieved independence on June 30, 1960.

In 1997 President Mabutu Sese-Seko was overthrown, and Laurent Desire Kabila came to power and the country's name was changed from Zaire to the Democratic Republic of the Congo. Joseph Kabila took over power when his father was killed in 2000. As of this writing, the country is considered unsafe for travel. Please get a current update on the situation before considering a visit there. The accommodations listed may or may not be open, depending on the security in the region.

The D. R. Congo is a country of gigantic untapped resources. Fifty percent of the land is arable and scarcely 2% is under cultivation or used as pasture. Much of the arable land, however, is covered in dense forest, and the D. R. Congo is still covered by one of the largest blocks of tropical forest in the world. Much of the soil in the Congo Basin is of very low nutrient content and would make exceedingly poor farmland. The country holds 13% of the world's hydroelectric potential. Copper accounts for about half of the country's exports, followed by petroleum, diamonds and coffee.

WILDLIFE AND WILDLIFE AREAS

Eight reserves cover 15% of the country's area. Over 1,000 species of birds have been recorded in the country, which makes it Africa's richest, but the majority are forest-dwelling and hard to see. In addition, the D. R. Congo is also a home of the rare okapi (giraffe-like ungulate), the highly elusive Congo peacock, and a number of other endemic species found nowhere else in the world.

Like Uganda and Rwanda, gorillas are a major attraction in the D. R. Congo. Should the region stabilize politically, mountain gorillas may be visited in Virunga National Park and eastern lowland gorillas in Kahuzi-Biega National Park.

Of the countries covered in this book, the D. R. Congo is the most difficult and unpredictable one in which to travel. Those not willing to put up with delays and constant last-minute changes in their itineraries should look elsewhere for adventure.

THE NORTHEAST (KIVU AREA)

GOMA
Goma is situated on the northern shores of Lake Kivu, one of the most beautiful lakes in Africa, with Mt. Nyiragongo and Mt. Nyamulagira (volcanoes) forming a dramatic backdrop to the north. It is the administrative center for Virunga National Park. Lake Kivu is suitable for swimming because there are no crocs or hippos.

Three boats per week depart Goma for Bukavu across Lake Kivu.

ACCOMMODATIONS – TOURIST CLASS * *Hotel Stella Matutina Lodge* has 12 rooms with ensuite facilities. * *Hotel Ihusi* has 19 rooms with ensuite bathrooms. *Hotel Ishango* has 17 ensuite rooms, a two-bedroom suite and a few apartments.

NORTH OF GOMA
On the drive from Goma northward you pass over the dramatic Kabasha Escarpment to Butembo. The route from the Kabasha Escarpment to Beni is one of the most beautiful in Africa and is properly named the "Beauty Route." The road passes through many picturesque villages, coffee, tea and banana plantations — the Africa that many of us have pictured in our minds.

VIRUNGA NATIONAL PARK
(PARC NATIONAL DES VIRUNGA)
Virunga National Park, previously called Albert Park, is one of the oldest reserves in Africa (created in 1925) and is the best wildlife reserve in the Congo. Altitudes range from 3,000 feet (915 m) on the grassy savannah to 16,794 feet (5,120 m) in the Ruwenzori Mountains, resulting in a tremendous variety of topography, flora and fauna.

Virunga is about 185 miles (300 km) long and 25 miles (40 km) wide and is divided into three sections, each requiring separate entrance fees. From south to north: 1) The Southern Sector, comprising the Nyiragongo and Nyamulagira Volcanoes, Tongo Chimpanzee Site, Bukima Gorilla Site and the Djomba Gorilla Site; 2) The Central Sector, including Rwindi, Ishango and Ishasha on the shores of Lake Edward; and 3) The Northern Sector, including the Semliki River, the Ruwenzori Mountains and Mt. Hoyo. Guides are compulsory and their services are included in the park entrance fees.

Unfortunately, as of this writing all of these areas within the park, and the accommodations, are either closed to tourism or considered too unstable for safe travel. This situation will hopefully change for the better soon.

Volcanoes

The region around Goma is a highly volcanic area of constant activity. On my first visit, I discovered that a new volcano had been recently born, and we hiked 10 miles (16 km) into the bush to see it. Because of the possibility of an eruption, we camped uphill from the volcano, which was scarcely 300 feet (915 m) high, and watched the fabulous fireworks all night. For some unknown reason, a new volcano usually pops up in this active region about every other year. I just missed visiting another lava-filled caldera in 1984, which cooled a few weeks before my arrival.

In the southern part of the park near Goma lie the active volcanoes of Nyiragongo and Nyamulagira, which do not require technical mountaineering skills to climb. If the volcanoes are active at the time of your visit, you may want to spend a night near the crater rim to enjoy the remarkable fireworks display.

The best time to climb is December-January and June, when the weather is most clear. February, July and August are also good.

Nyiragongo

Nyiragongo (11,384 ft./3470 m) erupted in 1977, spewing out miles (kilometers) of molten lava that destroyed the villages in its path. I visited the area three months later and could still feel heat radiating from the newly hardened lava. On the 17th of January, 2002, Nyiragongo erupted again, destroying a large portion of Goma and the surrounding area in the process.

Nyiragongo can be climbed in one day, if you begin climbing early in the morning. The guide and porter station is located at Kibati (6,400 ft./1950 m), 8 miles (13 km) north of Goma on the Rutshuru road. Hike four to five hours through submontane forest past lava flows to the summit. Have lunch on the crater rim while watching sulfurous gases escape from the crater below. Allow two to three hours to return to Kibati before dark.

It is better to take two days for the climb, overnighting at a hut (in poor condition) about a 30-minute walk below the summit. At dawn the next morning, hike to the crater rim and enjoy breathtaking views of Lake Kivu, Goma and the surrounding countryside.

Nyamulagira
Nyamulagira erupted in the year 2000 and several other times in recent years. If you are interested in wildlife, this is the better of the two volcanoes to climb. An armed guide accompanies each group, and porters may be hired. With luck, you may see forest elephant, chimpanzees, buffalo and duiker.

Nyamulagira (10,023 ft./3,055 m) is best climbed in three days. On the first day, you will hike about six hours through dense upland jungle, pass numerous lava flows and arrive at a basic lodge at 8,200 feet (2,500 m) altitude. Water is available at the lodge but must be purified.

On day two you reach the tree line after about an hour's hike and the crater rim about an hour after passing the tree line. The crater itself is about a mile and a half (2 km) in diameter. Within the crater is a blowhole with a huge, 1,300-foot- (400-m) diameter shaft. Descend into it and explore the crater, then return to the same lodge you slept in the night before. Hike down the mountain on the third day.

Nyamulagira is reached via Kakomero (5,900 ft./1800 m), 24 miles (39 km) north of Goma.

 ACCOMMODATIONS – CAMPING: Campsites are available at the Nyamulagira base camp.

Tongo Chimpanzee Site
Located north of Goma about 9 miles (15 km) west of the main Goma/Rutshuru road is Tongo, presently the best place in the D. R. Congo to see chimpanzees.

A chimpanzee trek from Tongo Lodge can be arduous, often lasting five to eight hours. The land has been covered by lava flows (probably centuries old) from Mt. Nyamulagira, leaving the surface very rough and resulting in a lot of up-and-down hiking. Highland forest grew over the lava flows, camouflaging the rugged surface underneath, and requiring trekkers to watch nearly every step to prevent falling or twisting an ankle.

Chimps are often found; however, they often move away after a few minutes and trekkers must be patient. Black-and-white colobus, red-tailed monkey and other primates may be seen. The park has an average altitude of about 3,930 feet (1,200 m).

 ACCOMMODATIONS – CLASS D: * *Tongo Lodge,* located on a hill overlooking the forest where the trekking for chimps occurs, has several rooms with private facilities.

Bukima Gorilla Site
The main attraction of Bukima is visiting mountain gorillas (*Gorilla gorilla beringei*), where the Lulengo and the Ndunguts gorilla groups have been habituated to visitors.

To reach Bukima from Uganda, drive from Ishasha to Rutshuru and turn off at the Park Headquarters at Rumangabo Station, or via Kisoro in Uganda, crossing the border at Bunagana. From Rwanda, go north on the Goma/Rutshuru road to the turnoff. You then hike uphill for about 40 minutes to Bukima Lodge while porters carry your luggage. Trekkers usually spend the night, and the following day they hike for about 90 minutes through cultivated land and near small villages to the edge of the forest in which the gorillas live. From there, gorillas may be found in less than an hour, or the search could take several hours.

For a description of gorillas and gorilla trekking in general, see "Bwindi Impenetrable Forest National Park" in the chapter on Uganda.

ACCOMMODATION – CLASS D: * *Bukima Lodge* is a small lodge (six beds) with shared facilities.

Djomba (Jomba) Gorilla Site
At the Djomba Gorilla Site, four groups of mountain gorillas have

been habituated to man's presence. Three of the groups reside in the area, but the Faida Group sometimes crosses the Rwanda border. Each group may be visited by up to eight people at a time. National Parks guides and armed guards must accompany each group.

Djomba Camp is the base from which gorilla trekking begins. To reach Djomba (also spelled Jomba), drive about 40 miles (65 km) north from Goma past Nyiragongo and Nyamulagira volcanoes. Two miles before reaching Rutshuru, turn right and continue 19 miles (30 km) to Park Headquarters. From there, visitors must hike for 30-45 minutes to Djomba Camp. Porters are available to carry luggage. Travelers can also overnight in Kisoro, Uganda, depart very early and visit Djomba on a day trip, returning to Kisoro at night.

Trekkers may visit with the gorillas for about an hour, as in Uganda and Rwanda.

Buffalo and elephant are also present in the sanctuary, so keep an eye out for them.

ACCOMMODATION – CLASS D: * *Djomba Camp* has several cabins, each with two double rooms with private facilities and a shared sitting room with a fireplace.

CLASS F: A self-service hut with two bedrooms (six beds total) is available. Bring your own food.

CAMPING: Campsites are available.

Rwindi

Continuing north toward Rwindi are the **Rutshuru Waterfalls** and **Maji Ya Moto** hot-water springs, both near Rutshuru.

Rwindi was formerly a good game viewing region of Virunga National Park and is predominantly composed of savannah plains and swamp. Unfortunately, most of the wildlife here has either been poached or has crossed the border to Uganda.

The Kabasha Escarpment rises up to 6,000 feet (1,830 m) above the plains below and provides a dramatic backdrop. The fishing village of **Vitshumbi**, located on the southern shores of Lake Edward, is worth a stop.

The main road from Goma to Butembo passes right through the park.

The best time to visit is during the dry season. Roads and tracks are poor in the rainy season. Rwindi Lodge, Park Headquarters and camping sites are located at Rwindi, 81 miles (121 km) north of Goma.

 ACCOMMODATION – CLASS D: * *Rwindi Lodge* has rondavels with private facilities (130 beds total) and a swimming pool.

CAMPING: Camping is allowed but not considered safe.

Ruwenzori Mountains

The third highest mountains in Africa (after Mts. Kilimanjaro and Kenya), the "Mountains of the Moon" are, in fact, the highest mountain chain on the continent. Permanently snow-covered at over 14,800 feet (4,500 m), these jagged peaks are almost perpetually covered in mist. For a map of the Ruwenzoris, see "Ruwenzori National Park" in the chapter on Uganda.

The mountain chain is approximately 60 miles (100 km) long and 30 miles (50 km) wide, and the highest peak, Margherita, is 16,762 feet (5,109 m) in altitude. A number of permanent glaciers and peaks challenge mountaineers. However, mountaineering skills are not needed for the hike itself — only for climbing the glaciers or peaks.

Unlike Mt. Kilimanjaro and many other mountains in east and central Africa, the Ruwenzoris are not volcanic in origin. The range forms part of the border with Uganda and can be climbed from either the D. R. Congo or Ugandan side. The trail on the D. R. Congo side of the Ruwenzoris is much steeper than the Ugandan side. Allow five days for the climb and longer if any peaks are to be attempted.

The Afro-alpine vegetation zones and Afro-alpine heathlands you pass through on the Ruwenzoris are the most amazing I have seen in the world. The nectar-filled flowers of massive lobelias and giant senecios attract jewel-like sunbirds while "Spanish moss" and ephiphytic orchids adorn gnarled tree branches. Colorful mosses look solid, but when probed with a walking stick (or your foot) often prove to cover a tangle of roots more than 6 feet (2 m) deep. Several plants that are commonly small in other parts of the world grow to gigantic proportions in the Ruwenzoris.

The **Butawu Route** is the only route regularly used on the D. R. Congo side of the Ruwenzoris. All other routes are so overgrown with vegetation that they are virtually impossible to climb.

On the first day, it takes five to six hours of hiking from the Park Headquarters at Mutsora (5,600 ft./1,700 m) through small fields of bananas, coffee and other crops to reach Kalonge Hut (7,015 ft./2,135 m). The hut sleeps 16 people, and there is room for tents nearby.

On the second day, you pass through areas with giant stinging nettles and bamboo forest over 100 feet (30 m) high. Soon you come to a resting spot where offerings are left for the mountain gods. Your guide will expect you to leave something (a few coins will do).

At about 8,500 feet (2,600 m), the sides of the slick, muddy path become lined with spongy mosses and heather 25 feet (8 m) tall. After about five hours of hiking (actually the most difficult part of the climb), you reach Mahangu Hut (10,860 ft./3,310 m). The hut has room for 16 people, and there is room for camping.

The third day, you finally hike past the upper tree line at about 12,500 feet (3,800 m) and enter a zone of giant groundsels over 16 feet (5 m) high and giant lobelia over 25 feet (8 m) high. Before completing the five-hour hike to Kiondo Hut (13,780 ft./4,200 m), you hike along an open ridge with fabulous views of Lac Noir (Black Lake). Kiondo Hut has room for 12, and there is room for tents nearby.

On day four of the hike, the Butawu Route continues on to Wasuwameso Peak (14,600 ft./4,450 m) for some fabulous views of Mt. Stanley. Climbers then return to Kiondo Hut and continue on down to Kalonge Hut for the night.

Alternatively, take a fabulous hike past Lac Vert (Green Lake) and Lac Gris (Grey Lake) to Moraine Hut (14,270 ft./4,350 m) at the foot of the glaciers. The hike to Moraine Hut from Kiondo Hut takes about five hours round-trip and requires a short bit of easy rock climbing with fixed ropes. Then return to either Kiondo Hut or Mahangu Hut for the night.

If you hike to Moraine Hut, be sure to return to Kiondo Hut early. My guide insisted there was plenty of time to reach Moraine Hut and return to Kiondo Hut the afternoon of the third day. We were so late returning that we were forced to return in the dark. Had I not brought a flashlight, we might still be up there.

On the fifth day, return to Mutsora — hopefully for a hot bath and a soft bed!

Many hikers prefer camping at Grey Lake instead of using dilapidated Moraine Hut, which leaks. There is space for only one tent near Moraine Hut. Experienced mountaineers may press on to conquer the glaciers and peaks of the Ruwenzori from either location. Allow a minimum of six or seven days total for the climb if you wish to attempt any summits.

For information on climbing the summits and glaciers, I recommend the *East Africa International Mountain Guide* by Andrew Wielochowski (1986) and *Guide to the Ruwenzori* by Osmaston and Pasteur (1972), both published by West Col Productions in England.

The best time to climb is from December to February; June to August is also good. To reach the Ruwenzoris, travel north from Goma through Butembo, and just before Beni turn east 28 miles (45 km) to Mutwanga. Park Headquarters is at Mutsora, about 1.5 miles (2.5 km) from Mutwanga.

A guide is required, and his fee is included in the park entrance fee; porters are available for a small fee. Both guides and porters expect cigarettes in addition to a tip. The guides know the path and where to find water enroute — but little else. All guides speak French; an English-speaking guide may not be available. Guides who speak English tend to know only a few words.

Guides are neither equipped for, nor experienced in glacier or rock climbing. Your group must be self-sufficient. There are none of the mountain rescue teams you would find in the Alps or the Rockies; needless to say, you must bring a comprehensive medical kit.

Huts have fireplaces, bunk beds and wood stoves. Guides and porters love to smoke and often share the huts with you; consider bringing your own tent. Also, bring a warm sleeping bag, pad, food, fuel and enough water to last two days. Most of the windows are broken; you may wish to bring some plastic with which to cover them to help keep out rain and the chilly night air.

See "Mt. Kilimanjaro" in the chapter on Tanzania for a more extensive equipment checklist and other preparations. Mt. Kilimanjaro is higher, but the trail up the Ruwenzoris is much steeper, slicker and more difficult to negotiate.

ACCOMMODATION – TOURIST CLASS: See "Butembo" or "Beni" below.

CLASS F: Rooms are available at a basic lodge at Park Headquarters.

CAMPING: Camping is allowed at Park Headquarters.

Ishango

The Ishango region of Virunga National Park is situated at the northern end of Lake Edward. This seldom-visited region of the park is predominantly open savannah, similar to the Rwindi area and the southern shores of Lake Edward. Wildlife is also similar to what you find in the Rwindi region, except there are few elephant. Water birds are prolific, especially where the Semliki River leaves Lake Edward.

From Beni, travel east past the turnoff to the Ruwenzori Mountains and onward toward the Ugandan border to Kasindi. Then turn right (south) and continue to Ishango.

ACCOMMODATIONS: None.

CAMPING: Campsites are available.

Mt. Hoyo

Fifty-seven miles (92 km) north of Beni and 12 miles (19 km) south of Komanda, take the track to the east, uphill for 9 miles (15 km), to the colonial-style Mount Hoyo Lodge (Auberge du Mount Hoyo).

Halfway up this track, I came upon a line of millions of safari ants crossing the road. Thousands of ants had joined their legs and formed a living tunnel across the road, protecting those that crossed beneath.

Mt. Hoyo has many attractions. The **Cascades of Venus** (l'Escaliers de Venus) is a stepped waterfall in a thick jungle setting of natural beauty. The cascades and the grottoes (caves) with stalagmites and stalactites can be easily visited in a half-day hike. Black-and-white colobus monkeys and chimpanzees may be seen in the forest.

A very interesting excursion is to join a few Balese (pygmy) hunters on a mock antelope hunt. Groups of up to three visitors follow these hunters, who are armed with bows and arrows, through thick jungle vegetation in search of game. The pygmies whistle to attract their "prey." When I visited, they proved to me the advantage of being

A pygmy family in front of their hut near Mt. Hoyo.

small — effortlessly walking under vines and limbs while I had to crawl on my hands and knees.

We feasted on honey, which they fished from a beehive in a tree trunk with their arrows, and they enjoyed another delicacy — termites from a large mound.

Be sure to visit a pygmy village while in the area. Villages along the main roads have become a bit "commercialized," so if you have time, have a guide take you to a village off the beaten track.

 ACCOMMODATION – CLASS D: * *Mount Hoyo Lodge (Auberge du Mount Hoyo)* has rooms with private facilities and good views of the jungle below.

CAMPING: Campsites with basic shower and toilet facilities are available.

LOYA RIVER

The Loya River crosses the main road a few miles south of the turnoff to Mt. Hoyo. Take a ride in a piroque (dugout canoe) through the thick, green Ituri Forest, past artificial dams created for fishing, and then into thick jungle. The Loya River flows into the Ituri River, which travels deep into the Ituri Forest.

Visit a pygmy village before returning. Be sure to bring a gift, such as pens or tobacco, especially if you want to take pictures.

BUTEMBO

This busy town with a population of over 100,000 is situated in the highlands along the "Beauty Route" just north of the equator, about halfway between Goma and Bunia. Many banana, coffee and tea plantations are in the area. Travelers driving from Rwindi often spend the night there before continuing on to Mt. Hoyo or the Ruwenzori Mountains.

 ACCOMMODATION – TOURIST CLASS: * *Auberge* has rooms with private facilities. * *Kikyu Hotel* has rooms with private facilities.

EPULU OKAPI STATION

At the Okapi Station at Epulu, you may see the rare okapi antelope roaming several large pens set in natural surroundings. In addition, 14 primate species have been seen in the forests near Epulu.

An interesting excursion for the adventurous is to go hunting with pygmies and camp in the forest for a night or two. The pygmies will build you a shelter for the night or you may bring a tent.

Pygmy villages that are seldom visited by overseas visitors may also be visited by hiking into the jungle with a guide.

The Epulu Okapi Station is situated on the banks of the Epulu River about a six- to seven-hour drive from Mt. Hoyo in the dry season (December-February and June-August), which is the best time to visit. Roads are often impassable in the rainy season. From Mt. Hoyo, drive north to Komanda, then west past Mambasa to Epulu. Alternatively, charter a plane to Mambasa and try to hire a vehicle for the 50-mile (80-km) drive to Epulu.

 ACCOMMODATION – CLASS F: There are three rondavels and a guest house (20 beds total) with an ablution block with toilets and showers (cold water only).

CAMPING: Campsites are available.

THE SOUTHEAST

KAHUZI-BIEGA NATIONAL PARK

This 2,300-square-mile (5960-km^2) mountain sanctuary, located 17 miles (27 km) northwest of Bukavu, is dedicated to preserving the eastern lowland gorilla (*Gorilla gorilla graueri*). Searching for these magnificent, rare and endangered animals is recommended only for travelers in fairly good physical condition.

The four groups of habituated gorillas have been named Maheshe, Mushamuka, Naninja and Mubalala. The search for these gorillas usually takes an hour or two of hiking to altitudes from 7,000 to 8,200 feet (2,135 to 2,500 m) through dense upland jungle and bamboo forests. However, it occasionally takes three or four hours to locate the gorillas. The park also includes swamp, woodland and extensive equatorial rain forest. The highest point in the park, Mt. Kahuzi (10,853 ft./3,308 m), can be climbed in about six hours.

On my visit to the park, I was the only tourist there to search for gorillas. I was accompanied by a guide and several cutters wielding pangas (machetes). As our search progressed, we found lairs where gorillas had spent the previous night.

After four hours of following their trail and cutting our way through dense tropical foliage, we finally located them. The silverback (dominant male) was one of the largest I have seen — estimated by the guide to weigh over 400 pounds (180 kg). Hanging vines and branches that blocked our view were cut until the silverback pounded his chest and charged — stopping just short of us and establishing his well-earned territory. In the background, an adult female and her young offspring were curiously watching us.

Other wildlife present in the park includes elephant, giant forest hog, duiker, chimpanzee and colobus monkey.

The park is managed by the Frankfurt Zoological Society. At present, a limit of eight people may visit a gorilla group at one time. Children under 15 years of age are not allowed to visit the gorillas.

Daytime temperatures average 50-65°F (10-18°C), and yearly average rainfall is high — about 70 inches (1,790 mm). The heaviest rainfall is in April and November. The best time to visit the park is in the dry season. Bring waterproof, lightweight hiking boots (you may have to wade through water), a sweater, waterproof cover jacket, lunch, snacks and a water bottle.

To reach the park, go north from Bukavu along the western side of Lake Kivu for 13 miles (21 km) to Miti, then turn left (west), traveling for 4 miles (6 km) to Station Tshivanga, the Park Headquarters.

As of this writing, the park is considered unsafe to visit.

ACCOMMODATION – CLASS C: * *Mbayo Cottage* has seven rooms (doubles) and is located on a tea plantation 6 miles (10 km) from the park gate. Gorillas are sometimes seen on the plantation.

CAMPING: Campsites are available at Park Headquarters.

BUKAVU

Bukavu, the region's capital, is situated on the southern shores of Lake Kivu near the Rwanda border. Bukavu is the nearest city to Kahuzi-Biega National Park.

Boats for Goma depart Bukavu and cross beautiful Lake Kivu to Goma three times per week.

ACCOMMODATION – TOURIST CLASS: * *Orchids Safari Club,* located on the shores of Lake Kivu, has 28 rooms with ensuite facilities. Cruises on Lake Kivu are offered. * *Riviera Hotel* has rooms with ensuite facilities.

BURUNDI

THE INTELLIGENT CHIMPANZEE

Chimpanzees resemble humans in many physical and behavioral aspects. As humans, we are fascinated by these similarities and love to compare the familiar actions of chimpanzees to our own.

Chimpanzees typically begin their day with an early morning snack, followed for a couple of hours by more selective feeding. They use twigs like we use knives and forks, as tools to find food, locate termites in decaying wood or as wooden hammers to crack nuts, and they use leaves as spoons to gather water or honey from within tree trunks. Chimpanzees are also known to eat meat and have been filmed hunting colobus and other monkeys in highly coordinated group attacks.

During their parents' midday rest, youngsters engage in many "human" play activities. They use their five-digit hands to play tug-of-war with plants and roots, to climb trees and to play with ball-shaped objects (e.g., wild fruits). They beat their chests when excited and often disturb their parents with squabbling, screeches and screams. Individuals have even been known to beat the flat-sided buttresses of forest trees as a means of communication with others of their kind.

Chimpanzees are naturally inquisitive creatures, and they show their curiosity and indecisive nature by scratching their heads or continuing to feed and pretending not to notice. They will wield a stick to defend themselves, and others, if attacked.

At dusk they build their nests in the higher branches of trees, 19-60 feet (6-18 m) above the ground. They often sleep on their backs, hands behind their heads, or on their sides with their knees drawn up to their bodies in the fetal position.

BURUNDI

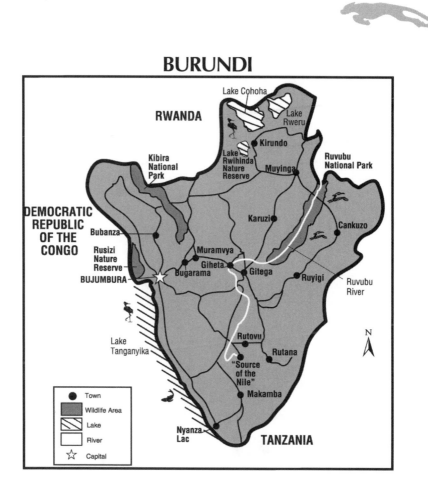

FACTS AT A GLANCE

AREA: 10,747 sq. mi. / 27,834 sq. km
APPROXIMATE SIZE: Vermont or Belgium
POPULATION: 6,054,714
CAPITAL: Bujumbura (pop. est. 400,000)
OFFICIAL LANGUAGES: Kirundi and French

BURUNDI

Burundi is one of the poorest and most densely populated countries in Africa. There are, however, some attractions that warrant a short visit, especially the prolific bird life, chimpanzees and other primates.

Burundi is a hilly country with altitudes ranging from 2,600 to 9,000 feet (790 to 2,745 m). The weather in Bujumbura and along the shores of Lake Tanganyika is warm and humid, with average temperatures ranging from 64 to 89°F (18 to 32°C); frost sometimes occurs at night in the highlands. Dry seasons are June-September and December-January; the principal rainy season is February-May.

The three major ethnic groups in the country are the Hutu, Tutsi and Twa (Pygmy). Hutus are primarily farmers and comprise more than half the population; their Bantu-speaking ancestors came to Burundi over 800 years ago. The Tutsi are a pastoral tribe and comprise less than a quarter of the population; they came to the region a few hundred years after the Hutus. The pygmy (Twa), who were the original inhabitants, presently comprise less than 2% of the population.

For centuries, the region that is now Burundi had a feudal social structure headed by a king. Although Europeans explored the region as early as 1858, Burundi did not come under European administration until it became part of German West Africa in the 1890s.

In 1916, Belgian troops occupied the country, and the League of Nations mandated it to Belgium as part of the Territory of Ruanda-Urundi in 1923. Ruanda-Urundi became a U.N. Trust Territory

Martial Eagle

under the administration of Belgium after World War II, and in 1962 became the independent country of Burundi.

As of this writing, it is not considered safe to travel in this country, due to the fighting between the Hutu and Tutsi tribes. Please get a current update on the situation before making arrangements to travel there. The accommodations listed may or may not be open, depending on the security in the region.

French and Kirundi are the official languages, and Swahili is also spoken. At the top hotels, restaurants and shops, some English-speaking staff are usually available to assist travelers; otherwise, very little English is spoken in the country. Most of the people are Catholic.

There are only two large cities in the country — Bujumbura and Gitega. Over 90% of the population are subsistence farmers. Burundi's major exports include coffee, tea, cotton and food crops, and coffee provide 80-90% of Burundi's foreign exchange earnings.

WILDLIFE AND WILDLIFE AREAS

The National Institute for the Conservation of Nature (INCN) has created several parks and nature reserves. Most of the parks and reserves lack access roads, camping sites and other facilities. Hunting is forbidden throughout the country.

Burundi's premier wildlife attraction is chimpanzees, along with crested mangabeys and red colobus monkeys. Other wildlife includes buffalo, several species of antelope, hyena, serval and a variety of bird life. Over 400 species of fish inhabit Lake Tanganyika, more than almost any other body of water in the world. Hippo and crocs are present in Lake Tanganyika and both the Rusizi and Ruvubu Rivers.

The combination of varying altitude and water creates a wide range of microclimates, giving rise to a great variety of flora.

RUSIZI NATURE RESERVE (RESERVE GEREE DE LA RUSIZI)
Entrances to this 35-square-mile (90-km²) reserve are located 9-16 miles (15-23 km) northwest of Bujumbura. The park has hippo, crocs, and a variety of bird life.

KIBIRA NATIONAL PARK (PARC NATIONAL DE LA KIBIRA)
Kibira National Park and the Kibira Forest are the best areas in Burundi to look for chimpanzees, red colobus monkeys and crested mangabeys.

This 155-square-mile (400-km²) park is situated 30 miles (48 km) or more to the north and northeast of Bujumbura and has a network of over 100 miles (160 km) of tracks (poor roads).

RUVUBU NATIONAL PARK
(PARC NATIONAL DE LA RUVUBU)
Ruvubu National Park is 193 square miles (500 km²) in size and covers a strip of land from one to six miles (1.5 to 10 km) wide along both sides of the Ruvubu River in eastern Burundi. Wildlife in the Ruvubu Basin and Parc National de la Ruvubu includes hippo, crocs, buffalo, leopard, antelope, monkeys and some lion. More than 425 bird species have been recorded. The closest road access to the park is 134 miles (216 km) from Bujumbura. The park has about 30 miles (50 km) of tracks.

LAKE RWIHINDA NATURE RESERVE
(RESERVE NATURELLE GEREE DU LAC RWIHINDA)

The Lake Rwihinda Nature Reserve and the other lakes in the northern part of the country, located approximately 125 miles (202 km) from Bujumbura, are called the "Lakes of the Birds" and include Lakes Cohoha, Rweru, Kanzigiri and Gacamirinda. They are a bird-watcher's paradise and can be explored by canoe.

BUJUMBURA

Founded in 1896 by the Germans, Bujumbura is the capital city, major port and commercial center of Burundi. The city has very good French and Greek restaurants. A fun restaurant and bar on Lake Tanganyika is Cercle Nautique, which also offers sailing, boating and fishing and has an abundance of hippos for entertainment.

There is a public beach called Kakaga, near Club du Lac Tanganyika (beware of crocodiles and hippos).

The ethnological **Musée Vivant** features a traditional Burundian village and daily traditional drum shows. The **Parc du Reptiles** is next door. The **Musée du Géologie du Burundi** has a good fossil collection. Jane Goodall operates a chimpanzee orphanage.

ACCOMMODATION – DELUXE: * *Novotel* has 110 air-conditioned rooms and 10 suites with ensuite facilities, restaurant, bar, swimming pool, business center, exercise room and tennis courts.

FIRST CLASS: * *Club du Lac Tanganyika*, situated just outside of town on Lake Tanganyika, has a swimming pool and air-conditioned rooms with ensuite facilities.

TOURIST CLASS: * *Hotel Burundi-Palace* has 29 rooms with ensuite facilities.

INLAND

The people outside Bujumbura seldom see tourists. Try to visit a village on market day to get a feeling of daily life in Burundi (be sure to check security in the area first).

Enroute to Gitega, you will pass **Muramvya**, the ancient city of the king and royal capital, and an active market at **Bugarama**.

Gitega, the former colonial capital, is situated on the central plateau in the middle of the country and is the second largest city. Sights include the National Museum, fine arts school, and beer market.

The artistic center of **Giheta**, seven miles (11 km) from Gitega, sells wood carvings, leather goods, baskets and ceramics. The southern-most possible source of the Nile is four miles (6 km) from the village of Rutovu and about 60 miles (97 km) from Gitega.

SOUTHERN AFRICA

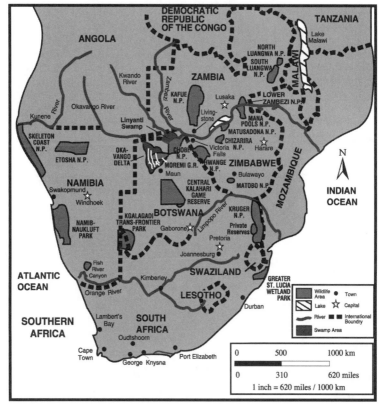

DEMOCRATIC REPUBLIC OF THE CONGO

TANZANIA

Lake Malawi

ANGOLA

NORTH LUANGWA N.P.
SOUTH LUANGWA N.P.

Kwando River

ZAMBIA

Zambezi River

KAFUE N.P.

Lusaka

LOWER ZAMBEZI N.P.

Okavango River

Livingstone

MANA POOLS N.P.

Kunene

River

Linyanti Swamp

MATUSADONA N.P.

SKELETON COAST N.P.

OKA-VANGO DELTA

CHOBE N.P.

Victoria Falls

CHIZARIRA N.P.

Harare

MALAWI

ETOSHA N.P.

MOREMI G.R.

HWANGE N.P.

ZIMBABWE

Maun

Bulawayo

MOZAMBIQUE

N

NAMIBIA

Swakopmund

Windhoek

CENTRAL KALAHARI GAME RESERVE

MATOBO N.P.

INDIAN OCEAN

NAMIB-NAUKLUFT PARK

KGALAGADI TRANS-FRONTIER PARK

BOTSWANA

Gaborone

Limpopo River

KRUGER N.P.

Private Reserves

Pretoria

Joannesburg

Fish River Canyon

SWAZILAND

ATLANTIC OCEAN

Orange River

Kimberley

LESOTHO

GREATER ST. LUCIA WETLAND PARK

Durban

SOUTHERN AFRICA

Lambert's Bay

SOUTH AFRICA

Oudtshoorn

Cape Town

George Knysna

Port Elizabeth

Wildlife Area • Town
Lake ☆ Capital
River ■■ International Boundary
Swamp Area

0	500	1000 km
0	310	620 miles

1 inch = 620 miles / 1000 km

BOTSWANA

THE ELEPHANT'S TRUNK

Watching a herd of elephant using their multipurpose trunks can provide hours of rewarding entertainment. The trunk is a combination of upper lip and nose, with the nostrils beginning at the tip and running the entire length. The trunk possesses thousands of muscles, and the tip of the trunk is covered by sensitive hairs.

The matriarchal elephant holds up her trunk in the air to pick up the scent of a nearby elephant herd. When the two groups come together, the elephants softly entwine their trunks, caress each other gently and place their trunks in each other's mouths as a greeting.

During feeding, an elephant's trunk will first touch the object and then the feeding begins. An elephant will pluck leaves, tufts of grass and branches, shake fruit off trees, tug at roots or strip tree bark. Its feet gently nudge away the roots of stubborn grass just before its trunk swishes and flaps the soil away, delicately placing the food in its small mouth for chewing.

Elephants expel air through their trunks to create the familiar trumpeting sound, which they use to chastise a playful calf, to greet another elephant or as a display of defense.

Young calves clumsily trip over their trunks, since they are too young to control the muscles. They also suck the tip of their trunk like a thumb. Best of all, they use their trunks to enjoy daily visits to a water hole.

An elephant trunk holds about 7.3 quarts (7 l) of water, and adults drink about 212 quarts (200 l) of water per day. They also cool themselves by spraying a fine mist of water over their bodies. They finish with a dust bath, which they accomplish by sucking dust into their trunks and blowing it all over themselves.

Elephants are sometimes seen resting their trunks over the tip of one of their tusks; after all, those muscles have been put to hard work smelling, touching, feeding, drinking and communicating!

BOTSWANA

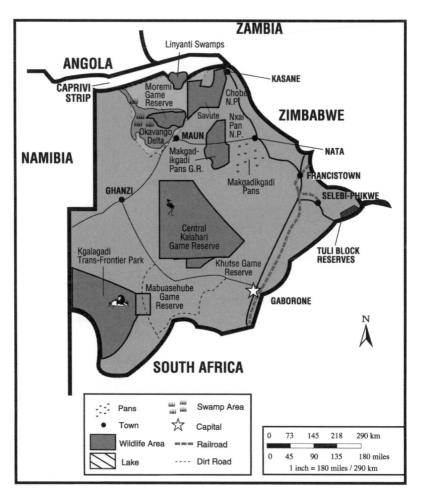

FACTS AT A GLANCE

AREA: 224,606 sq. mi. / 581,730 sq. km
APPROXIMATE SIZE: Texas or France
POPULATION: 1.6 million
CAPITAL: GABORONE (pop. est. 190,000)
OFFICIAL LANGUAGE: English
NATIONAL LANGUAGE: Setswana

BOTSWANA

In recent years, Botswana has earned a reputation as perhaps the finest safari destination in Africa. Very little of the country has been developed in any way, and the small population of less than two million people is concentrated in the eastern part of the country. The vast northern region of the Okavango Delta and the contiguous conservation areas of Moremi, Kwando, Linyanti and Chobe, along with nearby Nxai Pan and the Makgadikgadi Pans, are some of the planet's greatest wildernesses.

The best-selling book, *The Cry of the Kalahari* by Mark and Delia Owens (Houghton Mifflin), and the hilarious feature films, *The Gods Must Be Crazy* (I and II), feature stories in *National Geographic*, numerous documentaries on television and the production of many beautiful books have all helped Botswana to gain international recognition as a top safari destination.

More than four-fifths of the country is covered by the sands of the Kalahari, scrub savannah and grasslands. The land is basically flat with a mean elevation of 3,280 feet (1,000 m).

The Kalahari Desert is not a barren desert of rolling sand dunes as one might imagine. It is contains grasslands, bush, shrub and tree savannah, dry riverbeds and occasional rocky outcrops.

The "Pula" is not only Botswana's unit of currency, but also the Setswana word for rain, which is so critical to this country's wealth and survival. The rainy season is December-March, with the heaviest rains in January and February. Winter brings almost cloudless skies. January (summer) temperatures range from an average maximum of 92°F (33°C) to an average minimum of 64°F (18°C). July (winter) temperatures range from an average maximum of 72°F (22°C) to an average minimum of 42°F (6°C). Frost sometimes occurs in midwinter.

The Sotho-Tswana group of people comprise well over half of the country's population, and they all speak the Setswana language. English is spoken by most of the people, especially the youth. Cattle are their most important symbol of wealth and prestige. Ancestor worship was the chief form of religion until missionaries arrived in 1816 and converted large numbers of Batswana to Christianity.

The San, Basarwa or bushmen, were the first inhabitants of the area and may have come to southern Africa 30,000 years ago. Bechuanaland became a protectorate of the British Empire on September 30, 1885, and became the independent country of Botswana on September 30, 1966.

Today, very few of the people dress in their traditional costume, except for special celebrations. However, for many Batswana, tribal customs are still important in day-to-day life.

Botswana has a multi-party democracy and is one of the most economically successful and politically stable countries on the continent. Botswana's greatest foreign exchange earners are diamonds, tourism, cattle (there are three times as many cattle in Botswana as there are people) and copper-nickel matte.

WILDLIFE AND WILDLIFE AREAS

As far as wildlife is concerned, Botswana has been one of Africa's best-kept secrets. It is not surprising, though, because the country has set aside nearly 40% of its land area for wildlife. National parks and game reserves cover 17% of the country's area — one of the highest percentages of any country in the world. In addition, another 22% of the country has been set aside as wildlife management areas. These wildlife management areas adjoin the national parks and game reserves and form the core around which the safari industry operates. Most of the 22% of the wildlife land is leased out by the authorities to safari companies. In turn, they have created wonderful, private reserves (or concession areas as they are known locally) that

Taking a morning nap.

have incredible wildlife-viewing opportunities. These private reserves are what make Botswana's tourism today. Visitors are able to get away from crowds, as numbers are strictly regulated, and guests are able to enjoy probably the highest ratio of wildlife acreage per visitor of anywhere in Africa.

Botswana's combination of great game, uncrowded reserves, excellent small camps (most cater to 20 or fewer guests) and the use of open vehicles for day and night game viewing is difficult to beat.

The five main reserve areas most often visited by international tourists are all in the far northern reaches of the country. They are the Okavango Delta, Moremi Game Reserve (within the Okavango Delta), Linyanti/Kwando region, the Savute (southwestern part of Chobe National Park), and the Chobe River region in the northeastern part of Chobe National Park near Kasane.

The Linyanti/Kwando region, and the majority of the Okavango Delta outside of Moremi Game Reserve, has been divided into private concession areas that are feature limited numbers of camps, which can be visited by a limited number of guests. Only guests staying at the camps within each respective concession are allowed in these areas, guaranteeing exclusivity. Night game drives and limited, off-road driving are allowed in most of these areas, because the rules governing these concession areas are not as restrictive as in the national parks. Game viewing in many of these concessions is, in fact, as good or better than game viewing in some of the reserves themselves.

Because the five regions are each distinct in character, if time allows, a well-rounded wildlife safari to Botswana should include two to three days in each.

Chobe National Park, Moremi Game Reserve and Linyanti rank as three of the best wildlife areas in Africa. The Okavango Delta is the largest inland delta in the world. This "water in the desert" phenomenon has created a unique and fascinating ecosystem that is well worth exploring.

Generally speaking, game viewing for the Okavango Delta, Moremi, Linyanti, Chobe and Savute is good all year, although large numbers of elephant concentrate around the waterways and marshlands in the dryer months of April through November.

Calving season throughout the country is November-February, during the summer months. The abundance of young animals (babies) make for wonderful photographic opportunities from mid-November or December through March. The sight of warthog piglets and impala lambs, only a few days to a few months old, is too cute for words!

The rut, or season when impala males fight for dominance, provides plenty of action from April to May.

Fishing for tigerfish, bream, barbel and pike is very good, especially September–December.

Other northern attractions include Nxai Pan National Park and Makgadikgadi Pans Game Reserve. Game viewing in Nxai Pan is best in the wet summer season (November-April), and Makgadikgadi Pans is best January-April. Reserves in the south are, at times, excellent, but they are seldom visited by international travelers.

Many camps are accessed only by small aircraft, which allows visitors to minimize the time spent on roads between reserves and maximize the time viewing wildlife and enjoying the variety of other activities Botswana has to offer. Game activities are conducted by resident guides in the camps.

Game viewing by air is usually quite fruitful. On one flight from the

Savute to the Okavango Delta, we spotted four large herds of elephant, among numerous other species. Most charter flights have baggage limits of 26 pounds (12 kg) per person (unless you decide to "purchase" an extra seat on the plane for your extra luggage), so bring only what you need, and pack it in only soft-sided bags. Free laundry service and shampoo are available at all of the better camps.

Group and private luxury and first-class (full-service) and budget (participatory) mobile tented safaris are generally less expensive per day than flying safaris, and they are another excellent way to experience the reserves. On mobile tented programs, you generally have the same guide throughout the safari.

The Wildlife Department runs the parks. Driving in the parks is currently not allowed at night, but it is allowed in the private concession areas. However, it is expected — in the near future — that professionally licensed guides will be allowed to conduct night game drives in Moremi. Camping is allowed at designated spots. Some lodges and camps close January-February.

THE NORTH

MAUN
Maun is the safari center of the country's most important tourist region. Many travelers fly into Maun to join their safari; others begin their safari at Victoria Falls (Zimbabwe) or Kasane, Botswana, and end up in Maun.

TOURIST CLASS: * *Riley's Hotel* has air-conditioned rooms with ensuite facilities and a popular bar and restaurant. * *Island Safari Lodge* is located 9 miles (14 km) north of Maun on the western bank of the Thamalakane River and has brick-and-thatch bungalows with private facilities, campsites, swimming pool, bar and restaurant. * *Crocodile Camp* is located on the banks of the Thamalakane River, 8 miles (12 km) north of Maun on a tarred road. Chalets with ensuite facilities and campsites are available.

THE OKAVANGO DELTA
The Okavango, covering over 6,000 square miles (15,000 km²), is a natural mosaic of palm-fringed islands, open savannah, fast flowing rivers, crystal-clear lagoons and floodplains sprinkled with water lilies, and gigantic baobab and jackalberry trees.

OKAVANGO DELTA

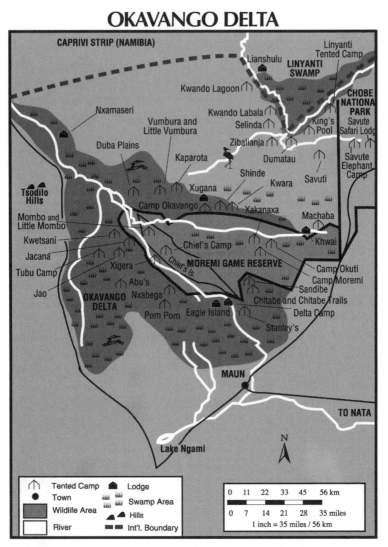

The Okavango River originates in the central African highlands about 600 miles (1,000 km) northwest of Botswana, then it fans out into the Kalahari Desert to create a vast system of thousands of waterways, separated by innumerable islands, and it eventually disappears into the Kalahari sands.

The opportunities to explore and experience the wonder of this inland delta and enjoy the primordial silence, unusual flora, bird life, hippo, crocs, and excellent fishing, are well worth the visit.

A young antelope leaping away from danger.

Game viewing for the larger land mammal species is excellent in many parts of the Delta. Large herds of buffalo, elephant, giraffe and a variety of antelope are often seen. Lion, leopard, cheetah and other predators are also frequently encountered.

Crocodiles are most heavily concentrated in the larger waterways and in the northern part of the Delta and the panhandle, where there is permanent, deep water. However, crocs are found throughout the Delta.

The Okavango, an ornithologist's and botanist's dream come true, is beautifully presented in *Okavango – Africa's Last Eden* (Hale Publishers)by Frans Lanting, *'Running Wild'* (Southern Book Publishers) by Nico McNutt and Dave and Helene Hamman, *Okavango: Sea of Land, Land of Water* (Struik Publishers) by Peter Johnson and Anthony Bannister, *Okavango: Jewel of the Kalahari* by Karen Ross (Macmillan Publishing) and *Okavango – Africa's Wetland Wilderness* (Struik Publishers) by Adrian Bailey.

Mother Nature must have smiled on this region, for the waters are highest during the peak of the dry season. It takes six months for the rainy season floodwaters to travel from their source in the Angolan highlands to the Delta.

Flying into the Delta gives you an overall perspective of the region and is an adventure in itself. Game can be easily spotted and photographed from the air.

Poling through the waterways of the Okavango Delta by mokoro.

A 150-mile- (240-km) long buffalo fence has been constructed along the southern and western edges of the Delta to keep cattle from moving into the pristine natural areas. The villages and their cattle are to the west and south of the fence; therefore, little game is found on the Maun (southern) side.

Calling the Okavango a "swamp" is a misnomer, since the waters are very clear and are continually moving. The clarity is mainly due to the fact that the waters carry little sediment. There is only about a 203-foot (63-m) drop in altitude over 150 miles (240 km) from the upper to the lower Delta. In addition, the larger stands of papyrus in both the panhandle and in the north act as a large filtration plant, filtering out impurities and helping to keep the waters crystal clear. Very little bilharzia (a snail-borne disease) exists in the area; the only real problem region is around Maun, where the waters can become stagnant.

Activities in the Delta include mokoro (dugout canoe) and modern canoe excursions, boat game drives, day and night vehicle game drives, nature walks on islands, bird watching, and fishing on request. Motor boats allow you to visit more distant attractions, and they must be used for fishing or where the water is too deep to pole a mokoro or canoe. Where there is access by land, a 4wd vehicle is necessary.

The best way to experience the majesty of the Okavango Delta waterways is by mokoro. Traveling by mokoro allows you to become a part of the environment. Sitting inches from the waterline, thoughts of

A leopard mum protecting her cub.

hippos or crocodiles overturning your boat cross your mind but soon pass with assurances from your guide and the peacefulness of the pristine environment.

Patterns of gold are created by the reflection of papyrus on the still waters of the narrow channels during early morning and late afternoon. You sometimes pass through channels that often appear to be narrower than the boat itself. Silence is broken only by the *ngashi* (boatman's pole) penetrating and leaving the water, by the cries of countless birds and by the movement of game along the Delta's banks. Tiny frogs chime to an unknown melody. Sunsets with rosy pink clouds reflect in the waters and create the illusion of floating in the sky. Life slows to a regenerative pace. This relaxed form of adventure and exploration is difficult to match anywhere in the world.

On one occasion, I tried poling our canoe across a small lagoon. My guide was right, it's definitely not as easy as it looks!

Guided excursions, ranging in length from a few hours to a full day, using mekoro (plural for mokoro), canoes or small motor boats, are offered by many camps in the Delta. Canoes are larger and therefore a little more comfortable, but mekoro harmonize better with the natural surroundings. To minimize cutting the large trees in the Delta, many camps use specially built fiberglass mekoro, which look and move like the real thing — without a cost to the woodlands. Mokoro trips for two or more days, during which you camp on remote islands in the Delta, are possible when booked in advance.

On one mokoro trip, we spotted an elusive sitatunga antelope running through the reeds. Sitatunga are rare, shy, solitary antelope that are not often seen, and a real highlight if spotted.

The islands in the Delta are created by many natural geological forces. Another of the causes for islands are termites, whose mounds have been built up over the eons. Because of the cement-like quality of termite mounds, the soil is sometimes dug up and used to build elevated paths in camps and even airstrips. Meanwhile, diamond prospectors inspect termite mounds closely. Since soil is brought up from quite a depth, it provides them with easily accessible core samples.

During a day game drive in the Jao Concession, we witnessed one of the most incredible sightings — a leopard stalking and killing a red lechwe antelope. As the leopard held on to the lechwe's neck, the antelope fought and tossed the leopard about for several minutes, until the lechwe finally succumbed. Later that day we spotted five lion, giraffe, a variety of other species — and hundreds of red lechwe - the ones that got away!

On yet another day game drive in the Delta, we saw a pride of 19 lion on a buffalo kill. On a night drive, we also observed an aardwolf and a large spotted genet, along with other general game. The next morning, by mokoro, we saw large herds of red lechwe, a hippo out of water, and myriad bird species. I had forgotten how relaxing it was!

That afternoon, on the way to the dock, we spotted two leopard. As we approached them, the leopard ran off, and we found a reedbuck kill they had abandoned. We then went by motorboat to an island for sundowners (drinks and snacks), and we traveled through channels surrounded by thick papyrus and reeds. From the looks of it, this could have been Tarzan and Jane's island.

We returned to the dock in the dark and drove to the location of the previous leopard sighting. Just as we drove up, we saw two leopard cubs run up a tree followed closely by their mother, who was chased about 20 feet up the tree by a female lion! The mother leopard came down the tree two more times, and was again chased up the tree by the lioness — seemingly to tease the lioness who had stolen their kill!

The following morning, on a game drive, we saw three giraffe, two cheetah males, a pride of four lion, wattled crane, lilac-breasted roller, tawny eagle, fish eagle and bateleur eagles.

One of the real highlights of any safari is to sight African wild dogs, and the Okavango is one of Africa's last refuges for this rare and endangered animal.

As might be expected of an inland delta, the Okavango is a haven for birds and a huge attraction for birdwatchers from around the world. There is a bewildering variety of aquatic species, and the Okavango boasts the highest concentration of African fish eagles on the continent. There are good numbers of the awe-inspiring Pel's fishing owl and the seasonally breeding African skimmers. On numerous occasions our guide waved a fish in the air and called to a fish eagle perched high in a tree over a half-mile away, then tossed the fish into the water about 30 feet (9 m) from the boat. Like magic, the eagle dived down at full speed and plucked the fish from the water. You must be fast with a camera to catch that on film!

Large, mixed aggregations of waterfowl are common during the dry winter months, when the Angolan floodwaters fill up the seasonal wetlands. It is not uncommon to see five or six species of heron alongside four or five varieties of stork, with ducks, waders, cormorants and kingfishers - all gathered in the shallows or surrounding vegetation. The beautiful African pygmy goose, lesser jacana, slaty egret, wattled crane and the goliath heron are among the most sought-after birds.

It is not only waterfowl that populate the Okavango Delta, for the surrounding savannah and riverine woodlands provide ideal habitats for a host of hornbills, parrots, woodpeckers, rollers, shrikes, plovers, waxbills, weavers and bee-eaters, among others. Northern Botswana (and, indeed, the whole country) is renowned as a stronghold for birds of prey, with substantial populations of martial eagle, bateleur, tawny eagle, white-headed vulture, to name just a few.

Bird species we spotted on a recent visit included the coppery-tailed coucal, purple heron, striped kingfisher, Meyer's parrot, black-collared barbet, yellow-fronted tinker barbet, hamerkop, red-billed woodhoopoe, saddle-billed stork, Dickinson's kestrel, lesser spotted eagle, grey lourie, carmine bee-eater (they are migrants that are found in the Okavango from late August to March), slaty egret (a real

Horseback safari, possibly the finest in Africa.

birder's highlight!), little egret, reed cormorant, wattled crane, green-backed heron, goliath heron, blacksmith plover, pied kingfisher, yellow-billed kite, western banded snake eagle, African darter, African jacana and numerous fish eagles.

Coasting along one afternoon in a small motorboat, we drove right by an 8-foot- (2.4-m) long crocodile. We went back for a closer look and discovered it was fast asleep. We maneuvered the boat within 5 feet (1.5 m) of it, and it still didn't wake up — and I'm glad it didn't!

Fishing is best in the northwestern part of the Delta. The best time of the year for catching tigerfish is September-November. For barbel, the best time is from the end of September through October, when the fish are running (migrating). Overall, the best time for fishing is September-December.

Horseback safaris, possibly the finest in Africa, last from two to 10 days. Four to six hours a day are spent in the saddle. Afternoons are often spent walking, swimming, fishing or on mokoro trips. Only experienced riders are allowed, because they must be able to confidently canter alongside herds of game, including zebra, giraffe and antelope. Accommodations are usually in mobile tented camps.

An elephant-back safari on an African elephant is a unique way of experiencing the bush. Guests can fly to Abu's Camp for a six-day

On elephant back – a unique safari in Botswana.

safari, during which they join Abu, the lead elephant, along with his family of several adults and youngsters. Another option is Stanleys Camp, where guests may walk with trained elephants.

If you wish to visit Tsodilo Hills (see below) to see the bushmen and rock paintings, consider making reservations in advance. By booking in advance, you can fly from your camp in the Okavango to the Nxamaseri or Shakawe airstrip and then be driven to the hills.

One issue to consider when visiting the Okavango Delta is the water levels and how they can affect a camp, its access and your activities. Each year the Okavango presents a different scenario to its inhabitants and its visitors. The changes are caused by the varying yearly rainfall in central Africa. The annual flood is an eagerly awaited event, and the levels of the incoming water have an enormous impact on the region. A safari camp, after a low flood, may be surrounded by huge, open grassland savannahs. The next year, that same camp may be surrounded by water as the result of an extremely high flood, and the game viewing areas will have moved. This is all part of the fun of traveling to the Okavango. It's a dynamic and constantly changing system!

When the floods arrive, much of the savannah is submerged – forcing the wildlife to concentrate on fewer and smaller islands. The area

Duba Plains, a permanent tented camp.

covered by game drives may be reduced; however, the drives are often more productive.

ACCOMMODATION – CLASS A+: * *Jao Camp*, one of the most luxurious camps in Botswana, is located in a private concession area west of the Moremi Game Reserve. This beautiful camp has nine large tented rooms with a lounge area and ensuite bathrooms, all under a thatched roof. Each room has an outdoor shower and a "sala" with mattresses under thatch, for great midday siestas. Activities include day and night game drives in open vehicles, boat game drives (usually May-October, depending on water levels), mokoro (dugout canoe) trips to explore the crystal-clear channels, islands and waterways, and walks. Guests staying for three or more nights may spend one night under the stars in a fly camp. * *Abu's Camp* is a 10-bed, deluxe tented camp with ensuite facilities. Elephant-back safaris, mokoro rides, walks and vehicular game drives are offered.

CLASS A: * *Duba Plains* accommodates a maximum of 12 guests in luxury tents with ensuite bathroom facilities, including inside and outside showers, and is located in a remote region of the Delta. Game drives, walks and mokoro excursions (depending on the water level) are available. There is a pool and a hide overlooking a waterhole at the back of the camp. One of Africa's highest concentrations of lion exist there, feeding off of the tremendous buffalo herds. * *Kwetsani Camp* is a

10-bed luxury tented camp, located in the same private concession area as Jao. The camp is raised on stilts beneath the shady canopy that overlooks the expansive plains. The five spacious tented "tree-house" chalets are built under a thatch roof, and all have ensuite facilities, including a shower, flush toilet, basin and outdoor shower. Guests staying three or more nights may spend one night in a fly camp. * *Little Vumbura Camp* offers a private location in the northern area of the Delta that borders Moremi. It has five large, luxury tented rooms, each with full ensuite facilities and outdoor shower. The main dining area has a decked lounge and a pool. It offers both water and land activities, including boat game drives, game viewing by mokoro, day and night game drives, and walks. * *Vumbura Camp* is located in the northern part of the Delta and has eight luxury tents with ensuite bathroom and an outdoor shower. Day and night game viewing by vehicle, mokoro excursions, walks, boat game drives and fishing are offered. * *Nxabega Okavango Safari Camp* has nine beautifully furnished East-African-style tents with ensuite facilities. Activities include game drives, walks and mokoro rides. * *Eagle Island Camp* at Xaxaba is situated in the Delta west of Chief's Island and has 12 reed-and-thatch chalets with ensuite facilities. Activities include mokoro rides, walks and sundowner cruises. * *Camp Okavango* is a 22-bed tented camp in the eastern Delta with private facilities located down a private walkway behind each tent. Activities include mokoro safaris, boat trips and walks.

CLASS A/B: * *Tubu Tree Camp*, situated in the Jao Concession, is a tree house-style tented safari camp built on to raised wooden platforms to take best advantage of the beautiful view over the floodplains. The camp sleeps a maximum of 10 guests in five large, comfortable tents, each with small, private decks, ensuite bathroom facilities and private outdoor shower. The main dining and lounge areas are also housed in large tents on raised platforms. Activities include day and night game drives in open 4wd vehicles, as well as walks with an armed guide. When the Okavango's annual flood is at its highest (normally May to late September), boating, fishing and mokoro trips are also offered. * *Kaparota* is a luxury camp (eight guests maximum) with tents raised on wooden decks overlooking the surrounding islands and floodplains. The bathrooms are ensuite and open-aired because the camp targets the slightly more adventurous traveler. Day and night game drives, guided walks, mekoros rides and boat game drives are offered. * *Pom Pom* has six deluxe tents (12 beds), with ensuite facilities, overlooking a lagoon in the central Delta. Activities include day and night game drives, walks

Stanley's Camp, elegantly photographed at dusk.

and mokoro rides. * *Jacana Camp,* an 8-bed camp set in the Jao Concession, is primarily a water camp that offers mokoro excursions, boat game drives and escorted walks. Day and night game drives are generally possible by vehicle September-May, when the water levels are lower. * *Shinde Island Camp* has eight deluxe tents (16 beds) with private facilities situated a few feet behind each tent, and a small swimming pool. Activities include mokoro trips, boat rides, fishing, walks and game drives. * *Xugana Island Camp* has eight reed chalets (16 beds) built on stilts, with ensuite facilities and a swimming cage. Xugana offers boat rides, mokoro trips, walks and fishing. * *Stanleys Camp* is a 16-bed tented camp offering game drives and mokoro excursions, when water levels allow it. For an additional fee, guests may spend time walking with trained elephants.

CLASS B: * *Nxamaseri Camp,* located in the panhandle of the Delta, is one of the top fishing camps in the Okavango. Boat game drives are also offered. * *Delta Camp* has eight reed chalets with ensuite facilities. Walks and mokoro excursions are offered. * *Xudum Camp* is a 16-bed tented camp with ensuite facilities. Day and night game drives, walks, fishing and mokoro excursions are offered. * *Starling's Camp* is a 16-bed tented camp with ensuite facilties offering day and night game drives and walks. Mokoro and boat game drives are offered seasonally.

TSODILO HILLS

Over 2,700 bushmen paintings are scattered through the rocky outcrops of Tsodilo Hills, one of the last places in Botswana where bushmen may be found. The largest of the four hills rises 1,000 feet (305 m) above the surrounding plain. Archeological evidence indicates that these hills may have been inhabited as long as 30,000 years ago.

Located west of the Okavango Delta, Tsodilo Hills is accessible by a flight from Maun (or from safari camps in northern Botswana) to the Nxamaseri or Shakawe airstrips, which is followed by either a short drive or a very long and rough day's ride from Maun by 4wd vehicle. There are no facilities, so travelers must be totally self-sufficient. Unfortunately, this site has become a little touristy, so don't expect to see bushmen living as they did thousands of years ago. However, the rock paintings are worth a visit. Because water is scarce in this area, be sensitive and do not drink in the presence of bushmen.

ACCOMMODATION: None.

MOREMI GAME RESERVE

Moremi is the most diversified of all the Botswana parks, in terms of wildlife and scenery, and many people feel it is the most beautiful. Located in the northeastern part of the Okavango Delta, Moremi contains over 1,160 square miles (3,000 km²) of permanent swamps, islands, floodplains, forests and dry land. The park's boundaries have been recently extended to the west and northwest, significantly enlarging its size.

In the floodplains, reedbuck, common waterbuck, red lechwe, tsessebe, ostrich, sable and roan antelope, crocodile, hippo and otter can be found. In the riparian forest, you may spot elephant, greater kudu, southern giraffe, impala, buffalo and Burchell's zebra, along with such predators as lion, leopard, ratel (honey badger), spotted hyena and cheetah.

Bat-eared fox, black-backed and side-striped jackals are often seen in the riparian forest, as well as in the floodplain. Seldom-seen species include pangolin, aardvark, porcupine and hedgehog.

The reserve has a large wild dog population, as creatively presented in the book *Running Wild: Dispelling the Myths of the African Wild Dog* by John McNutt and Lesley Boggs, with photography by Helene Heldring and Dave Hamman (Russel Friedman Books).

Cheetah are often seen in Moremi.

Game viewing is excellent during the drier months of May-November when the bush has thinned out, making wildlife sightings a bit easier. In parts of Moremi, game viewing is, in fact, excellent year-round.

On my last visit, I was honored to witness four white rhino being released in the wild at Mombo Camp. Eleven more rhino have since joined the group. The release is part of a grand, ongoing plan to repopulate the species in Botswana. At the ceremony, Lt. General Khama, Vice President of Botswana, spoke of the importance of the reintroduction of rhino to wildlife conservation and to the people of Botswana. You now have a chance of seeing the "Big Five" (lion, leopard, elephant, buffalo and rhino) once more on safari in Botswana!

Botswana and South Africa have an agreement to swap roan antelope from Botswana for white rhino from South Africa, and sable antelope from Botswana for black rhino from South Africa. Such efforts will form viable breeding nuclei to repopulate rhino throughout northern Botswana.

Other wildlife sightings during my November visit included over 30 lion, including a pair mating, 10 spotted hyena, cheetah, slender mongoose, giraffe, red lechwe, impala, tsessebe, large herds of elephant, and warthog piglets and impala calves only a day or two old!

One of the most hilarious sightings I have experienced was several juvenile lions confronting a water monitor. A lion would cautiously approach the monitor, and then beat a hasty retreat the second the monitor made a quick move. The monitor eventually walked away unharmed!

We enjoyed the fascinating sight of a male dung beetle rolling a huge ball of dung with the female riding on it. Once he got it to the right place, he buried the female along with the dung.

During a morning game drive on another visit, we saw two herds of sable antelope, elephant, greater kudu, tsessebe, impala and Burchell's zebra. That same afternoon and evening we saw a variety of game, including leopard, seven lion, cheetah, bat-eared fox, and several species of antelope.

The following afternoon we found leopard, and later a cheetah with her two cubs stalking a male impala. We also found two male cheetahs and a mother leopard with her two cubs.

In a single day we spotted leopard, three honey badgers, side-striped and black-backed jackal and a lioness that had chased a warthog into its hole and then dug it out for the kill. The lioness then kept going back to the hole, digging a bit deeper each time. Just as she moved a few feet away from the hole, a warthog shot out like a rocket and ran to safety.

On another game drive we saw giraffe, greater kudu, wildebeest, black-backed jackal and wattled cranes. Our group also spotted seven lion on a buffalo kill: three adult male, a female and three juveniles.

Elephant and buffalo are the only large animals that migrate. After the rains have begun, they move northward to the area between Moremi and the Kwando-Linyanti River systems. Other wildlife may move to the periphery of, or just outside, the reserve.

Moremi is also an ornithologist's delight. Fish eagles, kingfishers and bee-eaters abound. Other birds commonly seen include parrots, shrikes, egrets, jacanas, pelicans, bateleur eagles, hornbills, herons, saddle-billed storks, yellow-billed oxpeckers, wattled cranes, reed cormorants, spur-winged geese, long-tailed shrikes and flocks of thousands of red-billed quelea, which group together in the form of a sphere like a great spotted flying ball.

With the onset of the floods in May or June, waterfowl follow the progression of the floodwaters as they flow through the region.

Mombo Camp offers some of the best game viewing in Africa.

Under new park rules, which are expected to be in place in the near future, night game drives and escorted walks with an armed guide may be allowed in Moremi.

Moremi is open year-round; however, some areas may be temporarily closed due to heavy rains or floods. Four-wheel-drive vehicles are necessary. The South Gate is about 62 miles (100 km) north of Maun.

ACCOMMODATION IN MOREMI GAME RESERVE – CLASS A+:
* *Little Mombo* is an exclusive, luxury tented camp with only three tents (six beds) set on decks, with ensuite bathrooms, indoor and outdoor showers, private salas (lounging areas), separate lounge/dining room and plunge pool. Morning and afternoon game drives are conducted in open vehicles. * *Mombo Camp* is a luxury tented camp with nine large tents (18 beds total) set on decks with ensuite facilities, indoor and out-door showers, and a plunge pool. These two camps, along with Jao Camp in the Okavango Delta, have set the highest standard for luxury and service of all tented camps in Southern Africa. Both camps are situated in the reserve near the northern tip of Chief's Island, where the savannah meets the Okavango, in what is considered by many to be the best game viewing area in Southern Africa. Big game, including

Private mobile tenting provides an exclusive safari experience.

rhino, lion, leopard, cheetah and wild dog, is plentiful year-round in this concession area. This is one area where the "Big Five" can be seen. Activities include day and early evening game drives (up to a half hour after sunset) and walks. Night game drives are expected to be allowed from both camps soon.

ACCOMMODATION – CLASS A: * *Chief's Camp*, located on the northwest tip of Chief's Island, has 12 luxury tents with private viewing decks, ensuite bathrooms, and a swimming pool. The "Big Five" may be see in this area. * *Xigera Camp* is situated within the Moremi Game Reserve on a large island in the Delta. The camp has eight luxury tented rooms with ensuite facilities. Activities include mokoro rides, walks and game viewing by vehicle and by boat. * *Xakanaxa Camp* is a 22-bed tented camp with ensuite facilities. The camp is located within the park, overlooking the Xakanaxa Lagoon. Game drives and boat trips are offered.

CLASS A/B: * *Camp Moremi* is a 22-bed tented camp located overlooking Xakanaxa Lagoon within the reserve. Private facilities are situated a short walk down a secluded pathway behind each tent. Game drives are offered.

CLASS B: * *Camp Okuti*, located within the reserve, has brick-and-thatch chalets with ensuite facilities.

LINYANTI

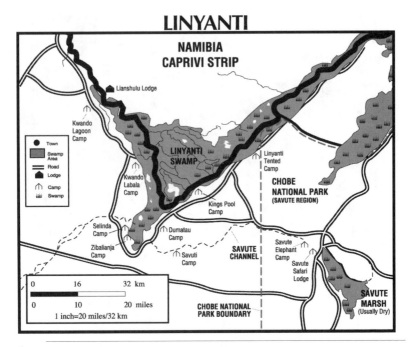

ACCOMMODATION ON THE PERIPHERY OF MOREMI GAME RESERVE – CLASS A:* *Chitabe Camp,* located on a private concession bordered by Moremi Game Reserve on three sides, has eight luxury tents set on wooden decks, with ensuite facilities and an additional outside shower. Day and night game drives and walks are offered. There are a number of hides in the area. * *Chitabe Trails,* located in the same private concession area as Chitabe Main Camp, has five luxury tents with ensuite facilities. Activities include day and night game drives and walks. * *Sandibe Camp,* also located on a private concession surrounded by Moremi Game Reserve on three sides, has eight thatched cottages with ensuite facilities. Activities include day and night game drives, escorted walks, mokoro trips and boat game drives. * *Khwai River Lodge,* situated outside the reserve, has 15 luxury tents (30 beds) under thatch with ensuite facilities and a swimming pool. Game drives are offered.

CLASS A/B: * *Kwara Camp,* situated just north of the reserve, has eight tents (16 beds) with ensuite facilities and offers day and night game drives, walks and mokoro rides. * *Machaba Camp* is located outside the reserve and has eight tents (16 beds) with ensuite facilities and a small swimming pool. The camp offers day and night game drives and walks outside the reserve.

CAMPING: * *South Gate Campsite* is located just outside the South Gate and has only toilet facilities. * *Third Bridge* is Moremi's most popular campsite and can be very crowded in peak season. This camp has only long-drop toilets. Water is available from the river. * *Xaxanaka* has no facilities. * *North Gate* campsite is situated just inside the reserve and has showers, toilet facilities and water. Because all of these campsites (and the permanent tented camps and lodges) are not fenced, beware of lion and other wild animals.

LINYANTI

The Linyanti, situated northeast of the Okavango Delta and northwest of the Savute marshes within Chobe National Park, is home to many crocodile, hippo, sitatunga, lechwe, elephant, buffalo, lion and spotted hyena. The Linyanti region is, in essence, a mini "Okavango Delta" with a lot of of big game. During the dry season this is, in fact, big elephant country with literally thousands in the region.

Two-thirds of the Savuti Channel is actually within the Linyanti Concession Area. The part of the channel within Chobe National Park is called Savute, and the area outside of the park is called Savuti.

On a recent visit we had an excellent leopard sighting, took a boat game drive and canoed among herds of elephant crossing the river channels, and we even walked up to a large bull elephant. On a night drive we saw lesser bushbaby, African wild cat, hyena, a pride of lion on a giraffe kill, a caracal that had killed a cattle egret, a giant eagle owl and a white-faced owl.

On another visit we saw large herds of elephant, zebra, several prides of lion, buffalo and bat-eared fox, along with a variety of other game. We stopped by a lagoon for a cool drink, and we watched two elephant playing in the water with the sun setting behind them. On a night game drive we saw six African wild dog on a greater kudu kill, a pride of 13 lion, leopard, serval, and a very vocal and aggressive confrontation between two adult female hyena and a sub-adult — the likes of which I have never seen!

The Kwando and Linyanti Rivers form the region's border with Namibia. The Kwando River flows southeast and then meets the end of the Great Rift Valley. This causes the river to flow northeast, and at this point its name changes to the Linyanti River and later to the Chobe River, which eventually meets the Zambezi River.

This region is prolific in bird life. Big game is most concentrated in this region during the dry season (May-November).

ACCOMMODATION – CLASS A: * *DumaTau* is a 16-bed tented camp with ensuite facilities, indoor and outdoor showers, family tent and plunge pool. It overlooks an enormous lagoon. DumaTau is located close to the source of the Savuti Channel and offers day and night vehicle game drives, boat game drives and walks in this private concession area. * *Kings Pool Camp*, located on a large private concession and overlooking a lagoon, has 10 luxury tents set on raised decks, ensuite facilities, indoor and outdoor showers, and a plunge pool. There is a family tent with an adjoining bedroom. Day and night vehicle game drives, boat game drives on a double-decker houseboat, and walks are offered. The hides are a great attraction at Kings Pool. There is a hide within the camp, and guests enjoy great viewing around midday. There are also a number of hides in the bush, including an underground hide where guests can enjoy viewing animals at water level (great for photography). * *Savuti Camp* has five luxury tents with ensuite facilities. It is located on the Savuti Channel (currently dry) about 10 miles (17 km) "downstream" from its source. A number of waterholes and hides are located along the channel. A waterhole in front of camp is a magnet for game in the dry season. Day and night game drives are offered.
* *Selinda Camp* is a 12- bed tented camp with ensuite facilities, set on a private concession. Activities include day and night game drives by vehicle, boat game drives (water levels permitting — usually July-October), morning walks and walking safaris for up to six guests and lasting two to three days. * *Kwando Lebala Camp* is located on a large concession area bordered for 50 miles (80 km) on the east by the Kwando River which flows into the Linyanti and Chobe Rivers. The camp has eight tents (16 beds) under thatch, with ensuite facilities. Day and night vehicle game drives, walks, boat game drives and fishing are offered. * *Kwando Lagoon Camp* is set on the banks of the Kwando River and has six tents (12 beds) under thatch, with ensuite facilities. Day and night vehicle game drives, boat game drives, walks and fishing are offered.

ACCOMMODATION – CLASS A/B: * *Linyanti Tented Camp* is located close to the western border of Chobe National Park in the Linyanti Concession area. The camp is sited on the banks of a stunning lagoon and consists of five luxury tents with ensuite facilities. The dining area is under canvas. Activities include day and night game drives, game and bird walks, canoeing on the large lagoons and boating on the smaller waterways. * *Zibalianja Camp*, located on the Selinda Concession, is an exclusive, six-bed camp with ensuite facilities. Day and night game drives and walks are offered.

SAVUTE (CHOBE NATIONAL PARK)

Savute is an arid region located in the southern part of Chobe National Park. The landscape ranges from sandveld to mopane forest, acacia savannah, marshlands (always dry) to rocky outcrops. The Savute Channel connects the grasslands or marshlands of the interior with the Linyanti River. However, the Savute River has not flowed since 1981, and the marshlands are currently dry. The Savute Channel changes its spelling as it arrives within Chobe National Park. Outside of the Chobe it is called the Savuti, and within the park it is known as the Savute.

The Savute, like the northern part of Chobe National Park, is famous for its lions and is seasonally known for its bull elephant herds. However, because the Savute Channel has dried up, the game is not as prolific as it used to be in the 70s and 80s. The area is also home to zebra, eland, kudu, roan antelope, sable antelope, waterbuck, tsessebe, wildebeest, impala and many other antelope, along with numerous predators, including leopard, cheetah, wild dog, spotted hyena, black-backed jackal and bat-eared fox.

The Savute region is greatly affected by the seasons, and is at its best in the wet season (November-March), or during the early dry season (April-May). When the rains fall, from November to April, the plains become green and large herds of zebra and tsessebe are present. From June to October, it is typically very dusty and dry, and bull elephants dominate the small, man-made waterholes. To secure access to a permanent water source, most antelope, along with breeding herds of elephant, migrate to and settle around the Linyanti Swamps at this time.

Game viewing along the Savute Channel, from the park's northern boundary to the Linyanti Swamps, is best from May to November. Burchell's zebra migrate from the Mababe Depression, which is south of the Savute Marsh, northward to the Linyanti Swamps in May, and they return to the Mababe Depression in November.

Approaching elephant from the water.

Bird watching is best during the wet season (November-April). Large flocks of dazzling carmine bee-eaters hawk insects, and large gatherings of white and Abdim's storks patrol the plains for grasshoppers. The world's heaviest flying bird — the kori bustard — is a common and conspicuous inhabitant of the area. Rollers, kestrels, plovers, sandgrouse, coursers, queleas and doves are among the other prominent groups.

 On a morning drive down the dry Savute Channel, we stopped for tea and watched a herd of 15 giraffe and a large herd of zebra cross the channel. There were many elephant in the area, and we were amazed by how many juvenile bateleurs we saw. We saw lion and bat-eared fox on numerous occasions.

On another game drive we spotted impala, five greater kudu, warthog, elephant, two black-backed jackals, steenbok, about 50 tsessebe, a herd of blue wildebeest, 12 bat-eared fox, tawny eagle, yellow-billed hornbill and kori bustard. We followed vultures to a warthog kill, where we found only part of the carcass remaining. A large male lion was hiding in the bush nearby.

Sometimes, during the dry season, 20-40 lone elephant bulls can simultaneously gather at a water hole. Females tend to stick close to permanent sources water, which are found to the west along the Linyanti River or up north along the Chobe River.

A few bushmen paintings may be found in this region. Four-wheel-drive vehicles are necessary for the Savute.

ACCOMMODATION – CLASS A: * *Savute Safari Lodge*, situated within the park on the banks of the Savute Channel, has 12 Swedish-style wood-and-thatch chalets with ensuite bathrooms. The lounge, dining area and plunge pool overlook the channel. Day game drives are conducted. * *Savute Elephant Camp* is located within the park and has 12 luxury tents with ensuite facilities. Only day game drives are offered.

ACCOMMODATION NEAR SAVUTE – CLASS A: * *Savuti Camp* is located in a private concession between the Savute region of Chobe National Park and the Linyanti Swamps. The camp overlooks the dry Savuti Channel and a water hole, which attracts enormous quantities of game in the winter months. This luxury tented camp, with ensuite facilities and a plunge pool, caters to a maximum of eight guests. Day and night game drives, walks and game viewing from hides are offered. Game viewing is excellent April-November.

CAMPING: A *National Parks Campsite* is located near Savute Elephant Camp. The site is very sandy, and there is little shade. Toilet and shower facilities are not always operational. Beware of wild animals.

CHOBE NATIONAL PARK
(CHOBE RIVER/NORTHERN REGION)

Famous for its large herds of elephant, Chobe National Park covers about 4,250 square miles (11,000 km²) and is beautifully depicted in *Chobe — Africa's Untamed Wilderness* (Southern Book Publishers), by Daryl and Sharna Balfour. The park is situated only about 50 miles (80 km) from Victoria Falls in Zimbabwe, and the Chobe River forms its northern and northwestern boundaries. Across the river is Namibia's Caprivi Strip. Bird life is prolific, especially in the riverine areas.

The four main regions of the park are the northeast near Kasane, the Corridor around Ngwezumba and Nogatsaa, a portion of the Linyanti Swamps in the northwest, and the Savute (discussed above) in the west.

Northern Chobe is famous for its huge elephant and buffalo populations, which number in the thousands. Lion are often seen. The ele-

CHOBE NATIONAL PARK

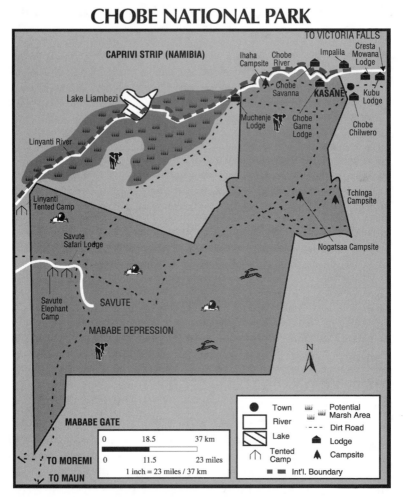

phant are some of the most vocal and active I've encountered on the continent, constantly trumpeting, making mock charges and sometimes sparring with each other. Great entertainment!

Game viewing by boat along the Chobe River can be spectacular, especially May-November in the dry season. Often large herds of elephant and a variety of other wildlife come down to the river to drink. On my last three visits we witnessed herds of 50-100 elephant swimming across the river at sunset. Mothers were assisting several babies in the herd to make it across. Once they reached the riverbank, the herds had dust baths and wandered off into the bush. This is an excellent park for boat game drives!

On a recent vehicle game drive we saw over 100 elephant, a pride of lion, greater kudu, hippo, sable antelope, fish eagles and crocs.

 Game viewing is actually very good during the mid-day at this park, as well as in the mornings and late afternoons. Animals can be seen making their way to the river to drink and may be seen along the river's edge at close range by both boat and vehicle.

Along the Chobe River, between the Chobe Game Lodge and the village of Kasane, you are likely to see numerous hippo, red lechwe, puku, common waterbuck, warthog and guinea fowl. Driving from the lodge toward the old Serondela Campsite, you can usually see giraffe, impala, zebra and occasionally kudu and Chobe bushbuck. Large monitor lizards are commonly seen.

The hot and dry Corridor (Ngwezumba to Nogatsaa) is one of the few areas in the country where oribi is found. Gemsbok, eland, ostrich and steenbok are sometimes seen. Prevalent species include giraffe, elephant, roan and sable antelope. The large populations of both resident and migratory elephant have inflicted severe damage on the riverine forest along the Chobe River, virtually eliminating the band of evergreen trees within the national park. Opinions vary as to whether this is a natural phenomenon or a result of too many elephants being hemmed in. As a consequence of the elephant browsing pressure, species dependent upon dense cover, such as the Chobe bushbuck and narina trogon, have become extremely rare.

One of the great highlights of the Chobe River is the breeding colonies (with up to 1,000 birds per colony) of carmine bee-eaters, which are active during the month of September and early October. These magnificent birds — dressed in pink and turquoise — provide a truly breathtaking spectacle. Other species found along the river are the rare rock pratincoles, African skimmer and large, mobile flocks of open-billed stork and spur-winged geese.

The northern region is accessible by 2wd vehicles, but 4wd vehicles are necessary for the rest of the park.

This is the only reserve in Botswana that may be crowded.

ACCOMMODATION – NORTHERN CHOBE – CLASS A: * *Chobe Chilwero Camp* has 15 luxurious air-conditioned cottages with ensuite facilities, balcony and outdoor shower. The lodge is located on an escarpment overlooking the park and Chobe River. Game viewing is by

Chobe Game Lodge, one of the most well-known lodges in Botswana.

vehicle and boat. * *Chobe Game Lodge* is a beautifully decorated, Moorish-style lodge, with 96 beds, set on the banks of the Chobe River within the park. The lodge has a large swimming pool and beautifully kept, spacious grounds. All rooms are air-conditioned and have ensuite facilities, and the four luxury suites have private swimming pools. Sundowner cruises and day game drives are offered.

CLASS A/B: * *Muchenje Safari Lodge* is located outside the western boundary of Chobe National Park on the Chobe River. The camp consists of 10 thatched chalets (20 guests) with ensuite facilities and swimming pool. Activities include game drives, boat trips and bush walks. * *Chobe Savanna Lodge*, located on the Namibian Banks of the Chobe River and overlooking the national park, has 12 stone-and-thatch cottages with private decks, air-conditioning, mini bars, ensuite bathrooms and swimming pool. Activities include early morning or evening game drives, sunset cruises, fishing and guided nature walks. * *Impalila Island Lodge,* situated on an island across from Chobe National Park in Namibia, has eight elevated chalets with ensuite facilities and swimming pool. Activities offered are mostly water based, including mokoro trips, boat game drives and fishing. * *Cresta Mowana Lodge* is located 5 miles (8 km) east of the park. All 112 rooms have ensuite facilities. Game drives by vehicle and by boat are offered.

CLASS B&C: * *Chobe Safari Lodge* has rooms and rondavels with private facilities, a swimming pool and boats for hire. A new wing of rooms has recently been built (Class B).

CLASS C: * *Kubu Lodge* has wood-and-thatch chalets with ensuite facilities, a swimming pool and spacious lawns. It is a 10-minute drive from the Chobe National Park gate.

CAMPING: The public campsites in Northern Chobe, Savute and Nogatsaa have toilets and showers, while the campsite at Tjinga has only a water tank. Ihaha, the new site for the public campsites in Northern Chobe (moved from Serondela), is often very crowded. The camps are accessible by 2wd vehicles and are close to Kasane. Beware of wild animals, including baboons, which may raid tents for food.

KASANE

Kasane is a small town only a few miles northeast of Chobe National Park about a two-hour drive from Victoria Falls (Zimbabwe). Many tourists are driven here from Victoria Falls and, after clearing customs at the border, begin their Botswana safari.

ACCOMMODATION – See "Chobe National Park" above.

CAMPING: Sites are available at * Chobe Safari Lodge and * Kubu Lodge.

NXAI PAN NATIONAL PARK

Nxai Pan National Park, well known for its huge springbok population, covers over 810 square miles (2,100 km²) and is located north of the Maun-Nata road in Northern Botswana.

The Nxai Pan is a fossil lake bed about 15 square miles (40 km²) in size; it is covered with grass during the rains. The landscape is dotted with baobab and acacia trees. Kgama-Kgama Pan is second to Nxai Pan in size.

In addition to southern giraffe, wildlife includes gemsbok, eland, greater kudu, blue wildebeest, red hartebeest, springbok, steenbok, brown and spotted hyena, cheetah and other predators. During the rains, elephant and buffalo may also be seen. After the first rains have fallen (December-April), game viewing can be good. Bird life is excellent during the rains.

Baines' Baobabs, situated in the park not far from the Maun-Nata road, were immortalized by the famous painter Thomas Baines in 1862. His painting, titled "The Sleeping Five," is of five baobabs, one

Makgadikgadi Pans.

of which is growing on its side. Seldom are baobab trees found growing so closely together. Baines' Baobabs were later painted by Prince Charles.

This park is seldom visited by international travelers because there are no permanent, fully catered camps. A 4wd vehicle is necessary.

ACCOMMODATION: None as of this writing. However, a permanent tented camp is expected to be built here in the near future.

CAMPING: There are two campsites, one of which has an ablution block. Water is usually available at both sites.

MAKGADIKGADI PANS GAME RESERVE

Makgadikgadi Pans Game Reserve includes a portion of the 4,600-square-mile (12,000-km²) Makgadikgadi Pans, which is the size of Portugal. The pans are nearly devoid of human habitation and give one a feeling of true isolation.

Once one of the world's largest prehistoric lakes, the Makgadikgadi Pans are now barren salt plains fringed with grasslands and isolated "land islands" of vegetation, baobab and palm trees. Scattered Stone Age tools have been found. Engravings left by explorers David Livingstone and Frederick Selous in the trunks of ancient baobab trees mark their passage through the region so many years ago.

Quad biking out from Jack's Camp.

The reserve itself covers about 1,550 square miles (3,900 km²) . It is located south of the Maun-Nata road in northern Botswana and borders Nxai Pan National Park to the north. Large herds of blue wildebeest, zebra, springbok, gemsbok and thousands of flamingos may be seen December-May. Other wildlife includes hyena, suricate and meerkat. A 4wd vehicle is highly recommended.

The highlight of my most recent visit was that I was able to see my first brown hyena. A den has been located near Jack's and San Camp, and the hyena have become habituated to human presence. This has to be one of the best places to see them in all of Africa!

The recently established **Nata Bird Sanctuary** is set on the eastern fringe of the Makgadikgadi Pans and provides a chance to view the aggregations of lesser and greater flamingos, white pelican, avocet, African spoonbill and other birds, which arrive here seasonally. Information on how to access the sanctuary and what birds might be present can be obtained at Nata Lodge. Thousands of flamingos may breed at Makgadikgadi but this is a highly unpredictable event and viewing is limited, because even the best-intentioned human observers can cause great disturbance, even nest desertion, by these sensitive birds.

 ACCOMMODATION: CLASS A: * *Jack's Camp* is a classic camp (16 beds) in the 40s safari style. The tents have private open-air bathrooms with flush toilets and bucket showers set behind each tent. Activities include day and night game drives, riding quad motorbikes on the pans, game walks with bushmen trackers and lectures by resident researchers. * *San Camp*, a 12-bed tented camp with private bush toilets and bucket showers, is set right on the edge of the pans, and it offers the same activities as Jack's Camp. The guides at both camps have university degrees in zoology, biology, anthropology or similar subjects. Adventurous two-night/three-day Kubu Island quad-bike trips are also offered.

ACCOMMODATION NEAR THE RESERVE: CLASS C: * *Planet Baobab* offers either traditional painted mud huts with ensuite facilities or grass huts and campsites with shared facilities. Cultural safaris and overnight fly camps to view fossil plates are offered. The Kalahari Surf Club offers a Pan experience — guests camp on the edge of the saltpans and take quad bike trips across the pans and escorted walks.

TOURIST CLASS: * *Nata Lodge*, located near the northeast border of the reserve just off the Nata/Francistown Road, has chalets and tents with ensuite facilities.

CAMPING: There are two camping areas with limited facilities. Travelers must be totally self-sufficient.

CENTRAL KALAHARI GAME RESERVE

This 20,000-square-mile (52,000-km²) reserve, one of the largest in the world, covers a portion of the Kalahari Desert. Wildlife is not abundant, but does include hartebeest, springbok, gemsbok, ostrich, eland, brown hyena, lion, cheetah and giraffe — especially during the rainy season (December-April).

Perhaps the best part of this gigantic reserve, from a visitor's perspective, is the Deception Valley area where American researchers Mark and Delia Owens were based during their work on the brown hyena. This drainage line is a hauntingly remote location, sparsely populated with mostly nomadic wildlife and thin vegetation.

ACCOMMODATION: CLASS A/B: * *Deception Valley Lodge*, located outside of the northern periphery of the reserve, has five large units with ensuite facilities and outside shower. Walks with bushmen guides offer an opportunity to learn about their hunting and survival skills, culture and crafts. Afternoon and night drives are available.

CAMPING: No facilities. Travelers must be self-sufficient and use 4wd vehicles.

KHUTSE GAME RESERVE

The Khutse Game Reserve shares its northern boundary with the Central Kalahari Game Reserve and is the closest reserve to Gaborone. Khutse covers 965 square miles (2,500 km²) of gently rolling savannah and pans (over 50) and is best known for its bird life.

Lion, leopard, cheetah and antelope have adapted to an arid environment. However, wildlife is seasonal and numbers depend on the rains. If there has been little rain, game is usually scarce. The best time to visit is after the rainy season has begun, usually December-April.

Khutse is a five-hour drive (136 miles/220 km) from Gaborone via Molepolole. The route is not well marked. Four-wheel-drive vehicles are essential.

ACCOMMODATION: None.

CAMPING: There is one public campsite with toilets. Water is available at the gate.

THE SOUTH

GABORONE

Gaborone, phonetically pronounced "Hab oh roni," is the capital of Botswana. In the center of town is the main shopping and commercial center - the Mall. Other than some shopping, there is little of interest for the international traveler, with the exception of the National Museum.

ACCOMMODATION – FIRST CLASS: * Grand Palm Hotel has 152 air-conditioned rooms, three restaurants, outdoor heated pool, fitness center, lighted tennis courts and business center. * The Gaborone Sun is located 1.5 miles (2 km) from the city center. This 203-room, air-conditioned hotel has a swimming pool, tennis and squash courts and casino. * The President Hotel is an air-conditioned hotel centrally located in the Mall.

Mashatu Main Camp, located in the Limpopo Valley.

NORTHERN TULI GAME RESERVE

In the remote southeastern corner of Botswana, at the confluence of the Limpopo and Shashe rivers, and at the junction of the borders of Botswana, South Africa and Zimbabwe, lies an area of approximately 180,000 acres (72,000 hectares). It is known historically as the Tuli enclave — a diverse wilderness of open grassland, mopane veld, riverine forest, semi-arid bush savannah, marshland, and sandstone outcrops.

Because the properties within the reserve are privately owned, they are generally less restricted than the private concession areas, reserves and national parks in Botswana, and may conduct activities such as off-road driving, walking with armed rangers, night game drives, horseback riding and mountain biking. This is a great reserve for the active traveler!

The Tuli is home to large herds of elephant, as well as lion, cheetah, eland, impala, wildebeest, giraffe and zebra. Bat-eared fox, African wild cat, hyena, jackal and leopard may be seen searching for prey.

The region is 5.5-hour drive from Johannnesburg and a six-hour drive from Gaborone. Alternatively, Air Botswana flies three times per week into the Limpopo Valley Airfield, which is situated within the Nothern Tuli Game Reserve. You may also fly by scheduled air charter from Johannesburg.

ACCOMMODATION – CLASS A: * *Mashatu Main Camp*, located on the Mashatu Game Reserve, accommodates a maximum of 34 guests in one suite, 11 twin superior rooms (with "his" and "her" bathrooms), and five standard rooms (all air-conditioned with ensuite facilities). The property has a floodlit waterhole and a swimming pool. Game viewing is conducted in open 4wd vehicles, on mountain bikes, on foot and on horseback. Fly camping is also offered. Mashatu Game Reserve, the largest and most diverse of the properties in the reserve with 70,000 acres (28,000 hectares) of privately owned land, is managed and owned by the same company that owns Mala Mala Game Reserve in South Africa. * *Nitani*, located in the northwest of the reserve on the banks of the Mojale River, has seven thatched ensuite chalets built on platforms with private swimming pools.

ACCOMMODATION – CLASS A/B: * *Tuli Safari Lodge*, situated on the banks of the Limpopo River, has 10 thatched chalets with ensuite facilities and swimming pool.

ACCOMMODATION – CLASS B: * *Mashatu Tent Camp*, set in a remote northern area of the Mashatu Game Reserve, accommodates up to 14 guests in seven fan-cooled tents, with ensuite facilities and plunge pool. Guests explore the reserve in 4wd vehicles, on foot, with mountain bikes and on horseback.

ACCOMMODATION – CLASS C: * *Tumelo*, located on the banks of the Limpopo River, has six fan-cooled ensuite thatched chalets and a family unit, and swimming pool. Day and night game drives and walks are offered.

ACCOMMODATION – CLASS D: * *Kolobe* is a basic tented camp (small tents) with separate ablution facilities, set on the northern bank of the Limpopo River. Game drives and walks are offered.

MABUASEHUBE GAME RESERVE

Mabuasehube is an extremely remote reserve in southwestern Botswana. Mabuasehube is about 695 square miles (1,800 km²) in size and shares its western border with Kgalagadi Transfrontier Park. The park has six large pans and sand dunes over 100 feet (30 m) high.

The best time to visit is during and just after the rainy season (December-April), when a variety of arid-adapted animals can be seen. Springbok are present in good numbers, while gemsbok, eland and red hartebeest are sparse, but are likely to be seen. This is an excellent locality for the elusive brown hyena, and impressive Kalahari lions are invariably present. Other interesting mammals seen here are the Cape fox, honey badger, aardwolf and aardvark. Among the many interesting birds here are the secretary bird, kori bustard, black-breasted snake eagle, crimson-breasted shrike and the swallow-tailed bee-eater. The huge communal nests of the sociable weaver are a feature of this pristine landscape. At sunset the sand-veld comes alive to the clicking sound of barking geckos, calling from their burrow entrances.

Mabuasehube is 333 miles (533 km) from Gaborone. A 4wd vehicle is needed, and the drive takes at least 11 hours.

 ACCOMMODATION: None.

CAMPING: No facilities. Water may be available at the Game Scouts Camp.

KGALAGADI TRANSFRONTEIR PARK
See "Kgalagadi Transfrontier Park" in the chapter on South Africa for details.

ZIMBABWE

THE ENDANGERED BLACK RHINO

This poor-sighted, bad-tempered mammal has been under intense poaching in the last few years due to the high price its hair-like horn fetches in the Yemen and Far East markets. The horn is used for dagger handles, which are a sign of wealth in Yemen, and for "medicinal" purposes in the Far East. To encourage its preservation, several programs have evolved in addition to working to lower demand.

Programs to dehorn rhinos have been conducted in some reserves to deter poaching, as the "value" of the rhino to poachers is its horn. However, there have been reports that poachers shoot the dehorned rhino as well. But since the rhinos' horns are used for defense, studies are being conducted to determine how the dehorning affects their behavior.

National parks have also employed antipoaching teams to patrol the parks, resulting in some protection to the rhino and the arrest of suspected poachers within the parks. Rhinos are creatures of habit; they return to the same drinking holes every day and can therefore be easily found by poachers.

So as not to be detected, black rhino may visit their drinking holes at night. This pattern of night drinking can interfere with their much-loved midday mud-wallow, where they will lie down in the mud to cool off.

In order to better protect the black rhino from poachers, many have been relocated into newly created IPZs (Intensive Protection Zones) within some national parks and in some private reserves which currently hold a large percentage of the existing population.

The relocation process involves tracking the animals for a distance and darting them with a sedative. Rhinos usually have the noisy red- or yellow-billed oxpeckers acting as their sentries — warning them of human approach. This makes it difficult for the darter to get close enough to shoot. Once under sedation, the rhinos are moved to their new (hopefully safer) homes.

Black rhino are exciting to track and, with luck, may be found on a morning's walk in certain reserves. Since the rhino has no natural enemy, there is no reason he should not survive if left alone by man.

ZIMBABWE

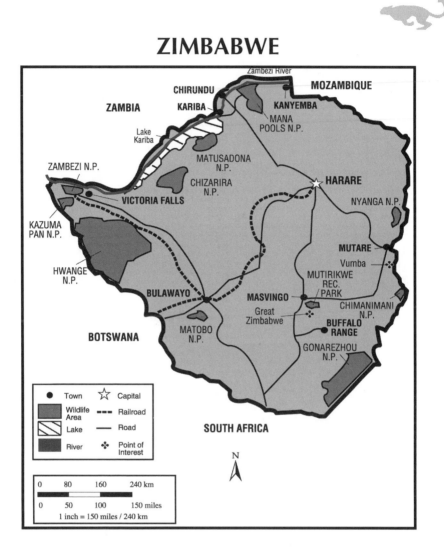

FACTS AT A GLANCE

AREA: 150,872 sq. mi. / 390,759 sq. km
APPROXIMATE SIZE: California or one and a half times
the size of Great Britain
POPULATION: 11.5 million
CAPITAL: Harare (pop. est. 2.0 million)
OFFICIAL LANGUAGE: English
OTHER: Shona and Ndebele

ZIMBABWE

Thought by some to be the land of King Solomon's mines, Zimbabwe (previously called Rhodesia) is a country blessed with good farmland, mineral wealth, beautiful and varied landscapes, and excellent game parks.

Most of Zimbabwe consists of a central plateau, 3,000-4,000 feet (915-1,220 m) above sea level. The highveld, or high plateau, stretches from southwest to northeast from 4,000 to 5,000 feet (1,220 to 1,525 m) with a mountainous region along the eastern border from 6,000 to 8,000 feet (1,830 to 2,440 m) in altitude.

The northern border is formed by the mighty Zambezi River, while the Limpopo River creates the division between Zimbabwe and South Africa in the south. The spectacular Victoria Falls were created by a fracture in the Zambezi Valley, which is an extension of the Great Rift Valley.

Zimbabwe is a land-locked country, but it is rich in biological diversity due to its proximity to the temperate south, tropical north and semi-arid west. Much of the country is a highland plateau at about 3,300 feet (1,000 m) above sea level on one of the world's oldest granite formations. In the north and south, the Zambezi and Limpopo River valleys, respectively, create hot lowlands as well as international boundaries. The granite shield forms the main watershed of the country, with numerous spectacular rock formations. This plateau is dominated by miombo woodland, but is also ideal farming country, so much of the natural vegetation has been replaced.

The so-called Eastern Highlands are a chain of sandstone and basalt mountains, characterized by a cooler, wetter climate. The highest peaks rise above 6,500 feet (2,000 m). Temperate forests occur in patches from Nyanga to Chimanimani, and sub-tropical forests are found in the humid lowlands of the Honde, Burma and Rusitu valleys, which enter Mozambique. In the western part of the country, on the border with Botswana, deep Kalahari sands dominate in places and create yet another unique environment for wildlife.

The climate is moderate on the central plateau, but hot in the low-lying Zambezi and Limpopo valleys. Seasons are reversed from the northern hemisphere. Winter days (May-August) are generally dry and sunny with day temperatures averaging 59-68°F (15-20°C). Summer daytime temperatures average 77-86°F (25-30°C), and October is the hottest month. The rainy season is December-March.

The major ethnic groups are the Mashona and Ndebele. About 50% of the population is syncretic (part Christian and part traditional beliefs), 25% Christian, 24% traditional and 1% Hindu and Muslim. Twenty-five percent of the population lives in urban areas, with half of that 25% residing in the cities of Harare and nearby Chitungwiza. English is understood by a majority of the population.

In the first century, the region was inhabited by hunters related to the San Bushmen. Cecil Rhodes and the British South Africa Company took control in 1890, and the area was named Southern Rhodesia, which became a British colony in 1923. Prime Minister Ian Smith and the white minority declared unilateral independence from Britain on November 11, 1965. Zimbabwe officially became independent on April 18, 1980, with Robert Mugabe as president.

Main foreign exchange earners are tobacco, minerals, agriculture and tourism.

Zimbabwe has had more than its share of political and economic woes during the last few years. As of this writing, security at Zimbabwe's major attractions (Victoria Falls, Hwange, Matobo, Matusadona and Mana Pools) has been fine, and tourists who have traveled there have been handsomely rewarded with excellent wildlife viewing and guiding in uncrowded parks.

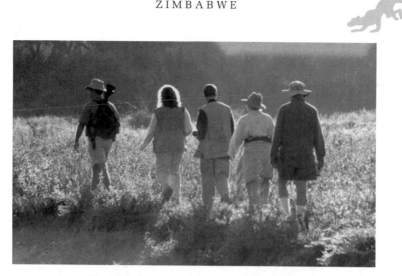

Zimbabwe has some of the best walking guides.

WILDLIFE AND WILDLIFE AREAS

Adventurers wishing to do more than view wildlife from a vehicle should seriously consider a safari in Zimbabwe. It offers the greatest variety of methods of wildlife viewing in Africa, including day and night game drives in open vehicles, boat game drives, walking, backpacking, canoeing, kayaking and travel by houseboat.

As mentioned earlier, the country is situated at the junction of three major climatic zones (temperate south, tropical northeast and semi-arid west), and there is a resultant diversity of wildlife. All of Africa's big-game species are here, as well as over 660 bird species and an amazing variety of reptiles, frogs and invertebrates. Plant life is equally impressive, from Afro-alpine proteas in the east to tropical baobabs in the hot valleys of the north and south. The distinctive miombo woodlands (dominated by *Brachystegia* trees) are characterized by a unique variety of plants and associated wildlife. Birdwatching is hugely rewarding and many ornithological groups visit the country.

Zimbabwe offers excellent and well-maintained parks and reserves. The country's three premier reserves, which also rate among the best in Africa, are Hwange, Mana Pools and Matusadona National Parks.

Hwange National Park is famous for its huge elephant population (over 25,000) and numerous large pans. Matusadona National Park, located along the southern shores of beautiful Lake Kariba, has enormous buffalo and elephant populations. During the dry season, Mana Pools on the Zambezi River has one of the highest concentrations of wildlife of any park on the continent.

Many of the safari camps cater to only six to 16 guests and offer personalized service, excellent accommodations and superb guiding. The professional guiding standards in Zimbabwe are, in fact, the highest of any country on the continent.

Instead of driving to the reserves, many people fly to the parks, taking advantage of scheduled charter flights connecting Victoria Falls, Hwange, Matobo Hills, Matusadona, Mana Pools and Harare. There are also a number of deluxe, first class and participation group or private mobile tented safaris available, during which guests are driven from park to park or combine driving and flying.

Game viewing is by open vehicle, and walking is allowed with a licensed Professional Guide who carries a high-caliber rifle at all times. Night game drives are conducted in some areas adjacent to the reserves and on some private concessions within the reserves.

THE WEST

VICTORIA FALLS NATIONAL PARK

Dr. David Livingstone became the first European man to see Victoria Falls on November 16, 1855, and named them after the British queen of his day. In his journal he wrote, "Scenes so lovely must have been gazed upon by angels in flight."

Victoria Falls is approximately 5,600 feet (1,700 m) wide, twice the height of Niagara Falls, and one and one-half times as wide. It is divided into five separate waterfalls: Devil's Cataract, Main Falls, Horseshoe Falls, Rainbow Falls and Eastern Cataract, ranging in height from 200 to 355 feet (61 to 108 m).

Peak floodwaters usually occur around mid-April when 150 million gallons (625 million *l*) per minute crash onto the rocks below, spraying water up to 1,650 feet (500 m) in the air. During March-April, so much water is falling that the spray makes it difficult to see the falls.

May-February is actually a better time to see them, but keep in mind that they are spectacular any time of the year.

Victoria Falls and the Zambezi River form the border between Zambia and Zimbabwe. The banks of the 1,675-mile- (2,700-km) long Zambezi River, the fourth largest river in Africa and the only major river in Africa to flow into the Indian Ocean, are lined with thick riverine forest.

A rainbow over the falls can often be seen during the day and a lunar rainbow within a two- to four-night period over a full moon.

Fortunately, the area around the falls has not been commercialized on the Zimbabwe side of the falls, and there are unobstructed views from many vantage points, which are connected by paved paths. An entry fee (currently US $20.00) is required. Be prepared to get wet as you walk through a luxuriant rain forest surrounding the falls, a result of the continuous spray. A path called the Chain Walk descends from near Livingstone's statue into the gorge of the Devil's Cataract, which provides an excellent vantage point.

Victoria Falls can also be viewed from Zambia. Zambian visas for day visits are generally available at the border for most nationalities. Generally speaking, the falls are more impressive on the Zimbabwean side.

Mammals that can be seen in close proximity to the falls include the beautifully marked bushbuck, vervet monkey and banded mongoose. Birds to look out for include the noisy trumpeter hornbill, green pigeon and Schalow's turaco, which feed on figs, and the rock pratincole, reed cormorant and giant kingfisher that may be found in the rapids above the falls. One of Africa's rarest birds of prey, the diminutive Taita falcon, is frequently seen on the cliffs below the falls, alongside peregrine falcon, augur buzzard and Verreaux's (black) eagle.

The **Zambezi Nature Sanctuary** has crocodiles up to 14 feet (4.3 m) in length and weighing close to 1,000 pounds (450 kg). The **Craft Village** in the middle of town has living quarters and other structures representing the traditional Zimbabwean life of the country's major tribes, and it features the best African dance show in town. Tribal dancing may also be seen at the Boma Restaurant at Victoria Falls

Victoria Falls, as seen from the Rain Forest.

Safari Lodge. **Big Tree** is a giant baobab over 50 feet (15 m) in circumference, 65 feet (20 m) high and 1,000 — 1,500 years old.

Sundowner cruises operate above the falls, where hippo may be spotted and elephant and other wildlife may be seen coming to the shore to drink.

The **"Flight of Angels,"** a flight over the falls by helicopter (best choice) or in a small plane, is highly recommended to acquire a feeling for the true majesty of the falls. Game-viewing flights, upstream from the falls along the Zambezi River and over Victoria Falls National Park, are also available. It is best to reserve seats in advance.

One of the world's highest commercially run **bungee jumps** is operated on the bridge crossing the Zambezi River. After falling over 300 feet (100 m), a member of the bungee staff is lowered to the jumper and connects a cable to his harness. The jumper is winched into the upright position and then winched back up onto the bridge.

Canoeing and kayaking safaris are a great way to explore the upper Zambezi, from near Kazungula to just above Victoria Falls. Adventurers pass numerous hippo, crocs, elephant and other wildlife as they paddle two-man kayaks or canoes on safaris ranging from a half-day to four days in length. No previous kayaking or canoeing experience is necessary. Accommodation is in tents with separate bush shower and toilet facilities.

Half and full-day **horseback rides** around the Victoria Falls area are available for novice and experienced riders, while multi-day horseback safaris are available only for experienced riders. Morning and afternoon **elephant back safaris** (African elephants) provide another interesting way to experience the bush and to view some game, and they are less expensive than those offered in Botswana.

White-Water Rafting

The upper Zambezi River offers one of the most exciting and challenging white-water rafting trips in the world. There are numerous fifth-class rapids, which are the highest class runable, and these can be experienced either with a professional oarsman at the helm or in a raft with everyone paddling.

One-, two-, three- and seven-day trips are operated on the Zambezi River below Victoria Falls from the Zambian and/or Zimbabwean side of the Zambezi River. No experience is required; just hang on and enjoy the ride! The one-day trip is rated as the wildest commercially run one-day trip in the world. For some travelers, this trip is a highlight of their safari.

For the even more adventurous, there is **boogie boarding** on the rapids. This is often done in conjunction with a half or full day of white-water rafting.

Around 8:30 a.m., rafters walk down into the gorge to the river's edge where the rafting safari begins. Rafts with up to eight paddlers, or up to eight riders and one oarsperson, disappear from sight as they drop into deep holes and crash into waves over 12 feet (3.5 m) high, and they are further dwarfed by sheer cliffs that often rise hundreds of feet on both sides of the canyon.

Each group is usually accompanied by a professional kayaker who helps "rescue" those who have fallen out of the rafts.

At the end of the trip, rafters have to climb back out of the gorge to the top of the escarpment, about 700 feet (213 m) above. For most people, this is the most difficult part of the excursion.

For the one-day trip, I would suggest you wear a swimsuit and take a hat, sunglasses with something to tie them onto yourself, a short-sleeve shirt, sunscreen and tennis shoes (tackies) or Tevas (a type of sandal). For longer trips, obtain a checklist from your tour operator.

The Victoria Falls Safari Lodge - one of the largest hotels under thatch.

One-day trips are offered year-round, water levels permitting. Longer rafting safaris (two to seven days) are usually run August-December. Rafters must be 16 years of age or older to participate.

Hippo and crocs are seen from the second day onward on multi-day trips. Kudu and other wildlife can be seen on the banks, especially during the dry season. Camp is made on sandy riverbanks, and all meals are prepared by the staff. These multi-day trips are not for those who wish to be pampered. There are no facilities enroute.

ACCOMMODATION: The Victoria Falls Hotel, The Kingdom and Ilala Lodge have the advantage of being located nearest to the falls.

DELUXE: * *Victoria Falls Hotel* has maintained much of its colonial elegance, including colonial architecture, spacious terraces and colorful gardens, and it is only a 10-minute walk from Victoria Falls. The hotel has 181 air-conditioned rooms and suites with ensuite facilities, swimming pool and tennis courts. From the hotel you can see the bridge and the Zambezi Gorge. * *Victoria Falls Safari Lodge*, located a five-minute drive from the falls, has 72 stylishly decorated air-conditioned rooms and suites with ensuite facilities, and a swimming pool. The lodge is built under thatch and overlooks a floodlit water hole where wildlife may be seen coming to drink. Optional excursions to a hide overlooking a waterhole are offered. A complementary hourly shuttle service is available to Victoria Falls town and to the entrance to the falls.
* *Elephant Hills Intercontinental* overlooks the Zambezi River a few miles upstream from Victoria Falls. The hotel has 276 rooms and suites with facilities ensuite, an exotic swimming pool, squash courts, tennis courts, a world-class 18-hole championship golf course, three restaurants and a conference center.

FIRST CLASS: * *Ilala Lodge*, a small, 32-room thatched lodge with ensuite facilities and a swimming pool, is located within walking distance to the falls. * *The Kingdom Hotel* is only a 10-minute walk from the falls and has 294 air-conditioned rooms with ensuite facilities, that are separated in two and three-story units, a casino, food court and swimming pool. This is a good hotel for families.

TOURIST CLASS: * *Sprayview Hotel* is a budget hotel with rooms with ensuite facilities located a little more than a mile (2 km) from the falls. * *Rainbow Hotel* is located near Victoria Falls village and has 88 air-conditioned rooms with private facilities and a swimming pool. * *The A-Zambezi River Lodge*, one of the largest buildings under traditional thatch on the continent, is located 1.5 miles (2.5 km) from town on the banks of the Zambezi River. The lodge has a swimming pool and 83 air-conditioned rooms with ensuite facilities. The hotel gives complementary scheduled transfers to the town and the falls.

CLASS D, F AND CAMPING: * *Victoria Falls Rest and Caravan Park* has self-catering cottages, a small hostel, camping and trailer (caravan) sites, swimming pool and restaurant.

ACCOMMODATION NEAR VICTORIA FALLS – CLASS A: * *The Stanley and Livingstone*, situated on a 6,075-acre (2430-hectare) private estate a 10-minute drive from the falls, has 10 suites with ensuite facilities. A raised patio overlooks nearby waterholes. * *Elephant Camp*, located on a private wildlife estate 15 miles (25 km) from Victoria Falls, offers morning and afternoon elephant rides (African elephants) and game drives. A maximum of eight guests are accommodated in four thatched cottages with ensuite facilities. *Sekuti's Drift* is a colonial-style 10-room lodge situated on top of a hill 9 miles (15 km) from Victoria Falls. * *Masuwe Lodge* is a 20-bed tented lodge located 4 miles (7 km) from Victoria Falls on a private game concession that adjoins Zambezi National Park. * *Matetsi Safari Lodge* and * *Matetsi Water Lodge* are situated on a private game reserve about a 45-minute drive from Victoria Falls. Matetsi Water Lodge has three riverside camps, each with six air-conditioned ensuite bedrooms, fan-cooled living rooms and private splash pools. Matetsi Safari Lodge consists of a tented camp with 12 air-conditioned luxury tents. Day and night game drives, walks, boat cruises, fishing and canoeing are offered. * *Imbabala Camp*, located on private land on the banks of the Zambezi River only a mile (2 km) from the Botswana border, has eight chalets (doubles) with ensuite facilities and a swimming pool. Day and night game drives by vehicle, boat game drives and fishing are offered.

NORTHWESTERN ZIMBABWE

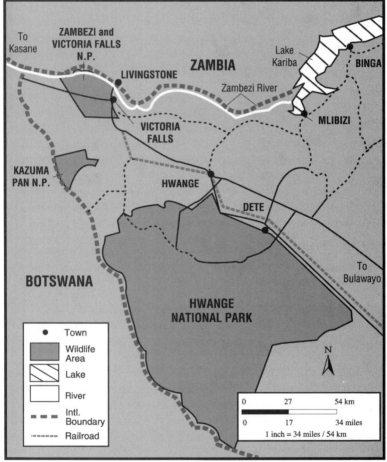

CLASS A/B: *Gorges Lodge*, located 15 miles (24 km) from Victoria Falls, overlooks the Zambezi Gorge and has six single and four double-story rooms with ensuite facilities and a swimming pool.

CLASS D: See "Zambezi National Park."

ZAMBEZI NATIONAL PARK

Victoria Falls National Park includes Victoria Falls as well as the 216-square-mile (560-km²) Zambezi National Park. The park is located west of the falls and extends for 25 miles (40 km) along the Zambezi River.

Zambezi National Park is well known for its abundance of sable antelope, among other species, such as elephant, zebra, eland, buffalo, giraffe, lion, kudu and waterbuck. Noteworthy birds include collared palm thrush, white-breasted cuckooshrike, racquet-tailed roller, African finfoot, Schalow's turaco, Pel's fishing owl and rock pratincole.

Day game drives, walks, canoeing and kayaking are offered from Victoria Falls. Fishing for tigerfish and tilapia is good. There are 30 sites along the river for picnicking and fishing (beware of crocodiles). Since the game reserve does not have all-weather roads, parts of it are usually closed during the rains from November 1 to May 1.

 ACCOMMODATION – CLASS A/B: * *Chamabondo Lodge*, located in the Chamabondo Valley within Zambezi National Park overlooking a waterhole, has nine thatched lodges with private bathrooms. Game drives, escorted walks, and tours of the falls and cultural visits are offered.

ACCOMMODATION – CLASS D: * *Zambezi National Park Lodges*, scenically situated on the banks of the Zambezi, consist of 15 self-service lodges, each catering to a maximum of six people.

KAZUMA PAN NATIONAL PARK
Located north of Hwange National Park in the Matetsi Safari Area, Kazuma Pan National Park is a small park (121 square miles/313 km²) that has a series of pans that flood in the rainy season. The eastern part of the park is wooded, with more water and a greater variety and concentration of wildlife than the western side of the park, which is predominantly grasslands. Lion and cheetah may be seen.

This is an outstanding park for birdwatchers during the rainy season, when large aggregations of ducks, geese, storks, ibises, herons and egrets forage in the seasonal wetlands.

The park is open to campers who are self-contained. Walking is allowed with a professionally licensed guide. As there are no facilities, visitors generally stay in mobile tented camps with their own private guides.

HWANGE NATIONAL PARK
Hwange (previously called Wankie), Zimbabwe's largest national

HWANGE NATIONAL PARK

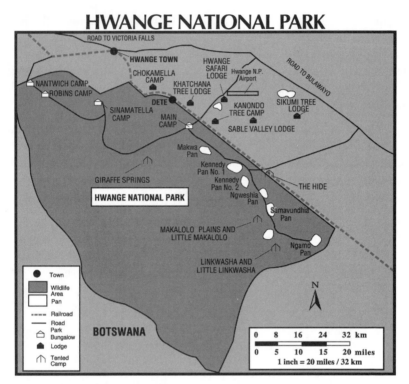

park, is famous for its large herds of elephant. Other predominant species include rhino, buffalo, giraffe, zebra, wildebeest, lion, wild dog and bat-eared fox. This is one of the best parks on the continent to see sable antelope.

Hwange is slightly larger than the state of Connecticut, covering 5,656 square miles (14,651 km²). The park is located in the northwest corner of the country, just west of the main road between Bulawayo and Victoria Falls. Hwange boasts over 100 species of mammals and 400 species of birds.

The park ranges from semi-desert in the south to a plateau in the north. The northern part of Hwange is mudstone and basalt, and the southern part is Kalahari sand veld. The park has an average altitude of 3,300 feet (1,000 m). Winter nights can drop to below freezing, and summer days can be over 100°F (38°C), while average temperatures range from 65 to 83°F (18 to 28°C).

There are no rivers and only a few streams in the north of the park, but waterholes (fed by wells) provide sources of water year-round for wildlife. During the dry season, these permanent water holes (pans) provide an excellent stage for guests to view wildlife performing day-to-day scenes of survival.

Generally, there are no seasonal animal migrations. The best time to see wildlife is during the dry season, from July to October, when the game concentrates near permanent water. Game viewing is good in May, June and November, and fair December through April. During the rainy season from January to March, game is widely dispersed in the mopane woodland. However, game viewing is actually good year-round in the Makalolo/Linkwasha region of the park.

An estimated population of 28,000 elephants lives in Hwange, although these animals move freely to the north and west into Botswana. Nevertheless, the browsing pressure of these great pachyderms is a threat to the extensive hardwood forests upon which other wildlife is dependent. Birdwatching is excellent, and numerous Kalahari-sand specialists are present in good numbers. Kori bustard, Bradfield's hornbill, crimson-breasted bushshrike, swallow-tailed bee-eater and scaly-feathered finch are all abundant. Hwange is an important refuge for birds of prey, with bateleur, martial eagle and white-headed vulture among the species that enjoy sanctuary here.

The wilderness area of Hwange in the southeastern part of the park is excellent for seeing a great variety of game and is much less crowded than the "Main Camp" area. There are only four safari camps in this private area — Makalolo, Little Makalolo, Linkwasha and Little Linkwasha. On a short visit we saw sable, giraffe, lion, bat-eared fox, hyena, buffalo, elephant, warthog, wildebeest and zebra. We took an evening game drive to Ngweshla Pan, a morning walk to Mbisa Pan, and another evening drive to Ngamo Flats, and we encountered only a few other vehicles from the Makalolo/Linkwasha family of camps. The combination of great game and exclusivity make this the best region in Hwange for an overall wildlife experience.

Wildlife commonly seen include elephant, rhino, giraffe, zebra, greater kudu, impala, buffalo, sable antelope, wildebeest, tsessebe, black-backed jackal, lion and hyena. On a recent visit in May, we saw sable antelope, lion, giraffe, hyena, buffalo, elephant, wildebeest,

Makalolo Plains Camp.

zebra and about a dozen bat-eared fox. On another visit we saw a very large, full-maned lion guarding a buffalo kill while a jackal darted in and out, snatching morsels as dozens of vultures waited their turn.

Another time we sat in a tree hide by a water hole and watched over 30 giraffe come to drink. From a ground-level hide, we watched as a herd of over 70 eland passed within 65 feet (30 m) and 10 buffalo came within 30 feet (9 m) of us.

Moonlight game viewing is best from one or two nights before and after a full moon, when park staff escort guests to the Nyamandhlovu (meaning "meat of the elephant") Platform near Main Camp. Morning walks with a national park game scout may be available. Camps that have Professional Guides on staff may also offer walks in certain regions of the park.

The area around Sinamatella Camp in the northern part of the park is good for spotting kudu, elephant, giraffe, impala, hippo, klipspringer, warthog, lion, hyena and leopard. The Bumbusi Ruins of ancient stone building are located behind Bumbusi Camp, 15 miles (24 km) northwest of Sinamatella Camp.

The northwestern part of the park near Robins Camp has a large lion population. Other species often seen include impala (which attract the lion), buffalo, greater kudu, sable antelope, roan antelope, waterbuck, elephant, giraffe, reedbuck, tsessebe, lion, side-striped jackal, cheetah and spotted hyena.

Hwange has 300 miles (480 km) of roads, some of which are closed during the rainy season. All-weather roads run through most of the park. Some roads near the main camp are tarmac, which detracts a bit from the feeling of being in the bush.

Vehicles must keep to the roads, and visitors are not allowed to leave their vehicles unless escorted by a licensed Professional Guide, or in designated areas, such as hides, game-viewing platforms or at fenced-in picnic sites. Open vehicles are allowed only for licensed tour operators.

Airstrips for small aircraft are available at Makalolo, Giraffe Springs and at Main Camp; large and small aircraft may land at Hwange Airport. The closest rail station is Dete Station, 15 miles (24 km) from Main Camp.

Luxury, first class and participation mobile tented camp safaris to the northern part of the park are also available.

ACCOMMODATIONS: Makalolo Plains, Little Makalolo, Linkwasha and Little Linkwasha are located in one exclusive area deep within the park. Only guests of those camps are allowed in this region of the park. Giraffe Springs Camp is also located in another exclusive area. The Hide is located on a private reserve; guests enter the park through the Kennedy Pan entrance. Sable Valley Lodge, Sikumi Tree Lodge, Khatshana Tree Lodge and Hwange Safari Lodge are all located in 60,000-acre (24,000-hectare) Dete Vlei (private reserve) bordering Hwange National Park, a 30-60-minute drive from Hwange National Park; guests of these camps and Kanondo Tree Camp enter the park through the Main Gate.

CLASS A: * *Makalolo Plains* has nine luxury tents, including a family tent with ensuite facilities, set on raised wooden platforms, and a plunge pool. Raised wooden walkways connect the sleeping tents with the lounge/dining room area. * *Little Makalolo* has five luxury tents with ensuite facilities. Both Makalolo and Little Makalolo have hides over-looking their respective camp water holes, and guests can overnight in these hides * *Linkwasha Camp* consists of seven tents with ensuite bath-rooms. * *Little Linkwasha* consists of three tents with ensuite bathrooms. Activities at all four of the above camps include day and night game drives, walks and visits to hides. * *The Hide* is a luxury tented camp only a 10-minute drive from the Kennedy Pan entrance to the park. The camp overlooks a water hole and has 10 large "Manyara" tents with ensuite facilities. Two guests may overnight in the Dove's Nest Treehouse. Day game drives are offered in the park; walks and night drives are offered on the private concession. * *Giraffe Springs Camp*, located in its own private concession area within the park, has 10 luxury tents with ensuite facilities and a swimming pool.

CLASS A/B: * *Sable Valley Lodge* overlooks a water hole and accommodates up to 30 guests in luxury thatched lodges with ensuite facilities. Day game drives and walks are offered. * *Sikumi Tree Lodge* has 14 thatched tree houses (32 beds) set in acacia trees, all with private facilities, and a swimming pool. Activities include day game drives and walks. Children are welcome. * *Khatshana Tree Lodge* has six tree houses, with ensuite facilities, overlooking a water hole.

CLASS B: * *Kanondo Tree Camp* accommodates a maximum of 14 guests in tree houses with ensuite facilities. * *Detema Lodge* has nine tree houses and four family rooms with ensuite facilities and a swimming pool. Day and night game drives and walks are offered. * *Hwange Safari Lodge* has 100 double rooms with ensuite facilities and a swimming pool, conference center and elevated game-viewing platform with a bar overlooking a waterhole. * *Chokamella Camp* has 10 brick chalets under thatch with private facilities and a small swimming pool.

CLASS D, F & CAMPING: There are seven National Park camps — Main Camp, Sinamatella Camp, Robins Camp, Bumbusi Camp, Lukosi Camp, Deka Camp and Nantwich Camp — all of which have lodge accommodation. Some rooms have ensuite facilities. Ablution blocks are available for campers and for people in rooms without ensuite facilities.

MATOBO (MATOPOS) NATIONAL PARK

Hundreds of kopjes supporting thousands of precariously balanced rocks give the 164-square-mile (424-km²) Matobo National Park one of the most unusual landscapes in Africa. One jewel of a park, it is a well-kept secret and is a highlight of many safaris. The park is divided into two sections — a general recreational area, with popular pony trails, and a game reserve.

Matobo National Park has the highest concentration of eagles in the world, with 58 pairs of black eagles, 45 pairs of African hawk eagle, 32 pairs of Wahlberg's eagle and five pairs of crowned eagle known to exist within the reserve.

Part of the park is an IPZ (Intensive Protection Zone) and contains one of the highest concentrations of black and white rhino in Africa. Leopard are plentiful but are seldom seen. Other wildlife includes a large population of sable antelope along with giraffe, zebra, civet, genet, black-backed and side-striped jackal, caracal and porcupine.

Elephant back excursion among the kopjes.

Other birdlife includes purple-crested lourie, boulder chat, and both peregrine and lanner falcon.

In addition to viewing game, on our most recent visit we visited rock painting sites, took an morning elephant back ride, and then visited a rural clinic, a primary school and an authentic African healer in her village. This is definitely one of the best areas to visit for a quality cultural experience.

The elephant ride was scenic, up through the kopjes to the top for a panoramic view of the rugged landscape. The clinic proved to be surprisingly clean. While visiting the primary school, several classes sang to us, and our kids really enjoyed the visit. During our meeting with the African healer, our guide served as the interpreter as we exchanged questions about how she works and how she came to be a healer. An extraordinary experience, we were fascinated by the interesting hut with animal skins, potions, etc., all over the walls.

The region has over 3,000 San Bushman rock paintings — more than any other place in Africa. **Nswatugi Cave** rock paintings include images of giraffe and antelope. For **Bambata Cave** rock paintings, allow one and one-half hours for the hike. **White Rhino Shelter** rock paintings are also worth a visit.

Cecil Rhodes was buried on a huge rock kopje called "**View of the World**," from which there are sensational panoramas of the rugged countryside, especially at sunrise. A colony of dazzling platysaurus flat lizards may be seen at Rhode's gravesite; the colorful reptiles provide great photographic opportunities.

ACCOMMODATION – CLASS A: * *Amalinda Camp*, attractively built into enormous kopjes, has 10 chalets with ensuite facilities, and a magnificent natural rock pool. Activities include game drives, walks and horseback riding in the park and on the game ranch, elephant riding, day visits to nearby villages and Bushman paintings. The camp is located about a 10-minute drive from the park.

CLASS A/B: * *Big Cave Lodge* has six chalets (12 beds) with ensuite facilities. Game drives, horseback riding within the reserve, visits to local villages and Bushman paintings are offered. * *Matobo Hills Lodge*, located in a beautiful "amphitheater" of rock kopjes about a 10-minute drive from the park, has 17 thatched chalets (doubles) and a swimming pool creatively built into the rocks. Game drives, walks, horseback riding and visits to Bushman paintings and local villages are offered.

ACCOMMODATION NEAR THE PARK – CLASS A/B: * *Malalangwe Lodge*, located on a 6,300-acre (2,500-hectare) ranch about an hour drive from the park, has seven luxury chalets (14 beds) with ensuite facilities. Game drives, walks and hikes to Bushman paintings on their private game farm as well as day trips to Matobo National Park are offered.

A bedroom built into the rocks at Amalinda Camp.

 CAMPING: Camping and caravan sites with ablution blocks are available at Maleme Dam and Toghwana Dam.

CLASSES D & F: * *National Park* bungalows with and without ensuite facilities are available.

BULAWAYO

Bulawayo is the second largest city in Zimbabwe and holds the **National Museum** and **Railway Museum** — both well worth a visit. Some visitors to Matobo National Park fly in to Bulawayo Airport.

Chipangali Wildlife Orphanage, 15 miles (24 km) southwest of Bulawayo on the Esigodini/Beit Bridge Road, cares for a variety of young animals, often including lion, leopard, genet, civet, elephant and chimpanzee. Chipangali is well known for its pioneering work on a variety of duiker species, some of which may be seen in captivity there.

 ACCOMMODATION – FIRST CLASS: * *Induna Lodge* has six rooms (12 beds) with ensuite facilities, swimming pool, sauna, personalized service and excellent food. * *Churchill Arms Hotel* is a modern Tudor-style hotel with 50 rooms with ensuite facilities, located 4 miles (6 km)

Sun – downers.

 from the city center. * *Holiday Inn Bulawayo* is located in the center of town and has 150 air-conditioned rooms with ensuite facilities.
* *Nesbitt Castle*, built in 1906 by a Scottish architect, has nine exclusive suites with ensuite bathrooms and is located only a few miles/kilometers from the city.

THE NORTH

KARIBA (TOWN)

Kariba is a gateway to both Matusadona and Mana Pools National Parks. Some people fly there from Harare, Victoria Falls, Hwange or Lusaka (Zambia) and are then transferred by aircraft, boat or vehicle to their respective camps. Most international travelers coming from within Zimbabwe, however, bypass Kariba and charter directly into Matusadona and Mana Pools. Kariba is a good place to meet Zimbabweans on vacation.

Sunset on Lake Kariba – nesting darters and cormorants

Kariba Dam, one of the largest in Africa, is a short distance from town. Water sports (beware of crocodile and hippo) and cruises on the lake are available.

ACCOMMODATION – TOURIST CLASS: * *Caribbea Bay Resort,* located on the shores of Lake Kariba, is a Sardinian-style resort with 83 rooms (some air-conditioned) with ensuite facilities, two swimming pools, a popular poolside bar and a casino. * *Cutty Sark Hotel* has 65 air-conditioned rooms with facilities ensuite and a swimming pool. * *Lakeview Inn* has 39 air-conditioned rooms with ensuite facilities and a swimming pool overlooking Lake Kariba. * *Kariba Breezes Hotel* has air-conditioned rooms with ensuite facilities, a swimming pool and marina.

CAMPING: * *M.O.T.H. Campsite* is located just below the Lakeview Inn.

LAKE KARIBA

Sunsets over the waters of island-dotted Lake Kariba are rated among the most spectacular in the world. One of the largest man-made lakes on earth, covering over 1,970 square miles (5,100 km²) , Kariba was formed in 1958 by damming the Zambezi River. The lake is 175 miles (280 km) long and up to 20 miles (32 km) in width and is surrounded, for the most part, by untouched wilderness.

When the dam was completed and the waters in the valley began to rise, animals were forced to higher ground, which temporarily became islands that were soon to be submerged under the new lake. To save these helpless animals, Operation Noah was organized by Rupert Fothergill. Over 5,000 animals, including 35 different mammal species, numerous elephant and 44 black rhino, were rescued and released in what are now Matusadona National Park and the Chete Safari Area.

Lights from commercial kapenta fishing boats are often seen on the lake at night. Fishing is excellent for tigerfish, giant vundu, bream, chessa and nkupi. October is the optimum month for tigerfishing (although very hot), and November-April for bream. Bird life, especially waterfowl, is prolific and superb viewing of African fish eagles is guaranteed. Cormorants and kingfishers are in abundance.

The Lake Kariba Ferry usually takes 22 hours to cruise from Mlibizi (a few hours drive from Victoria Falls) to Kariba Town. If you are thinking of taking a vehicle through Zimbabwe from Victoria Falls to Kariba, this ferry will save you over 775 miles (1,250 km) of driving.

MATUSADONA NATIONAL PARK
Situated on the southern shore of Lake Kariba and bounded on the east by the dramatic Sanyati Gorge and the west by the Umi River, this scenic 543-square-mile (1,407-km²) park has an abundance of elephant, lion, kudu, impala and buffalo — especially along the shoreline in the dry season (May-October). Other game includes sable antelope, roan antelope and waterbuck. Cheetah have been introduced into the area. Black rhino may be seen on walks, and leopard are occasionally spotted. Part of Matusadona is, in fact, an IPZ (Intensive Protection Zone) for rhino.

On my last visit, within 30 minutes of my first game drive, we spotted two sets of two black rhino from the vehicle — outstanding! Enroute to camp we stopped to see lion on a buffalo kill.

On an afternoon game drive during another visit, we spotted elephant, impala, buffalo and a large male lion, and had an interesting excursion out tracking black rhino.

During an afternoon boat ride, we spent more than half an hour watching two bull elephants frolicking in the water — locking tusks

MATUSADONA NATIONAL PARK

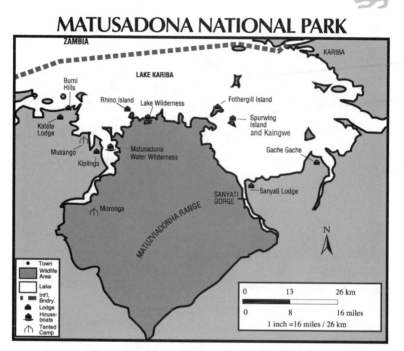

and at times completely submerging, then popping up with water hyacinth on their heads.

Game viewing by boat is a real attraction, and walking safaris are popular. Fishing is excellent, but beware of crocodiles. Private mobile tented safaris with Professional Guides are another great way to experience the bush. Motor yachts complete with captain, staff and Professional Guide provide private parties with great freedom and comfort in exploring the region. Multi-day hiking and backpacking trips provide other options for adventure.

ACCOMMODATION – CLASS A: * Matusadona Water Wilderness, located in a secluded area of the lake within the park, has one group of four and another group of five floating houseboats (18 beds) with facilities ensuite, moored near two central dining houseboats. Game walks, canoeing, vehicle game drives and sunset boat cruises are offered. * Rhino Island Safari Camp, situated near Elephant Point, has six chalets with ensuite bathrooms, and are set on wooden platforms with thatched roofs. Activities include game viewing drives and walks within the park and boat cruises on the lake along the Matusadona shoreline. * Sanyati Lodge, situated on the Sanyati Gorge, just outside the western border of the park, has 11 air-conditioned ensuite luxury lodges, including a

Matusadona Water Wilderness, a floating house boat.

Honeymoon Suite and Presidential Suite, and a gym and plunge pool. Boat and vehicle game drives and fishing are offered. Escorted walks can be arranged. * *Musango* has eight ensuite tents including two honeymoon tents with private plunge pools and a swimming pool. Walks, vehicle and boat game drives, canoeing, visits to dinosaur fossil sights, villages and the rhino orphanage are offered. * *Kiplings Lodge*, located at the mouth of the Ume River on the lake, has 10 rooms with ensuite facilities and a plunge pool. Day game drives, walks, canoeing, boat game drives and fishing are offered. * *Katete Lodge*, set on a hill west of the park, has 16 rooms with ensuite facilities and a swimming pool. Day and night vehicle game drives in a private wilderness area, boat game drives, walks and village visits are offered. * *Bumi Hills Lodge*, located on the western outskirts of the park on a hill overlooking the lake, has 20 well-appointed luxury rooms with ensuite facilities and a swimming pool. Walks, day and night game drives by vehicle in a private wilderness area, game drives by boat, fishing and village visits are offered.

CLASS B: * *Kaingwe Tented Camp* is a six-bed camp located at the tip of Spurwing Island, with ensuite flush toilets and bush showers. Walks and vehicle and boat game drives are offered. * *Maronga Tented Camp*, a 20-mile (30-km) boat transfer up from Musango Camp, has four tents with bucket showers and flush toilets, and caters to a maximum of six guests. * *Spurwing Island* is a 40-bed camp with tents, cabins and thatched chalets with ensuite facilities and a swimming pool. Walks, game drives by vehicle and by boat, and fishing are offered. * *Fothergill Island Safari Camp* has 10 A-frame thatched lodges (32 beds) with facilities ensuite and a swimming pool. Game viewing on foot, by boat and by vehicle is offered, as are fishing excursions. * *Gache Gache*, situated on Lake Kariba an hour east of Matusadona by boat, has 10 thatched lodges (20 beds) with ensuite facilities and a swimming pool. Game drives by boat and vehicle as well as walks in a private wilderness area are offered.

CLASS C: * *Lake Wilderness* has two houseboats with shared facilities, accommodating up to eight guests each, and a few smaller houseboats (doubles). Walks and game viewing by both boat and vehicle are offered.

CLASS D: The National Park has two self-service camps — Ume and Mbalabala; each camp may be booked by only one party.

CAMPING: The two National Park Campsites, Tashinga and Sanyati, have ablution blocks.

MANA POOLS NATIONAL PARK

During the dry season, Mana Pools National Park has one of the highest concentrations of wildlife on the continent. The park is situated on the southern side of the Lower Zambezi River downstream (northeast) of Lake Kariba and Victoria Falls.

This 845-square-mile (2,190-km²) park is uniquely characterized by fertile river terraces reaching inland for several miles from the slow-moving Zambezi River. Small ponds and pools, such as Chine Pools and Long Pool, were formed as the river's course slowly drifted northward. Reeds, sandbanks and huge mahogany and acacia trees near the river give way to dense mopane woodland to the park's southern boundary along the steep Zambezi Escarpment.

Mana Pools National Park covers part of the Middle Zambezi Valley, which is home for 12,000 elephant and 16,000 buffalo (with herds of over 500 each).

Mana Pools is one of the best parks in Africa for seeing African wild dog. Species commonly seen in the park include elephant, leopard,

MANA POOLS NATIONAL PARK

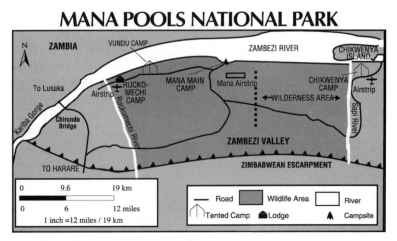

buffalo, waterbuck, greater kudu, zebra, eland, impala, bushbuck, lion and crocodile. Large pods of hippo are often seen lying on the sandbanks, soaking up the morning sun. Occasionally spotted are jackal, spotted hyena and the rare nyala. Large varieties of both woodland and water birds are present.

On my most recent visit we walked with our Professional Guide into a large herd of buffalo, and were, at one point, surrounded by them. Later in the walk we encountered lion, and an elephant that stood on its hind legs in an attempt to break off a large tree branch. In the afternoon we again tracked lion and approached the pride closely by a technique the Zimbabweans call "bum crawling" — sitting on your backside and using your arms to push you forward. Great fun!

On foot early the next morning we approached a large bull elephant and a younger male elephant. The younger elephant gave us a mock charge but was stopped by the older bull, which seemed quite comfortable with our presence. A short time later we approached the older bull so closely that I could have leaned out and touched his tusks. We even followed them across a small channel to spend more time observing them. This is the closest I have ever been to wild elephant (less that 6 ft./2m), and it was certainly one of the most exciting experiences I have had in my 25 years of visiting Africa. This kind of adventure is only safe and only possible with a top Professional Guide. Mana Pools is by far the best reserve in Africa for this level of interaction with elephants.

Also on this visit, I saw more greater kudu with magnificent horns than in any other reserve I can think of.

Canoe Safaris

For the adventurous traveler, this is one of the best ways to experience the African bush and is one of my favorite safaris on the entire continent.

Traveling silently by canoe, you can paddle closely to wildlife that has come to drink along the shore. Most importantly, you actively participate in the adventure!

Canoe safaris are available, lasting from three to nine days and covering different stretches of the river. They are operated from Kariba Dam downstream for up to 159 miles (255 km) past Mana Pools National Park to Kanyemba near the Mozambique border.

The river is divided into four canoeing segments: 1) from below Kariba Dam through the Kariba Gorge to Chirundu, 2) from Chirundu to the border of Mana Pools, 3) along Mana Pools National Park and 4) downstream (east) of the park through the rugged Mupata Gorge to Kanyemba. The section (3) along Mana Pools National Park is the best section for wildlife viewing. In addition, no motorized boats are allowed on the Zimbabwe side of this stretch of the river, making it all the more attractive.

Three different "levels" of canoe safaris are available:

(1) Budget (participation) canoe safaris do not have a support vehicle on land. Camping is often done on islands in the Zambezi where there are no facilities. Participants sleep in sleeping bags in small pup tents or under mosquito nets, and everyone pitches their own tents and helps with the chores. Walking inland is limited to 165 feet (50 m) from the riverbank.

(2) First class (full-service) canoe safaris are led by a Professional Guide licensed to escort you on walks. These safaris have a cook and camp attendants who take care of all the chores, which allows guests to spend all their time exploring the area and enjoying the bush. This option is far superior to the "Budget" option, because it allows you to canoe and go on vehicular game drives and walks. Guests are accommodated in comfortable tents (large enough to stand) with cots with mattresses, sheets and blankets. Bush shower tents and toilet

tents are set up for the group. Bucket shower and bush toilet tents are usually separate from the sleeping tents, or in some cases, bush toilets may be ensuite.

(3) Luxury (full-service) canoe safaris have all the benefits of the First Class option with the added attraction of larger sleeping tents that each have ensuite bush showers and toilets.

On the second day of a recent canoe safari, we pulled onto the riverbank for lunch. As we started walking up the bank, we were greeted by a young bull elephant coming down for a drink. He trumpeted, kicked dirt and shook his head a number of times before he backed off enough to let us by.

Later, as we were having lunch, another bull elephant paid us a visit, approaching within 15 feet (4.5 m) of us. That's close when the elephant is almost 10 feet (3 m) in height at the shoulder! As we were about to return to the canoes, the bull elephant that had almost kept us from coming ashore earlier apparently decided he wanted a mud bath and completely covered our canoes with mud in the process. Our guide approached him from the riverbank above in an attempt to persuade him to leave, and the elephant responded by using the tip of his trunk to throw a large blob of mud, just missing our guide by inches!

On a previous canoe safari along Mana Pools, as we canoed past two large bull elephant walking along the river's edge, our guide instructed us to pull into shore about 50 yards (50 m) downstream of them. The larger of the elephants continued walking toward us, eating apple ring acacia (*Acacia albida*) pods that had fallen from trees along the river.

Our guide and I crouched silently behind our canoe, with the rest of the group doing the same behind us. The elephant came closer and closer and closer until he was not more than 6 feet (2 m) from us. One step more and he would have stepped into the canoe. What a thrill! Eventually, after having a drink, he turned around and walked back down the shoreline that he came from.

Several times we saw elephant swimming from the mainland to islands in the Zambezi in search of food. We also saw hundreds of hippo, buffalo, waterbuck and impala and countless elephant, crocodile, lion and many other species.

Exhilarating canoe safari experience.

Although these canoe safaris are by no means marathons, participants must paddle their own canoes, which allows them to be more involved in the adventure. Your guide will instruct you on safety precautions. Previous canoe experience is not necessary. However, spending at least a few hours in a canoe before your African safari will allow you to feel more comfortable canoeing in a foreign environment.

Walking Safaris

The eastern part of Mana Pools has been designated a wilderness area in which only walking and canoeing along its shores are allowed. There are no roads or other signs of man.

Recently we joined a three-night/four-day walking safari (full service) escorted by a Professional Guide through the rich Mana Pools floodplains along the Zambezi River — an area teeming with wildlife. The only humans we saw for four days were canoeists off in the distance, paddling down the Zambezi River.

On the first day, we encountered a bull elephant that decided to mock charge us not once — but twice! On the first charge, it stopped about 30 feet (9 m) from us, and on the second charge — about 15 feet (4.5 m). Keep in mind that, as long as you do what your guide says, there is little danger — only a big rush of adrenaline!

Ivan Carter walking clients up to an elephant.

Shortly after the charge, we reached camp. Later, under a full moon, the same elephant approached our camp, and we walked out to meet it. The elephant trumpeted, then gave us a mock charge in the moonlight!

On the last day of the safari, we encountered so many breeding herds (females with their young) of elephant that we had to continuously backtrack and look for alternative paths between them in order to get to our pickup point.

Because it was late in the dry season and food was scarce, most of the large elephant herds had broken into several small ones. Our guide climbed several termite mounds to scout out the area. We even found ourselves walking through "adrenaline grass" — thick, golden grass often over 7 feet (2 m) in height that is so thick you would almost bump into a buffalo or elephant before seeing it.

Events like this are why walking safaris, and safaris in general, are so popular: You never know what is going to happen next!

Walking safaris like this one may sound a bit risky. They are, however, quite safe — as long as the safari is conducted by a fully licensed Professional Guide. Just use common sense and enjoy the adventure.

The best time to visit the park, for one of the finest exhibitions of wildlife on the continent, is at the end of the dry season (July-October) when large numbers of elephant, buffalo, waterbuck and impala come to the river to drink and graze on the lush grasses along its banks. Game viewing is also good in May, June and November. During the rainy season (December-March), many large land mammals move away from the river toward the escarpment. However, game viewing in the area near Chikwenya Camp is good year-round.

Because many roads within the park are closed during the rainy season, from early November until the end of April, the camps (except for Chikwenya) are also closed during that period. Charter flights operate into three airstrips in the park. Gasoline (petrol) is not available in the park, and powerboats are not allowed. Four-wheel-drive vehicles are recommended in the dry season and necessary in the rainy season.

ACCOMMODATION – CLASS A: * *Chikwenya Camp* is situated on the banks of the Zambezi River and at the eastern end of Mana Pools. The camp is protected by large mahogany trees that form a natural dining area. The nine luxury tents under thatch have ensuite bathrooms, and the lodge offers walking, canoeing, fishing, and game viewing by vehicle and by boat. Alternatively, you may sit in one of the hides and wait for the wildlife to come to you! The camp is open year-round. * *Ruckomechi Camp,* just outside the western boundary of the park, has 10 comfortable chalets including one family room (20 beds) with ensuite facilities. Game drives, walks, boat game drives, hides and canoeing are offered.

ACCOMMODATION – CLASS B: * *Vundu Tented Camp* is located within the park and has six large tents with ensuite, open-air bathrooms. From your camp you may take leisurely canoeing safaris, game drives and walks to explore and appreciate the rich floodplains and river channels.

CLASS D & F: National Parks accommodations include Musangu Lodge and Muchichiri Lodge.

CAMPING: * *Nyamepi Camp* has 29 caravan/camping sites and ablution blocks with hot and cold water. The exclusive camps, which are limited to one group at a time, are Mucheni Camp, Nkupe Camp, Ndungu Camp and Gwaya (Old Tree Lodge) Camp.

CHIZARIRA NATIONAL PARK

This remote, undeveloped park is situated on the Zambezi Escarpment overlooking the Zambezi Valley and the southern part of Lake Kariba. Chizarira covers 737 square miles (1,910 km²) of wild, untouched bush with plateaus, deep gorges, thick woodlands and riverbeds.

Chizarira is a park for the adventurer more interested in experiencing the wilderness than in seeing huge herds of animals. Walking is allowed if accompanied by a Professional Guide, and that is the best way to explore the park.

The best view of Lake Kariba and the Zambezi Valley is from Mucheni View Point, which is also a great spot for birdwatching — especially for birds of prey.

Roads are rough and gas (petrol) not available; a 4wd vehicle is recommended year-round and is necessary in the rainy season. Chizarira National Park is a day's drive from Matusadona National Park. Easiest access is by charter aircraft. Some luxury, first class and budget group camping safaris include Chizarira in their itineraries.

 ACCOMMODATION – CLASS A/B: * *Chizarira Lodge* has eight thatched chalets (16 beds) with ensuite facilities and a swimming pool. Activities include game drives, walks and overnight walking trails.

CLASS F & CAMPING: There are four exclusive national park campsites, Kasiswi Bush Camp, Mobola Bush Camp, Mucheni Gorge Camp and Busi Bush Camp. Each limited to one party (maximum 12 people).

THE EAST

NYANGA NATIONAL PARK

Most of this beautifully forested and mountainous park lies above 6,560 feet (2,000 m), rising to 8,504 feet (2,592 m). Mt. Inyangani is the highest mountain in Zimbabwe. Trout fishing, horseback riding, hiking and golf are just a few of the many sports enjoyed in the refreshing environment. The park covers 127 square miles (330 km²) and is located near the Mozambique border north of Mutare.

This is the northern limit of the Eastern Highlands and is also the most accessible. The upland grasslands are a refuge for endangered birds, such as the blue swallow and wattled crane, while smaller mammal species, such as the oribi, are not uncommon. Numerous rare and endemic plants are found here, and blue duiker and Samango monkey may be found in the indigenous forests.

On a recent visit in May we had a great time picnicking at **World's View**, horseback riding through the pine plantations and fishing for trout.

 ACCOMMODATION – TOURIST CLASS: * *Inn on Ruparara* is a lovely country inn that accommodates a maximum of 36 guests in 17 lodges. Activities on the grounds and in the area include horseback riding, fishing, golf and gambling at a nearby casino. * *Pine Tree Inn* is a small country inn; rooms have facilities ensuite. * *Troutbeck Inn,* a comfortable country resort with 70 rooms with ensuite facilities, offers horseback riding, trout fishing, lawn bowling, squash, tennis and golf. * *Montclair Hotel* has rooms with ensuite facilities, a golf course and casino.

CAMPING: Numerous camping and trailer (caravan) sites are available.

BVUMBA BOTANICAL GARDEN AND RESERVE

The Bvumba Highlands, situated about 15 miles (25 km) southeast of Mutare, is a cool and often misty area of major interest to naturalists. The beautiful Bvumba (formerly Vumba) Botanical Garden is a scenic and tranquil locality, not only for botanists but also for the general wildlife enthusiast. Excellent views of Samango monkeys can be enjoyed there, and it is a superb birdwatching locality for species such as silvery-cheeked hornbill and red-throated twinspot. Numerous small streams twist through the garden and there are breathtaking views out across Mozambique.

The nearby **Bunga Forest Reserve** supports large populations of the tiny blue duiker and the secretive Swynnerton's robin, among many others. Small footpaths wind among the tall forest trees.

 ACCOMMODATION – DELUXE: * *Leopard Rock Hotel* has 58 rooms with ensuite facilities, an 18-hole golf course (considered to be one of the most scenic in southern Africa), casino, swimming pool, tennis and squash courts. Horseback riding and fishing are available.

TOURIST CLASS: * *Inn on the Vumba* has 22 bedrooms with ensuite facilities. * *White Horse Inn* is a small hotel (20 beds) with rooms that have ensuite facilities. * *Eden Lodge* has 12 bedrooms, two luxury lodges and two family rooms, all with ensuite facilities.

CAMPING: Camp and trailer (caravan) sites are available.

CHIMANIMANI NATIONAL PARK

This rugged, mountainous 66-square-mile (171-km²) park with deep gorges and numerous streams includes most of the Chimanimani Mountain Range, which rises to 7,995 feet (2,437 m). This is an excellent park for hiking and backpacking. Eland, sable antelope and bushbuck are often seen.

This is undoubtedly the most beautiful and undisturbed part of Zimbabwe's Eastern Highlands. The hiking trail winds among huge sandstone boulders, sculpted by wind and rain into bizarre shapes and forms. Crusty lichens in various colors adorn the rocks, and numerous isolated forms of stunted Afro-montane plants (including protea and erica) are present.

Birding is good in the forest areas of the gorges where orange thrush and Chirinda apalis are among the interesting species present. Nectar-feeding sunbirds thrive in the heathlands and forest fringes, where bokmakierie and stone chat are also seen. A number of pairs of the endangered blue swallow breed in burrows on the upland grasslands.

 ACCOMMODATION NEAR THE PARK – TOURIST CLASS: * *Kiledo Lodge*, located 44 miles (70 km) from the park, has rooms with ensuite facilities and a swimming pool.

ACCOMMODATION – CLASS F: A mountain hut is available for refuge.

CAMPING: Camping is allowed in the park.

HARARE

Formerly called Salisbury, Harare is the capital and largest city in Zimbabwe. It is one of the cleanest and most modern cities on the continent. Points of interest include the National Art Gallery, Botanical Garden, Houses of Parliament and the Tobacco Auction Floors (the largest in the world). **Mbare Msika Market** is good for shopping for curios from local vendors.

Harare is an excellent place to shop for Shona carvings made of wood and soapstone, silverwork and paintings.

A beautiful park adjacent to the Intercontinental Hotel features a large variety of brilliant flora. Harare Botanical Gardens has indigenous trees and herbs.

Harare's best restaurants include Tiffany's, L'Escargot, Amanzi, The Bagatelle, 22 Victoria Street, La Chandelle, Wombles and La Francais. Imba Matombo Lodge also has a restaurant that is open to the public and serves excellent food.

The **Larvon Bird Gardens** and **Lake Chivero (McIlwane) Game Park** are a short drive west of Harare. Larvon provides the opportunity to see (and photograph) a host of African bird species close-up, and this park has gained many accolades for its educational work and ability to raise endangered species. Lake Chivero is a popular fishing and boating destination, but there is also lion, white rhino, spotted hyena, cheetah, elephant, bushpig, giraffe, zebra and a variety of antelope present. The tall miombo woodland is home to a variety of birds, including miombo rock thrush, spotted creeper and white-breasted cuckooshrike.

West of the capital city are the lovely **Ewanrigg Botanical Gardens**, famous for their collection of aloes, which are at their flowering peak between June and August. A huge variety of other African trees and other plants can be seen here.

ACCOMMODATION – DELUXE: * *Meikles Hotel,* one of the "Leading Hotels of the World," has 269 rooms and suites with ensuite facilities, a swimming pool, sauna, gym and traditional Old-World atmosphere. * *Imba Matombo,* located a 15-minute drive from Harare in the suburb of Glen Lorne, accommodates guests in rooms in a large home and chalets (20 beds total) with ensuite facilities. The property has a tennis court, swimming pool and excellent restaurant. * *Sheraton Hotel* has 325 air-conditioned rooms and suites with ensuite facilities, a swimming pool, tennis courts, and a sauna and gym. **Crowne Plaza Monomatapa* *Hotel* has 240 air-conditioned rooms with ensuite facilities, a swimming pool and convention facilities.

FIRST CLASS: * *Wild Geese Lodge,* located 20 minutes by road from the city center and 30 minutes from the airport, is a private guesthouse set in beautiful gardens, with nine chalets with ensuite facilities. The lodge is adjacent to a private conservancy, with plains game including blesbok, eland, kudu, tsessebe and zebra. * *Holiday Inn* has 200 air-conditioned rooms with ensuite facilities and a swimming pool. * *Best Western Jameson Hotel* has 128 air-conditioned rooms and suites with facilities ensuite and a swimming pool. * *Landela Lodge*, located 20 minutes by road from the airport in the suburb of Ruwa, has 10 rooms with ensuite facilities, a swimming pool, tennis court, horseback riding and temporary membership at the Ruwa Country Club (18-hole golf course).

TOURIST CLASS: * *Bronte Hotel* has 140 rooms and a swimming pool. * *Cresta Lodge* has 173 rooms. * *Oasis Hotel* has 84 rooms (including five family rooms) and a swimming pool.

ACCOMMODATION NEAR HARARE – CLASS A: * *Pamuzinda Safari Lodge*, located 53 miles (85 km) from Harare, is a private game ranch with 12 luxury bungalows (doubles) and a swimming pool. Game drives are offered.

THE SOUTH

GREAT ZIMBABWE

These impressive stone ruins, a World Heritage Site, located 11 miles (18 km) from Masvingo, look distinctly out of place in sub-Saharan Africa, where almost all traditional structures have been built of mud, cow dung, straw and reeds. The origin of these ruins is rather confusing, but it is now widely believed that they represent an important ceremonial and residential center for former Zimbabwean rulers. Evidence of artifacts from the Far East indicate that the site was part of a trading center that involved the export of ivory and gold. Some historians believe it was an 11th century Shona settlement.

In addition to the astonishing archaeological interest, the area's antelope and birdlife are also attractions to naturalists.

In 1890, Fort Victoria (now Masvingo) became the first settlement of whites in what is now Zimbabwe. The settlers first discovered the Great Zimbabwe Ruins in 1888.

The city was at its prime from the twelfth to fourteenth centuries. The Acropolis or Hill Complex, traditionally the King's residence, is situated high on a granite hill overlooking the Temple (a walled enclosure) and the less-complete restoration of the Valley complex.

This 33-foot (10 m) high conical tower is part of Great Zimbabwe.

ACCOMMODATION – FIRST CLASS: * *Lodge of the Ancient City* has been attractively built in the style of the ruins. The lodge has 20 rooms with ensuite facilities and a swimming pool.

TOURIST CLASS: * *Great Zimbabwe Hotel* is a country hotel, located a few minutes' walk from the ruins, with a swimming pool and 56 rooms with private facilities. * *The Inn on Great Zimbabwe*, located on a hillside minutes from Great Zimbabwe, has eight rooms with ensuite facilities, seven self-catering cottages and a campsite.

MUTIRIKWE (KYLE) RECREATIONAL PARK

Located 20 miles (32 km) southwest of Masvingo, this 65-square-mile (169-km²) park is a great place to go horseback riding among white rhino and a variety of other game. Rides on the pony trails are led by a park ranger into a fenced wildlife section of the park.

 ACCOMMODATION – TOURIST CLASS: See "Great Zimbabwe."

CLASSES D & F: * National Park lodges, some with private facilities and others without, are available.

CAMPING: Camping and trailer (caravan) sites with ablution blocks are located near the National Park office and at Sikato Bay Camp on the west bank of Lake Mutirikwe.

GONAREZHOU NATIONAL PARK

The second largest park in Zimbabwe, Gonarezhou borders the country of Mozambique in southeastern Zimbabwe and covers over 1,950 square miles (5,053 km²) of bush.

Gonarezhou means "the place of many elephants" and is definitely elephant country. Other species commonly seen are lion, buffalo, zebra, giraffe and a variety of antelope species. Nyala are regularly seen in riverine areas. Rarely seen are roan antelope and Liechtenstein's hartebeest.

The park is divided into two regions, the Chipinda Pools section, which includes the Runde and Save subregions, and the Mabalauta section. Game viewing is best in the Runde subregion.

Perhaps the most beautiful part of the reserve is the Chilojo Cliffs on the broad Runde River. These impressive cliffs are composed of oxide-rich sandstone, which is spectacularly colorful at sunset.

Much of the park is comprised of Mopane woodland and scrub, some of which has been drastically altered by the browsing activities of elephants. Gonarezhou was once home to some of the most magnificent baobab trees in Africa, but many of these were lost during a crippling drought in 1991-93.

Visited mostly by the more adventurous, this park provides a true wilderness experience. Among the birds to be seen here are giant eagle owl, lappet-faced vulture, woolly-necked stork, Bohm's spinetail, red-billed helmetshrike and golden-breasted bunting.

Gonarezhou has been earmarked for incorporation into the proposed Kruger-Gaza Transfrontier Reserve, but only time will tell if this gigantic conservation area will come to pass.

The park is usually only open in the dry season, May 1 to October 31. Winter temperatures are mild; however, summer temperatures can exceed 104°F (40°C).

From Masvingo, drive southwest to Chiredzi, then continue either 36 miles (58 km) to Chipinda Pools or 105 miles (170 km) to Mabalauta Camp. Four-wheel-drive vehicles are highly recommended. The nearest airstrip is Buffalo Range.

ACCOMMODATION – CLASS A/B: * *Chilo Gorge Safari Lodge,* set on the cliffs of the gorge overlooking the Save River, has 14 thatched lodges (doubles) with ensuite facilities. * *Mahenye Safari Lodge* is situated on the Save River bordering the reserve and consists of eight thatched lodges (doubles) with ensuite facilities.

CLASS F: * *Swimuwini,* which means "the place of baobabs," is located 5 miles (8 km) from the Warden's Office and has three self-service chalets and an ablution block.

CAMPING: * *Chipinda Pools Camping and Caravan Site* and * *Chinguli* have ablution blocks. Seven remote campsites with basic facilities are also available. * *Mabalauta* has five camping/trailer (caravan) sites.

ACCOMMODATION NEAR GONAREZHOU NATIONAL PARK – CLASS A: * *Pamushana* is a luxury lodge consisting of four large double and two spacious family air-conditioned villas with ensuite facilities, swimming pool and sauna. Activities include day and night game drives, walks, canoeing, bass and bream fishing and visits to San Bushman paintings. * *Nduna Lodge,* set on the 378-square-mile (980-km²) **Lone Star Reserve** bordering Gonarezhou National Park, has six air-conditioned luxury stone-and-thatch chalets (doubles) with ensuite facilities and a swimming pool. The lodge is nestled in a rock amphitheater on the edge of a lake. Elephant, buffalo, lion, black rhino, leopard and a variety of antelope may be seen. Activities include day and night game drives, canoeing, walks and viewing Bushman paintings. Easiest access is by private air charter. * *Senuko Lodge,* located in the **Save Valley Conservancy** approximately 44 miles (70 km) from Chiredzi, has eight chalets with a unique open-front design with rolldown canvas screens, and ensuite facilities and a swimming pool. Day and night game drives, walks and visits to local villages are offered.

ZAMBIA

THE LONESOME LEOPARD

This shy, solitary, secretive creature is an independent animal that moves silently and, by its intelligence, can adapt to any environment. Its presence is widespread, but sightings are uncommon. However, there are ways of increasing your chances of seeing a leopard in the bush.

Leopards wake early in the morning, often with their tails hanging from beneath the branches of trees, watching their prey before descending. They begin a short stalk, then chase and pounce on their victims and, finally, suffocate them with a death bite to the throat. Both their phenomenal neck and claw strength are used to drag their meal, step over step, back up the tree. Later in the morning, they find an open, sunny spot on a rock outcrop to warm and groom themselves.

The leopard's ability to feed on anything from termites and stranded fish, to lizards, baby giraffe and elephant carcasses is what allows it to live in so many different environments. Over most of its range, its principle prey is medium-sized mammals from hyrax to impala.

Leopards are natural swimmers and often supplement their diet with fish and other river species and may be seen taking a drink at a river or pool in the late afternoon. If baboons are nearby, the elusive leopard never goes undetected; the baboons move through the branches chattering and barking, creating a noise loud enough to deter an attack.

It is not uncommon for a leopard to initiate an attack on a baboon troop only to be attacked itself by the fierce troop and driven up a tree. There, the leopard is chided by baboons from above and below, and the great cat finds peace only when the baboons move off. Hyrax will also announce the presence of any leopard hiding in rocky outcrops.

Two of the biggest thrills on a safari are to hear the sound of a leopard's sawing grunt and to sight one on a game drive.

ZAMBIA

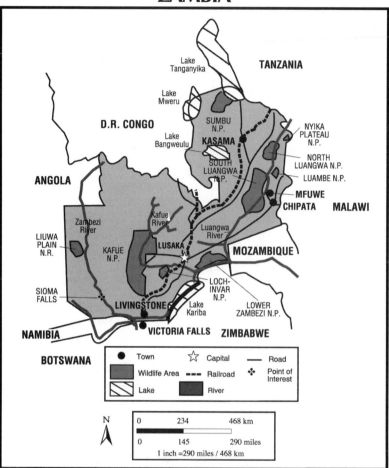

FACTS AT A GLANCE

AREA: 290,586 sq. mi. / 752,614 sq. km
APPROXIMATE SIZE: Larger than Texas or France
POPULATION: 10.3 million
CAPITAL: Lusaka (pop. est. 1.5 million)
OFFICIAL LANGUAGE: English

ZAMBIA

A country rich in wildlife, Zambia was named after the mighty Zambezi River, which flows through southern Zambia. The Zambezi River is fed by its Kafue and Luangwa tributaries, and forms the boundary between Zambia and Zimbabwe before flowing through Mozambique — eventually emptying into the Indian Ocean. The three great lakes of Bangweulu, Mweru and Tanganyika are in northern Zambia, and Lake Kariba is found along the southeastern border adjacent to Zimbabwe.

The country is predominantly a high plateau ranging in altitude from 3,000 to 5,000 feet (915 to 1,525 m), which is why it has a subtropical rather than a tropical climate. April-August is cool and dry, September-October is hot and dry, and November-March is warm and wet. Winter temperatures are as cool as 43°F (6°C) and summer temperatures exceed 100°F (38°C). The dry season, with clear sunny skies, is May-October.

The Zambian people are predominantly composed of Bantu ethnic groups who practice a combination of traditional and Christian beliefs. English is the official language and is widely spoken, in addition to 73 other languages and dialects. In contrast to most African countries, over 40% of the population lives in urban areas, due mainly to the copper mining industry.

In 1888, emissaries of Cecil Rhodes signed "treaties" with African chiefs ceding mineral rights of what was proclaimed Northern Rhodesia, which came under British influence. In 1953, Northern Rhodesia, Southern Rhodesia (now Zimbabwe) and Nyasaland (now Malawi) were consolidated into the Federation of Rhodesia and Nyasaland. The Federation was dissolved in 1963. Northern Rhodesia achieved its independence on October 24, 1964, as the Republic of Zambia.

Zambia's economy is based primarily on copper mined in the "Copper Belt" near the Congo border. Due to low copper prices over the last few decades, the economy was forced to diversify. More emphasis has since been placed on developing agriculture (exporting fruit, coffee, sugar), and the tourism industry, as greater sources of foreign exchange.

Since the elections in 1991, Zambia has a multiparty political system.

WILDLIFE AND WILDLIFE AREAS

Zambia provides fabulous options for the wildlife adventurer, including both night and day game drives by open vehicle, walking safaris using remote bush camps or mobile tented camps, canoe safaris and white-water rafting.

Zambia boasts 19 gazetted national parks covering over 24,000 square miles (60,000 km^2), and with the 34 game management areas adjacent to the parks, the country has set aside 32% of its land for the preservation of wildlife. However, some of the national parks and reserves are not open to the general public.

The country's four major parks are South Luangwa National Park, North Luangwa National Park, Lower Zambezi National Park and Kafue National Park. South Luangwa and the Lower Zambezi are the most popular of the four, largely due to their large concentrations of game.

Zambia is excellent for walking safaris, which are operated primarily in South Luangwa, North Luangwa, Lower Zambezi and Kafue National Parks. Virtually all of the camps offer morning walks and day and night game drives.

Fishing is very good for tigerfish in Lake Kariba and the Zambezi River, and for tigerfish, goliath tigerfish, Nile perch and lake salmon in Lake Tanganyika.

Visitors who have their own vehicles must return to the camps by nightfall, and, therefore, cannot conduct night safaris on their own;

neither may they leave the roads in search of game or walk in the park without the company of an armed wildlife guard.

The best time to visit South Luangwa, Lower Zambezi and Kafue National Parks is June-October, when the grass level is low and game is easier to see. Many of the rivers will have dried up and the game is concentrated around the lagoons and oxbow lakes — making game viewing all the more spectacular. Game viewing is fairly good in November, April and May. December-March is the hot and humid rainy season when foliage becomes thicker, making wildlife more difficult to spot.

THE NORTH AND NORTHEAST

SOUTH LUANGWA NATIONAL PARK

The natural beauty, variety and concentration of wildlife make this huge, 3,494-square-mile (9,050-km^2) park one of the finest in Africa. Game can be so prolific that Luangwa is called "The Crowded Valley."

South Luangwa is home to savannah, wetland and forest animals. The southern regions are predominantly woodland savannah with scattered grassy areas. Leopard, kudu and giraffe are numerous. To the north, the woodlands give way to scattered trees and open plains, where wildebeest and other savannah animals dominate the scene.

Thornicroft's giraffe are indigenous to the park. Lion, hyena, buffalo, waterbuck, impala, kudu, puku, bushbuck and zebra are plentiful. There are also small herds of Cookson's wildebeest, unique to Luangwa, while African wild dog are present in small numbers and rarely seen. Leopard are most commonly sighted on night game drives from July-October.

November, with the onset of the rains, is a time of rebirth with the calving of impala, wildebeest and other species. Most of the Palearctic migrants have arrived, along with large flocks of Abdim's and white storks.

Hippo and crocs abound in the muddy Luangwa River, a tributary of the Zambezi which runs along much of the park's eastern boundary and then traverses the southern part of the park.

Over 400 species of birds have been recorded, including sacred ibis, saddle-billed storks, yellow-billed storks, Egyptian geese, spur-

SOUTH LUANGWA NATIONAL PARK

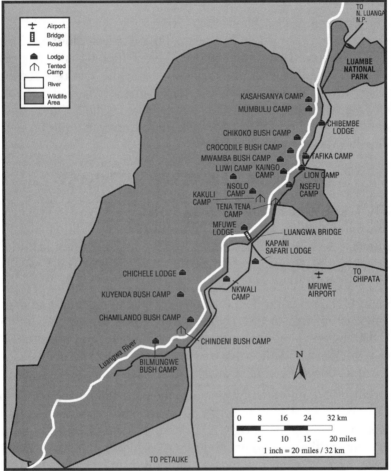

winged geese, fish eagles (Zambia's national bird), crowned cranes, carmine bee-eaters (spectacular breeding colonies September – November), woodland kingfishers, lilac-breasted rollers, bateleur eagles, Pel's fishing owl and long-tailed starlings. The best time for bird watching is November-April.

A real advantage of this great park is that visitors can experience day and night game drives in open vehicles, as well as participate in walking safaris ranging in length from a few hours to three or more days.

On my most recent visit we saw very good game, including a huge herd of over 500 buffalo, elephant (including a huge tusker), many hippo, including a large pod with several humorous juveniles, Thornicroft's giraffe, bushbuck, greater kudu, lion, serval and genet.

I took a **ultralight (microlight) flight** from Tafika Lodge over a wilderness region of the park. There were huge herds of elephant and buffalo, large pods of hippo, a variety of antelope species and even a lion. None of the wildlife even took note of us, except for crocs, which quickly fled to deep water. John, my pilot, surmised that they must have thought we were a pterodactyl. This is one of the most exciting adventures I have taken in Africa!

During a previous week's safari to South Luangwa, our wildlife sightings included buffalo, bushbuck, civet, eland, elephant, large-spotted genet, Thornicroft's giraffe, hippo, honey badger, spotted hyena, four leopard, over 20 lion, puku, Cookson's wildebeest, Crawshay's zebra, banded mongoose and white-tailed mongoose. Gray crowned crane, African darter, fish eagle, goliath heron, marabou stork, long-tailed glossy starling, brown snake eagle and a very large colony of open-billed storks were among the birds we saw.

Night Game Drives
South Luangwa is one of the best parks in Africa for night drives. On one of our visits, the night game drive started out slowly until we almost ran over a lion lying in the middle of the road. What a shock! We followed what turned out to be a pride of seven lion while they hunted.

We then followed a leopard at close range (20 ft./6 m), which all but ignored our presence. We had quite a thrill when the leopard jumped high into a bush after two sleeping doves. Other sightings on the night game drives included spotted hyena, Pel's fishing owl, several more leopard and lion, and a number of genet and civet.

Walking Safaris
Walking safaris were first pioneered in this park by Norman Carr, and are conducted by a licensed walking guide accompanied by an armed national parks game scout. Most lodges and camps offer morning and afternoon walks. Multi-day walks are also offered, during which guests hike from bush camp to bush camp or stay in

Night game drive.

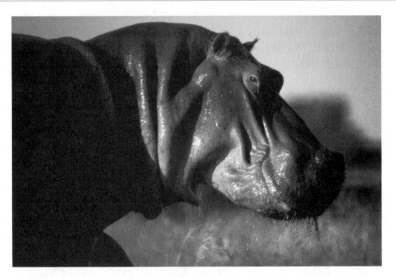

The Luangwa River has one of the largest hippo populations on the continent.

mobile tents. Walking safaris are only conducted from June-October during the dry season when the foliage has thinned out enough for safe walking. Children under the age of 12 are not allowed on walks.

Walking safaris are the highlight of many visitors' trips to Africa and are certainly one of my favorite ways of experiencing the bush. For

A room at the newly renovated Chichele Lodge.

those who would enjoy walking 3 to 7 miles (5–11 km) per day at a reasonable pace and wish to experience nature up close, walking safaris are highly recommended.

Many lodges have their own smaller bush camps, catering to a maximum of six or seven guests, set in remote regions of the park where walking is the main activity. However, bush camps are also excellent for those who do not want to do a lot of walking, but wish simply to relax and experience isolation in the bush.

Facilities in bush camps vary from comfortable chalets or tents with ensuite facilities to simple chalets or tents with separate shower and toilet facilities (see "Accommodations" below for details). In addition to walking, some bush camps also offer day and night game drives.

Some camps offer programs whereby guests may walk from one bush camp to another. Your luggage is carried ahead to the next bush camp by vehicle or by porters who walk separately from the group. Guests usually carry only their cameras and a little water. The terrain is fairly flat but often rugged.

On the first morning of a four-day walking safari, we walked for about two hours, at which point we paused while our tea-bearer prepared hot tea. Our guide showed us how to make fire with a piece of wood, a stick and dried elephant dung. He did an excellent job of answering our endless questions about spoor (animal footprints and droppings) and the flora and fauna of the bush. Watching a dung beetle at work, for instance, can be fascinating — an event that most likely would not be experienced from a vehicle.

After another one-and-one-half-hour walk, we reached our first camp. Scenically situated on the banks of the Luangwa River, there were more than 40 hippo in the water below and numerous crocs on the far shore.

After much-welcomed cold drinks, lunch and a short siesta, we regrouped at 3:30 p.m. for tea. At 4:00 p.m. we set off for another walk and returned just before dark. After everyone had a hot shower, dinner was served. Then we sat around the campfire, listening to the mysterious sounds of the night and gazing up at millions of stars.

Hippo, lion, hyena and elephant often come into camp at night, so it's not a good idea to leave your hut after everyone has gone to bed.

One night we were awakened by an elephant, silhouetted in the moonlight, standing next to our hut. One of the group took a flash photo and spooked the giant pachyderm, running it out of camp. I would have loved to have watched it longer, to have more fully experienced such an encounter with the wildlife that is Africa.

One afternoon as we were walking through an area with high golden grass, I commented to our guide that a lion could be 20 feet (6 m) from the path and we might not see it. Just as the guide agreed with me, we turned around and, standing not 50 feet (15 m) on the path behind us, was a large lioness! Once the lioness knew we were all aware of her presence, she ran off.

The following morning we walked to our next bush camp, then had another walk in the afternoon. Two days later we returned to main camp, after viewing numerous herds of impala, Burchell's zebra, puku, elephant and buffalo, along with Thornicroft's giraffe, baboon and lion. Most importantly, we felt a sense of accomplishment from having experienced the bush on more intimate terms, in the way that Livingstone, Stanley and other early African explorers confronted the challenge of the continent — on foot!

Nsefu Camp offers a great South Luangwa experience.

In addition to a walking safari, I suggest that you stay at least two additional nights in the park for day and night game drives by open vehicle; it will give you the opportunity to see many species that you might not have seen on your walking safari.

There are few all-weather roads in the park north of Mfuwe, so most of the northern camps are closed November-May, and the camps that stay open during that period are usually reachable only by motor-boat.

Guests of most camps usually have a game drive or walk in the early morning, and in the afternoon they take either a day game drive, departing about 3:30 p.m. and returning at dusk, or a late after-noon/night game drive, departing after 4:00 p.m. and returning around 8:00 p.m. Schedules will, of course, vary from camp to camp. Be sure to request the options of your choice (walks, night drives, etc.) when checking in or as soon as possible thereafter. Plans for the following day are usually discussed with your guide over dinner the night before.

Mfuwe International Airport is about an hour flight from Lusaka. South Luangwa's main gate is 433 miles (700 km) from Lusaka; driv-ing takes about 10 hours and is not recommended. Some international visitors fly into Mfuwe from Lilongwe (Malawi) and Kariba or Harare (Zimbabwe).

ACCOMMODATION IN CENTRAL AND SOUTHERN SOUTH LUANGWA (this region of the park has many all-weather roads and is usually open year-round) – CLASS A: * *Chichele Lodge,* the former Presidential hideaway recently transformed into an early colonial "Gentleman's Lodge," is set on a hill overlooking the surrounding plains. This Victorian lodge has a swimming pool and caters to 20 guests in cottages with facilities ensuite. Activities include day and night game drives and walks with a professional guide.

CLASS A/B: *Chindeni, Bilimungwe and Chamilandu* (Class A/B) and *Kuyenda* (Class B) bushcamps are all located south of Mfuwe within the park. Guests can base themselves at one or two of the camps or may walk from camp to camp. * *Chamilandu Bush Camp* overlooks the Luangwa River and consists of three grass-and-thatch chalets, built on wooden decks, with ensuite facilities. Walks and limited day and night game drives are offered. * *Chindeni Bushcamp* overlooks a permanent oxbow lagoon and has four luxury tents (maximum of six guests), on raised wooden decks, with ensuite facilities. Bush walks, as well as limited day and night game drives, are offered. * *Bilimungwe Bushcamp* is set on a permanent waterhole, and has four large reed-and-thatch chalets (maximum of six guests) with ensuite facilities. Walking safaris are the primary activity, but limited day and night game drives are offered. * *Nkwali Camp,* situated just outside the park on the eastern banks of the Luangwa River, is open year-round and has six chalets with ensuite facilities, and a swimming pool. Day and night game drives and walks are offered. * *Kapani Safari Lodge* has eight standard chalets and two suites, with small refrigerators and ensuite facilities, and a large swimming pool. Kapani was operated by the late Norman Carr, who introduced walking safaris to Zambia. The camp offers day and night game drives and walks. * *Mfuwe Lodge,* set on two picturesque lagoons, has 18 chalets (including two suites) with private decks and ensuite facilities, a huge bar/dining/deck area and a large swimming pool. Day and night game drives are offered. * *Puku Ridge,* set on a secluded ridge near Chichele Lodge, accommodates up to 12 guests in tented camp with ensuite facilities.

CLASS B: * *Kuyenda Bush Camp* has four grass chalets (maximum of 6 guests), set on the banks of the Manzi River, with ensuite bucket showers and flush toilets. Daily walks as well as day and night game drives are offered.

ACCOMMODATION: CLASS D AND F: * *Flatdogs*, located near Mfuwe Bridge outside the park, has catered and self-catered bungalows and campsites.

ACCOMMODATION IN *NORTHERN* SOUTH LUANGWA – Because this region has few all-weather roads, the camps usually open in June and close at the end of October, before the onset of the rains. This area is generally less crowded than Central South Luangwa near Mfuwe, and many of the camps offer multi-day walking safaris. Tafika, Tena Tena, Nsefu, Lion Camp and Kaingo are located in the Nsefu Sector of the park.

CLASS A: * *Tafika* Camp has four large thatched chalets and one two-bedroom family chalet — all with ensuite facilities. Day and night game drives, walks, village visits and exciting ultralight (microlight) flights are offered. Because this is the only northern camp open in November, guests of that period have the entire region virtually to themselves.
* *Tena Tena*, set on the banks of the Luangwa River inside the park, accommodates up to eight guests in five tents under thatch, with ensuite facilities. Day and night game drives, morning walks and six-day mobile tented walking safaris are offered.

ACCOMMODATION – CLASS A/B: * *Kaingo Camp* overlooks the Luangwa River and has five thatched chalets with ensuite facilities. Walks, day and night game drives, and photography from a hide are offered. * *Nsefu Camp*, located near the Luangwa River a 60- to 90-minute drive from Mfuwe Airport, has six tastefully decorated brick-and-thatch rondavels (12 beds) with open-roofed ensuite facilities. Day and night game drives and morning walks are offered. The bar overlooks a water hole. * *Chibembe Lodge*, located just outside the park on the Chibembe Channel of the Luangwa River, has six tents with ensuite facilities. Day and night game drives and afternoon walks are offered.

CLASS B: * *Chikoko Bush Camp* is located on the western bank of the Luangwa River in an area with no roads, so it is highly unlikely that you will not see other tourists. The area is specifically for walking. There are three tree chalets on raised platforms 10 feet (3m) above the ground with ensuite flush toilets, hand basins, and two separate showers. Access is from Tafika Camp by a banana boat ride across the Luangwa.
* *Crocodile Bush Camp* consists of three grass and pole chalets with

ensuite open-air bathrooms. The camp is located within the park, 2.5 miles (4 km) upstream from Tafika, and caters to a maximum of six guests. Walking safaris are conducted between Tafika, Crocodile Camp and Chikoko Bush Camp. * *Mwamba Bush Camp,* located on the banks of the Mwamba River a three-hour walk from Kaingo Camp, has three reed-and-thatch chalets with ensuite facilities. The chalets are uniquely designed with large skylights (protected by mosquito netting) to give you the feeling that you are sleeping "under the stars." Walks, as well as day and night game drives, are offered. * *Lion Camp* overlooks Lion Lagoon and has eight tents with ensuite facilities and a plunge pool. Game drives and walks are offered. * *Mchenja Camp,* set on the banks of the Luangwa River, has five A-frame chalets with thatched roofs and ensuite facilities. Day and night game drives and walks are offered. Nsolo Camp, Luwi Camp and Kakuli Camp are in association with Kapani Camp (see above). Walking safaris from camp to camp are available and are usually limited to six guests. * *Nsolo Camp,* situated near a permanent water hole, caters to a maximum of eight guests in four chalets, with ensuite facilities, set on decks overlooking an open vlei. The fronts of the chalets are completely open and are closed using tent material at night. There are some roads for game drives; however, walks are the most prominent activity. * *Luwi Camp* is located further inland than Nsolo and has four bamboo huts with ensuite facilities, accommodating a maximum of eight guests. Walking safaris from camp are offered, and some guests walk from this camp to Nsolo Camp. * *Kakuli Camp,* set on a riverbank overlooking the confluence of the Luangwa and Luwi Rivers, accommodates a maximum of 10 guests in tents with ensuite facilities. Day and night game drives as well as walks are offered. Chibembe's two bush camps, * *Kasansanya* and * *Mumbulu* each cater to a maximum of six guests in four chalets with ensuite flush toilets and bucket showers.

CAMPING: Camping is not allowed in the park except with a licensed tour operator.

NORTH LUANGWA NATIONAL PARK

As the name implies, this largely undeveloped 1,780-square-mile (4,636 km²) park lies north of South Luangwa National Park in the upper Luangwa Valley.

Mark and Delia Owens, coauthors of *Eye of the Elephant* and *Cry of the Kalahari* (Houghton Mifflan), conducted wildlife research here and were successful in reducing poaching and creating an infrastructure to attract tourists.

The park lies between the 4,600-foot-high (1,400-m) Muchinga Escarpment on the west and the Luangwa River on the east, with altitudes ranging from 1,640 to 3,610 feet (500 to 1,100 m). Vegetation includes miombo woodland, scrubland and riverine forest.

Wildlife includes lion, leopard, elephant, buffalo, zebra, eland, kudu, Cookson's wildebeest (much larger populations than in South Luangwa), impala, bushbuck, hippo, crocodile and a large population of spotted hyena. Black-maned lion are seen here more often than in South Luangwa. Nearly 400 species of birds have been recorded, including species not usually seen in South Luangwa, such as the half-collared kingfisher, long-tailed wagtail, white-winged starling, yellow-throated longclaw and black-backed barbet.

Walking is by far the primary activity, however, there are now enough roads (about 60 mi./100 km) in the park for productive game drive/walk combinations and limited night drives.

This park is visited by very few tourists. It is in fact unlikely that you will encounter any other groups.

On my most recent visit we walked from the airstrip for an hour and then crossed the crystal-clear, shallow Mwaleshi River (great for cooling off in hot weather) before coming to our camp. In the afternoon we began driving toward the confluence of the Mwaleshi and Luangwa rivers, when we spotted some vultures in the trees. We got out of the vehicle to investigate and found two lions on a buffalo kill, and after walking a bit more, found two more lion. Other game seen enroute included a large herd of eland, wildebeest, impala, Crawshay's zebra, and double-banded sandgrouse. When we arrived at the confluence, we walked down to the river to a pod of over 100 hippos. As we approached, more than 50 ran out of the shallow water across the dry riverbed to deep water a few hundred yards (meters) away. The sight of 50 one-ton "bums" of bouncing fat running together was too funny for words!

After sundowners, we drove back to the buffalo kill and checked out the lions on spotlight. After seeing the lions devouring their meal, we returned to our camp and fell upon our own finely prepared meals with equal gusto!

Mwaleshi Camp, North Luangwa.

The next morning we left camp at 6:00 a.m., after a small breakfast, and went for a five-hour walk along the Mwaleshi River. On the walk we saw impala, puku, wildebeest, zebra and brown snake eagle. We stopped for tea, and our porter reported hearing a roar that turned out to have come from a nine-foot croc hidden under some bushes high on the riverbank. In the afternoon we drove west on the road that goes toward the Mwaleshi Falls and saw more lion, white-tailed mongoose and wood owl, among other species.

Guests staying several days in the park may have time to visit the waterfalls located near the foot of the Muchinga Escarpment. The excursion involves a long drive and a two hour-walk. The water at the falls is so clear that you may see hippo and crocs swimming underwater. You can also swim (at your own risk) in some shallow pools nearby. Game seen enroute to the falls may include elephant, Lichtenstein's hartebeest, bushpig, roan antelope and blue monkey.

The rainy season is November–March. The best time to visit is June–October. Access to the park is best by a 45-minute or so charter flight from Mfuwe Airport; alternatively it is about a six-hour drive. I suggest spending at least seven nights divided between North and South Luangwa.

 ACCOMMODATION – CLASS B: * *Mwaleshi Camp* is a bush camp set on the banks of the Mwaleshi River with four reed-and-thatch chalets with ensuite facilities with showers and flush toilets. Escorted walks, day and night game drives are offered. An early morning walk from camp is often followed by a bush breakfast and a game drive back to camp. * *Kutandala Bush Camp* is set on the banks of the Mwaleshi River and has three reed-and-thatch chalets with ensuite facilities. Escorted walks and limited day and night game drives are offered.

CLASS C: * *Buffalo Camp* is a rustic, six-bed camp with separate facilities.

CAMPING: Campsites are not available.

LUAMBE NATIONAL PARK

This undeveloped, 99-square-mile (254-km²) savannah and woodlands park is located just northeast of South Luangwa National Park. Luambe has many of the same species and features of South Luangwa National Park, but has limited facilities to accommodate visitors.

ACCOMMODATION – CLASS B/C: * *Wilderness Camp* has four grass chalets with ensuite facilities. The units are available on a fully catered or self-catered basis.

CAMPING: Campsites are available at Wilderness Camp.

NYIKA PLATEAU NATIONAL PARK

The rolling highlands of Nyika are located in northeast Zambia and western Malawi. This 31-square-mile (80-km^2) park includes the small Zambian portion of the Nyika Plateau. This is a good park to visit for a keen naturalist or anyone wishing to escape the summer heat of the valleys below. Due to the high altitude, night temperatures sometimes drop below freezing May-September.

Montane grassland and relic montane forest dominate the scene. A great variety of orchid and butterfly species are present, along with Moloney's monkey, blue monkey, civet and a number of other small mammals. Roan antelope, reedbuck, bushbuck, eland and bushpig and even leopard are regularly seen, while serval are present but rarely seen. The spotted hyena populations have increased dramatically over the last five years, and due to the colder climate, have thicker coats than those found in the lowland areas. Interesting bird species in the area include the moustached green bulbul, olive thrush, white-tailed crested flycatcher and bar-tailed trogon. The best time for bird watching is November-June.

 ACCOMMODATION – See "Nyika National Park" in the chapter on Malawi.

NSUMBU NATIONAL PARK

Nsumbu National Park borders the huge inland sea of Lake Tanganyika in the extreme north of Zambia. Visitors come to this 780-square-mile (2,020-km^2) park mainly for fishing and water sports. This part of Lake Tanganyika is reputedly bilharzia-free, but be sure to check the current status.

Forest and wetland wildlife species are plentiful. In fact, visitors are often accompanied to the sandy beaches by wildlife guards. Elephant, lion, buffalo, eland, puku, roan antelope, blue duiker and Sharpe's grysbok may be seen. The shoreline is inhabited by hippo, crocodile and water birds. Savannah dominates the park inland.

Day and night game drives in open vehicles, guided walks, and day and night game viewing by boat for crocodile are available.

Fishing for goliath tigerfish, vundu (giant catfish), lake salmon and

Nile perch in Lake Tanganyika is excellent, especially December-April. The Zambia National Fishing Competition at Kasaba Bay is held every March or April, depending on the water level. Boats are available for hire.

ACCOMMODATION – CLASS B: * *Kasaba Bay Lodge* has 18 chalets (doubles) with ensuite facilities, a swimming pool and nine-hole golf course, and is located a few hundred yards from the beach. The lodge offers fishing, game viewing and boating.

ACCOMMODATION – CLASS C/D: * *Ndole Bay Lodge*, located just outside the park, has chalets (18 beds) with facilities ensuite; game viewing, fishing and boating are available. * *Nkamba Bay Lodge*, located 15 miles (24 km) from Kasaba Bay in the park on a hill overlooking the beach, has 10 chalets (doubles) with ensuite facilities. Activities include fishing, boating and game viewing.

BANGWELU SWAMPS

Lake Bangwelu, and the seemingly endless plains found to the east, have some unique mammal and bird species that, for some travelers, may be worth the effort of getting to this remote area. From May-July thousands of the endemic black lechwe are found in the wetlands. The rare and prehistoric looking shoebill and the shy sitatunga may be seen by boat or on foot in the swamps. Other game in the area includes oribi, tsessebe and side-striped jackal.

During the rainy season the floodplains are visited by over 370 species of migrant birds. Sightings may include the blue-breasted bee-eater, coppery-tailed coucal, white and pink-backed pelicans, herons, white storks, saddle-billed storks, ibises, pratincoles, Montagu's harrier, crowned cranes, jacanas and flamingos.

ACCOMMODATION – CLASS C: * *Shoebill Camp* has tents under thatch with separate facilities.

THE SOUTH AND WEST

LOWER ZAMBEZI NATIONAL PARK

Located along the Zambezi River across from Mana Pools National Park (Zimbabwe), the Lower Zambezi National Park extends 75 miles (120 km) along the Zambezi River between the Chongwe River on the west and nearly to the Luangwa River to the East, and approximately 20 miles (35 km) inland.

Walks, day and night game drives, and boat game drives are arranged to see elephant, buffalo, lion and a variety of antelope, and fishing is also offered. This is certainly one of the best parks in Africa!

While driving from the airstrip to camp on my most recent visit, we found a large male lion (Stumpy) with two females. Other game spotted during the day were five more lion, one leopard, large herds of elephant and buffalo, several bushbuck, common waterbuck and impala.

On the evening game drive we saw two civet, two genet, six lion killing an impala, mating porcupine, white-tailed mongoose, large grey mongoose, banded mongoose, side-striped jackal, giant eagle owl and barn owl.

The following evening we went for a sundowner upstream on the pontoon boat, and after dark, drifted downstream to spot game on shore.

The next day, on a three-hour fishing excursion, I caught over a dozen tigerfish weighing six to 10 pounds. For a half an hour I fought what I thought was a giant vundu — but later turned out to be a 6-foot croc. You can see that catch recorded in Chiawa Camp's record book!

One afternoon we canoed for two hours along the narrow, beautiful Chifungulu Channel downstream from Sausage Tree Camp. We encountered an abundance of game and had to wait about 15 minutes for a lone hippo to move downstream and out of our path before canoeing the last 200 yards (200m) to the pullout point. While driving to the airstrip the following morning, we drove through a breeding herd of 150 elephant that interestingly enough included a large number of bachelors, which in most regions are booted out of the herd at a much earlier age.

Game viewing is best July-October and is good in May and June. The best fishing months are September, October, and the first two weeks of November.

 ACCOMMODATION – CLASS A: * *Sausage Tree Camp* has seven tents with ensuite open-air bathrooms with bucket showers and flush toilets. Day and night game drives, boat game drives, fishing, walking

LOWER ZAMBEZI NATIONAL PARK

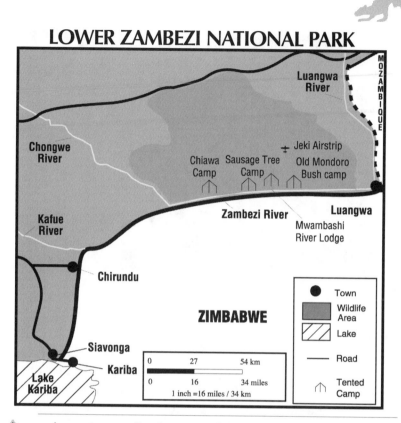

Luangwa River

Chongwe River

Jeki Airstrip

Chiawa Sausage Tree Camp Camp

Old Mondoro Bush camp

Kafue River

Zambezi River

Luangwa

Mwambashi River Lodge

Chirundu

ZIMBABWE

Siavonga

Kariba

Lake Kariba

0	27	54 km
0	16	34 miles

1 inch =16 miles / 34 km

● Town

Wildlife Area

Lake

— Road

Tented Camp

MOZAMBIQUE

and canoeing are offered. Guests call the office from their tents using old wind-up telephones to request escorts to the dining tent. * *Chiawa Camp,* located on the banks of the Zambezi River within the park, has eight new spacious tents under thatch with facilities ensuite, set on elevated wooden platforms. The charming thatched lounge/bar area has an upstairs observation deck and lounge, as well. Day and night vehicle game drives, day and night boat game drives, visits to the hide, fishing (it is excellent here), canoeing and walking are offered.

ACCOMMODATION – CLASS A/B: * *Old Mondoro Bushcamp,* located on the banks of the Zambezi River within the park, has four reed-and-pole rooms with canvas roofs and ensuite facilities. The focus is on walking trails; game drives, boat safaris and canoeing are also available. Many guests will spend a few nights here along with a few nights at either Chiawa or Sausage Tree camps, because they are located in different regions of the park and favor different activities. * *Mwambashi Camp* has eight tents with ensuite bathrooms. Day and night game drives, walks in the bush and boat game drives are offered.

Sausage Tree Camp.

LAKE KARIBA

Lake Kariba is one of the largest man-made lakes in the world — 180 miles (290 km) long and up to 20 miles (32 km) wide (see "Lake Kariba" in the chapter on Zimbabwe for full details). The Zimbabwe (southern) side of the lake is currently more developed than the Zambia (northern) side of the lake. Canoe safaris are offered downstream of Kariba Dam through the Kariba Gorge.

SIAVONGA

Siavonga is a small village situated on Lake Kariba just west of Lake Kariba Dam.

 ACCOMMODATION – TOURIST CLASS: * *Manchinchi Bay Lodge* is a 50-bed lodge with air-conditioned rooms and a swimming pool. Boating and fishing are offered.

LUSAKA

Attractions in Lusaka, the capital of Zambia, include the Luburma Market and Chieftainess Mungule's Village. Woodcarvings made by local craftsmen can be seen at Kabwata Cultural Center. A new shopping mall, Manda Hill, has recently opened with international stores from South Africa. There is also a museum near the city center. The international airport is 16 miles (26 km) from the city.

ACCOMMODATION – FIRST CLASS: * *Lusaka Inter-Continental Hotel* is an air-conditioned hotel with 402 rooms with facilities ensuite, 24-hour room service, three restaurants, a casino, gym and a swimming pool. * Taj *Pamodzi Hotel* is a 480-bed air-conditioned hotel with facilities ensuite, a swimming pool and gym. * *Holiday Inn* is an air-conditioned 215-bed hotel with facilities ensuite and a swimming pool.

ACCOMMODATION – TOURIST CLASS: * *Andrews Motel* is a 250-bed air-conditioned motel with a swimming pool.

ACCOMMODATION NEAR LUSAKA – CLASS A/B: * *Chaminuka* is a lodge situated near the airport, convenient for travelers needing to overnight before catching charter flights into the parks the following day. * *Protea Safari Lodge*, located about an hour's drive from the airport and overlooking Lechwe Lake, has 20 thatched chalets with facilities ensuite, private verandah and swimming pool. Kudu, sable, sitatunga, waterbuck and lechwe may be seen on the property.

LOCHINVAR NATIONAL PARK

Lochinvar is a birdwatcher's paradise, with over 400 recorded species. In addition, the park is host to about 30,000 Kafue lechwe (their stronghold), 2,000 blue wildebeest and 700 zebra. Greater kudu, buffalo, bushbuck, oribi, hippo, side-striped jackal, reedbuck and common waterbuck are also present.

Kafue lechwe are unique to the Kafue Flats and are related to the red lechwe of the Busanga Swamps of Kafue National Park.

Birdwatching in this 153-square-mile (410-km²) park is best February-March and also very good November-December and April-May. Water birds, such as the wattled crane, are especially abundant, and fish eagles are prolific. The park also encompasses part of Chunga Lake, which is fished by villagers living outside the park boundaries.

The park is open year-round and is located 145 miles (235 km) southwest of Lusaka, 30 miles (50 km) northwest of Monze off the Lusaka-Livingstone Road. A 4wd vehicle may be necessary in the rainy season.

ACCOMMODATION – CLASS A: * *Lechwe Plains Tented Camp* caters to a maximum of 12 guests in six luxury tents set on teak decks with ensuite facilities and a swimming pool. Canoeing, walking and limited game drives are offered.

KAFUE NATIONAL PARK

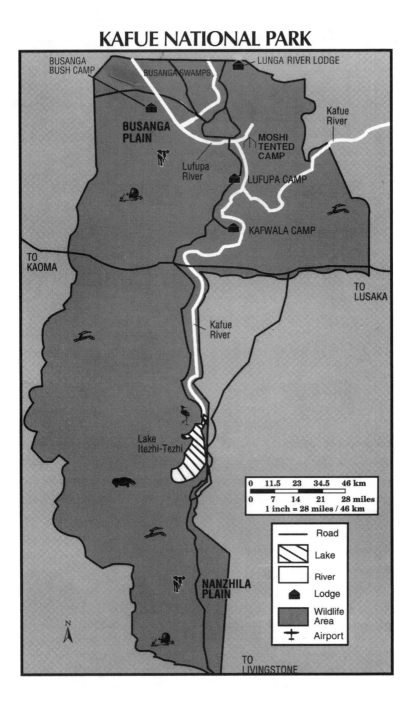

BUSANGA
BUSH CAMP

BUSANGA SWAMPS

LUNGA RIVER LODGE

BUSANGA
PLAIN

Kafue
River

MOSHI
TENTED
CAMP

Lufupa
River

LUFUPA CAMP

KAFWALA CAMP

TO
KAOMA

TO
LUSAKA

Kafue
River

Lake
Itezhi-Tezhi

0	11.5	23	34.5	46 km
0	7	14	21	28 miles

1 inch = 28 miles / 46 km

Road
Lake
River
Lodge
Wildlife
Area
Airport

NANZHILA
PLAIN

N

TO
LIVINGSTONE

ACCOMMODATION – CLASS C/D: * *Lochinvar House*, located within the park, is a self-catering lodge with several small chalets.

KAFUE NATIONAL PARK

Kafue National Park, one of the largest in Africa, covers 8,687 square miles (22,400 km²), making it two and one-half times the size of South Luangwa National Park and half the size of Switzerland.

Kafue has the largest number of different antelope species of any park in Africa. Many of the species, such as greater kudu and sable antelope, are said to be substantially larger than elsewhere in the country.

Visitors usually see a greater variety of species in Kafue, although not the quantity of wildlife that they might see in South Luangwa.

The southern and central parts are open all year, and the northern area is open only during the dry season (June-October/November). Game is especially difficult to spot in the rainy season.

Game drives in this park are sometimes a combination of riding in a vehicle and walking, according to the wishes of the group.

Lake Itezhi-Tezhi, formed as the result of a hydroelectric dam constructed at the southern end of the Kafue Flats, provides fishing, bird-watching and boating opportunities for visitors.

The Busanga Plains and marshes in the north have a greater number and variety of wildlife species. Animals are easier to spot here than in the dense woodland savannah in the south. This region is predominantly miombo forest, which gives way to savannah grasslands, along with rock hills, marshes and riverine forests. The Kafue River runs through the northern part of the park and along its east central border.

Large herds of red lechwe may be seen on the Busanga Plains. Sitatunga may be found in the Busanga Swamps on the northern border of the park. Lion are often seen on day and night game drives, with occasional encounters with cheetah and leopard. Also present on the plains are buffalo, elephant, puku, wildebeest, impala, roan antelope, sable antelope, greater kudu, Lichtenstein's hartebeest, waterbuck and hyena. More than 400 species of birds have been recorded.

Moshi Tented Camp.

On my last visit we encountered elephant, puku, impala and white-tailed mongoose, among other wildlife, on an afternoon/evening game drive.

The fact that Kafue has the largest number of antelope species of any park in Africa became immediately evident the following day on a three-hour morning drive from Lunga River Lodge to the Busanga Plains, during which we spotted nine species: impala, puku, common duiker, sable antelope (herd of 34), Lichtenstein's hartebeest, roan antelope, reedbuck, blue wildebeest and oribi.

To leave the forest and watch the expansive plains of Busanga open before our eyes was truly an amazing sight. The 350 square miles (900 km²) of plains are broken by numerous small palm "islands," and have a feel of the openness of the short grass plains of the south-eastern Serengeti coupled with the presence of water and landscape similar to Botswana's Okavango Delta.

We witnessed lion chasing a puku across the plains, and saw yellow baboon, buffalo, hippo, side-striped jackal, large grey mongoose, warthog, Defassa waterbuck, Burchell's zebra and zorilla. Birdlife was prolific.

During my last visit we only encountered a few other vehicles — most of which were from our own camp. This is definitely a park for anyone wanting to get off the beaten track!

There is little to be seen on the four-hour, 170-mile (275-km) drive from Lusaka; scheduled group charter flights from Livingstone, Lusaka and Lower Zambezi National Park are available and are a better alternative. Mobile tented safaris are another way to explore the park. Most safari camps are open from June to October or November.

 ACCOMMODATION – CLASS A: * *Moshi Tented Camp*, situated in the heart of the Busanga Plains, is an "old-fashioned" safari camp with eight luxury tents set on raised platforms with a small swimming pool.

CLASS A/B: * *Lunga River Lodge* has six thatched cabins with ensuite facilities. There is a swimming pool and steam bath, and a masseuse is available. Activities include walks, day and night game drives, canoeing and boating.

CLASS B: * *Busanga Bush Camp* has four thatched huts with ensuite facilities. Day and night game drives and walks are offered. Access to the camp is sometimes by canoe when water levels are high.

CLASS C: * *Kafwala Camp* overlooks the Kafwala Rapids and has chalets (some with ensuite facilities). Day and night game drives are offered. * *Lufupa*, situated in the center of the northern region near the confluence of the Kafue and Lufupa Rivers, has chalets (some with ensuite facilities) and offers day and night game drives, fishing and game viewing by boat.

VICTORIA FALLS
Called Mosi-Oa-Tunya, "the smoke that thunders," Victoria Falls is one of the seven natural wonders of the world. Visitors may walk along the **Knife Edge Bridge** for a good view of the Eastern Cataract and Boiling Pot.

A **sunset cruise** on the colonial *African Queen* is a very pleasant experience; hippo and crocodile are often seen. Fixed-wing aircraft flights over the falls are a great way to get a bird's eye view of Victoria Falls.

Canoe safaris are conducted upstream of the falls. Fishing for tigerfish on the Zambezi River is best from June to October (September is best), before the rains muddy the water.

One of the world's highest commercially run **bungee jumps** is operated on the bridge crossing the Zambezi River. After falling over 300

Rafting begins below Victoria Falls.

feet (100 m), a member of the bungee staff is lowered to the jumper and connects a cable to his harness. The jumper is winched into the upright position and then winched back up onto the bridge.

The Zambezi River below Victoria Falls is one of the most exciting **white-water rafting** experiences in the world. Numerous fifth-class rapids (the highest class runable) make this one of the most challenging rivers on earth. One-, two-, three- and seven-day trips are operated on the Zambezi River below Victoria Falls from the Zambia and/or Zimbabwe side of the Zambezi River. See the description of white-water rafting in the "Victoria Falls" section of the chapter on Zimbabwe for further details.

The falls are located about 3 miles (5 km) from Livingstone. See the chapter on Zimbabwe for a detailed description of the falls

MOSI-OA-TUNYA (SMOKE THAT THUNDERS) NATIONAL PARK

Much of the area around the Victoria Falls on the Zambian side is positioned within the 4-square-mile (10 km²) Mosi-Oa-Tunya National Park. Only a small section is fenced off into a game park that is well worth a visit. This small sanctuary protects five white rhino, plus sable, eland, warthog, giraffe, zebra, buffalo and elephant. There are two monuments within the park — one where the pioneers used to cross the river, and the other at the old cemetery. There are no large predators in the park.

ACCOMMODATION – CLASS A: * *Sussi & Chuma Tree Lodge*, a new luxury lodge built on the Zambezi River within Mosi-Oa Tunya National Park just a 10-minute drive above the Victoria Falls, has 10 large rooms with ensuite facilities and private decks. The main lodge consists of an upstairs sitting area and a nice downstairs patio area with a swimming pool. The camp offers tours to the Zambian side of Victoria Falls, Livingstone Museum visits, and a cultural tour to experience Zambian tribal villages, as well as game drives within Mosi-Oa-Tunya National Park.

LIVINGSTONE

Livingstone is a city of over 100,000 inhabitants, 5 miles (8 km) from the town of Victoria Falls. Driving from Lusaka takes five to six hours (295 miles/470 km) and flying takes a little over an hour.

The **Livingstone Museum** is the National Museum of Zambia and is renowned for its collection of Dr. Livingstone's memoirs. Other exhibits cover the art and culture of Zambia. The **Maramba Cultural Center** exhibits bandas from various districts in Zambia and presents colorful costumed performances by Zambian dancers. The **Railway Museum** has steam engines and trains from the late 1800s and 1900s.

Livingstone Zoological Park is a small, fenced park near Livingstone covering 25 square miles (65 km²). It is stocked with giraffe, buffalo, impala and other wildlife. The best time to visit is from June to October.

Tongabezi Honeymoon House.

ACCOMMODATION – DELUXE: * *The Royal Livingstone Hotel* has a total of 173 rooms including three standard suites, one Presidential Suite and two paraplegic (handicapped) rooms, restaurant and bar. All rooms have air-conditioning, satellite television, mini-bar and mini safe, and private balconies and terraces that offer spectacular views of the Zambezi River.

ACCOMMODATION – FIRST CLASS: * *Zambezi Sun* has a total of 212 rooms with private balconies and satellite TV including four suites and two paraplegic rooms, and a restaurant and bar focused around the central swimming pool.

TOURIST CLASS: * *Maramba River Lodge,* set on the banks of the Maramba River 2.5 miles (4 km) from the Victoria Falls, has thatched chalets with ensuite facilities, tents under thatch and campsites. Facilities include a swimming pool, bar and restaurant.

ACCOMMODATION NEAR LIVINGSTONE – CLASS A: * *The River Club* is located 12 miles (20 km) upstream from Victoria Falls and has a distinct Edwardian flavor with 10 luxury ensuite chalets overlooking the Zambezi River. Guests are usually taken to the lodge by boat.
* *The Islands of Siankaba*, two islands on the Zambian side of the Zambezi River 24 miles (38 km) upstream from the Victoria Falls, have six teak-and-canvas chalets on raised platforms with facilities ensuite and a swimming pool. The two islands are linked by a series of suspension bridges and overhead walkways. Activities include guided walks on the main island, fishing and sunset river cruises, as well as trips to the

Victoria Falls. * *Tongabezi Camp*, situated on the Zambezi River 12 miles (20 km) upstream from Victoria Falls, has five standard chalets with ensuite facilities, four ensuite luxury chalets, and a family chalet (Garden House) set away from the river, and a swimming pool hewn out of rock. Canoeing, boat excursions, fishing, croquet and flights over the falls are offered.

CLASS B: * *Sindabezi Island Camp*, located on an exclusive island in the Zambezi River 2 miles (3 km) downstream from Tongabezi Camp, has four thatched cottages with ensuite bush (bucket) showers and flush toilets. * *Songwe Village* is a stunning property perched 120 meters or nearly 400 feet above the Zambezi Gorge, just a short drive from the Falls. There are eight, comfortable thatched huts, built in the traditional style. * *Thorn Tree Camp*, located 6 miles (10 km) from Victoria Falls, has seven stone rooms under thatch and two wood suites under thatch with ensuite facilities. Activities include river cruises, tours of the Victoria Falls area and game drives.

CLASS B/C: * *Taita Falcon Lodge*, located 5 miles (7 km) downstream from the falls, overlooking the spectacular Batoka Gorge and the Zambezi River, has six chalets with verandahs and ensuite facilities. This is the only lodge overlooking the gorge.

CLASS D: * *Livingstone Island Camp is* a mobile tented fly-camp set on the edge of Victoria Falls in the midst of the thundering spray. The camp is open June-December.

SIOMA FALLS
Sioma Falls, located a six-hour drive and 185 miles (300 km) upstream (northwest) of Victoria Falls, is a magnificent series of six horseshoe-shaped falls stretching across the one and one-half-mile-wide Zambezi River. The best time to visit is July-January.

ACCOMMODATION – CLASS A/B: * *Maziba Bay Lodge* has six chalets with ensuite facilities and a swimming pool. Activities include fishing, white-water rafting, canoeing, game activities and microlighting.

LIUWA PLAIN NATIONAL PARK
Located in southwestern Zambia, this remote 1,413-square-mile (3,660-km²) park of open plains contains large numbers of wildebeest along with lion, hyena and spectacular numbers of migrating birds.

Wildlife, however, should be considered a plus and not the main reason for traveling to this seldom-visited park. It is a remote wilderness that is more suited for birdwatchers and for those interested in meeting African villagers who are uninfluenced by modern culture.

 ACCOMMODATION: As of this writing, a permanent camp is under construction. Mobile tented safaris are available.

NAMIBIA

THE HEAT-ADAPTED GEMSBOK

Gemsbok normally inhabit arid regions, and the key to their survival is their ability to exist without water. Also, various heat-resistant methods help the gemsbok exist in a dry environment.

They have splendid grey, white and black colorations, and their black face markings and dark leg and underpart markings may deflect heat and light away from their bodies. In extremely hot areas, gemsbok will use any form of shade. When none can be found, they are known to dig a small area in the sand and lie down to reduce the amount of hide exposed to the sun. If subjected to intense heat during the hottest part of the day, they can increase their body temperature by several degrees, thereby not using up precious body water in the form of perspiration or panting (evaporation). They will then slowly lower their temperature by radiation during the cooler desert nights.

The gemsbok, for an animal of its size, has a lower-than-normal body metabolism, which means that it requires less water. It has an extensive network of blood vessels, close to surface of the nose, which cools the blood flowing through the vessels by inhaled and exhaled air, thereby lowering the temperature of the blood returning to the brain. Its highly efficient kidneys are able to conserve valuable moisture, and waste products pass as only a few drops of concentrated urine.

Gemsbok have also adapted amazing digging techniques to find bulbs, roots and underground plants — including cucumber and Tsamma melon — to obtain much needed moisture. Their stomachs have a high moisture content (80%), and Bushmen are known to squeeze and strain gembok stomach contents for the water.

NAMIBIA

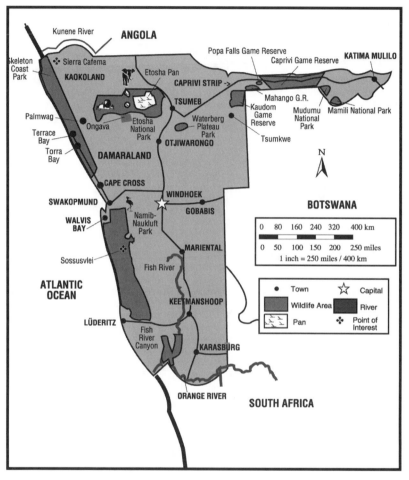

FACTS AT A GLANCE

AREA:	318,250 sq. mi.. / 824,268 sq. km
APPROXIMATE SIZE:	Texas and Oklahoma, or one and a half times the size of France
POPULATION:	1.8 million
CAPITAL:	Windhoek (pop. est. 170,000)
OFFICIAL LANGUAGE:	English

NAMIBIA

In addition to wildlife, Namibia has some of the most spectacular desert ecosystems in the world. It is famous for its stark beauty and diversity of tribes, and it is a geologist's and naturalist's paradise.

Essentially a desert land, Namibia is one of the most interesting and unusual of African countries. It may seem inhospitable in its dryness, but an astonishing variety of wildlife exists there, including unique, desert-adapted species, together with the big game of the savannah. Namibia has a sparse population of about 1.8 million, the majority of which live in Windhoek (the capital city) or in the far northern region of Ovamboland.

Namibia is situated in the sub-tropics, and flanked by the cold Atlantic Ocean. The cold Benguela current, which drifts northward from Antarctica, has a massive influence on the climate. Cool, dry air is pushed inland, creating a temperate coastline, and the extreme desert conditions of the Namib. Most of the country receives less than 10 inches (250 mm) of rain (the entire coastal region has less than 1 inch/25mm), 80% of which falls between November and March.

Namibia has a subtropical climate. Inland summer (October-April) days are warm to hot with cool nights. Summer is the "rainy" season, and most rainfall occurs in the north and northeast.

Namibia is one of the world's most sparsely populated countries. Its population is 86% black, 7% white and 7% colored (of mixed descent). Most people live in the northern part of the country where there is more water. Herero women, colorfully dressed in red and black, continue to wear conservative, impractical and extremely hot attire that was fashioned for them by puritanical, nineteenth century missionaries.

In 1884 much of the coast became German South West Africa until 1915, when South Africa took control during World War I. In 1920 the Union of South Africa received a mandate by the League of Nations to govern the region as if it were part of South Africa. The United Nations retracted the mandate in 1966 and renamed the country Namibia. The country became independent on March 21, 1990.

Namibia is one of the world's largest producers of diamonds and has the world's second largest uranium mine. Tsumeb is the only known mine to have produced over 200 different minerals.

WILDLIFE AND WILDLIFE AREAS

Namibia has set aside about 14% of its surface area to national parks. Etosha is the most famous, and it offers game viewing on a par with the Serengeti or Masai Mara. The Namib-Naukluft and Skeleton Coast parks protect unique desert ecosystems, and are an attraction for smaller life forms and landscapes, as well as low concentrations of desert-adapted big game. A number of smaller reserves exist in the far northern parts of the country, including the Caprivi Strip. In the south there is a movement to form a trans-frontier park by linking the country's Fish River Canyon reserve with the South African Richtersveld National Park.

May-November is the best time to visit the game parks and the central and northern regions. From May to August (winter), days are warm with clear skies and nights are cold. From September to November, days are hot and nights are cool.

Only open-sided, game-viewing vehicles registered to a few select tour operators are allowed in Etosha National Park. Open-sided vehicles are allowed in all other parks. Walking is allowed in all parks and reserves, except Etosha. Walking is not, however, recommended unless you are accompanied by an experienced guide. The parks are well organized and the facilities clean.

THE NORTH AND WEST

WINDHOEK

Windhoek is the capital and administrative, commercial and educational center of Namibia, situated in the center of the country at 5,410 feet (1650 m) above sea level.

Sights include the two Windhoek castles (Schwerinsburg and Sanderburg), built between 1913 and 1918, and the State Museum at the Alte Feste (Old Fort).

On a day trip from Windhoek you can visit the Ombo Ostrich Farm to see ostriches in all stages of development, from the egg to the grown bird, the historic Otjisazu Guest Farm, and you can meet the colorful Herero people at Ovitoto.

ACCOMMODATION – FIRST CLASS: * *Heinitzburg Hotel* is an old castle with 16 air-conditioned rooms and ensuite facilities. * *Windhoek Country Club Resort and Casino* has 152 air conditioned rooms with ensuite facilities, tennis courts, an 18-hole golf course and a swimming pool. * *Kalahari Sands Hotel and Casino*, located in the center of town, has 173 air-conditioned rooms and suites with ensuite facilities, a rooftop swimming pool and a fitness center. * *Hotel Safari* and *Safari Court*, located 2 miles (3 km) out of town, has 439 air-conditioned rooms with ensuite facilities, a swimming pool and free transport to and from Windhoek.

TOURIST CLASS: * *Hilltop House* is a luxurious bed and breakfast with commanding views over Windhoek, only a few minutes' walk from town. There is a swimming pool, and the rooms have facilities ensuite. * *Villa Verdi*, a small guest lodge located a few minutes walk from downtown, has 10 rooms with ensuite facilities and a swimming pool. * *Pension Kleines Heim* has 13 rooms with ensuite facilities. * *Hotel Thüringerhof* has 40 air-conditioned rooms with ensuite facilities and a beer garden. * *Continental Hotel* has 60 air-conditioned rooms, most with ensuite facilities.

CAMPING: * *Arebush*, located about 2.5 miles (4 km) from the city center, has campsites and budget, self-catering chalets. * *Daan Viljoen Game Park*, 17 miles (27 km) from Windhoek, has campsites available.

NAMIB-NAUKLUFT PARK

The consolidation of the Namib Desert Park and the Naukluft

Mountain Zebra Park along with the incorporation of other lands, including most of what was called "Diamond Area #2", created the largest park in Namibia and one of the largest in the world. Namib-Naukluft Park covers 19,215 square miles (49,768 km²) of desert savannah grasslands, gypsum and quartz plains, granite mountains, an estuarine lagoon, a canyon and huge, drifting apricot-colored dunes.

The Kuiseb River runs through the center of the park from east to west and acts as a natural boundary separating the northern grayish-white gravel plains from the southern deserts.

Herds of mountain zebra, gemsbok, springbok and flocks of ostrich roam the region.

Many small, fascinating creatures have uniquely adapted to this environment and help make this one of the most interesting deserts in the world. The dunes are home to numerous unique creatures, such as the translucent Palmato gecko, shovel-nosed lizard and Namib golden mole.

The five main regions of the park are the Namib, Sandvis, Naukluft, Sesriem and Sossusvlei areas.

The **Namib** may well be the world's oldest desert. The Welwitschia Flats lies on a dirt road about 22 miles (35 km) north of the Swakopmund-Windhoek road and is one of the best areas to see the prehistoric *Welwitschia mirabilis* plants. Actually classified as trees, many welwitschia are thousands of years old and are perfect examples of adaptation to an extremely hostile environment. The water holes at Hotsas and Ganab are good locations to spot game; Ganab and Aruvlei are known for mountain zebra.

If you plan to deviate from the main road through the park, a permit is required and is obtainable weekdays only at the Environment and Tourism Office in Swakopmund, Windhoek or Sesriem.

The **Sandvis** area includes Sandwich Harbour, 26 miles (42 km) south of Walvis Bay, and is accessible only by 4wd vehicles. Fresh water seeps from under the dunes into the saltwater lagoon, resulting in a unique environment. Bird watching is excellent September-March. Only day trips are allowed to the harbor. Permits are required and may be obtained from the Ministry of Environment and Tourism or from service stations in Walvis Bay.

NAMIB-NAUKLUFT PARK

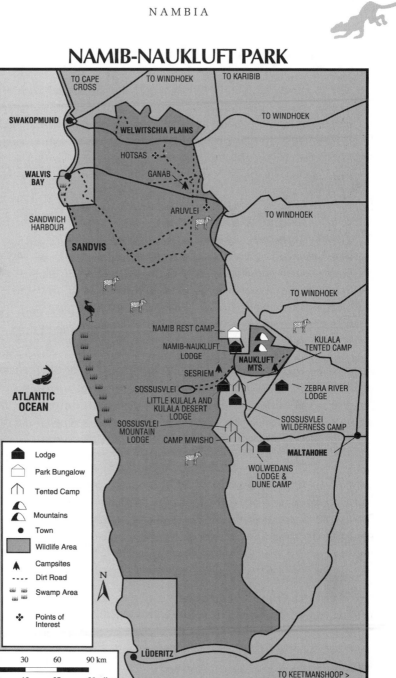

TO CAPE CROSS
TO WINDHOEK
TO KARIBIB

SWAKOPMUND
TO WINDHOEK

WELWITSCHIA PLAINS

HOTSAS

WALVIS BAY

GANAB

SANDWICH HARBOUR

ARUVLEI
TO WINDHOEK

SANDVIS

TO WINDHOEK

NAMIB REST CAMP

NAMIB-NAUKLUFT LODGE

KULALA TENTED CAMP

SESRIEM
NAUKLUFT MTS.

SOSSUSVLEI
ZEBRA RIVER LODGE

ATLANTIC OCEAN

LITTLE KULALA AND KULALA DESERT LODGE

SOSSUSVLEI WILDERNESS CAMP

SOSSUSVLEI MOUNTAIN LODGE

CAMP MWISHO

MALTAHOHE

WOLWEDANS LODGE & DUNE CAMP

Legend

- Lodge
- Park Bungalow
- Tented Camp
- Mountains
- Town
- Wildlife Area
- Campsites
- --- Dirt Road
- Swamp Area
- Points of Interest

N

LÜDERITZ

| 0 | 30 | 60 | 90 km |
| 0 | 19 | 37 | 56 miles |

1 inch = 56 miles / 90 km

TO KEETMANSHOOP >

431

The **Naukluft** region is an important watershed that is characterized by dolomitic mountains over 6,445 feet (1,965 m) in height with massive picturesque rock formations and thickly foliated riverbeds. Large numbers of mountain zebra, along with springbok, kudu, klipspringer, rock hyrax, baboon and black eagles are frequently sighted. Also present are cheetah and leopard.

There are several hiking trails from which to choose. One of the more interesting trails is the Naukluft Trail, 10.5 miles (17 km) in length, requiring six to seven hours of hiking. A 75-mile (120-km) trail, which takes eight days, may also be hiked April-October, with prior permission.

Sesriem Canyon is about 0.6 mile (1 km) long and is as narrow as 6 feet (2 m), with walls about 100 feet (30 m) high. In some places the canyon takes on a cave or tunnel-like appearance.

Sossusvlei has the highest sand dunes in the world, exceeding 1,000 feet (300 m). The base of the second highest sand dune in the world can be closely approached by vehicle.

The hike along the knife-edge rim to the top is strenuous, requiring 60–90 minutes of taking two steps up and sliding one step down. The view from the top into other valleys and of the mountains beyond is marvelous. Even up there, colorful beetles, ants and other desert critters roam about.

Driving back to camp from Sossusvlei, a gemsbok ran full speed beside our vehicle for several minutes, proving the strength and resiliency of these majestic animals.

Sunrise on these magnificent and colorful dunes is spectacular.

Ballooning safaris are offered by one company and can be booked from most lodges including Camp Mwisho, Kulala Desert Lodge, Little Kulala, Kulala Tented Camp, Sossusvlei Wilderness Camp and Sossusvlei Lodge.

At Sossusvlei, camping is not allowed and there are no accommodations.

 ACCOMMODATION – CLASS A+: * *Little Kulala* has eight thatch-and-canvas chalets or "Kulalas" (Swahili for resting place) with ensuite bathrooms set on wooden platforms, and private plunge pools. Guests may also sleep under the stars on the roof of their chalet — a private stargazing platform!

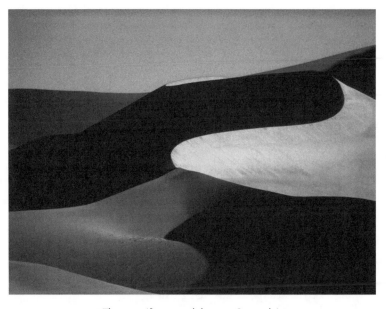

The magnificent sand dunes at Sossusvlei.

ACCOMMODATION – CLASS A: *Kulala Desert Lodge, Little Kulala, Kulala Tented Camp* and *Sossusvlei Wilderness Camp* are located on the scenic, 52,000-acre (21,000-hectare) Kulala Wilderness Reserve, which is on the boundary of the park. Close proximity to the park gate provides for quick access into the park. Activities include day visits to the Sossusvlei dunes, desert breakfasts under the camel-thorn acacia trees, visit to Sesriem Canyon, drives into the desert, ballooning, walking trails, horseback riding, and visits to Bushman paintings on the private reserve. * *Kulala Desert Lodge,* situated on the boundary of Sossusvlei, is a 24-bed tented camp with ensuite facilities. A rooftop sleeping area allows guests to enjoy a night under the spectacular desert sky.
* *Sossusvlei Wilderness Lodge* is built near the top of a mountain overlooking vast open plains. There are 10 bungalows with ensuite bathrooms. The main living area is under thatch * *Sossusvlei Mountain Lodge* has 10 spacious air-conditioned stone-and-glass suites with ensuite facilities. Activities include walks, ballooning, and scenic drives to Sossusvlei and the Sesriem Canyon. * *Wolwedans Dune Lodge,* set on the 463-square-mile (1,200-km^2) Namib Rand Game Ranch, has chalets with private balconies built on wooden platforms with facilities ensuite.

Kulala Desert Lodge, with Sossusvlei dunes in the background.

CLASS B: * *Kulala Tented Camp,* located on the Kulala Wilderness Reserve, has six tents with ensuite facilities. * *Wolwedans Dune Camp,* set on the 463-square-mile (1200-km²) Namib Rand Game Ranch, has six igloo tents with ensuite facilities. Activities include desert drives, game viewing and walking trails. * *Camp Mwisho,* located 30 miles (50 km) from Sesreim, has three large tents with ensuite facilities, one bungalow and a small swimming pool. Balloon safaris over the Namib Desert, followed by a champagne breakfast, and day and night nature drives are offered. * *Namib-Naukluft Lodge* is a 16-room lodge with ensuite facilities and a swimming pool. * *Zebra River Lodge* is located in the Tsaris Mountains and has seven rooms with ensuite facilities. Swimming, nature drives and hikes to five natural springs are offered on the farm. * *Sossusvlei Lodge,* located in the Sesriem area about 37 miles (60 km) from Sossusvlei, has 45 rooms with ensuite facilities.

CLASS C: * *Namib Rest Camp,* located about 37 miles (60 km) from Sesriem, has 13 rooms with ensuite facilities and a swimming pool.

CAMPING: * *Namib Campsites* have no firewood or water. * *Naukluft Campsites* have water, charcoal and ablution facilities. * *Sesriem Campsite* has two ablution blocks with hot and cold water and a swimming pool. Firewood and fuel are available.

Nicholas Nolting sitting behind a *Welwitschia mirabilis* plant, that may be more than 2000 years old.

SWAKOPMUND AND WALVIS BAY

The resort town of Swakopmund, located on the coast and surrounded by the Namib Desert, has many fine examples of German colonial architecture.

The coastal strip south of Swakopmund to Walvis Bay (a distance of about 20 mi./30 km) has the highest density of shorebirds in southern Africa and perhaps on the whole continent. In excess of 13,000 birds of more than 30 species feed on the nutrient-rich beaches. The majority are palearctic waders, including knot, Curlew sandpiper, turnstone and grey plover (present only between September and April). The threatened Damara tern and black oystercatcher may also be seen.

Walvis Bay plays an important role in Namibia's economy — an international seaport and entry point for many visitors, like ourselves, who embark on one of the many desert adventures the country has to offer. Another fun adventure for us all was quad biking into the dunes just outside of Swakopmund.

Some travelers base themselves at Swakopmund and take day trips to the many attractions in the area. Some of the more interesting excursions include a visit to **Walvis Bay Lagoon**, home to the greater and lesser flamingoes, a visit to the **Moon Valley** and the **Swakop River Canyon**, home to the world's oldest living fossil plant — the welwitschia — and the largest, man-made, offshore Guano Island, home to flocks of cormorants and Cape gulls, as well as pelicans. On the **Dolphin Cruise** you can enjoy champagne and oysters while having a very good chance to observe heavyside and bottlenose dolphins as they swim along side the boat, turtles, and the huge seal colony at Pelican Point.

On a recent visit with my wife and two boys (5 and 8 years old at the time) we were hardly through our introductions to our boat captain when Flipper, a sub-adult seal, hauled himself aboard our 22-foot boat. The captain invited the kids to come closer, and he explained all about the seals. Finally, the kids built up the courage to offer a fish to their new-found friend. Their eyes sparkled with the wonder that only small children can show as they proudly looked back at us while 500 pounds of lumbering Cape Fur Seal flopped over the side of the boat to be transformed to weightless grace.

The best time to visit the coast for sunbathing, fishing and surfing is from December to February; June-July is cold with some rain.

 ACCOMMODATION —FIRST CLASS: * *Swakopmund Hotel & Entertainment Centre,* built around the original colonial railway station, has 90 rooms with ensuite facilities, a swimming pool, tennis courts and a gym. Guests have use of the Rossmund Golf Course, one of only four desert golf courses in the world. * *The Hansa Hotel* is an attractive hotel with 58 rooms with ensuite facilities. * *The Sams Giardino House,* situated with a view of the dunes of the Namib Desert and within walking distance of the city center, has nine rooms with ensuite facilities.

TOURIST CLASS: * *The Strand Hotel* is located on the beachfront and has 45 rooms with private facilities. * *Hotel Schweizerhaus* has 24 rooms (some with seaview) with ensuite facilities.

CAPE CROSS SEAL RESERVE
Cape Cross Seal Reserve, home to the largest breeding seal colony in the southern hemisphere of approximately 200,000 seals, is open daily from 10:00 a.m. to 5:00 p.m.

 CLASS B: * *Cape Cross Lodge,* located 30 miles (50 km) north of Hentie's Bay and 73 miles (118 km) north of Swakopmund, has eight ensuite rooms with superb views of the bay, and a restaurant and wine cellar.

Whale bone on the Skeleton Coast.

SKELETON COAST PARK

Skeletons of shipwrecks and whales may be seen on the treacherous coast of this park, which stretches along the seashore and covers over 2,000 square miles (5,000 km²) of wind-sculpted dunes, canyons and jagged peaks of the Namib.

Skeleton Coast by Amy Schoeman (Southern Book Publishers) is a superb pictorial and factual representation of this fascinating region.

The freezing Benguela Current of the Atlantic flows from Antarctica northward along the Namibian coastline and meets the hot, dry air of the Namib Desert, forming a thick fog bank which often penetrates inland for over 20 miles (32 km) almost every day and often lingers until the desert sun burns it off at 9:00-10:00 a.m. When the winds blow from the east, there is instant sunshine.

The park is divided into southern and northern sections. The **southern section** is more accessible and lies between the Ugab and Hoanib Rivers. Permits and reservations (paid in advance) must be made with the Directorate of Tourism and Resorts for stays at either Torra Bay or Terrace Bay.

The **northern part** of the park has been designated as wilderness area and can be visited only with fly-in safaris.

The northern region has many unusual and fascinating attractions. One such attraction is the **Cape Frio Seal Colony**, which has grown to about 40,000 individuals.

A walk down the **roaring dunes** will give you the surprise of your life. Suddenly, everyone is looking up to spot the B-52 bomber that *must* be overhead. Apparently, the sand is just the right diameter and consistency to create a loud noise when millions of its granules slide down the steep dune. Incredible!

Driving through Hoarusib Canyon, you will witness striking contrasts of dark-green grasses against verdite canyon walls and near-vertical white dunes.

Big game is present in surprisingly large numbers for a desert environment and includes desert elephant, cheetah, leopard and baboon. Brown hyena are plentiful but rarely seen. Black-backed jackal, springbok and gemsbok are often sighted. On a rescent visit we encountered many small and fascinating desert creatures as well as desert elephant, black-backed jackal (over 30, in fact, near the seal colony), herds of majestic gemsbok, springbok, and even a brown hyena!

Birds too are sparse, but interesting. Small flocks of gray's lark forage off the gravel plains, while Ludwig's bustard, tractrac chat and bokmakierie are among the species likely to be seen near camps and on walks.

The east wind brings detritus (small bits of plant matter) providing much-needed compost for plants and food for lizards and beetles. The west wind brings the moisture on which most life depends in this desert — one that is almost completely devoid of water. The ancient "fossil" plant, *Welwitschia mirabilis*, is also found in the region.

On our last visit, my wife and I and the kids had the time of our lives. The activities included fascinating nature walks in the park. It supports some of the most harsh yet tranquil, inhospitable yet fragile environments in the world. Every participant in this unique ecosystem was carefully and cleverly designed for its role, be it the fog-gathering lichens or the water-independent gemsbok.

Our day trips included a visit to the nomadic and very tribal **Himba** people, bedecked in ritualistic jewelry and ochre skins, a fishing trip that did, in fact, provide supper, a visit to Cape Frio Seal Colony, where 30,000 lumps of fur and fat lie basking on the beach, a visit to the "Clay Castles" and an amethyst mine. Add to that a healthy dose

Vehicle at the Skeleton Coast on the Atlantic Ocean.

of the most fantastic and variable scenery you can imagine, and that's about 10% of what the area offers!

ACCOMMODATION – NORTHERN SKELETON COAST – CLASS A/B: * *Skeleton Coast Camp* has six stylishly appointed tents with ensuite facilities. Each tent is set on decking off the ground and has a veranda area with private view. Only guests staying at this camp may visit the exclusive 600,000 acre (240,000 hectare) northern region of the park. In addition to exploring the park, guests may also visit local Himba tribes. The camp is open year-round and only accessible by air.

ACCOMMODATION – SOUTHERN SKELETON COAST – CLASS D: * *Terrace Bay* is open year-round and offers full board and lodging in basic bungalows with private facilities. There is a landing strip for light aircraft.

CAMPING: * *Torra Bay* has campsites and caravan sites and is open only over the holidays (December 1 to January 31). You must be self-contained because supplies are not readily available.

ACCOMMODATION NEAR THE SKELETON COAST – CLASS C: * *Kuidas Camp, Purros Camp* and *Kunene Camp* accommodate guests in basic igloo huts with ensuite chemical toilets and separate bucket showers. Guests normally fly from camp to camp and go on walks and nature drives from the camps.

Giraffe at home in Damaraland.

DAMARALAND

Damaraland is a large region with many attractions and is located east of Skeleton Coast National Park and southwest of Etosha National Park. This is an arid, mountainous region of spectacularly rugged scenery. Damara herders can be seen throughout this region.

The **Brandberg** is a massive mountain covering an area of 19-by-14 miles (23-by-30 km) and rises 6,500 feet (1,980 m) above the surrounding plains to 8,440 feet (2,573 m) above sea level. Its special attraction is that it harbors thousands of rock paintings, including one of the most famous in the region — "The White Lady."

Twyfelfontein has rock engravings of wildlife, including rhino, elephant and giraffe, which are considered to be some of the best on the continent. The **Petrified Forest** has many broken, petrified tree trunks up to about 100 feet (30 m) in length. Welwitschia plants may also be seen here. **Burnt Mountain**, a colorful mountain composed of many shades of purple and red, glows as if on fire when it is struck by the rays of the setting sun.

Wildlife is sparse and should be considered a bonus. However, many consider the search for wildlife, which has adapted to a near-water-

A Himba family.

less environment, well worth the effort. Wildlife includes desert elephant, desert black rhino, lion, desert-dwelling giraffe and Hartmann's mountain zebra. Wildlife migrates east and west along the dry riverbeds in search of food and water.

Among the interesting birds of the region are Ludwig's bustard, Ruppell's korhaan and rosy-faced lovebird.

On a recent visit, some of our sightings included herds of desert elephant and giraffe. We searched for the elusive desert rhino and took nature walks that revealed much about this delicate and fascinating environment.

Damaraland is interesting to visit year-round, and the best time to see big game is April–December.

 ACCOMMODATION – CLASS A/B: * *Damaraland Camp*, an 18-bed, tented camp with ensuite facilities, rock pool and airstrip, is situated in the Huab River valley where desert-adapted elephants are often seen and desert rhino may also be seen. Activities consist of guided walks and nature drives in open vehicles. Twyfelfontein Rock Paintings are located nearby.

CLASS B: * *Palmwag Lodge* has two- and four-bed thatched bungalows (24 beds), and two swimming pools. Activities include hiking and guided tours into their massive 1,737-square-mile (4,500-km²) private reserve that has one of the largest populations of black rhino in Africa. A new luxury tented camp is planned to open in the Palmwag concession that will feature a camel-back rhino-trekking operation, run in conjunction with the "Save the Rhino Trust." This will give guests an opportunity to see conservation in action and to raise funds for the trust by being there. * *Vingerklip Lodge* has 22 comfortable bungalows with ensuite facilities, each with a view across the valley, and a swimming pool.

CLASS C: * *Etendeka Mountain Camp* is a tented camp (16 beds) with communal showers and flush toilets. Exploring the region by open 4wd vehicle and walks is offered. * *Khorixas Rest Camp* has rondavels with ensuite facilities.

CAMPING: * *Khorixas Rest Camp* and *Palmwag Rest Camp* have campsites with an ablution block. Campsites with shower and toilet facilities are also available at Aba Huab River near Twyfelfontein.

KAOKOLAND

This region of rugged mountain ranges interspersed with wide valleys is north of Damaraland and bordered on the west by Skeleton Coast National Park. Wildlife is sparse but includes elephant, giraffe, gemsbok, ostrich and some black rhino and lion. Himba tribes may be seen in the region.

If you wish to visit a Himba village, it is customary to wait a distance from the village until someone comes and invites you in. If you come across a village that is deserted, please do not take anything that you may find lying around. Due to their nomadic lifestyle, the Himba often leave possessions behind because they know they will return.

The best time to visit is May-December. A minimum of two fully self-contained 4wd vehicles per party is required, and a professional guide is highly recommended. There is no fuel in the western region.

 ACCOMMODATION – CLASS A:* *Sierra Cafema*, one of the most remote camps in all of Southern Africa, is located on the Kunene River in an area of incredible beauty. A new camp, built on the site of the old camp, and has six luxury tents with ensuite bathrooms. Walks, nature drives, boat game drives and visits to local Himba tribes are offered. Access is by air charter or on a guided tour.

Epupa Falls, Kunene River.

CLASS B: * *Sesfontein Lodge*, located between Skeleton Coast Park and Etosha National Park, is an old fort with rooms and suites with ensuite facilities. It is arranged around a swimming pool and central oasis-garden.

CLASS C: * *Epupa Camp*, located near Epupa Falls on the Angolan border, has nine tents with ensuite facilities.

ETOSHA NATIONAL PARK

Etosha — the "great white place" or "place of emptiness" — is one of Africa's greatest parks in both size and variety of wildlife species. The park covers 8,598 square miles (22,270 km^2) in the northern part of the country and lies 3,280-4,920 feet (1,000–1,500 m) above sea level.

The park's vegetation is mainly mixed scrub, mopane savannah and dry woodland that surrounds the huge Etosha (Salt) Pan. The pan is a silvery white, shallow depression, dry except during the rainy season. Mirages and dust devils play across what was once a lake fed by a river that long ago changed course. Along the edge of the pan are springs that attract wildlife during the dry winter season.

The eastern areas of the park experience the most rainfall and have denser bush than the northwestern region, which is mainly open grasslands. About 40 water holes spread out along 500 miles (800 km) of roads provide many vantage points from which to watch game.

ETOSHA NATIONAL PARK

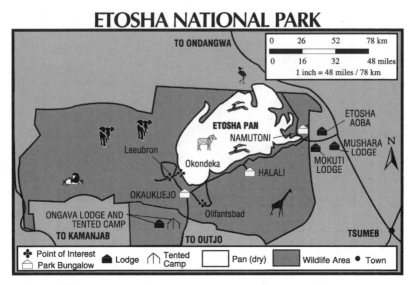

Etosha is famous for its huge elephant population, which is most visible July to September in the center of the park. Large numbers of elephant may also be seen in May, June and October. When the rains begin in January, some elephant herds migrate north to Angola and west to Kaokoland and begin returning in March. Large populations of zebra, blue wildebeest, springbok and gemsbok migrate westward from the Namutoni area in October-November to the west and northwest of Okaukuejo Camp, where they stay until around March-May. From June to August they migrate eastward again, past Okaukuejo and Halali Camps, to the Namutoni plains where there is water year-round. The calving season (which attracts predators) for a number of antelope species is November-April. The park is totally fenced, although this does not always stop the elephant from going where they please.

Lion are commonly seen, and zebra are often sighted way out on the barren pan where lions have no cover from which to launch an attack. Black-faced impala and Damara dikdik, one of Africa's smallest antelopes, are two distinctive species of this area. Black rhino occur throughout the park, with the best viewing opportunities at Okaukuejo. Leopard are seen fairly often.

During one visit, we spotted black rhino, elephant, lion, red hartebeest, greater kudu, giraffe, gemsbok, zebra, blue wildebeest, springbok, black-faced impala, black-backed jackal, honey badger, warthog

Etosha waterhole scene.

and mongoose. Other wildlife in the park includes brown hyena, spotted hyena, caracal, African wildcat, leopard, cheetah, aardwolf, Cape fox, bat-eared fox, eland, roan antelope and grey duiker.

A real attraction to photographers is that it is, in fact, common to see from five to eight or more mammal species at a waterhole at the same time.

Bird life is prolific, and 340 species have been recorded. The main pan is of importance as a regional breeding site for lesser and greater flamingos, as well as white pelicans. Over one million flamingos may gather to breed in the saline shallows of the salt pan, when conditions are suitable, but tourists are not given access to the breeding colonies of these sensitive birds. Birds of prey are particularly well-represented, with martial eagle, black-breasted snake eagle, bateleur, pale chanting goshawk, pygmy falcon and red-necked falcon among the most arresting. Other frequently seen species are red-billed teal, Namaqua sandgrouse, Burchell's sandgrouse, kori bustard, purple roller and crimson-breasted shrike.

Roads run along the eastern, southern and western borders of the Etosha Pan. The area around Namutoni Camp, in the eastern part of the park, receives more rain than the other regions of the park. Eland, kudu and Damara dikdik are often seen in the area. A good spot to see elephant is at Olifantsbad, a water hole between Halali and Okaukuejo Camps.

Okaukuejo Camp.

At the floodlit water hole at Okaukuejo Camp, we witnessed an hour-long standoff between a black rhino and two elephants over control of the water hole. A lioness also came for a drink. The flatulence of the elephants was almost deafening!

From Okaukuejo you can drive along the southwestern edge of the pan to Okondeka and west to the Haunted Forest, a dense concentration of eerie-looking African moringa trees. Etosha is a five-hour drive on good, paved roads or a one-hour charter flight from Windhoek.

 ACCOMMODATION – CLASS A: see *"Ongava Game Reserve" below.*

CLASS A/B: * *Mushara Lodge,* located on the eastern boundary of Etosha, has 13 rooms with air-conditioning, mini-bar, telephones and ensuite facilities. * *Etosha Aoba Lodge* accommodates up to 18 guests in thatched cottages with ensuite facilities and is located 7 miles (12 km) from the Van Lindequist Gate (near Namutoni Camp). * *Mokuti Lodge,* located 500 yards (500 m) from the Van Lindequist Gate, has 106 air-conditioned thatched bungalows with ensuite facilities, a swimming pool and an airstrip.

CLASS B/C, C & D: There are three National Park camps: *Namutoni,* *Halali* and *Okaukuejo.* All three camps have lodge accommodations, trailer (caravan) and camping sites, swimming pool, floodlit water hole, restaurant, store, petrol station and landing strip. The camps are fenced

Ongava Lodge, located adjacent to Etosha.

 for the visitors' protection. * *Namutoni Camp*, situated 7 miles (11 km) from the Van Lindequist Gate, features an attractive fortress built in 1903 that was converted to hotel rooms, many of which have private facilities. * *Halali Camp*, the most modern of the camps, lies halfway between Namutoni and Okaukuejo Camps at the foot of a dolomite hill. Some rooms have private facilities. * *Okaukuejo Camp*, situated 11 miles (18 km) from the Andersson Gate entrance, has chalets with private facilities.

ONGAVA GAME RESERVE

Ongava Game Reserve is a 115-square-mile (300-km²) private reserve along the southern boundary of Etosha near Andersson Gate. The reserve is the top privately owned rhino breeding area in the country, currently with 10 black and 19 white rhino, along with high concentrations of a variety of game.

Night game drives and walks, which are not allowed in Etosha, are allowed on the reserve. Guests staying on the reserve usually take morning game drives in Etosha and take afternoon game drives or walks and night game drives in the reserve. Birdwatching is good. Some of the key Namibian "specials" to be seen here include Hartlaub's francolin, white-tailed shrike, Monteiro's hornbill and bare-cheeked babbler.

ACCOMMODATION – CLASS A: * *Ongava Lodge*, situated on Ongava Game Reserve near Etosha's Andersson Gate, has 10 luxury air-conditioned rock-and-thatch chalets with ensuite facilities, overlooks a flood-lit waterhole, and has a swimming pool and a hide. * *Ongava Tented Camp*, also located on the reserve, has six large tents with ensuite facilities and a private water hole. Both Ongava Lodge and Ongava Tented Camp offer day and night game drives and walks on the reserve and day game drives in open-sided vehicles into Etosha.

KAUDOM GAME RESERVE

Situated in the extreme northeast section of the country on the Botswana border, Kaudom Game Reserve is a 1,480-square-mile (3,800-km²) park, composed primarily of Kalahari sand dunes and dry woodland savannah, and is one of the most remote reserves in Namibia.

Mammal species include elephant, lion, leopard, side-striped jackal, African wild dog, giraffe, wildebeest, eland, kudu, roan antelope and sable antelope.

During the dry season (June–October), game viewing can be good, especially at springs and water holes lying along dry riverbeds, which serve as "roads." However, wildlife is not nearly as concentrated as in Etosha National Park. Kaudom should be visited by primarily those seeking a wilderness experience in a reserve that they will most likely have to themselves.

Birdlife is most interesting between January and April, when aquatic species are attracted to the rain-filled pan systems. Large numbers of knob-billed duck, open-billed stork, black-winged stilt and glossy ibis, to name just a few, crowd the productive waterholes. Palearctic migrants can be numerous in some years, as can be sandpipers, pratincoles and harriers.

Access to the park is from Tsumkwe in the south or Katere in the north. A minimum of two 4wd vehicles are required for each party visiting the reserve.

ACCOMMODATION – CLASS D: * *Sigaretti*, located in the south of the reserve, has three thatched huts with shared facilities. * *Kaudom*, situated in the north of the park, has two huts.

CAMPING: Campsites are available at *Sigaretti* and *Kaudom*.

BUSHMANLAND

Tsumkwe, the unofficial capital of Bushmanland and home to the Bushmen (San) people, borders Botswana and is situated south of Kaudom and east of Grootfontein.

The Ju/'hoan people were the last independent hunters and gatherers in southern Africa, planting no crops and domesticating no animals until 1920. The 2000 or so Ju/'hoansi are now permanently settled in approximately 30 villages where they continue to hunt and gather within *n!oresi* — areas of 115-230 square miles (300-600 km) where different bands have rights to the natural resources. They also keep cattle and earn income through tourism and by selling traditional crafts. They speak the central of three dialects of !Kung — the language spoken by the northern Bushmen.

The Nyae Nyae Conservancy was formed in 1998 and gives the Ju/'hoansi the right to benefit from wildlife and tourism activities in the area. A 4wd vehicle is required to explore the area.

ACCOMMODATION – CLASS B/C: * *Tsumkwe Lodge* can accommodate up to 12 people in six thatched rooms with ensuite facilities. From here, the Nyae Nyae (Bushman) area and the Khaudum Game Reserve 30 miles (50 km) to the north can be explored. Guests are introduced to the cultures and traditions of the Ju/wasi Bushman group. The Ju/wasi show guests how they gather food and introduce them to their customs and beliefs. Guests may even be invited to join the Bushmen on hunt! Access to the camp is by road and air charter.

WATERBERG PLATEAU PARK

Situated south of Etosha National Park and east of the town of Otijiwarongo, this 156-square-mile (400-km²) park is the home of several scarce and endangered species, including black rhino, white rhino, roan antelope and sable antelope. Other species include brown hyena, eland, tsessebe, kudu, gemsbok, giraffe, impala, klipspringer and dikdik. Leopard are sometimes seen on the top of the plateau.

This is a prime area for seeing many of Namibia's near-endemic bird species, and a Mecca for birdwatchers from across the world. Hartlaub's francolin, Ruppell's parrot, white-tailed shrike, Monteiro's hornbill, rockrunner, bare-cheeked babbler and Bradfield's swift are all resident.

Waterberg Plateau Park also contains unique flora, along with rock paintings and engravings. Three trails lead up to the top of the sandstone plateau, which rises over 820 feet (300 m) above the surrounding plains, and one runs across the top. Walking on the plateau is restricted to organized, guided walking trails.

ACCOMMODATION – CLASS C & D: * *Bernarbe de la Bat Rest Camp* has a restaurant, swimming pool and bungalows with and without ensuite facilities.

CAMPING: Campsites with an ablution block are available.

ACCOMMODATION NEAR WATERBERG – CLASS B: * *Okonjima Guest Farm* is family-run and located on a private game reserve. The farm is the home of the Africat Foundation, which is committed to saving cheetah, leopard and lion. Accommodations are in rooms with ensuite facilities. Activities include bird watching, walks and watching orphaned wild animals adopted by the family roam freely about the farm. * *Okonjima Bush Camp*, situated in a wilderness area 2 miles (3 km) from the Main Camp, consists of eight, thatched African-style chalets with ensuite facilities. The main lodge area overlooks a waterhole, and there is a swimming pool. * *African Wilderness Trails* is a farmstead with five ensuite rooms, swimming pool and sauna. Game drives, hikes, and trips to the Waterberg Plateau Park and The Cheetah Conservation Fund project are offered.

THE CAPRIVI STRIP

The Caprivi Strip is the "panhandle" of Namibia, bordered by Angola and Zambia to the north and Botswana on the south.

Much of the wildlife in this region has been poached, especially during the conflict with Angola. However, wildlife populations are increasing, and the Caprivi is well worth a visit for anyone looking for a wilderness experience first, with wildlife as a bonus.

Mudumu National Park and Mamili National Park are similar to Botswana's Okavango Delta.

Access to the region is by scheduled flights to Katima Mulilo, private charter flights and by road.

MAHANGO GAME RESERVE

Mahango is a 96-square-mile (250-km^2) reserve of floodplain and

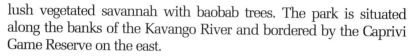

lush vegetated savannah with baobab trees. The park is situated along the banks of the Kavango River and bordered by the Caprivi Game Reserve on the east.

Wildlife includes elephant, hippo, crocs, buffalo, waterbuck, lechwe, reedbuck, bushbuck, kudu, tsessebe, impala and the rare sitatunga. Bird life includes fish eagle, wattled crane, crowned crane and African skimmer. Four-wheel-drive vehicles are required to explore the most remote regions of the park, but 2wd vehicles may be used on the main route.

 CAMPING: *Ngepi campsite,* situated next to a river, has ablution facilities with hot water, bar and restaurant.

ACCOMMODATION AND CAMPING NEAR MAHANGO: See "Popa Falls" below.

POPA FALLS GAME RESERVE

This small park features rapids (more so than "falls") of the Kavango River, which has numerous hippo and crocs. This is a good base from which to explore the Mahango Game Reserve and Caprivi Game Reserve.

ACCOMMODATION NEAR POPA FALLS – CLASS B/C: * *Ndhovu Safari Lodge,* situated close to Popa Falls on the Okavango River across from the Caprivi Game Park and a 1.5 miles (2 km) from Mahango Game Reserve, has tents with ensuite bathrooms, two wooden chalets, restaurant and bar. Boats are available for hire. * *Suclabo Lodge,* located 10 miles (16 km) from Mahango Game Reserve, has 12 chalets with bathrooms ensuite, swimming pool, restaurant and bar. Sundowner boat cruises and half-day excursions to Mahango are offered.

CLASS D: * *Popa Falls Government Camp,* located about 10 miles (16 km) north of the Mahango Game Reserve entrance, has thatched bungalows and ablution facilities.

CAMPING: Campsites with ablution facilities are available.

CAPRIVI GAME RESERVE

Wildlife in this park includes elephant, buffalo, hippo, crocs, roan antelope, sable antelope and plenty of waterfowl.

An all-weather gravel road runs through the park. Travelers are not allowed to leave the main road without permission. Four-wheel-drive vehicles are necessary off the main road.

ACCOMMODATION: None.

CAMPING: Campsites with no facilities are available.

MUDUMU NATIONAL PARK

This newly proclaimed park of floodplains, islands and bush is similar to the Okavango Delta (Botswana), but with not as much game. The Kwando River runs along the park's western border. On a recent visit while on walks we encountered elephant, impala and a number of other species. Other wildlife includes lion, hippo, crocs, roan antelope and sitatunga.

Birdwatching is tremendous. Coppery-tailed coucal, slaty egret, greater swamp warbler, swamp boubou and brown firefinch are all resident, and flocks of migratory carmine and blue-cheeked bee-eaters may be seen between December and April.

Game viewing by open vehicle and walks is allowed. Four-wheel-drive vehicles are recommended.

 ACCOMMODATION – CLASS A/B: *Lianshulu Lodge and its sister lodge, Lianshulu Bush Lodge, are located on the banks of the Kwando River. *Lianshulu Lodge has 10 thatched chalets (doubles) and one honeymoon suite, all with ensuite facilities, and a swimming pool. *Lianshulu Bush Lodge has eight rooms with ensuite bathrooms. Activities include game drives, walks, game viewing by boat, sunset cruises on a double-decker barge and excursions to Mamili National Park. Access is by scheduled flights to Mpacha, air charter and by road.

MAMILI NATIONAL PARK

This newly proclaimed park is predominantly floodplain and has similar wildlife as Mudumu National Park. The Linyanti River flows along its southeastern border, which it shares with Botswana. Wildlife is increasing in this park quite rapidly, and plenty of game is seen on the Botswana side of the river.

 ACCOMMODATION: None. See "Mudumu National Park" above.

CAMPING: Campsites with no facilities are available.

THE SOUTH

INTU AFRIKA

Situated near the town of Mariental, about a three-hour drive south of Windhoek, Intu Africa offers an insight into Bushman culture. A Bushman tracker takes guests into the Kalahari and shares secrets on survival in the bush. The walk usually covers less than a mile (1 km), and afterward guests may be taken to visit the tracker's family. Guests are also shown how the Bushmen make curios and weapons.

ACCOMMODATION – CLASS A: * *Dune Lodge* consists of five luxury chalets with ensuite bathrooms and lounge area. A private game ranger is included.

ACCOMMODATION – CLASS A/B: * *Zebra/Main Lodge* consists of eight air-conditioned colonial-type rooms with bathrooms ensuite.

CLASS B: * *Camelthorn Lodge* has 10 bungalows situated about a 10-minute walk away from the Zebra/Main Lodge. Each bungalow has an ensuite bathroom with shower and flush toilets, and electricity.

CLASS B/C: * *Surricate Camp* has bungalows with ensuite open-air bathrooms with bath and shower and flush toilets. Each tent has electricity. Game drives and Bushman excursions are offered.

FISH RIVER CANYON

Second in size only to the Grand Canyon, Fish River Canyon is 100 miles (161 km) in length, up to 17 miles (27 km) in width and up to 1,800 feet (550 m) deep. The Fish River cuts its way through the canyon to the Orange River, which empties into the Atlantic Ocean.

The vegetation and wildlife are very interesting. Many red aloes make the area appear like you might imagine the planet Mars. Baboons, mountain zebra, rock hyrax, ground squirrel and klipspringer are often seen, while kudu and leopard remain elusive. The river water is cold and deep enough in areas to swim.

There is a well-marked path into the canyon in the north of the park where the four-day hike begins. For those hiking into the canyon for the day, allow 45-60 minutes down and 90 minutes back up. Permission to walk down to the canyon floor must first be obtained from the ranger at Hobas.

The main hiking trail is 53 miles (86 km) in length and is open May-August. The going is tough because much of the walking is on the sandy, rock-strewn floor. No facilities exist enroute, so this hike is not for the tenderfoot. Water is readily available (bring purification tablets) from the many pools that join to become a river during the rainy summers. Hot sulfur springs are located about halfway through the hike.

A maximum group of 40 people is allowed per day. Permits must be obtained in advance from the Directorate of Tourism and Resorts. A medical certificate of fitness is also required. There are plans on the drawing board to link the Fish River Canyon National Park with the Richterveld National Park in South Africa, to create a vast Trans-frontier Peace Park conservation area.

ACCOMMODATION – CLASS A/B: * *Canyon Lodge*, located 12 miles (20 km) from the main viewpoint, has 28 thatched bungalows with ensuite facilities. The original farmhouse, built in 1910, serves as the restaurant.

ACCOMMODATION – CLASS C: * *Ai-Ais Hot Springs*, located at the southern end of the canyon at the end of the hiking trail, has rooms with private facilities, refrigerators and hot plates, a large thermally heated swimming pool and mineral baths. Ai-Ais is open from the second Friday in March through the end of October.

CAMPING: * *Ai-Ais* campsites have hot showers. * *Hobas* campsite, located at the trailhead in the north of the park, has hot showers and a swimming pool.

SOUTH AFRICA

THE TERRITORIAL WHITE RHINO

The population of white rhinos has, fortunately, increased from a precarious population of just 20 individuals at the beginning of the 20th century, to a current population of over 7,000 individuals that have repopulated areas where the species had become locally extinct. The male white rhino maintains a territory, whereas the cow moves across boundries, led by calves or sub-adult offspring. Territorial bulls are the only males that will mate with a female within a marked territory, and they have devised several ways of marking and maintaining their distinct boundaries.

The bull paws the ground and scuffles the dust with his feet, or he scrapes the bushes or the bark of a tree with his horns. Then, curling his tail back over his rump, he sprays urine backward between his legs onto his scentpost, impregnating it with his scent. Other bulls moving within the area will use the spot to urinate but will not spray-urinate because the area has already been reserved.

The territorial male also uses the same spot for defecating. These dung latrines are known as middens. Rhinos scrape their dung over the midden pile in a backwards motion with their feet, similar to the urination spraying.

Territories may overlap, however, and the territorial bull can be challenged by another bull that is looking for a new territory or following a female in estrus. If the territorial bull loses, he becomes a subordinate bull and moves out of the marked area to find a new one.

If a female in heat moves into a territory, the territorial bull tries to keep her by squealing and horn clashing and by physically preventing her from leaving.

When on conducted walks and tracking rhino spoor, territorial markings are signs of a bull's presence. These spoor can indicate how recently rhino have moved through the area, and they allow the guide to interpret how long ago they may have passed.

SOUTH AFRICA

Wildlife Area ☆ Capital
- - - Railroad ● Town
— Road

ZIMBABWE

BOTSWANA

WELGEVONDEN AND MARAKELE

SUN CITY AND PILANSBERG

PRIVATE RESERVES

KRUGER NATIONAL PARK

MOZAM-BIQUE

KGALAGADI TRANS-FRONTIER PARK

MADIKWE

JOHANNESBURG

PRETORIA

MBABAN

NAMIBIA

TSWALU

UPINGTON

SWAZILAND

PHINDA

GREATER ST. LUCIA WETLAND PARK

KIMBERLEY

HLUHLUWE UMFOLOZI PARK

MASERU

RICHARD'S BAY

NAMAQUALAND

LESOTHO

DURBAN

LAMBERTS BAY

INDIAN OCEAN

N

ATLANTIC OCEAN

CEDERBERG

ADDO

SHAMWARI

KWANDWE

EAST LONDON

OUDTSHOORN

CAPE TOWN

PORT ELIZABETH

PLETTENBERG BAY

HERMANUS

GEORGE

KNYSNA

CAPE AGULHAS

| 0 | 193 | 386 | 579 km |
| 0 | 90 | 180 | 360 miles |

1 inch = 360 miles / 579 km

FACTS AT A GLANCE

AREA: 471,445 sq. mi. /1,221,037 sq. km.

APPROXIMATE SIZE: Twice the size of Texas or Great Britain

POPULATION: 40.5 million

CAPITALS: Administrative — Pretoria (pop. est. 1.5 million); Legislative — Cape Town (pop. est. 2.5 million); Judicial — Bloemfontein (pop. est. 310,000)

OFFICIAL LANGUAGES: Afrikaans, English, isiNdebele, Sesotho sa Leboa, Sesotho, siSwati, Xitsonga, Setswana, Tshivenda, isiXhosa, and isiZulu.

SOUTH AFRICA

South Africa is commonly promoted as "The Rainbow Nation" and "A World In One Country", and with two oceans, subtropical savannah, arid scrubland, deserts, and the impressive Drakensberg Mountains, this is hard to deny. This large country is rich in natural beauty and wildlife diversity and covers about 4% of the continent's land surface. The southwestern corner (Cape Town and surroundings) is climatically and botanically unique. The country consists of a high-altitude central plateau surrounded by a rim of mountains, which are particularly impressive in the KwaZulu-Natal Drakensberg. Think of an inverted soup bowl, and you will have a rough idea of the country's landscape.

The plateau is temperate in climate, and it is there that most people live and where agriculture is most developed. In the south, the coastal plain is very narrow or non-existent, with cliffs often plunging directly into the sea. In the east, the lowlands are more extensive, most notably in the warm lowveld with the Kruger National Park and its rich wildlife. The country's largest river is the Orange, which rises in Lesotho and meanders some 600 miles (1,000 km) west to spill out into the Atlantic Ocean. A number of large rivers drain to the east and to the Indian Ocean, predominantly the Limpopo, Olifants, Sabie, Komati, Umfolozi, Tugela and Kei.

There are three distinct climatic zones within South Africa. The entire central plateau and eastern parts, including the lowveld, experience summer rainfall (October to March). It is warm to hot (depending upon altitude) in summer and cool to warm during winter (May to August). Nights can be cold, even at lower altitudes, in mid-winter. The southwestern corner, including Cape Town, experiences dry, warm summers and cool, wet winters — a Mediterranean climate not unlike California or southern France. The region east of the southwestern Cape, extending along the coast to East London, experiences rainfall throughout the year, but is prone to drought conditions.

Seventy percent of the population belong to four ethnic groups: Zulu (the largest), Xhosa, Tswana and Bapedi. Fifteen percent of the population is white, of which 60% is Afrikaner. English and Afrikaans are spoken throughout the country.

In 1488 Portuguese navigator Bartholomew Dias discovered the Cape of Good Hope. The first Dutch settlers arrived in 1652 and the first British settlers in 1820. To escape British rule, Boer (which means farmer) Voortrekkers (forward marchers) moved from Cape Town to the north and east, establishing the independent Republic of the Transvaal and Orange Free State.

Two very big economic breakthroughs were the discovery of diamonds in 1869 and, even more importantly, the discovery of gold in Transvaal shortly thereafter. Conflict between the British and Boers resulted in two separate Anglo-Boer Wars from 1899 and the ultimate British victory in 1902.

In 1910 the Union of South Africa was formed and remained a member of the British Commonwealth until May 31, 1961, when the Republic of South Africa was formed outside the British Commonwealth. On April 27, 1994, a national election open to all races was held and was won by the African National Congress (ANC) under the charismatic leadership of Nelson Mandela. Since that time, South Africa has been welcomed back into the international fold, and tourism has increased dramatically.

WILDLIFE AND WILDLIFE AREAS

In line with its numerous distinct geographic, altitudinal and climatic zones, South Africa supports a great diversity of wildlife and plants. In fact, well over 10% of all the world's plants and flowers occur in South Africa. Virtually all of Africa's great land mammals are to be found (mostly in the eastern lowlands), as well as whales, dolphins and other marine species in the surrounding oceans. In many places, large mammals have been reintroduced to locations where they were once hunted to extinction, with the white rhinoceros being perhaps the biggest success story.

Birdlife is outstanding throughout the country, with some 600 breeding species and close to 800 overall, including Eurasian migrants and seabirds. A good number of bird species are endemic (restricted) to South Africa, particularly in the Karoo, highveld grasslands and Cape fynbos regions, making this a highly popular destination among international birdwatchers.

Reptiles, frogs and other life forms are equally well represented. The Cape fynbos region is home to an astonishing 8500 plant species and is considered to be one of the world's eight Floristic Regions. The plants in this winter rainfall area are characterized by relatively small leaves and include many varieties of erica and protea. The Karoo is a semi-arid scrubland, but it is a botanist's dream because of its astonishing number of hardy and succulent plants. The much-celebrated Namaqualand region is renowned for its springtime (late August-early September) displays of colorful flowers. True forests are sparse in South Africa, with only small patches on the south coast near Knysna and Transkei, and along the Northern KwaZulu-Natal coast and in the eastern escarpment. Acacia, combretum and mopane dominate the sub-tropical lowlands, with taller, evergreen trees along rivers and watercourses.

South Africa has a good network of protected areas, with over 700 publicly owned reserves (including 19 national parks), which cover about 6% of the land surface. In addition to that, there are about 200 private game and wildlife reserves. The Kruger National Park is the largest park, and together with the second largest (Kgalagadi Transfrontier Park), accounts for about 40% of the total protected area. The great majority of the other parks and sanctuaries are quite small.

In recent years, South Africa has been the primary catalyst for a number of proposed Trans Frontier Conservation Areas (TFCAs), which link protected areas across national boundaries and form "corridors" to link separated parks. The idea is to have multi-use areas, which incorporate the needs of local people while safeguarding the natural resources over a larger area. The first of these areas to be formally promulgated was the Kgalagadi National Park, which is shared with Botswana, to embrace the Kalahari Gemsbok National Park. Other TFCAs are in various stages of negotiation and development in Mozambique, Swaziland, Namibia and Zimbabwe.

The Kruger and other national parks are ideally suited to self-drive visitors and are most popular with South African holiday-makers and larger coach-tour (40+ tourists) groups. Open vehicles are generally not allowed, although a few local companies are now allowed open sided and canvas-roofed vehicles. Visitors are required to stick to a designated road and track network.

Accommodation is mostly at large rest camps, although there are some smaller bush camps. Most campsites have ablution blocks (communal bathrooms) with hot and cold water, and many sites even have laundry facilities. Generally speaking, the major roads in the parks are tarred and the minor roads are constructed of good quality gravel, allowing for comfortable riding — and mass tourism. In contrast, a number of private reserves offer premier accommodation, superb food, day and night game drives in open vehicles and escorted walks.

Leopard, lion and other animals have become accustomed to game viewing vehicles at several of these comparatively small reserves, and local guides often know the territories or whereabouts of particular animals, which ensures more predictable and intimate encounters. Trained guides and trackers interpret the wildlife and ecosystem for guests. In a move toward partial privatization, the Kruger has recently allocated sites within the park for experienced operators to set up and manage more exclusive camps and lodges.

GAUTENG

JOHANNESBURG
Johannesburg began as a mining town when the largest deposits of gold in the world were discovered in the Witwatersrand in 1886. Since the Middle Ages, one-third of the gold mined in the world has come from the Witwatersrand field.

This "City of Gold," locally known as "Egoli," is now the country's largest commercial center and city and the country's main gateway for overseas visitors. The city itself has a population of approximately 2 million, while the total urban area including Soweto (SOuth WEstern TOwnships) has a population of approximately 4 million. Attractions include the Museum Africa, the Gold Mine Museum and Gold Reef City, a reconstruction of Johannesburg at the turn of the century, "Cradle of Mankind" anthropological excursions, and the De Wildt Cheetah Centre.

ACCOMMODATION – DELUXE: * *The Saxon Hotel*, located in the Sandhurst suburb of Sandton, makes a world-class statement of ethnic African elegance. Set in six acres of lush landscaped gardens, there are 26 suites overlooking the gardens. * *The Rosebank Grace*, located in Rosebank adjacent to The Mall, is surrounded by a variety of restaurants, boutiques and craft markets. The hotel, rated as "The Third Top Hotel in the World for Service" by Conde Naste Traveler Magazine in 2002, has 75 rooms with ensuite facilities, restaurant, sitting room with library and complimentary café and informal evening wine tastings, heated swimming pool and business center. A walkway connects the hotel directly to "The Mall" shopping center. * *The Michelangelo*, located on Sandton Square, has 242 rooms with ensuite facilities, restaurants, a heated swimming pool, steam bath, fitness center, business center and direct access to one of South Africa's best malls. * *The Westcliff Hotel*, located in the suburb of Westcliff Ridge, has 120 rooms and suites with ensuite facilities, a business center and a swimming pool. Some of the suites have private swimming pools. * *Sandton Sun and Towers Intercontinental* is located adjacent to one of the country's finest shopping malls. The hotel has 334 air-conditioned rooms with ensuite facilities and refrigerators; there is also a health club, swimming pool and five restaurants. * *Park Hyatt Johannesburg*, located in the suburb of Rosebank, has 239 rooms and suites with ensuite facilities, a heated swimming pool, sauna, steam rooms and a gymnasium. * *Johannesburg International Intercontinental* is a brand-new hotel located right across from arrivals and departures at the airport, and it features a restaurant, bar, fitness center and indoor pool. * *Palazzo Inter-Continental – Johannesburg Montecasino*, located in the heart of the Montecasino entertainment complex in the northern suburb of Fourways, has 243 rooms with ensuite facilities.

FIRST CLASS: * *The Emperor Hotel*, located a five-minute drive from Johannesburg International Airport, has 169 air-conditioned rooms with ensuite bathrooms in palatial-style buildings, with a health spa, tennis courts, swimming pool, bars and restaurants. * *Balalaika Hotel*, located in Sandton, has 60 rooms with ensuite facilities. * *Sandton Holiday Inn* has 249 rooms with ensuite facilities. * *Holiday Inn Johannesburg International* has 362 air-conditioned rooms with ensuite facilities and a swimming pool.

TOURIST CLASS: * *The Senator Hotel* has 80 air-conditioned ensuite rooms. Guests may use the facilities at The Emperor Hotel. * *Airport Holiday Inn Garden Court*, located less than a mile from Johannesburg International Airport, has 238 air-conditioned rooms with facilities ensuite, a swimming pool and a sauna. * *City Lodges* have simple rooms with ensuite facilities.

ACCOMMODATION NEAR JOHANNESBURG – DELUXE: * *Mount Grace Country House Hotel*, located in Magaliesburg less than an hour's drive from Johannesburg, has 80 luxuriously appointed rooms with ensuite facilities, swimming pools, a tennis court, lawn bowling, a croquet lawn, walking trail, and a world-class spa. Other activities include horseback riding, mountain biking and fly-fishing.

TOURIST CLASS: * *Lesedi Cultural Village*, located north of Johannesburg, has traditional villages. Guests may visit with families from the Xhosa, Zulu and Sotho cultures. Each traditional homestead at Lesedi is inhabited by a family of elders, wives and children. Guests are accommodated in 16 comfortable rooms with ensuite facilities.

PRETORIA

Pretoria is an attractive city and the administrative capital of South Africa. Points of interest include Paul Kruger's house, Voortrekker Monument, Natural History (Transvaal) Museum, Union Buildings, the State Opera House and Church Square.

ACCOMMODATION – DELUXE: * *Marvol House* of Tshwane is a luxury five-star hotel, styled after the Cape Dutch architecture, that offers 13 air-conditioned suites with ensuite facilities, swimming pool, jacuzzi, sauna, steam room and dining/bar area. * *Kievits Kroon Country Estate*, located 10 minutes north of Pretoria, is a Cape-Dutch themed hotel with 75 ensuite rooms, three restaurants, swimming pool and conference facilities. The Wellness Centre has a heated pool, jacuzzis, sauna, steam bath, gym and health bar. * *Sheraton Pretoria Hotel & Towers*, set opposite the Union Buildings in Pretoria, has 175 ensuite rooms in the Hotel section and seven suites in the Towers section. * *Illyria House* is a privately owned residence in an exclusive suburb of Pretoria with six rooms with ensuite facilities. * *Kloof House*, located in the suburb of Waterkloof, has seven rooms with ensuite or private facilities.

FIRST CLASS: * *Court Classique*, located in Arcadia (Pretoria), has rooms ranging from studios to two-bedroom suites with kitchenettes and ensuite bathrooms. * *Centurion Lake Hotel*, located outside Pretoria on a lake, has 160 rooms with ensuite facilities.

TOURIST CLASS: * *Holiday Inn Garden Court Pretoria – Hatfield* has 238 rooms and suites with ensuite facilities and a swimming pool.

THE BLUE TRAIN

The world-renowned luxurious Blue Train offers an experience that has all but disappeared in modern times. The train is promoted as "A Five-Star Hotel on Wheels," and that it is.

Two Blue Trains were built in South Africa and put into service in 1972. One train accommodates 74 guests in 37 suites while the other accommodates 82 guests in 41 suites. The suites have individual air-conditioning controls, television, radio and ensuite bathrooms with shower or bathtub. The luxury compartments are only about 3 feet (1 m) wider than the deluxe cabins and also contain CD and video players. Each train has 18 carriages and has 34 staff to take care of guests.

Five-star meals (two sittings for lunch and dinner) are served in the beautifully appointed dining car, which features exquisite table settings. Dress for lunch is "smart casual," and for dinner a jacket and tie are required for men and elegant dress for ladies.

The train runs overnight from Cape Town to Pretoria three times a week, and vice versa, year-round, and periodically there are two-night trips from Pretoria to Victoria Falls, and Cape Town to Port Elizabeth. Book well in advance because reservations are often difficult to obtain.

ROVOS RAIL

Rovos Rail has five restored luxury steam trains, each with 20 coaches accommodating up to 72 passengers, two dining cars and an observation car. The Deluxe Suites have ensuite showers, while the Royal Suites have ensuite showers and Victorian baths. Royal Suites are about 50% larger than Deluxe Suites. Jacket and tie are required for men and elegant dress for ladies at dinner.

Rovos Rail departing Cape Town.

On our journey we enjoyed the magical atmosphere of this restored vintage steam train and the scenery enroute, along with quality wines and five-star dining.

You have the choice of a two-night trip from Pretoria to Cape Town with a sightseeing stop in the old mining town of Kimberley and in the quaint village of Matjiesfontein; a two-night trip from Pretoria to Pietersburg, followed by a charter flight to Livingstone, Zambia, to see Victoria Falls; a two-night trip from Pretoria to Komatipoort (game drive in Kruger National Park), continuing to Swaziland (game drive in Mkhaya Game Reserve) and Zululand (game drive in Hluhluwe Umfolozi) ending in Durban; overnight trip along the Garden Route from Cape Town to Knysna via George; an occasional four-night safari from Pretoria to Kimberley, Upington, Windhoek and Swakopmund (Namibia); and a once-a-year, 11-night safari from Cape Town to Dar es Salaam (Tanzania), and vice versa.

MPUMALANGA AND LIMPOPO PROVINCES

KRUGER AND THE PRIVATE RESERVES

The most popular area in the country for wildlife safaris for international visitors is the private reserves that lie along Kruger National

Park's western border, possibly followed by Kruger National Park itself.

There is a tremendous difference in the variety and quality of experience between visiting Kruger National Park and staying in the National Park rest camps versus visiting the adjacent private reserves. In Kruger, which has over 500,000 tourists each year, only closed vehicles are allowed, and off-road driving is not allowed. Park rangers in open park vehicles conduct night game drives, but driving after dark in private vehicles are not allowed. Facilities are fair to basic.

In the adjacent private reserves, day and night game viewing is conducted in open vehicles, walking is allowed and facilities are excellent. In other words, visitors have a greater opportunity to experience the bush in the private reserves than in Kruger. However, a safari to Kruger National Park using national park camps is considerably less expensive than a safari of the same length in the private reserves.

The best game viewing in Kruger National Park is May-October, during the sunny, dry winter season, when the grass has been grazed down and the deciduous plants have lost their leaves. Game viewing in the private reserves is actually good year-round, because the guides are in radio contact with other vehicles (they can direct each other to the best sightings) and can drive off-road in search of game. Calving season is in early spring (September–October) for most game species.

Winter days (June-August) are usually warm, with an average maximum temperature of 73°F (23°C) and clear skies. Late afternoons are cool, while temperatures at night and in the early morning sometimes drop below freezing. From October to February there are light rains, with December, January and February receiving the heaviest downpours. Temperatures from October to February sometimes rise to over 100°F (38°C). March and April are cooler as the rains begin to diminish.

The best time to look for over 450 bird species in this region is October-March — just the opposite of the best game viewing periods. However, birdwatching is good year-round because less than half the bird population is composed of seasonal migrants.

KRUGER NATIONAL PARK

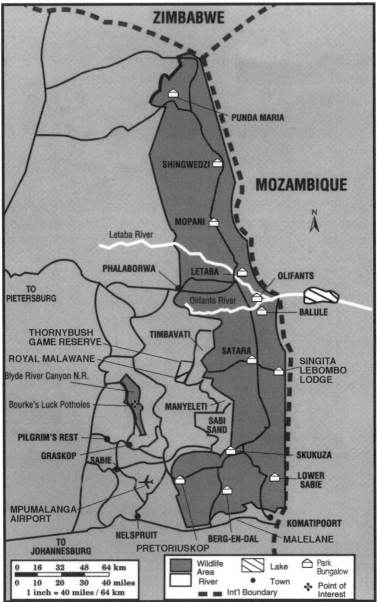

To get to the area from Johannesburg, many people take about an hour's flight to Mpumalanga, Hoedspruit, or an air charter directly to their camp. Alternatively, the drive from Johannesburg to Kruger (Skukuza) is about 250 miles (400 km) northeast on good tarred roads and takes five to six hours.

KRUGER NATIONAL PARK

Kruger is the largest South African park and has more species of wildlife than any other game sanctuary in Africa — 130 species of mammals, 114 species of reptiles, 48 species of fish, 33 species of amphibians and 468 species of birds.

The park is home to large populations of elephant (over 8,000), buffalo (over 25,000), Burchell's zebra (over 25,000), greater kudu, giraffe, impala, white rhino, black rhino, hippopotamus, lion, leopard, cheetah, wild dog and spotted hyena, among others.

Kruger's 7,523 square miles (19,485 km^2) make it nearly the size of the state of Massachusetts. The park is 55 miles wide at its widest point and 220 miles (355 km) long. It had been totally fenced until fairly recently, when the fences separating the park and the Timbavati and Sabi Sand Reserves were taken down, effectively increasing the size of the reserve by 15% and allowing the wildlife greater freedom of movement. However, the annual winter migration routes of antelope, zebra and various other species in search of water and better grazing are still cut off by fences. Several hundred windmills and artificial water holes have been constructed to provide the water that is so desperately needed in the dry season.

The park can be divided into three major regions: northern, central/southeastern and southwestern. Altitude varies from 650 feet (200 m) in the east to 2,950 feet (900 m) at Pretoriuskop in the southwest.

The northern region from the Letaba River to the Limpopo River is the driest. Mopane trees dominate the landscape, with the unique baobab (upside-down) trees becoming increasingly numerous toward Pafuri and the Limpopo River. From Letaba to Punda Maria is the best region for spotting elephant, tsessebe, sable and roan antelope. Elephant prefer this area since it is less developed than the other regions, making it easier to congregate away from roads and traffic, and mopane trees (their preferred source of food) are prevalent.

The central/southeastern region is situated south of Letaba to Orpen Gate and also includes the eastern part of the park from Satara southward, covering Nwanedzi, Lower Sabie and Crocodile Bridge. Grassy plains and scattered knobthorn, leadwood, and marula trees dominate the landscape. Lion inhabit most areas of the park but are most prevalent in this region, where there is also an abundance of zebra and wildebeest — their favorite prey. Cheetah and black-backed jackal are best spotted on the plains. Wild dogs are mainly scattered through flatter areas, with possibly a better chance of finding them in the Letaba-Malopene River area, Skukuza, and northwest of Malelane.

The southwestern part of the park, including a wide strip along the western boundary from Skukuza to Orpen Gate, is more densely forested with thorny thickets, knobthorn, marula and red bush-willow. This is the most difficult region in which to spot game — especially during the rainy season. Many of the park's 600 white rhino prefer this area.

Black rhino are scattered throughout the southern and central areas, often feeding on low-lying acacia trees. Although common, mostly nocturnal leopard are rarely seen. Buffalo roam throughout the park, while hippo prefer to inhabit the deeper parts of Kruger's many rivers by day. Among the most conspicuous of Kruger's birds are the raptors. Commonly encountered throughout the year are the tawny eagle, bateleur, brown snake eagle and martial eagle, while the migratory Wahlberg's eagle is present in large numbers between September and March. A hundred or more white-backed vultures commonly show up at carcasses of large mammals, with lappet-faced, white-headed and hooded vultures in smaller numbers. Even without a prior interest in birds, you'll soon become captivated by the abundant lilac-breasted rollers, yellow-billed hornbills, greater blue-eared starlings, long-tailed shrikes and fork-tailed drongos. Several species of francolin can be seen crossing roads, particularly in the late afternoon, and red-billed oxpecker are always found pecking ticks from the coats of antelope, rhino and giraffe. In the wet season, carmine bee-eater, woodland kingfisher and European roller are conspicuous roadside birds. Some of the best birdwatching is in the rest camps and picnic spots where you have a chance to walk around and listen. When out on the roads, it is advisable to switch

Open game drive vehicle used in a Private Reserve.

---

off the vehicle motor on a regular basis to just listen and wait — you'll soon be rewarded with sightings of a variety of birds.

During school holidays and long weekends, the number of day visitors to the park is limited and accommodations are almost impossible to obtain. Be sure to reserve in advance.

ACCOMMODATION WITHIN KRUGER NATIONAL PARK – CLASS A+: * *Singita Lebombo Lodge* is located on a 37,500-acre (15,000-hectare) private concession area within Kruger National Park, east of Satara along the Mozambique border. The lodge, situated on elevated outcrops overlooking the confluence of the Nwanetsi and Sweni rivers, has 21 luxurious air-conditioned suites (one cluster of 15 suites and one of six) with ensuite facilities and private plunge pools, health spa, gym and swimming pool. Day and night game drives and walks are offered.

CLASS A:* *Ngala Lodge* has 20 air-conditioned cottages with separate lounge and ensuite bathrooms and a swimming pool. Day and night game drives, walks, and three-day walking safaris are offered in a luxury mobile tented camp. * *Ngala Tented Safari Camp* has six spacious tents set on wooden platforms with ensuite facilities and a swimming pool. * *Jock Safari Lodge*, located on a private concession area within the southern part of Kruger, has 12 luxury suites with private salas (outdoor lounges) and a swimming pool. Day and night game drives are conducted.

Singita Boulders reception area.

 ACCOMMODATION – CLASS B/C, C, D & CAMPING: There are 16 National Park Rest Camps that offer a wide range of accommodations, including cottages with ensuite facilities, thatched huts, with or without private facilities, and campsites. The larger rest camps have licensed restaurants. Many of the cottages and huts have cooking facilities and refrigerators.

ACCOMMODATION NEAR KRUGER NATIONAL PARK – CLASS A/B: * *Malelane Intercontinental,* located near Kruger's southernmost gate, has 102 chalets and suites with ensuite facilities overlooking several water holes.

THE PRIVATE RESERVES IN SABI SANDS AREA

Along the western border of Kruger are found a number of privately owned wildlife reserves. Associations of ranchers have fenced the western boundary of their reserves but have not placed fences between their individual properties, allowing game to roam throughout the reserves and Kruger National Park. The private reserves, in general, have exceptionally high standards of accommodation, food and service.

A very important advantage private reserves have over national parks is that private reserves use open vehicles, which give not only a better view but also a much better feel of the bush. At most reserves,

SABI SANDS GAME RESERVE

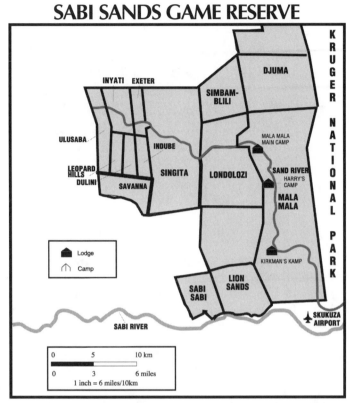

a game tracker sits on the hood or the back of each vehicle. Drivers are in radio contact with each other, greatly increasing the chances of finding those species that guests want to see most.

Vehicles may leave the road to pursue game through the bush. Night drives, which are only allowed in national park vehicles in Kruger, provide an opportunity to spot nocturnal animals rarely seen during the day. Walking safaris with an armed tracker are available.

ACCOMMODATION – SABI-SAND PRIVATE GAME RESERVE: Sabi-Sand Private Game Reserve is situated about a five-hour drive or one hour by air from Johannesburg. There is scheduled air service to Kruger Mpumalanga International Airport located about 87 miles (140 km) from the reserve. All the lodges have airstrips for private air charters. Lodges in the reserve include Singita (Boulders and Ebony camps), Mala Mala (Mala Mala Main Camp, Kirkman's and Harry's camps), Londolozi (Bateleur, Tree, Bush and Pioneer), Ulusaba (Rock and Safari Lodge) and Djuma (Vuyatela Lodge and Djuma Bush Lodge), Sabi Sabi

Mala Mala Main Camp

(Earth, Bush and Selati), Simbambili, Exeter, Inyati and Idube reserves. All of the camps offer day and night game drives and walks. Many guests take scheduled flights to Mpumalanga International Airport and are transferred to their respective camps. Others fly by private charter, drive or travel by tour bus to the camp of their choice.

CLASS A+: Singita was rated by Conde Naste Traveler Magazine as the best resort in the world in 2001. * *Singita Boulders Lodge* has nine air-conditioned suites with ensuite facilities, deck, fireplace and private plunge pool. * *Singita Ebony Lodge* has nine air-conditioned rooms with fireplace, deck, private plunge pool and ensuite facilities. Boulders and Ebony share a gym and spa center. * *Mala Mala* Main Camp is a luxurious camp with 25 air-conditioned, spacious thatched rondavels (each with two ensuite "his" and "hers" bathrooms) and a swimming pool. The lodge has won the "Best Hotel in the World" award from Travel and Leisure Magazine five times. * *Londolozi Pioneer Camp* has six large and luxurious air-conditioned suites with ensuite facilities and a swimming pool. * *Londolozi Tree Camp* has six luxury air-conditioned suites with ensuite facilities. Each suite has its own plunge pool and a private sala. The camp has a boma, swimming pool and lounge deck. * *Earth Lodge* (Sabi Sabi Reserve) has 12 air-conditioned suites with their own plunge pools and patios. The lodge has a wine cellar, health spa, library and swimming pool. * *Ulusaba Rock Lodge*, located on a hill 800 feet (244 m) high, with spectacular views of the reserve, has rooms with ensuite facilities, each with a private deck overlooking the savan-nah below. The lodge has a swimming pool surrounded by a natural waterfall, two tennis courts and a masseuse.

Djuma Vuyatela bedroom.

CLASS A: * *Vuyatela* (Djuma Game Reserve) has eight unique chalet suites, each with a private lounge separated from the bedroom by a beautiful teak deck, ending with a private plunge pool. The main lodge overlooks a water hole and has a suspended birdwatching tower. There is also a gym and relaxation room. * *Londolozi Bateleur Camp* has 10 luxury chalets and two suites (Class A+), each with their own private verandah and plunge pool.* *Londolozi Founders Camp* has six suites with ensuite facilities and a swimming pool. * *Kirkman's Kamp* (Mala Mala Reserve) overlooks the Sand River and has 18 air-conditioned rooms with ensuite facilities and a swimming pool. * *Simbambili Lodge*, located in the northern part of the reserve, has eight air-conditioned, thatched chalets with private facilities, plunge pools and salas. * *Lion Sands River Lodge* is located in the southern part of the reserve with 6 miles (10 km) of river frontage on the Sabie River. The lodge has 14 air-conditioned, thatched rooms with ensuite facilities, gym and heath spa, swimming pool, sala and four hides. * *Lion Sands South Camp* has six air-conditioned, thatched rooms with ensuite facilities, private decks, gym and health spa, swimming pool and two hides. Fishing is also offered. * *Sabi Sabi Bush Lodge* overlooks a water hole and has 22 air-conditioned rooms and five suites with ensuite facilities and a swimming pool. * *Harry's Camp* (Mala Mala Reserve) consists of 12 air-conditioned Ndebele-style rooms with ensuite bathrooms and a swimming pool * *Selati Lodge* (Sabi Sabi) has eight air-conditioned chalets (including a Presidential Suite with private vehicle/guide) with ensuite facilities and a swimming pool. * *Leopard Hills*, located in the western part of Sabi Sands, is built on a hill overlooking a waterhole and has eight air-conditioned suites with private plunge pools and swimming pool. * *Ulusaba Safari Lodge*, situated on the banks of the Mabrak River, has 10 luxurious "tree" chalets built on wooden stilts from which you can watch the game wander by the water hole in front of the lodge. A spa treatment center and tennis courts are shared with guests of Ulusaba Rock Lodge. * *Exeter* has 10 thatched air-conditioned, ensuite chalets set on the banks of the Sand River, and a swimming pool.

CLASS A/B: * *Djuma Bush Lodge* offers seven comfortable air-conditioned thatched-roof rondavels with ensuite facilities, a pool, bar and viewing deck. * *Idube Game Lodge* has nine air-conditioned chalets with ensuite facilities and a swimming pool. * *Inyati Game Lodge* has nine thatched chalets (doubles) with ensuite facilities and a swimming pool.

ACCOMMODATION – MANYELETI GAME RESERVE: Guests fly to Hoedspruit or by charter aircraft directly to their respective camps. CLASS B: * *Honeyguide Safari Camp* caters to a maximum of 24 guests in tents with ensuite facilities. Daily walking trails and night game drives are offered.

ACCOMMODATION – TIMBAVATI GAME RESERVE: Guests of the camps listed below fly to Hoedspruit or by charter aircraft directly to their respective camps. Day and night game drives and walks are offered. CLASS A/B: * *Kings Camp* has 10 air-conditioned, thatched bungalows with ensuite facilities and minibars, and a swimming pool. * *Motswari* has 15 rondavels with ensuite facilities and a swimming pool. * *Tanda Tula* Bush Camp has 12 tents with ensuite facilities.

ACCOMMODATION – OTHER RESERVES IN THE REGION – CLASS A+: * *Royal Malewane*, situated near Hoedspruit and adjacent to the Kruger National Park, has six regal suites including a two-bedroom Royal Suite with private vehicle and guide, providing a feel of original colonial elegance.

CLASS A: * *Thornybush Main Lodge*, located in the Thornybush Game Reserve adjacent to Kruger, has 20 glass-fronted air-conditioned suites including two family units with ensuite facilities and decks overlooking a waterhole, and a swimming pool.

CLASS A/B: * *Edeni Safari Lodge*, situated within the Karongwe Game Reserve, has 13 suites with ensuite facilities, air-conditioning, ceiling fans, a wooden deck overlooking the bush, and a swimming pool.

BLYDE RIVER CANYON, PILGRIM'S REST AND BOURKE'S LUCK POTHOLES

West of the Kruger National Park, the landscape rises abruptly in altitude. This dramatic escarpment, which separates lowveld from highveld, is formed by the imposing Drakensberg range. The best way to appreciate this area is by driving from Hoedspruit, up and through the Strydom Tunnel, to Graskop and then south to the town the Sabie. The Blyde River Canyon is an area of great scenic beauty, with the impressive red sandstone gorge rising half a mile (1 km) above the river below. Three isolated rock pinnacles, each capped with vegetation, have the appearance of traditional African huts and are known as the **Three Rondavels**. This is a good lookout point for birds such as Alpine swift, jackal buzzard and red-winged starling.

South of the Three Rondavels lookout are the astonishing **Bourke's Luck Potholes**. There, the sandstone bedrock has been carved out at the confluence of the Treur and Blyde rivers, to form a series of whirlpool-eroded potholes. Nearby, a number of beautiful waterfalls occur during the summer rainy season, and there are numerous lookout points and short walks. For the fit and enthusiastic, there are back-packing trails into the Blyde River Canyon itself.

The little village of **Graskop**, frequently covered in mist, is famous for its craft and coffee shops. The grasslands fringing the village are home to a few surviving pairs of South Africa's rarest bird — the blue swallow. To the west of Graskop is the picturesque village of **Pilgrim's Rest**, a living museum. This was the site of major alluvial gold panning and digging between 1873 and 1876. Some of the original buildings remain standing, while many others have been meticulously restored. There is certainly great Old World charm about the tin-and-wood buildings — now shops, bars or guesthouses. Explore the unusual and quaint shops, take a drive in a horse-drawn carriage through the village, play golf, fish for trout or go horseback riding.

Cybele Forest Lodge in White River.

The small village nature reserve supports a number of oribi and birds, such as bush blackcap and chorister robin.

South of Pilgrim's Rest is the town of **Sabie**, the center of the region's timber industry. This is the gateway to the winding Long Tom Pass — a smooth tarmac road meandering through highland meadows to the trout fishing havens of **Lydenburg** and **Dullstroom**. The modern road is set upon a wagon route that was charted in 1871, which allowed access to the lowveld and Indian Ocean for the isolated Boer Republic. The name of the pass is derived from a large field gun used by the Boers in a skirmish with the British in 1900.

ACCOMMODATION IN THE REGION – DELUXE: * *Cybele Forest Lodge* (White River) is a lovely lodge with luxuriously appointed rooms and cottages with facilities ensuite and a swimming pool. This forested area is great for walks, horseback riding, and trout fishing. The Spa in the Forest offers a range of health and beauty treatments. * *Blue Mountain Lodge* (White River), located on a 500-acre (200-hectare) estate, has 13 suites with ensuite facilities and a swimming pool. Activities include walking, bass fishing and birdwatching. * *The Coach House* (Tzaneen) has 42 rooms with ensuite facilities and a swimming pool.

FIRST CLASS: * *Hulala Lakeside Lodge* (White River) is set amongst great granite boulders and surrounded on three sides by a lake. The lodge has rooms and suites with ensuite facilities, log fireplaces and private terraces, and a swimming pool. * *Royal Hotel* (Pilgrims Rest) has bedrooms and suites with ensuite facilities.

TOURIST CLASS: * *Mount Sheba* (Pilgrim's Rest) has 25 rooms with ensuite facilities and a swimming pool.

ACCOMMODATION BETWEEN THE REGION AND JOHANNES-BURG – DELUXE: * *Mount Anderson Ranch* is an exclusive 20,000-acre (8,000-hectare) property with three rooms in a large ranch house with ensuite facilities. Trout fishing, horseback riding, nature drives and walks are offered. The lodge is booked out to one private party at a time. * *Walkersons Country Manor* resembles a Scottish highland estate because it is surrounded by lakes and rivers. The suites have log fireplaces and ensuite facilities. Mountain walks and trout fishing are the main attraction. * *Critchley Hackle* is a rustic stone-built complex with ensuite facilities.

WELGEVONDEN GAME RESERVE AND MARAKELE NATIONAL PARK

Located about two and a half hours northwest of Johannesburg, these reserves are destined to become one of South Africa's new wildlife hotspots. Welgevonden is an 85,000-acre (34,000-hectare) private game reserve that borders Marakele National Park's eastern boundary. When combined, these two parks are close to 250,000 acres (100,000 hectares) of wildlife, with all the "Big 5" found in a malaria-free area. The area is known as the "Valley of the Tuskers," because many of the elephant bulls have massive tusks with over 70 pounds (32 kg) of ivory on each side.

ACCOMMODATION – CLASS A: * *Shidzidzi* has five brick-and-thatch lodges with ensuite bathrooms and indoor and outdoor showers. The main lodge has the dining room, a lounge, a bar and a pool. Day and night game drives are conducted in open vehicles. * *Pitsi Laodge* has five ensuite rooms.

NORTH WEST PROVINCE

PILANESBERG NATURE RESERVE

An extinct volcanic crater was the site for one of the most ambitious wildlife restoration projects on the African continent. Officially opened in 1979, Pilanesberg Game Reserve was a joint project between the local community and the provincial administration to transform an area of marginal agricultural value into a productive wildlife estate. This was a highly controversial program at the time, but it proved to be a groundbreaking success. Livestock was removed, villages willingly relocated, and thousands of animals (only species known to occur historically) were reintroduced. The popularity of the neighboring Sun City resort ensured that visitors came from afar, and in good numbers, to fulfill the promise of an improved livelihood for the local community.

This beautiful reserve covers 212 square miles (550 km²) and is located within a 17-mile- (27-km) wide volcanic bowl that rises over the surrounding plains, and it offers good game viewing in a beautiful, hilly setting. Both white and black rhino are fairly common; elephant, eland, red hartebeest and sable antelope are frequently seen. Lion, cheetah and leopard occur in reasonable numbers, and the elusive brown hyena occurs alongside its more gregarious relative, the spotted hyena. Close to 400 species of birds have been recorded, with crimson-breasted shrike, grey hornbill, pearl-spotted owl and golden-breasted bunting among the characteristic residents. Day and night game drives and hot-air balloon safaris are conducted in the reserve.

ACCOMMODATION – CLASS A: * *Kwa Maritane* has 90 comfortable rooms with ensuite facilities and a swimming pool. * *Tshukudu* has six chalets and two cabins with ensuite facilities.

ACCOMMODATION – CLASS B: * *Bakubang* overlooks a hippo pool and has 76 air-conditioned ensuite rooms and 66 self-catering cabanas with ensuite bathrooms, conference center, restaurant, swimming pool and children's playground. Guests may take a 10-minute shuttle to Sun City.

CLASS C & D: * *Kololo,* * *Mankwe,* * *Manyane* and * *Metswedi* camps provide basic tented accommodation.

CAMPING: * *Manyane Caravan and Camping Site* has campsites and ablution facilities.

SUN CITY

Sun City is a premier entertainment vacation complex with Las Vegas-style floor shows, casinos, tennis and a variety of water sports. There are also two world-class golf courses. The Lost City Golf Course is an 18-hole Gary Player-designed course with desert style on the front nine holes and African bushveld on the back nine holes. The Gary Player Golf Course is an 18-hole bushveld course and is

The Palace Hotel of the Lost City, Sun City.

home of the annual Nedbank Golf Challenge. Sun City is a two-hour drive (116 mi./187 km) or a short flight from Johannesburg. Excursions to Pilanesberg Nature Reserve are offered by some of the hotels.

ACCOMMODATION – DELUXE: * *The Palace Hotel of the Lost City* has been constructed as a royal residence from an ancient civilization and is set in 62 acres (25 hectares) of lush gardens. This lavish property has 338 rooms with ensuite facilities, a pool with 6-foot (2-m) surfing waves, water chutes, several restaurants and bars and a world-class Gary Player golf course.

FIRST CLASS: * *The Cascades*, landscaped with lush gardens, waterfalls and a swimming pool, has 245 rooms with facilities ensuite. * *Sun City Hotel* has 340 rooms with ensuite facilities and a swimming pool.

TOURIST CLASS: * *Sun City Cabanas* has 284 cabanas with facilities ensuite.

MADIKWE GAME RESERVE

Following on the success of Pilanesberg, the Northwest provincial authorities embarked upon a similar transformation of a vast semi-arid area close to the Botswana border, known as Madikwe. A vast area of plains, interrupted in places by inselberg rock outcrops, Madikwe is dominated by acacias and sweet grasses. The absence of surface water limited agricultural development, but indigenous wildlife has thrived since "Operation Phoenix" translocated some

8,000 animals from other parks in South Africa, Namibia and Zimbabwe. Madikwe was the site for the first relocation of adult African elephants, moved from Gonarezhou in Zimbabwe in 1993. They have thrived to the point to which some have recently been translocated to Angola.

Two packs of the endangered wild dog occur in the 465-square-mile (750-km²) reserve, alongside lion, cheetah and leopard. Black and white rhino and a wide range of antelope are numerous.

Birdlife is outstanding, with numerous species characteristic of the Kalahari, such as violet-eared waxbill, swallow-tailed bee-eater and pied babbler.

A real plus for some travelers is that the area is malaria free.

 ACCOMMODATION – CLASS A: * *Jaci's Safari Lodge* has nine thatched chalets overlooking a waterhole, with ensuite bathrooms and fireplaces (including a family unit).

THE CAPE PROVINCES

KGALAGADI TRANSFRONTIER PARK

In May 2000 Kalahari Gemsbok National Park was officially merged with Botswana's Gemsbok National Park to form the Kgalagadi Transfrontier Park. The park is located in the northwest corner of South Africa and the southwest corner of Botswana, bordering Namibia to the west. This huge 13,900-square-mile (36,000-km²) park is predominantly semi-desert and open savannah. Scattered thorn trees and grasses lie between red Kalahari sand dunes. San Bushmen inhabited the area as far back as 25,000 years ago.

The most interesting (and productive from an animal-viewing perspective) habitat in the park is the fossil riverbeds. Tens of thousands of years ago, in a wetter era, the Auob and Nossob Rivers flowed into the Orange River, but today they are no more than furrowed drainage lines. They do, however, hold underground water, and once in a decade or so, they flow briefly after particularly heavy downpours. It is in the Auob and Nossob drainage lines that the largest camel thorn acacias grow, providing shade, nutrition and nesting sites for a host of creatures. Grasses grow taller and sweeter here, too. The two main roads in the park follow the Nossob and Auob (they are linked by the

KGALAGADI TRANSFRONTIER PARK

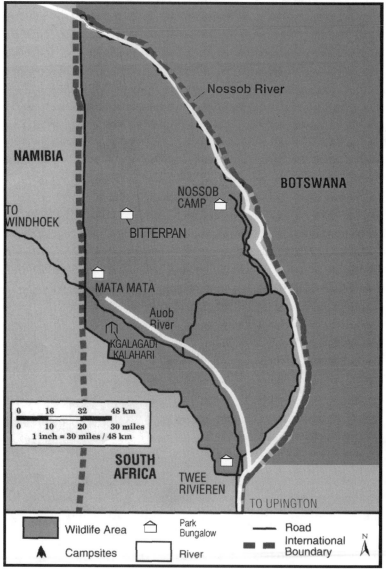

NAMIBIA

Nossob River

BOTSWANA

TO WINDHOEK

NOSSOB CAMP

BITTERPAN

MATA MATA

Auob River

KGALAGADI KALAHARI

| 0 | 16 | 32 | 48 km |
| 0 | 10 | 20 | 30 miles |

1 inch = 30 miles / 48 km

SOUTH AFRICA

TWEE RIVIEREN

TO UPINGTON

| | Wildlife Area | | Park Bungalow | | Road | N |
| | Campsites | | River | | International Boundary | |

so-called "Dune Road") where a much higher concentration of animals are seen than in the surrounding dunes.

The park is famous for the majestic gemsbok (oryx), which occur in abundance. This is also one of the best places to see and photograph the gazelle-like springbok, the national sporting emblem of South Africa. Blue wildebeest occur in small numbers — a mere remnant of a migratory population that may have once rivaled the famed Serengeti herds. Predator viewing is often quite good, with lion, leopard and particularly cheetah, seen with frequency. The Kalahari lions are among the most handsome in Africa, for there is little dense bush to scratch or damage their coats and manes. The elusive, mostly nocturnal brown hyena may be encountered in the early mornings or late afternoon. This park also offers wonderful opportunities to see less common creatures such as honey badger, aardwolf, bat-eared fox and African wild cat, which, though primarily nocturnal, are often active during the day, especially in the cooler winter months.

Birdwatchers will not be disappointed, for the Kalahari supports a wide variety of species not commonly seen elsewhere. The gigantic thatched nests of sociable weavers are unmistakable wonders of avian architecture. Built by the small, sparrow-sized weavers, the huge structures commonly grow to a size that breaks the branches of the tree in which they are built. Birds of prey thrive in the Kalahari, with pale chanting goshawk, gabar goshawk, bateleur, secretarybird, lanner falcon and the tiny pygmy falcon all very common. Giant eagle owl are regularly seen at their daytime roosts, while white-faced and pearl-spotted owls hunt about the rest camps after dark. Three species of sandgrouse can be seen quenching their thirst at waterholes, while the world's heaviest flying bird, the kori bustard, is extremely common.

Summer temperatures can exceed 104°F (40°C). Winter days are pleasant, but temperatures can drop below freezing at night. The animals have adapted to desert conditions by eating plants with high water content, such as wild cucumber and tsamma melon.

The southern entrance to the park is about 255 miles (411 km) north of Upington, which has scheduled air service from other major cities in the country.

ACCOMMODATION – CLASS B: * *Kgalagadi Kalahari Tented Camp*, set on a red sand dune overlooking a waterhole, has 15 tents, including four family units with ensuite facilities, and swimming pool. * *Bitterpan*, located a three-hour drive (4wd only) from Nossob, has four chalets on stilts with shared cooking facilities.

CLASS C&D: There are three rest camps with self-contained cottages with kitchens, huts with and without bathrooms, camping sites, stores, gas (petrol) and diesel. * *Twee Revieren* is located at the southern entrance to the park. The camp has a restaurant, swimming pool and a landing strip for small aircraft. * *Nossob*, located in the northeastern part of the park near the Botswana border, has bungalows with ensuite facilities and kitchens, as well as huts with separate facilities and communal kitchens. The camp has an information center for the plant and animal life in the park and has a landing strip for small aircraft. * *Mata Mata*, located on the western border of the park, has simple cottages with kitchens and ensuite facilities, and huts with separate facilities and a communal kitchen.

ACCOMMODATION NEAR THE PARK – CLASS B & C: * *Molopo Kalahari Lodge*, located 37 miles (60 km) from the park, has 10 air-conditioned rondavels with ensuite facilities and five chalets with separate facilities.

TSWALU PRIVATE DESERT RESERVE

Tswalu Private Desert Reserve is the largest privately owned game reserve in South Africa, covering 290 square miles (900 km²). Black rhino, roan and sable antelope may be seen, as well as up to 30 species of plains game.

The reserve is located west of Kuruman. Transfers are available from Kimberley or Upington; quickest access is by air charter.

ACCOMMODATION: CLASS A: * *Tswalu Lodge* accommodates 22 guests in air-conditioned luxury desert suites with ensuite facilities and double fireplaces. Guests may go on day and night game drives, track desert rhino, go horseback riding, or just relax around the swimming pool. Visits to the sable antelope breeding program can be arranged.

The "Big Hole" at Kimberley.

KIMBERLEY

Kimberley is the "diamond city," where one of the world's biggest diamond strikes occurred in 1868. Visit the open-air museum and the "Big Hole," where over 3 tons of diamonds were removed from the largest hole dug by man on earth.

 ACCOMMODATION – TOURIST CLASS: * *Holiday Inn Garden Court* has 114 rooms with facilities ensuite and a swimming pool.

CAPE TOWN

Sir Francis Drake once said of the Cape Town area, "The fairest cape we saw in the whole circumference of the globe." Today, Cape Town is still thought by many well-traveled people to be one of the most beautiful settings in the world. The Cape reminds me of the California coast — stark, natural beauty and a laid-back atmosphere.

An afternoon **Champagne Cruise** past islands with hundreds of seals, and featuring rocky cliffs and sandy beaches, allows a delightful perspective of the area.

The **Victoria and Alfred Waterfront** has a variety of shops, historical buildings, museums, waterfront walks, restaurants, nightclubs, luxury and first class hotels, three micro breweries, theater, boat trips,

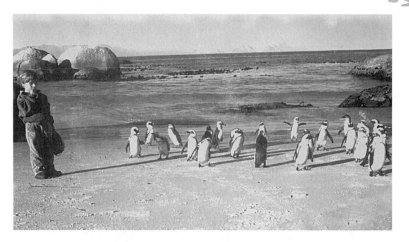

Miles Nolting's first encounter with African penguins.

helicopter rides and the **Two Oceans Aquarium**, which exhibits species from both the Atlantic and the Indian oceans.

Tours to **Robben Island**, where Nelson Mandela was held as a political prisoner for so many years, depart from the Nelson Mandela Gateway situated at the Clock Tower at the Victoria and Alfred Harbor. The boat transfer to the island takes about 30 minutes. An hour tour of the island includes a visit to Mandela's cell, a stone quarry, an old village and a drive around the island, where you may see African (jackass) penguins and have great views of the city.

The one-day excursion down the Cape Peninsula to the **Cape of Good Hope Nature Reserve** and **Cape Point** is one of the finest drives on the continent. The reserve has lovely picnic sites, a population of bontebok and a variety of beautiful wildflowers. Some people say this is where the Atlantic meets the Indian Ocean, but that actually happens at Cape Agulhas, the southernmost point of Africa.

On our recent visit, we saw bontebok and ostrich, while baboons at the ocean's edge were eating mussels they had picked off the rocks. Be sure to stop in **Simon's Town** enroute to visit the wonderful African penguin colony (formally called jackass penguins).

Whale watching in Table Bay, Hout Bay and False Bay is good July-August and best September-October. **Kirstenbosch National**

Botanical Gardens, one of the finest gardens in the world, has 9,000 of the 21,000 flowering plants of southern Africa. A recent addition to the gardens is a magnificent glass-house conservatory containing succulent plants from all over southern Africa, including an exquisite baobab tree.

The **Cableway** (or three-hour hike) up **Table Mountain**, with breathtaking views, is a must. The cable car can take 65 passengers at a time and does a full rotation on the way up. There is a good restaurant on the top of the mountain. Bring warm clothing because it is usually much cooler and windier on top. Table Mountain also offers the highest commercial **abseiling** or **rappelling** in the world.

A more active way to discover the area is by **kayaking** in single or double kayaks. Trips are available around Cape Point, from Table Bay to Clifton, in Hout Bay, in the Langebaan Lagoon and at Rietvlei (for birdwatching), and from Simons Town to Boulders Beach to see the penguin colony. **Horseback riding** on beaches at Hout Bay, on the beaches, dunes and lagoons at Noordhoek Valley, or in the winelands is another great option. **Mountain biking** off Table Mountain to The Cape of Good Hope Nature Reserve and in the winelands is popular. From the Victoria & Alfred Waterfront, you may go **Oceanrafting** in rubberducks (Zodiacs), which reach speeds in excess of 80 mph (120km/hr). **Wet bikes** and **jet skis** may be rented in Blouberg and Muizenberg. **Quad bikes** may be rented in Melkbos, 30 minutes from central Cape Town. **Sand boarding** is offered on some of the biggest sand dunes in the Cape, about an hour's drive out of Cape Town, either in Atlantis or Betty's Bay. **Thunder City** offers one-hour flights in fighter jets — with just you and the pilot!

The Atlantic Ocean and False Bay offer good angling and deep-sea **fishing**. Maasbanker and mackerel are numerous in the warmer waters in Table Bay in summer, while False Bay is one of the top angling areas with the Gordon Bay harbor as an entry point to the ocean. The fishing harbors of Kalk Bay and Hout Bay are excellent, particularly at the peak of the season around June and July. Simon's Town is the principle harbor for tuna boats, and there is a club for tuna fisherman and boats, which also offers boats for charter. At the Cape of Good Hope Nature Reserve, fishing is particularly good from the rocky vantage points on both sides of the Peninsula. The west coast offers good fishing at many points along the coast. At Bloubergstrand, fishing off the rocks is good. Fishing charters depart from the V&A Waterfront, Hout Bay, Simon's Town and Gordon's Bay and range from four hours to a full day.

Some of the finer **restaurants** include Quay 4, Quay West, the Atlantic Grill, Baia and Emilys (Victoria and Alfred Waterfront), Buitenverwachting, Constantia Uitsig, La Colombe and Cape Malay Kitchen (Constantia); Blue Danube (Tamboerskloof); Panama Jacks (Town Harbour); Leinster Hall (Gardens); Blues and Vilamoura (Camps Bay); The Restaurant, the Africa Café and Café Riteve (Cape Town city), Brass Bell (Kalk Bay); and La Perla (Sea Point). The Wooden Bridge, situated across Table Bay, is exceptionally nice in summer; guests may watch the sun set behind Table Mountain.

Cape Town has many fabulous **shopping** areas, including The Victoria and Alfred Waterfront small shops (excellent quality and variety), Greenmarket Square (local stalls featuring African Crafts, textiles and handmade goods, Mon.-Sat. only), Cape of Good Hope Fine Wine Exporters (will arrange to ship cases of wine home — you will probably have to pay duty), The Collector (Church Street — a small downtown gallery), Jewel Africa (City Centre — manufacturing jeweler, enormous variety of precious and semi-precious stones, also curios and craftwork), Uwe Koetter (manufacturing jeweler), Cape Gallery and Pan African Market (Church Street), Long Street Arcade (variety of antique and collectable dealers in one arcade) and La Cotte Wineshop (Franschhoek — noted for its extensive selection of older wines, shipping arranged).

February-March is the best time to visit the Cape because there is very little wind; October-January is warm and windy and is also a good time to visit. May-August is rainy and cool. However, this is one of the most beautiful cities in the world to visit any time of the year.

ACCOMMODATION – DELUXE: * *Ellerman House* is a grand old home with 10 suites with ensuite facilities and a swimming pool, gym and steam bath. It is an historical landmark situated in the suburb of Bantry Bay within walking distance of the famous Clifton Beach. * *Cape Grace* is an elegant hotel located in the Victoria and Alfred Waterfront on its own quay, with 104 rooms and suites with ensuite facilities, restaurant, lounge, "Bascule" whiskey bar and a swimming pool. It was voted by Conde Naste Traveler Magazine as the "Number One Hotel in the World" in 2001. * *Table Bay* is a 330-room hotel located in the Victoria and Alfred Waterfront with ensuite facilities, satellite television, a restaurant, conference facilities and a swimming pool, spa and health club. * *Mount Nelson* is an Old World British hotel set on seven land-scaped acres. The hotel is situated near the base of Table Mountain and has rooms with facilities ensuite and a swimming pool. * *Le Vendome*, situated in Sea Point, is an elegant hotel with 143 rooms and luxury suites, two restaurants and a swimming pool.

FIRST CLASS: * *Radisson Waterfront Hotel* (formerly the Villa Via Granger Bay Hotel), located a few minutes' walk or complementary hotel shuttle to the Victoria and Alfred Waterfront, has 187 rooms with ensuite facilities, two restaurants and a pool. Rooms either overlook the ocean in front or Table Mountain behind. * *Peninsula Hotel*, located in Sea Point facing the Atlantic Ocean, has 112 suites with one to three bedrooms and two swimming pools. * *Victoria and Alfred Hotel*, located in the Victoria and Alfred Waterfront, has 68 air-conditioned rooms with ensuite facilities.

TOURIST CLASS: * *The Commodore Hotel* is located a few minutes' walk from the Victoria and Alfred Waterfront and has 225 air-conditioned rooms. * *Portswood Hotel*, located a five-minute walk to the Victoria and Alfred Waterfront, has 104 air-conditioned rooms with ensuite facilities. * *The Cullinan Inn*, located near the entrance to the Victoria and Alfred Waterfront, has 416 rooms all with bath and separate shower, bar, swimming pool, gym and restaurant. * *Holiday Inn V&A Waterfront* has 546 air-conditioned rooms, restaurant, bar, gym and swimming pool. * *Holiday Inn Cape Town* is a downtown business hotel with a great view of the harbor; it has 362 rooms with facilities ensuite and a pool, health club and gym.

GUESTHOUSES: * *Kensington Place* is located within walking distance to Cape Town's trendy Kloof Street, with its diverse eating and shopping establishments. It has six suites with private balconies overlooking the bay and Table Mountain, and a swimming pool. * *Clarendon House* is an elegant guesthouse situated in Fresnaye, one of Cape Town's prime residential seafront suburbs. Each of the seven bedrooms has ensuite bathrooms. * *Welgelegen*, a beautiful double-story Victorian home in the popular suburb of Gardens within walking distance of Kloof Street, has ensuite bedrooms and a swimming pool.

ACCOMMODATION IN THE CAPE AREA – DELUXE: * *The Cellars-Hohenhort Hotel* is comprised of two luxury country houses with a swimming pool and is situated in the beautiful Constantia Valley, a 15-minute drive from Cape Town. All 38 rooms and 15 suites have ensuite facilities. * *Bay Hotel*, located on the beach at Camps Bay, a 10-minute drive out of Cape Town, has 70 rooms and suites with ensuite facilities and a swimming pool. * *Twelve Apostles Hotel* has 70 ensuite rooms, some with sea and some with mountain views, swimming pool and restaurant.

FIRST CLASS: * *Constantia Uitsig,* located on a 200-acre (80-hectare) private wine farm in the Constantia Valley, offers simple elegance with 16 garden suites with ensuite bathrooms, Uitsig and La Colombe (two of the top restaurants in South Africa) and a swimming pool.
* *Greenways,* located near Kirstenbosch Botanical Gardens, is a magnificent mansion with eight rooms and six suites with ensuite facilities, a swimming pool and a croquet lawn. * *The Palm House* is an elegant guesthouse with 11 rooms with ensuite facilities.

THE WINELANDS

From humble beginnings as an experimental vineyard, below Table Mountain, by the Dutch East India Company during the 17th Century, the wine industry in South Africa today has spread over a large and diverse area. Grapes are grown in nearly 60 officially declared appellations covering over 250,000 acres (100,000 hectares).

There are six important wine producing areas within a two-hour drive of Cape Town, offering an amazing array of different wine styles from the many estates, private wine cellars and cooperatives. A superb marine- and mountain-influenced climate, coupled with stunning scenery, makes this an attractive area to visit. Hundreds of restaurants serve interesting regional cuisine matched to the local wines, which helps to drive the continuing Cape wine renaissance. The areas close to Cape Town are 1) Constantia, 2) Durbanville, 3) Paarl, Wellington and Franschhoek, 4) Stellenbosch, 5) Swartland, and 6) Walker Bay. **Constantia** is sometimes referred to as the cradle of wine making in the Cape; Simon vander Stel was granted land here in 1685. Constantia is a leafy zone on the southeast of the Cape Peninsula facing the Atlantic Ocean. It is cooled by sea breezes from two sides, southeasterly from False Bay, and northerly gusts over the

Roggeland Country House in the Paarl Winelands area.

Constantiaberg mountain spine. Red and white wines are produced, but the area is recognized for whites, especially sauvignon blanc. **Durbanville** is an area in transition from rustic tradition to modern development. The area of rolling hills north of the city gets cooling nighttime mists and influences from both Table and False Bays. Wine farming dates from 1716, and the area was originally known for bulk wine production, but is now recognized for sauvignon blanc and merlot. **Paarl, Wellington and Franschhoek** have a variety of microclimates, soil types and grape varieties, with German and Huguenot heritage as well as the Dutch dating from the 17th Century. Paarl is noted for shiraz, and more recently viognier, while Franschhoek has become a center for food and wine appreciation. The area is better known for white wine styles, especially chenin and semillon, but some wonderful shiraz and "bordeaux style" red blends are also being produced. **Stellenbosch** is known to most as *the* red wine producing area in South Africa. However, the local estates produce great sparkling, white and fortified wines, as well. Cooler mountain slopes and cooling sea breezes from False Bay help moderate summer temperatures. The Simonsberg and Helderberg mountain areas fall within the Stellenbosch region. The area is recognized for cabernet, pinotage, shiraz and sparkling wines. **Swartland** is the wheat and tobacco farming area north of Cape Town, and it is traditionally associated with big red wines. Swartland is now producing very good white wines — especially in the Groenekloof area that provides cooling Atlantic ocean breezes. Swartland, along with the Malmesbury and Tulbagh areas, is recognized for pinotage, shiraz and sauvignon blanc. The age-old adage that the best wine is grown within sight of the ocean is true for

Walker Bay. Famous also for the winter whale watching, the area, which includes Elgin, is recognized for pinot noir, chardonnay and pinotage.

The main towns of the Cape Winelands are Stellenbosch, Paarl and Franschhoek. **Stellenbosch** is known for its unique Cape Dutch architectural heritage and the Stellenbosch (Maties) University. The town is also home to the Bergkelder wine complex, the Village Museum, and many galleries, specialty and antique shops. **Paarl** is the home of the Afrikaans Language Museum and the Taal Language Monument, and the KWV wine complex located in the Berg River Valley between the dramatic mountain scenery of the Paarlberg and the Klein Drakenstein Mountains. **Franschhoek**, nestled in the Valley of the Huguenots among spectacular mountains, is a charming village with many galleries, shops, cafes and fine restaurants and is also home to the Huguenot Monument and Museum.

There are four popular wine routes through the beautiful wine country northeast of Cape Town. The Stellenbosch Route covers 55 private cellars and cooperative wineries, including the Bergkelder, Blaauwklippen and Delheim, and the Van Ryn Brandy Cellar. The Paarl Route covers 26 cooperative wineries and estates, including Nederburg Estate and KWV Cooperative. The Franschoek Route covers 24 cooperative wineries and private wine estates, including Bellingham and Boschendal. The Worcester Route has 20 cooperative wineries and estates.

There are a number of excellent restaurants in the region, including 96 Winery Road, 33 and Auberge Paysan (Stellenbosch), Bosman's (Paarl) and La Petite Ferme, Haute Cabriere and the restaurant at Le Quartier Francais (Franschoek).

ACCOMMODATION – DELUXE: * *Grand Roche,* a luxury estate hotel located in Paarl, has 35 rooms and suites with ensuite facilities and a swimming pool, fitness center and tennis courts. Bosman's is one of the finest restaurants in the country. * *Le Quartier Francais,* a lovely country inn located in Franschhoek, has 15 deluxe rooms and two luxurious suites with fireplaces, excellent restaurant and swimming pool.
* *Lanzerac Manor & Winery* has 48 luxurious ensuite bedrooms and suites, authentic Cape Dutch architecture, restaurant, bar, Craven Lounge with a cigar bar, and three outdoor swimming pools. * *The Lord Charles Hotel,* located in Somerset West, has 196 rooms with ensuite facilities.

FIRST CLASS: * *D'Ouwe Werf,* located in Stellenbosch, is a beautiful old inn with 25 rooms with ensuite facilities, tennis courts and a swimming pool. * *Roggeland Country House* is a stately Cape Dutch farmhouse located near Paarl, with 10 bedrooms with ensuite facilities, and a swimming pool. * *La Provence,* a quaint country inn situated in the middle of the Franschoek Valley, has rooms with facilities ensuite, a restaurant and a swimming pool. * *Auberge Rozendal Wine Farm Country House,* a 140-year-old homestead located near Stellenbosch, has Victorian-style cottages with ensuite facilities and a swimming pool. Horseback riding is available. *La Couronne Hotel & Winery,* surrounded by the estates vineyards high on a mountain overlooking the Franschoek Manor, has 19 rooms with ensuite facilities, restaurant, swimming pool and sauna.

GUEST HOUSES: * *Rusthof Franschoek* is an exclusive country house in Franschoek with five air-conditioned rooms with ensuite facilities, and swimming pool. * *Residence Klein Olifantshoek,* is located in Franschoek and has six spacious ensuite bedrooms and saltwater swimming pool. * *River Manor* in Stellenbosch has 16 rooms with bathrooms ensuite, two swimming pools and a health spa.

NORTH OF CAPE TOWN

This region has attractions that easily rival those on the more well-known Garden Route. Fabulous mountain scenery, whale and bird-watching along the stark Atlantic Coastline and the magnificent proliferation of flowers in August and September make this a region well worth visiting.

The **West Coast Ostrich Farm** is located 20 minutes north of Cape Town on the way to the West Coast National Park.

West Coast National Park

West Coast National Park covers 107 square miles (276 km²) along the Atlantic Ocean about an hour's drive north of Cape Town and includes the Langebaan Lagoon, several islands and coastal areas.

Whales can be seen from the park's shoreline between July and November.

Langebaan Lagoon, a wetland of internationally recognized importance, often has populations of over 50,000 birds comprised of 23 resident species and dozens of migrants from northern Europe and

Asia. In total, over 250 different species have been recorded. Bird hides allow close view of the thousands of waders that migrate here in the summer months. Langebaan is also the site of a fossil footprint approximately 117,000 years old. Strandloper is an open-air restaurant on the beach serving a BBQ of the local seafood caught in the area.

During spring, the land is in full flower. The **Postberg Nature Reserve** section of the park is open for visitors to enjoy from mid-August until the end of September. Bontebok, Cape mountain zebra, eland and Cape grysbok can be seen. A special bird is the black harrier. At Geelbek there is a historic farm and national monument with a country-style restaurant. It also serves as National Park Headquarters.

Another attraction in the area is the **West Coast Fossil Park**, located in Langebaanweg. The park has a visitor center with fossil displays, laboratory and lecture room, coffee shop and tea garden.

ACCOMMODATION – GUESTHOUSES: * *Farmhouse Guest House*, located in Langebaan, has 10 rooms with ensuite facilities. * *Kersefontein* Guest House, located on a working farm on the Berg River, has six ensuite rooms and is a national monument.

ACCOMMODATION IN THE REGION: FIRST CLASS: * *Bartholomeus Klip Farmhouse*, located in the Swartland region, is a restored Victorian farmhouse with five bedrooms with facilities ensuite, set on an historic wheat and sheep farm combined with thousands of acres (hectares) of private nature reserve. Walks, mountain biking, and watersports at the dam are offered along with game drives to look for wildlife such as the Cape mountain zebra, and explore unique fynbos of the reserve. The lodge is located about a 75-minute drive from West Coast National Park and a three-hour drive from Lambert's Bay.

Lambert's Bay

Lambert's Bay is famous for the crayfish and fish industry. Bird Island (now more a peninsula than an island) is found near the entrance of the harbor and is the breeding ground of thousands of Cape gannets, cormorants, penguins and other seabirds. There is a new information center, restaurant and truly sensational bird hide which offers outstanding photographic oportunities.

Muisbosskerm is an open-air seafood restaurant on the beach. Meals are prepared on open fires behind a hedge of thorny shrubs that are traditionally used for building sheep pens. The west coast crayfish is excellent.

The Cedarberg

This rugged, mountainous 502-square-mile (1,300-km²) wilderness area dotted with interesting rock formations created by erosion, also features waterfalls, clear mountain pools, rock paintings and beautiful fynbos flora.

This is a fabulous area (along with Namaqualand to the north) in which to see millions of flowers blooming in the spring and is part of the "Wildflower Route." The best time to see wildflowers in the Cedarberg is August to early September.

There are over 250 marked hiking trails in the Cedarberg.

From the Cedarberg consider taking a day trip to Lamberts Bay to visit the gannet colony and see the whales in season.

The area is also known for the cultivation of unique products such as Rooibos Tea. There are a number of vineyards in the region, and tobacco is also cultivated, especially around the Rhenish Mission Station at Wupperthal. The nearby Biedouw Valley is famous for the profusion of wild flowers in spring (August and September) and the large variety of colorful vygies (mesembryanthemums) reaching right up to the mountains.

Clanwilliam, located 150 miles (240 km) from Cape Town, is the gateway to the Cederberg, via the Packhuis Pass, and much of the Karoo and the Maskam areas. It is famous for the Clanwilliam Dam (recreational water sports), the Ramskop Flower Reserve, Rooibos Tea factory and the many restored historic buildings.

 ACCOMMODATION – CLASS A: * *Bushmans Kloof Lodge*, a Relaix Chateaux property and a South African Natural Heritage site, is located on the 19,275-acre (7800-hectare) Bushmans Kloof Wilderness Reserve and provides a sanctuary for indigenous wildlife, birdlife and 755 species of plants. Wildlife on the reserve includes bontebok, red harte-beest, black wildebeest, Cape mountain and Burchell's zebra, eland and springbok. The lodge has seven rooms and nine suites with ensuite facilities, and a Manor House with four suites with its own chef, game ranger and vehicle. Besides the guided game drives, guests can go on guided rock art walks (more than 125 rock art sites, some dating back

10,000 years), botanical tours, mountain biking, hikes, abseiling and fly-fishing.

TOURIST CLASS: * *Saint Du Barry's Country Lodge*, located in Clanwilliam, has four rooms and one family unit with ensuite facilities and plunge pool.

GUESTHOUSES: * *Oudrif Guest House*, situated in the Cederberg on the banks of the Doring River, has five straw-baled, solar-powered cottages with ensuite bathrooms and a restaurant. This is more an "eco-lodge" than a B&B.

Namaqualand

Namaqualand is located north of the mouth of the Olifants River and south of the Orange River, and it is a place of rare and exquisite beauty, with vivid contrasts between vast expanses of space and brilliant displays of flowers in spring (August-early September). The area is largely semi-desert with warm dry temperatures year-round, and it has about 4,000 species of plants.

The flora of this region is unique. After a good rainy season there are not only carpets of annual flowers, but also a wide variety of geophytes (plants with bulbs, corms and tubers), dwarf shrubs and succulents that vary from creepers to large-stem succulents like the chubby kokerboom (*Aloe dichtoma*), a tree-succulent.

The reason for this unique flora is the region's low and sporadic winter rainfall, which gives rise to plant adaptations for survival during moist winters and to dry and very hot summers. In winter and spring the plant cover is high with perennials and many annuals, but in the summer Namaqualand becomes a barren scene. This winter-summer transformation is almost unimaginable and must be seen to be believed.

There are many towns in this region that are famous for their flowers. Nieuwodtville is home to many of the geophytes; Van Ryhynsdorp features many of the succulents in the area; and Gareis, Kamieskroon and Springbok become carpeted with wild flowers such as daisies, herbs, succulents and lilies in the springtime.

 ACCOMMODATIONS – TOURIST CLASS: * *O'Kiep Country Hotel*, located in O'Kiep, 5 miles (8 km) north of Springbok, is a comfortable country hotel with 18 air-conditioned rooms with ensuite facilities, restaurant and bar. * *Kamieskroon Hotel*, located in the heart of

Namaqualand, has 15 rooms with ensuite facilities, lounge, restaurant and bar. * *Masonic Hotel*, located in the center of Springbok, has 26 air-conditioned rooms with ensuite facilities, restaurant and bar.

EAST OF CAPE TOWN

Hermanus , Gansbaai and De Kelders

This beautiful region is located less than a two-hour drive from Cape Town or Franschoek (The Winelands). Explore this charming seaside town, walk in the Fernkloof Reserve with magnificent views over scenic Walker Bay and stroll along the cliff paths, and visit the Saturday Craft Market. The Hamilton Russell and Bouchard & Finlayson wineries have tasting facilities not far from Hermanus. There are also specialist wine shops in Hermanus that offer wine tastings to showcase the local wine estates in the Hermanus area.

Hermanus and the Walker Bay area, which encompasses Gansbaai, are some of the best land-based whale-watching sights in the world. The whales come into these waters from the Antarctic Convergence between July and November.

The southern right whale is eight times as big as a large bull elephant, and it reaches over 50 feet (15 m) in length and 50 tons in weight. It is so aware of its exact position that it is able to pass under, or next to your boat with its tail fluke curved around you. Breaching is an incredible sight and can only be likened to a missile being launched from a submarine.

Boat trips to Walker Bay and Gansbaai for whale watching, and to nearby Dyer Island to view Cape fur seals, African (jackass) penguins, thousands of cormorants and other seabirds, and to great white shark dive (see description under "Scuba Diving in the Southern Cape") are highly recommended. A visit to Grootbos Nature Reserve is also recommended (see the description that follows).

 HERMANUS – DELUXE: * *The Marine Hotel*, situated in Hermanus on a cliff overlooking Walker Bay, is a Relais & Chateaux hotel with 47 rooms and suites, two restaurants, a swimming pool and a heli-pad. Golf, tennis, bowls and squash are available at a nearby Country Club. * *The Western Cape Hotel and Spa* has 145 ensuite rooms and suites, golf courses, swimming pool, and Acquabella Spa and Wellness Centre.

Whale watching in Walker Bay (July – November).

TOURIST CLASS: * *Beach House,* located in Kleinmond, near Hermanus between Cape Town and Mossel Bay, has 197 rooms and suites with ensuite facilities.

GUEST HOUSES: * *Auberge Burgundy Guest House,* situated on Walker Bay, has 10 garden rooms, either sea or garden facing, three poolside rooms and three suites with sea views. The Burgundy Restaurant offers outstanding cuisine, featuring fresh local seafood. * *Sandbaai Country House,* located on the beachfront, has 10 rooms with ensuite bathrooms. **De Kelders* Bed and Breakfast, located near Gansbaai overlooking the cliffs of De Kelders and the sea, has three rooms with facilities ensuite. * *Anlo Guest House,* situated five minutes from Gansbaai in De Kelders, has eight ensuite rooms set back from the ocean with sea views.

Grootbos Nature Reserve

Grootbos is a private fynbos reserve located between Hermanus and Gansbaai about a two hour drive from Cape Town. This is an excellent place to stay if you plan to whale watch, take boat excursions to see seal colonies and dive with great white sharks.

Grootbos Nature Reserve has a diversity of fynbos vegetation with over 600 plant species and over 100 bird species. Activities available at Grootbos include nature drives, walks, horse rides, mountain biking, and walks along the 20 miles (30km) of beaches.

During our visit we were treated to the most interesting guided presentation of fynbos ecology that I have ever had. The next day we went whale watching on Walker Bay and came within a few yards (meters) of several southern right whales, which seemed to enjoy our presence. That same afternoon we boarded a 30-foot (9-m) rubber duck (Zodiac) and zoomed across the waves at speeds over 50 miles per hour (80 km/h) to Dyer Island, where we found a large seal colony and watched great white shark diving in action — and even had a great white at least 20 feet (6 m) in length swim right under our boat. That's enough to stop your heart for a few seconds!

 ACCOMMODATION: CLASS A: * *Grootbos* has 11 private luxury cottages each with separate lounge, ensuite bathroom, fireplace and mini-bar. There is a restaurant with central fireplace, full bar and lounge area with wooden deck overlooking Walker Bay, library and gift shop, large swimming pool, ecological interpretation and research center and Leica spotting scopes for whale watching. From the deck, you may have a vista all the way to Cape Point.

SCUBA DIVING IN THE SOUTHERN CAPE

The world's two great oceans, the cold south Atlantic and the warm Indo-Pacific, rub brawny shoulders along the southernmost curve of Africa. This contrast of temperatures produces two extremes in underwater habitats and at least three unique opportunities for the adventurous diver: the Southern Cape, Southern Natal Coast (Durban area) and Northern Natal Coast (near Sodwana Bay and Rocktail Bay).

For those seeking the ultimate underwater thrill, the Southern Cape offers the magnificent cold-water predator — the *great white shark*.

South Africa is one of the few places in the world where divers can encounter this formidable creature from the safety of a shark cage. The great white shark is a protected species in South Africa and reaches heroic proportions in these rich waters.

Dyer Island is believed to be one of the best places in the world to view the great white shark. The island is six nautical miles from Gansbaai and is a bird sanctuary and a breeding site of the African penguin. Adjoining the island is a smaller rocky island called Geyser

Grootbos is a lovely base for whale watching and great white shark viewing.

Rock, which supports a large seal population. Separating Geyser and Dyer Island is a channel named " Shark Alley" where the boats anchor hoping to sight these magnificent predators.

There have been a few licenses granted to commercial shark divers in the Southern Cape area, and all operations have experienced skippers and divers on board who supply all the necessary equipment required to enter the cages under the water. You need a diving qualification to enter the cage but non-divers can see the sharks from the boat because they come very close to the surface. The best time to see the great white sharks is between May and October. The probability of seeing a shark during January, February and March is about 50%.

The boats go out to sea between 7-9:00 a.m. and, depending on weather conditions, they reach the anchoring spot in about 20-25 minutes. The anchor is put down, the cage goes into the water and a scent trial is begun. Once final preparations for the diving are made, you settle down to spend the rest of the time watching, diving and enjoying the day. A light lunch and drinks are available on the boat, and there is a toilet on board.

The water temperature can be anywhere between 54° and 61° (12° and 16°). Visibility is usually 20-26 feet (6-8 m), but it can go up to 40-50 feet (12-15 m) on a good day and down to 7-10 feet (2-3 m) on a bad day.

Diving facilities, equipment and training in South Africa are generally excellent.

THE GARDEN ROUTE

One of the most beautiful drives on the continent, the Garden Route is lined with Indian Ocean coastal scenery, beautiful beaches, lakes, forests and mountains, with small country hotel accommodations and large resort hotels. The Garden Route runs between Mossel Bay (east of Cape Town) and Storms River (west of Port Elizabeth).

A number of tours and self-drive options are available from Cape Town to Port Elizabeth (or vice versa) for a minimum of two nights/three days. These programs visit a variety of areas and attractions. The **coastal route** from Cape Town passes through the winelands, Hermanus, Mossel Bay and the coastal areas of Wilderness, Knysna and Plettenberg Bay to Port Elizabeth. The **mountainous route** from Cape Town passes through the winelands, Caledon, Swellendam, over magnificent Tradouw Pass to Barrydale and Calitzdorp, and then to Oudtshoorn. Continue over the Outeniqua Mountains to Wilderness and through the coastal areas to Port Elizabeth. The **northern route** from Cape Town passes through the winelands, Matjiesfontein, and Prince Albert to Oudtshoorn. From there you can join the coastal areas route to Port Elizabeth.

Departing Cape Town, the better way to begin the **coastal route** is to drive to Somerset West, turn toward the coast at The Strand, and continue along False Bay passing Gordon's Bay, Betty's Bay (where there is a mainland colony of African penguins) and onward to Hermanus. The road down to the coast yields fine views of the rugged coastline. The southernmost vineyards in Africa are located nearby.

Southern right whales usually start arriving in Walker Bay (Hermanus) in June or July and usually depart by December, with the peak season being August and September. The best time for whale watching in general along the Garden Route is also August and September.

You may continue to **Cape Agulhas**, the southernmost tip of Africa, where the Atlantic and Indian oceans meet, and to **Waenhuiskrans** (Arniston), a 200-year-old fishing village. An interesting day visit from Arniston is the **De Hoop Nature Reserve**, which is a pristine reserve with magnificent, unspoiled beaches. It is the breeding ground of the African black oystercatcher and has a colony of Cape vultures. Other species seen include bontebok, eland and Cape mountain zebra.

Continue to the town of **Mossel Bay** and then drive north to **Oudtshoorn** where you can ride an ostrich — or at least watch them race — and tour an ostrich farm. Located about 16 miles (26 km) north of Oudtshoorn are the **Cango Caves**, the largest limestone caves in Africa, with colorful stalactites and stalagmites.

Return to the coast via **George**, an Old World town with oak-tree-lined streets set at the foot of the Outeniqua Mountains. A narrow-gauge steam train runs in the morning from George across the Knysna Lagoon to Knysna and back to George that same afternoon.

Continue east to the **Wilderness Area**, which encompasses a number of interlinking lakes, and onward to **Knysna**, a small coastal town with a beautiful lagoon excellent for boating. The Knysna Forest and the Tsitsikamma Forest together form South Africa's largest indigenous high forest.

Farther east lies **Plettenberg Bay**, the Garden Route's most sophisticated resort area. The new Boardwalk complex has many shops, restaurants and a casino. Whale-watching boat trips depart from the beach.

Nearby is **Tsitsikamma National Park** — a lushly vegetated 50-mile (80-km) strip along the coast. Wildlife includes the Cape clawless otter, grysbok, bushbuck and blue duiker. Over 275 species of birds have been recorded. The park has hiking trails, including the famous Otter Trail, and underwater trails for both snorkelers and scuba divers. At **Bloukran's Bridge**, about 25 miles (40 km) from Plettenberg Bay, is the highest bungee jump in the world — 708 feet (216 m)!

The northern route passes the Paarl winelands area through a portion of the Great Karoo (semidesert) to **Matjiesfontein**, a charming little town where the buildings and railway station have been preserved in their original Victorian style. From there the route runs southeast through Prince Albert to Oudtshoorn, where it meets the southern route.

From Plettenberg Bay you may continue to St. Francis Bay, Jeffrey's Bay (famous for surfing) and to Port Elizabeth.

 ACCOMMODATION – SOUTHWEST TO NORTHEAST:

WAENHUISKRANS – FIRST CLASS: * *The Arniston* has 29 rooms with ensuite facilities and a swimming pool. Whales are often seen May-October.

SWELLENDAM – FIRST CLASS: * *Klippe Rivier Homestead* is a Cape Dutch homestead in which the old wine house and stables have been converted into six luxury bedrooms and one honeymoon cottage with ensuite facilities.

OUDTSHOORN – FIRST CLASS: * *Rosenhof Country Lodge* has 12 rooms with ensuite facilities and a swimming pool.

TOURIST CLASS: * *De Opstal Farm*, a working ostrich farm located between Oudtshoorn and the Cango Caves, has air-conditioned rooms with ensuite facilities and a swimming pool. * *Queens Hotel* has 40 ensuite rooms and is located in downtown Oudtshoorn.

PRINCE ALBERT – TOURIST CLASS: * *The Swartberg Hotel*, located north of Oudtshoorn, is a charming 20-room hotel with facilities ensuite.

GEORGE – DELUXE: * *The Fancourt Hotel & Country Club Estate* is an elegant hotel (a National Monument) with 37 rooms and suites with ensuite facilities, four championship golf courses, swimming pool, tennis and a spa.

FIRST CLASS: * *Hoogekraal Country House*, an eighteenth century coastal estate, has 10 rooms with facilities ensuite.

WILDERNESS – TOURIST CLASS: * *Wilderness Hotel* is situated close to the ocean and the lagoon and has 160 rooms with ensuite facilities.

BETWEEN WILDERNESS AND KNYSNA – DELUXE: * *Lake Pleasant Hotel*, a converted 1840 manor house situated within a bird sanctuary on a natural freshwater lake, has 29 air-conditioned luxury rooms and four suites with ensuite bathrooms, restaurant, beautifully restored bar, wine cellar, indoor swimming pool, spa (wellness center), steam room, sauna and tennis courts.

KNYSNA – DELUXE: * *St. James Club* is located on the shores of the

Knysna Lagoon, with 11 suites with ensuite facilities, a swimming pool and floodlit tennis courts. * *Phantom Forest Lodge*, located on the Phantom Forest Eco Reserve, is situated on the Knysna River and offers guests a unique bio-diversity of Afro-montane forest, estuarine wetland and Cape coastal fynbos. The lodge has 12 tree suites that comprised of a sitting room, bedroom with private forest bathroom and an outside deck area. Activities include walking trails, canoeing and birdwatching.

FIRST CLASS: * *Belvidere Manor* has guest cottages with ensuite facilities. * *Ai Due Camini Guest House*, located on the eastern head of Knysna Lagoon, has five bedrooms with facilities ensuite and a swimming pool.

TOURIST CLASS: * *Yellowwood Lodge*, a restored Victorian house, has 10 rooms with ensuite facilities. * *Point Lodge*, set on the water's edge, has seven rooms with facilities ensuite and a swimming pool. * *Brenton-on-Sea*, located in the secluded Brenton Cliffs area, has rooms with ensuite facilities.

PLETTENBERG BAY – DELUXE: . * *Tsala Treetop Lodge* has 10 secluded suites built with natural stone, wood and glass set at the top of the canopy of the trees about 20 feet (6 m) above the forest floor. Each suite has an ensuite bathroom, outdoor shower and a plunge pool. * *Kurland*, a luxury country hotel established in old Cape Dutch tradition surrounded by polo fields, has eight large and beautifully furnished rooms with facilities ensuite situated around the swimming pool, and a health spa with fully equipped gymnasium, sauna and steam bath. * *Hunter's Country House* has 10 elegantly decorated thatched cottages with ensuite facilities. * *The Plettenberg*, formerly a magnificent nineteenth century mansion, has 40 elegant rooms and suites with ensuite facilities.

FIRST CLASS: * *Hog Hollow*, set on the edge of the forest with great views of the Tsitsikamma Mountains, has 12 suites (chalets) with ensuite facilities, private decks and fireplaces. * *Beacon Isle*, located on a peninsula jutting into the sea, has 192 rooms and eight suites with facilities ensuite, a swimming pool and a tennis court. Water skiing, scuba diving, deep-sea fishing and sailing are offered. * *Lodge on the Bay* has three standard rooms and three air-conditioned suites with ensuite bathrooms.

TOURIST CLASS: * *Formosa Inn*, an old established coach house, has 38 garden chalets with ensuite facilities. * *Country Crescent Hotel*, located just outside of Plettenberg Bay, has 26 rooms with facilities ensuite and a swimming pool.

STORMS RIVER – TOURIST CLASS: * *Tsitsikamma Forest Inn* has 34 Swiss-style chalets with facilities ensuite.

ST. FRANCIS BAY – FIRST CLASS: * *Jyllinge Lodge*, located on the beach in a charming coastal resort town, has eight rooms with facilities ensuite.

PORT ELIZABETH – DELUXE: * *Courtyard Suites Hotel*, a new hotel located on the beachfront in front of the new Boardwalk complex, has 64 suites and a swimming pool. * *Hacklewood Hill Country House*, built in 1898, is an elegant residence located in a suburb, with eight rooms with ensuite facilities, a swimming pool and tennis courts.

FIRST CLASS: * *Marine Hotel*, located near the beach, has 69 rooms with ensuite facilities and a swimming pool.

TOURIST CLASS: * *Edward Hotel*, a historical landmark, has 95 rooms with facilities ensuite and a swimming pool. * *Kings Beach Holiday Inn Garden Court* has 280 rooms with ensuite facilities and a swimming pool.

MATJIESFONTEIN (NORTHERN ROUTE) – TOURIST CLASS: * *The Lord Milner* is located just off the Cape Town-Johannesburg road (N1).

SHAMWARI PRIVATE GAME RESERVE
Shamwari is a 35,000-acre (14,000-hectare), malaria-free private game reserve located 47 miles (75 km) northeast of Port Elizabeth.

Wildlife on the reserve includes white rhino, black rhino, elephant, buffalo, lion, hippo and 17 species of antelope. Day and night game drives and walks are offered.

 ACCOMMODATION – CLASS A: * *Long Lee Manor* is an Edwardian mansion with 18 air-conditioned rooms with private balconies and ensuite facilities. * *Lobengula Lodge* has six air-conditioned suites with ensuite facilities. * *Riverdene* is a restored settler's home accommodating 18 guests with facilities ensuite. * *Bushman River Lodge* is also a restored settler's home, with four suites with ensuite facilities.

ADDO ELEPHANT NATIONAL PARK
This 29,000-acre (11,718-hectare) park, located in a malaria-free area

about 45 miles (72 km) north of Port Elizabeth, was formed to protect the last of the elephant and Cape buffalo in the Eastern Cape. Other wildlife in the park includes black rhino, greater kudu, eland, red hartebeest and bushbuck. By far the main attraction of the park is the opportunity for close encounters with elephants.

 ACCOMMODATION – CLASS A: * Gorah Elephant Camp, set on a private concession area in the park, has 10 luxurious tents with ensuite bathrooms. Gorah House, the main lodge building, was built in 1856 and has been restored to its colonial style.

FIRST CLASS: * Riverbend Country Lodge, located on a private game farm adjacent to the park, has eight rooms with bathrooms ensuite and a swimming pool. Walks on the farm and horseback riding are offered.

KWANDWE

Kwandwe is a 40,000-acre (16,000 hectare) private reserve of rolling hills and savannah located in the malaria-free Eastern Cape, about 20 minutes by road from Grahamstown and two hours from Port Elizabeth. The reserve includes 19 miles (30 km) of river frontage on the Great Fish River. Over 7,000 head of game was reintroduced into the reserve, including both black and white rhino, lion, elephant, cheetah, Cape buffalo and a variety of antelope.

 ACCOMMODATION – CLASS A: * Kwandwe Game Lodge overlooks the Great Fish River and has nine air-conditioned suites with bathrooms, indoor and outdoor showers, private plunge pools and salas, a swimming pool and wine cellar. Activities include day and night game drives, walks, fishing, rhino tracking, overnight fly-camping and visits to historical Grahamstown. * Uplands Homestead has three ensuite bedrooms, private game ranger, chef and butler, and is ideal for families and private parties.

KWAZULU-NATAL

KwaZulu-Natal is located in eastern South Africa along the Indian Ocean. The Drakensberg Mountains rise to 11,420 feet (3,482 m) and run roughly north and south along its western border, which it shares with Lesotho.

KwaZulu-Natal is the home of the Zulu. A large variety of wildlife concentrated in several small yet interesting reserves. Hiking in the Drakensberg Mountains is popular.

DURBAN

The largest city in KwaZulu Natal, Durban has a beachfront called **The Golden Mile** that features amusement parks, amphitheater, colorful markets and aquarium (Sea World). Rickshaws, with drivers in traditional Zulu costume, are available along the beachfront. The Victoria Market and Grey Street Mosque are evidence of the strong Indian influence in this area.

FIRST CLASS: * *Hilton Durban*, a 327-room business hotel located next to the International Convention Centre, has a restaurant, bar and swimming pool. * *Holiday Inn Crown Plaza* has 450 rooms and suites with ensuite facilities and two swimming pools.

TOURIST CLASS: * *Protea Edward Hotel*, a hotel with Old World charm and located on the beachfront, has 101 rooms with ensuite facilities and a swimming pool. * *The Royal Hotel*, located in the city center, has 250 rooms and 22 suites with ensuite facilities and swimming pool. * *Marine Parade Holiday Inn Garden Court* has 346 sea-facing rooms and suites with ensuite facilities and a swimming pool. * *Holiday Inn Garden Court North Beach* has 294 rooms and suites with facilities ensuite and a swimming pool.

ACCOMMODATION NEAR DURBAN – DELUXE: * *Zimbali Lodge*, located 26 miles (42 km) north of Durban, has been built in a forest and is surrounded by a championship 18-hole Tom Weiskopf golf course. The lodge has 76 rooms, colonial-style restaurant with views over the Indian Ocean, tennis courts, a private beach, outdoor pool, a health spa, conference facilities, golf club and pro shop. Nearby attractions include the traditional Zulu village of Shakaland, Crocodile Creek, Zulu Battlefields, Chaka's Rock and Hluhluwe Game Reserve. * *Beverly Hills*, located north of Durban on the beach at Umhlanga Rocks, has 88 rooms and suites with ensuite facilities and a swimming pool. * *Shorten's Country House*, an old colonial homestead built in 1905, is located a 20-minute drive from Durban and has chalets with ensuite facilities, an 18-hole golf course, squash and tennis courts and bowling greens. * *Selbourne Lodge and Golf Resort* is an English manor-style resort set close to the Indian Ocean, with 72 rooms and suites with ensuite bathrooms. Facilities include an 18-hole golf course, restaurant, private beach club, tennis courts and swimming pool.

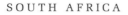

KWAZULU-NATAL

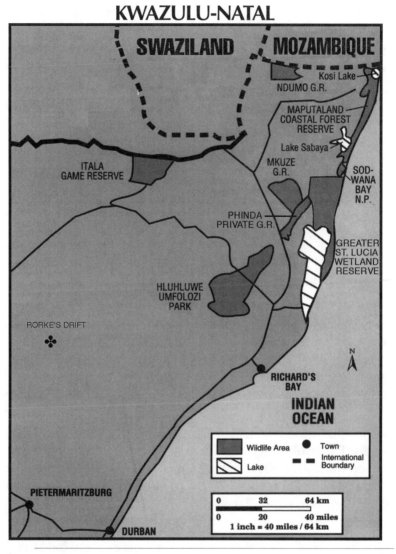

TOURIST CLASS: * *The Oyster Box* is on the beach, with 206 rooms with facilities ensuite and a swimming pool.

ZULULAND

This is the most tropical part of South Africa, with many plant and animal species typical of East Africa, extending south along what is a broad coastal plain. It is not surprising that Zululand also has the greatest concentration of wildlife areas and game ranches in the country. This is also the land of scenic hills and valleys, dotted with Zulu homesteads, many still in the traditional "beehive" style.

ACCOMMODATION – CLASS A/B: * *Shakaland,* a resort built on the movie set for the films *Shaka Zulu* and *John Ross,* offers a look into the Zulu culture. Take a walk through a typical Zulu village where you may be shown the art of bead making, spear throwing and beer brewing, visit the Sangoma (witch doctor) and enjoy a display of Zulu Dancing. Guests are accommodated in 48 traditional beehive huts with ensuite bathrooms.

CLASS B: * *Simunye Pioneer Settlement,* located between Durban and Hluhluwe Umfolozi Park, allows guests to experience contemporary Zulu culture. Accommodations are rock chalets built into the side of a cliff, with facilities ensuite and a rock pool. There is no electricity; lighting is supplied by lamps and candles. Guests may learn to drive a single-horse ox cart or horseback ride in the valley.

MIDLANDS – RORKE'S DRIFT

There are numerous Zulu War and Anglo-Boer War battle sites in the region, including Isandlwana and Rorke's Drift. Tour guides who are superb storytellers make the history of that day come alive, and long, family associations with the area and its people allow you some unique Zulu perspectives on the battles fought with the British soldiers.

Overlooking the Battlefield of Isandlwana, the 6,250-acre (2,500-hectare) **Fugitive's Drift Game Reserve** is 5 miles (8 km) from Rorke's Drift on the Buffalo River in KwaZulu Natal. Diverse and abundant wildlife includes giraffe, zebra, kudu, hartebeest and a host of smaller antelope, as well as 275 recorded bird species. The **Buffalo George** is a Natural Heritage Site where spectacular walks can be enjoyed.

ACCOMMODATION – CLASS B: * *Fugitives' Drift Lodge* consists of five "colonial-style" cottages with ensuite facilities. Most people who stay here are interested in tours of the Anglo/Zulu battlefields.   * *Three Tree Hill Lodge* overlooks the Anglo/Zulu battlefield of Spioenkop, and has six cottages with facilities ensuite, swimming pool and library. Tours of the battlefield are given.

HLUHLUWE UMFOLOZI PARK

The Hluhluwe and Umfolozi Reserves, the oldest reserves in Africa (proclaimed in 1895), were combined to form Hluhluwe Umfolozi Park — now the third largest reserve in South Africa. As there are no roads directly connecting Hluhluwe and Umfolozi, and each section of the park must be visited separately. The best time to visit is during the dry winter months (May-September). Game drives by open vehicle and walks with national park guides are available.

The **Umfolozi** section of the park is located about 165 miles (265 km) north of Durban. This 185-square-mile (478-km²) reserve of open grassland and savannah woodland is best known for having the world's largest concentration of white rhino — approximately 1,900.

Other species include black rhino, elephant, nyala, greater kudu, waterbuck, zebra, wildebeest, buffalo, giraffe, black-backed jackal, lion and cheetah. Over 400 species of birds have been recorded.

The 90 square miles (231 km²) of grassland, forest and woodland of the **Hluhluwe** section of the park is host to a variety of wildlife, including large numbers of white rhino, along with black rhino, elephant, buffalo, southern giraffe, wildebeest, Burchell's zebra, kudu, lion, cheetah, Samango monkeys, hippo and crocs. This is one of the best parks in Africa to see the splendid nyala antelope. Over 425 bird species have been recorded, with narina trogon, cinnamon dove and Natal robin among the more interesting species.

On one visit we spotted over 20 white rhino, 12 nyala and southern giraffe, along with buffalo and grey duiker, among other species.

The Hluhluwe section of the park is located about 18 miles (29 km) from St. Lucia and 175 miles (282 km) from Durban. The park contains walking trails.

ACCOMMODATION IN THE UMFOLOZI SECTION – CLASS C & D:
* The park has self-service chalets, huts and bush camps with ablution blocks.

ACCOMMODATION IN THE HLUHLUWE SECTION – CLASS B: *
Hilltop Camp, an attractive camp run by the park, has chalets with ensuite facilities and a restaurant.

CLASS C & D: The park has cottages with ensuite facilities and self-service huts with ablution blocks. A small self-service bush camp with an ablution block is also available.

CAMPING: None.

511

ACCOMMODATION NEAR THE PARK – CLASS A/B: * *Zululand Tree Lodge*, located on the Ubizane Game Reserve near the Hluhluwe entrance, has 24 fan-cooled tree-house-style chalets with ensuite facilities and a swimming pool. Game drives to Hluhluwe Umfolozi and Mkuzi Game Reserves, walks, horseback riding, local community visits and cruises on Lake St. Lucia are offered.

ITALA GAME RESERVE

This scenic 116-square-mile (300-km^2) reserve consists of open savannah, deep valleys, granite outcrops and rivers.

The reserve has a high concentration of wildlife, including black rhino, white rhino, giraffe, eland, kudu, tsessebe, waterbuck and cheetah. Over 300 bird species have been recorded, including birds of prey such as martial eagle, black eagle, Wahlberg's eagle and brown snake eagle.

Game drives by park rangers are in open vehicles; wilderness trails and guided day walks are also available. The park is located in northern Natal just south of the Pongola River.

 ACCOMMODATION – CLASS B: * *Ntshondwe Camp* has 39 thatched chalets with ensuite facilities, overlooking a water hole.

CLASS D: A small, self-service bush camp with separate facilities is available.

CAMPING: Campsites with ablution blocks are available.

PHINDA PRIVATE GAME RESERVE

Privately owned Phinda covers 58 square miles (150 km^2) of landscape, much of it reclaimed from former livestock and pineapple farms. The habitats are extremely diverse, with acacia and broad-leafed savannah, riverine woodland, marshes and rocky hillsides. Groves of unique sand-forest exist on ancient dunes, and this remarkable dry forest is home to rare plants and mammals such as suni, bushpig and nyala, and unusual birds, including African broadbill, Neergaard's sunbird and pink-throated twinspot.

Wildlife at Phinda includes white rhino, giraffe, elephant, hippo, zebra and buffalo, as well as the big carnivores — all reintroduced since 1991 and thriving in this reborn wilderness. Birdwatching is

Phinda Forest Lodge.

outstanding; among the more interesting species are crested guineafowl, gorgeous bushshrike, pygmy kingfisher, lemon-breasted canary and Eastern nicator.

Phinda operates along the lines of private reserves bordering Kruger, with day and night drives in open 4wd vehicles, bush walks and boma dinners. Additional experiences offered include boat cruises and canoeing on the Mzinene River, excursions to the nearby Indian Ocean, and flights to enjoy an aerial perspective of the region. Loggerhead turtles, bottlenose dolphins, whale sharks and rays are among the marine animals often seen from the air. Three-day walking safaris with overnights in a luxury mobile tented camp, and a Bush Skills Academy are also offered.

Phinda is very important from a regional perspective because it forms an ecological link between the St Lucia reserves and Mkuze Game Reserve — a vast area that is soon to have all fences removed. Phinda has also pioneered successful community development projects in the region, providing employment, skills development and infrastructures, such as clinics and schools, to a previously impoverished area. Guests are invited to visit nearby communities to see how the lives of many people have been transformed, thanks to the revenue earned from tourism.

ACCOMMODATION – CLASS A: * *Phinda Rock Lodge* has six air-conditioned suites nestled on the edge of a rocky cliff, each with ensuite bathroom, indoor and outdoor showers and plunge pool. * *Phinda Vlei Lodge* has six air-conditioned suites on stilts, each with their own bathroom and plunge pool. *Phinda Forest Lodge* has 16 air-conditioned chalets, surrounded on three sides by glass and built on stilts between the forest floor and the towering torchwood trees, and a swimming pool. The windows open up to the canopy beyond. * *Phinda Mountain Lodge* has 20 spacious air-conditioned chalets with ensuite facilities and a swimming pool.

MKUZE GAME RESERVE

This 131-square-mile (340-km²) park has a diversity of vegetation including riverine forest, savannah woodland and forests of large sycamore fig trees. Wildlife includes leopard, side-striped jackal, white rhino, black rhino, eland, kudu, nyala, bushbuck, reedbuck, klipspringer, hippo, crocs and a variety of aquatic birds.

Mkuze is second only to Ndumo as the country's best birdwatching locality, and most serious birders should visit both reserves (only a few hours drive apart). A particular highlight at Mkuze is the various observation hides (blinds), which overlook key points and provide unrivalled viewing and photographic opportunities, not only of birds such as purple-crested turaco and yellow weaver, but also of rhino, nyala and warthog quenching their thirst. The fig forest walk offers an outstanding chance to see Narina trogon, white-eared barbet and trumpeter hornbill, to name just a few.

 CLASS C & D: * *National Park* bungalows, an eight-bed bush camp with facilities ensuite, and huts with ablution blocks.

ST. LUCIA AND MAPUTALAND MARINE RESERVES

These two reserves combined form Africa's largest marine conservation area, covering 342 square miles (885 km²). The reserve runs along the coastline from 0.6 mile (1 km) south of Cape Vidal to the Mozambique border and 3.5 miles (5.6 km) out into the Indian Ocean.

Several species of turtles, including loggerhead and the endangered leatherback, lay their eggs on the northern beaches. St. Lucia includes the southernmost coral reefs in the world and is the only

breeding spot for pink-backed pelicans in South Africa. Flamingos migrate to the reserve, depending upon the salinity levels in the lakes and lagoons. Boat tours are available from the village of St. Lucia.

CLASS B: * *Makakatana Bay Lodge*, located within the Greater St. Lucia Wetland Park Reserve, has five air-conditioned suites with ensuite bathrooms, swimming pool, restaurant and bar.

CLASS D: * National Parks huts and log cabins with ablution blocks are available.

CAMPING: Campsites are available.

MAPUTALAND COASTAL FOREST RESERVE
The Maputaland Coastal Forest Reserve is a remote reserve containing very possibly the highest forested sand dunes in the world. No construction is allowed on the ocean side of these huge dunes. The beach is, in fact, rated as one of the most beautiful and pristine beaches in the world!

Maputaland is one of the best areas for scuba diving in southern Africa. The Indian Ocean "Big Five" — humpback whales, whale sharks, huge leather-back turtles, bottlenosed dolphins and ragged-tooth sharks — can be seen on dives.

Wildlife includes large spotted genet, water mongoose, hippos and turtles (in season). During our visit we saw a variety of birdlife, including scarlet-chested sunbirds and dusky flycatchers. KwaZulu locals are often seen collecting mussels and catching reef fish in the reserve.

Beach walking, snorkeling, surf casting and fly-fishing, and exploring the unique flora and bird life of this region provide visitors with plenty to do. **Black Rock**, a large sandstone protrusion into the Indian Ocean about 4 miles (6.7 km) from Rocktail Bay, is one of the few places in the world where pelagics may be fished from shore. **Lala Neck**, located south of Rocktail Bay, is very good for snorkeling. **Lake Sibaya**, the largest freshwater lake in South Africa, is separated from the Indian Ocean by only the coastal dunes.

ACCOMMODATION – CLASS A/B: * *Rocktail Bay Lodge* has 11 attractive wooden chalets and one family suite, with ensuite facilities and a swimming pool. Fishing, snorkeling, scuba diving, nature drives and excursions to Black Rock, Lala Neck and Lake Sabaya are offered.

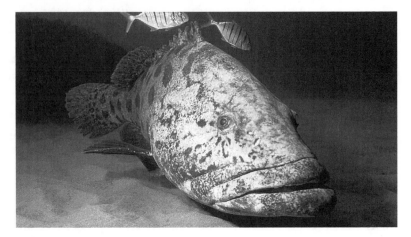

Scuba diving at Rocktail Bay.

NDUMO GAME RESERVE

Located in northeastern KwaZulu-Natal, on the border with Mozambique, Ndumo comprises a mosaic of woodland and wetland, and is known by some as the "Little Okavango" (in reference to the Okavango Delta in Botswana).

Although only 39 square miles (100 km²) in extent, this is undoubtedly one of the finest reserves in South Africa. The vegetation is dense and there are no large herds of game — and neither elephant nor lion — but the tropical setting and semi-aquatic wildlife is spectacular. Both black and white rhino occur, but it is hippo, nyala, suni and red duiker that are most often seen.

The beautiful Nyamithi Pan is a small lake ringed by ghostly fever trees and home to some massive Nile crocodiles. Nyamithi (and other pans) is also a haven for waterfowl, including white pelican, goliath heron, yellow-billed stork and black egret. Pied and malachite kingfishers feed in the shallows, alongside black-winged stilt and African jacana. In the woodlands and forests, birds such as tambourine dove, Natal robin, crowned hornbill and green coucal are fairly common. Known as the "birding Mecca" of South Africa, Ndumo has recorded over 60% of the 700 species found in the country.

Ndumo Wilderness Camp.

 ACCOMMODATION – CLASS A: * *Ndumo Wilderness Camp* has eight tents with ensuite facilities. Game drives and walks are offered.

CLASS D: * *National Parks* cottages with ablution facilities.

CAMPING: None.

SODWANA BAY NATIONAL PARK

Fishing (especially for marlin) and scuba diving are the main attractions of this 1.6-square-mile (4.1-km²) reserve.

 ACCOMMODATION – CLASS B/C: * *Sodwana Bay Lodge* has chalets with ensuite facilities and offers scuba diving and big-game fishing.

CAMPING: Campsites are available.

SCUBA DIVING – NATAL COAST

In the transition zone between Sodwana and Rocktail Bay's coral reefs and the Cape's kelp forests is the city of Durban and the southern Natal Coast. Aliwal Shoal, Lander's Reef and the *Produce* wreck are the diving focal points of the region.

Escorted boat dives to these rocky reefs are opportunities to view a wide variety of southern Africa's marine animals, including potato bass (a large grouper), eels, rays, turtles and myriad reef fish.

The best time to see Aliwal's famed "ragged tooth sharks" is June-July. A group of huge resident bridle bass (jewfish) and schools of dagger salmon make the nearby wreck of the *Produce* their home.

Zululand's semitropical coast has South Africa's warmest and clearest waters — ideal for scuba diving and snorkeling. Because the coral reefs are home to both warm- and cold-water fishes, there are more fish families to be found on the reefs off shore of Rocktail Bay and Sodwana Bay than in the whole of the Great Barrier Reef. Escorted boat dives are offered from Sodwana Bay and Rocktail Bay (see above).

Africa's most southern coral reefs are composed of hard and soft reefs. Named according to their distance from the Sodwana launch site, these reefs are called quarter-, two-, three-, four-, seven- and nine-mile (0.4-, 3.2-, 4.8-, 6.4-, 11.2- and 14.5-km) reefs. The reefs are home to many species of colorful Indian Ocean tropical fish, rock cods (groupers), kingfish (a large jack), barracudas and moray eels. Dolphins are sometimes sighted on the way to dive sites, and humpback whales migrate through the area in February and September. "Ragged tooth" sharks and enormous whale sharks (the world's biggest fish) are sometimes seen by divers in January-February. Manta rays and pelagics are also part of the fish mix. Loggerhead, green and leatherback sea turtles use the undeveloped coastline for nesting from December-March. Night drives and walks to see turtles nesting can be arranged.

Diving is possible year-round, with the best conditions February-June. Visibility ranges from 20 to 100+ feet (6 to 30+ m), depending on sea conditions, with an average of 65 feet (20 m). Water temperature ranges from 70 to 80°F (21 to 27°C). Most diving is conducted from 25 to 125 feet (8 to 38 m) below the surface.

MALAWI

HORSE-LIKE ANTELOPE-ROAN AND SABLE

Sable antelope are majestic animals that have long, scimitar-like horns. Males display glossy black coats with a long, upstanding mane, and they look far classier than their cousin the roan antelope. Roan have shorter horns, large floppy ears and are dun colored and rather reminiscent of an odd-looking donkey.

Sable antelope frequent broad-leaved deciduous woodlands, especially open miombo (brachystegia) woodlands with good grass cover, and they also favor mopane woodlands. Roan antelope prefer thinly treed areas and open grassed savannah. Sable and roan antelope are selective grazers of tall, often coarse grasses that are ignored by the majority of other grazing antelope.

Exclusively African, these antelope share a common ancestry with gazelles and goats and, like them, are adapted to dry conditions. They are grazers with molars well adapted to grinding hard grasses. They are specialists in exploiting zones with less nutritious grasses, preferring areas where there are few competitors and few predators.

Sable and roan develop intimate attachments to large home ranges. During the dry season, these antelope may move out of their wooded and grassland areas to valley bottoms or riverine grasslands, where water is more readily available.

Sable herds of up to 30 females and youngsters are controlled by a dominant cow, but during the rut, a bull dominates the herd and defends it aggressively from other males. Roan are not territorial, and in the breeding season a dominant bull maintains access to a female herd by defending it from intruders.

Both species of antelope have single calves. Young animals are exceptionally social, spending much of their time cavorting, running about and mock fighting. Adult antelope are unusual in that the horns of females are as long as the horns of the males. This enables females to resist attempts by males to limit their movements or threaten their youngsters.

MALAWI

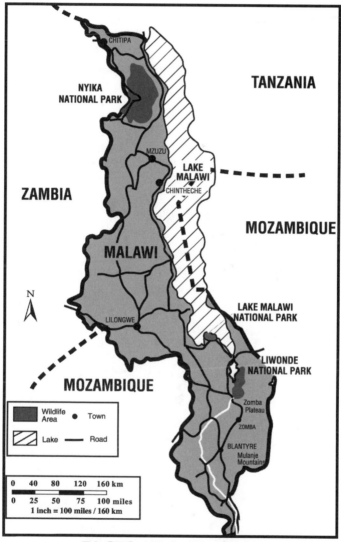

FACTS AT A GLANCE

AREA: 45,560 sq. mi. /118,000 sq km
APPROXIMATE SIZE: one-sixth the size of Texas
POPULATION: 10.4 million
CAPITAL: Lilongwe (pop. est. 350,000)
OFFICIAL LANGUAGE: English
NATIONAL LANGUAGE: Chichewa

MALAWI

Malawi, the warm heart of Africa, is a beautiful country with a variety of wildlife, cultural and holiday attractions of interest to the international traveler.

Geographically, the country is dominated by Lake Malawi, which stretches along the spine of the country. It is often referred to as the "calendar lake" because its surface dimensions are 365 miles (568 km) long and 52 miles (84 km) wide.

This freshwater lake, the southernmost in the Rift Valley chain, is the third largest in Africa. It is also one of the deepest of the Great Rift Valley lakes, over 2,296 feet (700 m) deep, with its deepest point 755 feet (230 m) below sea level. Lake Malawi has over 400 species of freshwater fish and the largest number of cichlid fish species in the world.

Malawi is bordered by Zambia to the west, Tanzania to the north and Mozambique to the east, southwest and south. From north to south, Malawi is about 560 miles (900 km) long. The dominant geographical features in the south of the country are the Shire River and the high plateau of Dedza, Zomba and the Kirk Mountain Range, reaching an altitude from 5,050 feet (1,540 m) to 8,000 feet (2,440 m) above sea level.

As a whole, the country ranges in altitude from 121 feet (37 m) in the lower Shire Valley in the south to a height of 9,847 feet (3,002 m) at Mt. Mulanje, also in the south. The northern lakeshore and adjacent low country rise steeply to the west. Several areas, the Misuku Hills, the Nyika Plateau (Nganda Point is the highest peak on the plateau at 8,551 ft./2,607 m) and the Viphya Plateau, dominate the areas of higher ground.

The dominant vegetation of Malawi is brachystegia or miombo woodlands. Malawi has a tropical climate with a rainy season extending from November to March in the south and November to April in the north. Its climate is influenced locally by the lake and by altitude. A curious weather effect, known as chiperoni — low clouds, condensation and a light drizzle, precipitated by a high-pressure system in Mozambique, forces moist cool air over higher ground — is a frequent occurrence during the dry season in the south of the country, particularly around Blantyre and Thyolo. Temperatures vary considerably, from a maximum of 104°F (40°C) in the low-lying Shire Valley (pronounced shirry) to below freezing on the plateaus, where frost may occur.

In the early fifteenth century, the area was inhabited by the Maravi people (a derivation of the word Malawi), who moved in from the west of the continent around the twelfth century. Arab slave traders were well established in the area by 1870 and were handling more than 20,000 slaves per year. David Livingstone first visited the area in 1859, and on his subsequent visits brought many British missionaries.

Nyasaland became a protectorate of the British Empire in 1891 and in 1953 joined the Federation of Northern (now Zambia) and Southern (now Zimbabwe) Rhodesia. Malawi became independent in 1964.

Chichewa is the national language, but English is the official language and is widely spoken. The most popular beer is Carlsberg, brewed according to Danish traditions. You may want to try some Malawi Gin, and do not miss out on Malawian cashew nuts, peanut butter and Mulanje Gold, an admirable substitute for Kahlua.

The country's economy is based on agriculture; 90% of its population is rural, and agriculture accounts for 40% of the gross domestic product and 90% of its export revenues. Almost 70% of agricultural produce comes from smallholder farmers, whose principal crops are maize, tobacco, tea, sugarcane, groundnuts and coffee. With a population in excess of 10 million, almost every available piece of arable land is cultivated.

Roan antelope on Nyika Plateau.

WILDLIFE AND WILDLIFE AREAS

Great importance has been attached to the protection of Malawi's natural heritage, which is reflected in the number of national parks and reserves within the country. Despite the burdens of overpopulation, almost 20% of Malawi's land area is set aside as either national park, game reserve or forest reserve.

Malawi's primary wildlife attractions are Liwonde National Park, Nyika National Park and Lake Malawi itself. Zambia is an excellent country to combine with Malawi, because South Luangwa National Park (Zambia) is easily accessible by air from Lilongwe.

NYIKA NATIONAL PARK

The Nyika Plateau is a wild, remote and spectacular area of rolling montane grasslands interspersed with pockets of evergreen forest. The upland area of the Nyika (which means wilderness in the local Tumbuka language) Plateau was designated as Malawi's first national park in 1966. An important extension to the park, effectively doubling its size, was gazetted in 1976. Today it is the country's largest park, encompassing a total area of 1,210 square miles (3,134 km²).

Game on the plateau is plentiful; reedbuck, common duiker and roan antelope are the dominant animals, along with eland and Burchell's zebra. Leopard, hyena and bushpig may seen on evening drives.

The flower-filled, rolling grasslands of the Nyika are home to wattled crane, Denham's bustard, churring and black-lored cisticolas, common quail, rufous-naped lark, red-tufted malachite sunbird and mountain nightjar. The evergreen forest pockets, often beginning in valley heads and following drainage lines, are sanctuary to the large checkered elephant shrew, bushpig and forest duiker. They are also home for a number of forest-dwelling birds such as moustached green tinkerbird, Fulleborn's black boubou, Sharpe's akalat, olive-flanked alethe, scaly francolin, white-tailed flycatcher and bar-tailed trogon.

The best time to visit the park for botanists (for wildflowers and orchids) is September-January. For birders, September-March is best, although the heavy rains in January-April can restrict access and activites in the park. Wildlife viewing is good throughout the year.

Horseback-Riding Safaris

Horseback safaris, ranging from day rides to three- and ten-day overnight trails for a maximum of six guests, are a great way to see the park. The horses are thoroughbred, part thoroughbred or cross breeds, and all stand between 14 and 17 hands in height. Tack is split-seat Western for comfortable riding over long distances.

Overnight trails are supported by pack horses or by vehicle, depending on the size of the group and length of the safari. The camp is full service and is set up in advance of the guests' arrival. Riders sleep in stand-up size tents, with a separate shower tent and long-drop toilet for the group. Meals are served in the dining tent or under the stars, depending on the weather. Riders are met in Mzuzu and transferred by road or air charter to Chelinda, where the horses are stabled.

A network of dirt roads meanders across the plateau. Access to the park is via Thazima Gate, 34 miles (55 km) from Rumphi and 81 miles (130 km) from Mzuzu. From Thazima Gate, it is about 37 miles (59 km) to the Malawian Parks Board Camp of Chelinda.

 ACCOMMODATION – CLASS A: * *Chelinda Lodge* has eight deluxe log cabins, each with private facilities, lounge with a fireplace, and balcony. Raised wooden walkways link the cabins to the central restaurant and lounge.

ACCOMMODATION – CLASS C: * *Chelinda Rest Camp* has four two-bedroom cottages with private facilities and kitchen, and six twin-bedded rooms with private facilities. Bring your own food and drink, and cottage attendants will prepare your meals as requested. There is a restaurant and bar nearby.

CAMPING: A campsite with pre-erected tents and limited ablution facilities is available. You may also bring your own tent.

LAKE MALAWI

Magnificent Lake Malawi is the country's largest tourist attraction. The huge lake supplies a seemingly endless number of protein-rich fish to the local people. Chambo, a sought after tilapia (freshwater bream), is a good-eating fish.

On the lake you will see fishermen in their *bwatus* (dugout canoes) fishing either with nets or with lines. Sometimes at night you will see the twinkling of lights on the lake from bwatus and boats with small outboard motors.

The mostly clear waters of the lake make this an inviting environment for recreational activities. The southern lakeshore hotels are best equipped for watersporst, and boardsailing, water skiing, sailing, snorkeling and scuba diving are all available.

Lake Malawi offers some of the best inland sailing in Africa. Although rough waters can suddenly develop with the onset of strong winds, there are no tides or currents in the lake. The prevailing wind is southeasterly, and the lake is at its calmest from April to November.

ACCOMMODATION – TOURIST CLASS: * *Chintheche Inn*, situated on a sandy beach just south of Nkhata Bay on the western shore of the lake, has 10 fan-cooled rooms with ensuite bathrooms, restaurant, and swimming pool. Snorkeling, scuba diving, sailing and windsurfing are available. Bird life of note in this area includes palm-nut vulture, green coucal, moustached warbler, Gunning's robin, narina trogon and purple-banded sunbird.

LAKE MALAWI NATIONAL PARK

Lake Malawi National Park is the first national park to provide protection to the freshwater life of a deep-water Rift Valley lake. The 34-square-mile (88-km^2) park is located in the southern part of the lake and includes 12 islands and most of the Nankhumba Peninsula. Its crystal clear waters and myriad colorful cichlid fish darting among

Livingstonia Beach Hotel.

the rocky shoreline entice one to don a mask and snorkel and join the fish in their daily activities. Day excursions to the park can be arranged from Nkopola and Club Makokola lodges.

Wildlife that may be seen includes bushbuck, klipspringer, crocs and hippos. Bird life includes fish eagles, trumpeter hornbill, white-breasted cuckooshrike, crowned and black eagles, golden-backed pytilia and mocking chat.

ACCOMMODATION ON THE SOUTHERN LAKESHORE – FIRST CLASS: * *Livingstonia Beach Hotel*, one of the finest hotels in Malawi, has 18 rooms and eight rondavels, all fan-cooled, with ensuite facilities, a restaurant and swimming pool. Sailboards, kayaks and boats are available for hire. * *Club Makokola*, set on a sand beach on the shores of Lake Malawi near Nkopola Lodge, has cottages and 55 rooms with ensuite facilities, two swimming pools, tennis courts, squash court, 9-Hole Mlambe Golf Course and a conference center. * *Nkopola Lodge* is set on a hillside on the shore of Lake Malawi about 12 miles (20 km) north of the town of Mangochi. The lodge has 55 air-conditioned rooms with ensuite facilities and a restaurant.

ACCOMMODATION ON MUMBO ISLAND – CLASS C: *Mumbo Island Camp* and *Domwe Island Camp* are rustic camps with tents set on raised wooden decks. Each two tents share a separate bathroom with a bucket shower and chemical toilet. Guests paddle their own kayaks out to the island, which is set off the Cape Maclear Peninsula. Activities include swimming, snorkeling, and exploring the local islands and lakeshore.

LILONGWE

Lilongwe became the capital in 1975. While you are there, you will hear people talk of the **Old Town** and the **New Town**. They are exactly that — the Old Town with its hustle and bustle, markets and buildings close together, and the New Town (also known as the Garden City), with its modern architecture, open pedestrian precincts and parklands.

A visit to the **market** in the Old Town is a worthwhile experience. There, one can buy anything from live chickens to used motorcar parts. The air is high with the aroma of dried fish, spices and fresh vegetables.

The **Lilongwe Nature Sanctuary**, located between the old and new towns, is a good place for seeing small mammals, such as porcupine, civet and vervet monkeys. It is also good for spotting birds, such as red-throated twinspot and perhaps African finfoot.

ACCOMMODATION – FIRST CLASS: * *Capital Hotel* is located in the New Town, adjacent to the commercial and diplomatic areas. The hotel has 185 air-conditioned rooms with ensuite facilities, two restaurants and a swimming pool.

TOURIST CLASS: * *Heuglin's Lodge*, an exclusive guesthouse with a large swimming pool set in a quiet area of the Garden Suburbs of New Town, has six bedrooms with ensuite facilities. The lodge has an excellent wildlife library and can arrange local sightseeing trips. * *Lilongwe Hotel*, situated on three acres of landscaped gardens in the heart of the Old Town, has 91 air-conditioned rooms with ensuite facilities, two restaurants and a swimming pool.

BLANTYRE

Blantyre, named after the birthplace of the great explorer David Livingstone, began as a mission station in 1876. Its position in the agriculturally rich highlands, which has a more temperate climate, made it attractive to the first commercial traders.

LIWONDE NATIONAL PARK

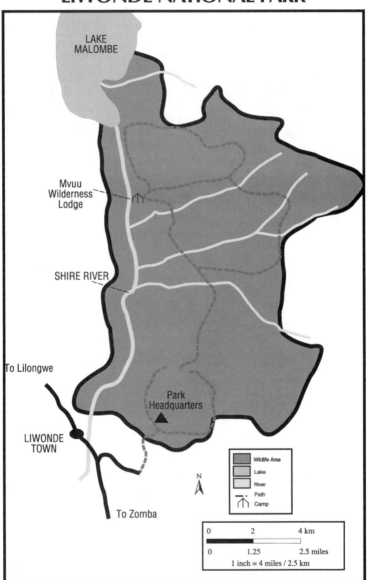

Today, Blantyre is the largest city in the country and is also the commercial and industrial center of Malawi. Historical sites include the **Blantyre Mission**, the beautiful church of **St. Michael's and All Angels,** and the **Mandala House**, the oldest building in the country (erected in 1882).

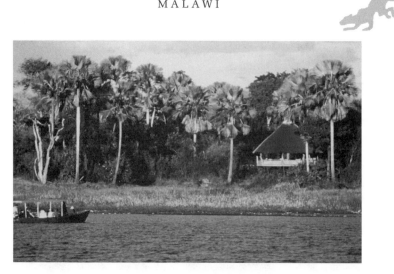

Mvuu Lodge, as seen from a boat game drive on the Shire River.

Blantyre's market is more modern and does not have quite the same appeal as that of Lilongwe. However, for six months of each year (April-September) the **Tobacco Auction Floors** in Lilongwe and the nearby city of Limbe are hives of activity as buyers gather from around the world. Those thinking of visiting the floors should call in advance.

ACCOMMODATION – DELUXE: * *Le Meridien Mt. Soche Hotel,* located very close to the city center, has 132 air-conditioned rooms with ensuite facilities, two restaurants and a swimming pool.

LIWONDE NATIONAL PARK
Established in 1973, the 212-square-mile (548-km²) Liwonde National Park was created to protect the important riverine vegetation and mopane woodland of the upper Shire Valley and is now Malawi's showpiece park.

A major feature of the park is the Shire River, which provides one of the last refuges in the country for hippo and Nile crocodile. The river flows out of Lake Malawi and forms the western boundary of the park. It forges its way southward over tumultuous rapids and falls to join the Zambezi River beyond Malawi's borders.

A recent cooperative project between the South African National Parks Board and the Government of Malawi helped fence the park

Guesthouse with Mt. Mulanje in background.

to prevent poaching, restocked it with species that were previously present in the region, and assisted in the construction of overnight accommodations that are suitable for tourists.

In Liwonde you have a good chance of seeing good numbers of impala, sable antelope, common waterbuck, warthog, hippo, elephant and crocodile. Lion are also seen.

This is a birder's paradise with over 400 species recorded, including Boehm's bee-eater, Lilian's lovebird, brown-breasted barbet, Pel's fishing owl, white-backed night heron and marsh tchagra.

The best time for game viewing is during the dry season, May-October. Birding is best November-April, but is very good year-round.

Liwonde National Park lies 75 miles (120 km) from Blantyre and 152 miles (245 km) from Lilongwe, via the town of Liwonde.

 ACCOMMODATION – CLASS A: * *Mvuu Wilderness Lodge*, set on a quiet backwater area of the Shire River, offers splendid views of the mighty river from its bar/dining deck. The lodge has five luxury tents with ensuite facilities, and offers day and night game drives in open vehicles, boat game drives and escorted walks.

CLASS C AND D: * *Mvuu Camp* is a 30-bed tented camp with a restaurant. Some of the tents have facilities ensuite and some have separate communal facilities.

CAMPING: Sites are available.

MULANJE

In the southeast of the country lies Mt. Mulanje, an impressive hunk of rock that juts out from the surrounding featureless plains. This is one of the finest scenic areas in the country. Sapitwa is the highest peak at 9,847 feet (3,002 m).

There are a number of forestry rest huts on the plateau, and there are trails leading from hut to hut. Several footpaths lead up to the massif from its base; the most popular is Likhabula, on the west side of the mountain. A Forestry Rest House at the foot serves as a base camp, and from there you can organize your climb. Porters may be hired to carry your gear because you must take all your supplies with you. The path is quite steep in places.

Mulanje is home to the coniferous Mulanje cedar, which is said to be one of the world's finest softwoods. Because the plateau is inaccessible by vehicles, all felled trees are carried off the plateau on the heads or shoulders of porters.

Mulanje is a flower-lover's paradise. A variety of soil types have resulted in a range of habitats from evergreen rain forests, with begonias on the sides of the plateau, to heath-like grasslands that are covered in ericas and giant lobelias at higher altitudes. Helichrysum daisies dominate the landscape in the spring, as do a number of species of iris and brilliantly colored red-hot pokers. Two interesting birds seen here are the cholo alethe and the yellow-streaked bulbul.

Unfortunately, most game animals have been eliminated, but Mulanje can be very rewarding for botanists and birders.

The mountain is subject to extremes of climate, so if you are planning to walk on Mulanje, it is best to avoid the rainy season, January-April. Daytime temperatures May-August (the southern winter) are cool, with the likelihood of heavy mists in the mornings and frost at night. Between August and November, it can get quite hot. Thunderstorms occur November-April.

ACCOMMODATION – CLASS F: * *Forestry Rest House* at Likhabula provides bedding. Forestry huts on the plateau have wooden bunks; you must bring all necessary equipment.

ACCOMMODATION NEAR MULANJE – CLASS C: * *Chawani Bungalow,* located on the Satemwa Tea Estate below Thyolo Mountain, has four rooms with separate facilities. Bring your own food and drink, and the cottage attendants will prepare your meals.

ZOMBA PLATEAU

The Zomba Plateau, decreed a forest reserve in 1913, rises 3,300 feet (1,000 m) above the surrounding plains. Although much of the plateau is covered in commercially planted Mexican pine (for the timber and wood pulp industries), the forest reserve protects some patches of exquisite indigenous forest and some extensive grassland.

A series of walking trails meander through the plateau. Those who are less energetic can drive, although some roads may become impassable during the wet season. The highest point on Zomba is Chiradzulu at 6,835 feet (2,084 m), and the climatic extremes are very similar to those on Mt. Mulanje. A narrow, one-way road leads to the top of the plateau from the town of Zomba, and another takes you down.

Clear, cool mountain streams drain the plateau. Trout fishing in these streams and dams on the plateau is a popular pastime. Indeed, Malawi's only fish-fly-making factory is found in Zomba, home to the University of Malawi and one-time capital of the country. Fishing licenses are required and can be obtained from the Ku-Chawe Inn.

 ACCOMMODATION – FIRST CLASS: * *Ku-Chawe Inn,* located on the top of the Zomba Plateau, has 40 rooms with ensuite facilities and a restaurant.

CLASS D: Self-service cottages are available.

CAMPING: Forestry campsites area available.

SWAZILAND

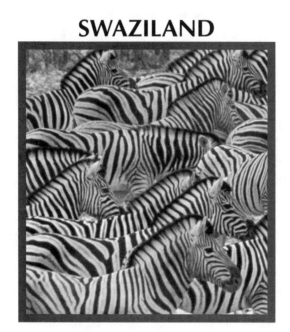

THE MIGRATING ZEBRA

Zebras' regal, black-and-white striped coats are a spectacle when they are assembled in herds during the annual dry-season migration. As they go in search of a new water source, the gregarious behavior of male and female animals is interesting to observe.

The rich and polished stripes of a zebra give the impression of a healthy animal, plump with plenty of fat reserves. But they do not have ruminant stomachs, and they need to eat nearly double the amount of grass as a wildebeest to give them enough protein. Zebra are odd-toed ungulates, related to rhino. They play an important role in the migratory herbivorous trail. Zebra graze the taller, upper parts of new grasses, while the wildebeest and other antelope species eat the shortened grasses.

Family groups are usually comprised of three or more related females and their most recent offspring, and a dominant stallion. Larger herds consist of family group aggregations, but the hierarchy within these units remains intact. Zebra breeding season is stimulated by the coming rains.

Stallions test female zebra for estrus (the cyclic period of sexual activity) by exhibiting flehmen. This is a characteristic act during which the male raises its head high, sniffs the mare's urine and curls back his lips, assessing her reproductive status. The estrus filly is also a cause for fighting among the males; the stallions rear, bare their teeth and bite, kicking and thumping each other with their hooves.

Young foals are usually born as migration begins, and their brown, furry faces and wobbly legs are a gorgeous sight to behold as they hurry to keep up with the mares. The foaling season coincides with the new growth of grass.

SWAZILAND

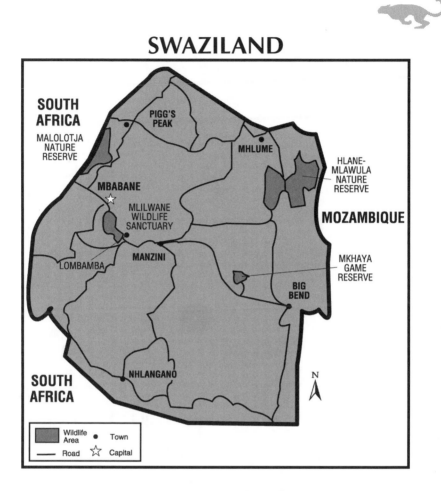

FACTS AT A GLANCE

AREA: 6,704 sq. mi. / 17,364 sq. km
APPROXIMATE SIZE: New Jersey or Wales
POPULATION: 1.1 million
CAPITAL: Mbabane (pop. est. 51,000)
OFFICIAL LANGUAGES: English and siSwati

SWAZILAND

The combination of friendly people, interesting culture, beautiful countryside and small game reserves makes Swaziland an attractive country to visit.

Swaziland, along with Lesotho and Morocco, is one of the last three remaining kingdoms in Africa. The country is deeply rooted in tradition — an important part of present-day life.

Although Swaziland is the second smallest country in Africa, within its boundaries is found a rich diversity of landscapes. Swaziland offers several wildlife reserves, fine examples of stone age San Bushmen rock paintings, international-class resorts and superb scenery.

Unlike most African countries, Swaziland has never been a totally subject nation. Although the British administered the country for 66 years, the people have always been governed by their own rulers according to their own traditions.

Swaziland has an excellent climate. The higher altitudes have a near-temperate climate, while the rest of the country is subtropical. Summers (November-January) are rainy, hot and humid. Winters (May-July) are crisp and clear, with occasional frosts in the highveld (higher altitudes). August is usually windy and dusty.

Geographically, the country is divided into four belts of about the same width that run roughly north to south: 1) the mountainous highveld in the west, 2) the hilly middleveld, 3) the lowveld bush, and 4) the Lubombo mountains, which are located along the eastern border with Mozambique.

Evidence suggests that Swaziland may have been inhabited by Bushmen between the early Stone Age and the fifteenth century. During the fifteenth century, descendants of the Nguni migrated to what is now Maputo, the capital of Mozambique, from the great lakes of Central Africa. Around 1700, the Nkosi Dlamini settled within the present-day borders of Swaziland.

Mswati II was proclaimed king of the people of the Mswati in 1840, forming the seed of a Swazi nation. By that time, the kingdom had grown to twice its present size, and whites (Europeans) began to secure valuable commercial and agricultural concessions. Dual administration of the country by British and Boer (Transvaal) governments failed. The Boers took over from 1895 until the Anglo-Boer War broke out in 1899. Swaziland became a High Commission Territory under the British after the war in 1903.

In 1921, Sobhuza II became king and remained on the throne until his death in 1982, making him the longest ruling monarch in history. The length of his reign gave Swaziland a higher level of political stability than experienced by most of the world. Only four rulers in modern times have reigned over 60 years: Sobhuza II, Queen Victoria of Great Britain, Louis XIV of France, and Karl Friedrich the Grand Duke of Badan.

Swaziland regained its independence on September 6, 1968. It was the last directly administered British colony in Africa. The Queen Regent, Indlovukazi ruled after the death of Sobhuza and until Prince Makhosetive was crowned king in 1986.

The mining of the highlands' (Ngwenya's) iron ore began as early as 26,000 B.C. and continued until 1980, when deposits were exhausted. In the late 1800s, the Swazi gold rush centered around Pigg's Peak and Jeppe's Reef and lasted for 60 years.

The people are called Swazi(s), most of whom are subsistence farmers, and most follow a mixture of Christian and indigenous beliefs. About 95 percent of the population is of Swazi descent. The rest are Zulu, European, Mozambiquean and mulatto. Most prefer to live in scattered homesteads rather than concentrating themselves in villages and cities. Much of Swazi tradition revolves around the raising of cattle.

More than 15,000 Swazis work outside the country, primarily in South African gold and platinum mines. The country's main crops are maize, sugar, citrus, cotton, pineapples and tobacco. Seventy-five percent of the population works in agriculture.

WILDLIFE AND WILDLIFE AREAS

Less than 100 years ago, Swaziland was abundant in most forms of wildlife. In recent times, however, the introduction of large-scale commercial plantations (timber, sugar and citrus), combined with a growing population of subsistence farmers, have transformed most of the country and displaced most of its wildlife. Fortunately, some small natural ecosystems remain and are protected within a few beautiful nature reserves.

The two most important protected areas are Malotoltja and Hlane-Mlawula. Malotoltja protects a host of restricted-range or threatened species. Eliminated by hunters in the middle of the last century, elephant, white rhino, black rhino and lion have all been reintroduced in recent years. Because potentially dangerous large mammals are limited to only a few areas, many of the Swaziland reserves are ideal for horseback riding and hiking. Populations of waterbuck and oribi have declined, but typical savannah species are well represented in the lowveld.

Close to 500 species of birds have been recorded in this tiny, land-locked country — a diversity that can be attributed to the altitudinal range discussed earlier. Bald ibis, blue crane, blue swallow, Stanley's bustard and ground woodpecker all breed in the mist-belt grasslands of Malolotja. Saddle-billed stork, bateleur, ground hornbill and pink-throated twinspot are among the notable species of the lowveld. There is a great diversity of reptiles and amphibians, with many endemic forms of lizards and frogs identified in recent years.

Remarkably, 6,000 plant species have been identified in Swaziland, including eight species of rare, primitive cycads. These living fossils date back to the age of dinosaurs and are the oldest known seed-bearing plants on the planet. Highly valued by illegal collectors, all species are protected by law.

THE NORTH

MALOLOTJA NATURE RESERVE

Malolotja is a 70-square-mile (180-km2) highland wilderness of rolling, boulder-strewn grassland, rivers and streams, deep gorges and tall, montane forests. The vistas are quite breathtaking; the reserve varies in altitude from 6,000 feet (1829 m) to 2,100 feet (640 m) along the Nkomati River. Tumbling some 300 feet (90 m), the **Malolotja Falls** are Swaziland's highest waterfall, and the reserve is also home to the world's oldest known mine — **Ngwenya** — where hematite was extracted for rituals and cosmetics around 41,000 B.C. Game such as wildebeest, zebra and blesbok have been reintroduced, to add to the already-present oribi, Vaal rhebok and mountain reedbuck.

Malolotja is possibly the best place in Africa to see the elusive aardwolf — a nocturnal, termite-eating member of the hyena family. Black-backed jackal and serval are the major predators, although leopard may be found in remote areas.

A total of 290 bird species have been recorded, including numerous grassland-dependent species. A small colony of the highly endangered blue swallow exists close to the reserve's tourist camp. Blue crane are often seen. A small colony of bald ibis breed on the cliffs opposite the Malolotja Falls. Characteristic flora include proteas, erica and other Cape fynbos varieties. Rock-dwelling streptocarpus and three species of cycad are found on Ngwenya Mountain.

Because of a limited number of roads, the park is best suited for walkers and backpackers. Well-marked wilderness trails that require hikes of one to seven days are available, and they require a permit to be hiked. Day trails may be used without first seeking a permit. Camping along the trail is allowed only at official sites; these sites have water but no facilities. Permits for backpacking and fishing must be obtained from the tourist office at the Forbes Reef Dam and Upper Malolotja River.

The best time to visit Malolotja is August-April; June-July is cold and windy. The main gate is located 22 miles (35 km) northwest of Mbabane on the road to Pigg's Peak.

ACCOMMODATION – CLASS C and D: * *National Park Cabins* features six fully furnished cabins, each with six beds, private facilities, crockery and cutlery. Bring your own food, bedclothes and towels.

CAMPING: Campsites with ablution blocks are available.

HLANE-MLAWULA GAME RESERVES

This 190-square-mile (484-km²) reserve complex is situated in northeastern Swaziland and includes both lowveld savannah and the Lubombo Mountains. Hlane was initially set aside by King Sobhuza II as a royal hunting ground, and it was proclaimed as a game reserve in 1967. Hlane is a fairly uniform, flat savannah dominated by knob thorn and marula trees.

The adjoining Mlawula Reserve, to the north, was established in 1980 and has more diverse topography, vegetation and wildlife. Impala, greater kudu and warthog are common larger mammals of open woodlands, while Sharpe's grysbok and mountain reedbuck are present in open grasslands on the Lebombo Heights, which provides wonderful views of the Mozambique coastal plain. The groves of Lubombo ironwood trees in the ravines of the Mbuluzi Gorge are fascinating in terms of their rare cycads and epiphytic orchids. Red duiker and samango monkey coexist with a variety of interesting birds, such as the African broadbill and narina trogon. Interestingly, some typically coastal birds from Mozambique, such as yellow weaver, yellow-spotted nicator and grey waxbill, may be seen along the Mbuluzi River.

The once-thriving population of white rhinos (originating from South Africa's Zululand reserves) crashed during the 1990s due to poaching, but it is slowly recovering. Reintroduced elephant are confined to select areas within Hlane. The complex is renowned for its abundance of birds of prey, including eagles, vultures and goshawks, and a lone family group of ground hornbills.

Game drives are best in Hlane, where waterholes provide excellent viewing in the dry winter months. The emphasis at Mlawula is on walking and backpacking on the network of trails.

 ACCOMMODATION - CLASS C: * *Sara Bush Camp* has three tents set on wooden decks with ensuite, open-air bathrooms.

CAMPING: * *Siphiso Camp* has campsites for caravans and tents, and an ablution block.

MLILWANE WILDLIFE SANCTUARY

The first modern nature reserve to be established in Swaziland, it is owned and operated by the well-known Reilly family. It is located in the Ezulwini Valley. Mlilwane means "little fire" and is named for the lightning that often strikes a nearby hill. This 17-square-mile (45-km²) game sanctuary has a variety of wildlife, including giraffe, hippo, zebra, crocodile, jackal, caracal, serval, civet, nyala, blue wildebeest, eland, kudu, waterbuck, blesbok, reedbuck, bushbuck, oribi, duiker and klipspringer. Not all of these species are indigenous to the area, so the reserve is really more of an animal sanctuary than a natural ecosystem.

The sanctuary setting is middleveld and highveld, with altitudes ranging from 2,200 to 4,750 feet (670 to 1,450 m). It is located on an escarpment that was once a meeting point of westerly and easterly migrations of animals. The result is the congregation of a large number of wildlife species.

The northern limits of Mlilwane stretch to the outskirts of Mbabane and are visited only by guided, overnight trips on horse, mountain bike or on foot. Landmarks in the park include the twin peaks of "Sheba's Breasts," and "Execution Rock" — a legendary peak (the siSwati name is Nyonyane), where common criminals were supposedly pushed to their deaths.

Over 60 miles of gravel roads run throughout the sanctuary. Guided tours in open vehicles, on foot, mountain bike or on horseback can be arranged in advance. A network of self-guided walking trials covers approximately 12 miles (20 km). The best time to visit is during the dry season, May-September.

ACCOMMODATION – CLASS A/B: * *Reilly's Rock Hilltop Lodge*, situated on the Mlilwane Hill inside the sanctuary, is an old homestead built at the turn of the century. It has been converted into a colonial-style lodge featuring only six rooms with ensuite facilities. Game drives, horseback riding, escorted walks and mountain bike tours are offered.

CLASS C AND D: * *Mlilwane Rest Camp* has thatched wooden huts with ensuite facilities and traditional "beehive" huts and an ablution block, a deck overlooking the hippo pool, and a restaurant. Traditional dancing is enjoyed by guests in the evening. * *Sondzela*, located inside the southern boundary of Mlilwane, caters primarily to backpackers, and it offers a variety of self-catering huts and dormitories, and a swimming pool.

CLASS D: * *Nyonyane Camp* has four self-catering log cabins with four to eight beds each.

CAMPING: Campsites are available.

EZULWINI VALLEY

The Ezulwini Valley, or "Place of Heaven," is the entertainment center of the country and is the most convenient area in which to stay when visiting the Mlilwane Wildlife Sanctuary.

ACCOMMODATION – DELUXE: * *The Royal Swazi Sun Hotel, Casino and Country Club*, situated on 100 acres (40 hectares), has 149 rooms with ensuite facilities, a swimming pool, a large al fresco spa, nearby mineral springs and sauna, casino, cinema, 18-hole championship golf course, horseback riding, tennis, squash, lawn bowling and a large convention center. Guests of the Ezulwini Sun and the Lugogo Sun may use the facilities of the more exclusive Royal Swazi Sun Hotel; a courtesy inter-hotel shuttle service is provided.

FIRST CLASS: * *Ezulwini Sun* has 60 air-conditioned rooms with private facilities, a swimming pool and tennis courts.

TOURIST CLASS: * *Lugogo Sun* has 202 air-conditioned rooms with ensuite facilities and a swimming pool.

LOBAMBA

Lobamba is the spiritual and legislative capital of the country. The Queen Mother's village is situated there. The King Sobhuza II Memorial and National Museum, concentrating on Swazi culture and traditions, and the House of Parliament are prime attractions. The country's two premier ceremonies are the Ncwala and Umhlanga, both of which take place at the Ludzidzini Royal Residence. The more important of the two ceremonies is the **Ncwala**, or First Fruit Ceremony, usually held in December and January. Its exact date depends on the phases of the moon as analyzed by Swazi astrologers. The Ncwala symbolizes the religious

Mother and her foal.

spirit uniting the Swazi people with their king. The Ncwala is spread over about a three-week period and involves the entire Swazi nation.

The famous week-long Umhlanga (**Reed Dance**) is a colorful ceremony in which hundreds of Swazi maidens gather reeds and march to the royal residence at Ludzidzini, where the reeds are used to repair the windbreakers around the residence of the Queen Mother, Indlovukazi. Traditionally, at the final dance, the king chooses a wife from among these performing maidens. The Umhlanga occurs in late August/early September. Photographs of these two ceremonies may be taken only with permission from the Swaziland Information

Services (P.O. Box 338, Mbabane, Swaziland, telephone: 011-268-4-2761).

PIGG'S PEAK

Pigg's Peak, located in one of the most scenic areas of the country, was named after William Pigg, who discovered gold there in January of 1884. Nearby is the country's most famous bushman painting, located at the **Nsangwini Shelter**. Ask the District Officer at Pigg's Peak to find a guide to take you there.

 ACCOMMODATION – FIRST CLASS: * *Protea Pigg's Peak Hotel & Casino*, located 9 miles (15 km) north of Pigg's Peak, has 102 rooms with ensuite facilities, a swimming pool, sauna, gym, tennis and squash courts, bowling green, clay pigeon shooting, cinema and casino.

MBABANE

Mbabane, the capital of Swaziland, is located in the mountainous highveld overlooking the Ezulwini Valley. Mbabane has a number of shops that sell local crafts. Most international visitors stay in Ezulwini Valley instead of Mbabane as the accommodations are superior. The international airport (Matsapha) is located about 15 miles (24 km) from Mbabane, between Mbabane and the industrial city of Manzini.

THE SOUTH

NHLANGANO

Nhlangano means "The Meeting Place of the Kings" and commemorates the meeting between King Sobhuza II and King George VI in 1947. Nhlangano is located in the southwestern part of the country in an unspoiled mountainous area and is the burial place of many Swazi kings.

ACCOMMODATION – FIRST CLASS: * *The Nhlangano Sun* is the best hotel in the area, with a casino, disco bar, swimming pool, tennis, and 47 comfortable, chalet-type rooms with ensuite facilities. Golf, squash and lawn bowling are available at the nearby country club.

MKHAYA GAME RESERVE

Swaziland's official refuge for endangered species, Mkhaya covers 25 square miles (65 km²) with sandveld savannah in the north and acacia-dominated savannah in the south. Altitude ranges from 6,170 to 1,150 feet (1,880 to 350 m). Winters are warm by day but cold at night; summers are hot, and temperatures exceed 100°F (38°C).

Mkhaya Game Reserve is a private enterprise of the Reilly family, who have set out to conserve and breed endangered species, such as black rhino and roan antelope. The Reillys have also devoted considerable attention to the breeding of pure Nguni cattle — a traditional, disease-free strain — which are considered to be in danger of becoming genetically polluted. The breed is considered a cornerstone of Swazi culture. Bird life at Mkaya is good and typical of the eastern lowveld.

Wildlife includes elephant, hippo, black and white rhino, zebra, roan antelope, sable antelope, buffalo, eland, wildebeest, red hartebeest, waterbuck, kudu, tsessebe, reedbuck, red duiker, grey duiker, steenbok, ostrich, spotted hyena, black-backed and side-striped jackal, and crocodile.

No self-driving is allowed in the reserve, and all visits must be booked in advance.

 ACCOMMODATION – CLASS B: * *Stone Camp* has semi-open, stone-and-thatch chalets with ensuite facilities. Game drives in open 4wd vehicles and walks are offered. White-water rafting is also available.

LESOTHO

THE WANDERING ELAND ANTELOPE

The cow-like eland are very mobile animals, within their chosen environment, and have adapted their feeding habits accordingly. Food availability dictates where they move within their local area, whether nomadically or migrating between areas. For their size (5.5 ft./1.5 m shoulder height) and weight (many over 1,500 pounds/680 kg), they are staggeringly good jumpers and will clear 7 feet (2 m) if a fence or other obstacle is in the way of their feeding path.

Eland browse during the winter months and have been known to eat 60 types of food plants, including 11 grasses. Feeding includes chewing twigs and branches (mopane, combretum, and lonchocarpus) up to 2 inches thick. They use their horns extensively to break the higher branches. They reach leaves (grewia, mopane, acacia), berries, flowering bushes (tagestes and bidens) and tasty fruit pods with their lips. In the summer months, eland graze new grass shoots to sustain their high-protein diet. In drier regions, if water is not readily available, they feed on succulent branches, acacia leaves and roots to take in enough moisture, and they also forage at night when grasses are laden with dew.

As they walk from feeding ground to feeding ground, eland bulls make a distinct castanet-like clicking sound, most likely caused by the slipping tendons in their knees and by the two toes of each hoof coming together as they are raised.

The eland was a sacred animal to the San Bushmen and features prominently in their characteristic rock art. Its sacred status did not prevent it from being hunted, and the feasts provided by this largest of all antelope were regarded as "Gifts from the Gods."

LESOTHO

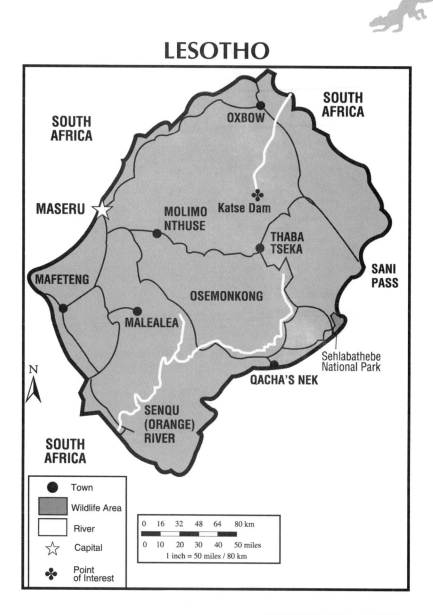

SOUTH AFRICA

OXBOW

SOUTH AFRICA

MASERU ☆

MOLIMO NTHUSE   Katse Dam

THABA TSEKA

SANI PASS

MAFETENG

OSEMONKONG

MALEALEA

Sehlabathebe National Park

QACHA'S NEK

N

SENQU (ORANGE) RIVER

SOUTH AFRICA

● Town
▨ Wildlife Area
▢ River
☆ Capital
♣ Point of Interest

| 0 | 16 | 32 | 48 | 64 | 80 km |
| 0 | 10 | 20 | 30 | 40 | 50 miles |

1 inch = 50 miles / 80 km

FACTS AT A GLANCE

AREA: 11,720 sq. mi./ 30,355 sq. km
APPROXIMATE SIZE: Maryland or Belgium
POPULATION: 2.15 million
CAPITAL: Maseru (pop. est. 170,000 million)
OFFICIAL LANGUAGES: English and Sesotho. English is
widely spoken.

LESOTHO

Lesotho is a rugged country with spectacular mountain scenery. Despite the cool climate and poor soils, the landscape has been intensively settled by subsistence farmers, and wildlife is restricted to hardy and adaptable species. This is certainly not a country to visit if you are looking for a big-game experience, but there are several rare and endemic birds and reptiles that will excite the genuine enthusiast. Infrastructure is limited. The countryside is best explored on pony treks and hiking trails, although a new, high-quality tar road allows access to the center of the country, and the legendary Sani Pass allows for 4wd vehicle access from South Africa's KwaZulu-Natal province.

Called the "Kingdom in the Sky," Lesotho's lowest point (4,530 ft./1,380 m above sea level) is higher than the lowest point of any other country. Most of the country lies above 6,000 feet (1,830 m).

Lesotho is an "island" surrounded by the Republic of South Africa, which makes it one of only three countries in the world (including The Vatican and the Republic of San Marino) surrounded entirely by only one other country.

The country is called Lesotho (pronounced *Lesutu*), a citizen is called Mosotho and the people Basotho. Many men wear multicolored, traditional blankets to keep them warm in the often-freezing air, and they also wear the traditional conical basket hats. The Basotho are, in fact, known as the "Blanket People."

The Basotho are the only Africans to adapt to below-freezing temperatures, which can drop to -8°F (-22°C). Snow can fall in the mountains any time of the year, and it falls in the lowlands between May and August. Summer temperatures seldom rise over 90°F (32°C). The rainy season is during the summer with 85% of the annual rainfall (about 28 in./710 mm) occurring October-April, making many roads impassable.

The western part of the country is "lowland," with altitudes of 5,000-6,000 feet (1,525-1,830 m). The eastern three-quarters of the country is highland, rising to 11,420 feet (3,482 m) in the Drakensberg Mountain Range, bordering the Natal Province of South Africa.

Bushmen (Qhuaique) inhabited Basutoland (now Lesotho) until the end of the sixteenth century. For the following 300 years the area was inhabited by refugees of numerous tribal wars in the region; these refugees formed the Basotho tribal group.

Moshoeshoe I reigned from 1823 to 1870, and his kingdom was powerful enough to keep even the warring Zulus at bay. Wars with South Africa, from 1823 to 1868, resulted in the loss of much land, now called "The Lost Territory." Lesotho asked to become a British protectorate to gain assistance in halting the encroachment of its lands by the Orange Free State (South Africa). Lesotho was a British protectorate from 1868 until its independence on October 4, 1966.

Lesotho is one of Africa's poorest countries, but it benefits from its proximity to South Africa and derives income from labor export and, most recently, from fresh water diverted from the Lesotho Highlands Water Project (LHWP) to the industrial and economic center of Johannesburg. Light manufacturing and tourism are also important foreign exchange earners.

The headwaters of the Senqu (Orange) River rise in Lesotho, and they cut deep gorges through the Drakensberg and Maluti Mountains. The mighty river, critical for development and agriculture in neighboring South Africa and providing the water requirements for Johannesburg, eventually empties into the Atlantic Ocean, some 600 miles (1,000 km) from its source. The LHWP has brought revenue and development to Lesotho. It harnesses water resources in a series dams, produces hydro-electric power and provides employment to both rural and urban people.

WILDLIFE AND WILDLIFE AREAS

Lesotho is notable for its Afro-alpine plants and animals, many of which are found nowhere else (endemic) or found only in other highlands of the continent. Among larger mammals, the eland, black wildebeest, mountain reedbuck and chacma baboon occur only in small numbers. Large predators have been eliminated by stock farmers, though leopard and brown hyena may survive in remote areas. The endangered Cape vulture breeds at several localities in cliff-face colonies, while the spectacular but solitary bearded vulture occurs at a higher density in the Drakensberg than anywhere else in Africa. Among the interesting smaller birds are the orange-breasted rock-jumper, sentinel rock thrush, Drakensberg siskin and mountain pipit. Good numbers of bald ibis are also found.

Sehlabathebe is the Lesotho's only national park, situated on the edge of the great escarpment on the eastern border and adjacent to South Africa's much bigger Natal Drakensberg Park.

PONY TREKKING

Lesotho is one of the best countries in the world for pony trekking. The Basotho pony is the chief means of transportation in the mountainous two-thirds of the country and the best way to explore this land of few roads. Bridle paths crisscross the landscape from one village or family settlement to the next.

The Basotho pony is perhaps the best pony in the world for mountain travel and was highly prized during wartime. It can easily climb and descend steep, rocky paths that other breeds of horses would not attempt. The riding style in Lesotho, as in most countries in Africa, is English.

PONY TREKKING FROM MOLIMO NTHUSE

Molimo Nthuse, located about an hour's drive (34 mi./54 km) on a good, tarred road from Maseru, is the center for pony trekking in this region. Escorted day trips to the refreshing rock pools of **Qiloane Falls**, and other rides of up to seven days in length, are offered. The ponies are well trained and a pleasure to ride.

Pony treks are conducted year-round — in summer "swimsuit" weather as well as in cold, snowy weather. Remember, the seasons

Stopping at a village during a pony trek.

are reversed from the northern hemisphere! When it's summer in Lesotho, it's winter in New York.

Accommodation on overnight treks is in Basotho huts or you can camp (bring your own tent).

 ACCOMMODATION – CLASS C: * *The Molimo Nthuse Lodge* offers 16 rooms with veranda and private facilities in a beautiful mountain setting.

PONY TREKKING FROM MALEALEA TO SEMONKONG

One of the most interesting pony treks in Lesotho (offered from September to April) is a four- to six-day ride from Malealea, in southwestern Lesotho, to Semonkong and Maletsunyane Falls.

The pony trek begins after examining some interesting Bushmen rock paintings and rock pools located near **Malealea**, about 50 miles (80 km) from Maseru. Riding east, the dark-blue skies are broken by high mountains in the distance. Basotho, wrapped in their traditional blankets and traveling on foot and by pony, offer friendly greetings and warm smiles. Riding in a cool breeze on a moonlit night in these remote mountains calms the soul and brings peace and harmony to one's spirit.

The nights are spent in traditional huts that are usually owned by the headman of the village. He provides firsthand knowledge of how the people live. Hikes to view **Ribaneng Falls** and **Ketane Falls** (495 ft./150 m) are made along the way.

The final destination is **Maletsunyane Falls**, a few miles and less than a half-hour ride (or a one and a half-hour walk) from Semonkong. Maletsunyane is one of the highest waterfalls in southern Africa, falling 635 feet (196 m) in a single drop. The impressive falls are best viewed from the bottom of the gorge, where camping is allowed overnight.

Semonkong, meaning "Place of Smoke" (probably from the mist from Maletsunyane Falls), is a dusty little town resembling America's "Wild, Wild West," with a general store, hitching posts, stables and horses providing the main means of transportation. Activities in the area, other than horse treks, include 4wd excursions, mountain bike and motorbike trails, hiking, bird watching and trout fishing.

ACCOMMODATION – CLASS D&F: MALEALEA: * *Malealea Lodge* is a small, self-service lodge featuring nine cottages with ensuite facilities, 11 ensuite bedrooms in the farmhouse, six Basotho huts with communal bathrooms and kitchens, eight budget rooms, and campsites. Day pony treks are available. The lodge specializes in horse treks from one hour to six days in length. CAMPING: Campsites are available at Malealea Lodge and Fraser Lodge (Semonkong).

ACCOMMODATION – CLASS D&F – SEMONKONG: * *Semonkong Lodge* has stone-and-thatch cottages with separate facilities, communal kitchen, bar and restaurant. * *Mountain Delight Lodge* is a small, self-service lodge with 10 beds.

THE MOUNTAIN ROAD

This route cuts through the center of Lesotho, from west to east, and through spectacular mountain scenery to "the roof of Africa." From Maseru, the road ascends over **Bushmen Pass** (Lekhalong la Baroa) to **Molimo Nthuse** ("God Help Me Pass"). Between December and March, colorful scarlet-and-yellow red-hot pokers (flowers) may be seen in this area.

Continue to **Thaba Tseka**, where the good road ends and 4wd is necessary to negotiate the tracks that pass small villages and isolated herd boys. After **Sehonghong**, the route descends into the **Orange (Senqu) River Canyon**, which is dotted with unusual rock formations, then it climbs over **Matebeng Pass** (9,670 ft./2,948 m), which had snow, sleet and icicles during my visit one April, and onward to Sehlabathebe National Park.

KATSE DAM

An incredible structure on the Malibamatso River, Katse Dam was completed on 1997 and is central to the Lesotho Highlands Water Project. The project funnels water through a series of tunnels through numerous ranges of the great Maluti Mountains, and it leads all the way to Gauteng (Johannesburg) and South Africa's industrial hub. The LHWP is one of the most ambitious, multi-purpose water schemes in the world and the dam (over 600 ft./185 m high) is second in size only to Ghana's Lake Volta Akosombo Dam. An interpretive center offers visitors a view of the impressive features of the dam, and they can go on tours through the dam wall. It is also a great area for water sports.

 ACCOMMODATION – CLASS C and D: * *Katse Lodge*, situated at the banks of Katse Lake close to the Katse Dam wall, has 10 single and 10 double rooms with ensuite bathrooms, plus two self-catering units of six bedrooms, each unit with its own kitchen, lounge with fireplace and communal ablutions.

OXBOW

Oxbow, a village set in the Mahlasela Valley at 10,570 feet (3,222 m) above sea level, is being developed into the largest ski resort in Southern Africa, with the longest ski lift on the continent. The resort is planned to open by July 2003 and will have ski lodges, restaurants and shops. Other activities available in the area include trout fishing, hiking, horseback riding and a variety of other outdoor activities.

 ACCOMMODATION: CLASS C: * *Oxbow Lodge* has 100 rooms with ensuite bathrooms. * *New Oxbow Lodge* has 27 rooms with ensuite bathrooms.

ACCOMMODATION NEAR OXBOW – CLASS A/B: * *Mountainview Estate* is located in the small village of Fouriesburg, across the border in South Africa, just over an hour's drive from Oxbow and three hours from Johannesburg. This 100-year-old homestead has luxury garden suites, with ensuite bathrooms, and beautiful views of the mountains. Guided tours of Lesotho and the surrounding areas are offered.

SEHLABATHEBE NATIONAL PARK

Sehlabathebe has the highest sandstone formations (including arches) in southern Africa. This park, situated on a high plateau with small lakes, offers tremendous views of the Drakensberg Mountains and Natal. Sehlabathebe means "Plateau of the Shield" and has an average altitude of over 8,000 feet (2,440 m). Three peaks, called "The Three Bushmen" (Baroa-ba-Bararo), dominate the skyline.

This small, 25-square-mile (65-km^2) fenced park is dominated by open grasslands, with evergreen shrubs forming thickets at the bases of cliffs. High-altitude shrubs form a heath landscape dominated by showy ericas. The meandering Tsoelikana River, marshlands and rock pools provide habitats for aquatic creatures. A small population of black wildebeest has been reintroduced and is faring well alongside oribi, eland and mountain reedbuck.

Bearded vulture (lammergeyer) may be seen soaring overhead, along with Cape vultures, lanner falcon and jackal buzzard. The strange, crab-eating aquatic river frog is fairly common in the cold waters of the Tsoelikana.

The best time to visit Sehlabathebe for game viewing, hiking and some of the best freshwater fishing in southern Africa is November-March. Quickest access is by charter flight. Land access is by a 185-mile (300-km) drive across Lesotho from Maseru or from South Africa via Qacha's Nek, Sani Pass, or a five- to six-hour hike (or three- to four-hour pony trek) of 15 miles (24 km) from Bushman's Nek Lodge.

ACCOMMODATION – CLASS D: * *Sehlaba Thebe Park Lodge* is a self-service lodge with four double rooms.

CLASS F: Dormitory accommodation is available.

CAMPING: Campsites are available near the lodge.

SANI PASS

The Sani Pass is in the Drakensberg Mountains on the border between the Republic of South Africa and Lesotho. It is the most famous of three road crossings through the Drakensbergs — the other two are Bushman's Nek and Qacha's Nek. The nearest town of any note in Lesotho is Mokhotlong (31 mi./50 km), and the nearest city in the Republic of South Africa is Pietermaritzberg.

Sani Pass is a very steep and twisting road pass that can be driven only in a 4wd vehicle, or walked. The pass drops (or climbs, if you are heading into Lesotho) over 2,600 feet (800 m) in just under 5 miles (8 km) — an average grade of 1:10.

> ACCOMMODATION – CLASS D: * *Sani Top Chalet*, set right on top of the pass at 9,425 feet (2,874 m), and home to the highest pub in Africa, has four basic rooms and a dorm.

MASERU

Maseru is the capital and largest city, located in the western lowlands. Sights include the Cathedral and the Royal Lesotho Carpet Factory, where some of the world's finest, hand-woven, woolen carpets may be bought. The tourist office is next to the Victoria Hotel.

Some interesting day excursions from Maseru include **Thaba-Bosiu** (The Mountain at Night), the table mountain fortress that is 19 miles (30 km) from Maseru, where the Basotho fought off the Boers, and the **Ha Khotso** rock paintings, considered to be some of the finest in southern Africa, located 28 miles (45 km) from Maseru off the mountain road.

> ACCOMMODATION – DELUXE: * *The Lesotho Sun* is situated on a hill overlooking Maseru, with 194 rooms and suites with ensuite facilities, a swimming pool, tennis courts, health club, casino, tenpin bowling, several restaurants and conference facilities.

> FIRST CLASS: * *Maseru Sun* has 112 rooms with ensuite facilities, tennis courts, a swimming pool, conference rooms and a casino.

SEYCHELLES

ESMERALDA — THE GIANT ALDABRAN TORTOISE

Esmeralda has a safe haven on Bird Island, where he (yes, he) slowly ambles around the lodge, introducing himself to surprised guests.

Though the giant Aldabran tortoise (*Geochelone gigantea*) originated in the Aldabran Islands, a small breeding colony was set up in the Seychelles islands to ensure its chance of survival.

Giant Aldabran tortoises can grow a carapace as long as 56 inches (140 cm). They can live to be 150 years of age, as with Esmeralda, who is believed to be one of the oldest in the world. The tortoises found on mainland Africa are smaller than these island giants and are found mostly in tropical areas. They are primarily herbivores.

The raised shell of terrestrial tortoises, such as the Aldabran, probably evolved from the flatter shell of their aquatic ancestry for two reasons: 1) as a defense against predators, who otherwise might have been able to crush the reptile in their jaws, and 2) to provide for increased lung capacity, since they have proportionately larger lungs than do turtles.

SEYCHELLES

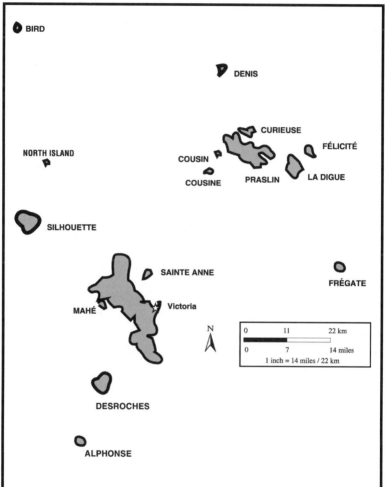

FACTS AT A GLANCE

AREA: 171 sq. mi. / 433 sq. km
APPROXIMATE SIZE: 1/7 the size of Rhode Island
POPULATION; 79,326
CAPITAL: Victoria (pop. est. 25,000)
OFFICIAL LANGUAGE: Creole, English and French are
widely spoken

SEYCHELLES

The Seychelles are unspoiled islands that have a charm all their own, complemented by the genuine friendliness of the people. To help maintain the unspoiled nature of the islands, construction of new hotels (additional beds) is strictly limited. The beauty and variety of the islands make the Seychelles a vacation in itself or an excellent add-on to any safari. With numerous scheduled flights it is easy to hop from island to island. The Seychelles is certainly a fabulous place for a honeymoon.

The Seychelles comprise 115 islands spread over an Exclusive Economic Zone (EEZ) of no less than 500,000 square miles (1.3 million km²) in the Western Indian Ocean, situated northeast of Madagascar and approximately 1,100 miles (1,800 km) east of Kenya. Mahé, the largest of the islands, is located 4° south of the equator.

Forty granitic and 75 coraline islands make up the Seychelles. The granitic group is mountainous islands with peaks rising up to 2,970 feet (905 m) and surrounded by narrow coastal strips. These include the three main and most visited islands of Mahé, Praslin and La Digue. Félicité, Frégate, Silhouette and North Island are smaller granite islands with only one resort on each island. Many of the islands in the coraline group, or "outer islands," are only about 3 feet (1 m) above sea level. Visitors should consider including at least one granite and one coral island in their stay.

The people of the Seychelles are a mixture of African, Asian and European cultures. About 85% of the population resides on Mahé, the largest and the most economically important island in the Seychelles archipelago. About 89% of the population is Roman Catholic, 7% belongs to the Church of England, and the balance divided among Pentecostal, Seventh-Day Adventists, Jehovah's Witnesses, Hindus and Muslims.

Creole cuisine, like the origins of the racially mixed backgrounds, brings together a concoction of interesting recipes from the far corners of the world. Delicate local touches, such as varieties of curries with wonderful spices from India, stir fries and rice from Asia, and garlic-flavored dishes from France, are all enjoyed on the Seychelles. Locally brewed beers are Seybrew and Eku.

The Seychelles is very diverse, with something to suit a great variety of travelers. Accommodations vary from comfortable five-star hotels and island resorts to the less expensive family-owned guest houses, most with fewer than 15 rooms.

The Seychelles offers a tropical climate, which is generally warm and humid year-round. There are two tradewinds: The Southeast Tradewinds blow from May to September, during which it is relatively dry (although possibility of rain is all year round), and the Northwest Tradewinds blow from November to March. The rainy season starts at the end of November and continues until the beginning of February. The temperature throughout the year varies between 75-90° F (24°-32° C). The average monthly rainfall in January is 15.2 inches (386 mm) and in July is 3.3 inches (84 mm). Fortunately, the Seychelles lies outside the cyclone belt.

There is much speculation about the early discovery of the Seychelles by Arab traders but no documentary evidence exists. Vasco de Gama visited part of the archipelago, the islands known as the Amirantes, in 1502. In 1756, the French were the first to colonize the islands, on which they established spice plantations. The English conquered the islands in 1794 and abolished slavery in 1835. In 1903 it became a British Crown Colony and claimed it's independence in 1976. Tourism is the major foreign exchange earner.

WILDLIFE AND WILDLIFE AREAS

Seychelles exhibits unique flora and fauna, due to its geographic isolation. Nearly 50% of the land area has been set aside for national parks, nature reserves and World Heritage sites. The Aldabra Atoll is a World Heritage site, boasting a population of 150,000 giant land tortoises—more than can be found on the Galapagos. The Seychelles has five species of frogs (four are endemic), including the smallest frog in the world, which rarely reaches 1 inch (2 cm,) at maturity. Marine life is prolific, and places like Alphonse and Desroches provide some of the best diving in the world.

Birdwatchers will be well entertained by 10 endemic species and 17 endemic sub-species, which are found on the granitic islands, plus three endemic ones found on the coraline islands. The flora is as exotic and unique as the islands themselves. The most exotic and strangest palm in the world is the famous "coco-de-mer," which has the largest and heaviest seed in the world.

There are seven established walking trails in the Seychelles — six on Mahé Island and one on La Digue Island. These walks offer great opportunities to enjoy the flora and fauna unique to these beautiful islands.

BIRD LIFE

The Seychelles are the "Galapagos" of the Indian Ocean. Many tropical species of birds are not afraid of man and can be approached from within a few feet (less than a meter). Colonies of over 200,000 sooty terns can be found nesting on some of the islands. For twitchers (keen birders), these islands offer an opportunity to add several species to their lists. Two species found only in the Seychelles are the rare black parrot (found only on Praslin) and the Seychelles black paradise flycatcher (found only on La Digue). Other rarities include magpie robins and the Seychelles fody.

FLY FISHING

The Seychelles Islands are a superb saltwater fly-fishing destination for both "flats" and blue water species. The coral islands to the south of the main island at Mahe is the area where most of the flats are to be found. St. Josephs, Poivre, the Amirantes, Farquar and Cosmeledo groups all offer excellent fishing for bonefish and is rated by experts as one of the best bonefish destinations in the world. The area's potential has only recently been recognized, and a reasonable fisherman can expect to catch in excess of 20 of these elusive fish per day. Deeper water fishing on the drop-off, using heavier faster sinking lines, is productive. Several species of trevally are to be found in one spot off of Alphonse. Other species to be found are bonito, rainbow runner, dogtooth tuna, dorado, wahoo and sailfish.

Access to the best areas is not easy. Places like Alphonse have a lodge where fishermen can be based and from which all the different types of fishing are available. To reach the rest of the areas, live-aboard sailing or motor yachts are the answer. The distances are formidable but the rewards are great.

MAHÉ ISLAND

Mahé is the largest and most developed island, and it is the economic and political center of Seychelles. The island covers 59 square miles (152 km²) and is 17 miles (27 km) long and 8 miles (12 km) wide. It offers a variety of hotels and guesthouses and many lovely beaches. Both the international airport and major harbor (Victoria) are found on Mahé.

The interior of the island is mountainous, rising to 2,668 feet (905 m) at Morne Seychellois. One of the most scenic drives on the island is from Victoria through the highlands, south of Morne Seychellois National Park, to Port Glaud on the west coast. **Île Thérèse**, located off the west coast of Mahé, is the island home to a colony of giant tortoises.

There are 75 white sandy beaches, the most popular of which is **Beau Vallon Beach**, a 2-mile (3-km), crescent-shaped beach on the northwest coast. **Grand' Anse** is a good beach for surfing. **Anse Royale** is a 2-mile (3-km) beach protected by a coral reef and located on the southeast coast of the island. There is a better opportunity to find deserted beaches on the south side of the island than on the more developed north side.

Mahé provides hikers several trails, including 1) Victoria to Beau Vallon Bay to Victoria, 2) The Trois Freres Trail, which runs through Morne Seychellois National Park to the summit, 3) La Réserve and Brulee, which lead through a palm forest, 4) Danzil, which takes you to the secluded beach Anse Major, 5) Val Riche to Copolia, which runs through Morne Seychellois National Park, and 6) the Tea Factory, which goes to Morne Blanc in Morne Seychellois National Park.

VICTORIA

Victoria is the capital city and the major port of the Seychelles. Places of interest include the market, the Capuchin House, built in colonial Portuguese style, the State House, a fine example of Seychelles architecture, the Cathedral of the Immaculate Conception, the National Museum and the Botanical Gardens. The "Pirates Arms" bar and restaurant is a popular meeting point.

MORNE SEYCHELLOIS NATIONAL PARK

This 11-square-mile (30-km²) park covers much of northwest Mahé, with altitudes ranging from sea level to 2,969 feet (905 m). There are hiking trails from Sans Souci Road to Copolia (1,630 ft./497 m), Morne Blanc (2,188 ft./667 m) and Trois Freres (2,293 ft./699 m).

Bird life includes the blue pigeon, Seychelles bulbul, Seychelles kestrel, cave swiftlet and Seychelles white-eye.

Flora in the park includes five different species of palm trees, the vanilla orchid (*Vanilla phalaenopsis*), the extremely rare jellyfish tree (*Medusagyne oppositifolia*) and the bwa-d-fer (*Vateria seychellarum*).

SAINTE ANNE MARINE NATIONAL PARK

Located east of Victoria, Sainte Anne Marine National Park includes six small islands and the waters that surround them. Île Ronde (Round Island), Île au Cerf and Île Moyenne islands have lovely coral beds and are excellent for snorkeling or exploring in glass-bottom boats. Among the granite islands, Sainte Anne Island, which is closed to visitors, is the most important nesting site for hawksbill turtles.

 ACCOMMODATION ON MAHÉ – DELUXE: * *Banyan Tree*, located on the southwest coast overlooking Anse Intendance, has 36 air-conditioned, luxury villas with private swimming pools and sundecks, gym, spa, three restaurants and a main swimming pool. The Beach Villas are more spacious, and have an outdoor Jacuzzi, steam shower room and feature larger private swimming pools than the Hillside Villas.

FIRST CLASS: * *Le Meridien Fisherman's Cove*, located on Beau Vallon Bay in the northwest part of Mahé Island, has 48 air-conditioned rooms and cottages with their own private balcony or terrace, plus 14 new suites — all with ensuite facilities. The hotel offers two restaurants, a bar overlooking the bay, swimming pool, tennis court and many other recreational activities. * *The Plantation Club*, located on Baie Lazare in southwest Mahé, has 200 air-conditioned rooms and suites with ensuite facilities, each with split-level bedroom and living areas facing the sea or fresh water lagoon. Facilities include three restaurants, bars, a swimming pool, tennis courts, casino, children's club and free water sports, including snorkeling, wind surfing, canoeing, paddleboats and rowboats.* *Sunset Beach Hotel*, situated on Mahé's northwest coast, offers a good standard of accommodation, particularly in the junior suites. The hotel is set on a rocky promontory with a pathway that leads down to a secluded sandy cove. It has 29 air-conditioned rooms with baths, and the junior suites have sitting areas. Facilities include a restaurant, bar, boutique and swimming pool.

TOURIST CLASS: * *Sun Resort* is a short stroll from Beau Vallon Beach. It has 20 air-conditioned rooms with shower, sitting area, and a balcony or patio overlooking the swimming pool. The restaurant serves Creole and international dishes, and there is a small bar and coffee shop.
* *Lazare Picault* overlooks Baie Lazare on the southwest coast and has 14 rooms, with ensuite facilities, perched on the hillside.

PRASLIN ISLAND

Praslin, a granite island located 25 miles (40 km) northeast of Mahé, is the second largest island in the archipelago. Praslin is 6.5 miles (10.5 km) long and 2.3 miles (3.7 km) wide. The island is less mountainous than Mahé but still has hills over 1,150 feet (350 m) high. Beaches are less crowded than on Mahé, and **Anse Lazio** is considered the best beach on the island. Praslin is home to the famous Vallée de Mai National Park, which was declared a World Heritage Site by UNESCO in 1984.

VALLÉE DE MAI NATIONAL PARK

The Vallée de Mai National Park contains over 4,000 coco-de-mer palm trees that grow in excess of 100 feet (30 m) in height and have a unique double-lobed coconut in the provocative shape of the human female pelvic region. At 20 pounds (9 kg), this is considered to be the world's largest fruit and takes over 10 years to ripen! Many myths and legends have arisen from the presence of this fruit, thought by some to be the original "forbidden fruit," and the island is considered the proverbial "Garden of Eden."

Allow two or three hours for your walk in this lovely park. The sale of the coco-de-mer (a unique souvenir, indeed) is strictly controlled, and a specimen may be purchased at the park or from other shops on the island. We were also amazed at the gigantic size of some of the palm fans and were lucky enough to spot the rare black parrot on our visit.

CURIEUSE MARINE NATIONAL PARK
Curieuse Marine National Park includes the waters between Curieuse Island and the northwestern coast of Praslin. The park covers 5 square miles (14 km²) and reaches depths of 100 feet (30 m). A large colony of giant land tortoises is protected in Laraie Bay.

ACCOMMODATION ON PRASLIN – DELUXE: * *Lemuria Resort* is situated in the northwest, straddling two beaches — Anse Kerlan and Petite Anse Kerlan. This luxury resort has 88 suites with sea-facing balconies or patios. Facilities include a choice of three restaurants, bars, lounge, health spa, boutique, children's club, swimming pool, tennis courts, 18-hole championship golf course and water sports.
* *L'Archipel* has 21 air-conditioned rooms with ensuite facilities, two restaurants, lounge, bar, swimming pool, gym, boutique, and free water sports including windsurfing, canoeing and snorkeling. * *La Réserve*, located on Anse Petite Cour, has four elegant air-conditioned suites and 30 air-conditioned rooms with ensuite facilities and balconies or patios. The hotel offers a weekly Sundown and Discovery Cruise.

ACCOMMODATION – FIRST CLASS: * *Hotel Coco de Mer*, located on Anse Takamaka, has 40 air-conditioned rooms with ensuite facilities, sitting area and terrace. Facilities include a restaurant, two bars, swimming pool, tennis and water sports, including wind surfing and canoeing. The hotel's yacht, *Charming Lady*, is available for charter. **Hotel Acajou*, named after the timber used in its log cabin-style accommodation, is located on the Cote D'Or beach. It has 28 air-conditioned rooms with balconies facing the sea. Facilities include a restaurant, bar, beach snack bar, cocktail lounge and a swimming pool. Diving and bicycle hire can be arranged.

TOURIST CLASS: * *Maison des Palmes*, located in the Grand Anse beach, has 12 thatched-roof cottages (24 rooms) with ensuite facilities, a swimming pool, tennis court and water sports, including wind surfing and sailing.

COUSINE ISLAND

Cousine, not to be confused with Cousin Island (listed below), is a privately owned, 175-acre (70-hectare) island situated between Praslin and Mahé islands. The island has large granitic outcrops, open plains and pristine sandy-white beaches with beautiful coral reefs just offshore.

Wildlife above and below the sea is superb; many rare and endangered species, such as brush warblers and giant tortoises, may be found on and around the island.

At certain times of the year, turtles come ashore during the day and night to lay their eggs. Over 200,000 noddy terns plus a host of other interesting seabirds, such as tropicbirds and frigatebirds, roost and breed on the island.

Access to the island is only by helicopter.

 ACCOMMODATION – DELUXE: * *Cousine Island Lodge* caters to a maximum of eight guests in luxurious villas with ensuite facilities. Resident scientists conducting research on the island act as your guides. No day-trippers are allowed — which guarantees an intimate meeting with nature for guests. Activities include nature walks and lectures, beach walking, boating, fishing, snorkeling and scuba diving.

COUSIN ISLAND

Cousin Island is located 2 miles (3 km) from Praslin. It was bought by the International Council for Bird Preservation with assistance from the World Wildlife Fund to establish a bird sanctuary to protect endangered species, including the Seychelles fody and Seychelles brush warbler. Between May and October, thousands of seabirds can be seen nesting on the island.

The island can be visited only on Tuesdays, Thursdays and Fridays, with groups limited to 20 people.

LA DIGUE ISLAND

La Digue is a granite island that has spectacular rock formations and secluded beaches. The best way to travel around this, the fourth largest island in the archipelago, is by foot, bicycle or ox cart. There are only a few vehicles on the island.

Rock formations on a secluded beach, La Digue.

The highest point on this small 2-by-3 mile (3-by-5 km) island is 1,092 feet (333 m). A lovely walking trail from La Passe to Grand' Anse can be completed on foot or by bicycle. We spent three days exploring the island by bicycle and on foot, and would have loved to have stayed longer.

The island is reached by a 30-minute boat ride from Praslin.

ACCOMMODATION – FIRST CLASS: * *La Digue Island Lodge*, located on the west coast, has 60 air-conditioned rooms, either garden villas or thatched roofed chalets (rondavel or 'A' frame), with ensuite facilities. Amenities include a beachfront restaurant, bar, boutique, swimming pool, wind surfing, snorkeling and a dive center.

TOURIST CLASS: * *Fleur de Lys*, located abut 150 yards (150 m) from the ferry jetty and about the same distance from Anse Reunion Beach, has four air-conditioned bungalows with kitchens and ensuite facilities. * *Patatran Village*, located on the northwest coast, has 18 air-conditioned, chalet-style rooms with ensuite facilities. It has a restaurant and bar and a small beach close by.

FÉLICITÉ ISLAND

Félicité, a small granite island with white sand beaches, is reached by a 30-minute boat ride from Praslin or La Digue. This is an exclusive island with only one hotel.

ACCOMMODATION – FIRST CLASS: * *Félicité Island Lodge* is a
restored, old French plantation with eight air-conditioned guestrooms
with ensuite facilities, tennis court and swimming pool. Activities
include fishing, snorkeling, diving and yacht sailing.

BIRD ISLAND (ILE AUX VACHES)

Bird Island is a small coral island (1.5-by-0.5 mi./2.5-by-1 km) that is
located about 60 miles (100 km) north of Mahé — about a 30-minute
flight. A leisurely walk around this pristine island, with stops for an
occasional swim and snorkel, takes about two to three hours.

Over 500,000 sooty terns nest on the island, an event that usually
occurs May-October. We also encountered "Esmeralda" — one of the
largest giant tortoises in the world — thought to be over 150 years
old.

 ACCOMMODATION – FIRST CLASS: * *Bird Island Lodge*, the only
property on the island, has 24 fan-cooled, spacious and comfortable
bungalows with ensuite facilities. Facilities include a restaurant, bar,
lounge, boutique and the use of snorkeling equipment.

DESROCHES ISLAND

Desroches, a coral island 6 miles long and 1.5 miles wide (10-by-2
km), is the largest island in the Amirantes group. It is situated an
hour by air from Mahé. This is an excellent island for those who
enjoy water sports. Scuba diving, big game fishing and fly-fishing are
excellent.

 ACCOMMODATION – DELUXE: * *Desroches Island Lodge*, the only
lodge on the island, has 20 air-conditioned rooms with ensuite facilities.
Water sports include Hobie Cat sailing, snorkeling, scuba diving, wind
surfing and deep-sea fishing.

DENIS ISLAND

This small (350-acre/140-hectare) coral island is only 25 minutes by
air north of Mahé, and is often thought of as the "perfect desert
island." Denis is located on the edge of the Seychelles Bank, where
water depths quickly reach over 6,500 feet (2,000 m). Deep-sea fishing for barracuda, dog-tooth tuna, marlin and sailfish is excellent.
There is only one exclusive lodge on the island.

ACCOMMODATION – FIRST CLASS * *Denis Island Lodge* has 25 large, spacious individual cottages (some with air-conditioning) with ensuite facilities and a restaurant. Water sports include wind surfing, snorkeling, diving, fly-fishing, bottom and deep-sea fishing.

FRÉGATE ISLAND

Frégate Island, historically a haven for pirates, is a granite island that is 1.5 miles long and a quarter-mile wide (2.5-by-0.4 km). It is situated about 20 minutes east of Mahé by air. The island has magnificent beaches and a variety of flora and bird life, including the Seychelles magpie robin and Seychelles blue pigeon.

ACCOMMODATION – DELUXE: * *Frégate Island Private*, the only accommodation on the island, has16 air-conditioned villas with ensuite facilities. Each Indonesian-style villa overlooks the sea and consists of a separate bedroom and lounge divided by a foyer. The sun deck includes a private jacuzzi and sunbeds. Facilities include water sports, scuba diving, snorkeling and deep-sea fishing.

SILHOUETTE ISLAND

Located 15 minutes northwest of Mahé by helicopter, this unspoiled granite island is the third largest island in the Seychelles and can be seen from the north coast of Mahé. Mountains rise to 2,427 feet (740 m) on this thickly forested, round island, which is approximately 3 miles (5 km) in diameter.

ACCOMMODATION – FIRST CLASS: * *Silhouette Island Lodge*, the only lodge on the island, has 12 bungalows with ensuite facilities. Activities include nature walks, snorkeling and diving.

ALPHONSE ISLAND

Alphonse Island is located in the Amirantes Group some 300 miles (500 km) and an hour by plane from Mahé. It boasts 2 miles (3 km) of reef-protected coastline and a tranquil lagoon.

ACCOMMODATION – DELUXE: * *Alphonse Island Lodge* has 30 air-conditioned rooms with king size beds, ensuite bathroom and an outside showers. More spacious executive villas feature a separate sitting area and jacuzzi bath. Facilities include a restaurant, bar, swimming pool, non-motorized water-sports, tennis, bicycles, PADI Dive Center, big game fishing and world-class fly fishing.

North Island, view of East Beach.

NORTH ISLAND

North Island is over 1,000 acres (400 hectares) in size, with four wonderful white sand beaches, mountains and freshwater lakes. One of the world's most progressive island rehabilitation and conservation programs is underway; alien fauna and flora is being removed, and the Seychelles' rarest fauna and flora are being reintroduced. Great snorkling and scuba diving is a specialty.

For the fisherman, blue water fishing is excellent, both on fly and conventional tackle. The drop off is close to the shoreline and working from a boat is the most productive method of fishing. Trevally, dorado, bonito, tuna and sailfish are all found in the area.

ACCOMMODATION – DELUXE: * *North Island Lodge*, the only property on the island, has 12 large (approximately 4,500 sq. ft./420 m^2) , magnificent guest villas — providing a "Robinson Crusoe," barefoot luxury experience for guests. Each villa has an ensuite sunken bath, indoor and outdoor shower, bidet, private rock pool, study and "sala." Activities include snorkeling, scuba diving, abseiling, rock climbing, fly fishing, health spa treatments, interactions with the scientists on the island and visits to neighboring Silhouette Island.

MAURITIUS

THE EXTINCT DODO

"Dead as a dodo" is a popular saying, in memory of this island bird. The name "dodo" stems from Portuguese for "foolish" or "simple." Mistakenly thought to be related to the swan, the dodo, of which there were two known varieties, actually belonged to the pigeon family Columbiformes. Though it did have small wings, it had no flight feathers, and it had a large, fat body. The crop under its chin held stones, which broke up the nuts and grains of its diet.

Unable to fly, the dodo was doomed to be game meat for visiting sailors, and dodos provided them with a much-sought-after change of diet. Sadly, between Dutch settlers' domestic animals and the ships' rats, the dodos' one-egg nests were completely plundered — the dodo became nothing more than a legend.

MAURITIUS

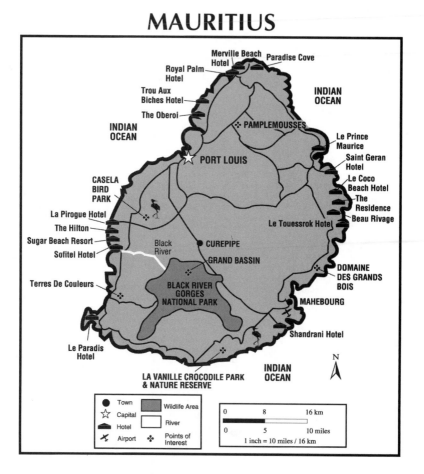

Map labels:
- Merville Beach Hotel
- Paradise Cove
- Royal Palm Hotel
- Trou Aux Biches Hotel
- The Oberoi
- INDIAN OCEAN
- INDIAN OCEAN
- PAMPLEMOUSSES
- Le Prince Maurice
- Saint Geran Hotel
- Le Coco Beach Hotel
- PORT LOUIS
- The Residence
- Beau Rivage
- CASELA BIRD PARK
- La Pirogue Hotel
- The Hilton
- Sugar Beach Resort
- Sofitel Hotel
- Black River
- Le Touessrok Hotel
- CUREPIPE
- GRAND BASSIN
- DOMAINE DES GRANDS BOIS
- Terres De Couleurs
- BLACK RIVER GORGES NATIONAL PARK
- MAHEBOURG
- Le Paradis Hotel
- Shandrani Hotel
- LA VANILLE CROCODILE PARK & NATURE RESERVE
- INDIAN OCEAN
- N

Legend:
- Town
- Capital
- Hotel
- Airport
- Wildlife Area
- River
- Points of Interest

Scale:
- 0 — 8 — 16 km
- 0 — 5 — 10 miles
- 1 inch = 10 miles / 16 km

FACTS AT A GLANCE

AREA: 720 sq. mi. / 1,865 sq km
APPROXIMATE SIZE: Rhode Island or Luxembourg
POPULATION: 1,205,665
CAPITAL: Port Louis (pop. est. 146,319)
OFFICIAL LANGUAGE: English. French and Creole predominate

MAURITIUS

If you have come from half-way around the world to explore Africa, you may wish to consider visiting Mauritius, which lies east of the coast of southern Africa. Mauritius is a favorite destination for jet-setters, celebrities and royalty from around the world. The combination of a cosmopolitan atmosphere, virgin-white beaches, crystal-clear waters, chic hotels with service to match — along with exquisite Creole, Indian, Chinese and European cuisine — is difficult to beat.

This mountainous island paradise lies in the middle of the Indian Ocean in the tropics about 1,200 miles (1,935 km) east of Durban (South Africa), 1,100 miles (1,775 km) southeast of Mombasa (Kenya), 2,900 miles (4,675 km) southwest of Bombay (India) and 3,700 miles (5,970 km) west of Perth (Australia). Combining a visit to this remote island with a safari on the African mainland or an around-the-world vacation should be considered.

The most appropriate and frequently heard phrase on this island is, "No problem in paradise." Unlike the populations of many other "paradises," most of the people in Mauritius have maintained their genuine and refreshing friendliness in the face of tourism.

The 720-square-mile (1,865-km²) island features a central plateau, with the south more mountainous than the north. Much of the lush, native vegetation has been destroyed in favor of sugarcane and other crops.

The population of just over one million consists of Indians, Creoles, French and Chinese. Hindu, Muslim, and Christian festivals are frequent. English is the official language, and French is widely spoken, but most of the native people prefer to speak Creole. Creole cooking, which emphasizes the use of curries, fresh seafood and tropical fruits, is often served. Mauritian beer and rum are popular.

The island is known for the awkward dodo, which, living on an island free of large predators, never needed to evolve the ability to fly. This evolutionary trait ironically contributed to its demise; the dodo was easily hunted to extinction during Dutch rule in the 1800s.

Mauritius has a tropical, oceanic climate. The best time to visit for a beach holiday is from September through mid-December and from April through June, when the days are sunny and the temperatures are warm. From mid-December through March is the cyclone season, which brings occasional tropical rains. June-August (winter) nights are cool and the temperatures along the coastline are pleasant. The average daily maximum temperature in January is 86°F (30°C) and in July is 75°F (24°C). Surf temperatures around the reefs average 74°F (23°C) in winter and 81°F (27°C) in summer.

The first known discovery of Mauritius was by colonizers from Iran in 975 A.D., but they chose not to settle. They moved on to what is now Mombasa and Pemba Island. In the sixteenth century, the Portuguese used the island as a staging post along their trade route to India.

The Dutch came in 1598, led by Wybrandt van Warwyck, who named the island Mauritius after Prince Maurice of Nassau. However, the Dutch did not settle on the island until 1638. In 1710 they left the island to be replaced by the French in 1715, and the French renamed it Isle de France. The island then became a "legal" haven for pirates who preyed on British cargo ships during the war between Britain and France. In fact, this type of pirating was viewed by many at the time as a respectable business.

After 95 years of French control and influence, the British took over Mauritius in 1810. Slavery was abolished in 1835. As the emancipated slaves no longer wished to work on the sugar plantations, thousands of indentured Chinese and Indian workers were brought in to fill their places.

Mauritius became an independent member of the British

Commonwealth in 1968. Mauritius has a parliamentary democracy, holding elections every five years. Republic Day was proclaimed on March 12, 1992.

Industrial products and sugar are the country's major exports.

SCUBA DIVING/SNORKELING

The 205-mile (330-km) coastline of Mauritius is almost completely surrounded by coral reefs, making it an excellent destination for snorkeling and scuba diving. You can dive on the colorful coral reefs and over 50 wrecks, which harbor a great variety of sea life.

The best conditions for scuba diving and sailing are during the period from October through March. Most of the larger beach hotels offer dive excursions and lessons, and they rent equipment. Spearfishing while snorkeling or diving with scuba equipment is prohibited.

BIG-GAME FISHING

Big-game fish, including blue marlin (plentiful), black marlin, yellowfin tuna and skipjack tuna, jackfish, wahoo, barracuda, sea bass and many species of shark can be caught. Fishing is excellent only a few miles offshore; the ocean drops to over 2,300 feet (700 m) in depth just one mile from shore! The best fishing is from December to March and is sometimes good as late as May. An international fishing tournament is held every year in December.

The largest fleets of deep-sea fishing boats are based at the Centre de Pêche at Rivière Noire (Black River) and at the Organization de Pêche du Nord at Trou-aux-Biches. Boats can be hired through your hotel or through travel agencies and should be booked well in advance during the prime fishing season. Fishing in the lagoons during this same period is also very good.

WILDLIFE AND WILDLIFE AREAS

Mauritius' major wildlife attractions are found both on land and below the surface of the Indian Ocean.

View from the pool at the Oberoi.

BIRD LIFE

Mauritius has a number of endemic species of birds — many of which are found nowhere else in the world. Ornithologists or keen birders who wish to add unique species to their lists will find the long journey to this birder's paradise well worthwhile.

The pic-pic (Mauritian grey white-eye) is the only commonly seen bird of the island's nine known remaining endemic species. The pink pigeon is thought to be the rarest pigeon in the world, and the echo parakeet is the world's rarest parrot, with approximately 40 birds alive. The Mauritius kestrel is also one of the rarest birds in the world; only four were known to exist in 1974. Fortunately, due to conservation efforts, populations of all the rare bird species are increasing. The other endemic species include the flycatcher, parakeet, Mauritius fody, olive white-eye, the merle and the cuckoo shrike. In total, about 45 species are found on the island. *Birds of Mauritius*, a book by Claude Michel, is available in many Mauritius shops.

CASELA BIRD PARK

This peaceful, 25-acre (10-hectare) park harbors over 140 varieties of birds from five continents, including the Mauritian pink pigeon.

BLACK RIVER GORGES NATIONAL PARK

Proclaimed as the country's first national park in 1994, this 25-square-mile (65-km²) park covers 3.5% of the island and protects much of its remaining native forests. Nine endemic bird species, including the pink pigeon and Mauritius kestrel, are present.

The Black River Gorges are located in the highest mountain chain on the island and offer splendid views of the countryside. There are several scenic hiking trails, including a 4-mile (7-km) hike to the Macchabee Forest and a 9-mile (15-km) hike through the gorges to the Black River.

DOMAINE DES GRANDS BOIS

Introduced stags, deer, wild boar and African monkeys roam this 2,000-acre (800-hectare), forested park, located north of Mahebourg on the east coast.

LA VANILLE CROCODILE & TORTOISE PARK

Located in the south, this farm breeds Nile crocodiles from Madagascar. There is also a small zoo, featuring the wild animals found on Mauritius, and a nature walk.

PORT LOUIS

Port Louis, the chief harbor and capital city, is partially surrounded by mountains and is multifaceted in character. The city has a large **market** where indigenous fruits and vegetables, spices, pareos (colorful cloth wraps) and other clothing and souvenirs are sold. Just off the main square along Place d'Armes are some eighteenth century buildings, including the **Government House** and **Municipal Theatre**. The Caudan Waterfront and the Port Louis Waterfront are good areas for shopping. There are also a few movie houses and numerous eateries.

CUREPIPE

Curepipe, a large town located on the central plateau, is a good place to shop and cool off from the warm coast. An extinct volcano, Trou aux Cerfs, may be visited nearby.

PAMPLEMOUSSES

The world-renowned botanical gardens of Pamplemousses have

Le Touessrok Hotel, located at Trou d'eau Douce.

dozens of bizarre plants and trees including the talipot palm — at age 60 it blooms only once, then it dies. Giant water lilies imported from Brazil are also found here.

TERRES DE COULEURS

On sunny days, the land takes on the colors of the rainbow at Terres de Couleurs (the colored earth), located in the southwest mountains near Chamarel.

GRAND BASSIN

Grand Bassin is a lake in an extinct volcano's caldera; it is the holy lake of the Hindus, who celebrate the Maha Shivaratree, an exotic festival held yearly in February or March.

ACCOMMODATION

BEACH HOTELS

The beaches, water sports, fabulous holiday hotels and exquisite dining are by far the major attractions of the island.

Hotels are spread out, so visitors spend most of their time enjoying the many activities and sports their particular hotel has to offer. In many of the top hotels, most water and land sports, with the exception of scuba diving, horseback riding and big-game fishing, are free,

Sugar Beach Resort.

including wind surfing, water skiing, sailing, snorkeling, volleyball, golf and tennis. Small sailboats are available at most resorts. Casinos are operated at the Saint Géran, La Pirogue, and Trou aux Biches, as well as at the Casino of Domaine Les Pailles in Pailles and the Casino de Maurice. If you wish to visit the island during the high season (December-February and July-August) and Easter, I suggest that you book your trip several months in advance. Demand for accommodation in the top hotels is high year-round.

DELUXE: * *Le Prince Maurice*, set in 60 acres (24 hectares) of private land, tropical gardens and sheltered beaches on the northeast coast of the island, has 88 air-conditioned junior and senior suites. The hotel has two a la carte restaurants — one of which is a "floating" restaurant — two bars, health and fitness centers, and water sports. *The Oberoi*, located at Baie of Tortues on the northwest coast, has 76 luxuriously furnished rooms with sunken baths. Facilities include two restaurants, bar, two ocean-front swimming pools, gym, health spa, tennis courts and water sports. * *The Hilton Mauritius*, located on the island's western coast, has 193 richly decorated rooms with butler service. The hotel has four restaurants, fitness club, jacuzzi and sauna, hairdressing salon, water sports and 9-hole golf course nearby. * *The Residence*, set on a lovely stretch of beach on the east coast of the island, has 171 luxury air-conditioned rooms and suites with balconies or terraces. Facilities

include two restaurants, snack bar, health center, beauty salon and water sports. * *Royal Palm Hotel* is an elegant, 84-room, deluxe hotel located on Grand Bay on the northwest tip of the island. * *Le Saint Géran*, located on Pointe de Flacq on the east coast of the island, has four restaurants, Givenchy Spa, a casino, nine-hole golf course, sailing and scuba diving. All 175 rooms are air-conditioned with ensuite facilities. * *Le Touessrok*, situated on the east coast at Trou d'Eau Douce, is currently undergoing a major renovation. It will offer approximately 200 air-conditioned rooms with ensuite facilities, spa, swimming pools, restaurants, shops, *Ilot Mangenie* (a private "Robinson Crusoe"-style island retreat), and *Ile de Cerfs* — Le Touessrok's offshore water-sport playground, which also offers secluded coves for sunbathing.
* *Le Paradis* is located in the southwest of the island on a lagoon at the foot of the dramatic Le Morne Mountain. The hotel has 286 air-conditioned rooms and 13 villas, all with facilities ensuite, a swimming pool, a casino, a disco, nightly entertainment and a fleet of deep-sea fishing boats.

FIRST CLASS: * *Beau Rivage*, situated at Belle Mare on the east coast, has 174 air-conditioned rooms, four restaurants, bars, swimming pool, gym, sauna, flood-lit tennis courts and water sports * *Paradise Cove Hotel*, located at Anse La Raie on the north coast, has 67 air-conditioned rooms with ensuite facilities, two restaurants, bars, swimming pool and water sports. * *Sugar Beach Resort* is a plantation-style resort, set on the west coast of the island, with a total of 238 air-conditioned rooms with ensuite facilities located in the Manor House and 16 Creole-style beach villas. Guests may enjoy a variety of water sports and the island's largest landscaped swimming pool, and they may also use the amenities of the nearby sister hotel, La Pirogue. * *La Pirogue* is located on a fine, white beach at Flic-en-Flac on the island's west coast. Thatched cottages spread out from the main building that features a distinctive, sail-like roof. There is a casino, and all 248 rooms are air-conditioned with ensuite facilities. * *Shandrani Hotel* is conveniently located 4 miles (6 km) from the international airport on Blue Bay on the southeastern coast. This 327-room hotel has three separate beaches, all the usual water sports and tennis. All rooms are air-conditioned with ensuite facilities. * *Trou aux Biches Hotel*, located on Trou aux Biches on the northwest coast, has 200 air-conditioned rooms with ensuite facilities and offers the usual water sports, golf, tennis and a dive center.

TOURIST CLASS: * *Le Coco Beach* is located on the east coast and has 337 air-conditioned rooms with ensuite facilities. Water sports and famiy entertainment activities are offered. * *The Merville Beach Hotel* is a comfortable hotel, situated on Grand Bay near the northern tip of the island, with 169 air-conditioned rooms with private facilities, a swimming pool and the usual water sports. * *Sofitel Imperial*, located at Flic-en-Flac on the island's west coast, has 145 air-conditioned rooms with ensuite facilities, three restaurants, a piano bar and the usual water sports.

SAFARI PAGES

We have endeavored to make the information that follows as current as possible. However, Africa is undergoing constant change.

My reason for including the following information, much of which is likely to change, is to give you an idea of the right questions to ask — not to give you information that should be relied on as gospel. Wherever possible, a resource has been given to assist you in obtaining the most current information.

AIRPORT DEPARTURE TAXES

Ask your African tour operator, call an airline that serves your destination, or the tourist office, embassy or consulate of the country(ies) in question, for current international and domestic airport taxes that are not included in your air ticket and must be paid with cash before departure. International airport departure taxes often must be paid in U.S. dollars or other hard currency, such as the Euro or British pounds. Be sure to have the exact amount required — often change will not be given. Domestic airport departure taxes are usually payable in local currency.

At the time of this writing, international airport departure taxes for the countries in this guide are listed below.

AIRPORT DEPARTURE TAXES

Country	Taxes due	Country	Taxes due
Botswana	*	Namibia	*
Burundi	$20.00	Rwanda	$20.00
Congo	$20.00	Seychelles	$40.00 approx
Egypt	*	South Africa	*
Kenya	*	Swaziland	$3.00
Lesotho	$30.00 approx	Tanzania	$30.00
Madagascar	$20.00	Uganda	*
Malawi	$20.00	Zambia	$30.00
Mauritius	$15.00 approx	Zimbabwe	*
Mozambique	$20.00		

* Incuded in price of air ticket.

BANKS
Barclays and Standard Chartered Banks are located in most of these countries.

BANKING HOURS
Banks are usually open Monday-Friday mornings and early afternoons, sometimes on Saturday mornings, and closed on Sundays and holidays. Most hotels, lodges and camps are licensed to exchange foreign currency. Quite often, the best place to exchange money is at the airport upon arrival.

BIRDWATCHING TIPS
Many guides are avid birders and are only too delighted to have interested guests to show around. If your guide is not a keen birdwatcher, and if you are, you obviously need to let him know this to ensure that you do not rush after large mammals all of the time.

As many birdwatchers know, the number of species counted on a safari will directly depend on the number of habitats visited. This means that if you are a serious *twitcher* and want to log as many new 'ticks' as possible, you should move a great deal throughout the safari. Africa, with its varying landscapes, lends itself well to this and in most cases you can visit two or three habitats while staying in the same camp. As mentioned before, some birding trips will take you to areas with less game and more birds — such as some of the forest areas, so a balance is important.

If you are a serious birder, it is very important to let your agent know about it. Many companies have one or two guides who are particularly knowledgeable and, with prior notice, a private birding guide can be booked for your safari.

A lot of birding is very close range, so a close-focusing pair of binoculars is an important asset. A minimum of 8-power and preferably 10-power (10-by-40) works well for birds, as the finer details are important for identification. For the ultra keen, a spotting scope and tripod will definitely come in handy — especially for waders and bird life around lakeshores — but carrying this equipment can be cumbersome so it is recommended for only the specialist.

Checklists are very important but will most often be provided by your guide, but don't forget a reliable pencil to carry along with that. Many people take a small dictaphone to record sightings and then translate them to a written list each evening in the camp. This saves fumbling around with complicated checklists while the guide is rattling off all those new and exciting species!

If you are keen on photographing birds, a minimum of a 400mm lens, with a beanbag for the vehicle and a tripod for the land, should be used. See the section on "Photography" that follows for more information.

There are several excellent illustrated field guides and references to the birds of Africa. The best identification guides are *Newman's Birds of Southern Africa* by Kenneth Newman, (Struik), *Sasol Field Guide to Birds of Southern Africa* (Struik), *Birds of Kenya and Northern Tanzania* by Zimmerman, Turner and Pearson (A&C Black), and *Field Guide to the Birds of East Africa* by Terry Stevenson and John Fanshawe (Academic Press). The compact *Illustrated Checklist: Birds of Southern Africa* by von Perlo (Collins) is useful in that it covers Zambia and Malawi, as well as the region south of the Zambezi River. For visitors to Seychelles, Mauritius or Madagascar, the *Birds of the Indian Ocean Islands* by Sinclair and Langrand (Struik) is indispensable.

Among the groups of birds best represented in Africa are the herons (22 species), plovers (30), storks (8), bustards (21), francolins (36), eagles (23), vultures (11), doves (41), sandgrouse (12), turacos (23), barbets (44), hornbills (25), kingfishers (14) and shrikes (79).

Some of the most spectacular bird sights are the vast flocks of flamingos on East Africa's Rift Valley lakes, the hundreds of vultures which gather at the remains of kills, the breeding colonies of carmine bee-eaters on the Zambezi River, and the comical hornbills that often approach to within arm's reach. Add to this the world's largest bird (the ostrich), the world's heaviest flying bird (the kori bustard), jewel-like sunbirds, iridescent starlings and dazzling rollers, and you'll have an idea of what awaits you!

Between the months of November and March, Africa is visited by an estimated five million migratory birds from Europe and Asia. Among these are swallows, storks, kestrels, waders and warblers. At the same time, the majority of Africa's resident birds are breeding so they are most vociferous, and may often be seen at their nests or with young. It follows that this is the best time to visit if you are specifically interested in birds, but a trip at any time of year may yield sightings of hundreds of different species.

BOOKING A SAFARI

When booking a safari, there are a number of issues that should be considered:

1. How long has the company been in business? Companies that have been in business since 1990 or earlier have weathered travel downturns for more than a dozen years. This says a lot for the financial stability of a company.
2. Does the company take credit cards for deposits as well as final payments on land and air arrangements? I am still amazed at the number of companies (some quite well-known) that do not take credit cards.
3. Does the company offer the "type" of safari that best fits what you are looking for? Many tour companies cater to "niche" markets. Even though the company may come highly recommended to you, it may not be the best company for the experience for which you are looking.
4. Does the person or persons working for the company with which you are speaking have extensive personal experience traveling in the areas you intend visiting? For instance, someone who knows South Africa well may not be qualified to give advice on Kenya or Tanzania.
5. Does the tour operator have an in-house air department? Air schedules within Africa change, and having the same company book your land and your air arrangements is the best way to go. If there are any changes in your air schedule, the operator is notified and they can then assist in getting you back on track. If your air is purchased elsewhere, then that company probably has little obligation or interest in helping you.
6. Does the company have liability insurance (ie. $1,000,000)? Many small tour operators do not have insurance.
7. Does the company offer tours to Africa only, or do they offer tours to other destinations, as well? I suggest you look more seriously at companies that either offer Africa only, or for which Africa is their

primary destination. Go with a company that focuses its attention and resources on the continent you wish to visit.

8. Will the operator provide you with references of clients who have recently traveled with them? This may give you a better idea of the quality of the operation, and also may give you some insight into the experience you might have on a similar safari.
9. Are you enjoying working with the tour operator? Planning a safari should be enlightening, educational and fun!
10. Are real benefits received by the local communities in which they operate, and do they operate with a sensitivity to the environment?
11. How qualified are the guides they use on safari? A good guide is absolutely crucial to the success of your African experience.
12. Is the tour company you have contracted providing you with a number of safari destinations and accommodation options from which to choose? Most people that love their African adventures rave about the excellent guides they had and the fact that their accomodations matched or exceeded their expectations.

CONSERVATION IN AFRICA
Africa is blessed with some of the most extensive wilderness areas on planet Earth — the Serengeti, Okavango and Congo Basin are among the most spectacular. A look at any map will show that a large proportion of land has been set aside as national parks or game reserves in many countries, with Botswana (39%) and Tanzania (15%) among those with the greatest percentage of land devoted to wildlife.

In most cases, these national parks were founded by colonial governments prior to 1960; although there are some notable exceptions such as in Uganda where three new national parks were established in 1993. Many of the national parks were initially set aside as hunting reserves for settlers. Rural people, most of whom were dependent upon wildlife for their sustenance, were deliberately excluded. It was because wildlife was primarily seen as something to pursue, kill and hunt that the word "game" (as in "fair game") came into use, and that is why wildlife reserves are still today known as game reserves (even though hunting is prohibited). In time, hunting came to an end in the national parks, because the wildlife resource was seen to be finite, and a "conservation" ethic took root.

In most cases, the early national parks were run along military lines, and local people who attempted to capture "game" were regarded as the enemy — poachers to be punished and jailed. This approach to national parks undoubtedly safeguarded large areas of wild land (for which modern-day conservationists can be grateful), but, at the same time, it alienated local communities who came to regard the reserves — and sometimes even the animals themselves — as symbols of repression.

To the credit of many African nations, the sanctity of most national parks has remained intact since the wave of independence during the 1960s — sometimes in the face of great pressure from rural communities. But while the boundaries of the parks were unchanged, the animals within were subjected to intensive hunting, either for food or for skin, horn and ivory. In numerous instances the poaching (for it was still illegal) involved the very staff who were charged with the responsibility of safeguarding the wildlife.

The 1970s and 1980s were decades of decimation in many African parks, because human populations grew and global marketplaces for rhino horn and elephant tusks opened up. Corruption, often at a high level, facilitated the illegal export of wildlife products to the Far East and elsewhere. At this time, too, the parks and reserves became ever more isolated as agriculture and settlements encroached upon the boundaries of protected areas.

In the 1990s, conservation philosophy in Africa swung towards initiatives that brought communities and wildlife closer together. Two things had become obvious. First, even the largest national parks contained only portions of ecosystems; many species extended their range beyond the boundaries. Second, a protectionist approach dictated to local people by governments or enthusiastic foreign environmentalists would have very little chance of succeeding in the absence of any real incentives.

While the borders of most national parks remain intact, innovative community-based programs encourage local people to develop sustainable resource utilization in adjoining areas. This concept serves to maintain natural ecosystems beyond the borders of protected areas, as opposed to the establishment of marginal farming activities that generally destroy or displace all wildlife.

Non-consumptive utilization, such as ecotourism, provides jobs and financial returns to communities, while the harvesting of thatching grass, honey, wood and wildlife, such as antelope and fish, provides direct sustenance. In some regions, trophy hunting, regulated by government permits, brings large sums of cash into communities. In essence, these programs set out to restore ownership and responsibility for wildlife to the local people. In areas of low seasonal rainfall (much of eastern and southern Africa) the financial returns from wildlife have proven to exceed most forms of agriculture or livestock farming.

Perhaps the most interesting development in recent years are the so-called trans-frontier initiatives, such as Peace Parks, which link existing protected areas across national boundaries. These potentially massive areas not only allow for greater expansion of wildlife but also provide developing countries with growth points for ecotourism and stimulate greater economic cooperation between neighbors.

There can be little doubt that ecotourism has made a significant contribution to the conservation of wildlife in Africa, through job creation and the stimulation of local economies. Another important benefit is that many young African people have been reconnected to the wildlife that their grandparents interacted with and depended upon, because they have become skilled and articulate guides, hosts and hostesses.

At the start of the new millennium, there is much to be positive about for the future of African wildlife. As many governments recognize the value of ecotourism, many rural people are deriving real benefits from sustainable resource use, and protected areas are actually increasing in size. But conservation is not just about elephants and other large mammals — it is about the land itself. Much still has to be achieved outside of Africa's savannah biome, because rainforests, temperate grasslands and specialized ecosystems, such as mangroves, shrink daily and rare, geographically isolated species face extinction.

CREDIT CARDS
Major international credit cards are accepted by most top hotels, restaurants, lodges, permanent safari camps and shops. Visa and MasterCard are most widely accepted. American Express and

Diner's Club are also accepted by most first-class hotels and many businesses. However, American Express is not often taken in more remote areas and camps. ATM's are in many locations in South Africa but are found in few other countries covered in this book.

CURRENCIES

The currencies of Namibia, Lesotho and Swaziland are on a par with the South African Rand. The South African Rand is widely accepted in Namibia, Lesotho and Swaziland; however, the currencies of Namibia, Lesotho and Swaziland are not accepted in South Africa.

Current rates for many African countries can usually be found in the financial section of large newspapers, in periodicals such as Newsweek and on the Internet.

U.S. $100.00 bills are not generally accepted; smaller denominations should be carried.

The currencies used by the countries included in this guide are as follows:

Botswana	1 Pula = 100 thebe
Burundi	1 Burundi Franc = 100 centimes
Congo, D. R.	1 Zaire = 100 makutas
Kenya	1 Kenya Shilling = 100 cents
Lesotho	1 Loti = 100 licente
Malawi	1 Kwacha = 100 tambala
Mauritius	1 Mauritius Rupee = 100 cents
Namibia	1 Namibian Dollar = 100 cents
Rwanda	1 Rwanda Franc = 100 centimes
Seychelles	1 Seychelles Rupee = 100 cents
South Africa	1 Rand = 100 cents
Swaziland	1 Lilangeni = 100 cents
Tanzania	1 Tanzania Shilling = 100 cents
Uganda	1 Uganda Shilling = 100 cents
Zambia	1 Kwacha = 100 ngwee
Zimbabwe	1 Zimbabwe Dollar = 100 cents

CURRENCY RESTRICTIONS

Some African countries require visitors to complete currency declaration forms upon arrival; all foreign currency, travelers checks and other negotiable instruments must be recorded. These forms must be surrendered on departure. When you leave the country, the amount of currency you have with you must equal the amount with which you entered the country less the amount exchanged and recorded on your currency declaration form.

For some countries in Africa, the maximum amount of local currency that may be imported or exported is strictly enforced. Check for current restrictions by contacting the tourist offices, embassies or consulates of the countries you wish to visit.

In some countries, it is difficult (if not impossible) to exchange unused local currency back to foreign exchange (i.e., U.S. dollars). Therefore, it is best not to exchange more than you feel you will need.

CUSTOMS

AUSTRALIAN CUSTOMS:
The Customs Information Centre: tel. (61 2) 6275 6666 (from outside Australia) and 1300 363 263 (from inside Australia); Monday-Friday, 8:30 a.m.-5:00 p.m.

CANADIAN CUSTOMS:
For a brochure on current Canadian customs requirements, ask for the brochure *I Declare* from your local customs office, which will be listed in the telephone book under "Government of Canada, Customs and Excise."

NEW ZEALAND CUSTOMS:
Custom House, Box 29, 50 Anzac Ave., Auckland; tel. 09 359 6655, fax 09 359 6735, www.customs.govt.az

UNITED KINGDOM:
HM Customs and Excise, Kent House, Upper Ground, London SE1 9PS

U.S. CUSTOMS:
For current information on products made from endangered species of wildlife that are not allowed to be imported, contact Traffic (U.S.A.), World Wildlife Fund, 1250 24th St. NW, Washington, DC 20037, tel. (202) 293-4800, and ask for the leaflet *Buyer Beware* for current restrictions.

DIPLOMATIC REPRESENTATIVES OF AFRICAN COUNTRIES

IN AUSTRALIA:

Kenya: Sixth Floor, QBE Building, 33-35 Ainslie Ave., P.O. Box 1990, Canberra City, ACT 2601, Australia; tel. (02)62 474788/62 474722/62 474688 or 62 474311, fax (02) 62 576613; Monday-Friday, hours 9 a.m.-4 p.m.

Mauritius: 2 Beale Crescent Deakin, ACT 2600, Australia; tel. (612) 6281-1203 or (612) 6282-4436 or (612) 6285-3896, fax (612) 6282 3235, email: mhccan@cyberone.com.au; Monday-Friday, hours 8:45 a.m.-3:15 p.m.

Seychelles: 12th floor West Clock, Wisma, Selangor Dredging, 142C Jalan Ampang, 50450 Kuala Lumpur, Malaysia; tel. (60-3)21305726 or (60-3)21635727, fax (60-3)21635729

Zambia and Zimbabwe: High Commissioner, 11 Culogoa Circuit, O'Malley, ACT 2606, Canberra, Australia; tel. (02) 62862700 or (02) 6286 2281 or (02) 62862303, fax (02) 62901680

IN CANADA:

Burundi: 325 Dalhousie St., Suite 815 Ottawa K1N 7G2

Congo, Democratic Republic of: 18 Range Rd., Ottawa, Ontario K1N 8J3, Canada; tel. (613) 232-3983

Kenya: tel. Kenya High Commission, 415 Laurier Ave. East, West Ottawa, Ontario K1N 6R4, Canada; tel. (613) 563-1773/6/8, fax (613) 233-6599, email: kenrep@on.abn.com

Malawi: 7 Clemow Ave., Ottawa, K1S 2A9, Canada; tel. (613) 236-8931, fax (613) 236-1054, email: Malawi-highcommission@sympatico.ca

Rwanda: 121 Sherwood Dr., Ottawa, Ontario K1Y 3V1, Canada; tel. (613) 722-5835, fax (613) 722-4052, email: embarwa@sympatico.ca

South Africa: High Commission of the Republic of South Africa, 15 Sussex Dr., Ottawa, Ontario K1M 1M8; tel. (613) 744-0330, fax (613) 731-1639, email: safrica@ottawa.net

Swaziland: 130 Albert St., Suite 1204, Ottawa, Ontario K1P 5G4, Canada; tel. (613) 567-1480, fax (613) 567-1058, email: shc@direct-internet.net

Tanzania: 50 Range Rd., Ottawa, Ontario K1N 8J4, Canada; tel. (613) 232-1500, fax (613) 232-5184, email: tzottowa@synapse.net

Uganda: 231 Coburg St., Ottawa, Ontario, K1N 8J2, Canada; tel. (613) 233-7797, fax (613) 232-6689

Zimbabwe: 332 Somerset St. West, Ottawa, Ontario K2P 0J9, Canada; tel. (613) 237-4388/9, fax (613) 563-8269, email: zim.highcomm@sympatico.ca

HIGH COMMISSIONS IN THE UNITED KINGDOM:

Botswana: 6 Stratford Place, London W1N 9AE, England; tel. (020) 7499 0031, fax (020) 7495 8595

Burundi: 1000 Bruxelles, LE Square Marie-Louise, 46 Brussels; tel. (00 322) 230 5 35, fax (00 322) 230 78 83

Congo, Democratic Republic of: 38 Holne Chase, London N2 0QQ, England; tel. (020) 8458 0254, fax (020) 8458 0254

Kenya: 45 Portland Place, London W1N 4AS, England; tel. (020) 763 62371/5, fax (020) 732 36717

Lesotho: 7 Chesham Place, Belgravia, London SW1 8HN, England; tel. (020) 7235 5686, fax (020) 7235 5023, email: lesotholondonhighcom@compuserve.com

Malawi: 33 Grosvenor St., London W1X ODE, England; tel. (020) 7491 4172, fax (020) 7491 9916

Mauritius: 32/33 Elvaston Place, London SW7 5NW, England; tel. (171) 581 0294/5, fax (171) 823 8437, email: Londonmhc@btinternet.com

Namibia: 6 Chandos St., London W1M 0LQ, England; tel. (020) 7636 6244, fax (020) 7637 5694, email: Namibia.hicom@btconnect.com

Rwanda: 58-59 Trafalgar Square, London WC2N 5DX, England; tel. (020) 7930 2570, fax (020) 7930 2572, email: ambarwanda@compuserve.com

Seychelles: 2nd floor, Eros House, 111 Baker St., London W1M 1FE, England; tel. (020) 7224 1660, fax (020) 7487 5756

South Africa: South Africa House, Trafalgar Square, London WC2N 5DP, England; tel. (020) 7930 4488, fax (020) 7451 7284, email: general@southafricahouse.com

Swaziland: 20 Buckingham Gate, London SW1E 6LB, England; tel. (020) 7630 6611, fax (020) 7630 6564

Tanzania: 43 Hertford St., London W1Y 7DB, England; tel. (020) 7499 8951, fax (020) 7491 9321, email: tanzarep@tanzania-online.gov.uk

Uganda: 58-59 Trafalgar Square, London WC2N 5DX, England; tel. (020) 7839 5783, fax (020) 7839 8925

Zambia: 2 Palace Gate, Kensington, London W8 5NG, England; tel. (020) 7589 6655, fax (020) 7581 1353

Zimbabwe: 429 Strand, London WC2R 0QE, England; tel. (020) 7836 7755, fax (020) 7379 1167, email: zimlondon@callnetuk.com

IN THE UNITED STATES:

Botswana: Intelstat Building, Suite 7M, 3400 International Dr. NW, Washington, DC 20008; tel. (202) 244-4990/1, fax (202) 244-4164

Burundi: Suite 212, 2233 Wisconsin Ave. NW, Washington, DC 20007; tel. (202) 342-2574, fax (202) 342-2578

Congo, Democratic Republic of: 1800 New Hampshire NW, Washington, DC 20009; tel. (202) 234-7690/1, fax (202) 686-3631

Kenya: 2249 R St. NW, Washington, DC 20008; tel. (202) 387-6101, fax (202) 462-3829

Lesotho: 2511 Massachusetts Ave. NW, Washington, DC 20008; tel. (202) 797-5533, fax (202) 234-6815, email: lesotho@afrika.com

Malawi: 2408 Massachusetts Ave., Washington, DC 20008; tel. (202) 797-1007, fax (202) 265-0976

Mauritius: 4301 Connecticut Ave. NW, Suite 441, Washington, DC 20008; tel. (202)244-1491/2, fax (202)966-0983; email: Mauritius.embassy@prodigy.net

Namibia: 1605 New Hampshire Ave. NW, Washington DC 20009; tel. (202) 986-0540, fax (202) 986-0443

Rwanda: 1714 New Hampshire Ave. NW, Washington, DC 20009; tel. (202) 232-2882, fax (202) 234-4544

Seychelles: Embassy of the Republic of the Seychelles and Tourist Office, Suite 900F, 820 Second Ave., New York, NY 10017; tel. (212) 972-1785, fax (212) 972-1786

South Africa: 4031 Connecticut Ave. NW, Suite 220, Washington, DC 20008; tel. (202) 274-7990, fax (202) 232-3402

Swaziland: 3400 International Dr. NW, Suite 3M, Washington, DC 20008-3006; tel. (202) 362-6683, fax (202) 244-8059

Tanzania: 2139 R St. NW, Washington, DC 20008; tel. (202) 726-7100, fax (202) 797-7408

Uganda: 5911 16th St. NW, Washington, DC 20011; tel. (202) 726-7100, fax (202) 726-1727, email: ugembassy@aol.com

Zambia: 2419 Massachusetts Ave. NW, Washington, DC 20008; tel. (202) 265-9717/8/9, fax (202) 332-0826

Zimbabwe: 1608 New Hampshire Ave. NW, Washington, DC 20009; tel. (202) 332-7100, fax (202) 483-9326, email: zimemb@erols.com

MISSIONS TO THE UNITED NATIONS OR CONSULATES IN NEW YORK:

Botswana: 103 East 37th St., New York, NY 10016; tel. (212) 889-2277, email: Botswana@un.int

Burundi: 336 East 45th St., New York, NY 10017; tel. (212) 687-1180, email: Burundi@un.int

Congo, Democratic Republic of: 14 East 65th St., New York, NY 10021; tel. (212) 754-1966, fax (212) 744-7975, email: Cogun@undp.org

Kenya: 866 United Nations Plaza, Room 486, New York, NY 10017; tel. (212) 421-4740, fax (212) 486-1985, email: Kenya@un.int

Lesotho: 204 East 39th St., New York, NY 10016; tel. (212) 661-1690, fax (212) 682-4388, email: Lesotho@un.int

Mauritius: 211 East 43rd St.-Suite 1502, New York, NY 10017; tel. (212) 949-0190, fax (212) 697-3829, email: Mauritius@un.int

Malawi: 600 3rd Ave., 21st Floor, New York, NY 10016; tel. (212) 949-0180, fax (212) 599-5021, email: mwiun@undp.org

Namibia: 135 East 36th St., New York, NY 10016; tel. (212) 685-2003, fax (212) 685-1561, email: Namibia@un.int

Rwanda: 124 East 39th St., New York, NY 10016; tel. (212) 808-9330, fax (212) 679-9133, email: rwaun@undp.org

Seychelles: 800 Second Ave., Suite 400-C, New York, NY 10017; tel. (212) 972-1785, fax (212) 972-1786, email: Seychelles@un.int

South Africa: 333 East 38th St., New York, NY 10016; tel. (212) 213-5583, fax (212) 692-2498, email: southafrica@un.int

Swaziland: 408 East 50th St., New York, NY 10022; tel. (212) 371-8910, fax (212) 754-2755, email: Swaziland@un.int

Tanzania: 205 East 42nd St., 15th Floor, New York, NY 10017; tel. (212) 972-9160, email: Tanzania@un.int

Uganda: Uganda House, 336 East 45th St., New York, NY 10017; tel. (212) 949-0110, email: Uganda@un.int

Zambia: 800 Second Ave., 9th Floor, New York, NY 10017; tel. (212) 972-7200, email: Zambia@un.int

Zimbabwe: 128 East 56th St., New York, NY 10022; tel. (212) 980-5084, fax (212) 308-6705, email: Zimbabwe@un.int

DIPLOMATIC REPRESENTATIVES IN AFRICA

AUSTRALIAN HIGH COMMISSIONS:

Kenya: Riverside Dr., P.O. Box 39341, Nairobi, Kenya; tel. (254 2) 44 5034, fax (254 2) 44 4718

Mauritius and Seychelles: Rogers House - 2nd floor, 5 President John Kennedy St., P.O. Box 541, Port Louis, Mauritius; tel. (230) 208 1700, fax (230) 208 8878, email: austhe@intnet.mi

South Africa: (three locations)
292 Orient St., Arcadia, Pretoria 0083 South Africa; Private Bag X150 Pretoria 0001; tel. (27 12) 342 3781, fax (27 12) 342 8442

Fourteenth Floor, 1 Thibault Square, 8001 Cape Town, South Africa; tel. (27 21) 419 5425, fax (27 21) 419 7345

Fourth Floor, Norwich Life Towers, 13 Fredman Dr. (Sandton), Johannesburg, South Africa tel. (27 11) 784 0620, fax (27 11) 784 0446

Zimbabwe: 29 Mazowe St., The Avenues, P.O. Box 4541, Harare, Zimbabwe; tel. (263 4) 253 661, fax (263 4) 253 679

CANADIAN HIGH COMMISSIONS:

Botswana: Consulate of Canada, Plot 182, Queens Road, Gaborone, Botswana; tel. (26 731) 304411, fax (26 731) 304411

Congo, Democratic Republic of: Canadian Embassy, 17, Avenue Pumbu, Commune Gombe, Kinshasa, Democratic Republic of Congo; tel. (243) 884 1276, fax (243) 884 1277

Kenya: Canadian High Commission, Comcraft House, Haile Selassie Ave., P.O. Box 30481, Nairobi, Kenya; tel. (254) 2 214804, fax (254) 2 226987

Malawi: P.O. Box 51146 B;andyre-LIMBE, Malawi; tel. (265) 645441 or 645004, fax (265) 6430446, email: KOKHAI@Malabiz.com

Mauritius: Canadian High Commission,18 Jules Koenig St., Port Louis, Mauritius; tel. (230) 212 5500, fax (230) 208 3391, email: canada@intnet.mu

Seychelles: Canadian High Commission, 38 Mirambo St., P.O. Box 1022, Dar es Salaam, Tanzania; tel. (255 51) 20651, fax (255 51) 46005

South Africa: Canadian High Commission, Private Bag X13, 1103 Arcadia St., Hatfield 0028, Pretoria, South Africa; tel. (27 12) 442 3000, fax (27 12) 442 3052, email: pret@dfait-maeci.gc.ca

Tanzania: Canadian High Commission, 38 Mirambo St., P.O. Box 1022, Dar es Salaam, Tanzania; tel. (255 22) 2112831, fax (255 22) 2116897, email: dslam@dfait-maeci.gc.ca

Uganda: Canadian High Commission, IPS Building, Parliament Ave., Kampala, Uganda; tel. (256 41) 258141, fax (256 41) 234518, email: canada.consulate@infocom.co.ug

Zambia: Canadian High Commission, 5199 United Nations Ave., P.O. Box 31313, Lusaka, Zambia; tel. (260 1) 250 833, fax (260 1) 254 176, email: 1usaka@dgait-maeci.gc.ca

Zimbabwe: Canadian High Commission, 45 Baines Ave., P.O. Box 1430, Harare, Zimbabwe; tel. (263 4) 252181, fax (263 4) 252186, email: harare@dfait-maeci.gc.ca

UNITED KINGDOM HIGH COMMISSIONS:

Botswana: British High Commission, Private Bag 0023, Gaborone, Botswana; tel. (267 31) 352841, fax (267 31) 356105, email: british@bc.bw

Burundi: British Liaison Office, 43 Ave. Bubanza, B.P. 1344, Bujumbura, Burundi

Permanent staff in Kinshasa, Democratic Republic of the Congo; tel. (257) 223711

Congo, Democratic Republic of: British High Commission, Avenue des Lemera 83, B.P. 8049, Kinshasa, Gombe, Democratic Republic of the Congo; tel. (243 12) 34775/8, fax (871) 144 5470, email: ambrit@ic.cd

Kenya: British High Commission, Upper Hill Road, P.O. Box 30465, Nairobi, Kenya; tel. (254 2) 714699, fax (254 2) 719082, email: bhcinfo@lesoff.co.za

Lesotho: British High Commission, P.O. Box MS 521, Maseru 100, Lesotho; tel. (266) 313961, fax (266) 310120, email: hcmaseru@lesoff.co.za

Malawi: British High Commission, P.O. Box 30042, Lingadzi House, Lilongwe 3, Malawi; tel. (265) 782400, fax (265) 782657, email: britcomm@malawi.net

Mauritius: British High Commission, Les Cascades Building, Edith Cavell St., P.O. Box 1063, Port Louis, Mauritius; tel. (230) 211 1361, fax (230) 211 1369, email: bhc@bow.intnet.mu

Namibia: British High Commission, P.O. Box 22202, 116 Robert Mugabe Ave., Windhoek 9000, Namibia; tel. (264 61) 223022, fax (264 61) 228895

Rwanda: British Embassy, Parcelle No 1131, Boulevard de l'Umuganda, Kacyiru-Sud, Kigali, Rwanda; tel. (250) 84098, fax (250) 82044, email: britemb@rwanda1.com

Seychelles: British High Commission, Oliaji Trade Centre, Francis Rachel St., P.O. Box 161, Victoria, Mahe, Seychelles; tel. (248) 225 225, fax (248) 225 127

South Africa: British Consulate, Dunkeld Corner, 275 Jan Smuts Ave., Dunkeld West 2196, Johannesburg, South Africa; tel. (27 11) 327 0015

Swaziland: British High Commission, Allister Miller St., Mbabane, Swaziland; tel. (268) 4 2581, fax (268) 4 2585

Tanzania: British High Commission, Hifiadhi, Samora Ave., P.O. Box 9200, Dar es Salaam, Tanzania; tel. (255 51) 117659, fax (255 51) 112951, email: bhc.dar@raha.com

Uganda: British High Commission, 10-12 Parliament Ave., P.O. Box 7070, Kampala, Uganda; tel. (256 41) 257054 or (256 41) 257304, email: bhcinfo@starcom.co.ug

Zambia: British High Commission, Independence Ave. 15101, P.O. Box 50050, Lusaka, Zambia; tel. (260 1) 251133, fax (260 1) 253798, email: brithc@zamnet.zm

Zimbabwe: British High Commission, Corner House, corner of Samora Machel Ave. and Leopold Takawira St., P.O. Box 4490, Harare, Zimbabwe; tel. (263 4) 72990, fax (263 4) 774617

UNITED STATES EMBASSIES:
Botswana: United States Embassy, P.O. Box 90, Gaborone, Botswana; tel. (267 31) 353982/3/4, fax (267 31) 356947, email: usembgab@mega.bw

Burundi: United States Embassy, B.P. 1720, Ave. du Zaire, Bujumbura, Burundi; tel. (257) 223454, fax (257) 222926

Congo, Democratic Republic of: B.P. 697, Unit 31550, 310 Ave. des Aviateurs, Kinshasa - Gombe, Democratic Republic of the Congo; tel. (243 88) 43608, fax (243 88) 43467

Kenya: United States Embassy, P.O. Box 30137, Mombasa Road near St James Hospital, Nairobi, Kenya; tel. (254 2) 537800, fax (254 2) 537810

Mauritius: United States Embassy, Rogers Bldg., Fourth Floor, John Kennedy St., Port Louis, Mauritius; tel. (230) 202 4400, fax (230) 208 9834, email: usembass@intnet.mu

Namibia: United States Embassy, Ausplan Bldg., 14 Lossen St., Private Bag 12029, Ausspannplatz, Windhoek 9000, Namibia; tel. (264) 61 22 1601, fax (264) 61 22 9792, email: windhoek@pd.state.gov

Seychelles: U.S. Consular Agency, Victoria House, 1st Floor, Room 112, P.O. Box 251, Victoria, Seychelles; tel. (248) 255 256, fax (248) 225 189

South Africa: United States Embassy, P.O. Box 9536, 877 Pretorius St., Pretoria 0001, South Africa; tel. (27 12) 342 1048, fax (27 12) 342 2244

Swaziland: United States Embassy, Embassy House, Allister Miller St., P.O. Box 199, Mbabane, Swaziland; tel. (268) 404 0677, fax (268) 404 5846, email: dnmlambo@usembassy.org.sz

Tanzania: United States Embassy, 140 Msese Road, Kinondon District, P.O. Box 9123, Dar es Salaam, Tanzania; tel. (255 22) 2666010/5, fax (255 22) 2666701, email: usembassy-dar1@catsnet.com

Zambia: Corner of Independence and United Nations Ave., Lusaka, Zambia; tel. (260) 1 250 955, fax (260) 1 252 225, email: usembcon@zamnet.zm

Zimbabwe: P.O. Box 3340 172 Herbert Chitepo Ave., Harare, Zimbabwe; tel. (263 4) 250 593, fax (263 4) 796 488

DUTY-FREE ALLOWANCES

Contact the nearest tourist office or embassy for current, duty-free import allowances for the country(ies) that you intend to visit. The duty-free allowances vary; however, the following may be used as a general guideline: 1-2 liters (approximately 1-2 qt./33.8-67.4 fl. oz.) of spirits, one carton (200) of cigarettes or 100 cigars.

ELECTRICITY

Electric current is 220–240-volt AC 50 Hz. Adapters: Three-prong square or round plugs are most commonly used.

FRESHWATER FISHING

The Nile Perch, the largest freshwater species in Africa, can attain a weight of well over 200 pounds (90 kg). These giants, like huge bass, are fished for in a similar way and fight in a similar style. They will jump, run and fight in the most spectacular manner. Most anglers fish with a 40-pound rig and large "crankbaits," and some have even caught them on fly. Nile Perch have been introduced to many large lakes in Central and East Africa, including Lake Victoria, Lake Turkana and Lake Tanganyika.

Possibly the best freshwater fighting fish in the world, the tigerfish, comes in two varieties: the regular tigerfish and the goliath tigerfish. Many different methods are used to catch this fearsome toothed, aggressive fish, ranging from cast and retrieve of spinners and lures, trawling spinners and lures, drifting with live bait, and drifting with fish fillets. Possibly the most exciting thing about tigerfishing is the high-speed strike and the manner in which they leap and jump out of the water when hooked. Classic places for tigerfishing are Lake Kariba in Zimbabwe and the Zambezi River between Zimbabwe and Zambia. Goliath tigerfish occur farther north on the Congo River and many of the lakes in that region, including Lake Tanganyika. Tigerfish attain a weight of up to 25 pounds (11 kg), though this is rare and one can expect more around 5-10 pound (2.3-4.5 kg) mark, while the goliath tigerfish can get well over 100 pounds (45 kg), but is a lot harder to catch.

There are no natural trout in Africa; however, many dams, lakes and rivers have been stocked over the years and can provide some very entertaining fishing. The best areas in Africa for trout are the Eastern Highlands of Zimbabwe, the Drakensberg foothills and high-altitude grasslands east of Johannesburg in South Africa, and the Kenyan Highlands, where they are fished with many of the classic British flies.

Most often, tackle will be provided, which saves you the trouble of carrying the stuff halfway around the world only to find it unsuitable. The exception to this is fly-fishing, where you must bring your own equipment.

Most freshwater fishing requires a license, which can usually be obtained from your hotel, lodge or camp for a small fee.

GETTING TO AFRICA

BY AIR:

Most travelers from North America flying to the countries listed in this guide must pass through Europe, with the exception of South African Airways, which flies New York to Johannesburg and Atlanta to Cape Town or Johannesburg. Airfares and air routings to Africa are continuously changing. For special discount air fares, please call The Africa Adventure Company at 1-800-882-9453 (U.S.A. and Canada) or (954) 491-8877, fax (954) 491-9060, email noltingaac@aol.com or visit the World Wide Web pages at http://www.AfricanAdventure.com.

BY ROAD:
From Egypt to Sudan and Ethiopia to Kenya and southward; trans-Sahara through Algeria, Niger, Nigeria or Chad, Cameroon, Central Africa Republic, Democratic Republic of the Congo, Rwanda or Uganda and eastern and southern Africa. Allow several months because the roads are very bad.

BY SHIP:
Some cruise ships stop along the coasts of Kenya, Tanzania and South Africa, and at Mauritius and the Seychelles.

GETTING AROUND AFRICA
See each country's map for details on major roads, railroad lines and waterways.

BY AIR:
Capitals and major tourist centers are served by air. There is regularly scheduled air service to the following destinations within Africa:

Botswana: Gaborone, Maun, Francistown and Kasane.
Burundi: Bujumbura.
Congo, Democratic Republic of: Kinshasa.
Kenya: Kisumu, Malindi, Mombasa, Lamu and Nairobi.
Scheduled charter services are available to Amboseli, Masai Mara, Nanyuki and Samburu.
Lesotho: Maseru
Malawi: Blantyre, Lilongwe, Mzuzu.
Mauritius: Plaisance International Airport.
Namibia: Windhoek, Luderitz, Swakopmund and Walvis Bay.
Rwanda: Kigali.
Seychelles: Mahe and Praslin.
South Africa: Bloemfontein, Cape Town, Durban, Eastgate (Hoedspuit), East London, George, Johannesburg, Kimberley, Nelspruit, Port Elizabeth, Richards Bay, Mpumalanga (replaced Skukuza), Umtata and Upington.
Tanzania: Kilimanjaro International, Dar es Salaam and Zanzibar.
Uganda: Entebbe.
Zambia: Lusaka, Livingstone (Victoria Falls), Mfuwe (South Luangwa National Park) and Ndola.
Zimbabwe: Bulawayo, Harare, Hwange, Kariba and Victoria Falls.

BY ROAD:

Major roads are tarmac (paved) and are excellent in Namibia, South Africa, Botswana and Zimbabwe. Most major roads are tarmac in fair condition in Kenya, Tanzania, Uganda, Zambia, Rwanda, Malawi and Swaziland. Burundi, Lesotho and the D. R. Congo have very few tarmac roads. Many dirt roads (except in Namibia) are difficult, and many are impassable in the rainy season (especially the D. R. Congo), often requiring 4wd vehicles.

Gas (petrol) and diesel are readily available in the main towns and cities of Botswana, Kenya, Lesotho, Malawi, Mauritius, Namibia, South Africa and Swaziland; may be difficult to obtain in Burundi, Rwanda, parts of Tanzania, Zambia and Zimbabwe; and they are very difficult to obtain in the D. R. Congo.

Taxis are available in the larger cities and at international airports. **Service taxis** travel when all seats are taken and are an inexpensive but uncomfortable means of long-distance travel. **Local buses** are very crowded, uncomfortable and are recommended for only the hardiest of travelers. Pickup trucks (matatus in East Africa), often crammed with 20 passengers, luggage, produce, chickens, etc., and are used throughout the continent. Be sure to agree on the price before setting off.

BY RAIL:

Trains in South Africa are excellent (especially the luxurious Blue Train and Rovos Rail). The so-called "Lunatic Express" from Nairobi to Mombasa in Kenya, as of this writing, is in poor condition. See the chapters on Kenya and South Africa for further details. Otherwise, train travel is slow and not recommended except for those who are on an extremely low budget or who have plenty of time to spare. Train travel is possible from Arusha (Tanzania) through Zambia, Zimbabwe and Botswana to Cape Town, South Africa. Railway lines are depicted on the maps of each country in this guide.

BY BOAT:

Steamer service on Lake Tanganyika serves Bujumbura (Burundi), Kigoma (Tanzania), Mpulungu (Zambia) and Kalemie (D. R. Congo) about once a week; steamers on Lake Victoria service Kisumu (Kenya), Musoma and Mwanza (Tanzania) and Kampala-Port Bell (Uganda); the *Ilala* and *Mtendere* steamers circumnavigate Lake Malawi.

HEALTH

Malarial risk exists in all of the countries included in this guidebook (except for Lesotho and much of South Africa), so be sure to take your malaria pills (unless advised by your doctor not to take them), as prescribed before, during and after your trip. Contact your doctor, an immunologist or the Centers for Disease Control and Prevention in Atlanta (toll-free tel. 1-888-232-3228, fax 1-888-232-3299, Web site: www.cdc.gov) for the best prophylaxis for your itinerary. Use an insect repellent. Wear long-sleeve shirts and slacks for further protection, especially at sunset and during the evening.

Bilharzia is a disease that infests most lakes and rivers on the continent but can be easily cured. Do not walk barefoot along the shore or wade or swim in a stream, river or lake unless you know for certain it is free of bilharzia. Bilharzia does not exist in salt water or in fast flowing rivers or along shorelines that have waves. A species of snail is involved in the reproductive cycle of bilharzia, and the snails are more often found near reeds and in slow-moving water. If you feel you may have contracted the disease, go to your doctor for a blood test. If diagnosed in its early stages, it is easily cured.

Wear a hat and bring sunblock to protect yourself from the tropical sun. Drink plenty of fluids and limit alcohol consumption at high altitudes.

In hot weather, do not drink alcohol and limit the consumption of coffee and tea unless you drink plenty of water.

For further information, obtain a copy of Health Information for International Travel from the U.S. Government Printing Office, Washington, DC 20402.

INOCULATIONS

See "Visa and Inoculations Requirements" on page 628.

INSURANCE

Travel insurance packages often include a combination of emergency evacuation, medical, baggage, and trip cancellation. I feel that it is imperative that all travelers to Africa cover themselves fully with an insurance package from a reputable provider. Many tour operators require at least emergency evacuation insurance as a requirement for joining a safari. The peace of mind afforded by such insurance far outweighs the cost. Ask your Africa travel specialist for information on relatively inexpensive group-rate insurance.

MAPS

Before going on safari, obtain good maps for each country you intend to visit. This will increase your awareness of the areas you want to see and enhance your enjoyment of the trip. For a free catalog of difficult-to-find country maps, regional maps and mountain maps, see the catalog at the end of this book or contact The Africa Adventure Company, 5353 N. Federal Highway, Suite 300, Fort Lauderdale, FL 33308, tel. (954) 491-8877 or 1-800-882-9453. It is best to purchase maps before arriving in Africa, because they may not be readily available upon your arrival.

METRIC SYSTEM OF WEIGHTS AND MEASURES

The metric system is used in Africa. The U.S. equivalents are listed in the conversion chart below.

MEASUREMENT CONVERSIONS

1 inch	= 2.54 centimeters (cm)
1 foot	= 0.305 meter (m)
1 mile	= 1.60 kilometers (km)
1 square mile	= 2.59 square kilometers (km2)
1 hectare	= 2.47 acres
1 quart liquid	= 0.946 liter (l)
1 ounce	= 28 grams (g)
1 pound	= 0.454 kilogram (kg)
1 cm	= 0.39 inch (in.)
1 m	= 3.28 feet (ft.)
1 km	= 0.62 mile (mi.)
1 km2	= 0.3861 square mile (sq. mi.)
1 l	= 1.057 quarts (qt.)
1 g	= 0.035 ounce (oz.)
1 kg	= 2.2 pounds (lb.)

TEMPERATURE CONVERSIONS

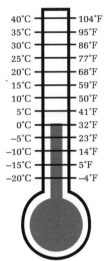

40°C	104°F
35°C	95°F
30°C	86°F
25°C	77°F
20°C	68°F
15°C	59°F
10°C	50°F
5°C	41°F
0°C	32°F
−5°C	23°F
−10°C	14°F
−15°C	5°F
−20°C	−4°F

TEMPERATURE CONVERSION FORMULAS
To convert degrees Centigrade into degrees Fahrenheit:
Multiply Centigrade by 1.8 and add 32.
To convert degrees Fahrenheit into degrees Centigrade:
Subtract 32 from Fahrenheit and divide by 1.8.

MONEY

One way to obtain additional funds is to purchase additional traveler's checks through your American Express or other credit card. Other options include having money sent by telegraph international money order (Western Union), telexed through a bank or sent via international courier (i.e., DHL). Do not count on finding ATM machines, except in South Africa.

PASSPORT OFFICES

To obtain a passport in the United States, contact your local post office for the passport office nearest you. Then call the passport office to be sure you will have everything on hand that will be required.

PHOTOGRAPHY

Capturing aspects of a safari on film is uppermost in the minds of many travelers. This could very well be the trip of a lifetime, and you want to record as much of it as possible. For those who have not photographed wildlife before, there are two primary things to take into account — technology and technique.

Camera technology has become so advanced in recent years that it is easier than ever for amateurs to take professional-quality photographs. The versatile 35mm camera is still the most appropriate and popular equipment, but digital zooms and video camcorders with freeze-frame options are so easy to use that they are preferred by a growing number of people.

You need to ask yourself what you are going to do with the photographs you take on safari. If you are going to try and sell them to a magazine or book publisher, then you need high-quality optics and good quality transparency (color slide) film. If you are going to make an electronic album to email to friends, then a reasonably priced digital zoom will be ideal. Print film is preferable to slides, if you plan to make an album, but the old-fashioned home slide show still has great appeal for many. Many people prefer the idea of capturing movement and sound, and with video camcorders being so compact and easy to use, this is an obvious choice.

The huge advantage of digital cameras is the tiny size of the picture-storing apparatus — this eliminates the need for bags and bags of film. In addition, unwanted frames can be deleted right away, making room for all the other great shots you need to take.

Video cameras and camcorders in themselves are great fun, and many a happy memory can be captured on the video that would simply be impossible to depict with a 'still' camera. Another great advantage is that they operate very well in low-light conditions. One danger of having a video is that often one is tempted to try and film too much and a huge proportion of your safari is seen through the viewfinder!

For the traditional approach for the serious photographer, a reliable 35mm body (preferably two bodies) should be complimented by two lenses: one for scenery and a telephoto for more distant subjects. A 200mm lens is the smallest you'll get away with for larger mammals (300-400mm is preferred), while bird photography requires 400mm or larger (500mm or larger is preferred). Auto-focus zoom lenses come in a variety of ranges, and a 28-70mm and 100-300 or 100-400mm would provide a good, balanced system. Lenses with built-in digital stabilizers, such as the Canon 100-400mm, are highly recommended. Fixed-length lenses are generally more expensive and, of course, have less flexibility, but they have the advantage of better light-gathering qualities than zoom lenses can provide. Also consider purchasing a teleconverter that will increase the power of your lens by a multiple of 1.4, 1.7, 2.0 etc. — depending on what you purchase. The downside is that they lose the same proportion of light as well (i.e. a 1.7 converter will lose you 1.7 "stops" of light).

Compact cameras with a small, built-in zoom lens and flash are great for pictures of your tents, the vehicles, people on safari, etc., but because of their limited zoom and light-gathering properties, generally their use in wildlife photography is very limited, and the results can be somewhat disappointing. In addition to your 35mm equipment, consider bringing along a compact camera and a small camera that takes panoramic shots.

Digital photography generally is not quite the same quality as 35mm slides or prints. However, this is changing fast, and in a couple of years digital cameras will almost certainly overtake traditional slide and print photography. The very latest digital cameras (like the Canon 1D and the Canon D60) are able to produce just about the same quality photographs (up to about 8.5 x 11 inch/A4 paper size) as traditional slides or print cameras. The advantage with these new digital cameras is that they use the same lenses as the normal Canon SLR cameras, but you have the advantage of instant feedback and you can correct your mistakes on the spot while shooting in the field. When you get home you already know you have perfect photos.

Here are a couple of digital photography tips: 1) take a lot of extra batteries and a battery charger. Digital photography can chew up batteries fast, 2) take an extra-large memory card for the camera so that you don't run out of storage space for your photographs (a 1GB microdrive is recommended), 3) try to shoot your photos with the camera settings that offer the greatest quality (ie. shoot in a large/fine quality format), and 4) shoot like crazy in all sorts of different settings and then delete the photos you don't like.

Digital photography has the advantage of being able to give you all sorts of light settings and a range of ASA settings, so you can even shoot indoors and in very low light situations. Having said that, try to shoot in the 100 to 200 ASA range, unless you have to shoot at 800 or 1600 ASA when the light is low.

Many cameras have a built-in flash system, but you'll need a more powerful, add-on unit for serious nighttime photography of nocturnal animals. Space and weight restrictions may limit you carrying a tripod, but a small cloth bag filled with rice or dry beans provides a wonderful support to reduce camera shake (the greatest cause of blurred images). Simply pack an empty bag, and fill it when you get to Africa. Another primary cause of blurred photographs is vibration from a running car motor, so always ensure that your guide or driver switches off when you are taking pictures. This is also true for video work where you want to capture the natural sounds of the bush, not a diesel engine!

If you will be on safari in a roof-hatch vehicle, consider bringing a small tripod to help steady your camera when shooting from the roof of your vehicle. Monopods (one-legged support) are also useful, especially in open vehicles and on walking safaris.

Generally, a clearer, sharper, truer image can be produced with color slide film than with print film. Slides can be made into prints later, should you wish, but at added expense. Print film must be of good quality, so choose a well-known brand and buy a lower ASA-rated film. The lab that develops your film could make a big difference in the quality of the final product.

ASA 64 and 100 are best during the day, when there is plenty of light. ASA 200-ASA 400 is often needed in early mornings and late afternoons, especially when using telephoto or zoom lenses. With very low light, use a flash or ASA 1000 or higher film. ASA 1600 may be necessary when photographing gorillas in the dark forests. Please, when you are buying film, think how much you are spending on your safari, and pay that little extra for the better quality film — it will definitely pay off!

Be careful about your 800 ASA film and higher because the airport x-ray machines will probably damage the film. Carry your film in x-ray protective bags, and try to get these films hand-searched.

Pack as much film (or blank video cassettes) as you possibly can, because it is generally much more expensive in Africa, if obtainable at all. Take at least two rolls of 36 exposures per person for each day on safari. You must bring all of your own spares, filters (UV and polarizing are recommended), batteries, charging units and so on.

A polarizer helps cut glare and is especially effective when you have a lot of sky and water in the photo.

If you bring a camcorder or video recorder, be sure to bring at least three extra batteries and a charging unit and converter (Africa uses 220-240 volts). Batteries can usually be recharged at your lodge or permanent camp while the generator is running or from your vehicle while you are being driven around.

In terms of technique, you need to develop as quick a response as possible. Much of the animal action you will want to try and capture will happen suddenly, so you need to be ready at all times. Familiarization with your equipment is critical to this end, so make sure you test out a new camera or video well before you get to Africa. Dust and heat are the biggest enemies to your equipment, but since it needs to be by your side (or in your lap) at all times, it is advisable to loosely wrap it in a T-shirt or plastic bag. Store the camera bodies and lenses in zippered plastic bags when not in use.

Light is what makes or breaks a photograph, and light is always best when the sun is lower in the sky. Softer, warmer light and less intense shadows exist between 6:00 a.m. and 9:00 a.m. and again after 4:00 p.m. Photographs taken in the middle of the day are invariably disappointing, but you never know what may turn up unexpectedly. If, for example, you want to try and photograph ALL of the mammal species you see, then it is advisable to photograph the common/frequently seen species (your guide will tell which these are in a particular place) only when the light is at its best, whereas you'll photograph the rarities whenever the opportunity presents itself.

From a compositional point of view, the most interesting photographs are very often those that depict the animal in its natural habitat, and for this reason it is important to pay attention to some fundamentals of picture composition:

1. Avoid "placing" the subject in the dead center of the picture frame (a common mistake) because this can result in a lifeless picture. A subject set on one side of the frame suggests movement — the viewer's eye automatically drifts from the point of interest to the space and back again.

2. Maneuver yourself, or the vehicle that you are in, in such a way that the background does not clash with the subject. For instance, if there is a beautifully shaped acacia tree directly behind a group of zebra, move forward until the animals are to one side of the tree; this will also create a sense of distance. Checking your background is very important because a photo is often spoiled by a pole, a sign, animal or vehicle being where it should not be.

3. One of the most wonderful things about Africa is the huge skies — often deep blue and cloudless, or piled with dramatic cloud formations. By getting back from your subject, or using a wide-angle lens, you can make these skies part of the picture in such a way that they add atmosphere without competing with the main subject.

Look for and photograph the small or less obvious things as well: butterflies, flowers, clouds or even tree bark textures. Incorporate them deliberately into your compositions. Take note of your horizon at all times; a photo is often ruined by a sloping horizon. In low light, your shutter speed should be at least as high as your focal length (1/250 of a second at 250mm); if not, use your monopod or beanbag. When you photograph a sunset, and to create a silhouette, meter off the sky or sun and focus on the subject you want silhouetted. Never let your film get hot or leave it or your camera in the sun. When photographing a living creature that is close, try to get the eye in focus — the rest does not matter so much. When taking a picture of scenery or a subject with interesting light — try to bracket (take a few pictures at different exposures), because this will help assure that one will be great.

The photography of traditionally dressed people is a sensitive issue, and you should talk to your guide about any intentions you have. While it may be tempting to take candid, "natural" photographs of tribal people going about their lives, this is regarded as rude and unacceptable by the majority of rural communities. Many people expect to receive a small fee for having their photograph taken, but this often results in a frozen, "staged" expression. A good approach is to settle on a reasonable fee for multiple photographs at a whole village, and then spend a fair amount of time waiting for relaxed expressions. Many people who have their picture taken request a print to be sent to them in due course, and this is a good way of developing and maintaining trust in the long term.

African governments are highly sensitive about certain structures being photographed or filmed, so do not take pictures of airports, bridges, military or police installations and personnel, or telecommunications installations.

Finally, a word of caution. Photography can be great fun, but be careful that you do not become pre-occupied with your camera or video equipment on safari. Some people spend their safari wrestling with lenses and cursing at dials, when they should be relaxing and absorbing the wilderness atmosphere. Possibly the best advice I can give is to have fun taking photographs!

SAFARI TIPS

Read the "Safari Glossary" to become familiar with the terminology used in the bush. Once on safari, you will notice that when you ask people what animals they saw on their game drive, they might reply, "elephant, lion, leopard and oryx," when in fact they saw several members of each species. This use of the singular form, when more than one of that species was seen, is common. However, one exception to this rule is saying *crocs* for *crocodile*. This form of "Safariese" will be used throughout this guide to help separate you from the amateur.

Put your valuables in a safety deposit box at your lodge or hotel.

Do not call out to a person, signaling with an index finger. This is insulting to most Africans. Instead, use four fingers with your palm facing downward.

Wear colors that blend in with your surroundings (brown, tan, light green or khaki). Do not wear perfume or cologne while game viewing. Wildlife can detect unnatural smells for miles and unnatural colors for hundreds of yards (meters), making close approaches difficult.

The very few tourists who get hurt on safari are almost always those travelers who ignore the laws of nature and most probably the advice and warnings of their guides. Common sense is the rule.

Do not wade or swim in rivers, lakes or streams unless you know for certain they are free of crocodiles, hippos, and bilharzia (a snail-borne disease). Fast-moving areas of rivers are often free of bilharzia, but can still be a bit risky. Bilharzia, fortunately, is not the dreaded disease that it once was; if detected early it can be easily cured.

Do not walk along the banks of rivers near dawn, dusk or at night. Those who do so may inadvertently cut off a hippo's path to its water hole, and the hippo may charge.

Malaria is present in almost all the parks and reserves covered in this guide. Malarial prophylaxis (pills) should be taken and must be prescribed by a physician. Because most malaria-carrying mosquitoes come out from dusk until dawn, during this period you should use mosquito repellent and wear long pants and long-sleeve shirt or blouse, shoes (not sandals) and socks. For further information see the section on "Health" in the "Safari Pages" section of this book.

Because of the abundance of thorns and sharp twigs, wear closed-toed shoes or boots at night and also during the day if venturing out into the bush. Bring a flashlight and always have it with you at night.

Don't venture out of your lodge or camp without your guide, especially at night, dawn or dusk. Remember that wildlife is not confined to the parks and reserves in many countries, and, in fact, roams freely in and around many camps and lodges.

Resist the temptation to jog or walk alone in national parks, reserves or other areas where wildlife exists. To lion and other carnivores, we are just "meat on the hoof" like any other animal — only much slower and less capable of defending ourselves.

SEMINARS ON AFRICA

Contact the Africa Adventure Company to arrange a seminar by Mark Nolting, author of this guidebook. Tel. (954) 491-8877 or 1-800-882-9453, fax (954) 491-9060, email: noltingaac@aol.com

SHOPPING

If you like bartering, bring clothing (new denims and T-shirts are great) or pens to trade for souvenirs. This works particularly well at roadside stands and in small villages in East and Central Africa, although the villagers are becoming more discerning in their tastes.

SOME SHOPPING IDEAS

Botswana: Baskets, wood carvings, pottery, tapestries and rugs. There are curio shops in many safari camps, hotels and lodges.

Burundi: Crafts available in numerous shops.

Congo, Democratic Republic of: Wood carvings, malachite, copper goods, semiprecious stones and baskets.

Kenya: Makonde and Akomba ebony wood carvings, soapstone carvings, colorful kangas and kikois (cloth wraps). In Mombasa, Zanzibar chests, gold and silverwork, brasswork, Arab jewelry and antiques.

Lesotho: Basotho woven carpets are known worldwide, tapestry weaving and conical straw hats.

Malawi: Wood carvings, woven baskets.

Mauritius: Intricately detailed, handmade model sailing ships of camphor or teak, pareos (colorful light cotton wraps), knitwear, textiles, T-shirts, Mauritian dolls, tea, rum and spices.

Namibia: Semiprecious stones and jewelry, karakul wool products, wood carvings, ostrich eggshell necklaces and beadwork.

Seychelles: Coco-de-mer nuts (may be purchased with a government permit that is not difficult to obtain), batik prints, spices for Creole cooking and locally produced jewelry, weaving and basketry.

South Africa: Diamonds, gold, wood carvings, dried flowers, wire art, wildlife paintings and sculpture, and wine.

Swaziland: Beautiful hand-woven tapestries, baskets, earthenware and stoneware, and mouth-blown, handcrafted glass animals and tableware.

Tanzania: Makonde carvings, meerschaum pipes and tanzanite.

Uganda: Wood carvings.

Zambia: Wood carvings, statuettes, semiprecious stones and copper souvenirs.

Zimbabwe: Carvings of wood, stone and Zimbabwe's unique verdite, intricate baskets, wildlife paintings and sculpture, ceramicware and crocheted garments.

SHOPPING HOURS

Shops are usually open Monday-Friday from 8:00 or 9:00 a.m. until 5:00 to 6:00 p.m. and from 9:00 a.m. until 1:00 p.m. on Saturdays. Shops in the coastal cities of Kenya and Tanzania often closed midday for siesta. Use the shopping hours given above as a general guideline; exact times can vary within the respective country.

THEFT

The number one rule in preventing theft on vacation is to leave all unnecessary valuables at home. What you must bring, lock in safety deposit boxes when not in use. Theft in Africa is generally no worse than in Europe or the United States, but consider leaving showy gold watches and jewelry at home. One difference is that Africans are poorer and may steal things that most American or European thieves would consider worthless. Be careful in all African cities (like most large cities in North America) and do not go walking around the streets at night.

TIME ZONES

EST = Eastern Standard Time (east coast of the United States)
GMT = Greenwich Mean Time (Greenwich, England)

EST + 3/GMT – 2
Cape Verde
EST + 4/GMT – 1
Guinea-Bissau
EST + 5/GMT
Algeria
Ascension
Burkina-Faso
The Gambia
Ghana
Guinea
Ivory Coast
Liberia
Mali
Mauritania
Morocco
St. Helena
São Tomé &
Principe
Senegal
Sierra Leone
Togo
Tristan de Cunha

EST + 6/GMT + 1
Angola
Benin
Cameroon
Central African
Republic
Chad
Congo
Democratic
Republic of the
Congo (western)
Equatorial Guinea
Gabon
Niger
Nigeria
Tunisia
EST + 7/GMT + 2
Botswana
Burundi
Democratic
Republic of the
Congo (eastern)
Egypt
Lesotho

Libya
Malawi
Mozambique
Namibia
Rwanda
South Africa
Sudan
Swaziland
Zambia
Zimbabwe
EST + 8/GMT + 3
Comoros
Djibouti
Eritrea
Ethiopia
Kenya
Madagascar
Somalia
Tanzania
Uganda
EST + 9/GM T + 4
Mauritius
Reunion
Seychelles

TIPPING

A 10% tip is recommended at restaurants for good service where a service charge is not included in the bill. For advice on what tips are appropriate for guides, ask the Africa specialist booking your safari.

TOURIST INFORMATION

In addition to the addresses below, information may also be available through embassies or consulates of the countries in question. See "Diplomatic Representatives" above.

OFFICES IN AFRICA

Botswana: Division of Tourism, Private Bag 0047, Gaborone, Botswana; tel. (267) 353024, fax (267) 308675, email: botswana-tourism@gov.bw

Burundi: National Office of Tourism, Liberty Ave., P.O. Box 902, 2 Ave des Euphorbes, Bujumbura, Burundi; tel. (257) 222023, fax (257) 229390

Congo, Democratic Republic of: 15 Ave des Clinques, B.P. 12348, Kinshasa-Gombe, Congo tel. (243) 30235, fax (243) 32668

Kenya: Kenya Tourist Board, 7th floor KenyaRe Towers, Regati Road, Upper Hill, P.O. Box 30630, Nairobi, Kenya; tel. (254) 724042, fax (254) 724180

Lesotho: National Tourist Board, P.O. Box 1378, Maseru 100, Lesotho; tel. (266) 32 3896, fax (266) 31 0108

Malawi: P.O. Box 402, Blantyre, Malawi; tel. (265) 620 300, fax (265) 620 947

Mauritius: Mauritius Government Tourist Office, Emmanuel Anquetil Building, Sir Seewoosagur Ramgoolam St., Port Louis, Mauritius; tel. (230) 201 1703, fax (230) 212 5142

Namibia: Ministry of Environment & Tourism, Private Bag 13346, Windhoek 9000, Namibia; tel. (264) 220 241, fax (264) 221 930

Rwanda: Office Rwandais du Tourisme et des Parcs Nationaux (ORTPN), B.P. 905, Kigali, Rwanda; tel. (250) 76514. fax (250) 76512

Seychelles: P.O. Box 47, Independence House, Victoria, Mahe, Seychelles; tel. (248) 225 313, fax (248) 224 035

South Africa: Tourism Board, Private Bag X10012, Sandton 2146, Bojanala House, 12 Rivonia Road, Illovo Johannesburg 2196, South Africa; tel. (27 11) 778 8000, fax (27 11) 778 8001

Swaziland: Government Tourist Office, P.O. Box 451, Mbabane, Swaziland; tel. (268) 42531

Tanzania: Tanzania Tourist Board, P. O. Box 2485, Dar es Salaam, Tanzania; tel. (255) 26680 fax (255) 46780

Uganda: Ministry of Tourism, Wildlife and Antiquities, P.O. Box 7211, Parliament Ave., Kampapa, Uganda; tel. (256) 41 242 196, fax (256) 41 242 188

Zambia: Century House, Cairo Road, P.O. Box 30017, Lusaka, Zambia tel. (260) 1 229 087 fax (260) 1 225 174

Zimbabwe: Tourist Development Corporation (ZTDC) P.O. Box 8052, Harare, Zimbabwe; tel. (263) 793 666, fax (263) 793 669

OFFICES IN AUSTRALIA
South Africa: Level 6, 285 Clarence St. Sydney, NSW 2000 Australia; tel. (61) 2 9261 3424, fax (61) 2 9261 3414

OFFICES IN CANADA
South Africa: (two offices) Suite 1001, 20 Eglington Ave. West, Toronto, Ontario, M4R 1K8, tel. (416) 283 0563, fax (416) 283 5465
Suite 205, 4117 Lawrence Ave. East, Scarborough, Ontario M1E 2S2

OFFICES IN THE UNITED KINGDOM
Botswana: Botswana High Commission; 6 Stratford Place, London W1N 9AE, England; tel. 020 7499 0031, fax 020 7495 8595

Democratic Republic of Congo: Embassy of the Democratic Republic of the Congo; 38 Holne Chase, London N2 0QQ, England; tel. 020 8458 0254, fax 020 8458 0254

Kenya: Kenya High Commission; 45 Portland Place, London W1N 4AS, England: Tel. 020 7636 2371 fax 020 7323 6717

Lesotho: High Commission for the Kingdom of Lesotho; 7 Chesham Place, Belgravia, London SW1 8HN, England; tel. 020 7235 5686, fax 020 7235 5023

Malawi: High Commission for the Republic of Malawi; 33 Grosvenor St., London W1K 4QT, England; tel. 020 7491 4172, fax 020 7491 9916

Mauritius: Mauritius High Commission; 32/33 Elvaston Place, London SW7 5NW, England; tel. 020 7581 0294, fax 020 7823 8437

Namibia: High Commission for the Republic of Namibia; 6 Chandos Street, London W1G 9LU, England; tel. 020 7636 2924, fax 020 7636 2969

Rwanda: Embassy of the Republic of Rwanda; 58/59 Trafalgar Square, London WC2N 5DW, England; tel. 020 7930 2570, fax 020 7930 2572

Seychelles: High Commission for the Seychelles; 2nd Floor, Eros House, 111 Baker Street, London W1U 6RR, England; tel. 020 7224 1660, fax 020 7487 5756

South Africa: South African High Commission; South Africa House, Trafalgar Square, London WC2N 5DP, England; tel. 020 7451 7299, fax 020 7451 7280

Swaziland: Kingdom of Swaziland High Commission; 20 Buckingham Gate, London SW1E 6LB, England; tel. 020 7630 6611, fax 020 7630 6564

Tanzania: High Commission for the United Republic of Tanzania; 43 Hertford Street, London W1Y 7DB, England; tel. 020 7499 8951, fax 020 7491 9321

Uganda: Uganda High Commission; Consular & Tourism Department, 58/59 Trafalgar Square, London WC2N 5DX, England; tel. 020 7839 5783, fax 020 7839 8925

Zambia: High Commission for the Republic of Zambia; 2 Palace Gate, Kensington, London W8 5NG, England; tel. 020 7589 6655, fax 020 7581 1353

Zimbabwe: High Commission for the Republic of Zimbabwe; Zimbabwe House, 429 The Strand, London WC2R 0QE, England; tel. 020 7836 7755, fax 020 7379 1167

OFFICES IN THE UNITED STATES

Kenya: 2249 R St. NW, Washington, DC 20008; tel. (202) 387-6101, fax (202) 462-3829

Mauritius: 8 Haven Ave., Port Washington, NY 11050; tel. (516) 944-3763, fax (516) 944-8458

Seychelles: 235 East 40th St. #24A, New York, NY 10016; tel. (212) 972-1785, fax (212) 972-3970

South Africa (two locations): Office of Tourism. 9841 Airport Blvd., Suite 1524, Los Angeles, CA 90045; tel. (213) 641-8444 or (800) 782-9772, fax (213) 641-5812.

Suite 2040, 500 Fifth Ave., New York, NY 10110; tel. (212) 730-2929 or (800) 822-5368, fax (212) 764-1980

Tanzania: 205 East 42nd St., Room 1300, New York, NY 10017; tel. (212) 972-9160

Zambia: 2419 Massachusetts Ave. NW, Washington, DC 20008; tel. (202) 265-9717/8/9, fax (202) 332-0826

Zimbabwe: Tourist Office, 1270 Avenue of the Americas, Suite 412, New York, NY 10020; tel. (800) 421-2381 or (212) 332-1090, fax (212) 332-1093

TRAVELERS CHECKS

American Express, Thomas Cook's, MasterCard and Visa travelers checks are widely accepted. Stay away from lesser-known companies; you may have difficulty cashing them.

VACCINATIONS

Check with the tourist offices or embassies of the countries you wish to visit for current requirements. If you plan to visit one or more countries in endemic zones (i.e., in Africa, South America, Central America or Asia), be sure to mention this when requesting vaccination requirements. Many countries do not require any vaccinations if you are only visiting the country directly from the United States, Canada or Western Europe; but, if you are also visiting countries in endemic zones, there may very well be additional requirements.

Then check with your doctor, and preferably an immunologist, or call your local health department or the Centers for Disease Control in Atlanta, Georgia (toll-free tel. 1-888-232-3228, toll-free fax 1-888-232-3299, Web site: www.cdc.gov) for information. They will probably recommend some vaccinations in addition to those required by the country you will be visiting.

Make sure you carry with you the International Certificate of Vaccinations showing the vaccinations you have received.

Malarial prophylaxis (pills) is highly recommended for all the countries included in this guide, except for Lesotho. However, international travelers must at least pass through South Africa enroute to Lesotho.

VISA AND INOCULATION REQUIREMENTS

Travelers from most countries must obtain visas to enter some of the countries included in this guide. Apply for visas with the closest diplomatic representative or through a visa service well in advance (but not so early that the visas will expire before your journey ends) and check for all current requirements (see "Diplomatic Representatives" on the next page).

Travelers must obtain visas and have proof that they have received certain inoculations for entry into some African countries.

COUNTRY	U.S.	CANADA	U.K.	INOCULATIONS
Botswana	No	No	No	Yellow fever (4)
Burundi	Yes	Yes	Yes	Yellow fever, cholera
Congo, D.R.	Yes	Yes	Yes	Yellow fever, cholera
Egypt	Yes	Yes	Yes	Yellow fever (4)
Kenya	Yes	Yes	Yes	Yellow fever (4)
Lesotho	No	No	No	Yellow fever (4)
Malawi	No	No	No	Yellow fever (4)
Mauritius	No	No	No	Yellow fever (4)(9)
Namibia	No	No	No	Yellow fever (4)
Rwanda	No	No	No	Yellow fever
Seychelles	No	No	No	Yellow fever (4)(8)
South Africa	No	No	No	Yellow fever (4)(10)
Swaziland	No	No	No	Yellow fever (4)
Tanzania	Yes	Yes	Yes	Yellow fever (4)(5)
Uganda	Yes	Yes	Yes	Yellow fever
Zambia	Yes	No	Yes	Yellow fever (4)
Zimbabwe	Yes	No	No	Yellow fever (4)(6)

NOTES:

1. Some optional vaccinations include: a) hepatitis A, b) hepatitis B, c) typhoid, d) tetanus, e) meningitis, f) oral polio.
2. Anti-malaria: It is not mandatory but is strongly urged. Anti-malaria is a tablet, not an inoculation. Malaria exists in all of the countries listed above.

3. Cholera: The cholera vaccination is not a guaranteed inoculation against infection, and most countries do not require a cholera vaccination for direct travel from the United States. Check with your local doctor and with embassies of the respective countries. Some require proof of a cholera vaccination, even if you are arriving directly from the United States.
4. Yellow fever**: Only if arriving from infected area (i.e., Nigeria).
5. Tanzania: Zanzibar requires yellow fever.
6. Zimbabwe: Visa may be obtained on arrival by paying a visa fee (currently US $30.00).
7. Complete necessary visa forms and return with your valid passport (valid for at least six months after travel dates) to the embassy or consulate concerned or use a visa service.
8. Seychelles: requires yellow fever vaccinations if arriving from Kenya.
9. Mauritius: requires yellow fever vaccinations if arriving from an infected area.
10. South Africa: requires yellow fever vaccinations if arriving from Kenya and Tanzania.

WHAT TO WEAR – WHAT TO TAKE

Countries close to the equator (Kenya, Tanzania, Uganda, Rwanda and Burundi) have small differences in seasonal temperatures, with June-August being the coolest time of the year; the main factor affecting temperature is altitude.

Countries in southern Africa (Botswana, Zambia, Zimbabwe, Namibia, South Africa, Swaziland, Lesotho and Malawi) have more pronounced seasons, often cold (sometimes freezing) in winter (June-August) and hot in summer (October-February).

Casual clothing is usually worn by day. Dresses for ladies and coats and ties for men are only required in a few top restaurants in Kenya, South Africa and Zimbabwe. In some restaurants, gentlemen's coats are available on request.

Bring at least one camera and a lot of film, binoculars, sun block, electric converter and adapter, a copy of the *African Safari Journal*, alarm clock, insect repellent, brown- khaki- or green-cotton clothing, including at least two pairs of long pants and two long-sleeve shirts, wide-brimmed hat, rain gear, good walking shoes, flashlight and extra batteries, two pairs of sunglasses, two pairs of prescription glasses (one for contact-lens wearers) and a copy of the prescription with a letter from your doctor verifying your need, medical summary from your doctor if medical problems exist, Band-aids (plasters), motion-sickness tablets, medicine for traveler's diarrhea, anti-malarial prophylaxis (malaria pills), decongestant tablets, laxative, headache tablets, throat lozenges, antacid, and antibiotic ointment.

Bring along a comfortable pair of walking shoes. If you are going on walking safaris, be sure to have a pair of earth-colored boots (not white tennis shoes!) for your walks.

Each person going on safari should definitely have his or her own pair of binoculars. I am amazed at the number of Africa travelers who have paid thousands of dollars each for a game viewing safari, yet take with them a poor-quality pair of binoculars which limits the enjoyment of the primary function of the trip. If your budget will allow, I suggest spending from $150 to $700 or more for a medium- to high-quality pair of binoculars that could be used on subsequent Africa safaris and safaris to other continents, and which can possibly provide you with a lifetime of use. I recommend binoculars with 8 to 10 power, such as Steiner 8x30 Safaris or 10x30 Predators; the 10x42 Predators are fabulous. Swarovski, Zeiss, Leitz and Leica are the top-of-the-line brands and generally cost in the $800-$1,200 range, depending on the power and field of vision.

Leave your dress watch at home and buy an inexpensive (under U.S. $50) waterproof watch with a light and alarm. Do not wear or bring any camouflage clothing; in many countries this is reserved for the military.

For a more comprehensive packing list and trip organizer for your safari, obtain a copy of the *African Safari Journal*. To receive a catalog of valuable books, maps, binoculars and safari clothing, see the order form at the end of the book.

WILDLIFE ASSOCIATIONS

African Wildlife Foundation, 1400 16th St. NW, Suite 120, Washington, DC 20036; tel. (202) 939-3333

The African Wildlife Foundation (AWF) is one of the leading international conservation organizations working in Africa. It is also one of the most experienced U.S.-based conservation organizations dedicated solely to Africa. AWF works with people — its supporters worldwide and its partners in Africa (local, national, and international partners, including communities, government at all levels, NGO's, research and training institutions, and donor agencies) — to craft and deliver creative solutions for the long-term well-being of Africa's remarkable species, their habitats and the people who depend upon them. AWF has been working with the people of Africa since 1961. Most of its staff is based in Africa, spread between eight countries, working at a grass-roots level with park managers and communities to safeguard wildlife and wilderness areas. AWF focuses on the big picture while achieving concrete results, helping African nations design successful long-term strategies for conserving their magnificent natural treasures. For more information on AWF and its programs, visit www.AWF.org

Birdlife International has conservation partnerships with many African countries. www.birdlife.net Email: birdlife@birdlife.org.uk

Dian Fossey Gorilla Fund, 45 Inverness Dr. East, Englewood, CO 80112-5480; tel. (303) 790-2345. website: www.gorillafund.org

East African Wildlife Society
One of the most effective conservation agencies in Kenya, Tanzania and Uganda. USA Representative: c/o P Bakker, 175 West 79th street, New York, NY10024. website: www.eawildlife.org

Endangered Wildlife Trust, c/o Mike Delvin, 346 Smith Ridge Road, New Canaan, CT 06840; tel. (203) 966-1981. website: www.ewt.org.za

Mauritius Wildlife Foundation, 4th floor, Ken Lee Building, Edith Cavell St., Port Louis, Mauritius; tel. (230) 211-1749, fax (230) 211-1789

Save the Rhino Trust, P.O. Box 2159, Swakopmund, Namibia; tel. and fax (64) 403829; email: srtrhino@iafrica.com.na

The Save the Rhino Trust (SRT) mission is to "actively promote and maintain the welfare of the people by adopting policies aimed at the maintenance of ecosystems, essential ecological processes and biological diversity of Namibia and utilization of living natural resources on a sustainable basis for the benefit of all Namibians both present and future."

SAFARI GLOSSARY

Ablution block: A building that contains showers, toilets and sinks, most often with separate facilities for men and women.

Acacia: Common, dry-country trees and shrubs armed with spines or curved thorns; they also have tiny, feathery leaflets.

Adaptation: The ability, through structural or functional characteristics, to improve the survival rate of an animal or plant in a particular habitat.

Aloe: A succulent plant of the lily family with thick, pointed leaves and spikes of red or yellow flowers.

Arboreal: Living in trees.

Avifauna: The birdlife of a region.

Banda: A basic shelter or hut, often constructed of reeds, bamboo, grass, etc.

Boma: A place of shelter, a fortified place, enclosure, community (East Africa).

Browse: To feed on leaves.

Calving season: A period during which the young of a particular species are born. Not all species have calving seasons. Most calving seasons occur shortly after the rainy season begins. Calving seasons can also differ for the same species from one park or reserve to another.

Camp: Camping sites; also refers to lodging in chalets, bungalows or tents in a remote location.

Canopy: The uppermost layer of a tree.

Caravan: A camping trailer.

Carnivore: An animal that lives by consuming the flesh of other animals.

Carrion: The remains of dead animals.

Crepuscular: Active at dusk or dawn.

Diurnal: Active during the day.

Endangered: An animal that is threatened with extinction.

Endemic: Native, and restricted to a particular area.

Estrus: A state of sexual readiness in a female mammal when she is capable of conceiving.

Gestation: The duration of pregnancy.

Grazer: An animal that eats grass.
Habitat: An animal's or plant's surroundings that offers everything it needs to live.
Habituated: An animal that has been introduced to and has accepted the presence of human beings.
Herbivore: An animal that consumes plant matter for food.
Hide: A camouflaged structure from which one can view wildlife without being seen.
Home range: An area familiar to (utilized by) an adult animal but not marked or defended as a territory
Kopje (pronounced kopee): Rock formations that protrude from the savannah, usually caused by wind erosion (southern Africa).
Koppie: Same as kopje (east Africa).
Kraal: Same as boma (southern Africa).
Mammal: A warm-blooded animal that produces milk for its young.
Migratory: A species or population that moves seasonally to an area with predictably better food/grazing or water.
Midden: Usually, an accumulation of dung deposited in the same spot as a scent-marking behavior.
Nocturnal: Active during the night.
Omnivore: An animal that eats both plant and animal matter.
Pan: A shallow depression that seasonally fills with rainwater.
Predator: An animal that hunts and kills other animals for food.
Prey: An animal hunted by a predator for food.
Pride: A group or family of lions.
Rondavel: An African-style structure for accommodation.
Ruminant: A mammal with a complex stomach which therefore chews the cud.
Rutting: The behavioral pattern exhibited by male of the species during a time period when mating is most prevalent, e.g., impala, wildebeest.

Savannah: An open, grassy landscape with widely scattered trees.

Scavenger: An animal that lives off of carrion or the remains of animals killed by predators or which is dead from other causes.

Species: A group of plants or animals with specific characteristics in common, including the ability to reproduce among themselves.

Spoor: A track (i.e., footprint) or trail made by animals.

Symbiosis: An association of two different organisms in a relationship that may benefit one or both partners.

Tarmac: An asphalt-paved road.

Termitarium: A mound constructed by termite colonies.

Territory: An area occupied, scent-marked and defended from rivals of the same species.

Toilet, long-drop: A permanent bush toilet or "outhouse" in which a toilet seat has been placed over a hole that is dug about 6 feet (2m) deep.

Toilet, short-drop: A temporary bush toilet, usually a toilet tent used on mobile tented safaris in which a toilet seat is placed over a hole that has been dug about 3 feet (1 m) deep.

Tracking: Following and observing animal spoor by foot.

Tribe: A group of people united by traditional ties.

Troop: A group of apes or monkeys.

Ungulate: A hooved animal.

Veld: Southern African term for open land.

Wallow: The art of keeping cool and wet, usually in a muddy pool (i.e., rhinoceros, buffalo and hippopotamus).

LATIN/SCIENTIFIC NAMES OF MAMMALS AND REPTILES

MAMMALS

Aardvark (antbear)	*Orycteropus afer*
Antelope, roan	*Hippotragus equinus*
Antelope, sable	*Hippotragus niger*
Baboon [olive]	*Papio cynocephalus anubis*
Baboon, [chacma]	*Papio cynocephalus ursinus*
Blesbok/Bontebuck	*Damaliscus dorcas*
Bongo	*Tragelaphus euryceros*
Buffalo	*Syncerus caffer*
Bushbaby, greater	*Galago crassicaudatus*
Bushbuck	*Tragelaphus scriptus*
Bushpig	*Potamochoerus porcus*
Caracal	*Caracal caracal*
Cheetah	*Acinonyx jubatus*
Chimpanzee	*Pan troglodytes*
Civet, African	*Civettictis civetta*
Colobus, black-and-white or guereza	*Colobus guereza*
Colobus, Zanzibar red	*Procolobus kirkii*
Dikdik, Kirk's	*Madoqua kirki*
Dog, African wild	*Lycaon pictus*
Duiker, blue	*Cephalophus monticola*
Duiker, grey (bush)	*Sylvicapra grimmia*
Duiker, red/forest	*Cephalophus natalensis/harveyi*
Eland, (Patterson's)	*Taurotragus (Tragelaphus) oryx*
Elephant, African	*Loxodonta africana*
Fox, bat-eared	*Otocyon megalotis*
Fox, Cape	*Vulpes chama*
Gazelle, Grant's	*Gazella granti*
Gazelle, Thomson's	*Gazella thomsoni*
Gemsbok	*(see oryx, southern)*
Genet, large-spotted and small-spotted	*Genetta tigrina/genetta*
Gerenuk	*Litocranius walleri*
Giraffe, Maasai	*Giraffa camelopardalis tippelskirchi*
Giraffe, reticulated	*Giraffa camelopardalis reticulata*
Giraffe, Rothschild's	*Giraffa camelopardalis rothschildi*
Giraffe, southern	*Giraffa camelopardalis camelopardalis*
Gorilla, lowland [Western]	*Gorilla gorilla gorilla*
Gorilla, Grauer's	*Gorilla beringei graueri*
Gorilla, mountain [Eastern]	*Gorilla beringei beringei*
Hare, African	*Lepus capensis*
Hare, spring	*Pedetes capensis*

Hartebeest, Lichtenstein's	*Sigmoceros lichensteini*
Hartebeest, red	*Alcelaphus buselaphus*
Hippopotamus	*Hippopotamus amphibius*
Hog, giant forest	*Hylochoerus meinertzhageni*
Hyena, brown	*Hyaena brunnea*
Hyena, spotted	*Crocuta crocuta*
Hyena, striped	*Hyaena hyaena*
Hyrax, bush	*Heterohyrax brucei*
Hyrax, rock	*Procavia johnstoni*
Hyrax, tree	*Dendrohyrax arboreus*
Impala	*Aepyceros melampus*
Jackal, black-backed	*Canis mesomelas*
Jackal, golden	*Canis aureus*
Jackal, side-striped	*Canis adustus*
Klipspringer	*Oreotragus oreotragus*
Kob	*Kobus kob*
Kongoni	*Alcelaphus buselaphus*
Kudu, greater	*Tragelaphus strepsiceros*
Kudu, lesser	*Tragelaphus imberbis*
Lechwe	*Kobus leche*
Leopard	*Panthera pardus*
Lion	*Panthera leo*
Mongoose, banded	*Mungos mungo*
Mongoose, dwarf	*Helogale parvula*
Mongoose, slender	Galerella sanguinea
	Herpestes san-guineus
Mongoose, water (marsh)	*Atilax paludinosus*
Mongoose, white-tailed	*Ichneumia albicauda*
Mongoose, yellow	*Cynictis penicillata*
Monkey, de Brazza's	*Cercopithecus neglectus*
Mangabey, crested	*Cercocebus galeritus*
Mangabey, gray-cheeked	*Cercocebus albigenia*
Monkey, L'Hoest's	*Cercopithecus l'hoesti*
Monkey, Patas	*Erythrocebus patas*
Monkey, vervet	*Cercopithecus aethiops*
Monkey, blue (or Syke's or samango)	*Cercopithecus mitis/albogularis*
Nyala	*Tragelaphus angasi*
Oribi	*Ourebia ourebi*
Oryx, fringe-eared	*Oryx beisa*
Oryx, southern	*Oryx gazella*
Otter, Cape clawless	*Aonyx capensis*
Otter, spotted-necked	*Lutra maculicollis*
Pangolin, Temminck's ground	*Manis temmincki*
Porcupine (southern or northern African)	*Hystrix africaeaustralis/cristata*
Puku	*Kobus vardoni*
Ratel (Honey Badger)	*Mellivora capensis*
Reedbuck, bohor	*Redunca redunca*
Reedbuck, common	*Redunca arundinum*
Reedbuck, mountain	*Redunca fulvorufula*
Rhinoceros, black	*Diceros bicornis*
Rhinoceros, white	*Ceratotherium simum*
Serval	*Leptailurus serval*

Sitatunga	*Tragelaphus spekei*
Springbok	*Antidorcas marsupialis*
Springhare	*Pedetes capensis*
Steenbok	*Raphicerus campestris*
Topi	*Damaliscus korrigum*
Tsessebe	*Damaliscus lunatus*
Waterbuck, common	*Kobus ellipsiprymnus ellip-siprymnus*
Waterbuck, Defassa	*Kobus ellipsiprymnus defassa*
Wildebeest	*Connochaetes taurinus*
Zebra, Burchell's	*Equus burchelli*
Zebra, Grevy's	*Equus grevyi*
Zebra, Cape mountain	*Equus zebra zebra*
Zebra, Hartmann's mountain	*Equus zebra hartmannae*
Zorilla	*Ictonyx striatus*

REPTILES

Chameleon, flap-necked	*Chamaelo dilepis*
Crocodile, Nile	*Crocodylus niloticus*
Monitor, Nile	*Varanus niloticus*
Python, African Rock	*Python sebae*

SUGGESTED READING LIST

GENERAL/WILDLIFE/AFRICA

Africa, John Reader, 2001 (USA: National Geographic)

Africa A Continent Revealed, Rene Gordon, 1997 (U.K.: New Holland)

Africa An Artists Journal, Kim Donaldson, 2001 (U.K.: Pavilion; USA: Watson Guptil)

Africa in History, Basil Davidson, 2001 (U.K.: Phoenix Pres)

Africa Timeless Soul, Wilby, 1996 (U.K.: Pan MacMillian)

Africa, Biography of the Continent, John Reader, 1998 (U.K.: Penguin)

African Ceremonies, Carol Beckwith and Angela Fisher, 1999 (USA: Harry N Abrams)

African Elephants, Daryl and Sharna Balfour, 1997 (South Africa: Struik)

African Folklore, Best of, A. Savoury, 1972 (South Africa: Struik)

African Game Trails, T. Roosevelt, 1983 (USA: St. Martins Press)

African Insect Life, A. Skaiffe, John Ledger and Anthony Barnister, revised 1997 (South Africa: Struik)

African Laughter, Doris Lessing, 1992 (U.K.: Flamingo)

African Magic, Heidi Holland, 2001 (U.K.: Viking/Allen Lane)

African Nights, K. Gallmann, 1995 (U.K.: Penguin Books)

African Predators, Gus Mills, 2001 (South Africa: Struik)

African Trilogy, P. Matthiessen, 2000 (U.K.: Harvill Press)

Africa's Big Five, William Taylor, Gerald Hinde, 2001 (South Africa: Struik)

Africa's Elephant, A Biography, Martin Meredith, 2001 (U.K.: Hodder & Stoughton)

Behaviour Guide to African Animals, Richard Estes, 1995 (South Africa: Russel Friedman Books; USA: University California Press)

Birds of Kenya & Tanzania, Zimmerman, Turner and Pearson, 1996 (U.K.: A & C Black)

Birds of the Indian Ocean Islands, I. Sinclair and O. Langrand, 1998 (South Africa: Struik)

Creatures of Habit, Peter Apps and Richard du Toit, 2000 (South Africa: Struik)

Elephant Memories, Cynthia Moss, 1999 (USA: Chicago University Press)

Elephants for Africa, Randall Moore, 2000 (South Africa: Abu Publications)

Field Guide to the Larger Mammals of Southern Africa, Chris and Tilde Stuart, 1996 (South Africa: Struik)

Field Guide to the Mammals of Southern Africa, Chris and Tilde Stuart, 1996 (South Africa: Struik)

Field Guide to the Reptiles of East Africa, S. Spawls, K. Howell, R. Drews and J. Ashe, 2002 (U.K.: Academic Press)

Gorilla: Struggle for Survival in the Virungas, Michael Nichols, 1989 (USA: Aperture Press)

Guide's Guide to Guiding, The, Garth Thompson, 2001 (Russel Friedman Books, South Africa)

I Dreamed of Africa, K. Gallman, 1991 (USA: Penguin Books)

Island Africa: The Evolution of Africa's Rare Animals and Plants by Jonathan Kingdon, 1990 (U.K.: William Collins)

The Kingdon Field Guide to African Mammals, Jonathan Kingdon, 1997 (U.K.: Academic Press)

Last Edens of Africa, Francois Odendaal, 1999 (South Africa: Southern Books)

Malaria , A Layman's Guide, Martine Maurel, 2001 (South Africa: Struik)

Night of the Lions, K. Gallman, 2000 (U.K.: Penguin Books)

North of South, Shiva Naipaul, 1994 (U.K.: Penguin)

Once We Were Hunters: A Journey with Africa's Indigenous People by P. Weinberg, 2001 (David Philip, South Africa)

Origins Reconsidered, R. E. Leakey and R. Lewin, 1992 (USA: Doubleday) (O/P)

Roberts Birds of Southern Africa, Gordon Maclean, 1993 (South Africa: Voelcker Trust)

Running Wild, John McNutt and Lesley Boggs, 1996 (South Africa: Southern Book Publishers)

Safari Companion, A Guide to Watching African Mammals, Richard D. Estes, 2001 (South Africa: Russel Friedman Books; USA: Chelsea Green Publishing)

Sasol Birds of Southern Africa, Ian Sinclair, 2002 (South Africa: Struik)

Scramble for Africa, 1876-1912, Pakenham, 1992(USA: Avon Books/ U.K.: Phoenix)

Smithers Mammals of Southern Africa, Peter Apps, 1996 (South Africa: Southern)

Southern, Central, and East African Mammals, A Photographic Guide Chris and Tilde Stuart, 2000 (South Africa: Struik)

The African Adventurers, Peter Capstick, 1992 (USA: St. Martins Press)

The Behavior Guide to African Mammals, Richard Despard Estes, 1991 (South Africa: Russel Friedman Books; USA: University of California Press)

The Blue Nile, Alan Moorehead, 1983 (U.K.: Penguin)

The End of the Game, Peter Beard, 1996 (USA: Chronicle Books, U.K.: Thames & Hudson)

The Great Migration, Harvey Croze, 1999 (U.K.: Harvill Press)

The Kingdon Field Guide to African Mammals, Jonathan Kingdon, 1997 (U.K.: Harcourt Brace)

The White Nile, Alan Moorehead, 1973 (U.K.: Penguin)

Through a Window, J. Goodall, 2000 (U.K.: Phoenix Press)

Time With Leopards, Dale Hancock, 2000 (South Africa: Black Eagle Publications)

Vanishing Africa, Kate Klippensteen, 2002 (USA: Abbeville Press)

When Elephants Weep, Emotional Lives of Animals, Jeffrey Masson, 1996 (U.K.: Vintage)

Wild Africa, Patrick Morris, et al, 2001 (U.K.: BBC Books)

Wildest Africa, Paul Tingay, 1999 (New Holland, U.K.)

SOUTHERN AFRICA

Complete Book of South African Birds, Peter Ginn, revised 1996 (South Africa: Struik)

Complete Book of South African Mammals, Gus Mills and Lex Hes, 1997 (South Africa: Struik)

Discovering Southern Africa, TV Bulpin, 2000 (South Africa: Tafelberg)

Field Guide to Mammals of Southern Africa, C. and T. Stuart, 1991 (South Africa: Struik Publishers)

Field Guide to Snakes and Reptiles of Southern Africa, Bill Branch, 1992 (South Africa: Struik)

Guide to Nests & Eggs of Southern African Birds, Warwick Tarboton 2001 (South Africa: Struik)

I'd Rather Be On Safari, Gary Clark, 2001 (USA: Baranski)

Illustrated Guide Game Parks and Nature Reserves of Southern Africa, 1999 (South Africa: Readers Digest)

In the Footsteps of Eve, Lee Berger, 2001 (USA: National Geographic)

Living Deserts of Southern Africa, Barry Lovegrove, 1993 (Capetown, South Africa: Fernwood Press)

Long Walk to Freedom, Nelson Mandela, 1995 (Abacus, Little Brown, U.K.)

Lost World of the Kalahari, Laurens van der Post, 2001 (U.K.: Vintage)

Majestic Southern Africa, Land of Beauty and Splendour, Bulpin 1999 (South Africa: Readers Digest)

National Parks & other Wild Places of Southern Africa, Nigel Dennis, 2000 (South Africa: Struik)

Newman's Birds of Southern Africa, Kenneth Newman, 2002 (South Africa: Struik)

Peoples of the South, Derek De La Harpe, 2001 (South Africa: Sunbird)

Raconteur Road, Shots into Africa, Obie Oberholzer, 2000 (South Africa: David Phillip Publishers)

Smithers Mammals of Southern Africa: A Field Guide, R. H. N. Smithers, 1999 (South Africa: Struik)

Southern Africa Revealed, Elaine Hurford, 2000 (South Africa: Struik Publishers)

Southern African Trees A Photographic Guide, Piet van Wyk, 1993 (South Africa: Struik)

Southern African Wildlife, Essential Illustrated Guide, 2002 (South Africa: Readers Digest)

Tracing the Rainbow, Art & Life in Southern Africa, Eisenhofer, 2001 (Germany: Arnoldsche)

Trees of Southern Africa, Keith Coates Palgrave, 1977 (South Africa: Struik)

Walk with a White Bushman, Laurens van der Post, 2002 (U.K.: Vintage)

Wildlife of Southern Africa a Field Guide, V. Carruthers, 1997 (South Africa: Southern)

Zambezi River of the Gods, Jan and Fiona Teede, 1990 (South Africa: Russel Friedman Books)

BOTSWANA

Chobe, Africa's Untamed Wilderness, Balfour, 1999 (South Africa: Struik)

Common Birds of Botswana, Kenneth Newman, 1998 (South Africa: Southern)

Cry of the Kalahari, Mark and Delia Owens, 1984 (USA: Houghton Mifflin)

Hunting with Moon, The Lions of Savuti, Derek and Beverley Joubert, 1998 (USA: National Geographic)

Miracle Rivers, The Chobe & Okavango Rivers of Botswana, Pickford, 1999 (South Africa: Struik)

Okavango — Sea of Land, A. Bannister, 1996 (South Africa: Struik)

Okavango: Africa's Wetland Wilderness, A. Bailey, 2000 (South Africa: Struik)

Okavango: African's Last Eden, Frans Lanting, 1993 (USA: Chronicle U.S.)

Okavango: Jewel of the Kalahari, Karen Ross (USA: Macmillan)

Panoramic Journey through Botswana, Alfred le Maitre 2000 (South Africa: Struik)

Plants of the Okavango Delta, Karen and William Ellcry, 1997 (Kwa-Zulu Natal, South Africa: Tsaro)

Prides: The Lions of Moremi by C. Harvey and P. Kat, 2000 (South Africa: Struik)

Running Wild, John McNutt and Lesley Boggs, 1996 (South Africa: Southern Book Publishers)

Shell Field Guide to the Common Trees of the Okavango Delta, Veronica Roodt, 1993 (Botswana: Shell)

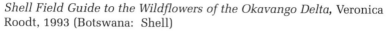

Shell Field Guide to the Wildflowers of the Okavango Delta, Veronica Roodt, 1993 (Botswana: Shell)

The Africa Diaries, Derek and Beverley Joubert, 2000 (USA: National Geographic)

The Bushmen, P. Johnson, A. Bannister and A. Wallenburgh, 1999 (South Africa: Struik Publishers)

The Heart of the Hunter, Laurens Van der Post, 2002 (U.K.: Vintage)

The Kalahari: Survival in a Thirstland Wilderness, Knight, Joyce, 1999 (South Africa: Struik)

The Lions and Elephants of the Chobe, Bruce Aitken, 1986 (South Africa: Stramill)

This is Botswana, Peter Joyce, 2000 (South Africa: Struik)

Wild Botswana, Adrian Bailey and Robyn Keene-Young, 2000 (South Africa: Sunbird)

Wildlife of the Okavango: Common Animals and Plants by D. Butchart, 2000 (South Africa: Struik)

ZAMBIA AND ZIMBABWE

African Laughter, Doris Lessing, 1992 (U.K.: Harper Collins)

Bitter Harvest, Ian Smith, 2001 (U.K.: Collins)

Don't Lets Go the Dogs Tonight, An African Childhood, Fuller, 2001 (USA: Random House)

Eye of the Elephant, Mark and Delia Owens, 1992 (USA: Houghton Mifflin)

Guide to the Wildlife of the Luangwa Valley, Norman Carr (BP Zambia Ltd.)

Hwange, Retreat of the Elephants, Nick Greaves, 1996 (South Africa: Struik Publishers)

Kakuli, Norman Carr, 1995 (U.K.: Corporate Brochure Co.) (O/P)

Luangwa, Zambias Treasure, Mike Coppinger, 2000 (South Africa: Inyathi Publishers)

Mukiwa, Peter Godwin, 1996 (U.K.: Picador)

The Leopard Hunts in Darkness (and other series), Wilbur Smith, 1992 (U.K.: MacMillan)

The Spirit of the Zambezi, Jeff and Veronica Stutchbury, 1991 (U.K.: The Corporate Brochure Company)

This is Zimbabwe, Gerald Cubitt and Peter Joyce, 1992 (South Africa: Struik)

Zambezi — A Journey of a River, Michael Main, 1990 (South Africa: Southern Book Publishers) (O/P)

Zambezi — The River of the Gods, Jan and Fiona Teede, 1991 (U.K.: Andre Deutsch)

Zambezi, L. Watermeyer, J. Dabbs and Y. Christian, 1988 (Zimbabwe: Albida Samara Pvt. Ltd.)

Zambia Landscapes, David Rodgers, 2001 (South Africa: Struik)

Zambia Tapestries, David Rodgers, 2001 (South Africa: Struik)

Zambia, African Adventurers Guide, Plewman, 2001 (South Africa: Struik)

Zambia, Ian Murphy and Richard Vaughan, 1992 (U.K.: Corporate Brochure Company)

Zambia Travel Guide, David Else, 2002 (Australia: Lonely Planet)

Zimbabwe Travel Guide, Tione Chinula, 2002 (Australia: Lonely Planet)

Zimbabwe, Ian Murphy and Richard Vaughan, 1993 (U.K.: Corporate Brochure Company)

MALAWI

Malawi, Lake of Stars, Vera Garland, 1998 (Malawi: Central Africana)

Malawi Travel Guide, David Else, 2001 (U.K.: Lonely Planet)

NAMIBIA

Desert Adventure, Paul Augustinus, 1997 (South Africa: Acorn Books)

Desertscapes of Namibia, Jean Du Plessis, 2002 (South Africa: Struik)

Etosha A Visual Souvenir, Daryl and Sharna Balfour, 1998 (South Africa: Struik)

Heat, Dust and Dreams, Exploration People & Environment Kaokoland & Damaraland, Rice, 2001 (South Africa: Struik)

Himba — Nomads of Namibia, Margaret Jacobsen, 1991 (South Africa: Struik)

Namibia African Adventurers Guide, W. and S. Olivier, 1999 (South Africa: New Holland)

Namibia Africa's Harsh Paradise, A. Bannister and P. Johnson, 1978 (South Africa: Struik Publishers)

Panoramic Journey through Namibia, Alfred le Maitre, 2000 (South Africa: Struik)

Sands of Silence, On Safari in Namibia, P. Capstick, 1991 (USA & U.K.: St. Martins Press)

Scenic Namibia, Thomas Dreschler, 2000 (South Africa: Tafelberg)

Sheltering Desert, Henno Martin, 1996 (South Africa: Ad Donker)

Skeleton Coast, a Journey through the Namib Desert, Benedict Allen, 1997 (U.K.: BBC)

Skeleton Coast, Amy Schoeman, 1999 (South Africa: Southern Book Publishers)

This is Namibia, Gerald Cubitt and Peter Joyce, 2000 (U.K. & South Africa: New Holland)

SOUTH AFRICA

Cape Floral Kingdom, Colin Paterson-Jones, 2000 (South Africa: Struik)

History of South Africa, Frank Welsh, Revised and Updated, 2000 (U.K.: HarperCollins)

Kruger National Park, Wonders of an African Eden, Nigel Dennis, 1997 (USA: BHB International/South Africa and U.K.: New Holland)

Long Walk to Freedom, Nelson Mandela, 1995 (U.K.: Abacus, Little Brown)

Magnificent Natural Heritage of South Africa, Knobel, 1999 (South Africa: Sunbird.)

Magnificent South Africa, Hurford and Joyce, 1996 (South Africa: Struik)

My Traitor's Heart, Rian Malan, 2000 (USA: Moon Publications)

Presenting South Africa, Peter Joyce, 1999 (South Africa: Struik)

Rock Paintings of South Africa, Stephen Townley Bassett, 2002 (South Africa: David Philip)

Rough Guide to South Africa, Donald Reid, 2002 (U.K.: Rough Guides)

Somewhere over the Rainbow, Travels in South Africa, Gavin Bell, 2001 (U.K.: Abacus, Little Brown.)

South Africa, Lesotho & Swaziland Travel Guide, Simon Richmond, 2001 (Australia: Lonely Planet),

The Covenant, James A. Michener, 1980 (USA: Random House)

The Heart of the Hunter (series), Laurens Van der Post, 1987 (U.K.: Vintage)

The Washing of the Spears: The Rise and Fall of the Zulu Nation, Donald R. Morris, 1995 (U.K.: Pimlico)

This is South Africa, Peter Borchert, 2000 (South Africa: Struik)

Twentieth Century South Africa, William Beinart, 2002 (U.K.: Oxford University Press)

When the Lion Feeds, (series) Wilbur Smith, 1986 (U.K.: MacMillan)

Wild South Africa, Lex Hes. Alan Mountain, 1998 (U.K.: New Holland)

Wildlife of the Cape Peninsula: Common Animals and Plants by D. Butchart, 2001 (South Africa: Struik)

Wildlife of the Lowveld: Common Animals and Plants by D. Butchart, Struik, 2001 (South Africa: Southern)

World That Made Mandela, L. Callinicos, 2001 (South Africa: STE Publishers)

EAST AFRICA

A Guide to the Seashores of Eastern Africa by M.D. Richmond (Ed.), 1997, (Sweden: Sida; Zanzibar: Sea Trust)

A Primates Memoir, Love, Death and Baboons in East Africa, Robert Sapolsky, 2001 (U.K.: Jonathan Cape)

Africa's Great Rift Valley, Nigel Pavitt, 2001 (USA: Harry N. Abrams)

African Trilogy, Peter Matthiessen, 1999 (U.K.: Harvill Press)

Among the Man-eaters, Stalking the Mysterious Lions of Tsavo, Philip Caputo, 2002 (USA: National Geographic)

Birds of Kenya & Tanzania, Zimmerman, Turner and Pearson, 1996 (U.K.: A & C Black) (South Africa: Russel Friedman Books)

Field Guide to the Birds of East Africa, Terry Stevenson and John Fanshawe, 2002 (U.K.: Academic Press)

Field Guide to the Reptiles of East Africa, Stephen Spawls, 2002 (U.K.: Academic Press)

Guide to Mt. Kenya and Kilimanjaro, edited by Iain Allen, 1981 (Nairobi, Kenya: Mountain Club)

Illustrated Checklist Birds of East Africa, B. von Perlo, 1995 (U.K.: Collins)

In the Shadow of Kilimanjaro, Rick Ridgeway, 2000 (U.K.: Bloomsbury)

Pink Africa, Nigel Collar, 2000 (U.K.: Harvill Press)

Portraits in the Wild: Animal Behavior in East Africa, Second Edition, Cynthia Moss, 1982 (University of Chicago Press) (O/P)

Safari Guide to Common Birds of East Africa, D. Hosking, 1996 (U.K.: Collins)

Safari Guide to Larger Mammals of East Africa, D. Hosking, 1996 (U.K.: Collins).

White Hunters, Golden Age of African Safaris, Brian Herne, 1999 (USA: Henry Holt)

KENYA

Big Cat Diary, Brian Jackson and Jonathan Scott, 1996 (U.K.: BBC)

Birds of Kenya & Tanzania, Zimmerman, Turner and Pearson, 1996 (U.K.: A & C Black; South Africa: Russel Friedman Books)

Born Free Trilogy, Joy Adamson, 2000 (U.K.: Macmillan)

Elephant Memories, Portraits in the Wild, Cynthia Moss, 1999 (USA: Chicago University Press)

F/G Birds of Kenya & Northern Tanzania, Dale A Zimmerman, Donald A. Turner & David J Pearson, 1999 (U.K.: A & C Black) (South Africa: Russel Friedman Books)

Flame Trees of Thika: Memories of an African Childhood, Elspeth Huxley, 1998 (U.K.: Pimlico)

I Dreamed of Africa, Kuki Gallman, 1991 (U.K.: Penguin)

Illustrated Checklist Birds of East Africa, B. von Perlo, 1995 (U.K. Collins).

Journey Through Kenya, M. Amin, D. Willetts and B. Tetley, 1982 (U.K.: Camerapix)

Kenya Pioneers, Errol Trzebinski, 1991 (U.K.: Mandarin)

Kenya the Beautiful, Brett Michael, 1997 (USA: BHB International/South

Africa: Struik)

Kingdom of Lions, Jonathan Scott, 1992 (U.K.: Kyle Cathie; South Africa: Russel Friedman Books).

Out in the Midday Sun, Elspeth Huxley, 2000 (U.K.: Pimlico)

Out of Africa, Isak Dinesen, 1989 (U.K.: Penguin Books)

Samburu, Nigel Pavitt, 2002 (U.K.: Kyle Kathie)

The Great Safari — The Lives of George and Joy Adamson, William Morrow, 1993 (New Jersey, USA: Adrian House) (O/P)

The Ukimwe Road: from Kenya to Zimbabwe, Dervla Murphy, 1995 (U.K.: Flamingo)

Wildlife Wars, Battle to Save Africa's Elephants, Richard Leakey, 2001 (U.K.: Macmillan)

Vanishing Africa, The Samburu of Kenya, Kate Klippensteen, 2002 (USA: Abbeville Press)

TANZANIA

Cheetahs of the Serengeti Plains, TM Caro, 1994 (USA: University Chicago Press)

Golden Shadows, Flying Hooves, George B. Schaller, 1989 (Chicago, IL, USA: University of Chicago Press)

In the Dust of Kilimanjaro, David Western, 2000 (USA: Island Press)

Journal of Discovery of the Source of the Nile, John Hanning Speke, 1996 (USA: Dover Publications)

Kilimanjaro, A Journey to the roof of Africa, Audrey Salkeld, 2002 (USA: National Geographic)

Kilimanjaro: The White Roof of Africa, Harald Lange, 1985 (USA: Mountaineers Books). Large photo book (O/P)

Mara Serengeti, A Photographers Paradise, Jonathan Scott, 2000 (U.K.: Newpro U.K. Ltd)

Ngorongoro Great Game Park. Chris Stuart, 1995 (South Africa: Struik)

Serengeti Lions, Predator Prey Relationships, GB Schaller, 1976 (USA: University Chicago Press)

Serengeti: Natural order on the African Plain, Mitsuaki Iwago, 1996 (USA: Chronicle Books)

Serengeti Shall Not Die, Bernard and Michael Grzimek, 1960 (U.K.: Hamish Hamilton)

Snows of Kilimanjaro, Ernest Hemingway, 1994 (U.K.: Arrow)

Tanzania, Portrait of a Nation, Paul Joynson-Hicks, 1998 (U.K.: Quiller Press)

The Chimpanzees of Gombe, Patterns of Behavior, Jane Goodall 1986 (USA: Harvard University Press). Chimpanzee research.

Thorns to Kilimanjaro, Ian McCallum, 2000 (South Africa: David Philip Publishers)

RWANDA

Across the Red River, Rwanda, Burundi and the Heart of Darkness, Christian Jennings, 1999 (U.K.: Indigo Paperbacks)

Gorillas in the Mist, Dian Fossey, 2001 (U.K.: Phoenix)

In the Kingdom of Gorillas, Bill Weber and Amy Veder, 2002 (U.K.: Aurum Press)

Lake Regions of Central Africa, Richard Burton, 2001 (USA: The Narrative Press)

Rwanda The Bradt Travel Guide, Janice Booth, Philip Briggs, 2001 (U.K.: Bradt Guides)

UGANDA

Bonobo, The Forgotten Ape, Frans De Waal, 1997 (USA: University of California Press)

Ecology of an African Rain Forest, Thomas Struhsaker, 1998 (USA: University Florida Press)

Forest of Memories, Tales from the Heart of Africa, Donald McIntosh, 2001 (U.K.: Little Brown)

Guide to the Ruwenzori, H. A. Osmaston and D. Pasteur, 1972 (Reading, Berks, U.K.: West Col Productions)

Rwenzori Mountain National Park, Uganda, H A. Osmaston and Joy Tukahirwa, 1999 (Makerere University Press, Uganda)

Uganda, Ian Leggett, 2001 (U.K.. Oxfam)

Uganda/Rwenzori, David Pluth, 1997 (Stafa, Switzerland: Little Wolf)

Uganda: Pearl of Africa, Paul Joynson-Hicks, 1994 (U.K.: Quiller Press)

Where to Watch Birds in Uganda, Rossoux, 2000 (Uganda)

CONGO

Congo Journey, Redmond O'Henlon, 1996 (U.K.: Hamish Hamilton)

The Forest People, Colin Turnbull, 1994 (Herts, U.K.: Pocket Books). On pygmies of the Ituri Forest.

The Mountain People, Colin Turnbull, 1987 (U.K.: Pocket Books)

The Road from Leopold to Kabila, A Peoples History. Nsongola-Ntalaja, 2002 (U.K.: Zed Books)

Facing the Congo, Jeffrey Taylor, 2001 (U.K.: Little Brown)

Travels in the White Mans Grave, Memoirs from West & Central Africa. Donald McIntosh, 2001 (U.K.: Abacus)

In the Footsteps of Mr. Kurtz, Living on the Brink of Disaster in the Congo, Michaela Wrong, 2001 (U.K.: Fourth Estate)

King Leopold's Ghost, Story of Greed & Heroism in Colonial Africa, Adam Hochschild, 2000 (U.K.: Macmillan)

PLACES AND PEOPLE INDEX

ANIMALS AND PLANTS INDEX

ACCOMMODATIONS INDEX

MAPS

CHARTS

ANIMAL PROFILES

PHOTO CREDITS

Thanks to all the Africa camps and companies, guides and Africa Adventure Company travelers.

Color photos:

Front Cover	Ivan Carter	
	Wilderness Safaris	
Spine	Cheli and Peacock	
Back cover	Mike Myers	
	Wilderness Safaris	
Pg 239	Bob Lipsky	
Pg 240	upper Sarah Taylor	
Pg 240	lower GeneEckhart	
Pg 241	upper Willis Okech	
Pg 241	lower Willis Okech	
Pg 242	upper Bob Lipsky	
Pg 242	lower Ivan Carter	
Pg 243	upper Governors Camps	
Pg 243	lower Cheli and Peacock	
Pg 244	upper Michael Poliza	
Pg 244	lower Ivan Carter	
Pg 245	upper Gene Eckhart	
Pg 245	lower Gene Eckhart	
Pg 246	upper Governors Camp	
Pg 246	middle Nomad Safari Guides	
Pg 246	lower Heritage Hotels	
Pg 247	Serena Hotels	
Pg 248	upper Wilderness Safaris	
Pg 248	lower CCAfrica	
Pg 249	upper Serena Hotels	
Pg 249	lower CCAfrica	
Pg 250	Wilderness Safaris	
Pg 251	upper Wilderness Safaris	
Pg 251	lower Wilderness Safaris	
Pg 252	upper Wilderness Safaris	
Pg 252	lower Wilderness Safaris	
Pg 253	upper Rovos Rail	
Pg 253	lower Wilderness Safaris	
Pg 254	upper Wilderness Safaris	
Pg 254	lower Ol Donya Waus	
Pg 255	Gene Eckhart	
Pg 256	upper Gene Eckhart	
Pg 256	lower Ivan Carter	
Pg 257	upper Wilderness Safaris	
Pg 257	lower Mitchell May	
Pg 258	Tom Milleson	
Pg 259	upper Dave	

	Christiansen	
Pg 259	lower Charles Secor	
Pg 260	Wilderness Safaris	
Pg 261	Wilderness Safaris	
Pg 262	Martin Grable	
Pg 263	upper left Tom Milleson	
Pg 263	upper right Gene Eckhart	
Pg 263	lower Michael Poliza- Wilderness Safaris	
Pg 264	upper left Abby Lazar-	
Pg 264	upper right Wilderness Safaris	
Pg 264	lower Cheli and Peacock	
Pg 265	Abby Lazar	
Pg 266	Wilderness Safaris	
Pg 267	upper Gene Eckhart	
Pg 267	lower Robin Pope Safaris	
Pg 268	Gene Eckhart	
Pg 269	Gene Eckhart	

Black and White Photos

Pg 13	Mike Appelbaum	
Pg 15	Mike Appelbaum	
Pg 25	Zimbabwe Sun	
Pg 26	Wilderness Safaris	
Pg 27	Wilderness Safaris	
Pg 28	Wilderness Safaris	
Pg 32	Mark Nolting	
Pg 34	Wilderness Safaris	
Pg 35	Sefofane	
Pg 36	Bob Lipsky	
Pg 38	Helena Spencer	
Pg 40	Mike Appelbaum	
Pg 41	Julio Teigell	
Pg 42	Africa Under Canvas	
Pg 44	Robin Pope Safaris	
Pg 48	Wilderness Safaris	
Pg 52	Alison Nolting	
Pg 60	Marilyn Ritz	
Pg 61	Gene Eckhart	
Pg 62	J&B Pratt	
Pg 63	Mike Myers	
Pg 69	Ivan Carter	
Pg 73	Ivan Carter	
Pg 77	Mark Nolting	
Pg 80	Alison Nolting	
Pg 83	Gloriann Liu	
Pg 85	Kikoti	
Pg 86	Gloriann Liu	
Pg 89	Iva Spitzer	
Pg 94	Ivan Carter	

Pg 96	CC Africa	
Pg 102	Mark Nolting	
Pg 103	Serena Hotels	
Pg 104	CC Africa	
Pg 105	Mike Yuhl	
Pg 106	Mike Appelbaum	
Pg 119	Mark Nolting	
Pg 129	Mark Nolting	
Pg 130	Selous Safari Camp	
Pg 136	Mahale/Greystoke	
Pg 140	Serena Hotels	
Pg 145	Alison Nolting	
Pg 149	Alison Nolting	
Pg 150	Mike Appelbaum	
Pg 151	P. Adamson	
Pg 152	Lonrho Hotels	
Pg 157	Ranger Safaris	
Pg 158	Cheli and Peacock	
Pg 159	Cheli and Peacock	
Pg 164	Galdessa Camp	
Pg 165	East African Ornithological	
Pg 166	Cheli and Peacock	
Pg 169	Cheli and Peacock	
Pg 170	Savannah Lodges	
Pg 171	Cottars 1920's	
Pg 177	East African Ornithological	
Pg 178	Cheli and Peacock	
Pg 181	Kenya Tourist Board	
Pg 184	Alison Nolting	
Pg 188	Loisaba	
Pg 195	East African Ornithological	
Pg 198	Virginia Misoff	
Pg 199	Heritage Hotels	
Pg 205	Alison Nolting	
Pg 209	Alison Nolting	
Pg 218	Mantana	
Pg 220	Alison Nolting	
Pg 222	Mantana	
Pg 227	Bob Lipsky	
Pg 231	Bob Lipsky	
Pg 238	Mark Nolting	
Pg 271	Lee Wosk	
Pg 275	Lee Wosk	
Pg 286	Mark Nolting	
Pg 291	Monica Andriacchi	
Pg 295	Monica Andriacchi	
Pg 296	Mike Appelbaum	
Pg 303	Ivan Carter	
Pg 307	Ivan Carter	
Pg 309	Tom Milleson	
Pg 313	Bob Lipsky	
Pg 314	CC Africa	

PHOTO CREDITS

Pg 315 Mike Myers
Pg 318 Donna Johnstone
Pg 319 Abus Camp
Pg 320 Wilderness Safaris
Pg 322 Sanctuary Lodges
Pg 324 David Manwaring
Pg 326 Wilderness Safaris
Pg 327 Africa Under Canvas
Pg 332 Wilderness Safaris
Pg 336 Desert and Delta
Pg 338 Uncharted Africa
Pg 339 Uncharted Africa
Pg 342 Rattray Reserves
Pg 345 Willis Okech
Pg 349 Willis Okech
Pg 351 Sarah Taylor
Pg 354 Zimbabwe Sun
Pg 356 Victoria Falls Safari
        Lodge
Pg 362 Brian Worsley
Pg 365 Garth Thompson
Pg 367 Amalinda Camp
Pg 368 Ivan Carter
Pg 372 Wilderness Safaris
Pg 377 Garth Thompson
Pg 378 Tim Best
Pg 385 Zimbabwe Tourist
        Board
Pg 389 Mark Nolting
Pg 393 Mark Nolting
Pg 398 Upper: Andrew Taylor
        Lower: Alison Nolting
Pg 399 Star of Africa

Pg 401 Robin Pope Safaris
Pg 406 Mwaleshi Camp
Pg 412 Sausage Tree Camp
Pg 416 Star of Africa
Pg 418 Kwando
Pg 420 Tongabezi
Pg 423 P & S Brady
Pg 427 P & S Brady
Pg 433 Gene Eckhart
Pg 434 Kulala Desert Lodge
Pg 435 Alison Nolting
Pg 437 Mark Nolting
Pg 439 Wilderness Safaris
Pg 440 P & S Brady
Pg 441 Wilderness Safaris
Pg 443 J & B Pratt
Pg 445 J & B Pratt
Pg 446 P & S Brady
Pg 447 Mike Myers
Pg 455 Pat Chase
Pg 459 Pat Chase
Pg 466 Rovos Rail
Pg 471 Rattray Reserves
Pg 472 Singita
Pg 474 Rattray Reserves
Pg 475 Djuma Vuyatela
Pg 478 Cybele Forest Lodge
Pg 481 Sun International
Pg 486 SATOUR
Pg 487 Mark Nolting
Pg 492 Roggeland
Pg 499 Mark Nolting
Pg 501 Grootbos

Pg 502 Mike Myers
Pg 513 CC Africa
Pg 516 Wilderness Safaris
Pg 517 Wilderness Safaris
Pg 519 Mark Nolting
Pg 523 Mark Nolting
Pg 525 Wilderness Safaris
Pg 528 Livingstonia Beach
        Hotel
Pg 531 Wilderness Safaris
Pg 532 Wilderness Safaris
Pg 535 Bob Lipsky
Pg 539 Bob Lipsky
Pg 546 Mary Lippold
Pg 549 Mark Nolting
Pg 553 Mark Nolting
Pg 556 Mark Nolting
Pg 561 Mark Nolting
Pg 565 Mark Nolting
Pg 573 Alison Nolting
Pg 576 Wilderness Safaris
Pg 577 Mauritius Tourist
        Office
Pg 581 Mauritius Tourist
        Office
Pg 584 Oberoi Hotel
Pg 586 Sun International
Pg 587 Sun International
Pg 671 Ivan Carter

ACKNOWLEDGEMENTS

The completion and accuracy of this guide would not have been possible without the assistance of many people. Many thanks to all who have contributed to this project, including the following: Roselyne Hauchler, Werabe Emmanuel of ORTPN, Moses S. Walubita, Omary Mnyangala, Willis Okech, Mel Ogola, Dave Bennett, Phil Ward, Praveen Moman, Pratik Patel, Stefano Cheli, Mike Myers, Mark Houldsworth, Hamish Grant, Nick Murray, Josiah Mkengwa, Peter Jones, Richard Salmon, Tim Farrell, Russel Friedman, and Ken Perna; to all the guides in the field that have shared their in depth knowledge of wildlife in Africa, and to our clients who have provided us with comprehensive trip reports on their African adventures.

Special thanks to Colin Bell, Dave van Smeerdijck, Brian Worsley, Keith Vincent, Chris Badger, Hilton Walker, Trevor Earl, Tessa Redman, Yvonne Christian, David Evans, Ivan Carter, Duncan Butchart, John Coppinger, Lis Farrell, Craig Sholley, Annette Lanjouw, Steve Turner, Peter Jackson, Shakir and Abbas Molindina, and Anita Warrener for their assistance; to my staff at The Africa Adventure Company including Bill Rivard, Sherri Perals, Irene Groden, Kinda Blomberg, Sarah Taylor, Kathy Berry, Gareth Quin and Karen Liza; and especially to my wife, Alison, for her assistance on the entire project.

ABOUT MARK NOLTING, AUTHOR AND AFRICA EXPERT

Mark Nolting wanted adventure. He found it as an Olympic sportscaster, international businessman, oil engineer and Hollywood actor. But it wasn't until he traveled through Africa that he found the excitement he was looking for.

Mark Nolting heads up The Africa Adventure Company, Ft. Lauderdale, Florida. He is the author of two award-winning books, *Africa's Top Wildlife Countries* and the *African Safari Journal*.

Known as the "Travel Expert of Africa" in the industry, Nolting and his experienced staff arrange safaris for travelers who want to experience the beauty and drama of Africa in exciting ways.

It all began in 1975. Nolting graduated from Florida State University the previous year with a degree in business administration and minors in chemistry, physics, math and biology. For a year and a half, he worked for a south Florida marketing firm, but the call of the wild beckoned.

"One morning," said Nolting, "I just woke up and realized I wanted to travel around the world. And I decided, if I don't go, I'll always regret it, and if I don't go now, I never will."

Two weeks later, he departed for Luxembourg. During the 1976 Winter Olympics in Innsbruck, Austria, he worked for ABC Sports. Next he found a job in middle management with the world's third-largest mail order catalog house, located in Germany.

But Nolting wasn't trying to become a European businessman. He was out to see the world. Although his itinerary called for him to head for India, Nepal and the Far East, he took a six-month detour through Africa and traveled across the Sahara Desert and on through central and east Africa. He toured several parks and reserves and fell in love with the "safari experience."

Then he found his way to the Mideast and was fast-tracked through a program for oil-drilling engineers. He eventually came back to the United States — Los Angeles. It occurred to Nolting that he'd never tried acting, so he decided to give it a shot and wound up working for four years.

Yet the yearning for more in-depth travel through Africa was still with him. He couldn't shake the memory of the wildlife and the spectacular terrain he had seen there. And so, once again, he was off, heading for Africa with a purpose in mind.

He returned to Africa and traveled for two years through 16 countries, from Cairo to Cape Town, gathering material for his books and establishing contacts with safari companies and tour guides. On his return to the United States in 1985, he wrote his books and established The Africa Adventure Company.

In July 1992 he married Alison Wright, whom he had met a few years previously at a safari camp she was running in Zimbabwe. In July, 1993, they had their first child, Miles William Nolting, and in 1996, their second child, Nicholas Hamilton Nolting.

His many visits have included touring the antiquities of Egypt and scuba diving off the Sinai Peninsula; crossing Lake Nasser and the deserts of Sudan; experiencing the multitude of lodge safaris and authentic African mobile tented safaris in the wildlife reserves of Kenya and Tanzania; climbing Mt. Kenya, Mt. Kilimanjaro in Tanzania and the Ruwenzoris in the Democratic Republic of the Congo; visiting the beautiful Kenyan coast; gorilla trekking and mountain climbing in Rwanda; hunting with Pygmies, gorilla trekking and game viewing in the Democratic Republic of the Congo; and taking the ferry from Bujumbura (Burundi) to Kigoma (Tanzania).

In southern Africa his adventures have included walking safaris from bush camp to bush camp and day and night game drives in Zambia; one- and seven-day, white-water, rafting safaris (fifth class) on the Zambezi River; viewing Victoria Falls at different times of the year; kayak safari upstream of Victoria Falls; several canoeing safaris on the lower Zambezi River; walking with top professional guides and game viewing by boat and open vehicle on day and night game drives in Zimbabwe; flying safaris to the major reserves of Botswana; mokoro safaris in the Okavango Delta; a fly-in safari to the Skeleton Coast and visiting Etosha Pan and other parks in Namibia; driving the Garden Route, sightseeing in Cape Town and visiting the private reserves and parks in South Africa; pony trekking in Lesotho; traveling through Swaziland; and holidaying in the beautiful island countries of Mauritius and the Seychelles.

Mark continues to travel to Africa yearly to update information and explore new areas. Hard-to-find information on Africa is always at his fingertips, and he loves to take the time to talk to people about the many adventures that can be found on the continent.

The Publishers

BUSH TAILS

Our passion is travel and we've been "on the road" for thirty-two years. In fact, one of the things that attracted us to each other thirty-two years ago was our common love of the wanderlust. We have recently discovered an affinity for Africa to which we've returned for the eighth consecutive year. For us, there is no other travel destination, which combines such high measures of adventure, comfort, a sense of history (both past and presently in the making), comradeship of fellow travelers, and graciousness that is found in Africa.

A noted guide during our second safari recommended Mark and Alison Nolting to us. Since then, The Africa Adventure Company has indulged us with experiences far beyond expectations for our last six safaris. We have become smitten with the incredible African wildlife, varied environments, and dramatic sunsets. They planned a Zambezi canoe safari that proved to be our grand adventure complete with adrenaline-raising encounters with wildlife on both land and water. They have made possible the realization of a long dreamed-about date with the mountain gorillas of Uganda and enabled us to enjoy the unearthly remoteness of Namibia's Skeleton Coast. They were instrumental in our experiencing the grandeur of the Ngorongoro Crater and spending magical nights under the star-filled sky of the paradise called Mana Pools. The jewel that is the Okavango Delta remains in our hearts and minds because of their recommendation.

We have been privileged to enjoy the companionship and expertise of the most well known guides of Southern and Eastern Africa, enjoyed the most gracious hosts in extraordinary camps and lodges, and we have been able to experience the prime game regions of Africa. In short, our travels to Africa are the treasured memories of a lifetime.

As a result of our collaborative planning with The Africa Adventure Company every safari has been sheer perfection. Our experiences have been a meticulous consideration of our interests and desires thoughtfully merged with their unmatched knowledge of Africa. Their wonderful staff leaves nothing to chance. We say to anyone bound for Africa — "The Africa Adventure Company will plan and create a flawless and magical safari experience."

June and William Tu, New York

I have been traveling to Africa regularly for the past ten years, and The Africa Adventure Company is the reason my trips are the great adventures I am seeking when I go. As a single woman, traveling alone, I need to know that all my arrangements and accommodations will give me a sense of security and comfort, while still wanting the "true bush" experience. As my preferences change with each trip, their knowledge allows me to dig deeper into the African landscape and all it has to offer. The Africa Adventure Company has the experience and the tools, which helps to create your own personal "African adventure."
Iva Spitzer, New York

Thank you for your welcome home letter, which awaited us when we got back. It was a fabulous trip with memorable encounters with wildlife. The density and variety of game and birds in the Masai Mara were mind blowing — thousands and thousands of wildebeest and zebra, two lionesses stalking and nearly catching a giraffe, a pack of hyenas catching and nearly killing a wildebeest (which was then chased half-heartedly by a rather full black maned lion), mating lions and nearly 200 bird species, etc., etc.

We booked this trip because, as you know, we wanted to do a trip with Ivan Carter and he is an outstanding guide attentive to everyone's smallest needs as well as having the big picture vision and the depth of knowledge we so much admired when we first met him last year.

Indeed all the administration was impeccable from start to finish. We had complete confidence that everything was well under control and that our guides would take care of anything that might arise. So thank you for planning and organizing an event, which justifies your strapline of "The Safari of a Lifetime".
Parry and Juliet Rogers, United Kingdom

This trip has been a part of my life for the past year. I can't believe that it is now in the wonderful memory category. Before departing, I thought this trip would certainly satisfy our desire to experience Africa once again, but now we find ourselves already thinking about another trip someday. I will certainly book it with you. Many thanks again for all your assistance in putting this trip together.
Alice & Ed Lowe, California

I'm in London. It's 7a.m. London time. I've just arrived from Nairobi and am having tea and a bite to eat while awaiting my connecting flight to Boston. What can I say? And where do I begin? Firstly the best thing

I did was read Mark Nolting's book. Secondly was my phone call to book my trip. I placed all my trust and faith in them and their judgment. And as a result, I can say that I've truly had a trip that will live on in my heart forever. Now I can say that Africa is in my soul and will always be a part of me. In the meantime thank you so much for everything you did to help make this a life altering experience for me.
Michelle Sweeney, Massachusetts

I wanted to thank everyone at The Africa Adventure Company for putting together a dream honeymoon trip for us!! We had the greatest time of our lives. Everything exceeded our high expectations...the safaris, the camps, the food, the hospitality. What an adventure. We will surely send our friends your way and look forward to future trips to Africa! Till next time.
Justin and Tristin Rumack, New York

I especially want to thank you for the private guide you selected for us. He was outstanding in every way and was absolutely wonderful with our eight year old. I know you think highly of him too, but I wanted to pass on our highest praise. We also were so pleased with the private camping experience for two days in Tarangire — it was utterly decadent having so much staff to support the three of us, but we loved just sleeping in a tent in the middle of the game park. Thank you for suggesting that and using it as our initial stay.

So all in all, we loved it! And our eight year old TV-watching, Nintendo-playing, roller-blader, who really resisted the idea of going to Africa, totally got into it, had the best time, and was not bored a minute.
L & D Becker, Maryland

I just wanted to thank you for organizing my safari trip on such short notice — less than 1 week; I had the most fantastic time. Traveling alone can often mean missing out on some things, however the camp staff went out of their way to make me feel included in every activity. The game viewing was unbelievable and the accommodations were just what I needed to relax and unwind. I put you in a spot to clean up the jam another company left me in and you could not have done a better job. I have been recommending your services to everyone who is interested in traveling to South Africa. Thank you again for one of the best vacations in my life.
Donna Johnson, Kansas

How can we ever thank you? We had the most wonderful fabulous trip! I want to close my eyes and listen for the hippos and baboons and night sounds of Africa and see those stars in the sky. Pat and I want to thank you for encouraging us. What were we so afraid of? This trip has given us back that satisfaction that we so missed from traveling. Thank you for awakening our spirits again. There is no place like Africa!
Nancy and Pat Scully, Florida

Uganda was spectacular. Our guide was fantastic. He was extremely knowledgeable and I only wish I knew all that he did about his country, the animals, birds, etc. What I loved about my trip to Uganda was that we got to cover a lot of ground by vehicle, which made it wonderful to learn about the people, the communities, the land, and all the culture. I wouldn't have changed that for anything. I always plan these trips as a photographic safari of animals, but always come back pleasantly surprised by how much the local people and culture have impacted my life. The gorilla hikes were phenomenal from beginning to end. Many people asked me if I felt safe in Uganda and the answer is completely! I can't thank you all enough for making this trip such a wonderful experience. I recognize and truly appreciate all the organizational efforts you go through to make every segment of a trip such as mine come together flawlessly...THANK YOU! You can be assured, on my next trip to Africa (and there WILL be a next trip in my future), I will be using AAC without question.
Monica Andriacchi, California

Pat and I would like to thank you and your staff for the wonderful arrangements you made for our trip to Botswana, Zambia and South Africa, and for the consideration and understanding you showed us when we had to postpone our trip last September. For us, it was truly the trip of a lifetime. Everything, from start to finish, ran like clockwork and was efficiently and courteously handled. We could not imagine anything so well done. Our accommodations were excellent, and the people at all of the camps were enthusiastic. The pilots were great, and the wildlife we saw exceeded our expectations. Pat did not want to come home. You can be rest assured we will recommend you to any of our friends who are thinking of an African trip.
Frank and Patrica Miller, Kentucky

Our tour with Africa Adventure Company could not have been more perfectly planned. I know this is your business, and you do it with excellence. Each stop on our magical tour complimented the previous stop. Such a variety of accommodations, but all gave us the opportunity to experience a closeness with the wildlife and scenery we had come so far to see.

I have waited my entire life to make this trip, and it was everything and more than I could ever have hoped for. I now have treasured memories, hopefully some good photos, but there is also a glimmer of hope deep inside me that I will somehow be able to see Africa again in my lifetime. I will end by saying thank you so very much to you and the Africa Adventure Company for making the dream of a lifetime a vivid and treasured experience and memory. I will now be glued to Big Cat Diary and my photo album until I can return to Africa.
Karen Marshall, California

My husband, son and I recently went on an Africa Adventure Company trip. It was the best vacation we have ever taken, even better than the Galapagos Islands. My 13 year old son actually shed tears in the plane from Maun to Johannesburg because he didn't want the safari to be over. The way that tourism is handled in Botswana is amazing and certainly commendable. The airport transfers were perfect. Our guide and hostess for the safari were wonderful and helped to make our safari a trip of a lifetime. We appreciated their knowledge, consideration, and care. They were very kind to our son, who loved the trip. We are all three ready to go back.
Joy, Larry and Drew Wiltse, Kansas

I can't believe what a fabulous trip this was!!!! I can't thank you enough for helping us plan what was probably the best trip we've been on to date. It's true what they say, you expect a game viewing trip to Africa to be good, then you get over there and find that it greatly exceeds your expectations. EVERYTHING was excellent: the food, the accommodations, the service, the animal sightings, the rangers, how smoothly all our transfers were, the places we visited. . .etc., etc., etc. You're the best. Thanks for everything and I hope to work with you again.
Christine Snovell, Virginia

Thank you so much for arranging a perfect safari for me. Everything went along according to the itinerary so I knew at all times just where I would be. It was so nice to be met at each airport by someone holding a piece of paper with my name on it. The lodges and tent camps were surprisingly modern and comfortable, and the food was excellent. I was so impressed with the staff at each facility; they were friend-

ly, polite and spoke different languages. My compliments to the guiding service around Tanzania. The guide was exceptional and really made the trip worthwhile. Driving across the Serengeti has been a dream since my childhood, and it came true. All the wildlife parks seen on TV documentaries were right there, and they are so beautiful. Wildlife sightings were everything I hoped for and more. Saw the "Big Five" and many others. I have many happy memories and met so many wonderful people. Thank you again. It was wonderful. I cried when I left.
Lue Rae Erickson, Alaska

Well, we made it back from the "Dark Continent" after a wonderful month visiting our daughter and wanted to let you know that the safaris that you arranged were fantastic. Our first trip was to Namibia, which we loved. The desert landscape was so haunting, especially in contrast to Cape Town and the Garden Route. Thanks for helping give us such great memories. I hope we can go back to Africa again. If so, we'll look forward to working with you.
Dawn Johnson, California

I returned home last night from the BEST trip EVER! The first trip will always be very special, as it was the first safari and it truly was wonderful. However, this third visit to Africa was quite amazing in diversity of experiences, quality of game viewing, and people with whom we got to interact. I was sure this would be my last trip to Africa, but before I left, I already wanted to return. Zimbabwe was a favorite. Zambia is dear to my heart, and I would love to visit there again. Thanks for planning a WINNER!
Marie Sullivan, Colorado

The feedback you will get from us is all positive — we were completely satisfied with our trip in every respect. It was even better than we had imagined. Everything went as expected which was a shock to us given we were traveling in developing countries. I think our expectations were appropriate because of the excellent job your materials did in preparing us for our trip. We felt very well prepared as a result of the information you provided us. Our ground operators, guides and accommodations were all first rate. With regard to wildlife sightings, we were more than pleased with our experience. We saw nearly everything that we hoped for including a leopard on Mitzi's 40th birthday (of all days). The gorilla experience, by far, was the highlight of our trip. It really thrilled Mitzi who has dreamed of such a thing for years. We will be going back to Africa in the future and plan to use your serv-

ices for our next trip. We have recommended you to several friends already. Thanks to all of you for making our dream trip a reality.
Jeffrey and Mitzi Richardson, Kentucky

We can't tell you how wonderful our trip was. It was perfect in so many ways that we plan to recommend your company to anyone who wants to go to Africa. To start with, the guides you gave us were THE best. We all fell in love with all three of them in the bush and in Cape Town and Victoria Falls. Thank you so much for making our vacation the best it could be. We never worried because you thought of every detail and were right on top of everything and everyone.... Thanks for advising Matthew about the ring for his engagement to Michelle. You were so right. His surprise announcement was just the cherry on top of a wonderful vacation. Thank you again.
Harriet and Ray Levy, New Jersey

You've done it once again! Just when I'm thinking that the last several trips couldn't be equaled, I'm proven very wrong! Our Skeleton Coast experience was the BEST! It was my favorite part of the entire trip. On to Botswana...I can see why this is a major wildlife destination. We had close encounters with animals we'd never seen in our previous visits to the continent. This time, we spent lots of time with the animal babies...it must be the season! Baby leopards, baby lions, baby cheetah, baby elephants and baby giraffe...incredible sights. The Okavango Delta was every bit as exciting and prolific as I had read!

Our final time at Singita was living in the lap of luxury! The "camp" was the most incredible place we had ever stayed (accommodation-wise). We were also fortunate enough to see some spectacular sightings...many of them with animals babies and their parent(s) playing together. The staff was wonderful as was the food.

All in all, the trip was fantastic! Rest assured, I'll be in touch in the next year to 18 months to plan for the next trip! Thanks so much for your marvelous plans, advise, patience and gifts. All are so appreciated!
Abby Lazar, New York

Two weeks ago we arrived home from our African Safari. We had high expectations of a journey of adventure and thanks to you and your staff those expectations were fulfilled. We were extremely impressed with the professionalism at all times by your staff and representatives.

Again we thank you, for helping us in the final days of our big decision of 'to go or not to go' after the terrorist attack on the World Trade Center.

It WAS a big decision for us to make. We are so glad we went on with the trip! It was a very exciting and wonderful experience. WE LOVED IT! All of our needs and concerns were covered from "A to Z" thanks to you and The Africa Adventure Company. You are to be highly recommended by us.

Darlene and George Durand, Iowa

Thank you so much for the time you spent planning and organizing our safari to Kenya and Tanzania. We had a fabulous vacation. The permanent tented camps, lodges, parks, animals, people and food exceeded our expectations. We had three guides who went out of their way to show us a good time and teach us about the animals and their countries. Something unique and exciting occurred every day. Everyone agreed that this was truly the adventure of a lifetime.

Two thumbs up for the Africa Adventure Company. I would recommend you and your staff to anyone interested in a first class safari to Africa. We look forward to traveling with you again. Asante sana.

Tom, Paula & Ashley Trainer, Minnesota

Just returned from our AMAZING ADVENTURE to UGANDA and KENYA — it was fantastic and we are so pleased with AAC. In Uganda our guide did a great job — spent many extra hours trying to make our time in Uganda perfect and he did. In the Mara, our guide and driver was really very good at Mara River Camp. Probably our favorite staff was here. They took excellent care of us. We will travel with AAC again!

Jim, Carolyn & Cheri Johnson, California

We returned from our incredible trip or should I say experience on Thursday. I just wanted to thank you for the wonderful itinerary you put together for us. I don't know how you were able to take the information I gave you and recommend what was the perfect diversity for our 3 1/2 weeks in Africa. You really took the time to listen to the type of "adventure" I was looking for in Africa. I would highly recommend you and your staff to anyone who is planning their trip to Africa! Thanks again,

Sheila and John Ducci, Florida

We just can't stop talking about our most recent travel in Southern Africa. We are buried in photos/slides and videos and enjoying every minute of it. Your planning was super as usual. We enjoyed the unique experiences offered by each camp in Zambia and the posh River Club.

The Zambian view of the falls is spectacular. We had a super guide in Moremi and Little Mombo exceeded our most extravagant expectations. Our guide was entertaining and informative. We can't wait to go back! The Cellars and Grand Roche made our re-entry to the real world a smooth and luxurious one. Your experience in African travel was evident throughout our adventure.
Dan and Fran Arnold, Florida

Just wanted to give you an update on our safari. In one word — it was WONDERFUL. We thoroughly enjoyed ourselves. All of the camps were very nice — and the staff were great as well. I would say that Sausage Tree was our favorite camp. We had animals outside of our tent non-stop since we were right beside their path to the water. It was absolutely amazing. We saw a variety of animals — most importantly the hippos since they're my favorite... Tim and I want to thank you for all of your help in planning this trip as well as making all of the last minute changes to the airline tickets. When we plan our next African trip, we'll be sure to contact you.
Mary Kendall and Tim Tuggle, Virginia

We can't thank enough the folks at The Africa Adventure Company (AAC). We traveled with our two children, ages 13 and 11, throughout four countries in eastern and southern Africa over five weeks. The planning and detail necessary for such a trip is extensive. Yet, AAC had everything arranged perfectly. It all went like clockwork! We had an incredible experience! Our children would never have had the benefit of touring such exotic places in the bush if we did not believe in the staff, and their efforts to put everything in place. Africa is a magnificent land! We are already making our plans to return through AAC. Thank you for a job well done!
Terri Williams and Chuck Jakway, Minnesota

We are currently planning our 7th trip to Africa for later this year. Our last 4 Safaris have been with The Africa Adventure Company.

We are looking forward to introducing our two boys (ages 4 and 2) to Africa. Their sister, age 5 a safari and eclipse veteran, has told them what a great time they will have. She has also made it clear that they need to be quiet around the lions.

The Africa Adventure Company is an unbelievable resource for anyone planning to travel to Africa with kids. In many cases they can advise parents based on their extensive first hand knowledge of traveling Africa with children.

We have also had the pleasure of referring numerous friends to The Africa Adventure Company. Their professionalism and the highly qualified staff have allowed us the confidence to make these referrals.
Michael and Wendy Maloon, California

This is just a note to tell you our trip to Africa met and even exceeded our expectations. Not an easy feat when you consider how hyped up we were about it. The culture and the people were as fascinating as the animals. We were very well looked after and, for the most part, the tourist industry in North America could take a lesson from their African counterparts. The mobile tented camp in the Serengeti was certainly one of the high points.

Our guide in Tanzania deserves a special mention for doing an outstanding job. His driving and guiding skills are top notch, but the service he provided went beyond these duties. He is a personable and capable individual and it was a privilege to spend our time in Tanzania in his company.

Thank you for all your assistance.
Bruce Nairn, Canada

Your contacts in Africa are so solid, so dependable, so resourceful, and so knowledgeable, that I always felt like I was in good hands, and I always felt safe and comfortable. This is an essential when you're about as far from home as you can get...what's more, in spite of the fact that I have a disability and use a scooter to get around, you spared no effort to make sure that every contingency was covered, from the plane that flew us to the Serengeti to the larger land rover (to make room for my scooter) that carried us all the way back to Kilimanjaro...this was a fabulous trip, one of the truly great experiences. The Africa Adventure Company was truly wonderful in ensuring that our whole family was truly accommodated in the fullest sense of the word, and we thoroughly loved the experience.
Judy and Atis Folkmanis, California

As a professional photographer going to Africa I was determined to get some great wildlife shots while we were there. The Africa Adventure Company did a stellar job of making our travels virtually seamless. AAC arranged for private guides and vehicles and made special arrangements to accommodate my heavy equipment when we took small charter flights. We never once had a problem and I got more amazing shots than I could have hoped for.
Dick and Linda Dickinson, Florida

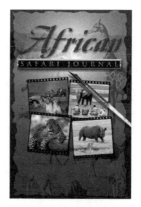

AFRICAN SAFARI JOURNAL

Revised and Greatly Expanded 4th Edition

The AFRICAN SAFARI JOURNAL is the perfect book to take on safari as it is a wildlife/botany guide, trip organizer, safari directory, phrase book, safari diary, map directory and wildlife checklist all in one!

This handsome 288-page safari journal with its colorful leatherette cover will stand up against the roughest of safaris. Key safari information is always at your fingertips. Record details of your exciting adventures so that they may be relived time and time again!

VALUABLE AFRICAN SAFARI JOURNAL
CONTENTS INCLUDE:

A **Wildlife/Botany Guide** with over 175 illustrations and descriptions of mammals, reptiles, birds and trees

A **Language Guide** (phrasebook) including useful words and phrases with phonetics in Swahili, Shona, Tswana, Zulu and French

A **Trip Organizer** ("Getting Ready for Safari") to help you prepare for your safari

A **Safari Directory** ("The Safari Pages") providing a veritable gold mine of safari tips and difficult-to-find information on Africa

A **Map Directory** including over 50 maps of African countries, parks and reserves, as well as constellation maps of the southern skies

A **Checklist** for recording your sightings of mammals, reptiles, birds and trees

A Journal ("Journal Pages") a personal diary to record the key events of your safari of a lifetime.

Why carry several cumbersome resource books when the African Safari Journal has it all!

Mark Nolting has explored and researched the African continent for over 25 years and is also the author of *Africa's Top Wildlife Countries,* an award winning travel guide currently in its sixth edition. Having spent hours in preparation for each of his earlier safaris, and in the end having to carry with him several heavy resource books on mammals, reptiles, birds and trees, as well as maps, phrase books and a diary, the idea of consolidating all this vital information into one book, the African Safari Journal was formed.

Many safaris have very strict baggage limitations (i.e. 25-33 lbs.) making this an all-the-more-valuable resource.

The AFRICAN SAFARI JOURNAL is the perfect Africa companion. Don't go on safari without it!

SPECIAL SALES

Discounts for bulk purchases available.

SPECIAL OFFER

Have the name and/or logo of your travel agency, tour company, safari group, organization, etc., gold-stamped on the cover!

For details please contact the publisher at: phone: 954-491-8877 or 1-800-882-9453, fax 1-954-491-9060

e-mail: safaribooks@aol.com or write to
Global Travel Publishers, Inc.
5353 North Federal Highway, Suite 300
Ft. Lauderdale, FL 33308 USA

AFRICAN SAFARI JOURNAL, 4TH EDITION

$16.95. ISBN# 0-939895-08-0 Travel. 177 B&W illustrations

54 maps, 8 charts, 288 pp., 5 x 8 leatherette (Kivar) 4-color cover

ORDER FORM

Please send me...

_____Copies of **African Safari Journal** @ $16.95 per copy.

_____Copies of **Africa's Top Wildlife Countries** @ $19.95 per copy.

Make checks and money orders payable to **Global Travel Publishers, Inc.**

Mail to: **Global Travel Publishers, Inc.,**
5353 N. Federal Highway, Suite 300,
Ft. Lauderdale, FL 33307-0067 USA,
Call Toll-free 1-800-882-9453 (1-800-882-WILD) or 954-491-8877. Fax your order to 954-491-9060. E-mail: safaribooks@aol.com or visit our website at: www.AfricanAdventure.com and charge to Visa/MasterCard/American Express.

☐ Check/M.O. enclosed

☐ Visa   ☐ MasterCard   ☐ American Express

Card No: _____ Exp: _____

Tel. Day: _____ Home:_____

Signature: _____

Name: _____

Company: _____

Street Address: _____

City: _____ State:_____ Zip:_____

African Safari Journal @ $16.95 per copy ....$ _____

Africa's Top Wildlife Countries, 6TH Edition @ $19.95 per copy.$ _____

Purchase Total ....$ _____

Sales Tax* ....$ _____

Shipping & Handling** ....$ _____

TOTAL ....$ _____

* Florida residents add 6% sales tax.
** **FREE SHIPPING** for books shipped within the USA. For books shipped to Canada, add $2.00 for one book and $1.00 for each additional book. For shipping and handling overseas orders, please call for rates.

_____Please send me your catalog of difficult to find books, maps, audiotapes, binoculars and other safari-related products.

_____Please put me on your mailing list and send me a complimentary copy nof your newsletter, the "Galloping Gnus".

_____ We would like one of your Africa travel experts to contact us to discuss safari options for our vacation, expedition, business, group or incentive trip (please include a daytime telephone number where you can be reached). If you have an idea of what you would like your safari to include please enclose details. We can also be reached Monday—Friday 9.00am—5.30pm Eastern Time toll free at 800-882-9453 or 954-491-8877, by fax at 954-491-9060, by e-mail at noltingaac@aol.com, or visit our website at www.AfricanAdventure.com and e-mail us a completed questionaire.

_____We would like Mark Nolting to speak to our club, organization, business, etc. We have enclosed a brief description of our request.

Name _____

Company _____

Address _____

Daytime
Telephone No. _____

Fax _____

E-mail _____